For Reference

Not to be taken from this room

D0741915

San Diego Christian College
Library
Santee, CA

San Diego Christian College
Library
Santee, CA

HISTORICAL DICTIONARY

The historical dictionaries present essential information on a broad range of subjects, including American and world history, art, business, cities, countries, cultures, customs, film, global conflicts, international relations, literature, music, philosophy, religion, sports, and theater. Written by experts, all contain highly informative introductory essays of the topic and detailed chronologies that, in some cases, cover vast historical time periods but still manage to heavily feature more recent events.

Brief A–Z entries describe the main people, events, politics, social issues, institutions, and policies that make the topic unique, and entries are cross-referenced for ease of browsing. Extensive bibliographies are divided into several general subject areas, providing excellent access points for students, researchers, and anyone wanting to know more. Additionally, maps, photographs, and appendixes of supplemental information aid high school and college students doing term papers or introductory research projects. In short, the historical dictionaries are the perfect starting point for anyone looking to research in these fields.

HISTORICAL DICTIONARIES OF SPORTS

Jon Woronoff, Series Editor

R
796.357
S738h

Historical Dictionary of Baseball

Lyle Spatz

The Scarecrow Press, Inc.
Lanham • Toronto • Plymouth, UK
2013

Published by Scarecrow Press, Inc.
A wholly owned subsidiary of The Rowman & Littlefield Publishing Group, Inc.
4501 Forbes Boulevard, Suite 200, Lanham, Maryland 20706
http://www.scarecrowpress.com

10 Thornbury Road, Plymouth PL6 7PP, United Kingdom

Copyright © 2013 by Lyle Spatz

All rights reserved. No part of this book may be reproduced in any form or by any electronic or mechanical means, including information storage and retrieval systems, without written permission from the publisher, except by a reviewer who may quote passages in a review.

British Library Cataloguing in Publication Information Available

Library of Congress Cataloging-in-Publication Data

Spatz, Lyle, 1937-
Historical dictionary of baseball / Lyle Spatz.
p. cm.
Includes bibliographical references.
ISBN 978-0-8108-7812-9 (cloth : alk. paper) -- ISBN 978-0-8108-7954-6 (ebook) 1. Baseball--History--Dictionaries. I. Title.
GV862.3.S63 2013
796.357--dc23
2012030409

♾️™   The paper used in this publication meets the minimum requirements of American National Standard for Information Sciences Permanence of Paper for Printed Library Materials, ANSI/NISO Z39.48-1992.

Printed in the United States of America

Contents

Editor's Foreword

Most all sports are played around the world, and the very idea that there should be something such as an "American" sport might appear out of place. Yet, the connection between the United States and baseball is amazingly strong and games are followed in the stadiums or on television by countless millions of Americans, to whom this is a particularly meaningful pastime. Indeed, many of them were introduced to it as kids, playing it on a vacant lot or a more suitable ball field at school, college, or the workplace. Admittedly, through the years, baseball has caught on in a growing circle of other countries, particularly Japan and Cuba, where it is also a national sport, and some parts of Latin America, Europe, and, of course, Canada. But baseball is still dominated—especially professionally—by the United States, which trains and develops its own players and attracts some of the best from abroad. That is where the most exciting games are played, where the teams achieve an impressively loyal following and, especially, where records are made and broken. So this volume does focus more heavily on the United States than most in the series, and rightly so.

Historical Dictionary of Baseball does look into the past, which is its historical slant, but it also follows the sport up until the latest season available to survey the current state of the game. This long view is clearly seen in the chronology, which traces the major stages over a long trajectory. The broader view is reflected by the introduction, which explains what the game is about, where it originated, where it is played today, and who plays it, not only professionals, but also amateurs, young and old, men, and, increasingly, women. The bulk of the information, however, appears in the dictionary section, which consists of numerous detailed entries on such universally known players as Babe Ruth or Jackie Robinson, and hundreds of others, on all of the teams that have emerged and, in some cases, disappeared, in all of the various leagues of today and yesteryear, as well as some of the essential organizations and indispensable technical terms. These entries are overflowing with facts and figures and are supplemented by an impressive array of statistical and other appendixes. For those looking for additional sources, the bibliography contains a comprehensive listing of suitable reading on the history of baseball and its players, teams, and leagues, among other topics.

This volume was written by someone who knows baseball inside out. His interest in the sport was first aroused more than 60 years ago, and, for the past three decades, Lyle Spatz has been researching and writing on the subject. The results are quite impressive, as he has authored several books, including his most recent compilations, *Dixie Walker: A Life in Baseball* and *1921: The Yankees, the Giants, and Battle for Baseball Supremacy in New York*, which he coauthored with Steve Steinberg, and which won the 2011 Seymour Medal for best book of baseball history or biography. He has also edited several books, made contributions to other works, and written biographical and other articles for various encyclopedias. This time he has beat his own record with an entire book, and a large and informative one at that, on the American sport, with mention of its impact elsewhere. Even in this day of instant feedback on the Web, this book contains a plethora of information that readers cannot readily find elsewhere. It is a must-have for baseball fans.

Jon Woronoff
Series Editor

Preface

Because organized baseball has been around for more than 150 years, and the roots of the game go back even further, I have limited my entries to those I feel are most important. I selected all players, managers, and executives already in the National Baseball Hall of Fame or likely to gain admission and others who are not Hall of Famers but have had a significant impact on the game.

Any team that has ever had major league status, however brief it may have been, is included, as well as some of the more prominent teams from the Negro Leagues. Also included are entries for Minor League Baseball and college baseball, as well as for several countries other than the United States. There are entries for various awards, organizations, rules, fielding positions, and major statistical categories. The statistical data used is through the 2012 season and comes from Baseball-Reference.com and *The Elias Book of Baseball Records*. The biographical data also comes from Baseball-Reference.com. The players' weights used were recorded at a specific point and, in all likelihood, changed over time.

To facilitate the rapid and efficient location of information and make this book as useful a reference tool as possible, extensive cross-references are provided in the dictionary section. Within individual entries, terms that have their own entries appear in **boldface type** the first time they appear. Related terms that do not appear in the text are indicated in the *See also* section that appears at the end of applicable entries. *See* refers to other entries that deal with the topic.

I am grateful to fellow members of the Society for American Baseball Research who were gracious in answering questions in their individual fields of expertise. I would also like to thank Michael M. Spatz for his diligence in fact checking the various entries. Any errors that remain are, of course, mine.

Acronyms and Abbreviations

1B	first baseman/single
1G	first game of a doubleheader
2B	second baseman/double
2G	second game of a doubleheader
3B	third baseman/triple
A	assists
AA	American Association
AAGPBL	All-American Girls Professional Baseball League
AB	at-bats
AL	American League
ALCS	American League Championship Series
ALDS	American League Division Series
ASA	Amateur Softball Association of America
ASG	All-Star Game
BA	batting average
BB	bases on balls/bats both right-handed and left-handed
BBWAA	Baseball Writers' Association of America
BF	batters faced
BK	balk
BL	bats left-handed
BR	bats right-handed
C	catcher
CBHFM	Canadian Baseball Hall of Fame
CEB	Confederation of European Baseball
CF	center field/center fielder
CG	complete games
CH	chances
CI	catcher interference
CS	caught stealing
DH	doubleheader/designated hitter

DL	disabled list
DP	double play
DS	Division Series
E	error
EBH	extra-base hit
ECL	Eastern Colored League
ER	earned run
ERA	earned run average
FC	fielder's choice
FL	Federal League
FP	fielding percentage/force play
G	games played
GF	games finished
GIDP	grounded into double plays (sometimes shown as GDP)
GM	general manager
GS	games started
H	hit
HBP	hit by pitch
HOF	Hall of Fame
HP	home plate
HR	home run
IBAF	International Baseball Federation
IBB	intentional base on balls
IL	International League
IOC	International Olympic Committee
IP	innings pitched
K	strikeout (also SO)
KBO	Korea Baseball Association
L	lost/losses
LCS	League Championship Series
LDS	League Division Series
LF	left field/left fielder
LH	left-handed
LP	losing pitcher
MLB	Major League Baseball

MLBPA	Major League Baseball Players Association
MVP	Most Valuable Player
NA	National Association
NABBP	National Association of Base Ball Players
NAIA	National Association of Intercollegiate Athletics
NAL	Negro American League
NAPBBP	National Association of Professional Base Ball Players
NBLM	National Baseball Library and Museum
NCAA	National Collegiate Athletic Association
NL	National League
NLBM	Negro League Baseball Museum
NLCS	National League Championship Series
NLDS	National League Division Series
NNL	Negro National League
O	outs
OBP	on-base percentage
OF	outfield/outfielder
OPS	on-base percentage plus slugging percentage
P	pitcher
PA	plate appearances
PB	passed ball
PCT	percentage
PH	pinch hitter
PL	Players' League
PO	putouts
PR	pinch runner
R	runs
RBI	runs batted in
RF	right field/right fielder
RH	right-handed
ROY	Rookie of the Year
SABR	Society for American Baseball Research
SB	stolen bases
SF	sacrifice fly

SH	sacrifice hit/switch-hitter
SHO	shutouts
SLG	slugging percentage
SO	strikeouts (also K)
SS	shortstop
SV	saves (sometimes shown as S)
TB	total bases
TC	total chances
TP	triple play
UA	Union Association
W	wins or won/walks
W-L%	win-loss percentage
WAR	wins above replacement
WBC	World Baseball Classic
WHIP	walks plus hits divided by innings pitched
WP	wild pitch/winning pitcher
WS	World Series

Chronology

1791 5 September: Baseball is formally mentioned for the first time in the United States at a town meeting in Pittsfield, Massachusetts. A law is passed making it illegal to play baseball and other sports within 80 yards of the town hall to prevent the breaking of windows.

1838 4 June: The first recorded game of baseball in Canada is played near Beachville, Ontario. The rules include five bases, three strikes, and three outs.

1845 23 September: Alexander Cartwright suggests the formation of the Knickerbocker baseball club of New York. Cartwright designs rules to distinguish the New York brand of baseball from other forms played throughout the country. **21 October:** The New York club defeats the Brooklyn club, 24–4, in a "friendly match" played at Elysian Fields in Hoboken, New Jersey.

1846 19 June: Alexander Cartwright umpires the first game played under his "New York rules." The New York club defeats the Knickerbockers, 23–1, at Elysian Fields.

1849 24 April: The New York Knickerbocker club is the first team to wear uniforms—blue woolen pantaloons, a white flannel shirt, and a straw hat.

1856 5 December: The *New York Mercury* refers to "base ball" as the national pastime. **13 December:** The *New York Clipper* states that the "game of base ball is generally considered the national game amongst Americans."

1857 22 January: The first formal baseball convention is held in New York City. The rule is changed to make games nine innings rather than ending when one team scores 21 runs. **10 March:** The National Association of Base Ball Players is formed at Cooper Union in New York City.

1859 15 March: At the annual meeting of the National Association of Base Ball Players, a rule is amended to read that, "No party shall be competent to play in a match who receives compensation for his services." **1 July:** Amherst defeats Williams, 66–32, in the first collegiate baseball game.

1861 Henry Chadwick writes that America's Civil War "has laid an embargo on outdoor sports, especially ball playing."

1862 15 May: The Union Baseball Grounds in Brooklyn becomes the first enclosed ball field to charge an admission fee.

1864 14 December: The National Association changes the rule for outs recorded. A batted ball must be caught on the fly rather than the first bounce.

1865 13 December: Ninety clubs are represented at the ninth convention of the National Association of Base Ball Players, held at Cooper Union. In 1864, primarily due to the constraints of the Civil War, there was only one-third that amount.

1869 31 May: The Cincinnati Red Stockings, baseball's first admittedly all-professional team, leaves for a month-long, 25-game Eastern tour.

1870 June: The Brooklyn Atlantics defeat the Cincinnati Red Stockings, 8–7, at Brooklyn's Capitoline Grounds, ending Cincinnati's 27-game winning streak.

1871 17 March: The National Association of Professional Base Ball Players (NAPBBP), more commonly known as the National Association, is formed in New York at a convention called together by Henry Chadwick. Teams represented at the convention include the Athletics of Philadelphia; Boston Red Stockings; Chicago White Stockings; Eckford of Brooklyn; Forest Citys of Cleveland; Forest Citys of Rockford, Illinois; Mutuals of New York; Nationals of Washington, D.C.; Olympics of Washington; and Union Club of Troy, New York, known as the Haymakers.The Atlantics of Brooklyn and Kekiongas of Fort Wayne, Indiana, do not attend but are members of the National Association. **4 May:** The NAPBBP's first game, between the Fort Wayne Kekiongas and Forest Citys of Cleveland, is played at Fort Wayne, Indiana. The Forest Citys win, 2–0. **30 October:** The Athletics of Philadelphia defeat the Chicago White Stockings, 4–1, at the Union Grounds in Brooklyn, to win the first National Association championship.

1874 27 February: Albert G. Spalding's plan to bring baseball to England is realized when a match takes place at the Kennington Oval Cricket Field in London.

1876 2 February: William Hulbert organizes a meeting at the Grand Central Hotel in New York to establish a new organization, the National League of Professional Baseball Clubs. The National League (NL) will consist of eight teams: Boston, Chicago, Cincinnati, Hartford, Louisville, New York, Philadelphia, and St. Louis. **22 April:** In the NL's first game, Boston defeats Philadelphia, 6–5, at Athletic Park.

1877 Tommy Bond of the Boston Red Stockings leads the NL in wins, earned run average, and strikeouts to win the Triple Crown for pitchers. **20 February:** The first minor league, the International Association, is formed in

Pittsburgh. The league consists of eight teams, six in the United States and two in Canada. **22 March:** The NL publishes its 1877 game schedule, the first leaguewide schedule ever issued. **24 November:** The *New York Mercury* predicts that, "The baseball mania is getting so bad that every city will soon have a mammoth structure like the Roman Coliseum to play in. This will be illuminated by electric lights so that games can be played at night, thus overcoming a serious objection at present existing."

1878 Paul Hines of the Providence Grays leads the NL in batting average, home runs, and runs batted in to win the Triple Crown for batters. **29 December:** The Professional Baseball League of Cuba is founded in Havana.

1879 6 December: The American College Baseball Association is founded in Springfield, Massachusetts, consisting of Harvard, Yale, Princeton, Amherst, Dartmouth, and Brown.

1880 12 June: Lee Richmond of the Worcester Ruby Legs pitches a perfect game against the Cleveland Blues, the NL's first perfect game. **17 June:** John Montgomery Ward of the Providence Grays pitches a perfect game against the Buffalo Bisons.

1881 2 November: The American Association of Professionals is founded as a major-league rival to the NL. The members are St. Louis, Cincinnati, Louisville, the Alleghenys, the Athletics, and the Atlantics. **23 December:** The Western Inter-collegiate Base Ball Association is formed by Northwestern, University of Michigan, and Racine College.

1882 2 May: The American Association (AA) begins play. It employs the first salaried umpiring staff.

1883 6 September: Both Tom Burns and Ned Williamson of the Chicago Colts set a major-league record by scoring three runs in an inning. **12 October:** A third major league, the Union Association (UA), is formed in Pittsburgh.

1884 Following the season, the Providence Grays of the NL defeat the New York Metropolitans of the AA in a postseason series. These series will continue through 1890. Charlie Radbourn of the Providence Grays leads the NL in wins, earned run average, and strikeouts to win the Triple Crown for pitchers. Radbourn's 59 wins are the most ever by a major-league pitcher. Guy Hecker of the Louisville Colonels leads the AA in wins, earned run average, and strikeouts to win the Triple Crown for pitchers. **17 April:** The UA begins play. **1 May:** Moses Fleetwood Walker becomes the first black in the major leagues when he plays for the Toledo club in the AA. **7 June:** Charlie Sweeney of the Providence Grays strikes out 19 Boston Beaneaters batters in a nine-inning game. **7 July:** Hugh Daily of the Chicago Browns of the UA strikes out 19 Boston Reds batters in a nine-inning game. **19 July:** Dupee Shaw of the Boston Reds of the UA strikes out 18 St. Louis Maroons batters in a nine-inning game. **3 October:** Henry Porter of the Milwaukee Brewers of the UA strikes out 18 Boston Reds batters in a nine-inning game.

1885 15 January: At a UA meeting held in Milwaukee, the league decides to disband. **25 June:** George Strief of the Philadelphia Athletics of the AA hits four triples in a game. **1 October:** The Cuban Giants, the first black professional team, is organized.

1886 17 March: *Sporting News* publishes its first issue. **15 August:** Guy Hecker of the Louisville Colonels of the AA is the first and only player to score seven runs in a major league game. **11 December:** The Executive Council of the Brotherhood of Professional Base-Ball Players, formed the previous year, meets and chooses John Montgomery Ward as president.

1887 Tip O'Neill of the St. Louis Browns leads the AA in batting average, home runs, and runs batted in to win the Triple Crown for batters. **16 March:** Chicago announces the sale of Mike "King" Kelly to Boston for $10,000, more than twice the amount ever paid for a player prior to that date. **12 December:** A baseball reporters' association is organized.

1888 Tim Keefe of the New York Giants leads the NL in wins, earned run average, and strikeouts to win the Triple Crown for pitchers. **4 September:** Pud Galvin of the Pittsburgh Alleghenys wins his 300th game. **18 December:** Albert Spalding and a group of players sail for Australia to begin an around-the-world baseball tour. **20 December:** The Joint Rules Committee reduces the number of balls required for a batter to walk from five to four, establishing the four balls and three strikes count that is still in effect today.

1889 John Clarkson of the Boston Beaneaters leads the NL in wins, earned run average, and strikeouts to win the Triple Crown for pitchers. **16 December:** The Players League (PL) is formed by the Brotherhood of Professional Base-Ball Players as a major league. The league will not allow player transfers without the player's consent, and excess profits will be split between owners and players.

1890 19 April: The PL begins its first and only season. **4 June:** Tim Keefe of the New York Giants (PL) wins his 300th game. **11 August:** Mickey Welch of the New York Giants (NL) wins his 300th game.

1891 14 May: Charlie Radbourn of the Cincinnati Reds wins his 300th game. **17 December:** The AA is dissolved. Four of its teams, Baltimore, Louisville, St. Louis, and Washington, join the NL, creating a 12-team league.

1892 6 June: President William Henry Harrison becomes the first U.S. president to attend a major-league game when he attends the Cincinnati–Washington game in Washington. **10 June:** Wilbert Robinson of the Baltimore Orioles gets seven hits in a nine-inning game, setting a major-league record for most hits in a game. **21 September:** John Clarkson of the Cleveland Spiders wins his 300th game.

1893 7 March: The NL eliminates the pitching box and adds a pitcher's rubber five feet behind the previous back line of the box, establishing the modern pitching distance of 60 feet, 6 inches.

1894 Amos Rusie of the New York Giants leads the NL in wins, earned run average, and strikeouts to win the Triple Crown for pitchers. **26 February:** Two new rules are added: The infield fly rule is instituted, and foul bunts will now be called strikes. **30 May:** Bobby Lowe of the Boston Beaneaters hits four home runs in a game.

1895 3 June: Roger Connor of the St. Louis Browns hits the 122nd home run of his career to become the all-time leader. **10 September:** Joe Harrington of the Boston Beaneaters hits a home run in his first major league at-bat.

1896 13 July: Ed Delahanty of the Philadelphia Phillies hits four home runs in a game.

1897 18 May: Bill Joyce of the New York Giants hits four triples in a game. **29 June:** The Chicago Colts score a major-league record 36 runs in defeating the Louisville Colonels.

1898 8 January: The NL reverts to a 154 game schedule, after five years at 132 games. **1 March:** The team owners unanimously pass a resolution to "suppress obscene, indecent, and vulgar language on the ball field by players." **21 April:** Bill Duggleby of the Philadelphia Phillies hits a grand slam in his first major league at-bat.

1899 25 February: The NL Committee on Rules recommends that umpires be given authority to fine unruly players $10 for a first offense. **15 April:** John McGraw makes his managerial debut by leading the Baltimore Orioles to a 5–3 win over the New York Giants. **2 November:** Henry Chadwick visits President William McKinley in Washington to propose that U.S. Army regiments be provided with baseball equipment.

1900 8 March: The NL cuts four teams, Baltimore, Cleveland, Louisville, and Washington, to again become an eight-team league. **7 September:** Kid Nichols of the Boston Beaneaters wins his 300th game. **15 December:** The Cincinnati Reds trade pitcher Christy Mathewson to the New York Giants for pitcher Amos Rusie.

1901 Nap Lajoie of the Philadelphia Athletics leads the American League (AL) in batting average, home runs, and runs batted in to win the Triple Crown for batters. Cy Young of the Boston Americans leads the AL in wins, earned run average, and strikeouts to win the Triple Crown for pitchers. **29 January:** The AL, led by Ban Johnson, declares itself a major league. The league has teams in eight cities, including Baltimore, Boston, Chicago, Cleveland, Detroit, Milwaukee, Philadelphia, and Washington. The AL actively recruits NL players, setting off a bidding war. **27 February:** The Rules Committee decrees that all fouls are to count as strikes, except after two strikes. Only the NL utilizes this rule. **24 April:** Chicago defeats Cleveland in the first AL game. **3 July:** Cy Young of the Boston Americans wins his 300th game. **3 December:** The AL moves its Milwaukee franchise to St. Louis for the 1902 season.

1902 9 December: The AL Rules Committee adopts the NL rule that all fouls are to count as strikes, except after two strikes.

1903 10 January: The AL moves its Baltimore franchise to New York. The two leagues agree to end the bidding war. **1 October:** Pittsburgh of the NL and Boston of the AL meet in the first game of the first modern "World Series." Boston wins the scheduled nine-game Series, five games to three.

1904 5 May: Cy Young of the Boston Americans pitches a perfect game against the Philadelphia Athletics, the AL's first perfect game. **10 October:** New York, champion of the NL, refuses to play Boston, champion of the AL, in the World Series.

1905 Christy Mathewson of the New York Giants leads the NL in wins, earned run average, and strikeouts to win the Triple Crown for pitchers. Rube Waddell of the Philadelphia Athletics leads the AL in wins, earned run average, and strikeouts to win the Triple Crown for pitchers. **9 October:** The New York Giants defeat the Philadelphia Athletics, four games to one, as World Series play resumes under a new seven-game format.

1906 12 April: Johnny Bates of the Boston Braves becomes the first 20th-century player to hit a home run in his first major league at-bat. **4 September:** The New York Highlanders win their fifth consecutive doubleheader.

1907 16 April: Cy Young of the Boston Americans wins his 400th game.

1908 Christy Mathewson of the New York Giants leads the NL in wins, earned run average, and strikeouts to win the Triple Crown for pitchers. **2 October:** Addie Joss of the Cleveland Naps pitches a perfect game against the Chicago White Sox.

1909 Ty Cobb of the Detroit Tigers leads the AL in batting average, home runs, and runs batted in to win the Triple Crown for batters. **12 April:** During the first game played in Philadelphia's Shibe Park, Athletics catcher Mike Powers crashes into a wall while chasing a foul pop-up. Two weeks later, he dies from complications from three intestinal surgeries. **19 July:** Shortstop Neal Ball of the Cleveland Naps executes an unassisted triple play.

1910 14 April: President William Howard Taft begins a presidential tradition by throwing out the first ball at the Washington Senators opening game. **19 July:** Cy Young of the Cleveland Naps wins his 500th game.

1911 14 February: A new cork-centered ball is introduced, which will cause both batting averages and earned run averages to rise dramatically. **4 April:** The idea of selecting a Most Valuable Player (MVP) is introduced. Hugh Chalmers, the automobile maker, offers a new car to the player in each league chosen MVP by a committee of baseball writers. **13 December:** For the first time in history, a woman, Mrs. H. H. Britton, owner of the St. Louis Cardinals, attends a major-league meeting.

1912 20 April: Fenway Park, in Boston, the oldest major-league park still in use, opens, with the Red Sox defeating the New York Yankees, 7–6, in 11 innings. **28 June:** Christy Mathewson of the New York Giants wins his 300th game.

1913 Walter Johnson of the Washington Senators leads the AL in wins, earned run average, and strikeouts to win the Triple Crown for pitchers.

1914 14 April: The eight-team Federal League (FL), a challenger to the two established major leagues, opens its first season. **9 June:** Honus Wagner of the Pittsburgh Pirates gets his 3,000th hit. **27 September:** Nap Lajoie of the Cleveland Naps gets his 3,000th hit.

1915 Grover Alexander of the Philadelphia Phillies leads the NL in wins, earned run average, and strikeouts to win the Triple Crown for pitchers. **11 September:** Eddie Plank of the St. Louis Terriers wins his 300th game. **22 December:** The FL dissolves.

1916 Grover Alexander of the Philadelphia Phillies leads the NL in wins, earned run average, and strikeouts to win the Triple Crown for pitchers.

1917 14 February: Dave Fultz, president of the Players Fraternity, calls off a strike set to begin within the week. One of the demands of the union was to abolish the 10-day clause, in which a team ceases to pay a injured player after he has been out of action for 10 days. Organized Baseball officially severs relations with the union, leaving the players without representation.

1918 Hippo Vaughn of the Chicago Cubs leads the NL in wins, earned run average, and strikeouts to win the Triple Crown for pitchers. Walter Johnson of the Washington Senators leads the AL in wins, earned run average, and strikeouts to win the Triple Crown for pitchers.

1919 Because of the world war, the major leagues reduce their schedules to 140 games. **5 February:** Charges brought in 1918 by Reds owner Garry Herrmann and manager Christy Mathewson against Hal Chase for betting against his team and throwing games in collusion with gamblers are dismissed by NL president John Heydler. Heydler decides that Chase's sometimes indifferent play was due to "carelessness." **19 April:** A bill legalizing Sunday baseball in the state of New York is signed by Governor Al Smith. **9 October:** The Cincinnati Reds defeat the Chicago White Sox in the World Series. Eight Chicago players are later charged with deliberately losing the Series.

1920 Grover Alexander of the Chicago Cubs leads the NL in wins, earned run average, and strikeouts to win the Triple Crown for pitchers. **5 January:** The New York Yankees announce the purchase of Babe Ruth from the Boston Red Sox. **12 January:** A plan is finally adopted whereby the annual drafting of players from the minor leagues will be done in inverse order to the teams' final standings. **13 April:** A meeting held in Kansas City, Missouri, establishes the Negro National League and its governing body, the National Association of Colored Professional Baseball Clubs. **1 May:** The Brooklyn Robins and Boston Braves play a 26-inning 1–1 tie, the longest game in major-league history. Brooklyn's Leon Cadore and Boston's Joe Oeschger each pitch complete games. **14 May:** Walter Johnson of the Washington Senators wins his 300th game. **16 August:** Carl Mays of the New York Yankees hits Cleveland Indians shortstop Ray Chapman in the head with a pitched ball. Chapman dies the next day from his injuries. **28 September:** An Illinois grand jury indicts eight Chicago White Sox players for conspiring to lose the 1919 World Series to the Cincinnati Reds. **10 October:** Second baseman Bill Wambsganss of the Cleveland Indians executes an unassisted triple play in Game 5 of the World Series. **12 November:** Judge Kenesaw Landis begins serving as the commissioner of baseball. **17 December:** Major-league baseball outlaws the spitball but allows 17 designated pitchers who used the spitball in 1920 to continue using it.

1921 12 March: Baseball commissioner Kenesaw Landis suspends the eight Chicago White Sox players accused of conspiring to fix the 1919 World Series. All eight—Eddie Cicotte, Happy Felsch, Chick Gandil, Joe Jackson, Fred McMullin, Swede Risberg, Buck Weaver, and Lefty Williams—are later permanently banned from baseball. **19 August:** Ty Cobb of the Detroit

Tigers gets his 3,000th hit. **20 December:** The World Series, which had been a best-of-nine for the past three seasons (1919–1921) is returned to a best-of-seven beginning in 1922.

1922 Rogers Hornsby of the St. Louis Cardinals leads the NL in batting average, home runs, and runs batted in to win the Triple Crown for batters. **30 April:** Charlie Robertson of the Chicago White Sox pitches a perfect game against the Detroit Tigers.

1923 18 April: Yankee Stadium opens, with an announced attendance of more than 74,000. **14 September:** First baseman George Burns of the Boston Red Sox executes an unassisted triple play. **6 October:** Shortstop Ernie Padgett of the Boston Braves executes an unassisted triple play. **6 December:** While in Paris, John McGraw announces plans for a tour of Europe by the New York Giants and Chicago White Sox in 1924, as world interest in baseball grows.

1924 The New York Giants become the first NL team to win four consecutive pennants. Dazzy Vance of the Brooklyn Robins leads the NL in wins, earned run average, and strikeouts to win the Triple Crown for pitchers. Walter Johnson of the Washington Senators leads the AL in wins, earned run average, and strikeouts to win the Triple Crown for pitchers. **20 September:** Grover Alexander of the Chicago Cubs wins his 300th game. **10 December:** The two major leagues agree on a permanent rotation for World Series play proposed by Charles Ebbets: The first two games will be played at one league's park, the next three at the other league's park, and last two, if needed, back at the first league's park, with openers to alternate between leagues.

1925 Rogers Hornsby of the St. Louis Cardinals leads the NL in batting average, home runs, and runs batted in to win the Triple Crown for batters. **7 May:** Shortstop Glenn Wright of the Pittsburgh Pirates executes an unassisted triple play. **17 May:** Tris Speaker of the Cleveland Indians gets his 3,000th hit. **1 June:** Lou Gehrig of the New York Yankees begins his record consecutive games-played streak. **6 June:** Eddie Collins of the Chicago White Sox gets his 3,000th hit.

1926 12 May: Walter Johnson of the Washington Senators wins his 400th game. **20 December:** The two best second basemen in the NL are traded for one another, as Frankie Frisch goes from the New York Giants to the St. Louis Cardinals in exchange for Rogers Hornsby.

1927 30 May: Shortstop Jimmy Cooney of the Chicago Cubs executes an unassisted triple play. **31 May:** First baseman Johnny Neun of the Detroit Tigers executes an unassisted triple play. **18 July:** Ty Cobb of the Philadelphia Athletics gets his 4,000th hit. **30 September:** Babe Ruth of the New York Yankees hits his 60th home run of the season, breaking the record of 59 he had set in 1921.

1928 14 February: The Major League Advisory Council allots $50,000 to develop a national championship program run by the American Legion.

1929 22 January: The New York Yankees announce that they will put numbers on the backs of their uniforms, becoming the first baseball team to start continuous use of the numbers. A few weeks later, the Cleveland Indians announce that they too will put numbers on their uniforms. By 1931, all AL teams will use them; it will be 1933 before all NL players are numbered. **11 August:** Babe Ruth of the New York Yankees hits his 500th home run.

1930 Lefty Grove of the Philadelphia Athletics leads the AL in wins, earned run average, and strikeouts to win the Triple Crown for pitchers. **28 September:** Hack Wilson of the Chicago Cubs drives in his 191st run of the season, a still-standing major league record. Wilson's 56 home runs for the year sets a NL record.

1931 Lefty Grove of the Philadelphia Athletics leads the AL in wins, earned run average, and strikeouts to win the Triple Crown for pitchers. Lou Gehrig sets the AL record for most runs batted in in a season, with 184. **21 August:** Babe Ruth of the New York Yankees hits his 600th home run. **2 November:** A major league team arrives in Japan, where they will win all 17 games they play.

1932 3 June: Lou Gehrig of the New York Yankees hits four home runs in a game. **10 July:** Johnny Burnett of the Cleveland Indians gets nine hits in a 16-inning game, a major-league record for most hits in a game.

1933 Chuck Klein of the Philadelphia Phillies leads the NL in batting average, home runs, and runs batted in to win the Triple Crown for batters. Jimmie Foxx of the Philadelphia Athletics leads the AL in batting average, home runs, and runs batted in to win the Triple Crown for batters. **6 July:** The first major league All-Star Game is played at Comiskey Park as part of the Chicago World's Fair.

1934 Lou Gehrig of the New York Yankees leads the AL in batting average, home runs, and runs batted in to win the Triple Crown for batters. Lefty Gomez of the New York Yankees leads the AL in wins, earned run average, and strikeouts to win the Triple Crown for pitchers. **13 July:** Babe Ruth of the New York Yankees hits his 700th home run. **21 October:** An American team led by Babe Ruth and Connie Mack sails on tour to Hawaii and Japan. Players include Lou Gehrig, Jimmie Foxx, Charlie Gehringer, Lefty Gomez, Earl Averill, and Lefty O'Doul. **11 December:** The NL votes to permit night baseball, authorizing a maximum of seven games per team. **26 December:** Matsutaro Shoriki, head of Yomiuri Newspapers, announces the official formation of Japan's first professional team, the Tokyo-based Yomiuri Giants.

1935 25 May: The Cincinnati Reds host the Philadelphia Phillies in the first major-league night game, winning 2–1 before a crowd of 24,422. President Franklin D. Roosevelt throws a switch from the White House to turn on the lights. Babe Ruth, playing for the Boston Braves, hits three home runs against Pittsburgh to finish his career with 714.

1936 2 February: Ty Cobb, Walter Johnson, Christy Mathewson, Babe Ruth, and Honus Wagner are selected by the Baseball Writers' Association as the first players named to the new Baseball Hall of Fame. **10 July:** Chuck Klein of the Philadelphia Phillies hits four home runs in a game.

1937 Joe Medwick of the St. Louis Cardinals leads the NL in batting average, home runs, and runs batted in to win the Triple Crown for batters. Lefty Gomez of the New York Yankees leads the AL in wins, earned run average, and strikeouts to win the Triple Crown for pitchers. **27 February:** The Negro American League announces the schedule for its first season.

1938 13–20 August: The first Baseball World Cup, originally called the Amateur World Series, is held in Great Britain. Only two teams compete, with Great Britain defeating the United States. **2 October:** Bob Feller of the Cleveland Indians strikes out 18 Detroit Tigers batters in a nine-inning game.

1939 The New York Yankees become the first team to win four consecutive World Series. Bucky Walters of the Cincinnati Reds leads the NL in wins, earned run average, and strikeouts to win the Triple Crown for pitchers. **2 May:** Lou Gehrig of the New York Yankees voluntarily benches himself, ending his consecutive games-played streak at 2,130. **16 May:** At Shibe Park in Philadelphia, the Athletics defeat the Cleveland Indians, 8–3, in 10 innings in the AL's first night game. **17 May:** Princeton plays Columbia at New York's Baker Field in the first televised baseball game. **12 June:** The Baseball Hall of Fame is dedicated at Cooperstown, New York.

1940 Bob Feller of the Cleveland Indians leads the AL in wins, earned run average, and strikeouts to win the Triple Crown for pitchers. **16 April:** Bob Feller pitches a 1–0 no-hitter against the Chicago White Sox, which remains the only Opening Day no-hitter in history. **24 September:** Jimmie Foxx of the Boston Red Sox hits his 500th home run.

1941 Joe DiMaggio of the New York Yankees compiles a record-setting 56-game hitting streak. Ted Williams of the Boston Red Sox bats .400, the last major league player to reach that mark. **25 July:** Lefty Grove of the Boston Red Sox wins his 300th game.

1942 Ted Williams of the Boston Red Sox leads the AL in batting average, home runs, and runs batted in to win the Triple Crown for batters. **15 January:** President Roosevelt gives baseball the go-ahead to play despite the outbreak of war the previous month. The president says, "I honestly think it would be best for the country to keep baseball going." He encourages more night baseball so that war workers may attend. **19 June:** Paul Waner of the Boston Braves gets his 3,000th hit.

1943 The All-American Girls Professional Baseball League is formed and exists through the 1954 season.

1944 10 June: Fifteen-year-old pitcher Joe Nuxhall of the Cincinnati Reds becomes the youngest player to appear in a major-league game.

1945 Hal Newhouser of the Detroit Tigers leads the AL in wins, earned run average, and strikeouts to win the Triple Crown for pitchers. **24 April:** Albert "Happy" Chandler begins serving as the commissioner of baseball. **1 August:** Mel Ott of the New York Giants hits his 500th home run, the first National Leaguer to do so. **23 October:** Branch Rickey announces the signing of Jackie Robinson by the Brooklyn Dodgers organization. Robinson signs a contract to play for the International League's (IL) Montreal Royals in 1946.

1946 12 January: The first professional league game is played in Venezuela, launching the newly constituted four-team Liga de Beisbol Profesional de Venezuela. **17 March:** In Daytona Beach, Florida, the Brooklyn Dodgers take the field against their minor-league farm team, the Montreal Royals. With Jackie Robinson in the lineup for Montreal, the game marks the first appearance of an integrated team in Organized Baseball in the 20th century. **30 March:** Several major-league players sign to play in the Mexican leagues, leading to their suspensions from Organized Baseball.

1947 Ted Williams of the Boston Red Sox leads the AL in batting average, home runs, and runs batted in to win the Triple Crown for batters. **1 February:** Commissioner Happy Chandler announces the creation of a pension plan for major leaguers. Players with five years of experience will receive $50 a month at age 50 and $10 a month for each of the next five years. The plan extends to coaches, players, and trainers active on Opening Day. The plan will be funded by $650,000, with the teams providing 80 percent and the players the remaining 20 percent. **9 April:** Commissioner Happy Chandler suspends Brooklyn Dodgers manager Leo Durocher for one year for conduct "detrimental to baseball." **15 April:** Jackie Robinson of the Brooklyn Dodgers becomes the first African American to play in a major-league game in the 20th century. **5 July:** In a game against the Chicago White Sox, Larry Doby of the Cleveland Indians becomes the first African American to play in the AL.

1948 16 July: The New York Giants fire manager Mel Ott and replace him with Brooklyn Dodgers manager Leo Durocher. Burt Shotton, who managed the Dodgers during Durocher's 1947 suspension, returns to Brooklyn. **18 July:** Pat Seerey of the Chicago White Sox hits four home runs in a game.

1949 7 February: Joe DiMaggio signs with the New York Yankees for $100,000, the first six-figure contract in the major leagues. **12 December:** By a 7–1 vote, the AL rejects a proposal to bring back the legal spitball. The Rules Committee also alters the strike zone to constitute the space between the armpits and the top of the knees. The new rule eliminates the batter's shoulders from being within the strike zone.

1950 The home team no longer has the option to bat first or last; it must bat last. **7 February:** Ted Williams of the Boston Red Sox becomes the highest-paid player in history, by signing for $125,000. **18 April:** The St. Louis Cardinals defeat the Pittsburgh Pirates, 4–2, in the major leagues' first night-time Opening Day game. **31 August:** Gil Hodges of the Brooklyn Dodgers hits four home runs in a game.

1951 20 September: Ford Frick begins serving as the commissioner of base-ball. **3 October:** Bobby Thomson of the New York Giants hits the most famous home run in history, off Ralph Branca. His "shot heard 'round the world" in the bottom of the ninth inning of the third and deciding playoff game defeats the Brooklyn Dodgers, 5–4, and wins the pennant for the Giants.

1952 The Little League, begun in 1939, with eight teams in two leagues, now has more than 1,800 leagues in 44 states and several foreign countries. **14 June:** Warren Spahn of the Boston Braves strikes out 18 Chicago Cubs batters in an extra-inning game.

1953 The New York Yankees become the first team to win five consecutive World Series. **20 February:** The U.S. Court of Appeals rules that Organized Baseball is a sport and not a business, affirming the 25-year-old Supreme Court ruling. **18 March:** The NL's Boston Braves move to Milwaukee, the first major-league franchise shift since 1903. **18 June:** Sammy White of the Boston Red Sox ties a major-league record by scoring three runs in an inning. **3 November:** The Rules Committee restores the 1939 rule, which says a sacrifice fly is not charged as a time at bat. The committee also votes for the "no gloves on the field rule."

1954 The AL's St. Louis Browns move to Baltimore and are renamed the Baltimore Orioles. **13 April:** The newly renamed Baltimore Orioles play their first game. **31 July:** Joe Adcock of the Milwaukee Braves hits four home runs in a game.

1955 The Philadelphia Athletics move to Kansas City. **12 April:** The newly minted Kansas City Athletics play their first game. **3 October:** The Brooklyn Dodgers defeat the New York Yankees to win their first World Series after seven previous Series losses.

1956 Mickey Mantle of the New York Yankees leads the AL in batting average, home runs, and runs batted in to win the Triple Crown for batters. **8 October:** Don Larsen of the New York Yankees pitches a perfect game against the Brooklyn Dodgers in Game 5 of the World Series. **20 November:** The Rules Committee adopts a new requirement of 477 plate appearances instead of the 400 official times at bat.

1957 1 February: Club owners approve a new five-year player pension plan, effective 1 April. It offers more liberal benefits and includes all players, coaches, and trainers eligible for the 1947 plan. The owners reject the players' request to raise the minimum salary from $6,000 to $7,500.

1958 The Brooklyn Dodgers move to Los Angeles, and the New York Giants move to San Francisco. **15 April:** The Los Angeles Dodgers play the San Franciso Giants at San Francisco's Seals Stadium in the first major-league game played on the West Coast. **13 May:** Stan Musial of the St. Louis Cardinals gets his 3,000th hit.

1959 26 May: Harvey Haddix of the Pittsburgh Pirates pitches a perfect game against the Milwaukee Braves for 12 innings but loses the game in the 13th inning. **10 June:** Rocky Colavito of the Cleveland Indians hits four home runs in a game. **21 July:** Pumpsie Green makes his major-league debut, as the Boston Red Sox become the final team to use an African American player. **31 August:** Sandy Koufax of the Los Angeles Dodgers strikes out 18 San Francisco Giants batters in a nine-inning game.

1960 13 March: The Chicago White Sox unveil new road uniforms with the players' names above the number on the back. **17 June:** Ted Williams of the Boston Red Sox hits his 500th home run.

1961 The AL expands to 10 teams by adding the Los Angeles Angels and Washington Senators. (The original Washington Senators move to Minnesota and become the Minnesota Twins.) **30 April:** Willie Mays of the San Francisco Giants hits four home runs in a game. **11 August:** Warren Spahn of the Milwaukee Braves wins his 300th game. **1 October:** Roger Maris hits his 61st home run of the season to set a new major-league record and a still-standing AL record.

1962 The NL expands to 10 teams by adding the Houston Colt .45s and New York Mets. **24 April:** Sandy Koufax of the Los Angeles Dodgers strikes out 18 Chicago Cubs batters in a nine-inning game. **12 September:** Tom Cheney of the Washington Senators strikes out 21 Baltimore Orioles batters in an extra-inning game.

1963 Sandy Koufax of the Los Angeles Dodgers leads the NL in wins, earned run average, and strikeouts to win the Triple Crown for pitchers. **13 July:** Early Wynn of the Cleveland Indians wins his 300th game.

1964 21 June: Jim Bunning of the Philadelphia Phillies pitches a perfect game against the New York Mets.

1965 Sandy Koufax of the Los Angeles Dodgers leads the NL in wins, earned run average, and strikeouts to win the Triple Crown for pitchers. **12 April:** The Astrodome, in Houston, Texas, becomes the first indoor stadium used by a major-league team when the Houston Astros host the Philadelphia Phillies. **June:** The first Amateur Draft is held. The first pick is outfielder Rick Monday, chosen by the Kansas City Athletics. **9 June:** Sandy Koufax of the Los Angeles Dodgers pitches a perfect game against the Chicago Cubs. **14 June:** Jim Maloney of the Cincinnati Reds strikes out 18 New York Mets batters in an extra-inning game. **13 September:** Willie Mays of the San Francisco Giants hits his 500th home run. **2 October:** Chris Short of the Philadelphia Phillies strikes out 18 New York Mets batters in an extra-inning game. **17 November:** William "Spike" Eckert begins serving as the commissioner of baseball.

1966 The Milwaukee Braves move to Atlanta. Frank Robinson of the Baltimore Orioles leads the AL in batting average, home runs, and runs batted in to win the Triple Crown for batters. Sandy Koufax of the Los Angeles Dodgers leads the NL in wins, earned run average, and strikeouts to win the Triple Crown for pitchers.

1967 Carl Yastrzemski of the Boston Red Sox leads the AL in batting average, home runs, and runs batted in to win the Triple Crown for batters. **14 May:** Mickey Mantle of the New York Yankees hits his 500th home run. **14 July:** Eddie Mathews of the Houston Astros hits his 500th home run.

1968 8 May: Catfish Hunter of the Oakland Athletics pitches a perfect game against the Minnesota Twins. **14 July:** Hank Aaron of the Atlanta Braves hits his 500th home run. Don Wilson of the Houston Astros strikes out 18 Cincinnati Reds batters in a nine-inning game. **30 July:** Shortstop Ron Hansen of the Washington Senators executes an unassisted triple play.

1969 The AL expands to 12 teams by adding the Kansas City Royals and Seattle Pilots. The NL expands to 12 teams by adding the Montreal Expos, the first team from outside the United States, and the San Diego Padres. Both leagues split into two divisions, with each division winner playing a best-of-five Series to determine the pennant winner. **4 February:** Bowie Kuhn begins serving as commissioner of baseball. **15 September:** Steve Carlton of the St. Louis Cardinals strikes out 19 New York Mets batters in a nine-inning game. **22 September:** Willie Mays of the San Francisco Giants hits his 600th home run.

1970 The Seattle Pilots move to Milwaukee and are renamed the Milwaukee Brewers. **22 April:** Tom Seaver of the New York Mets strikes out a record 10 consecutive San Diego Padres batters and a total of 19 in a nine-inning game. **12 May:** Ernie Banks of the Chicago Cubs hits his 500th home run. **17 May:** Hank Aaron of the Atlanta Braves gets his 3,000th hit. **18 July:** Willie Mays of the San Francisco Giants gets his 3,000th hit.

1971 The first annual Caribbean Series (Serie del Caribe) is held. The series is a round-robin tournament featuring the winners from the Winter Leagues of the Dominican Republic, Mexico, Puerto Rico, and Venezuela. **27 April:** Hank Aaron of the Atlanta Braves hits his 600th home run. **10 August:** Harmon Killebrew of the Minnesota Twins hits his 500th home run. **13 September:** Frank Robinson of the Baltimore Orioles hits his 500th home run.

1972 The Washington Senators move to Texas and are renamed the Texas Rangers. Steve Carlton of the Philadelphia Phillies leads the NL in wins, earned run average, and strikeouts to win the Triple Crown for pitchers. **30 September:** Roberto Clemente of the Pittsburgh Pirates gets his 3,000th hit.

1973 6 April: The AL plays its first games using the new designated hitter rule. **21 July:** Hank Aaron of the Atlanta Braves hits his 700th home run.

1974 8 April: Hank Aaron of the Atlanta Braves hit his 715th home run off Al Downing of the Los Angeles Dodgers, moving him past Babe Ruth as the all-time home run leader. **14 June:** Nolan Ryan of the California Angels strikes out 19 Boston Red Sox batters in an extra-inning game. **12 August:** Nolan Ryan of the California Angels strikes out 19 Boston Red Sox batters in a nine-inning game. **20 August:** Nolan Ryan of the California Angels strikes out 19 Detroit Tigers batters in an extra-inning game. **24 September:** Al Kaline of the Detroit Tigers gets his 3,000th hit.

1975 The reserve clause is successfully challenged, and the era of free agency for players begins. The Committee on African American Baseball is established to honor contributions to the game by Negro League and pre–Negro League players, managers, and executives. The committee lasts two years and elects 17 individuals to the Hall of Fame. **4 May:** Bob Watson of the Houston Astros scores the major leagues' (National and American only) one millionth run. **16 September:** Rennie Stennett of the Pittsburgh Pirates gets seven hits in a nine-inning game, tying the major-league record for most hits in a game.

1976 17 April: Mike Schmidt of the Philadelphia Phillies hits four home runs in a game. **25 June:** Toby Harrah of the Texas Rangers becomes the first and only major-league shortstop to play both games of a doubleheader without an official chance. **20 July:** Hank Aaron of the Milwaukee Brewers hits his 755th and final home run. **23 July:** Sadaharu Oh of the Yomiuri Giants hits his 700th home run. **10 September:** Nolan Ryan of the California Angels strikes out 18 Chicago White Sox batters in a nine-inning game.

1977 The AL expands to 14 teams, adding the Seattle Mariners and Toronto Blue Jays, the AL's first team from Canada. **8 June:** Nolan Ryan of the California Angels strikes out 19 Toronto Blue Jays batters in an extra-inning game.

1978 5 May: Pete Rose of the Cincinnati Reds gets his 3,000th hit. **30 June:** Willie McCovey of the San Francisco Giants hits his 500th home run.

1979 17 June: Ron Guidry of the New York Yankees strikes out 18 California Angels batters in a nine-inning game. **13 August:** Lou Brock of the St. Louis Cardinals gets his 3,000th hit. **12 September:** Carl Yastrzemski of the Boston Red Sox gets his 3,000th hit.

1980 3 May: Ferguson Jenkins of the Texas Rangers defeats the Baltimore Orioles, 3–2, to join Jim Bunning, Gaylord Perry, and Cy Young as the only pitchers to win 100 games in each league. **10 September:** Bill Gullickson of the Montreal Expos strikes out 18 Chicago Cubs batters in a nine-inning game.

1981 15 May: Len Barker of the Cleveland Indians pitches a perfect game against the Toronto Blue Jays. **12 June:** A strike by major-league players begins, leading to the cancellation of 713 games. The games resume on 10 August. Because of the split season, the first-place teams from each half in each division meet in a best-of-five divisional playoff series. The four survivors then move on to the two best-of-five League Championship Series. **23 June:** The IL Pawtucket Red Sox defeat the Rochester Red Wings, 3–2, in professional baseball's longest game. The game lasts 33 innings, with the first 32 having been played on 18–19 April.

1982 6 May: Gaylord Perry of the Seattle Mariners wins his 300th game. **30 May:** Cal Ripken of the Baltimore Orioles plays the first game of his record consecutive games-played streak of 2,632.

1983 23 September: Steve Carlton of the Philadelphia Phillies wins his 300th game.

1984 13 April: Pete Rose of the Montreal Expos gets his 4,000th hit. **17 September:** Reggie Jackson of the California Angels hits his 500th home run. **1 October:** Peter Ueberroth begins serving as the commissioner of baseball.

1985 The AL and NL Championship Series move from a best-of-five format to a best-of-seven. Dwight Gooden of the New York Mets leads the NL in wins, earned run average, and strikeouts to win the Triple Crown for pitchers. **4 August:** Tom Seaver of the Chicago White Sox wins his 300th game. Rod Carew of the California Angels gets his 3,000th hit. **8 September:** Pete Rose of the Cincinnati Reds gets his 4,190th hit, breaking the record previously held by Ty Cobb. **6 October:** Phil Niekro of the New York Yankees wins his 300th game.

1986 29 April: Roger Clemens of the Boston Red Sox strikes out 20 Seattle Mariners batters in a nine-inning game. **4 June:** Barry Bonds of the Pittsburgh Pirates hits his first major-league home run. **18 June:** Don Sutton of the California Angels wins his 300th game. **6 July:** Bob Horner of the Atlanta Braves hits four home runs in a game.

1987 18 April: Mike Schmidt of the Philadelphia Phillies hits his 500th home run.

1988 6 May: Kerry Wood of the Chicago Cubs strikes out 20 Houston Astros batters in a nine-inning game. **16 September:** Tom Browning of the Cincinnati Reds pitches a perfect game against the Los Angeles Dodgers.

1989 1 April: Bart Giamatti begins serving as commissioner of baseball. **13 September:** Fay Vincent begins serving as commissioner of baseball.

1990 22 May: Andre Dawson of the Chicago Cubs receives a record-setting five intentional walks in a 16-inning game. **4 June:** Ramon Martinez of the Los Angeles Dodgers strikes out 18 Atlanta Braves batters in a nine-inning game. **11 June:** Nolan Ryan of the Texas Rangers pitches his sixth no-hitter.

17 July: The Minnesota Twins become the first and only major-league team to execute two triple plays in a game. **31 July:** Nolan Ryan of the Texas Rangers wins his 300th game.

1991 28 July: Dennis Martinez of the Montreal Expos pitches a perfect game against the Los Angeles Dodgers. **6 October:** David Cone of the New York Mets strikes out 19 Philadelphia Phillies batters in a nine-inning game.

1992 7 September: Allan "Bud" Selig begins serving as the commissioner of baseball. **9 September:** Robin Yount of the Milwaukee Brewers gets his 3,000th hit. **20 September:** Second baseman Mickey Morandini of the Philadelphia Phillies executes an unassisted triple play. **27 September:** Randy Johnson of the Seattle Mariners strikes out 18 Texas Rangers batters in a nine-inning game. **30 September:** George Brett of the Kansas City Royals gets his 3,000th hit.

1993 The NL expands to 14 teams by adding the Colorado Rockies and Florida Marlins. **7 September:** Mark Whiten of the St. Louis Cardinals hits four home runs in a game. **9 September:** The major leagues vote to divide each league into three divisions for the 1994 season and add another round of playoffs featuring a wild-card team in each league. **16 September:** Dave Winfield of the Minnesota Twins gets his 3,000th hit.

1994 Each league is restructured into an Eastern Division, a Central Division, and a Western Division. **15 February:** Ila Borders becomes the first woman to pitch in a college game. Appearing for Southern California College of Costa Mesa, she five-hits Claremont-Mudd-Scripps, 12–1. **8 July:** Shortstop John Valentin of the Boston Red Sox executes an unassisted triple play. **28 July:** Kenny Rogers of the Texas Rangers pitches a perfect game against the California Angels. **12 August:** Major-league players go out on strike, prematurely ending the season. The dispute with owners centers on a salary cap, salary arbitration, free agency, and minimum salaries.

1995 With both leagues now split into three divisions, a wild card is added to the playoff scenario. **26 April:** With the strike settled, the season opens, with the schedule reduced to 144 games. **30 June:** Eddie Murray of the Cleveland Indians gets his 3,000th hit.

1996 6 September: Eddie Murray of the Baltimore Orioles hits his 500th home run. **16 September:** Paul Molitor of the Minnesota Twins gets his 3,000th hit. **18 September:** Roger Clemens of the Boston Red Sox strikes out 20 Detroit Tigers batters in a nine-inning game.

1997 Interleague play begins. Roger Clemens of the Toronto Blue Jays leads the AL in wins, earned run average, and strikeouts to win the Triple Crown for pitchers. **24 June:** Randy Johnson of the Seattle Mariners strikes out 19

Oakland Athletics batters in a nine-inning game. **8 August:** Randy Johnson of the Seattle Mariners strikes out 19 Chicago White Sox batters in a nine-inning game.

1998 The AL adds the Tampa Bay Devil Rays; however, the move of the Milwaukee Brewers from the AL to the NL keeps the total number of AL clubs at 14. In addition to adding the Milwaukee Brewers, the NL adds the Arizona Diamondbacks, raising the total number of NL clubs to 16. Mark McGwire of the St. Louis Cardinals hits 70 home runs for the season, to set a new major-league record. Roger Clemens of the Toronto Blue Jays leads the AL in wins, earned run average, and strikeouts to win the Triple Crown for pitchers. **17 May:** David Wells of the New York Yankees pitches a perfect game against the Montreal Expos. **25 August:** Roger Clemens of the Toronto Blue Jays strikes out 18 Kansas City Royals batters in a nine-inning game.

1999 The office of the NL and AL presidents are abolished after the conclusion of the season. Pedro Martinez of the Boston Red Sox leads the AL in wins, earned run average, and strikeouts to win the Triple Crown for pitchers. **23 April:** Fernando Tatis of the St. Louis Cardinals becomes the first and only major leaguer to hit two grand slams in the same inning. **18 July:** David Cone of the New York Yankees pitches a perfect game against the Montreal Expos. **5 August:** Mark McGwire of the St. Louis Cardinals hits his 500th home run. **6 August:** Tony Gwynn of the San Diego Padres gets his 3,000th hit. **7 August:** Wade Boggs of the Tampa Bay Devil Rays gets his 3,000th hit.

2000 15 April: Cal Ripken of the Baltimore Orioles gets his 3,000th hit. **29 May:** Second baseman Randy Velarde of the Oakland Athletics executes an unassisted triple play.

2001 17 April: Barry Bonds of the San Francisco Giants hits his 500th home run. Bonds finishes the season with 73 home runs to set a new major-league record. **8 May:** Randy Johnson of the Arizona Diamondbacks strikes out 20 Cincinnati Reds batters in an extra-inning game. **7 October:** Rickey Henderson of the San Diego Padres gets his 3,000th hit.

2002 Randy Johnson of the Arizona Diamondbacks leads the NL in wins, earned run average, and strikeouts to win the Triple Crown for pitchers. **2 May:** Mike Cameron of the Seattle Mariners hits four home runs in a game. **23 May:** Shawn Green of the Los Angeles Dodgers hits four home runs in a game and sets a major-league record, with 19 total bases. **8 August:** Barry Bonds of the San Francisco Giants hits his 600th home run.

2003 4 April: Sammy Sosa of the Chicago Cubs hits his 500th home run. **11 May:** Rafael Palmeiro of the Texas Rangers hits his 500th home run. **13 June:** Roger Clemens of the New York Yankees wins his 300th game. **29**

July: Bill Mueller of the Boston Red Sox becomes the first and only major leaguer to hit two grand slams in a game, one right-handed and one left-handed. **10 August:** Shortstop Rafael Furcal of the Atlanta Braves executes an unassisted triple play. **25 September:** Carlos Delgado of the Toronto Blue Jays hits four home runs in a game.

2004 16 May: Ben Sheets of the Milwaukee Brewers strikes out 18 Atlanta Braves batters in a nine-inning game. **18 May:** Randy Johnson of the Arizona Diamondbacks pitches a perfect game against the Atlanta Braves. **4 June:** Forty-five-year-old Julio Franco of the Atlanta Braves becomes the oldest major-league player to hit a grand slam. **20 June:** Ken Griffey Jr. of the Cincinnati Reds hits his 500th home run. **7 August:** Greg Maddux of the Chicago Cubs wins his 300th game. **17 September:** Barry Bonds of the San Francisco Giants hits his 700th home run.

2005 The Montreal Expos move to Washington, D.C., and are renamed the Washington Nationals. **2 March:** Jackie Robinson is posthumously awarded a Congressional Gold Medal, more than half a century after breaking baseball's color barrier. **15 July:** Rafael Palmeiro of the Baltimore Orioles gets his 3,000th hit.

2006 Johan Santana of the Minnesota Twins leads the AL in wins, earned run average, and strikeouts to win the Triple Crown for pitchers. **17 February:** A committee of 12 baseball historians elects 17 candidates to the National Baseball Hall of Fame. The electees include seven Negro Leagues players, five pre–Negro leagues players, four Negro Leagues executives, and one pre–Negro Leagues executive. Effa Manley, one of the Negro Leagues executives, becomes the first woman elected to the Baseball Hall of Fame.

2007 Jake Peavy of the San Diego Padres leads the NL in wins, earned run average, and strikeouts to win the Triple Crown for pitchers. **29 April:** Shortstop Troy Tulowitzki of the Colorado Rockies executes an unassisted triple play. **20 June:** Sammy Sosa of the Texas Rangers hits his 600th home run. **28 June:** Frank Thomas of the Toronto Blue Jays hits his 500th home run. Craig Biggio of the Houston Astros gets his 3,000th hit. **4 August:** Alex Rodriguez of the New York Yankees hits his 500th home run. **5 August:** Tom Glavine of the New York Mets wins his 300th game. **7 August:** Barry Bonds of the San Francisco Giants hit his 756th home run off Mike Bacsik of the Washington Nationals, moving him past Hank Aaron as the all-time home run leader. **5 September:** Barry Bonds hits his 762nd and final home run. **16 September:** Jim Thome of the Chicago White Sox hits his 500th home run.

2008 12 May: Second baseman Asdrubal Cabrera of the Cleveland Indians executes an unassisted triple play. **31 May:** Manny Ramirez of the Boston Red Sox hits his 500th home run. **9 June:** Ken Griffey Jr. of the Cincinnati Reds hits his 600th home run.

2009 17 April: Gary Sheffield of the New York Mets hits his 500th home run. **4 June:** Randy Johnson of the San Francisco Giants wins his 300th game. **23 July:** Mark Buehrle of the Chicago White Sox pitches a perfect game against the Tampa Bay Rays. **23 August:** Second baseman Eric Bruntlett of the Philadelphia Phillies executes an unassisted triple play.

2010 9 May: Dallas Braden of the Oakland Athletics pitches a perfect game against the Tampa Bay Rays. **29 May:** Roy Halladay of the Philadelphia Phillies pitches a perfect game against the Florida Marlins. **4 August:** Alex Rodriguez of the New York Yankees hits his 600th home run.

2011 Clayton Kershaw of the Los Angeles Dodgers leads the NL in wins, earned run average, and strikeouts to win the Triple Crown for pitchers. Justin Verlander of the Detroit Tigers leads the AL in wins, earned run average, and strikeouts to win the Triple Crown for pitchers. **9 July:** Derek Jeter of the New York Yankees gets his 3,000th hit. **15 August:** Jim Thome of the Minnesota Twins hits his 600th home run.

2012 Major League Baseball's new postseason format will feature the two Wild Card teams in the American League and National League playing in a single-elimination game with each winner advancing to compete with the three division champions from its League in the Division Series. Miguel Cabrera of the Detroit Tigers leads the AL in batting average, home runs, and runs batted in to win the Triple Crown for batters. **17 April:** Forty-nine-year-old Jamie Moyer of the Colorado Rockies defeats the San Diego Padres to become the oldest pitcher to win a major league game. **21 April:** Philip Humber of the Chicago White Sox pitches a perfect game against the Seattle Mariners. **8 May:** Josh Hamilton of the Texas Rangers hits four home runs in a game and sets the American League record with 18 total bases. **13 June:** Matt Cain of the San Francisco Giants pitches a perfect game against the Houston Astros. **15 August:** Felix Hernandez of the Seattle Mariners pitches a perfect game against the Tampa Bay Rays. **27 September:** Doug Fister of the Detroit Tigers sets an American League record by striking out nine consecutive Kansas City Royals batters. **3 October:** The Houston Astros play their final game as a National League franchise. **5 October:** In the first-ever wild card "play-in" games, the St. Louis Cardinals defeat the Atlanta Braves in the National League, and the Baltimore Orioles defeat the Texas Rangers in the American League."

Introduction

Like no other sport, baseball "hooks you" when you are young and then continues to hold you throughout your life. Attendance at major-league games in 2012 topped the 74.8 million mark, while millions more attended minor-league and non-professional games, watched on television, or listened on radio. The rise in recent years of social media, fantasy baseball, and new analytic tools developed to judge players' value has greatly increased fan interest. So, too, have the expanded playoffs in the major leagues, making more teams in each league eligible for the postseason. As John Thorn, the official historian of Major League Baseball, wrote, "We have a peculiar country in which we do not have a national creed, we do not have a king, we have no national set of beliefs. Baseball became a secular religion."

BASEBALL'S BEGINNINGS

Baseball is unlike basketball, whose founding can be traced directly to one man, James Naismith. The origins of the game we know today are clouded by myths and traceable to many sources. Historians have repeatedly shown that the once-popular theory that baseball was invented by Abner Doubleday in Cooperstown, New York, in 1839, is just a nationalistic fable.

In fact, most historians now accept the premise that the game evolved through the years, in many increments and in many places. They contend that baseball directly evolved from such English games as rounders and cricket and that it has even earlier roots in bat and ball games stretching as far back as 2500 B.C. in Egypt. They have discovered a form of baseball played in England in the late 1700s, and the two-base game of wicket, an early off-shoot of cricket, in New England in the early 1800s. Cricket, rounders, one o'cat, town ball, and other nascent forms of baseball had rules for batting, pitching, fielding, base running, and scoring that slowly evolved into the "New York Game," a more recognizable form of baseball played in the mid-19th century in New York City, Brooklyn, and nearby areas. The New York game eventually beat out the "Massachusetts Game," another form of early baseball that featured no foul territory and between seven and 14 fielders.

Rather than one inventor, like Naismith with basketball, we now recognize several men who played major roles in advancing the game of baseball toward its modern version. Among the most prominent in the years before and after America's Civil War are Alexander Cartwright, Henry Chadwick, Daniel "Doc" Adams, William Wheaton, and Louis Wadsworth.

Cartwright is credited with developing many rules of the modern game in New York City in the 1840s, and with helping to form the Knickerbocker Base Ball Club of New York, baseball's first organized club. Chadwick was a journalist who perfected the box score, introduced the scoring system to baseball, and edited the earliest baseball guides. Adams, a Knickerbockers player, was elected president of the first Base Ball Convention in 1857. He also headed the Committee on Rules and Regulations that year, which instituted the following rules: nine equal innings for a full game, five equal innings for a complete game, a 90-foot distance between the four bases, and nine men to comprise a team. Wheaton was one of baseball's first umpires and is the likely author of the first standardized rules of the game. Wadsworth is credited with establishing the number of players per side at nine and setting nine as the number of innings required to complete a game.

BASIC RULES OF BASEBALL

The rules of baseball continue to have tweaks and adjustments, but the basic rules, at almost every level, are that it is a game between two teams of nine players each, under the jurisdiction of one or more umpires. A team wins by scoring more runs than its opponent. The playing field is divided into three main sections: The infield contains four bases: first base, second base, third base, and home plate. The bases are 90 feet apart and form a square. The outfield is the grassed area beyond the infield grass line between the foul lines and bounded by a wall or fence. Foul territory is the entire area outside the foul lines. The pitcher's mound is located in the center of the infield. Near the center of the mound is the pitching rubber, a rubber slab positioned 60 feet, 6 inches from home plate. The pitcher must have one foot on the rubber at the start of every pitch to a batter, but the pitcher may leave the mound area once the ball is released.

Professional and college baseball games are played in nine-inning segments in which each team gets a turn at bat and tries to score runs. The teams switch every time the defending team gets three players of the batting team out. The winner is the team with the most runs after nine innings. If the home team is ahead after the top of the ninth, play does not continue into the bottom half. In the case of a tie, additional innings are played until one team comes out ahead at the end of an inning. If the home team takes the lead anytime during the bottom of the ninth or of any inning thereafter, play stops and the home team is declared the winner.

The basic contest is always between the pitcher for the fielding team and a batter. The pitcher throws the ball toward home plate, where the catcher for the fielding team waits to receive it. Behind the catcher stands the home plate umpire. The batter stands in one of the batter's boxes and tries to hit the ball with a bat. The catcher's job is to receive any pitches that the batter does not hit. Each pitch begins a new play, which might consist of nothing more than the pitch itself.

Each half inning, the goal of the defending team is to get three members of the other team out. There are many ways to get batters and base runners out; some of the most common are catching a batted ball in the air, tag outs, force outs, and strikeouts. After the fielding team has put out three players from the opposing team, that half of the inning is over and the team in the field and the team at bat switch places; there is no upper limit to the number that may bat in rotation before three outs are recorded. A complete inning consists of each opposing side having a turn (three outs) on offense.

The goal of the team at bat is to score more runs than the opposition; a player may do so only by batting, then becoming a base runner, touching all the bases in order (via one or more plays), and finally touching home plate. To that end, the goal of each batter is to enable base runners to score or to become a base runner himself. The batter attempts to hit the ball into fair territory—between the baselines—in such a way that the defending players cannot get them or the base runners out. In general, the pitcher attempts to prevent this by pitching the ball in such a way that the batter cannot hit it cleanly, or, ideally, at all. A base runner who has successfully touched home plate without being tagged out after touching all previous bases in order scores a run. In an enclosed field, a fair ball hit over the fence on the fly is normally an automatic home run, which entitles the batter and all runners to touch all the bases and score.

The goal of the defensive team, the one in the field, is to prevent the base runners from scoring. There are nine defensive positions, but only two have a mandatory location (pitcher and catcher). The location of the other seven fielders is not specified by the rules, except that at the moment the pitch is delivered, they must be positioned in fair territory and not in the space between the pitcher and catcher. The nine positions (with the number score-keepers use) are as follows: pitcher (1), catcher (2), first baseman (3), second baseman (4), third baseman (5), shortstop (6), left fielder (7), center fielder (8), and right fielder (9).

THE EVOLUTION AND GROWTH OF ORGANIZED BASEBALL IN THE UNITED STATES

At a meeting in New York City, in March 1857, a group of amateur teams, primarily from the Northeastern and Midwestern United States, formed the National Association of Base Ball Players. By the spring of 1859, its membership had grown to 50 teams, including the Brooklyn Atlantics, Brooklyn Eckfords, Cincinnati Red Stockings, and New York Mutuals. In 1869, the association began allowing professional members, and, the Red Stockings, whose record was 57–0 that season, are generally recognized as the first all-professional team; however, the professionalism of some clubs eventually led to the demise of the association. In 1871, the National Association of Base Ball Players was replaced by the National Association of Professional Base Ball Players (NAPBBP).

More commonly known as the National Association, the NAPBBP was baseball's first professional league. Nine teams participated in the National Association's first season, including Boston, Chicago, Cleveland, Fort Wayne (Indiana), New York, Philadelphia, Rockford (Illinois), Troy (New York), and Washington. Many more teams moved in and out of the league during the next four seasons, some playing as few as six games. The National Association's lack of franchise stability and a central authority, severe financial problems, and the influence of gamblers led to its demise after the 1875 season. While most historians recognize the association as baseball's first major league, others do not, citing the lack of franchise stability and uneven schedules.

Those who do not recognize the National Association point to the National League (NL) as baseball's first true major league. Spearheaded by William Hulbert, owner of the National Association's Chicago White Stockings, the National League, officially the National League of Professional Baseball Clubs, was formed in 1876 and has been in continuous existence ever since. The league's charter members were Boston, Chicago, Cincinnati, Hartford (Connecticut), Louisville, New York, Philadelphia, and St. Louis. By 2012, the NL consisted of 16 teams in three divisions: Atlanta, Arizona, Chicago, Cincinnati, Colorado, Houston (scheduled to move to the American League [AL] in 2013), Los Angeles, Miami, Milwaukee, New York, Philadelphia, Pittsburgh, St. Louis, San Diego, San Francisco, and Washington.

Three leagues formed in the late 19th century to challenge the NL's monopoly. Two, the Union Association (1884) and the Players' League (1890) lasted just one season, while the American Association (AA) was a more formidable challenger, existing for the 10 seasons from 1882 through 1891. In seven of those 10 seasons, the winners of the AA and NL pennants participated in an early version of the modern World Series.

Only the AL was successful in challenging the NL. The league, officially the American League of Professional Baseball Clubs, declared itself a major league in 1901, establishing teams in Baltimore, Boston, Chicago, Cleveland, Detroit, Milwaukee, Philadelphia, and Washington. It fought the resistance of the NL by signing some of the NL's biggest stars, causing the older league to sign a peace agreement in 1903. That same year, the winners of the AL and NL pennants began participating in the World Series, a postseason series of games to determine the champions of Major League Baseball. By 2012, the AL consisted of 14 teams in three divisions: Baltimore, Boston, Chicago, Cleveland, Detroit, Kansas City, Los Angeles, Minnesota, New York, Oakland, Seattle, Tampa, Texas, and Toronto. Houston is scheduled to move to the AL in 2013, giving each league 15 teams.

Through the years, the game has changed both on and off the field, but the basic two-league structure remains intact. During the first 20 years of the 20th century, most games were low scoring, relying more on bunts, stolen bases, and strategy than power hitting and home runs. That all changed in 1920, when Babe Ruth was sold from the Boston Red Sox to the New York Yankees. Ruth's power hitting and previously unimagined home run totals changed the way the game was played. The new emphasis on home runs was extremely popular with the fans. Attendance increased, and the seating capacities of ballparks were expanded.

The power game remained dominant for the next quarter century, although all the skills of baseball were in relatively short supply when so many of the stars of the game went off to serve in World War II. In 1947, the Brooklyn Dodgers brought Jackie Robinson to the major leagues, breaking the long unwritten ban on African American players. Many great black stars followed, bringing speed back to the game, along with a new source of power hitters. Pitching thoroughly dominated the game in the 1960s and 1970s, leading the AL to introduce the designated hitter in 1973.

The geographic setting of the game, unchanged since 1903, began to change in the 1950s. The Boston Braves moved to Milwaukee in 1953, the St. Louis Browns moved to Baltimore in 1954, and the Philadelphia Athletics moved to Kansas City in 1955. The 1958 moves of the Brooklyn Dodgers to Los Angeles and the New York Giants to San Francisco brought Major League Baseball to the West Coast and made the game truly national. The eight-team structure of the two leagues began changing for the AL in 1961 and the NL in 1962, and each league will have 15 teams by 2013.

With the expansion to 12 teams in each league in 1969, each league split into two divisions, with the winner of the Series between the two champions claiming that league's pennant. Further expansion led to three divisions and a playoff system first involving one wild card team, and now two wild cards. Because these changes have proven popular with the fans, it is safe to assume that some kind of tinkering will continue. The revelations of several star players using performance enhancing drugs marred their accomplishments of the late 1990s and early 2000s and hurt the game, but just as the fans came back after the Black Sox scandal of 1919 and the players strike that canceled the 1994 World Series, they have come back again. One reason is that a fan from 100 years ago would have little trouble recognizing the game of today, a fact that helps account for the special bond baseball fans have had across the generations.

THE BUSINESS OF BASEBALL

When the National Association, baseball's first professional league, was founded in 1871, the league charged a $10 franchise fee. By 1998, the franchise fee for Tampa Bay and Arizona to join the major leagues had risen to $130 million. Baseball is big business and has been for many years. The most recent reminder was the May 2012 sale of the Los Angeles Dodgers for $2 billion.

When professional baseball began, most teams were owned by one individual, a family, or a partnership, but never a corporation. The owner was often someone with a financial interest in a related business, such as a brewery. Today, most are owned by conglomerates, major corporations, or a wealthy individual. This transition began to occur when the tax benefits of owning a baseball team became significant enough that they were worth more to a wealthy conglomerate than a family owner.

When Shibe Park, the home of the Philadelphia Athletics, opened in 1909, it was baseball's first steel-and-concrete stadium. Similarly built parks soon followed in Boston, Chicago, Detroit, and Brooklyn, opening a new era of bigger ballparks. These parks were built by their owners, unlike today, when many of the new parks are fully or partially financed by local governments. They generate a great source of revenue to the club at the expense of the taxpayer.

The commercial aspect of baseball has always been with us, dating back to the advertisements that adorned outfield walls in the 19th century. Now, not only do the walls have ads, the stadiums themselves are advertisements for the companies who paid for the "naming rights." Petco Park in San Diego, Minute Maid Park in Houston, Comerica Park in Detroit, and PNC Park in Pittsburgh are only a few of the corporate names that adorn major-league parks. For the players, the endorsement of products has always served as a source of additional income.

From the beginning, major league owners have banded together to limit competition from new leagues and hold down players' salaries. The reserve clause bound a player to a single team, with no freedom to change teams unless he was given his unconditional release or traded. The clause was successfully challenged in 1975, ending more than 80 years of the reserve system thereby allowing players to become free agents after their contract with a team has expired. This has caused salaries to rise astronomically. As a result, there has been an extremely steep rise in ticket prices. The average ticket price for such teams as the Boston Red Sox, New York Yankees, Philadelphia Phillies, and Chicago Cubs is more than $100, with many premium and club suite locations costing much more. Nevertheless, most of a team's revenue comes from the sale of radio and television rights to broadcast their games.

The first team of baseball players to be openly paid was the 1869 Cincinnati Red Stockings. By 1877, the second year of the NL, the league's highest-paid player was pitcher Joe Borden of the Boston Red Stockings, at $2,000. It took another 26 years before a player reached a salary of five figures, as Willie Keeler of the New York Highlanders was paid $10,000 for the 1903 season. Babe Ruth earned $20,000 in his first year with the Yankees, 1920, eventually rising to a high of $80,000 in 1930.

The first player to earn $100,000 for a season was Hank Greenberg of the 1947 Pirates. In the next few seasons, he was joined in the $100,000-plus category by Joe DiMaggio and Ted Williams. The advent of free agency allowed Reggie Jackson to earn close to $600,000 for the 1977 Yankees. In 1980, Nolan Ryan was the first player to sign a million-dollar contract, and the number of millionaire players has steadily increased. After the 2007 season, the Yankees signed Alex Rodriguez to a 10-year contract worth $275 million. Salaries for all other players have also shown a significant rise in recent decades. The minimum salary, which was $12,000 in 1970, was $480,000 in 2012. The average salary climbed from $29,300 in 1970 to more than $3,000,000 in 2012.

Fantasy baseball, sometimes played for fun, but mostly as a form of gambling, is now played by millions of fans, competing with others while testing their skills at picking players for their teams. A more serious form of gambling on baseball, whether legal, in places like Las Vegas, or illegal, has always been a part of the game. In the years before World War I, open betting on games or specific outcomes was common at the ballparks, as well as at betting parlors. Professional gamblers soon began attempting to bribe players to lose games against teams that they had bet on to win. The fan's suspicions about the "throwing of games" reached a climax when charges were made that eight Chicago White Sox players deliberately lost the 1919 World Series to the Cincinnati Reds. Newly installed baseball commissioner Kenesaw Landis banned the eight men, along with several others under suspicion, from the game. The bribing of players has rarely been a problem since.

BEYOND THE MAJOR LEAGUES

Boys and, increasingly, girls begin playing some form of baseball as young as six years old. They play it casually in backyards or city streets, or more formally in T-ball leagues. They advance to well-organized Little Leagues, and, for those who are good enough, to Babe Ruth leagues, American Legion leagues, high schools, and colleges.

College baseball is played under the auspices of the National Collegiate Athletic Association (NCAA) or the National Association of Intercollegiate Athletics (NAIA). The final rounds of the NCAA tournaments are known as the College World Series, one for each of the three levels of competition sanctioned by the NCAA. The playoff bracket for Division I consists of 64 teams, with four teams playing at each of 16 regional sites. The 16 winners advance to the Super Regionals at eight sites. The eight winners then advance to the College World Series. Two finalists play a best-of-three series to determine the Division I national champion. The Division II College World Series has been played since 1968. The Division III College World Series has been played since 1976.

The best college players, high school players, or other amateurs from the United States and other nations are selected by the 30 major-league teams. Those who choose to sign professional contracts almost always begin with one of that team's minor-league affiliates. The minor leagues are professional leagues below the level of the major leagues. Class AAA is the highest minor-league level. Class AAA leagues are the International League, Pacific Coast League, and Mexican League (Liga Mexicana de Beisbol). Unlike all other minor-league teams, Mexican League teams are not affiliated with specific major-league teams.

Below Class AAA leagues, in descending order of readiness for the major leagues, are Class AA leagues, which include the Eastern League, Southern League, and Texas League; Class A-Advanced leagues, which include the California League, Carolina League, and Florida State League; Class A leagues, which include the Midwest League and South Atlantic League; Class A-Short Season leagues, which include the New York–Penn League and Northwest League; and Rookie leagues, which include the Appalachian League, Arizona League, Dominican Summer League, Gulf Coast League, Pioneer League, and Venezuelan Summer League.

BASEBALL AROUND THE WORLD

The popularity of baseball, long known as America's national pastime, has now spread to countries in all parts of the world. At the start of the 2012 season, major-league rosters included players from 18 different nations on five continents. In all of these countries, and others, the game is played by both males and females at all age levels, beginning in childhood and, in some cases, continuing through one's senior years. In the United States, and increasingly in other countries, almost every community has some variation of a sandlot league or Little League for boys and girls, and almost every high school and college fields a men's team and, in many cases, a women's team. Softball, a close variant of baseball, is also played by millions of males and females of all ages.

There are several international baseball tournaments held on a regularly scheduled basis, some annually, and others at specific intervals. Among the most notable of these competitions is the Baseball World Cup, an international tournament first held in 1938, in which national teams from around the world compete. There have been 39 Baseball World Cups to date, and Cuba has won the tournament the most times. The most recent Baseball World Cup, won by the Netherlands, was held in Panama in 2011.

The Caribbean Series (Serie del Caribe) is a round-robin tournament that, since 1971, has featured the winners from the winter leagues of the Dominican Republic, Mexico, Puerto Rico, and Venezuela. The tournament is played every year, usually in February, with each country taking turns as host. The 2013 Caribbean Series is scheduled to be played in Hermosillo, Mexico.

The European Baseball Championship is the main championship tournament between national baseball teams in Europe. The tournament is held every other year, in even-numbered years. The most recent European Baseball Championship was held from 7 September to 16 September 2012, with the Netherlands acting as the host nation.

The World Baseball Classic is an international baseball tournament sanctioned by the International Baseball Federation and created by Major League Baseball and other professional baseball leagues and their players' associations around the world. The tournament, begun in 2006 and held every three years, is the first of its kind to allow national baseball teams to use professional players from the major leagues.

Baseball at the Summer Olympics had its unofficial debut at the 1904 Summer Games, and it has a long history as an exhibition/demonstration sport. The International Olympic Committee (IOC) granted the sport medal status at the 1992 games, but at the IOC meeting in July 2005, baseball and softball were voted out of the 2012 Summer Olympics in London, England.

In April 2011, the International Baseball Federation and the International Softball Federation announced that they were preparing a joint proposal to revive play of both sports at the 2020 Summer Olympics.

The leading baseball-playing nations aside from the United States include Canada, where Canadians have been playing baseball almost as long as Americans, with the first game recorded in 1838. Canada has been the site of more than 75 minor-league teams through the years; however, the major leagues did not include a Canadian team until 1969, when the Montreal Expos joined the NL. The first AL team based in Canada was the Toronto Blue Jays, who joined the league in 1977. In 1990, Canada hosted the Baseball World Cup.

The largest growth in baseball-playing nations has occurred in Latin America and Asia. Although baseball has been played in Cuba since the 1860s, the government abolished all professional sports on the island after Fidel Castro seized power in the 1960s. Since then, Cuban amateur teams have continued their long domination of international competition, including the Baseball World Cup, Intercontinental Cup, Pan-American Games, Central American and Caribbean Games, and World Baseball Challenge.

Professional baseball has been played in the Dominican Republic since the early 1920s. Currently, the Dominican league consists of six teams. The league champion advances to the Caribbean Series to play against the champions of Mexico, Venezuela, and Puerto Rico. The Leones de Escogido team, representing the Dominican Republic, was the 2012 winner of the Caribbean Series.

The people of Mexico have played baseball since the late 19th century. The professional game began with the formation of the Mexican League in 1925. A member of the International Baseball Federation, Mexico competes in the Baseball World Cup and also the Caribbean Games, which will be played in Hermosillo, Mexico, in 2013.

Baseball, Nicaragua's national game, has been played in that country since the 19th century. The Nicaraguan Professional Baseball League (La Liga Nicaragüense de Beisbol Profesional) has four teams. Nicaragua's team competes in the Baseball World Cup, Pan-American Games, Central American Games, Central American and Caribbean Games, and World Baseball Classic.

Panamanians have been playing baseball since the late 19th century. In 1945, the Professional Baseball League of Panama was organized, and Panama became one of the four key national groups that formed the Caribbean Series. The Panama national baseball team also competes in the Baseball World Cup and World Baseball Classic.

The first organized baseball game in Puerto Rico was played in January 1898. The Puerto Rico Baseball League consists of four teams, with the winner advancing to the Caribbean Series to play against the champions of the Dominican Republic, Mexico, and Venezuela.

The Venezuelan Professional Baseball League (Liga Venezolana de Béisbol Profesional) began play in 1946. The champion of the eight-team league moves on to the Caribbean Series to face the champions of the baseball leagues of the Dominican Republic, Puerto Rico, and Mexico. Venezuela has won the Caribbean Series seven times

Japan and South Korea are symbolic of the popularity of baseball in Asia. Japanese baseball dates to the mid-1870s. Nippon Professional Baseball, founded in the mid-1930s, currently consists of two six-team leagues: the Central League and Pacific League. Japan has won the World Baseball Classic both times the tournament has been played, defeating Cuba in 2006 and South Korea in 2009.

The Korea Baseball Association is the governing body for the amateur baseball competitions. The Korea Baseball Organization is the governing body for the professional leagues of baseball in South Korea. The Korea Baseball Organization is a member of the International Baseball Federation and is responsible for the national baseball team for the World Baseball Classic.

Of the European countries, the Netherlands, more specifically Holland, has been the most dominant team. The playing of baseball began there in 1911, with the first professional league starting in 1922. The Netherlands National Baseball Team, which is consistently ranked in the top 10 of the International Baseball Federation's world rankings, has won the European Baseball Championship 20 times. In the most recent Baseball World Cup, held in 2011, the Netherlands won the championship, becoming the first European team to win since 1938.

A

AARON, HENRY LOUIS "HANK". B. 5 February 1934, Mobile, Alabama. Hank Aaron was 17 years old when he began playing baseball professionally for the Indianapolis Clowns of the **Negro National League**. In 1952, he was signed by the **Boston Braves** of the **National League (NL)**. After two years as a minor-league **shortstop**, he joined the **Milwaukee Braves** (relocated from Boston in 1953) as an **outfielder**. The 6-foot, 180-pound Aaron played for the Braves in Milwaukee from 1954 through 1965 and for the **Atlanta Braves** from 1966 through 1974. He finished his career with the 1975–1976 **Milwaukee Brewers** of the **American League**.

Aaron, who played in 24 **All-Star Games**, was the NL's **Most Valuable Player** in 1957 and the **Major League Player of the Year** in 1956 and 1963. He played in two **World Series**, both against the **New York Yankees**, in 1957 and 1958, hitting a combined .364 in 14 games. Aaron set many records during his 23 years as a major leaguer, including the record for most **home runs** in a career (755), later broken by **Barry Bonds**. His 715th home run, which moved him past **Babe Ruth** as the all-time leader, came off Al Downing of the **Los Angeles Dodgers** on 8 April 1974, at Atlanta's **Fulton County Stadium**. He remains the career home-run leader among right-handed **batters**.

Aaron led the NL in home runs**, slugging percentage**, and **runs batted in (RBI)** four times, and he twice led in **batting average** and **hits**. He had a lifetime batting average of .305 and a slugging percentage of .555, and he continues to rank at or near the top in numerous offensive categories. In addition to ranking second in home runs, he is first in RBI (2,297), **extra-base hits** (1,477), and **total bases** (6,856); second in **at-bats** (12,364); third in hits (3,771) and **games played** (3,298); tied for fourth in **runs** (2,174); and tenth in **doubles** (624). In 1982, he was elected by the **Baseball Writers' Association of America** to the **National Baseball Hall of Fame**. In 2002, Aaron was honored with the Presidential Medal of Freedom. After his playing days were over, he served the Atlanta Braves as director of player development and senior vice president and assistant to the president.

ADAMS, DANIEL LUCIUS "DOC". B. 1 November 1814, Mount Vernon, New Hampshire. D. 3 January 1899, New Haven, Connecticut. Doc Adams was a medical doctor who began playing baseball in 1839, with a group called the New York Base Ball Club. That club evolved into the **Knickerbocker Base Ball Club**, with Adams elected president in 1846. Two years later, he headed the Committee to Revise the Constitution and By-Laws, with **Alexander Cartwright** serving under him.

Adams has been credited with "inventing" the **shortstop** position in 1849 or 1850. The position evolved because the baseballs used were too light to be thrown far. A nonbase-tending player was needed to retrieve balls from the **outfielders** and return them to the **pitcher**. Under Adams's presidency (1846–1862), the Knickerbocker Club became the model upon which all early clubs were organized.

Adams was elected president of the first Base Ball Convention in 1857. He also headed the Committee on Rules and Regulations that year, which instituted the following rules: nine equal **innings** for a full game, five equal innings for a complete game, a 30-yard distance between the four **bases**, a pitching distance of 45 feet, and nine men to comprise a team. Adams was later elected chairman of the Committee on Rules and Regulations during the March 1858 Base Ball Convention, during which the **National Association of Base Ball Players** was formed.

AFRICAN AMERICANS IN BASEBALL. Fleetwood Walker and his brother, Welday Walker, who played for the **Toledo Blue Stockings** of the **American Association** in 1884, have long been thought to be the first African Americans to play in the **major leagues**. (Recent research by the **Society for American Baseball Research** suggests that William Edward White, who played in one game for the 1879 **Providence Grays** of the **National League**, may actually have been the first.) After the 1884 season, a faction of other owners and players demanded that the Walker brothers be removed from the league. While there was no written policy at the highest level of baseball organization barring black players, a tacit understanding among the leagues and various clubs developed over the years that kept baseball all-white. After the Walkers, no African Americans played major league baseball again until **Jackie Robinson** joined the **Brooklyn Dodgers** in 1947.

In the interim, African Americans formed their own leagues, which existed roughly from 1885 until the 1950s, when the integration of the major leagues made them much less attractive to black fans. There were numerous leagues formed during these years, but most were poorly administered. Three leagues that did have success and produced many outstanding players were the **Eastern Colored League**, **Negro American League**, and **Negro National League**.

Among the more prominent teams in the Negro leagues were the Bacharach Giants, **Baltimore Elite Giants**, Birmingham Black Barons, **Chicago American Giants**, Cleveland Buckeyes, Hilldale Daisies, **Homestead Grays**, the Indianapolis Clowns, **Kansas City Monarchs**, Memphis Red Sox, **New York Cubans, Newark Eagles, Philadelphia Stars, Pittsburgh Crawfords**, and **St. Louis Stars**.

Segregated baseball produced many great African American players whose ability would have made them stars in the major leagues had they been given the opportunity. Foremost among them were **Cool Papa Bell, Oscar Charleston, Ray Dandridge, Rube Foster, Josh Gibson, Judy Johnson, Buck Leonard, John Henry Lloyd, Biz Mackey, Satchel Paige, Bullet Rogan, Hilton Smith, Turkey Stearnes, Mule Suttles, Willie Wells**, and **Joe Williams**.

Along with Brooklyn, two other major-league teams broke the color line in 1947. The **Cleveland Indians** signed **Larry Doby** as the first African American to play in the **American League**, and, later in the year, Hank Thompson played for the **St. Louis Browns**. The last of the 16 teams to integrate were the **New York Yankees** (Elston Howard in 1955), the **Philadelphia Phillies** (John Kennedy in 1957), the **Detroit Tigers** (Ossie Virgil in 1958), and the **Boston Red Sox** (Pumpsie Green in 1959).

Jackie Robinson and Larry Doby paved the way for many of the African American stars that have been a part of baseball ever since. Among the greatest have been **Hank Aaron, Ernie Banks, Barry Bonds, Roy Campanella, Andre Dawson, Bob Gibson, Ken Griffey Jr., Tony Gwynn, Rickey Henderson, Reggie Jackson, Derek Jeter, Barry Larkin, Willie Mays, Willie McCovey, Joe Morgan, Eddie Murray, Kirby Puckett, Frank Robinson, Ozzie Smith, Frank Thomas**, and **Billy Williams**.

Frank Robinson, with the 1975 Cleveland Indians, was the first African American to manage in the major leagues; Bill Lucas of the 1976 **Atlanta Braves** was the first African American **general manager**; and Cito Gaston of the 1992 **Toronto Blue Jays** was the first African American manager to win a **World Series**.

ALEXANDER, GROVER CLEVELAND "PETE". B. 26 February 1887, Elba, Nebraska. D. 4 November 1950, St. Paul, Nebraska. Grover Alexander's first season with the **Philadelphia Phillies**, in 1911, was perhaps the greatest **rookie** season ever by a **pitcher**. He led the **National League (NL)** with 28 **wins**, 31 **complete games**, and seven **shutouts**. Alexander remained with the Phillies through the 1917 season, while establishing himself as the NL's best pitcher. For four consecutive seasons (1914–1917), he led the league each season in wins, complete games, **innings pitched**, and **strikeouts**. During that stretch, he also led in shutouts three times (1915–1917) and **earned run average (ERA)** twice (1915–1916).

Figure 1.1.   Josh Gibson of the Homestead Grays in a Negro National League game at Washington's Griffith Stadium. *National Baseball Hall of Fame Library, Cooperstown, N.Y.*

In 1915, Alexander's 31 wins and 1.22 ERA led Philadelphia to its first-ever NL pennant. The Phillies lost the **World Series** to the **Boston Red Sox** in five games. Alexander's 3–1 victory in Game One was Philadelphia's only win. Alexander won the pitchers **Triple Crown** in 1915 by leading in wins, ERA, and strikeouts, but he was even better in 1916, when he again won the Triple Crown. The 6-foot, 1-inch, 185-pound right-hander pitched 389 **innings**, threw 38 complete games, and had 33 wins and 16 shutouts—all career highs. His 16 shutouts are still the **major-league** record.

The entry of the United States into World War I led the Phillies to trade the draft-eligible Alexander to the **Chicago Cubs** in December 1917. He pitched in three games for the Cubs in 1918, but spent most of the season with a field artillery unit in France. While no longer the dominant pitcher he had been with Philadelphia, Alexander had two 20-win seasons with Chicago, including a third Triple Crown in 1920. On 22 June 1926, the Cubs sold the now 39-year-old pitcher to the **St. Louis Cardinals**. Alexander won nine games for the Cardinals and two more in the World Series against the **New York Yankees**. His relief appearance in the seventh inning of Game Seven, when he struck out **Tony Lazzeri** with the **bases** loaded, is among baseball's most memorable moments. He won 46 games during the next three years to raise his lifetime total to 373, tied with **Christy Mathewson** for the most ever in the NL.

During his 20-year career, Alexander led the NL in wins six times, in innings pitched seven times, complete games six times, shutouts five times, and ERA four times. His 90 shutouts are second only to **Walter Johnson** and are the most ever for a National Leaguer. In 1938, the **Baseball Writers' Association of America** elected Alexander to the **National Baseball Hall of Fame**.

ALL-AMERICAN GIRLS PROFESSIONAL BASEBALL LEAGUE (AAGPBL). The All-American Girls Professional Baseball League (AAGPBL) was a league for **women** that existed from 1943 to 1954. During its 12 years, the league's official title changed from All-American Girls Softball League to All-American Girls Baseball League (mid-season 1943), to All-American Girls Professional Ball League (1944–1945), to All-American Girls Baseball League again (1946–1950), and finally to American Girls Baseball League (1951–1954). The league's title changes occurred with changes in league administrative thinking or ownership. The league's current identity as the All-American Girls Professional Baseball League was coined by the players when they incorporated as the All-American Girls Professional Baseball League Players Association in the fall of 1987, to petition recognition by the **National Baseball Hall of Fame**, which was granted 5 November 1988.

Each AAGPBL season extended from May to mid-September, and teams played 100 to 112 games per season. With only a few exceptions, girls' baseball was the same game being played in the **major leagues** by men's professional baseball players. All in all, the rules, strategy, and general play were the same. Differences were only the distances between the **bases**, the distance from the **pitching mound** to **home plate**, the size of the ball, and pitching styles. All-American Girls Baseball began in 1943, with a 12-inch ball, which was pitched underhand at a distance of 40 feet. The base paths were 65 feet in length—five feet longer than regulation softball to compensate for allowing runners to lead off. Ball sizes were reduced from 12 inches to 11 1/2 (mid-season 1944), to 11 inches (1946), to 10 3/8 inches (1948), to 10 inches (1949, with red seams), and finally to 9 inches (1954). Base paths were extended from 65 feet to 68 (1944), to 72 feet (1946), to 75 feet (1953), and finally to 85 feet (1954). **Pitchers** had to adapt to throwing longer distances in 1945 (42 feet), 1946 (43 feet), 1948 (50 feet, with overhand pitching), 1949 (55 feet), 1953 (56 feet), and 1954 (60 feet). They also had to adjust from underhand pitching (1943–1947) to sidearm pitching (allowed in

1946 and 1947), to overhand pitching (1948–1954). The game progressed from modified fast-pitch **softball** played with baseball rules, including leading off bases.

The four original teams in 1943 were the Kenosha (Wisconsin) Comets, Racine (Wisconsin) Belles, Rockford (Illinois) Peaches, and South Bend (Indiana) Blue Sox. Over the next 11 years, the numbers of teams in the league often changed but never exceeded 10. Beyond the original four, the following teams played at least one season in the AAGPBL: the Milwaukee Chicks, Minneapolis Millerettes, Fort Wayne (Indiana) Daisies, Grand Rapids (Michigan) Chicks, Muskegon (Michigan) Lassies, Peoria (Illinois) Redwings, Chicago Colleens, Springfield (Illinois) Sallies, Battle Creek (Michigan) Belles, and Kalamazoo (Michigan) Lassies.

The AAGPBL's "Players of the Year," an award first recognized in 1945, included Grand Rapids' Connie Wisniewski (underhand pitcher, 1945) and Alma Ziegler (overhand pitcher/**shortstop**, 1950) Racine's Sophie Kurys (**second baseman**, 1946), Muskegon's Doris Sams (**outfield**, 1947 and 1949), Kenosha's Audrey Wagner (outfield, 1948), South Bend's Jean Faut (overhand pitcher, 1951 and 1953), and Fort Wayne's Betty Weaver Foss (**first base**, 1952) and her sister, Joanne Weaver (outfield, 1954). Rockford's perennial All-Star at first base, Dorothy "Kammie" Kamenshek, who played 10 of the league's 12 years, was considered the league's best player by most of her peers.

ALL-STAR GAME (ASG). The **major league** All-Star Game matches the best players in the **American League (AL)** against the best players in the **National League (NL)**. The first All-Star Game was played at **Comiskey Park** on 6 July 1933, as part of the Chicago World's Fair, called the Century of Progress Exposition. The game, played most often on the second Tuesday in July, has continued on an annual basis, with two exceptions. The 1945 game was canceled because of travel restrictions related to World War II, and two games were played each season from 1959 to 1962.

The original plan was that the leagues would host the game in alternate years, with each of the 16 teams playing host. The alternating years' tradition is still mostly in effect, but **expansion**, relocation, and the building of many new **stadiums** has led to the All-Star Game being played at numerous different venues. **Roster** sizes have increased steadily, beginning with 18 in 1933, to the current 34. The way in which the players are chosen has also changed throughout the years. Currently, the fans are allowed to select the eight starters and the 34th and final player on each squad, with the **managers** picking the rest of the team.

Through 2012, the NL had a 43–38 lead over the AL, with two ties. **Hank Aaron**, **Willie Mays**, and **Stan Musial** have appeared in the most games (24). Mays and Musial have the most **extra-base hits** (8) and **total bases**

(40). Mays also has the most **hits** (23), the most **runs** scored (20), and the most **stolen bases** (6). Musial has the most **home runs** (6), while **Ted Williams** has the most **runs batted in** (12) and the most walks (11). Among the **pitchers, Roger Clemens** has been in the most games (10). **Lefty Gomez, Robin Roberts**, and **Don Drysdale** have the most **games started** (5), and Gomez has the most **wins** (3).

For each All-Star Game since 1962, a committee of sportswriters has chosen the game's **Most Valuable Player (MVP)**. The winner received what was originally called the Arch Ward Memorial Award, named in honor of the All-Star Game's creator, Chicago sportswriter Arch Ward. In 1970, the award was renamed the Commissioner's Trophy, but, in 1985, the original name, the Arch Ward Memorial Award, was restored. The name was changed again in 2002, and since then the MVP in the All-Star Games earns the Ted Williams MVP Award.

In 1985, baseball began staging a Home Run Derby the night before the game. The contest features a group of sluggers from each league competing to see who can hit the most home runs off batting practice pitchers throwing surprisingly "lively" balls. In 2003, in an attempt to make the game more meaningful to both fans and players, Commissioner **Bud Selig** decided to award home-field advantage in the **World Series** to the league that wins the All-Star Game.

ALOMAR, ROBERTO (VELAZQUEZ). B. 5 February 1968, Ponce, **Puerto Rico**. Roberto Alomar, who played for seven teams in his 17-year big-league career, was baseball's best **second baseman** during the 1990s. Alomar played in the **National League (NL)** for the **San Diego Padres** (1988–1990), **New York Mets** (2002–2003), and **Arizona Diamondbacks** (2004). In the **American League (AL)**, where he had his best years, Alomar played for the **Toronto Blue Jays** (1991–1995), **Baltimore Orioles** (1996–1998), **Cleveland Indians** (1999–2001), and **Chicago White Sox** (2003–2004).

A 6-foot, 184-pound **switch-hitter**, Alomar had nine full seasons with a .300 or better **batting average** and eight seasons with 30 or more **stolen bases**. He was an All-Star for 12 consecutive seasons, from 1990 to 2001, and the winner of the **All-Star Game's Most Valuable Player (MVP) Award** in 1998. Alomar played on Toronto's **World Series** winners in 1992 and 1993; he batted .480 in the 1993 Series win over the **Philadelphia Phillies**. He had a combined .316 average in five **American League Championship Series (ALCS)** and was the MVP of the 1992 ALCS.

In addition to four **Silver Slugger Awards**, Alomar won 10 **Gold Glove Awards**, the most ever by a second baseman. Alomar, who had a .300 career batting average, with 2,724 **hits** and 474 stolen bases, was elected to the **National Baseball Hall of Fame** by the **Baseball Writers' Association of America** in 2011.

ALSTON, WALTER EMMONS "SMOKEY". B. 1 December 1911, Venice, Ohio. D. 1 October 1984, Oxford, Ohio. Walter Alston's **major-league** playing career consisted of one game at **first base** for the 1936 **St. Louis Cardinals**. After 13 seasons of managing in the **minor leagues**, the **Brooklyn Dodgers** appointed him as their **manager** in 1954. Alston managed the Dodgers for 23 years, from 1954 to 1957, in Brooklyn, and from 1958 to 1976, in Los Angeles. His overall record with the Dodgers was 2,040–1,613.

The Dodgers won seven **National League** pennants under Alston (1955–1956, 1959, 1963, 1965–1966, and 1974) and won the **World Series** four times, in 1955 and 1963 against the **New York Yankees**, in 1959 against the **Chicago White Sox**, and in 1965 against the **Minnesota Twins**. He was given the major league **Manager of the Year Award** by the *Sporting News* in 1958, 1959, and 1963. The **Veterans Committee** elected Alston to the **National Baseball Hall of Fame** in 1983.

ALTOONA (PENNSYLVANIA) MOUNTAIN CITYS. The Altoona Mountain Citys, also known as the Altoona Unions, were a team in the **Union Association (UA)** in 1884, the one year of the UA's existence. The team, which played in the smallest-ever major-league city, disbanded after 25 games, with a 6–19 record.

AMATEUR DRAFT. The Amateur Draft, also known as the First-Year Player Draft or the Rule 4 Draft, allows **major-league** teams to select amateur players, mostly from high schools and **colleges**. Teams choose in the reverse order of their record in the previous season. The team with the worst record picks first. Additional picks are given to teams to compensate for any **free agents** they lost in the previous off-season. Held in June, the draft usually contains at least 50 rounds. In the first Amateur Draft, in 1965, the first pick was **outfielder** Rick Monday, chosen by the **Kansas City Athletics**.

AMERICAN ASSOCIATION (AA). The American Association (AA) existed as a **major league** from 1882 to 1891. In seven of its 10 seasons, the AA and the previously established **National League (NL)** participated in an early version of the **World Series**. The AA differed from the more structured NL by allowing each team to set its own admission prices, which were generally cheaper. They also allowed the sale of alcohol at their games, which earned them the derogatory nickname, "The Beer and Whiskey League." During its existence, many different teams were members of the AA. The following six teams participated in the AA's first season, in 1882: the **Baltimore Orioles**, **Cincinnati Red Stockings**, **Louisville Colonels**, **Philadelphia Athletics**, **Pittsburgh Alleghenys**, and **St. Louis Browns**.

During the next nine years, the following additional teams were members of the AA for at least a part of one season: the **Boston Reds**, Brooklyn Bridegrooms, **Brooklyn Gladiators**, **Cincinnati Porkers**, **Cleveland Blues**, **Columbus (Ohio) Colts**, **Columbus (Ohio) Solons**, **Indianapolis Hoosiers**, **Kansas City Cowboys**, **Milwaukee Brewers**, **New York Metropolitans**, **Richmond Virginias**, **Rochester Hop Bitters**, **Syracuse Stars**, **Toledo Blue Stockings**, **Toledo Maumees**, **Washington Nationals**, and **Washington Statesmen**. The move to the NL by some of the AA's members and competition from the **Players League**, a third major league formed in 1890, drove the AA out of existence following the 1891 season.

AA pennant winners were: the Cincinnati Red Stockings (1882), Philadelphia Athletics (1883), New York Metropolitans (1884), St. Louis Browns (1885–1888), Brooklyn Bridegrooms (1889), Louisville Colonels (1890), and Boston Reds (1891). Notable players from the AA included **Dan Brouthers**, **Pete Browning**, Bob Caruthers, **Hugh Duffy**, Dave Foutz, Guy Hecker, Matt Kilroy, Silver King, Denny Lyons, Sadie McMahon, Ed Morris, Tip O'Neill, Dave Orr, **Harry Stovey**, Tommy Tucker, and Will White.

AMERICAN LEAGUE (AL). The American League (AL), officially the American League of Professional Baseball Clubs, is one of two leagues, along with the **National League (NL)**, that comprise the **major leagues**. Originally called the Western League, league president **Ban Johnson** renamed it the American League in 1900 and declared it a major league in 1901. The eight charter members of the league were the **Baltimore Orioles**, Boston Americans (now the **Boston Red Sox**), **Chicago White Sox**, **Cleveland Blues** (now the **Cleveland Indians**), **Detroit Tigers**, **Milwaukee Brewers**, **Philadelphia Athletics**, and **Washington Senators**. In 1902, the Milwaukee Brewers moved to St. Louis and became the **St. Louis Browns**. In 1903, the Baltimore Orioles moved to New York and became the New York Highlanders (now the **New York Yankees**).

The number of franchises and their locations remained stable until 1954, when the St. Louis Browns moved to Baltimore and became the Baltimore Orioles. The next year, 1955, the Philadelphia Athletics moved to Kansas City and became the **Kansas City Athletics**. In 1961, the league expanded for the first time, adding two new teams, the **Los Angeles Angels** and a new Washington Senators team. The original Senators relocated to Minnesota that year and became the **Minnesota Twins**.

In 1969, both leagues expanded from 10 teams to 12. The new teams in the AL were the **Kansas City Royals** and **Seattle Pilots**, but the Pilots were a failure and moved to Milwaukee in 1970 and became the **Milwaukee Brewers**. Then, in 1972, the second Washington Senators moved to Texas and became the **Texas Rangers**. Both leagues expanded again in 1977. The two new teams in the AL, which now totaled 14, were the **Seattle Mariners** and **Toronto Blue Jays**, the AL's first team from outside the United States. In 1998, the AL added the Tampa Bay Devil Rays (now the **Tampa Bay Rays**). That same year, the Milwaukee Brewers moved to the NL, keeping the number of teams in the AL at 14.

The league is made up of three divisions. The Eastern Division has the Baltimore Orioles, Boston Red Sox, New York Yankees, Tampa Bay Rays, and Toronto Blue Jays. The Central Division has the Chicago White Sox, Cleveland Indians, Detroit Tigers, Kansas City Royals, and Minnesota Twins. The Western Division has the Los Angeles Angels, Oakland Athletics, Seattle Mariners, and Texas Rangers. In 2013, the **Houston Astros** will move from the NL to the Western Division of the AL so that each league can have 15 teams.

Ban Johnson, the AL's original president, served until 1927. He was succeeded by Ernest Barnard (1927–1931), **Will Harridge** (1931–1959), **Joe Cronin** (1959–1973), **Lee MacPhail** (1973–1984), Dr. Bobby Brown (1984–1994), and Gene Budig (1994–1999). The office of league president was abolished after the 1999 season.

AMERICAN LEAGUE CHAMPIONSHIP SERIES (ALCS). The American League Championship Series (ALCS) is now the second round of the postseason playoffs in the **American League (AL)**. The ALCS began in 1969, when the AL expanded to 12 teams and split into an Eastern Division and a Western Division. At that time, the winners of each division played a best-of-five series to determine who would advance to the **World Series**. In 1985, the format changed from a best-of-five to a best-of-seven.

In 1994, the league was restructured into an Eastern Division, a Central Division, and a Western Division. Beginning in 1995, the three division winners and a **wild-card** team advanced to a new first round of playoffs called the **American League Division Series (ALDS)**. The two ALDS winners advance to the ALCS, with the winner of the best-of-seven ALCS going on to represent the AL in the World Series.

AMERICAN LEAGUE DIVISION SERIES (ALDS). The American League Division Series (ALDS) was first played in 1995, one year after the 14-team **American League (AL)** was restructured into an Eastern Division, a Central Division, and a Western Division. From 1995–2011, the ALDS consisted of two best-of-five series, featuring the winners of the three divisions plus a **wild-card** team, the second-place team with the best record. Beginning with the 2012 season, the wild card team is the winner of a "play-in" game between the two non-division winners with the best record. That team will become the fourth qualifier for the ALDS. The two ALDS winners then advance to the **American League Championship Series (ALCS)**, with the ALCS winner going on to represent the AL in the **World Series**. An ALDS was played during the strike-season of 1981, matching the pre-strike leaders and the post-strike leaders in each Division.

AMERICAN LEAGUE PARK. *See* WASHINGTON SENATORS (AL) 1901–1960.

AMERIQUEST FIELD IN ARLINGTON. *See* RANGERS BALLPARK IN ARLINGTON.

ANAHEIM ANGELS. *See* LOS ANGELES ANGELS OF ANAHEIM.

ANAHEIM STADIUM. *See* ANGEL STADIUM OF ANAHEIM.

ANDERSON, GEORGE LEE "SPARKY". B. 22 February 1934, Bridgewater, South Dakota. D. 4 November 2010, Thousand Oaks, California. Sparky Anderson played one season as a **major league second baseman**. The 5-foot, 9-inch, 170-pound Anderson batted .218 in 152 games for the 1959 **Philadelphia Phillies**. In 1970, following five years as a **manager** in the **minor leagues**, he was chosen to manage the **Cincinnati Reds**. In nine seasons, Anderson's Reds won four pennants (1970, 1972, 1975, and 1976) and two **World Series**, defeating the **Boston Red Sox** in 1975 and the **New York Yankees** in 1976. After second-place finishes in 1977 and 1978, Anderson was fired. He signed to manage the **Detroit Tigers** during the 1979 season and remained in Detroit through 1995. In 1984, he captured his third World Series title, when the Tigers downed the **San Diego Padres**.

The **Baseball Writers' Association of America** named Anderson **Manager of the Year** for the **American League (AL)** in 1984 and 1987, and the *Sporting News* gave him its AL Manager of the Year Award in 1987. Anderson had his uniform number 11 retired by both the Reds and Tigers. His combined record in 26 years as a big-league manager was 2,194–1,834. In 2000, the **Veterans Committee** elected Anderson to the **National Baseball Hall of Fame**.

ANGEL STADIUM OF ANAHEIM. Angel Stadium of Anaheim, located in Anaheim, California, is the home field of the **Los Angeles Angels of Anaheim** of the **American League**. Before moving into Angel Stadium of Anaheim, the team played its home games at Los Angeles's Wrigley Field in 1961, and at **Dodger Stadium**, which they called Chavez Ravine, from 1962 to 1965. The Angels have played at Angel Stadium of Anaheim since 1966, when the newly built park was called Anaheim Stadium. It was renamed Edison International Field of Anaheim in 1998 and Angel Stadium of Anaheim in 2004. The current seating capacity of Angel Stadium of Anaheim is approximately 46,000. The stadium hosted the **major league All-Star Game** twice—in 1967, when it was called Anaheim Stadium, and in 2010.

ANSON, ADRIAN CONSTANTINE "CAP," "POP". B. 17 April 1852, Marshalltown, Iowa. D. 14 April 1922, Chicago, Illinois. Cap Anson's record-long 27-year career (1871–1897) coincides with the first 27 years of Major League Baseball. He played in the National Association (NA) during the five years of its existence, for the **Rockford (Illinois) Forest Citys** in 1871, and for the **Philadelphia Athletics** from 1872 to 1875. Anson batted .359 for his five NA seasons. The Chicago White Stockings of the newly formed **National League (NL)** signed Anson for the 1876 season. He remained with the Chicago franchise, which later was called the Colts and was the forerunner of today's **Chicago Cubs**, for 22 seasons. In 1890, he chose to remain in the NL when many of that league's stars were defecting to the **Players League**, a decision that earned him the enmity of many of the defectors. The 6-foot, 227-pound Anson, who threw and batted right-handed, played every position during his career, including **pitcher**, but he was primarily a **first baseman**. His NL **batting average (BA)** was .331, giving him a combined lifetime BA of .334. He batted above .300 in 24 of his 27 seasons, accumulated 3,435 **hits** (423 in the NA and 3,012 in the NL), and was the first player to reach 3,000 hits. Anson led the NL in batting twice and in **runs batted in** eight times.

During the 1879 season, Anson was named **manager** of the White Stockings and remained a **player-manager** for the rest of his time in Chicago. (He also managed briefly for the **New York Giants** in 1898.) He led Chicago to five NL pennants, in 1880 through 1882 and 1885 and 1886. In 1885 and 1886, the White Stockings played the **St. Louis Browns** of the **American Association** in a championship series that was a predecessor to the modern **World Series**. In 1885, they won three, lost three, and tied one, and, in 1886, they lost to the Browns, four games to two. The **Old Timers Committee** elected Anson to the **National Baseball Hall of Fame** as a player in 1939. Yet, despite having one of baseball's most productive careers, Anson is often remembered for his prominent role in barring **African Americans** from playing in the **major leagues**.

APARICIO, LUIS ERNESTO (MONTIEL) "LITTLE LOUIE". B. 29 April 1934, Maracaibo, **Venezuela**. Luis Aparicio was an **American League (AL) shortstop** for 18 seasons. "Little Louie," as the 5-foot, 9-inch, 160-pound Aparicio was called, played for the **Chicago White Sox** (1956–1962, 1968–1970), **Baltimore Orioles** (1963–1967), and **Boston Red Sox** (1971–1973). Aparicio, the AL's **Rookie of the Year** in 1956, led the league in **stolen bases** in each of his first nine seasons, a **major-league** record. A right-handed **batter**, Aparicio's career **batting average** was only .262, and he surpassed the .300 mark just once (.313 in 1970); however, his value came not only from his speed on the bases, but from his great play at shortstop. He led AL shortstops in **fielding percentage** six times, **assists** seven times, and **putouts** four times.

Aparicio was selected to the **All-Star** team 10 times. At his retirement, he was the all-time major-league leader for most **games played**, assists, and **double plays** by a shortstop, and the AL all-time leader for putouts and **total chances** by a shortstop. His nine **Gold Glove Award**s set an AL record for shortstops that was later tied by **Omar Vizquel**. Aparicio's 2,583 games played at shortstop stood as the major-league record for the position until it was surpassed by Vizquel. In 1984, the **Baseball Writers' Association of America** elected Aparicio to the **National Baseball Hall of Fame**.

APPLING, LUCIUS BENJAMIN "LUKE". B. 2 April 1907, High Point, North Carolina. D. 3 January 1991, Cumming, Georgia. Luke Appling played 20 seasons for the **Chicago White Sox**, from 1930 through 1943, and from late 1945 to 1950. (He missed all of 1944 and most of 1945 while serving in the military.) In all but a few of those seasons, the 5-foot, 10-inch, 183-pound right-handed **batter** was Chicago's **shortstop** and **leadoff hitter**. Appling led the **American League (AL)** in **batting average** in 1936, with a .388 average, and in 1943, with a .328 mark. In both seasons, he finished second in the voting for the **Most Valuable Player Award**. He also had 128 **runs batted in** in 1936, scored 111 **runs**, had 204 **hits**, and compiled a 27-game hitting streak. His 1936 batting championship was the first won by a shortstop in the AL, and his .388 batting average was the highest by a major-league shortstop in the 20th century.

Appling was a seven-time **All-Star**, and he exceeded the .300 mark in 13 seasons as a full-time player. Noted for his ability to **foul** off potential third **strikes**, he garnered 1,302 **bases on balls** in his 20 seasons, as opposed to just 528 **strikeouts**. He finished with 2,749 hits and a .310 batting average. Defensively, Appling led AL shortstops in **putouts** twice and **assists** seven times. In 1964, he was elected by the **Baseball Writers' Association of America** to the **National Baseball Hall of Fame**. Three years after his election, he returned to the AL to **manage** the 1967 **Kansas City Athletics** for 40 games.

ARIZONA DIAMONDBACKS. The Arizona Diamondbacks are a team in the Western Division of the **National League (NL)**. They entered the NL in 1998 as part of a two-team major-league **expansion**, with the Tampa Bay Devil Rays joining the **American League**. The team played its home games at Bank One Ballpark before the name was changed to **Chase Field** in 2006.

The Diamondbacks reached the **National League Division Series (NLDS)** in 1999, their second year of existence, but the team lost to the **New York Mets** in the **National League Championship Series (NLCS)**. They also lost in the NLDS in 2002 and 2011, and in the NLCS in 2007. The Diamondbacks won their only NL pennant in 2001, and then defeated the **New York Yankees** in seven games to win the **World Series**. Winning the Series in only their fourth season was the earliest ever by an expansion franchise.

No Arizona Diamondbacks player has won the NL's **Most Valuable Player Award**. **Cy Young Award** winners are **Randy Johnson** (1999–2002) and Brandon Webb (2006). No Diamondbacks player has won the **Rookie of the Year Award**.

No Diamondbacks **batter** has led the league in **batting average**. No Diamondbacks batter has led the league in **home runs**. No Diamondbacks batter has led the league in **runs batted in**.

Diamondbacks **pitchers** who have led the league in **wins** are Curt Schilling (2001), Randy Johnson (2002), Brandon Webb (2006, 2008), and Ian Kennedy (2011). Randy Johnson led in **earned run average (ERA)** in 1999, 2001, and 2002. Johnson also led in **strikeouts** from 1999 through 2002 and in 2004. By leading in wins, ERA, and strikeouts in 2002, Johnson won the **Triple Crown** for pitchers.

Other notable players and **managers** in Diamondbacks' history include Bob Brenly, Craig Counsell, Stephen Drew, Steve Finley, Kirk Gibson, Luis Gonzalez, Dan Haren, Orlando Hudson, Bob Melvin, Wade Miley, Mark Reynolds, Buck Showalter, Chad Tracy, Justin Upton, Jose Valverde, Matt Williams, Tony Womack, and Chris Young.

ARLINGTON STADIUM. *See* TEXAS RANGERS.

ASHBURN, DON RICHARD "RICHIE". B. 19 March 1927, Tilden, Nebraska. D. 9 September 1997, New York, New York. Richie Ashburn was a speedy left-handed-hitting center fielder in the **National League (NL)** from 1948 to 1962. He batted .333 and had a league-leading 32 **stolen bases** as a **rookie** for the 1948 **Philadelphia Phillies**. His 23-game **hitting streak** that season set a NL rookie record. An outstanding **leadoff hitter** during his 12 years with the Phillies, the 5-foot, 10-inch, 170-pound Ashburn had eight seasons of batting above .300. He won batting championships in 1955 (.338) and 1958 (.350) and led the league in **hits** and walks three times each.

Ashburn was traded to the **Chicago Cubs** in 1960, where he again led the league in walks and **on-base percentage**. Ashburn played his final season for the **New York Mets** in 1962. Despite a .306 **batting average** for the **expansion** Mets in their first year of existence, he chose to retire after the season. In 1963, he became a broadcaster for the Phillies, a position he held until his death in 1997. Ashburn had a lifetime batting average of .308, with 2,574 hits. He led all NL **outfielders** in **assists** three times and **putouts** in nine of the 10 years between 1949 and 1958. In 1995, the **Veterans Committee** elected Ashburn to the **National Baseball Hall of Fame**.

ASSISTS (A). An assist is awarded to every defensive player who fields or touches the ball after it has been hit by the **batter** prior to the recording of a **putout**, even if the contact was unintentional. A **fielder** can receive a maximum of one assist per **out** recorded. An assist is also awarded if a putout would have occurred, had not another fielder committed an **error**.

ASTRODOME. The Astrodome, the first indoor stadium used by a **major-league** team, is located in Houston, Texas. The **Houston Astros** of the **National League** played their first official game at the Astrodome on 12 April 1965, and their last on 9 October 1999. Prior to moving to the Astrodome, the Houston team, then called the Houston Colt .45s, played at Colt Stadium (1962–1964). Since 2000, the Astros have played at **Minute Maid Park**, called Enron Field in 2000 and 2001. The Astrodome hosted the major league **All-Star Game** in 1968 and 1986.

See also STADIUMS.

AT-BATS (AB). A **batter** is charged with an at-bat when he reaches base on a **hit**, an **error**, or a **fielder's choice**, or if he makes an **out** other than as part of a **sacrifice hit** or **sacrifice fly**. The **major league** single-season leader in at-bats is Jimmy Rollins of the 2007 **Philadelphia Phillies**, with 716. The single-season **American League** leader is Willie Wilson of the 1980 **Kansas City Royals**, with 705. The career leader is **Pete Rose**, with 14,053. Rose played for the **Cincinnati Reds** (1963–1978, 1984–1986), Philadelphia Phillies (1979–1983), and **Montreal Expos** (1984).

AT&T PARK. AT&T Park, located in San Francisco, California, is the home field of the **San Francisco Giants** of the **National League**. The Giants played their first game at AT&T Park, known as Pac Bell Park from 2000 to 2003, and SBC Park from 2004 to 2006, on 11 April 2000. They had previously played at Seals Stadium in 1958 and 1959, and at **Candlestick Park** from 1960 through 1999. AT&T Park, which has a seating capacity of approximately 41,900, hosted the **major league All-Star Game** in 2007.

See also STADIUMS.

ATLANTA BRAVES. The Atlanta Braves are a team in the Eastern Division of the **National League (NL)**. The Braves franchise was located in Boston from 1876 to 1952, and in Milwaukee from 1953 to 1965. The move to Atlanta in 1966 made the Braves the first **major-league** team in the South. The team played at **Fulton County Stadium** from 1966 through 1996. Home games have been played at **Turner Field** since 1997.

Since moving to Atlanta, the Braves have finished first in their division 16 times, including 11 straight seasons (1995–2005) under **manager Bobby Cox**. They reached the **World Series** five times, but won only once, in 1995, against the **Cleveland Indians**. Atlanta's four Series losses were to the **Minnesota Twins** in 1991, the **Toronto Blue Jays** in 1992, and the **New York Yankees** in 1996 and 1999. Atlanta was the loser in the **National League Division Series** six times, and in the **National League Championship Series** six times. In 2012, Atlanta lost to the **St. Louis Cardinals** in the National League's first **wild card** "play-in" game.

Atlanta Braves who have won the NL's **Most Valuable Player Award** are Dale Murphy (1982–1983), Terry Pendleton (1991), and **Chipper Jones** (1999). **Cy Young Award** winners are **Tom Glavine** (1991, 1998), **Greg Maddux** (1993–1995), and **John Smoltz** (1996). **Rookie of the Year** winners are Earl Williams (1971), Bob Horner (1978), David Justice (1990), Rafael Furcal (2000), and Craig Kimbrel (2011).

Atlanta players who have led the league in **batting average** are Rico Carty (1970), Ralph Garr (1974), Terry Pendleton (1991), and Chipper Jones (2008). **Home run** leaders are **Hank Aaron** (1966–1967), Dale Murphy (1984–1985), and Andruw Jones (2005). **Runs batted in** leaders are Hank Aaron (1966), Dale Murphy (1982–1983), and Andruw Jones (2005).

Atlanta **pitchers** who have led the league in **wins** are **Phil Niekro** (1974, 1979), Tom Glavine (1991–1993, 1998, 2000), Greg Maddux (1994–1995), John Smoltz (1996, 2006), Denny Neagle (1997), and Russ Ortiz (2003). **Earned run average** leaders are Phil Niekro (1967), Buzz Capra (1974), and Greg Maddux (1993–1995, 1998). **Strikeout** leaders are Phil Niekro (1977) and John Smoltz (1992, 1996).

Other notable players and managers in Atlanta Braves' history include Steve Avery, Dusty Baker, Jeff Blauser, Darrell Evans, Julio Franco, Freddie Freeman, Rafael Furcal, Ron Gant, Gene Garber, Marcus Giles, Tommy Hanson, Jason Heyward, Glenn Hubbard, Tim Hudson, Jair Jurrjens, David Justice, Ryan Klesko, Mark Lemke, Javy Lopez, Brian McCann, Fred

McGriff, Kris Medlen, Kent Mercker, Kevin Millwood, Otis Nixon, Martin Prado, John Rocker, Mike Stanton, **Joe Torre**, Dan Uggla, and Mark Wohlers.

ATLANTIC. *See* BROOKLYN ATLANTICS (NA).

ATLANTIC BASEBALL CLUB OF BROOKLYN. *See* BROOKLYN ATLANTICS (NA).

AVERILL, HOWARD EARL. B. 21 May 1902, Snohomish, Washington. D. 16 August 1983, Everett, Washington. **Outfielder** Earl Averill made his big-league debut with the **Cleveland Indians** on 16 April 1929. Averill hit a **home run** in his first **at-bat**, becoming the first future member of the **National Baseball Hall of Fame** to accomplish that feat. Averill, a 5-foot, 9-inch, 172-pound left-handed batter, had his best season in 1936, when he batted .378 and led the **American League (AL)** in **hits** and **triples**. Cleveland traded him to the **Detroit Tigers** late in the 1939 season, enabling him to participate in his only **World Series**, in 1940. Averill ended his career with the **Boston Braves** in 1941, after playing in just eight early season games. His last few years as a player were marred by a back injury suffered in 1937. Coincidentally, it was in that year's **All-Star Game** that Averill's line drive struck **Dizzy Dean's** toe, breaking it and eventually shortening the career of the **St. Louis Cardinals** top **pitcher**. In all, Averill was selected to the AL All-Star team six times. He batted above .300 eight times and had a career **batting average** of .318. He is still Cleveland's all-time leader in **runs batted in, extra-base hits, runs**, triples, and **total bases**. In 1975, the **Veterans Committee** elected Averill to the National Baseball Hall of Fame.

B

BABE RUTH AWARD. The Babe Ruth Award is presented after each **World Series** to the player judged to have been the outstanding performer in the postseason. The judges for the award are from the New York chapter of the **Baseball Writers' Association of America**. The award, which is similar to but not the same as the World Series **Most Valuable Player Award**, was created after **Babe Ruth's** death in 1948. The first winner was Joe Page of the 1949 **New York Yankees**. The most recent winner, in 2011, was David Freese of the **St. Louis Cardinals**.

BAGWELL, JEFFREY ROBERT "JEFF". B. 27 May 1968, Boston, Massachusetts. Jeff Bagwell played his entire 15-year **major-league** career (1991–2005) as the **first baseman** for the **Houston Astros**. The 6-foot, 195-pound right-handed slugger was the **Rookie of the Year** in 1991 and the **Most Valuable Player** in 1994. Bagwell, who was also voted the **Major League Player of the Year** in 1994, batted .368 in that strike-shortened season, while leading the **National League (NL)** in **runs batted in**, **runs** scored, **total bases**, and **slugging percentage**. Bagwell won three **Silver Slugger Awards** and led NL first basemen in **games played** four times and **assists** five times. He finished his career with a .297 **batting average** and 449 **home runs**. Bagwell became eligible for the **National Baseball Hall of Fame** in 2011.

BAKER BOWL. *See* PHILADELPHIA PHILLIES.

BAKER, JOHN FRANKLIN "FRANK," "HOME RUN". B. 13 March 1886, Trappe, Maryland. D. 28 June 1963, Trappe, Maryland. Frank Baker made his big-league debut with the **Philadelphia Athletics** late in the 1908 season. The 5-foot, 11-inch, 173-pound left-handed-hitting Baker played **third base** in Philadelphia's "$100,000 infield," which also had Stuffy McInnis at **first base**, **Eddie Collins** at **second base**, and Jack Barry at **shortstop**. Baker led the **American League** in **home runs** for three consecutive seasons, in 1911, 1912, and 1913, with 11, 10, and 12, respectively, and in **runs**

batted in in 1912 and 1913. Under **manager Connie Mack**, the Athletics won pennants in 1910, 1911, 1913, and 1914. In three of those years, the A's won the **World Series**, defeating the **Chicago Cubs** in 1910 and the **New York Giants** in 1911 and 1913. Baker earned the nickname "Home Run" in the 1911 Series, when he hit dramatic late-inning home runs in successive games against Giants' aces **Rube Marquard** and **Christy Mathewson**.

Although heavily favored to win again in 1914, the Athletics were swept in four games by the **Boston Braves**. Following that defeat, Mack sold off many of his stars, including Baker. After sitting out the 1915 season, Baker played for the **New York Yankees** from 1916 to 1919, and in 1921–1922. (He also sat out the 1920 season.) Baker had a .307 **batting average** for his 13 **major-league** seasons and, despite the nickname, a total of only 96 home runs. In 1955, the **Veterans Committee** elected Baker to the **National Baseball Hall of Fame**.

BALK (BK). A balk is an illegal act by the **pitcher** with a **runner** or runners on **base**, entitling all runners to advance one base. It is a balk when the pitcher, while touching the pitching rubber, makes any motion naturally associated with his pitch and fails to make such delivery; the pitcher, while touching the pitching rubber, feints a throw to **first base** and fails to complete the throw; the pitcher, while touching the pitching rubber, fails to step directly toward a base before throwing to that base; or the pitcher, while touching the pitching rubber, throws, or feints a throw, to an unoccupied base, except for the purpose of making a play.

BALL. The **umpire** at **home plate** will call a pitch a ball if it does not enter the **strike zone** in flight and is not struck at by the **batter**. In 1876, the first year of the **National League**, it took nine balls for a batter to be awarded a **base on balls**. That number was gradually reduced during the course of the next 13 years, until it was fixed at four in 1889.

BALTIMORE CANARIES. The Baltimore Canaries, also called Lord Baltimore and the Baltimore Yellow Stockings, were members of the National Association from 1872 through 1874. The most notable players for the Canaries included **Candy Cummings**, Davy Force, George Hall, **Bobby Mathews**, and **Lip Pike**.

BALTIMORE ELITE GIANTS. The Baltimore Elite Giants were a **Negro National League (NNL)** team that played in several cities, most famously in Baltimore from 1938 to 1948. They were the NNL champions in 1939.

Among the notable players who went on to the **major leagues** from the Elite Giants were future **Brooklyn Dodgers** Joe Black, **Roy Campanella**, and Jim Gilliam.

BALTIMORE MARYLANDS. The Baltimore Marylands were members of the National Association from 14 April 1873 to 11 July 1873. During that stretch, they played six games and lost all six.

BALTIMORE MONUMENTALS. The Baltimore Monumentals were a team in the **Union Association (UA)** in 1884, the one year of the UA's existence. Baltimore finished with a 58–47 record. **Pitcher** Bill Sweeney of the Monumentals led the league in **wins**, with 40.

BALTIMORE ORIOLES (AA). The Baltimore Orioles were charter members of the **American Association (AA)**. They played in the AA from 1882 to 1889, dropped out in 1890, but returned in midseason to replace the **Brooklyn Gladiators**. In 1892, Baltimore joined the **National League** after the AA folded following the 1891 season. The Orioles never won an AA pennant. Their most successful year was 1887, when they finished third. Notable players and **managers** for the Orioles included Billy Barnie, Oyster Burns, Matt Kilroy, Sadie McMahon, and Tommy Tucker.
   See also BALTIMORE ORIOLES (NL).

BALTIMORE ORIOLES (AL) 1901–1902. The Baltimore Orioles were a team in the **American League (AL)** in 1901, the first year the AL was recognized as a **major league**, and in 1902. Managed by **John McGraw** in 1901, and John McGraw and **Wilbert Robinson** in 1902, the Orioles finished in the second division in both seasons. McGraw moved to the **New York Giants** of the **National League** in mid-1902, and lured Orioles' stars **Roger Bresnahan**, Dan McGann, and **Joe McGinnity** to New York. Before the start of the 1903 season, the franchise was moved to New York and renamed the New York Highlanders; it was eventually renamed the **New York Yankees**. Other notable players for the Orioles were Mike Donlin, Bill Keister, Cy Seymour, Kip Selbach, and Jimmy Williams.

BALTIMORE ORIOLES (AL) 1954–. The Baltimore Orioles are a team in the Eastern Division of the **American League (AL)**. The franchise began as the **Milwaukee Brewers**, entering the league as a charter member in 1901. The franchise was moved to St. Louis in 1902, where it played as the **St. Louis Browns** until moving to Baltimore in 1954. The Orioles played their home games at **Memorial Stadium** from 1954 through 1991. Since 1992, they have played their home games at **Oriole Park at Camden Yards**.

Baltimore has appeared in the **World Series** six times, winning three and losing three. The wins were against the **Los Angeles Dodgers** (1966), **Cincinnati Reds** (1970), and **Philadelphia Phillies** (1983). The losses were to the **New York Mets** (1969) and **Pittsburgh Pirates** (1971, 1979). The Orioles have lost in the **American League Championship Series** four times. In 2012, Baltimore defeated the **Texas Rangers** in the American League's first wild card "play-in" game." The team then lost to the **New York Yankees** in the **American League Division Series**.

Baltimore Orioles who have won the AL's **Most Valuable Player Award** are **Brooks Robinson** (1964), **Frank Robinson** (1966), Boog Powell (1970), and **Cal Ripken** (1983, 1991). **Cy Young Award** winners are Mike Cuellar (1969), **Jim Palmer** (1973, 1975–1976), Mike Flanagan (1979), and Steve Stone (1980). **Rookie of the Year** winners are Ron Hansen (1960), Curt Blefary (1965), Al Bumbry (1973), **Eddie Murray** (1977), Cal Ripken (1982), and Gregg Olson (1989).

Frank Robinson, in 1966, is the only Orioles player to lead the league in **batting average**. Leaders in **home runs** are Frank Robinson (1966) and Eddie Murray (1981). Leaders in **runs batted in** are Jim Gentile (1961), Brooks Robinson (1964), Frank Robinson (1966), Lee May (1976), Eddie Murray (1981), and Miguel Tejada (2004). By leading the AL in batting average, home runs, and runs batted in, Frank Robinson won the **Triple Crown** for **batters** in 1966.

Orioles **pitchers** who have led the league in **wins** are Chuck Estrada (1960), Mike Cuellar (1970), Dave McNally (1970), Jim Palmer (1975–1977), Mike Flanagan (1979), Steve Stone (1980), Dennis Martinez (1981), Mike Boddicker (1984), and Mike Mussina (1995). **Earned run average** leaders are **Hoyt Wilhelm** (1959), Jim Palmer (1973, 1975), and Mike Boddicker (1984). Bob Turley, in 1954, is the only Orioles pitcher to lead the league in **strikeouts**.

Other notable players and **managers** in Orioles history include Jerry Adair, **Roberto Alomar**, Joe Altobelli, Brady Anderson, **Luis Aparicio**, Steve Barber, Hank Bauer, Don Baylor, Mark Belanger, Paul Blair, Don Buford, Wally Bunker, Rich Dauer, Storm Davis, Doug DeCinces, Rick Dempsey, Andy Etchebarren, Bobby Grich, J. J. Hardy, Elrod Hendricks, Chris Hoiles, Davey Johnson, Jim Johnson, Adam Jones, John Lowenstein, Nick Markakis, Tippy Martinez, Scott McGregor, Bob Nieman, Johnny Oates, **Rafael Palmeiro**, Milt Pappas, Paul Richards, Brian Roberts, Gary Roenicke, Buck Showalter, Ken Singleton, Sammy Stewart, Gus Triandos, Eddie Watt, **Earl Weaver**, and Matt Wieters.

BALTIMORE ORIOLES (NL). The Baltimore Orioles were a team in the **National League (NL)** from 1892 to 1899. The Orioles had played in the **American Association (AA)** from 1882 to 1891, although they briefly dropped out in 1890. When the AA folded following the 1891 season, Baltimore was one of the four AA franchises the NL added in their expansion from an eight-team league to a 12-team league. After two poor seasons, the Orioles finished first in three consecutive years, from 1894 to 1896, and then second in 1897 and 1898. They participated in each of the four **Temple Cup** championship series, a seven-game series between the NL's first-place and second-place finishers. They lost the Temple Cup series to the **New York Giants** in 1894 and the **Cleveland Spiders** in 1895, but won it against Cleveland in 1896 and against the Boston Beaneaters in 1897.

In 1899, a syndicate formed that controlled both the Brooklyn and Baltimore franchises, with the best players winding up in Brooklyn. So, despite their great success, and now legendary status, when the NL went back to eight teams in 1900, the Baltimore franchise was one of the four eliminated. Under **manager Ned Hanlon**, the Orioles were known for their aggressive— some said dirty—style of play and their ability to outhustle and outsmart their opponents. Among their many notable players were **Dan Brouthers, Hughie Jennings, Willie Keeler, Joe Kelley, John McGraw,** and **Wilbert Robinson**, all future members of the **National Baseball Hall of Fame**, as well as Steve Brodie, Jack Doyle, Bill Hoffer, and Sadie McMahon.

BALTIMORE TERRAPINS. The Baltimore Terrapins were a team in the **Federal League (FL)** in 1914–1915, the two seasons the FL existed as a **major league**. The Terrapins finished in third place in 1914, but fell to eighth in 1915, despite adding **Chief Bender**, the former star **pitcher** of the **Philadelphia Athletics**. In addition to Chief Bender, other notable players for the Terrapins included Benny Meyer, Jack Quinn, George Suggs, and Jimmy Walsh.

BALTIMORE YELLOW STOCKINGS. *See* BALTIMORE CANARIES.

BANCROFT, DAVID JAMES "DAVE," "BEAUTY". B. 20 April 1891, Sioux City, Iowa. D. 9 October 1972, Superior, Wisconsin. Dave Bancroft was a speedy, slick-fielding **shortstop** who played for four **National League (NL)** teams in a 16-year **major-league** career. Bancroft played for the **Philadelphia Phillies** from 1915 until June 1920, when he was traded to the **New York Giants**. He was a key contributor, as **manager John McGraw's** Giants won pennants the next three seasons. The Giants played the **New York Yankees** in the **World Series** all three years, winning in 1921 and 1922, and losing in 1923. As a member of the Phillies, the **switch-hitting** Bancroft had batted .294 against the **Boston Red Sox** in the 1915 Series, but he hit only a combined .145 in the three Series against the Yankees.

Following the 1923 season, McGraw traded him to the **Boston Braves**, where he was a **player-manager** from 1925 through 1927. Bancroft later played for the Brooklyn Robins in 1928–1929, and a final season with the Giants in 1930. The 5-foot, 9-inch, 160-pound Bancroft batted better than .300 five times, while leading the NL in **putouts** four times and **assists** three times. From 1948 through 1950, Bancroft managed in the **All-American Girls Professional Baseball League**. In 1971, the **Veterans Committee** elected him to the **National Baseball Hall of Fame**.

BANK ONE BALLPARK. *See* CHASE FIELD.

BANKS, ERNEST "ERNIE," "MR. CUB". B. 31 January 1931, Dallas, Texas. Ernie Banks was playing for the **Kansas City Monarchs** of the **Negro National League** when the **Chicago Cubs** signed him in 1953. Banks, an affable, pleasant man, earned the name "Mr. Cub" in his 19 seasons with the team. The 6-foot, 1-inch, 180-pound Banks was the Cubs' **shortstop** through 1961, and their **first baseman** from 1962 to 1971. Banks, a right-handed hitter, slugged more than 40 **home runs** five times and led the **National League (NL)** twice. His high was 47 in 1958. He also led that year in **slugging percentage**, **total bases**, and **runs batted in (RBI)**, and he was voted the NL's **Most Valuable Player (MVP)**. He led in RBI again in 1959 and earned his second consecutive MVP award.

Whether at shortstop or **first base**, Banks rarely missed a game. He led NL shortstops in **games played** five times and NL first basemen in games played once, in 1965. As a shortstop, he led in **fielding percentage** and **assists** twice and **putouts** once. As a first baseman, he led in fielding percentage once, assists three times, and putouts five times. Banks, an 11-time **All-Star** and winner of the **Lou Gehrig Memorial Award** in 1967, had a career **batting average** of .274, with 512 home runs and 1,636 RBI. In 1977, the **Baseball Writers' Association of America** elected Banks to the **National Baseball Hall of Fame**.

BARLICK, ALBERT JOSEPH "AL". B. 2 April 1915, Springfield, Illinois. D. 27 December 1995, Springfield, Illinois. Al Barlick was an **umpire** in the **National League** from 1940 through 1971. His career was interrupted for service in the U.S. Coast Guard during World War II and for medical problems in 1956 and 1957. Barlick umpired in 4,232 **major-league** games, seven **All-Star Games**, and seven **World Series**. The **Veterans Committee** elected him to the **National Baseball Hall of Fame** in 1989.

BARNES, CHARLES ROSCOE "ROSS". B. 8 May 1850, Mount Morris, New York. D. 5 February 1915, Chicago, Illinois. The 5-foot, 8-inch, 145-pound Ross Barnes played for the **Boston Red Stockings** of the National Association (NA) from 1871 to 1875, the span of the league's existence. During that time, the right-handed-hitting **second baseman** and sometime **shortstop** led the league in **batting average, slugging percentage**, and **doubles** twice, and he had the most **hits** and **runs** scored three times. He is the NA's all-time leader in hits and runs scored.

In 1876, Barnes joined the Chicago White Stockings of the newly formed **National League (NL)**. He was the league's first-year leader in batting average, slugging percentage, **on-base percentage**, runs, hits, doubles, **triples**, and **walks**. In addition, Barnes is credited with hitting the first **home run** in the new league. He played with the White Stockings again in 1877, the **Cincinnati Reds** of the NL in 1879, and the Boston Red Stockings of the NL in 1881. Barnes, who was expert at the **fair-foul hit**, batted above .400 four times and finished with a lifetime batting average of .360. As a second baseman, he led his league in **fielding percentage** three times and **assists** four times.

BARROW, EDWARD GRANT "ED". B. 10 May 1868, Springfield, Illinois. D. 15 December 1953, Port Chester, New York. Ed Barrow was a **manager** in the **American League (AL)** for the **Detroit Tigers** (1903–1904) and **Boston Red Sox** (1918–1920). In 1918, he led the Red Sox to a **World Series** win over the **Chicago Cubs**. Before managing the Tigers, he had been a manager, **general manager (GM)**, and owner in the **minor leagues**, where he helped develop **Honus Wagner**. Barrow is also credited with converting **Babe Ruth** from a **pitcher** to an **outfielder**. In 1920, Barrow became the GM of the **New York Yankees**, who had yet to win their first AL pennant. Barrow became the team's president in 1939, after **Jacob Ruppert** died, and he remained with the Yankees until 1945. During his tenure, New York won 14 pennants and 10 World Series. In 1953, the **Veterans Committee** elected him to the **National Baseball Hall of Fame**.

BASE. A base is one of four points—**first base, second base, third base**, and **home plate**—that a **runner** must touch to score a **run**.

BASE COACH. A base coach is a team member in uniform, almost always not an active player, who is stationed in the coach's box at **first base** or **third base** to direct the **batter** and **base runners**.

BASE RUNNER. A base runner, sometimes called a **runner**, is an offensive player who is advancing toward, or touching, or returning to any **base**.

BASEBALL WORLD CUP. The Baseball World Cup, originally called the Amateur World Series, is an international tournament in which national teams from around the world compete. There have been 39 Baseball World Cups to date, and **Cuba** has won the tournament the most times. The first one, held in 1938, had only two teams, with Great Britain, the host, defeating the United States. The most recent Baseball World Cup, held in 2011, in **Panama**, included 16 teams from four continents. The winner was the **Netherlands**, which defeated Cuba, 2–1, in the championship game. The Netherlands was the first European team to win since Great Britain in 1938.

BASEBALL WRITERS' ASSOCIATION OF AMERICA (BBWAA). The Baseball Writers' Association of America (BBWAA) is an organization of more than 700 men and women who cover the **major leagues** on a regular basis for newspapers, magazines, and major websites. The organization, which now has chapters in each major-league city, was formed during the 1908 **World Series** as a way to improve working conditions for reporters covering games.

Those who have been members of the BBWAA for 10 consecutive seasons are authorized to vote on players eligible for selection to the **National Baseball Hall of Fame**. Two active members from each city also vote in the yearly selections in each league for the winners of the **Most Valuable Player Award**, the **Cy Young Award**, the **Rookie of the Year Award**, and **Manager of the Year**.

BASES ON BALLS (BB). A base on balls, also known as a "walk" is an award of **first base** granted to a **batter** who, during his time **at bat**, receives four "**balls**," that is, four pitches outside the **strike zone**. In 1876, the first year of the **National League (NL)**, it took nine balls for a batter to be awarded a base on balls. That number was gradually reduced during the span of the next 13 years, until it was fixed at four in 1889. Bases on balls became an official statistic in the NL in 1910, and in the **American League (AL)** in 1913.

For batters, the **major league** single-season leader in bases on balls is **Barry Bonds** of the 2004 **San Francisco Giants**, with 232. The single-season leader in the AL is **Babe Ruth** of the 1923 **New York Yankees**, with 170. The career leader is Barry Bonds, with 2,558. Bonds played for the **Pittsburgh Pirates** from 1986 through 1992, and for the San Francisco Giants from 1993 through 2007.

For **pitchers**, the major league single-season leader in allowing the most bases on balls prior to 1893, when the pitching distance was extended to its current 60 feet, 6 inches, is **Amos Rusie** of the 1890 **New York Giants**, who allowed 289. The single-season leader after the change in the pitching distance is also Amos Rusie, who allowed 218 for the 1893 New York Giants. The single-season leader in the AL is **Bob Feller** of the 1938 **Cleveland Indians**, with 208.

The career leader in allowing the most bases on balls is **Nolan Ryan**, with 2,795. Ryan pitched for the **New York Mets** (1966, 1968–1971), California Angels (1972–1979), **Houston Astros** (1980–1988), and **Texas Rangers** (1989–1993).

BATTER. A batter is an offensive player who takes his position in the **batter's box** to face the opposing **pitcher**.
See also BATTING ORDER.

BATTER'S BOX. The batter's box, introduced in 1874, is the area marked out in chalk lines within which the **batter** shall stand during his time at bat. There are two batter's boxes, one for right-handed hitters and one for left-handed hitters. Each is adjacent to **home plate**. The current dimensions of the batter's box, which date from 1885, are 6 feet by 4 feet and 6 inches from home plate.

BATTERY. The battery consists of the **pitcher** and **catcher**.

BATTING AVERAGE (BA). Batting average is calculated by dividing a **batter's** total **hits** by his total **at-bats**. An example is a player with 165 hits and 534 at-bats has a batting average of .309. Although Levi Meyerle batted .492 for the **Philadelphia Athletics** of the National Association in 1871, the generally recognized **major league** single-season leader in batting average is **Hugh Duffy**, who batted .440 for the 1894 Boston Beaneaters of the **National League**. The **American League (AL)** single-season leader is **Nap Lajoie** of the 1901 **Philadelphia Athletics**, with a .426 average. The career leader is **Ty Cobb**, at .366. Cobb played in the AL for the **Detroit Tigers** from 1905 through 1926, and for the Philadelphia Athletics in 1927 and 1928.

BATTING ORDER. A team's batting order is the sequence in which the nine members of the offense take their turns in batting against the opposing **pitcher**. The batting order is set by the **manager** before the game begins.
See also BATTER.

BECKLEY, JACOB PETER "JAKE". B. 4 August 1867, Hannibal, Missouri. D. 25 June 1918, Kansas City, Missouri. Jake Beckley, a left-handed-batting and throwing **first baseman**, began his **major-league** career in June 1888, by batting .343 in 71 games for the **Pittsburgh Alleghenys** of the **National League (NL)**. After batting .301 in 1889, he, like many of his contemporaries, jumped to the **Players League (PL)** in 1890. Playing for the **Pittsburgh Burghers**, the 5-foot, 10-inch, 200-pound Beckley batted .324 and led the PL with 22 **triples**. It was the only time he ever led his league in any offensive category. When the PL folded after one season, Beckley returned to the NL with his original Pittsburgh club, now called the **Pittsburgh Pirates**. He had his best season in 1894, reaching career highs with a .345 **batting average** and 122 **runs batted in**.

In mid-1896, the Pirates traded Beckley to the **New York Giants**, who released him early in 1897. Beckley then signed with the **Cincinnati Reds**, for whom he had five consecutive seasons (1899–1903) of batting above .300. The **St. Louis Cardinals** purchased his contract in 1904, and he spent his final four seasons in St. Louis. Beckley was a lifetime .308 hitter, with 2,934 **hits**. He led NL first basemen in **assists** for four consecutive seasons (1891–1894) and **putouts** a major-league high six times. His career total of 23,731 putouts is the most ever by a first baseman. In 1971, the **Veterans Committee** elected Beckley to the **National Baseball Hall of Fame**.

BELL, JAMES THOMAS "COOL PAPA". B. James Thomas Nichols, 17 May 1903, Starkville, Mississippi. D. 7 March 1991, St. Louis, Missouri. Cool Papa Bell was a **switch-hitting**, left-handed throwing center fielder who played in the **Negro Leagues** and in Latin America from 1922 to 1946. Bell, who stood 5 feet, 11 inches tall and weighed 150 pounds, is reputed to be the fastest runner ever to play in the Negro Leagues. He played for nine different teams in the Negro Leagues, including the **St. Louis Stars** (1922–1931), **Kansas City Monarchs** (1932–1934), **Homestead Grays** (1932, 1943–1946), and **Pittsburgh Crawfords** (1933–1938). From 1938 through 1941, he played in the Mexican League. In 1974, a special **Negro Leagues Committee** elected Bell to the **National Baseball Hall of Fame**.

See also AFRICAN AMERICANS IN BASEBALL.

BELLAN, ESTEBAN "STEVE". B. 1 October 1849, Havana, **Cuba**. D. 8 August 1932, Havana, Cuba. Esteban Bellan, who was half Irish and half Cuban, was the first Latin-born player in the **major leagues**. The 5-foot, 8-inch, 154-pound **third baseman** played in the National Association (NA) from 1871 to 1873, the first three years of the NA's existence. Bellan played for the **Troy Haymakers** in 1871 and 1872, and for the **New York Mutuals** in 1873. He played in a total of 60 games and batted .251.

BENCH. The bench and **dugout** are seating facilities reserved for players, substitutes, and other team members in uniform when they are not actively engaged on the playing field.

BENCH, JOHNNY LEE. B. 7 December 1947, Oklahoma City, Oklahoma. Johnny Bench joined the **Cincinnati Reds** late in the 1967 season and played with them through 1983. During that time, he was recognized as the best **catcher** in the **National League (NL)**, if not in all of baseball. Bench won the **Rookie of the Year Award** in 1968 and the **Most Valuable Player (MVP) Award** in 1970 and 1972. In both those years, he led the NL in **home runs** and **runs batted in (RBI)**. He led in RBI again in 1974. In 1970, he was also named the **Major League Player of the Year**.

The Reds were the dominant team in the NL in the 1970s, playing in six **National League Championship Series** and four **World Series**. Overall, Bench batted .266 with 10 home runs in postseason play. Bench, a 6-foot, 1-inch, 197-pound right-handed hitter, was the winner of the **Lou Gehrig Memorial Award** in 1975, the World Series MVP and **Babe Ruth Award** in 1976, and the **Hutch Award** in 1981. He was a member of 14 **All-Star** teams and won 10 **Gold Glove Awards** for his outstanding defensive abilities. Bench had a .267 career **batting average**, with 389 home runs and 1,376 RBI. The **Baseball Writers' Association of America** elected him to the **National Baseball Hall of Fame** in 1989.

BENDER, CHARLES ALBERT "CHIEF". B. 5 May 1884, Crow Wing County, Minnesota. D. 22 May 1954, Philadelphia, Pennsylvania. Chief Bender, a 6-foot, 2-inch, 185-pound right-handed **pitcher**, joined the **Phila-delphia Athletics** of the **American League (AL)** in 1903. He pitched for the Athletics, managed by **Connie Mack**, for the next 12 seasons, winning 193 games, including 23 in 1910 and 21 in 1913. He also led the AL in **winning percentage** in 1910, 1911, and 1914. Bender left the Athletics to play for the **Baltimore Terrapins** of the **Federal League (FL)** in 1915. Bender's 4–16 record for the Terrapins was the worst of his career, and when the FL folded following the season, he returned to Philadelphia to pitch for the **Philadel-phia Phillies** of the **National League** in 1916–1917. He made one final appearance with the 1925 **Chicago White Sox**.

Bender ended his big-league career with a lifetime record of 212–127, a 2.46 **earned run average**, and 40 **shutouts**. He pitched in five **World Series** for the Athletics (1905, 1910, 1911, 1913, and 1914), winning six games and losing four. Bender later pitched and managed in the **minor leagues**, served as a **coach** for the White Sox in 1925–1926, and acted as a **scout** for the Athletics in the late 1940s. In 1953, the **Veterans Committee** elected him to the **National Baseball Hall of Fame**.

BENNETT, CHARLES WESLEY "CHARLIE". B. 21 November 1854, New Castle, Pennsylvania. D. 24 February 1927, Detroit, Michigan. Charlie Bennett was the league's best defensive **catcher** during his 15 seasons in the

National League (NL). The 5-foot, 11-inch, 180-pound Bennett played with the **Milwaukee Grays** in 1878 and the **Worcester Ruby Legs** in 1880; however, the bulk of his career was with the **Detroit Wolverines**, from 1881 until they folded after the 1888 season, and then the Boston Beaneaters (1889–1893). The right-handed-hitting Bennett batted .301, .301, and .305 in his first three seasons with Detroit, but he never came close to batting .300 again. Defensively, however, he led NL catchers in **fielding percentage** seven times and **double plays** and **putouts** three times each. Bennett's career ended in January 1894, when a train accident led to both his legs being amputated.

BENNETT PARK. *See* DETROIT TIGERS.

BERRA, LAWRENCE PETER "YOGI". B. 12 May 1925, St. Louis, Missouri. The **New York Yankees** were not sure whether Yogi Berra was a **catcher** or an **outfielder** when he first joined them in 1946. They eventually decided he was a catcher, and, with the help of former Yankees catcher **Bill Dickey**, Berra became one of the greatest catchers ever. He led all **American League (AL)** catchers in **games played** each season from 1950 to 1957, **putouts** eight times, runners **caught stealing** four times, **assists** three times, and **fielding percentage** twice.

Although he stood only 5 feet, 7 inches, the 185-pound left-handed-hitting Berra generated tremendous power. He hit 20 or more **home runs** 11 times and reached the 100 **runs batted in (RBI)** mark five times. Berra was the Yankees RBI leader each season from 1949 through 1955. Although he never led the AL in any offensive category, he was selected to the **All-Star** team 15 times and won the league's **Most Valuable Player Award** three times, in 1951, 1954, and 1955. He was second in the voting twice and third once. Berra played in 14 **World Series** with the Yankees and holds numerous Series records, including games played (75), **hits** (71), **doubles** (10), and catcher putouts (457).

Berra's final season as a player with the Yankees was 1963. He was the club's **manager** in 1964 and led them to a pennant but was fired after losing to the **St. Louis Cardinals** in the World Series. He played in four games for the **New York Mets** in 1965, and then remained with the team as a **coach** until 1972, when he was named manager after the death of Gil Hodges. The Mets won the **National League** pennant in 1973, but lost a seven-game World Series to the **Oakland Athletics**. Berra was fired during the 1975 season. He later managed the Yankees again in 1984, and for 16 games in 1985. His career record as a manager was 484–444. As a player, Berra had a

.285 **batting average**, 358 home runs, and 1,430 runs batted in. He was elected to the **National Baseball Hall of Fame** by the **Baseball Writers' Association of America** in 1972.

BIGGIO, CRAIG ALAN. B. 14 December 1965, Smithtown, New York. Craig Biggio was the first-round choice of the **Houston Astros** in the 1987 **Amateur Draft**. He made his debut with the Astros in 1988 and spent the next 20 seasons in Houston. Originally a **catcher**, the Astros moved him to **second base** in 1992, the position he played for most of his career. In 2003–2004, the versatile Biggio was used as an **outfielder**. A 5 feet, 11 inches, 185 pounds right-handed hitter, Biggio had a .281 career **batting average**, with 3,060 **hits**, 414 **stolen bases,** and 668 **doubles** (fifth all-time). He led the **National League (NL)** in doubles three times, **runs** scored twice, and being **hit by pitch** five times. Biggio's career 285 hit-by-pitch total trails only **Hughie Jennings**, who had 287.

Biggio, a seven-time **All-Star**, won five **Silver Slugger Awards** and four **Gold Glove Awards**. He led NL second basemen in **games played** eight times, **assists** six times, and **putouts** five times. His honors include the **Branch Rickey Award** (1997), **Hutch Award** (2005), and **Roberto Clemente Award** (2007). Biggio, whose last active season was 2007, is likely to be elected to the **National Baseball Hall of Fame** when he becomes eligible.

BLYLEVEN, RIK AALBERT "BERT". B. 6 April 1951, Zeist, Netherlands. Bert Blyleven **pitched** for five **major-league** teams in a career that lasted 22 seasons. He pitched for the **Minnesota Twins** (1970–1976, 1985–1988), **Texas Rangers** (1976–1977), **Cleveland Indians** (1981–1985), and California Angels (1989–1990, 1992) in the **American League**, and for the **Pittsburgh Pirates** (1978–1980) in the **National League**. The 6-foot, 3-inch, 200-pound right-hander was a 20-game winner only once, with the 1973 Twins, but he had double-digit **win** totals in 17 of his 22 seasons. Using an exceptionally good **curveball**, he struck out 200 or more **batters** in eight seasons. Blyleven had a combined 5–1 record and 2.47 **earned run average** in 47.1 **innings pitched** in league championship and **World Series** play. His 1979 Pirates and 1987 Twins were both World Series winners. Blyleven retired with a career record of 287–250, with 3,701 **strikeouts**—behind only **Nolan Ryan** and **Steve Carlton** at the time—and 60 **shutouts**, ninth best all-time. He was elected by the **Baseball Writers' Association of America** to the **National Baseball Hall of Fame** in 2011.

BOGGS, WADE ANTHONY. B. 15 June 1958, Omaha, Nebraska. Wade Boggs was a **third baseman** for the **Boston Red Sox**, **New York Yankees**, and Tampa Bay Devil Rays from 1982 to 1999. While playing for Boston

(1982–1992), he won five **American League** batting titles, led in **on-base percentage** six times, and had 200 **hits** or more in seven consecutive seasons. He also led in **doubles, walks,** and **runs,** twice each, and scored 100 runs or more in seven consecutive seasons. He was the first **major-league** player to have four consecutive seasons with 200 or more hits and 100 or more walks.

After the 1992 season, Boggs, a 6-foot, 2-inch, 190-pound left-handed hitter, signed as a **free agent** with the Yankees. He topped the .300 mark in four of his five seasons in New York and then again declared free agency and played the 1998 and 1999 seasons for the Devil Rays. In 1999, he recorded his 3,000th hit, the first player to do so with a **home run.** Boggs, a 12-time **All-Star,** was the winner of eight **Silver Slugger Awards** (the most by any third baseman) and two **Gold Glove Awards.** He batted a combined .286 in his two **World Series** appearances, a 1986 loss to the **New York Mets,** when he was with Boston, and a 1996 win over the **Atlanta Braves,** when he was with the Yankees. His career **batting average** was .328, and he finished with 3,010 hits and 1,513 runs. The **Baseball Writers' Association of America** elected Boggs to the **National Baseball Hall of Fame** in 2005.

BOND, THOMAS HENRY "TOMMY". B. 2 April 1856, Granard, Ireland. D. 24 January 1941, Boston, Massachusetts. Tommy Bond spent only 10 seasons in the **major leagues,** during which time he **pitched** for seven different teams in four different leagues. He pitched in the National Association for the **Brooklyn Atlantics** (1874) and **Hartford Dark Blues** (1875); in the **National League** for the Hartford Dark Blues (1876), Boston Red Stockings (1877–1881), and **Worcester Ruby Legs** (1882); in the **Union Association** for the **Boston Reds** (1884); and in the **American Association** for the **Indianapolis Hoosiers** (1884).

Bond, a right-hander who stood only 5 feet, 7 inches tall and weighed 160 pounds, had his best seasons with the Red Stockings. He led the National League (NL) with 40 **wins** in both 1877 and 1878 for the pennant-winning Red Stockings and added 43 more wins in 1879. He was twice the league's leader in **earned run average (ERA)** and **strikeouts,** and, in 1877, he won the first pitcher's **Triple Crown** by leading the NL in wins, ERA, and strikeouts. Bond's career record is 234–163.

BONDS, BARRY LAMAR. B. 24 July 1964, Riverside, California. Barry Bonds was the first-round choice of the **Pittsburgh Pirates** in the 1985 **Amateur Draft.** He made his debut the next year as a center fielder and remained in Pittsburgh through 1992, although he was later moved to left field. Bonds joined the **San Francisco Giants** as a **free agent** for the 1993 season and played 15 years for the Giants. During his 22-year career, the 6-foot, 1-inch, 185-pound Bonds set many single-season and career batting records.

Bonds set a new single-season **home run** mark with 73 in 2001, and he also holds the career home-run record, with 762. He led the **National League (NL)** in walks 12 times, including a single-season record 232 times in 2004 and a career record of 2,558 overall. He also led in intentional walks 12 times, with a single-season record 120 in 2004 and a career record of 688 overall. He won two batting championships and led in **on-base percentage** 10 times and **slugging percentage** seven times.

Bonds was a 14-time **All-Star** and the winner of 12 **Silver Slugger Awards** and eight **Gold Glove Awards**. He was the **Major League Player of the Year** in 1990, 2001, and 2004, and the winner of the NL's **Hank Aaron Award** in 2001, 2002, and 2004. Bonds was the NL's **Most Valuable Player** an astonishing seven times, in 1990, 1992, and 1993, and in four straight seasons from 2001 to 2004.

In addition to his 762 home runs, Bonds had a .298 career **batting average**, 2,935 **hits**, 2,227 runs (third all-time), 1,996 **runs batted in** (fourth all-time), a .444 on-base percentage, a .607 slugging percentage, and 514 **stolen bases**. Bonds retired after the 2007 season, but charges that he used performance-enhancing drugs in the latter stages of his career could affect his election to the **National Baseball Hall of Fame**.

BOSTON AMERICANS. *See* BOSTON RED SOX.

BOSTON BEANEATERS. *See* BOSTON BRAVES.

BOSTON BEES. *See* BOSTON BRAVES.

BOSTON BRAVES. The Boston Braves, then called the **Boston Red Stockings**, entered the newly formed **National League (NL)** as a charter member in 1876. The Red Stockings had played in the National Association from 1871 through 1875. They remained in Boston until the franchise was shifted to Milwaukee in 1953. The team was called the Boston Beaneaters from 1883 to 1906, the Boston Doves from 1907 to 1910, the Boston Rustlers in 1911, and finally the Braves in 1912. The name Braves has remained until the present, with the exception of 1936 to 1940, when the team was called the Boston Bees. The club played its home games at the Congress Street Grounds, the South End Grounds, and briefly at **Fenway Park**, before moving to **Braves Field**, on 18 August 1915. The team played at Braves Field through the 1952 season.

Boston was one of the NL's dominant clubs in the 19th century, winning pennants in 1877, 1878, 1883, 1891, 1892, 1893, 1897, and 1898. The Boston Braves won two pennants in the 20th century. In 1914, they upset the heavily favored **Philadephia Athletics** in a four-game **World Series** sweep, and, in 1948, they lost the Series in six games to the **Cleveland Indians**. Just before the start of the 1953 season, the Braves became the first **major-league** team to relocate since 1903.

Boston Braves players who won the NL's **Most Valuable Player Award** were **Johnny Evers** in 1914 and Bob Elliott in 1947. The **Cy Young Award** came into existence in 1956, after the Braves had left for Milwaukee. **Rookie of the Year** winners include Alvin Dark in 1948 and Sam Jethroe in 1950.

Boston players who led the NL in **batting average** were **Deacon White** (1877), **Dan Brouthers** (1889), **Hugh Duffy** (1894), **Rogers Hornsby** (1928), and **Ernie Lombardi** (1942). **Home run** leaders include Charley Jones (1879), **Jim O'Rourke** (1880), **Harry Stovey** (1891), Hugh Duffy (1894, 1897), **Jimmy Collins** (1898), Herman Long (1900), Dave Brain (1907), Fred Beck (1910), Wally Berger (1935), and Tommy Holmes (1945). **Runs batted in** leaders were Deacon White (1877), Charley Jones (1879), John O'Rourke (1879), and Wally Berger (1935).

Boston **pitchers** who led the NL in **wins** were **Tommy Bond** (1877–1878), Jim Whitney (1881), **John Clarkson** (1889), **Kid Nichols** (1896–1898), Johnny Sain (1948), and **Warren Spahn** (1949–1950). **Earned run average (ERA)** leaders were Tommy Bond (1877, 1879), John Clarkson (1889), **Vic Willis** (1899), Jim Turner (1937), Warren Spahn (1947), and Chet Nichols (1951). **Strikeouts** leaders were Tommy Bond (1877–1878), Jim Whitney (1883), John Clarkson (1889), Vic Willis (1902), and Warren Spahn (1949–1952). By leading in wins, ERA, and strikeouts, Tommy Bond won the first **Triple Crown** for pitchers in 1877. By leading in wins, ERA, and strikeouts, John Clarkson won the Triple Crown for pitchers in 1889.

Other notable players and **managers** for the Boston Braves included **Dave Bancroft**, Wally Berger, Charlie Buffinton, **Billy Hamilton**, **King Kelly**, Bobby Lowe, **Tommy McCarthy**, **Bill McKechnie**, **Rabbit Maranville**, Billy Nash, Togie Pittinger, Lance Richbourg, Dick Rudolph, **Frank Selee**, **Billy Southworth**, Chick Stahl, George Stallings, Eddie Stanky, **Casey Stengel**, Jack Stivetts, Fred Tenney, Tommy Tucker, and **Harry Wright**.

BOSTON DOVES. *See* BOSTON BRAVES.

BOSTON RED SOX. The Boston Red Sox are a team in the Eastern Division of the **American League (AL)**. The Red Sox have been members of the AL since 1901, the first year the AL was recognized as a **major league**. The team was called the Boston Americans from 1901 through 1907. The Red Sox played their home games at the Huntington Avenue Baseball Grounds from 1901 to 1911. They currently play at **Fenway Park**, which opened on 20 April 1912, making it the oldest major-league park still in use.

In 1903, the Boston Americans represented the AL in the first modern **World Series**, defeating the **Pittsburgh Pirates** of the more established **National League**, five games to three. The Red Sox were baseball's dominant team in the decade of the 1910s, winning the World Series against the **New York Giants** in 1912, **Philadelphia Phillies** in 1915, Brooklyn Robins in 1916, and **Chicago Cubs** in 1918. But after a sixth-place finish in 1919, owner Harry Frazee sold **Babe Ruth**, his best player, to the **New York Yankees**. The sale of several other star players followed, mostly to New York, and it was not until 1934 that Boston would again finish as high as fourth place.

The Red Sox did not reach the World Series again until 1946, when they lost in seven games to the **St. Louis Cardinals**. Their next pennant was in 1967, with the same result, a seven-game Series loss to the Cardinals. Two more seven-game Series losses followed, to the **Cincinnati Reds** in 1975 and the **New York Mets** in 1986. In 2004, after 86 years, the Sox won another world championship when they swept the Cardinals in four games. They won again in 2007, sweeping the **Colorado Rockies**. A frequent playoff participant, the Red Sox have lost in the **American League Division Series** four times and in the **American League Championship Series** five times.

Red Sox players who have won the AL's **Most Valuable Player Award** are **Tris Speaker** (1912), **Jimmie Foxx** (1938), **Ted Williams** (1946, 1949), Jackie Jensen (1958), **Carl Yastrzemski** (1967), Fred Lynn (1975), **Jim Rice** (1978), **Roger Clemens** (1986), Mo Vaughn (1995), and Dustin Pedroia (2008). **Cy Young Award** winners are Jim Lonborg (1967), Roger Clemens (1986–1987, 1991), and **Pedro Martinez** (1999–2000). **Rookie of the Year** winners are Walt Dropo (1950), Don Schwall (1961), **Carlton Fisk** (1972), Fred Lynn (1975), Nomar Garciaparra (1997), and Dustin Pedroia (2007).

Red Sox players who have led the league in **batting average** are Dale Alexander (1932, part of season with **Detroit Tigers**), Jimmie Foxx (1938), Ted Williams (1941–1942, 1947–1948, 1957–1958), Billy Goodman (1950), Pete Runnels (1960, 1962), Carl Yastrzemski (1963, 1967–1968), Fred Lynn (1979), Carney Lansford (1981), **Wade Boggs** (1983, 1985–1988), Nomar Garciaparra (1999–2000), **Manny Ramirez** (2002), and Bill Mueller (2003). Leaders in **home runs** are Buck Freeman (1903), Jake Stahl (1910), Tris Speaker (1912), Babe Ruth (1918–1919), Jimmie Foxx (1939), Ted Williams (1941–1942, 1947, 1949), Tony Conigliaro (1965), Carl Yastrzemski (1967), Jim Rice (1977–1978, 1983), Dwight Evans (1981), Tony Armas (1984), Manny Ramirez (2004), and David Ortiz (2006). Leaders in **runs batted in** are Buck Freeman (1902–1903), Babe Ruth (1919), Jimmie Foxx (1938), Ted Williams (1939, 1942, 1947, 1949), Vern Stephens (1949–1950), Walt Dropo (1950), Jackie Jensen (1955, 1958–1959), Dick Stuart (1963), Carl Yastrzemski (1967), Ken Harrelson (1968), Jim Rice (1978, 1983), Tony Armas (1984), Mo Vaughn (1995), and David Ortiz (2005–2006). In 1942 and 1947, Ted Williams led the AL in batting average, home runs, and runs batted in to win the **Triple Crown** for **batters** both years. By leading the AL in batting average, home runs, and runs batted in, Carl Yastrzemski won the Triple Crown for batters in 1967.

Red Sox **pitchers** who have led the league in **wins** are **Cy Young** (1901–1903), Joe Wood (1912), Wes Ferrell (1935), Tex Hughson (1942), Mel Parnell (1949), Frank Sullivan (1955), Jim Lonborg (1967), Roger Clemens (1986–1987), Pedro Martinez (1999), Curt Schilling (2004), and Josh Beckett (2007). **Earned run average (ERA)** leaders are Cy Young (1901), Hubert "Dutch" Leonard (1914), Joe Wood (1915), Babe Ruth (1916), **Lefty Grove** (1935–1936, 1938–1939), Luis Tiant (1972), Roger Clemens (1986, 1990–1992), and Pedro Martinez (1999–2000, 2002–2003). **Strikeouts** leaders are Cy Young (1901), Tex Hughson (1942), Jim Lonborg (1967), Roger Clemens (1988, 1991, 1996), Pedro Martinez (1999–2000, 2002), and Hideo Nomo (2001). By leading in wins, ERA, and strikeouts in 1901, Cy Young won the Triple Crown for pitchers. By leading in wins, ERA, and strikeouts in 1999, Pedro Martinez won the Triple Crown for pitchers.

Other notable players and **managers** in Red Sox history include Marty Barrett, **Ed Barrow**, Ellis Burks, Rick Burleson, Bill Carrigan, **Jimmy Collins**, Ray Collins, Doc Cramer, **Joe Cronin**, Johnny Damon, Ike Delock, Dom DiMaggio, Bill Dinneen, Joe Dobson, **Bobby Doerr**, Jacoby Ellsbury, **Rick Ferrell**, Dave Ferris, Terry Francona, Larry Gardner, Rich Gedman, Adrian Gonzalez, Mike Greenwell, **Harry Hooper**, Bruce Hurst, Bob Johnson, Roy Johnson, Sam Jones, Ellis Kinder, Bill Lee, John Lester, Duffy Lewis, Derek Lowe, Mike Lowell, Sparky Lyle, Frank Malzone, Carl Mays, **Joe McCarthy**, John McNamara, Bill Monbouquette, Trot Nixon, Jonathan Papelbon, Freddy Parent, Herb Pennock, Johnny Pesky, Rico Petrocelli, Jimmy Piersall, Dick Radatz, Jerry Remy, Wally Schang, Everett Scott, George Scott, Ernie Shore, Reggie Smith, Bob Stanley, Mike Timlin, Jason Varitek, Sammy White, **Dick Williams**, Jimy Williams, George Winter, and Kevin Youkilis.

BOSTON RED STOCKINGS (NA). The Boston Red Stockings, also known as the Red Caps, were a team in the National Association (NA) from 1871 to 1875. Managed by **Harry Wright**, they were the NA's most successful team, winning four pennants (1872–1875) in the NA's five-year existence. In 1876, the Red Stockings became charter members of the new **Na-**

tional League. Notable players for the Red Stockings included **Ross Barnes**, Andy Leonard, Cal McVey, **Jim O'Rourke**, **Al Spalding**, **Deacon White**, and **George Wright**.

BOSTON RED STOCKINGS (NL). *See* BOSTON BRAVES.

BOSTON REDS (AA). The Boston Reds moved to the **American Association (AA)** in 1891 from the **Players League (PL)**, where they had won the pennant in 1890, the PL's only year of existence. They won again in the AA in 1891, the AA's final year. Among the notable players on the 1891 Boston Reds were **Dan Brouthers**, Tom Brown, Charlie Buffinton, **Hugh Duffy**, and George Haddock.

BOSTON REDS (PL). The Boston Reds were a team in the **Players League (PL)** in 1890, the one year of the PL's existence. Boston finished in first place, with a 81–47 record. In 1891, the team joined the **American Association**, where they repeated as pennant winners. Hardy Richardson led the PL in **runs batted in**, with 146. Other notable players on the 1890 Boston Reds were **Dan Brouthers**, **King Kelly**, **Charlie Radbourn**, and **Harry Stovey**.

BOSTON REDS (UA). The Boston Reds were a team in the **Union Association (UA)** in 1884, the one year of the UA's existence. Boston finished with a 58–51 record.

BOSTON RUSTLERS. *See* BOSTON BRAVES.

BOTTOMLEY, JAMES LEROY "JIM," "SUNNY JIM". B. 23 April 1900, Oglesby, Illinois. D. 11 December 1959, St. Louis, Missouri. Jim Bottomley played **first base** for four **National League (NL)** pennant winners during his 11 seasons with the **St. Louis Cardinals** (1922–1932). He batted .345 in the Cardinals win over the **New York Yankees** in the 1926 **World Series**, but his overall Series average for 24 games was a lowly .200. Known as "Sunny Jim," for his pleasant manner, the 6-foot, 180-pound Bottomley also played for the **Cincinnati Reds** from 1933 to 1935, and for the **St. Louis Browns** in 1936 and 1937. He was the **manager** of the Browns for the second half of the 1937 season. The left-handed-hitting Bottomley had outstanding seasons in 1923, when he batted .371, and in 1925, when he batted .367 and led the NL in **hits** (227) and **doubles** (44). But his best overall season was in 1928. Bottomley led the league that year in **triples** (20), **home runs** (31), and **runs batted in** (136), and he won the **Most Valuable Player Award**.

Bottomley had a lifetime **batting average** of .310, and he drove in more than 100 **runs** in six consecutive seasons. He twice had six hits in a game, and, on 16 September 1924, he set a **major-league** record (since tied) by driving in 12 runs in one game. While with the Browns in 1936, he set the single-season record for a first baseman with eight unassisted **double plays**. In 1974, the **Veterans Committee** elected Bottomley to the **National Baseball Hall of Fame**.

BOUDREAU, LOUIS, "LOU". B. 17 July 1917, Harvey, Illinois. D. 10 August 2001, Olympia Fields, Illinois. Lou Boudreau played in the **American League (AL)** from 1938 (one game) to 1952 (four games). For the years 1940 to 1950, he played **shortstop** for the **Cleveland Indians**. In 1942, when he was only 24 years of age, he was named **manager** of the Indians, making him the youngest man ever to manage a full season in the **major leagues**. A 5-foot, 11-inch, 185-pound right-handed hitter, Boudreau led the AL in **doubles** three times and won the AL batting championship in 1944, with a .327 **batting average**. He had his greatest season, however, in 1948, when he batted .355 and was voted the **Major League Player of the Year** and the AL's **Most Valuable Player**. He was the star of the game as his Indians defeated the **Boston Red Sox** in a one-game playoff to determine the AL pennant winner. The Indians then defeated the **Boston Braves** in the **World Series** to give Cleveland its first Series championship since 1920.

Boudreau was released by the Indians after the 1950 season. He played for the Red Sox in 1951 and 1952 and managed the Boston club from 1952 to 1954. For the next three seasons, he managed the **Kansas City Athletics**, before a final managerial stint with the 1960 **Chicago Cubs**. Boudreau, who had a lifetime batting average of .295, was voted to the **All-Star** team eight times. Defensively, he led AL shortstops in **fielding percentage** for 10 consecutive seasons, from 1940 to 1949. His record as a manager was 1,162–1,224. Boudreau was elected by the **Baseball Writers' Association of America** to the **National Baseball Hall of Fame** in 1970.

BRANCH RICKEY AWARD. The Branch Rickey Award is given annually to a **major-league** player, owner, **manager**, front-office member, **scout**, etc., in recognition of his or her exceptional community service. The award was created by the Rotary Club of Denver, Colorado, with the following criteria: The winner should be an outstanding individual currently involved in Major League Baseball. He or she must be a role model for young people, as evidenced by baseball accomplishments, coupled with high ethical standards. He or she must be an unselfish contributor to the community whose volunteer activities exemplify Rotary International's motto, "Service above Self." The first winner, in 1992, was **Dave Winfield** of the **Toronto Blue**

Jays. The most recent winner, in 2012, was R. A. Dickey of the **New York Mets,** in recognition of his work distributing baseball equipment and medical supplies in Central and South America.

BRAVES FIELD. Braves Field, located in Boston, Massachusetts, was the home of the **Boston Braves** of the **National League** from 18 August 1915 to 21 September 1952. In 1953, the Braves moved to Milwaukee, where they became the **Milwaukee Braves.** When Braves Field opened, it was the first park to have a seating capacity of more than 40,000. Braves Field hosted the **major league All-Star Game** in 1936.

See also STADIUMS.

BRESNAHAN, ROGER PHILLIP "DUKE OF TRALEE". B. 11 June 1879, Toledo, Ohio. D. 4 December 1944, Toledo, Ohio. Roger Bresnahan, a right-handed **batter** and thrower, began his **major-league** career as a **pitcher,** going 4–0 for the 1897 **Washington Senators** of the **National League (NL).** He eventually played every position during his 17 years in the big leagues, but he is best remembered as a **catcher.** The 5-foot, 9-inch, 200-pound Bresnahan was known for his ability to handle pitchers and his innovative mind; he is credited with being the first catcher to use shin guards. Bresnahan played in two games for the 1900 Chicago Orphans of the NL, after which **John McGraw,** the **manager** of the **Baltimore Orioles** in the new **American League,** signed him for the 1901 season. In mid-1902, McGraw left to manage the NL's **New York Giants** and brought Bresnahan and several of his Orioles teammates with him.

Because of Bresnahan's speed, McGraw played him primarily in center field in 1903 and 1904, before returning him to the catching position in 1905. The Giants won the pennant that year and defeated the **Philadelphia Athletics** four games to one in the **World Series.** Bresnahan, known as the "Duke of Tralee," batted .313 in the Series and caught four **shutout** victories for the Giants, three by **Christy Mathewson** and one by **Joe McGinnity.** Traded to the **St. Louis Cardinals** in December 1908, Bresnahan played for St. Louis through 1912, while also serving as manager. He finished his career with the 1913 to 1915 **Chicago Cubs,** whom he also managed in 1915. Bresnahan had a career **batting average** of .279 and a won-lost record of 328–432 as a manager. He was elected to the **National Baseball Hall of Fame** by the **Old Timers Committee** in 1945.

BRETT, GEORGE HOWARD. B. 15 May 1953, Glen Dale, West Virginia. During most of his 21-year career with the **Kansas City Royals** (1973–1993), George Brett was the premier **third baseman** in the **American League (AL).** Brett, a 6-foot, 185-pound left-handed hitter, bettered the .300

mark 11 times. He was a three-time AL batting champion, with a career high .390 **batting average** in 1980. Brett also led the AL with a .454 **on-base percentage** and a .664 **slugging percentage** that year. The Royals won the pennant, and Brett was named the **Major League Player of the Year**, the winner of the **Hutch Award**, and the AL's **Most Valuable Player (MVP)**. In 1986, he won the **Lou Gehrig Memorial Award**.

Brett led the league in **hits**, **triples**, and slugging percentage three times, and in **doubles** twice. He was a 13-time **All-Star** and the winner of three **Silver Slugger Awards**, including one at **first base** in 1988. (Late in his career, the Royals used Brett at first base and as a **designated hitter**.) Always dependable, he was a great hitter in the postseason, batting .340 in 27 **American League Championship Series (ALCS)** games, and .373 in 13 **World Series** games. He was the MVP of the 1985 ALCS. Brett had a career batting average of .305, with 3,154 hits, the most ever by a third baseman, and his 665 doubles are sixth best all-time. He was the first player to accumulate 3,000 hits, 300 **home runs**, 600 doubles, 100 triples, 1,500 **runs batted in**, and 200 **stolen bases**. In 1999, the **Baseball Writers' Association of America** elected Brett to the **National Baseball Hall of Fame**.

BRIGGS STADIUM. *See* TIGER STADIUM.

BROCK, LOUIS CARL "LOU". B. 18 June 1939, El Dorado, Arkansas. Lou Brock began his **major-league** career in 1961 with the **Chicago Cubs**. On 15 June 1964, the Cubs traded him to the **St. Louis Cardinals** in what turned out to be a very one-sided trade in favor of St. Louis. The 5-foot, 11-inch, 170-pound Brock played 16 seasons for the Cardinals, while becoming the greatest base stealer in modern **National League (NL)** history. His 118 **stolen bases** in 1974 broke Maury Wills's single-season major-league record. Brock's record was broken in 1982 by **Rickey Henderson** of the **Oakland Athletics**, who had 130 stolen bases; however, Brock still holds the NL single-season record, and his career total of 938 is also a record for the NL. Overall, Brock led the league in steals eight times.

A left-handed-hitting left fielder, Brock had 200 **hits** or more four times. He was a six-time **All-Star** who helped lead the Cardinals to three pennants and batted .391 with 14 stolen bases in 21 **World Series** games. In addition to his 938 stolen bases, Brock had a .293 **batting average** and 3,023 hits. His honors included the **Babe Ruth Award** in 1967, **Major League Player of the Year** in 1974, **Roberto Clemente Award** in 1975, **Lou Gehrig Memorial Award** in 1977, and **Hutch Award** in 1979. In 1985, the **Baseball Writers' Association of America** elected Brock to the **National Baseball Hall of Fame**.

BROOKLYN ATLANTICS (NA). The Brooklyn Atlantics, also called Atlantic or the Atlantic Baseball Club of Brooklyn, were established in 1855. In 1857, they were a founding member of the **National Association of Base Ball Players**, consisting of amateur teams primarily from the Northeastern and Midwest. The Atlantics won several championships, and, in 1869, the team was one of the first clubs to move from an amateur to a professional status. The Atlantics were members of the National Association from 1872 through 1875, after which the league folded. Notable players for the Atlantics included **Tommy Bond** and **Bob Ferguson**.

BROOKLYN BRIDEGROOMS (AA). *See* BROOKLYN TROLLEY DODGERS (AA).

BROOKLYN BRIDEGROOMS (NL). *See* BROOKLYN DODGERS.

BROOKLYN DODGERS. The Brooklyn Dodgers, then known as the Brooklyn Bridegrooms or the Brooklyn Trolley Dodgers, entered the **National League (NL)** in 1890 after jumping from the **American Association (AA)**. Winners of the AA pennant in 1889, the club repeated as NL pennant winners in 1890. Brooklyn played the **Louisville Colonels**, the 1890 AA pennant winner, in a championship series that was a predecessor to the modern **World Series**. Each team won three games and lost three, and one game ended in a tie. Playing as the Brooklyn Superbas when **Ned Hanlon** was **manager**, the club won back-to-back pennants in 1899 and 1900. Playing as the Brooklyn Robins during **Wilbert Robinson's** tenure as manager, they won pennants in 1916 and 1920. Brooklyn lost the World Series to the **Boston Red Sox** in 1916 and the **Cleveland Indians** in 1920.

The Dodgers did not win another pennant until 1941, with a team revitalized by **Larry MacPhail**, the club's president and **general manager**. Another Series loss followed, this time to the **New York Yankees**. **Branch Rickey**, who succeeded MacPhail, built a team that won six pennants after World War II and faced the Yankees in the World Series each time. The Yankees won five (1947, 1949, 1952, 1953, and 1956), with the Dodgers winning their only world championship in Brooklyn in 1955. The Dodgers played their home games at various incarnations of Washington Park from 1890 to 1912, and at **Ebbets Field**, named for owner **Charlie Ebbets**, from 1913 through 1957. In 1958, owner **Walter O'Malley** moved the Dodgers to Los Angeles, where they became the **Los Angeles Dodgers**.

Brooklyn Dodgers players who won the NL's **Most Valuable Player Award** were Jake Daubert (1913), **Dazzy Vance** (1924), Dolph Camilli (1941), **Jackie Robinson** (1949), **Roy Campanella** (1951, 1953, 1955), and

Don Newcombe (1956). In 1956, Don Newcombe won the first **Cy Young Award**. **Rookie of the Year** winners were Jackie Robinson (1947), Don Newcombe (1949), Joe Black (1952), and Jim Gilliam (1953).

Brooklyn players who led the league in **batting average** were **Dan Brouthers** (1892), Jake Daubert (1913–1914), **Zack Wheat** (1918), Lefty O'Doul (1932), Pete Reiser (1941), Dixie Walker (1944), Jackie Robinson (1949), and Carl Furillo (1953). **Home run** leaders were Oyster Burns (1890), Jimmy Sheckard (1903), Harry Lumley (1904), Tim Jordan (1906, 1908), Jack Fournier (1924), Dolph Camilli (1941), and **Duke Snider** (1956). **Runs batted in** leaders were Oyster Burns (1890), Dan Brouthers (1892), Hi Myers (1919), Dolph Camilli (1941), Dixie Walker (1945), Roy Campanella (1953), and Duke Snider (1955).

Brooklyn **pitchers** who led the league in **wins** were Jim Hughes (1899), **Joe McGinnity** (1900), Bill Donovan (1901), **Burleigh Grimes** (1921), Dazzy Vance (1924–1925), Kirby Higbe (1941), Whit Wyatt (1941), and Don Newcombe (1956). **Earned run average (ERA)** leaders were Dazzy Vance (1924, 1928, 1930) and Johnny Podres (1957). **Strikeouts** leaders were Burleigh Grimes (1921), Dazzy Vance (1922–1928), Van Mungo (1936), and Don Newcombe (1951). By leading in wins, ERA, and strikeouts, Dazzy Vance won the **Triple Crown** for pitchers in 1924.

Other notable players and managers in Brooklyn Dodgers history included **Walter Alston**, Ralph Branca, Leon Cadore, Hugh Casey, Watty Clark, Billy Cox, Bill Dahlen, Tom Daly, Curt Davis, **Leo Durocher**, Carl Erskine, Fred Fitzsimmons, Augie Galan, Mike Griffin, Luke Hamlin, Babe Herman, **Billy Herman**, Gil Hodges, Jimmy Johnston, Fielder Jones, **Joe Kelley**, Brickyard Kennedy, Clem Labine, Harry Lavagetto, Bill McGunnigle, **Joe Medwick**, Otto Miller, Ivy Olson, Mickey Owen, Jeff Pfeffer, Babe Phelps, **Pee Wee Reese**, Preacher Roe, Nap Rucker, Burt Shotton, Eddie Stanky, **Casey Stengel**, and **Arky Vaughan**.

BROOKLYN ECKFORDS. The Brooklyn Eckfords were established in 1855, as the Eckford Club of Brooklyn. In 1857, they were a founding member of the **National Association of Base Ball Players**, consisting of amateur teams primarily from the Northeast and Midwest. In 1869, the Eckfords were one of the first clubs to move from an amateur to a professional status. They played in the National Association for part of one season (1872).

BROOKLYN EXCELSIORS. The Brooklyn Excelsiors were an early amateur baseball team, originally formed in 1854. Among the Excelsiors' most notable players were Asa Brainard, **Jim Creighton**, and **Candy Cummings**.

BROOKLYN FEDERALS. *See* BROOKLYN TIP-TOPS.

BROOKLYN GLADIATORS. The Brooklyn Gladiators played part of the 1890 season as members of the **American Association (AA)**. They had a 26–72 record when they disbanded in midseason. They were replaced by the **Baltimore Orioles**, who had played in the AA from 1882 to 1889, but had dropped out after the 1889 season.

BROOKLYN GRAYS. *See* BROOKLYN TROLLEY DODGERS (AA).

BROOKLYN HARTFORDS. *See* HARTFORD DARK BLUES.

BROOKLYN ROBINS. *See* BROOKLYN DODGERS.

BROOKLYN SUPERBAS. *See* BROOKLYN DODGERS.

BROOKLYN TIP-TOPS. The Brooklyn Tip-Tops, also called the Brooklyn Federals or BrookFeds, were a team in the **Federal League (FL)** in 1914 and 1915, the two seasons the FL existed as a **major league**. The Tip-Tops finished in fifth place in 1914, but the team fell to seventh in 1915, despite the addition of Benny Kauff. Kauff, who had led the league in **batting average** in 1914 with the **Indianapolis Hoosiers**, repeated as batting champion in 1915, with a .342 average. He also led the league in **stolen bases**, with 55. In addition to Kauff, other notable players for the Tip-Tops included Steve Evans, Ed Lafitte, Lee Magee, Tom Seaton, and Al Shaw.

BROOKLYN TROLLEY DODGERS (AA). The Brooklyn Trolley Dodgers, who also played as the Brooklyn Grays, and, in 1888 and 1889, as the Brooklyn Bridegrooms, were a team in the **American Association (AA)** from 1884 through 1889. In 1889, they won the AA pennant but lost to the **New York Giants** of the **National League (NL)**, six games to three, in a championship series that was a predecessor to the modern **World Series**. In 1890, the Brooklyn team jumped to the NL, where they repeated as pennant winners. Notable players for Brooklyn's AA team included Oyster Burns, Bob Caruthers, Dave Foutz, Darby O'Brien, and Adonis Terry.
   See also BROOKLYN DODGERS

BROOKLYN TROLLEY DODGERS (NL). *See* BROOKLYN DODGERS.

BROOKLYN WONDERS. The Brooklyn Wonders were a team in the **Players League (PL)** in 1890, the one year of the PL's existence. The team was sometimes called Ward's Wonders, in honor of their **manager** and star **shortstop, John Montgomery Ward**. Brooklyn finished in second place, 6

1/2 games behind the pennant-winning **Boston Reds**. In addition to Ward, other notable players on the Wonders were Dave Orr, George Van Haltren, and Gus Weyhing.

BROTHERHOOD OF PROFESSIONAL BASE-BALL PLAYERS. *See* PLAYERS' LEAGUE (PL).

BROUTHERS, DENNIS JOSEPH "DAN". B. 8 May 1858, Sylvan Lake, New York. D. 2 August 1932, East Orange, New Jersey. Dan Brouthers, a 6-foot, 2-inch, 207-pound left-handed-hitting **first baseman**, is recognized as the greatest slugger of the 19th century. Brouthers entered the **major leagues** in 1879 with the **Troy Trojans** of the **National League (NL)**. He reached stardom after joining the **Buffalo Bisons** of the NL in 1881. Brouthers was part of Buffalo's "big four," along with Hardy Richardson, Jack Rowe, and **Deacon White**. The four players were sold to the **Detroit Wolverines** of the NL on 16 September 1885. In 1887, they led Detroit to its first pennant. Beginning in 1889, Brouthers spent three consecutive seasons playing for the Boston franchise in three different leagues: the Boston Beaneaters of the NL in 1889, the **Boston Reds** of the **Players' League** in 1890, and the **Boston Reds** of the **American Association** in 1891.

Brouthers returned to the NL in 1892 and spent the rest of his career there. He was with the Brooklyn Bridegrooms in 1892–1893, **Baltimore Orioles** in 1894 (his last full season) and part of 1895; **Louisville Colonels** in 1895, and **Philadelphia Phillies** in 1896. While in Baltimore, he befriended teammate **John McGraw**. In 1904, he appeared in two games for the **New York Giants**, then managed by McGraw, and later served as a **coach** and **scout** for the Giants, and for many years in various capacities at the **Polo Grounds**. Brouthers had a lifetime **batting average** of .342 and led his league in batting five times. He led in **slugging percentage** seven times, including six consecutive seasons from 1881 to 1886; **on-base percentage** five times; and **hits** three times. In 1945, the **Old Timers Committee** elected Brouthers to the **National Baseball Hall of Fame**.

BROWN, MORDECAI PETER CENTENNIAL "THREE FINGER," "MINER". B. 19 October 1876, Nyesville, Indiana. D. 14 February 1948, Terre Haute, Indiana. Mordecai Brown, often called "Miner" or "Three Finger"—his right hand was damaged in a farm accident when he was a child—was a **pitcher** for 12 seasons in the **National League (NL)** and two seasons in the **Federal League (FL)**. Brown was with the **St. Louis Cardinals** in 1903, but he is best remembered for his time with the **Chicago Cubs**, from 1904 to 1912. He was with the **Cincinnati Reds** in 1913, before jumping to the FL in 1914–1915, where he pitched for the **St. Louis Terriers, Brooklyn**

Tip-Tops, and **Chicago Whales**. He also served as **manager** of the Terriers in 1914. When the FL folded, he returned to the Cubs for a final season in 1915.

During his years with the Cubs, the 5-foot, 10-inch, 175-pound right-hander was second only to his great rival, **Christy Mathewson**, of the **New York Giants**, among NL pitchers. He was a 20-game winner for six consecutive seasons (1906–1911), and his retroactively computed **saves** show him as the NL leader from 1908 through 1911. His record in four **World Series** with the Cubs was 5–4. Brown had a career record of 239–130, for a .648 **winning percentage**. He had 55 **shutouts**, and his 2.06 **earned run average** is the lowest for pitchers with at least 200 victories. In 1949, the **Old Timers Committee** elected Brown to the **National Baseball Hall of Fame**.

BROWN, RAYMOND "RAY". B. 23 February 1908, Alger, Ohio. D. 8 February 1965, Dayton, Ohio. Ray Brown was a right-handed **pitcher** who spent most of his career (1932–1945, 1947–1948) as the ace of the staff for the **Homestead Grays** of the **Negro National League**. The 6-foot, 1-inch, 195-pound Brown was a **switch-hitter** who often played the **outfield** when he was not pitching. After leaving the Grays, he played professionally in **Mexico** and **Canada**. In 2006, Brown was elected to the **National Baseball Hall of Fame** in a special election conducted by the **Committee on African American Baseball**.

See also AFRICAN AMERICANS IN BASEBALL.

BROWN, WILLARD JESSIE. B. 26 June 1915, Shreveport, Louisiana. D. 4 August 1996, Houston, Texas. Willard Brown was a 6-foot, 200-pound right-handed-hitting **outfielder** who played for the **Kansas City Monarchs** of the **Negro American League** from 1935 to 1948. Brown, who also starred in winter ball in **Puerto Rico**, is reputed to have hit some of the longest **home runs** in the **Negro Leagues**. In 1947, he played in 21 games for the **St. Louis Browns** of the **American League (AL)**. He batted just .179, but, on 13 August, he became the first **African American** to hit a home run in the AL. In 2006, Brown was elected to the **National Baseball Hall of Fame** in a special election conducted by the **Committee on African American Baseball**.

BROWNING, LOUIS ROGERS "PETE". B. 17 June 1861, Louisville, Kentucky. D. 10 September 1905, Louisville, Kentucky. Pete Browning was an **outfielder** for six teams in three **major leagues** from 1882 to 1894. He spent his first eight seasons (1882–1889) with the **Louisville Colonels** of the **American Association**. He played for the **Cleveland Infants** of the **Players' League** in 1890, and in the **National League** for the **Pittsburgh Pirates**

(1891), the **Cincinnati Reds** (1891–1892), the **Louiville Colonels** (1892–1893), and two games for the St. Louis Browns and one for the Brooklyn Bridegrooms in 1894. Browning, a 6-foot, 180-pound right-handed hitter, won three batting championships—two with Louisville, in 1882 and 1885, and one with Cleveland in 1890—and had a career **batting average** of .341.

BRUSH STADIUM. *See* POLO GROUNDS.

BUFFALO BISONS (NL). The Buffalo Bisons were a team in the **National League (NL)** from 1879 to 1885. They finished in third place in four of their seven seasons, but never higher. On 17 September 1885, the Bisons sold their "big four," **Dan Brouthers**, Hardy Richardson, Jack Rowe, and **Deacon White**, to the **Detroit Wolverines** of the NL and went out of business at season's end. Other notable players for the Bisons were **Pud Galvin** and **Jim O'Rourke**.

BUFFALO BISONS (PL). The Buffalo Bisons were a team in the **Players League (PL)** in 1890, the one year of the PL's existence. The team was the league's worst, finishing in last place, with a record of 36–96. Notable players for the Bisons were Ed Beecher, Dummy Hoy, and Sam Wise.

BUFFALO BLUES. The Buffalo Blues, also called the Buffalo Federals or BufFeds, were a team in the **Federal League (FL)** in 1914 and 1915, the two seasons the FL existed as a major league. The Blues finished in fourth place in 1914 and sixth place in 1915. Buffalo **first baseman** Hal Chase led the FL in **home runs** in 1915, with 17. In addition to Chase, notable players for the Blues included Hugh Bedient, Howard Ehmke, Russ Ford, and Baldy Louden.

BUFFALO FEDERALS. *See* BUFFALO BLUES.

BULKELEY, MORGAN GARDNER. B. 26 December 1837, East Haddam, Connecticut. D. 6 November 1922, Hartford, Connecticut. Morgan Bulkeley served as president of the **Hartford Dark Blues** of the National Association from 1874 to 1875. When the **National League (NL)** was formed in 1876, he was elected its president, unanimously. Bulkeley agreed to serve one year and is credited with helping reduce gambling and drinking at NL games. In 1937, the **Centennial Commission** elected him to the **National Baseball Hall of Fame**.

BUNNING, JAMES PAUL DAVID "JIM". B. 23 October 1931, Southgate, Kentucky. Right-hander Jim Bunning never pitched for a pennant winner; nevertheless, he was the first **pitcher** since **Cy Young** to **win** 100 games and record 1,000 **strikeouts** in both the **American League (AL)** and **National League (NL)**. Bunning pitched in the AL for the **Detroit Tigers** from 1955 to 1963, and in the NL for the **Philadelphia Phillies** from 1964 to 1967 and 1970 to 1971. He also pitched briefly in the NL in 1968 and 1969 for the **Pittsburgh Pirates** and **Los Angeles Dodgers**.

The 6-foot, 3-inch, 190-pound Bunning threw a **no-hitter** in each league, including a **perfect game** against the **New York Mets** on 21 June 1964, the first perfect game in the NL in the 20th century. He led his league in strikeouts three times and **shutouts** twice and had a 1.00 **earned run average** in eight **All-Star** games. Bunning's career won-lost record was 224–184. His 2,855 strikeouts at his retirement were second only to **Walter Johnson**. He later became a United States congressman and senator from Kentucky, and, in 1996, he was elected by the **Veterans Committee** to the **National Baseball Hall of Fame**.

BUNT. A bunt is a batted ball not swung at, but intentionally met with the bat and tapped slowly within the infield. It may be for the purpose of getting a **hit** or moving **base runners** up a **base**.

BURKETT, JESSE CAIL "THE CRAB". B. 4 December 1868, Wheeling, West Virginia. D. 27 May 1953, Worcester, Massachusetts. Jesse Burkett was a left-handed-hitting and throwing **outfielder** who had a .338 career **batting average** and accumulated 2,850 **hits** during the span of 16 **major-league** seasons. The 5-foot, 8-inch, 155-pound Burkett began his big-league career with the 1890 **New York Giants** of the **National League (NL)**. He was purchased by the **Cleveland Spiders** in 1891, where he remained through the 1898 season. Known as "The Crab" for his sour disposition, Burkett won back-to-back batting championships, with a .405 mark in 1895, and a .410 mark in 1896. After being assigned to the St. Louis Perfectos of the NL in 1899, he won a third batting title in 1901. As he had in 1895 and 1896, he also led the league in hits.

In 1902, Burkett jumped to the **St. Louis Browns** of the new **American League (AL)**. He spent 1905, his final season, with the Boston Americans of the AL. After his playing career ended, he spent many years as an owner and **manager** in the **minor leagues**. Burkett, who had nine seasons of 100 or more **runs** scored, six 200-hit seasons, and 389 **stolen bases**, was elected to the **National Baseball Hall of Fame** by the **Old Timers Committee** in 1946.

BUSCH STADIUM (II). Busch Stadium (II), located in St. Louis, Missouri, was the home of the **St. Louis Cardinals** of the **National League** from 12 May 1966 to 19 October 2005, when they moved to **Busch Stadium (III)**. Before moving to Busch Stadium (II), the Cardinals played their home games at **Sportsman's Park**, which was renamed Busch Stadium in 1954 in honor of new Cardinals owner August Busch. Busch Stadium (II) hosted the **major league All-Star Game** in 1966.

See also STADIUMS.

BUSCH STADIUM (III). Busch Stadium (III), located in St. Louis, Missouri, has been the home field of the **St. Louis Cardinals** of the **National League** since 10 April 2006. Prior to that, the Cardinals played their home games at **Sportsman's Park** and **Busch Stadium (II)**. Busch Stadium (III), which has a seating capacity of approximately 44,000, hosted the **major league All-Star Game** in 2009.

See also STADIUMS.

C

CABRERA, JOSE MIGUEL (TORRES). B. 18 April 1983, Maracay, Aragua, **Venezuela**. Miguel Cabrera was 20 years old when he joined the Florida
Marlins in 2003. He played for the Marlins through 2007, batting a combined
.313 for his four and a half seasons. In what proved to be a terrible mistake
for the Marlins, they traded him to the **Detroit Tigers** in December 2007. In
his five seasons with the Tigers (2008–2012), the right-handed-hitting Cabrera has twice led the **American League (AL)** in **batting average**, **home runs**,
runs batted in (RBI), **on-base percentage**, and **total bases**. In 2012, his
.330 batting average combined with his league-leading 44 home runs and 139
RBI, earned him the **Triple Crown**, the first Triple Crown in the **major
leagues** since 1967. He was also voted the Most Valuable Player in the AL
for 2012.

The 6-foot, 4-inch, 240-pound Cabrera is a seven-time **All-Star** and winner of three **Silver Slugger Awards**. Originally a left fielder, he has also
played **third base** and **first base**. He led AL first basemen in **games played**
and **assists** in 2009, and AL **third basemen** in games played and **putouts** in
2012. Through the 2012 season, Cabrera has a career .318 batting average for
his 10 seasons, with 321 home runs and 1,123 runs batted in.

CALIFORNIA ANGELS. *See* LOS ANGELES ANGELS OF ANAHEIM.

CAMPANELLA, ROY "CAMPY". B. 19 November 1921, Philadelphia,
Pennsylvania. D. 26 June 1993, Woodland Hills, California. Roy Campanella, son of an Italian father and an **African American** mother, began his
professional career at the age of 15 as a **catcher** for the **Baltimore Elite
Giants** of the **Negro National League**. He caught for Baltimore from 1937
to 1945, when **Branch Rickey** signed him to play for the **Brooklyn Dodgers**
of the **National League (NL)**. After spending 1946, 1947, and part of 1948
helping to integrate the **minor leagues**, the 5-foot, 9 1/2-inch, 205-pound
Campanella played a half season with Brooklyn in 1948. He remained with
the Dodgers through the 1957 season, before an automobile accident, on 28
January 1958, left him completely paralyzed.

During his 10-year career, Campanella, a right-handed **batter**, set many offensive and defensive records for catchers. He was the NL's **Most Valuable Player** three times: in 1951; 1953, when he led the NL with 142 **runs batted in**; and 1955. He was a member of eight NL **All-Star** teams and four of *Sporting News*'s Major League All-Star teams. Campanella played in five **World Series**, all against the **New York Yankees**. In 1969, the **Baseball Writers' Association of America** elected him to the **National Baseball Hall of Fame**.

CANADA. The first baseball game recorded in Canada was played in Beachville, Ontario, on 4 June 1838. While baseball is widely played in Canada, the **major leagues** did not include a Canadian team until 1969, when the **Montreal Expos** joined the **National League**. In 2004, the Expos relocated to Washington, D.C., where they became the **Washington Nationals**. The first **American League** team based in Canada was the **Toronto Blue Jays**, who joined the league in 1977.

Canada has, however, been the site for more than 75 minor-league teams throughout the years, most famously the Montreal Royals and Toronto Maple Leafs of the International League. The Canadian cities of Ottawa, Winnipeg, Calgary, Edmonton, and Vancouver have all hosted Class AAA teams, and many more Canadian cities were in leagues of lower classifications. Currently, the only Canada-based minor-league team is the Vancouver Canadians of the Class A Northwest League, although Ottawa is scheduled to have a team in 2013. In 1990, Canada hosted the **Baseball World Cup**.

The most notable players, **managers**, **umpires**, and front-office personnel born in Canada include Jason Bay, Paul Beeston, Reggie Cleveland, Rheal Cormier, Ryan Dempster, Russ Ford, Dick Fowler, Jeff Francis, George Gibson, Jack Graney, Jeff Heath, John Hiller, Arthur Irwin, **Ferguson Jenkins**, Phil Marchildon, Kirk McCaskill, Jim McKean, Doug Melvin, Justin Morneau, Tip O'Neill, Frank O'Rourke, Bill Phillips, Terry Puhl, Paul Quantrill, Sherry Robertson, Goody Rosen, Allan Roth, George Selkirk, Matt Stairs, Larry Walker, William Watkins, and George Wood.

The Canadian Baseball Hall of Fame and Museum, which opened in 1998, is located in St. Marys, Ontario. The Canadian Hall of Fame has inducted such individuals as **Roberto Alomar**, **Sparky Anderson**, Paul Beeston, Joe Carter, Jim Fanning, Tony Fernandez, Cito Gaston, Tom Henke, Steve Rogers, Dave Stieb, Larry Walker, and Ernie Whitt.

CANDLESTICK PARK. Candlestick Park, located in San Francisco, California, was the home field of the **San Francisco Giants** of the **National League** from 1960 through 1999. In 1958 and 1959, the Giants' first two

CAREY, MAX GEORGE • 63

seasons in San Francisco, they played at Seals Stadium. Since 2000, the Giants have played at **AT&T Park**. Candlestick Park hosted the first of the two **major league All-Star Games** played in 1961 and also the 1984 game. *See also* STADIUMS.

CAREW, RODNEY CLINE "ROD". B. 1 October 1945, Gatun, Canal Zone. Rod Carew played 19 seasons and 2,469 games in the **American League (AL)**, almost equally split between **first base** and **second base**. The 6-foot, 170-pound Carew, who batted left-handed and threw right-handed, was the AL **Rookie of the Year** as a member of the 1967 **Minnesota Twins**. In 1969, Carew won the first of his seven batting championships. He added four consecutive batting titles from 1972 through 1975 and won again in 1977 and 1978. Carew batted .334 in 12 seasons with the Twins; nevertheless, in February 1979, he was traded to the California Angels, where he spent seven seasons, compiling a .314 **batting average**. Carew's career batting average was .328; he led the league in **hits** three times and finished with a total of 3,053. He was selected to the **All-Star** team in each of his first 18 seasons and was voted the AL's **Most Valuable Player** and the **Major League Player of the Year** in 1977, when he hit a career-high .388. Carew's uniform number 29 was retired by both the Twins and the Angels. In 1991, the **Baseball Writers' Association of America** elected Carew to the **National Baseball Hall of Fame**.

CAREY, MAX GEORGE. B. Maximillian Carnarius, 11 January 1890, Terre Haute, Indiana. D. 30 May 1976, Miami, Florida. During his 20-year career, Max Carey was the premier base stealer in the **National League (NL)**. Playing for the **Pittsburgh Pirates** from 1910 through mid-1926 and the Brooklyn Robins from late 1926 to 1929, Carey stole 738 bases, still the ninth-highest total ever. Between 1913 and 1925, the 5-foot, 11-inch, 170-pound Carey led the NL in **stolen bases** 10 times, including six seasons in which he stole 50 or more. His best offensive season was in 1925, when Carey, a **switch-hitter**, batted .343 and then hit .458 in Pittsburgh's seven-game **World Series** victory over the **Washington Senators**.

In addition to his base-stealing ability, Carey was known for his defensive prowess in center field. He led NL **outfielders** in **assists** four times and **putouts** nine times. His career putouts total of 6,363 was a NL record for outfielders until it was broken by **Willie Mays**. Carey had a .285 lifetime **batting average**, with 2,665 **hits** and 1,040 **walks**. He managed the **Brooklyn Dodgers** in 1932 and 1933, finishing third and sixth, respectively. Carey was elected to the **National Baseball Hall of Fame** by the **Veterans Committee** in 1961.

CARIBBEAN SERIES. The Caribbean Series (Serie del Caribe) is a round-robin tournament that, since 1971, has featured the winners from the winter leagues of the **Dominican Republic, Mexico, Puerto Rico,** and **Venezuela.** The tournament is played every year, usually in February, with each country taking turns as host. It has a double round-robin format in which each of the four teams plays the other clubs twice. The 2012 Caribbean Series was held at Estadio Quisqueya in Santo Domingo, Dominican Republic. The Dominican Republic's Leones de Escogido was the winner. Indios de Mayaguez from Puerto Rico was second, Tigres de Aragua from Venezuela was third, and Yaquis de Obregon from Mexico was fourth. The 2013 Caribbean Series is scheduled to be played in Hermosillo, Mexico.

CARLTON, STEVEN NORMAN "STEVE," "LEFTY". B. 12 December 1944, Miami, Florida. **Pitcher** Steve Carlton spent his first seven seasons (1965–1971) with the **St. Louis Cardinals** and his last three (1986–1988) bouncing between the **San Francisco Giants, Chicago White Sox, Cleveland Indians,** and **Minnesota Twins.** But it was while pitching for the **Philadelphia Phillies,** from 1972 to mid-1986, that the 6-foot, 4-inch, 210-pound left-hander established his greatness. In 1972, his first year in Philadelphia after being traded from St. Louis, Carlton had his best season. Pitching for the last-place Phillies, he won the pitchers **Triple Crown** by leading in **wins** (27), **earned run average** (1.97), and **strikeouts** (310), earning Carlton his first **Cy Young Award.** He captured the award again in 1977, 1980, and 1982, making him the first four-time winner. He was also the *Sporting News*'s choice as **Pitcher of the Year** in the **National League (NL)** those four seasons.

As a member of the Phillies, Carlton later led the NL in wins three more times and strikeouts four more times. Overall, in Philadelphia, he had five 20-win seasons and led the league in **innings pitched** five times. A 10-time **All-Star** during his career, Carlton had a 4–2 record in five **National League Championship Series.** He appeared in four **World Series,** two each with the Cardinals and the Phillies, winning two games and losing two. Carlton had a career record of 329–244, with 4,136 strikeouts. His 329 wins are second only to **Warren Spahn**'s 363 among left-handers, and his strikeouts total is fourth all-time. Carlton was elected by the **Baseball Writers' Association of America** to the **National Baseball Hall of Fame** in 1994.

CARTER, GARY EDMUND "KID". B. 8 April 1954, Culver City, California. D. 16 February 2012, West Palm Beach, Florida. Gary Carter was a **catcher** in the **National League (NL)** for the **Montreal Expos** (1974–1984, 1992), **New York Mets** (1985–1989), **San Francisco Giants** (1990), and **Los Angeles Dodgers** (1991). Carter, who was known for playing with great enthusiasm, caught more than 100 games in 14 different seasons, including 12 straight from 1977 to 1988. The 6-foot, 2-inch, 205-pound right-handed hitter had four seasons in which he drove in 100 or more **runs**. His career-high 106 **runs batted in** with the 1984 Expos led the NL.

Carter was traded to the Mets after the 1984 season, and, in 1986, he helped lead them to a pennant and a **World Series** victory over the **Boston Red Sox**. Carter was an 11-time **All-Star** and the game's **Most Valuable Player** in 1981 and 1984. He had a .262 career **batting average**, with 324 **home runs** and 1,225 **runs batted in**. Defensively, Carter led NL catchers in **games played** every season from 1977 to 1982, in **putouts** eight times, and in **assists** five times. The **Baseball Writers' Association of America** elected him to the **National Baseball Hall of Fame** in 2003.

CARTWRIGHT, ALEXANDER JOY, JR. B. 17 April 1820, New York, New York. D. 12 July 1892, Honolulu, Hawaii. Alexander Cartwright began playing baseball with other young lawyers and bankers at Madison Square in New York City in 1842. In 1848, Cartwright was a member of the Committee to Revise the Constitution and By-Laws of Baseball, a committee led by his **Knickerbocker Base Ball Club** teammate **Doc Adams**. Cartwright went to California during the gold rush of 1849, before eventually settling in Hawaii. The **Centennial Commission** elected him to the **National Baseball Hall of Fame** in 1938. Although his plaque reads "Father of Modern Baseball" in recognition of the many innovations credited to him, recent research has shown that credit for those innovations actually belongs to others.

CATCH. A catch is the act of a **fielder** getting secure possession in his hand or glove of a ball in flight and firmly holding it, providing that he does not use his cap, protector, pocket, or any other part of his uniform in getting possession.

CATCHER (C). The catcher is the defensive player on the team who receives the ball from the **pitcher**. He is positioned behind **home plate**, behind the **batter**, and in front of the home plate **umpire**. In the numbering system used to record defensive plays, the catcher is assigned the number 2.

The **major-league** career leader in **games played** by a catcher is 2,427, by **Ivan Rodriguez** (1991–2011). The major league career leader in **fielding percentage** (minimum 500 games) is Chris Snyder (2004–2012 and still active), at .9976.

The single-season leader in **putouts** by a catcher is Johnny Edwards of the 1969 **Houston Astros**, with 1,135. The **American League (AL)** single-season leader is Dan Wilson of the 1997 **Seattle Mariners**, with 1,051. The career leader is Ivan Rodriguez (1991–2011), with 14,864.

The single-season leader in **assists** by a catcher is Bill Rariden of the 1915 **Newark Peppers** of the **Federal League**, with 238. The **National League** single-season leader is Pat Moran of the 1903 Boston Beaneaters, with 214. The AL single-season leader is Oscar Stanage of the 1911 **Detroit Tigers**, with 212. The career leader is Deacon McGuire (1884–1888, 1890–1908, 1910, 1912), with 1,860.

CATCHER INTERFERENCE (CI). The **home-plate umpire** will call catcher's interference when the **catcher** hinders the **batter's** ability to hit a pitched ball by touching his bat. The call is automatic as long as the batter was standing inside the **batter's box**. The ball is dead, the batter is awarded **first base**, and **base runners** advance only if forced to. The catcher is charged with an **error**, and the batter is charged with neither an **at-bat** nor a **plate appearance**.

CAUGHT STEALING (CS). A **base runner** is charged with being caught stealing when he attempts to steal a **base**, that is, to advance from one base to another without the ball being batted and is tagged out on a throw from the **catcher** to a **fielder** while making the attempt.

The **major league** single-season leader in being caught stealing is **Rickey Henderson** of the 1982 **Oakland Athletics**, with 42. The single-season leader in the **National League (NL)** is George Burns of the 1913 **New York Giants**, with 35. The career leader is Rickey Henderson, with 335. Henderson played in the **American League** for the **Oakland Athletics** (1979–1984, 1989–1995, 1998), **New York Yankees** (1985–1989), **Toronto Blue Jays** (1993), Anaheim Angels (1997), **Seattle Mariners** (2000), and **Boston Red Sox** (2002). He played in the NL for the **San Diego Padres** (1996–1997, 2001), **New York Mets** (1999–2000), and **Los Angeles Dodgers** (2003).

CENTENNIAL COMMISSION. The Centennial Commission was a committee of high-ranking baseball officials that existed in 1937 and 1938. They were charged with the selection of inductees into the **National Baseball Hall of Fame** "for outstanding service to base ball apart from playing the game." **Morgan Bulkeley, Ban Johnson, Connie Mack, John McGraw,** and **George Wright** were chosen in 1937, and **Alexander Cartwright** and **Henry Chadwick** were chosen in 1938.

CENTER FIELDER (CF). *See* OUTFIELDER (OF).

CEPEDA, ORLANDO MANUEL (PENNES) "THE BABY BULL". B. 17 September 1937, Ponce, **Puerto Rico**. Orlando Cepeda had a .297 **batting average** with 379 **home runs** and 1,365 **runs batted in (RBI)** in his 17-year big-league career. The 6-foot, 2-inch, 210-pound right-handed-hitting Cepeda was a **first baseman** and sometime **outfielder** for six different teams. Most of his success came in his first 15 seasons in the **National League (NL)**, with the **San Francisco Giants** (1958–1966), **St. Louis Cardinals** (1966–1968), and **Atlanta Braves** (1969–1972). He finished with three **American League** teams: three games with the **Oakland Athletics** in 1972, and a season each with the 1973 **Boston Red Sox** and the 1974 **Kansas City Royals**. Cepeda was used solely as the **designated hitter** by the Red Sox and Royals.

Cepeda was the **Rookie of the Year** in 1958, when at age 20, he batted .312 for San Francisco and led the NL with 38 **doubles**. In 1961, he led the league in home runs (46) and runs batted in (142) and was second in voting for the **Most Valuable Player Award**. Six years later, he won that award, batting .325, with a league-leading 111 RBI for the pennant-winning Cardinals. A seven-time **All-Star**, Cepeda was elected to the **National Baseball Hall of Fame** by the **Veterans Committee** in 1999.

CHADWICK, HENRY. B. 5 October 1824, Exeter, England. D. 29 April 1908, Brooklyn, New York. Henry Chadwick was a journalist who wrote about early baseball in newspapers, magazines, pamphlets, and books. Beginning around 1856, until his death, Chadwick reported on the games, rules, and skills necessary to play baseball, while campaigning against the drinking and gambling associated with the game. Chadwick, a pioneer of early baseball, perfected the box score, introduced the scoring system to baseball, and edited the earliest baseball guides. The **Centennial Commission** elected Chadwick to the **National Baseball Hall of Fame** in 1938.

CHALMERS AWARD. The Chalmers Award was Major League Baseball's first **Most Valuable Player Award**. The Chalmers Automobile Company awarded a new Chalmers automobile to the one player in each **major league** "who should prove himself as the most important and useful player to his club and to the league at large in point of deportment and value of services rendered."

American League winners of the Chalmers Award were **Ty Cobb** of the **Detroit Tigers** (1911), **Tris Speaker** of the **Boston Red Sox** (1912), **Walter Johnson** of the **Washington Senators** (1913), and **Eddie Collins** of the **Philadelphia Athletics** (1914).

National League winners of the Chalmers Award were Frank Schulte of the **Chicago Cubs** (1911), Larry Doyle of the **New York Giants** (1912), Jake Daubert of the **Brooklyn Dodgers** (1913), and **Johnny Evers** of the

Boston Braves (1914). The award's failure to be as effective at advertising their automobiles as Chalmers had hoped, and the rule forbidding any player to win more than once, led to it being discontinued after 1914.

CHANCE, FRANK LEROY "THE PEERLESS LEADER". B. 9 September 1876, Fresno, California. D. 15 September 1924, Los Angeles, California. Frank Chance played **first base** for the **Chicago Cubs** from 1898 to 1912. The 6-foot, 190-pound Chance teamed with **Johnny Evers**, the **second baseman**, and **Joe Tinker**, the **shortstop**, to form one of baseball's most memorable **double-play** combinations. In mid-1905, he was appointed the team's **manager** as well. Chance led the Cubs to four pennants (1906–1908, 1910) and **World Series** victories over the **Detroit Tigers** in 1907 and 1908, earning him the nickname "The Peerless Leader."

Chance resigned after the 1912 season because of a dispute with owner Charles Murphy and signed to manage the **New York Yankees**. His overall managerial record with the Cubs was an impressive 768–389. But Chance could not duplicate his Cubs' success in New York. The Yanks finished seventh in 1913 and sixth in 1914. In 1923, Chance managed the **Boston Red Sox** to an eighth-place finish. He was to have managed the **Chicago White Sox** in 1924, but ill health interfered and he died prematurely that year. As a player, the right-handed-hitting Chance had a lifetime **batting average** of .296, with 1,274 **hits**. In 20 World Series games, he batted .300 and had 10 **stolen bases**. In 1946, the **Old Timers Committee** elected him to the **National Baseball Hall of Fame**.

CHANDLER, ALBERT BENJAMIN "HAPPY". B. 14 July 1898, Corydon, Kentucky. D. 15 June 1991, Versailles, Kentucky. Happy Chandler was a former governor and senator from Kentucky who succeeded **Kenesaw Landis** in 1945 to become Major League Baseball's second **commissioner**. Chandler made headlines in 1947, when he suspended **Leo Durocher**, the **manager** of the **Brooklyn Dodgers**, for one year because of "conduct detrimental to baseball." That same year, he oversaw the integration of the **major leagues**, when **Jackie Robinson**, an **African American**, joined the Dodgers. Chandler also acted decisively in dealing with players who left for the Mexican League; however, his taking of the players' side against the owners in several other disputes caused the owners to lose confidence in him, and, in 1951, Chandler resigned as commissioner. In 1982, the **Veterans Committee** elected him to the **National Baseball Hall of Fame**.

CHANGEUP. The changeup, also called an off-speed pitch, is a pitch that is slower than a **fastball**. A **pitcher** will throw the changeup with the same arm action as a fastball, but at a lower speed due to his holding the ball with a different grip.

CHARLESTON, OSCAR MCKINLEY. B. 14 October 1896, Indianapolis, Indiana. D. 5 October 1954, Philadelphia, Pennsylvania. Oscar Charleston was a player and later a **manager** in the **Negro Leagues** from 1915 to 1941. He played for several teams, including the Harrisburg Giants of the **Eastern Colored League** from 1924 to 1927, and the **Pittsburgh Crawfords** of the **Negro National League**, whom he also managed, from 1932 to 1937. An outstanding defensive **outfielder** who later became a **first baseman**, the 6-foot, 190-pound Charleston was a left-handed **batter** who hit for a high average and with power. He was also extremely fast on the **bases** and is considered by many to be the best all-around player ever in the Negro Leagues. In 1976, a special **Negro Leagues Committee** elected Charleston to the **National Baseball Hall of Fame**.
See also AFRICAN AMERICANS IN BASEBALL.

CHASE FIELD. Chase Field, located in Phoenix, Arizona, is the home field of the **Arizona Diamondbacks** of the **National League**. The **stadium** opened in 1998 as Bank One Ballpark. The name was changed to Chase Field in 2006. The current seating capacity of Chase Field is approximately 48,600. The field, which has a retractable roof, hosted the **major league All-Star Game** in 2011.

CHESBRO, JOHN DWIGHT "JACK," "HAPPY JACK". B. 5 June 1874, North Adams, Massachusetts. D. 6 November 1931, Conway, Massachusetts. **Pitcher** Jack Chesbro spent his first four **major-league** seasons with the **Pittsburgh Pirates**, from 1899 through 1902. His total number of victories improved each season, rising from six, to 15, to 21, to 28. Chesbro's 28–6 record in 1902 made him the **National League (NL)** leader in **wins** and **winning percentage**. He also led in **shutouts** for the second consecutive season. In both 1901 and 1902, the Pirates won the NL pennant. Chesbro, whose nickname was "Happy Jack," left Pittsburgh in 1903 to join the New York Highlanders of the **American League (AL)**. The Highlanders, later to become the **New York Yankees**, were playing their first season in New York after the **Baltimore Orioles** franchise had been moved there.

Chesbro, the Highlanders Opening-Day pitcher, won 21 games, just more than half of what he would win a year later. In 1904, the 5-foot, 9-inch, 180-pound right-hander set a still-standing AL record by winning 41 games (41–12), with a 1.82 **earned run average**. He led the league with 51 **games**

started, 48 **complete games**, and 454 2/3 **innings pitched**. Chesbro's 41 wins are the most by a major-league pitcher post-1893, when the pitching distance was extended to its current 60 feet, 6 inches. His 12th loss came against the Boston Americans on the final day of the season, allowing Boston, rather than New York, to win the AL pennant. Boston's game-winning run scored when Highlanders **catcher** Red Kleinow was unable to handle one of Chesbro's **spitballs**. Chesbro remained a solid pitcher for the next four seasons, before ending his career in 1909 with one game pitched for the **Boston Red Sox**. His 198–132 record earned him election by the **Old Timers Committee** to the **National Baseball Hall of Fame** in 1946.

CHICAGO AMERICAN GIANTS. The Chicago American Giants were the most dominant team in any of the **Negro Leagues** from 1910 until the mid-1930s. They were owned by **Rube Foster**, who was also the team's **manager** and, for many years, its best **pitcher**. Chicago won five **Negro National League** pennants between 1920 and 1927. In addition to Foster, other notable players for the American Giants included **Pete Hill**, **John Henry Lloyd**, and Ted "Double Duty" Radcliffe.

CHICAGO BROWNS. The Chicago Browns were a team in the **Union Association (UA)** in 1884, the one year of the UA's existence. Chicago had a 34–39 record in August, after which they moved to Pittsburgh and became the **Pittsburgh Stogies**.

CHICAGO COLTS. *See* CHICAGO CUBS.

CHICAGO CUBS. The Chicago Cubs are a team in the Central Division of the **National League (NL)**. Chicago entered the newly formed NL as a charter member in 1876, and it is the oldest continuous one-city franchise in Major League Baseball. The team was called the Chicago White Stockings from 1876 to 1889, the Chicago Colts from 1890 to 1897, the Chicago Orphans from 1898 to 1902, and the Cubs since 1903.

The Cubs have played their home games at **Wrigley Field** since 1916. Wrigley Field was originally called Weeghman Park until 1919, and then Cubs Park from 1920 to 1926. Prior to 1916, the Cubs played at the Twenty-Third Street Grounds (1876–1877), Lakefront Park (1878–1884), and West Side Park (1885–1915). They also played some home games at South Side Park in 1891, 1892, 1893, and 1897.

Led by **manager** and **pitcher Al Spalding**, Chicago won the first NL pennant in 1876. They won five more pennants during the 1880s (1880–1882, 1885–1886) under manager and **first baseman Cap Anson**. Following the pennant-winning seasons of 1885 and 1886, Chicago played the **St. Louis Browns**, the **American Association** pennant winner, in a championship series that was a predecessor to the modern **World Series**. In 1885, each team won three, lost three, and tied one. In 1886, the Browns defeated the White Stockings, four games to two.

The Cubs reached their greatest glory under **player-manager Frank Chance**, winning four pennants in the five years from 1906 to 1910. They split their four World Series appearances, losing to the **Chicago White Sox** in 1906 and the **Philadelphia Athletics** in 1910, and defeating the **Detroit Tigers** in 1907 and 1908. In the more than 100 years since the 1908 win over the Tigers, the Cubs have never won another World Series. After the 1910 loss to the Athletics, they have been defeated in six more Series: in 1918 by the **Boston Red Sox**, in 1929 by the Athletics, in 1932 and 1938 by the **New York Yankees**, and in 1935 and 1945 by the Tigers. The Cubs have not won a pennant since 1945, losing three times in the **National League Division Series** and three times in the **National League Championship Series**.

Chicago Cubs who have won the NL's **Most Valuable Player Award** are Frank Schulte (1911), **Rogers Hornsby** (1929), **Gabby Hartnett** (1935), Phil Cavarretta (1945), Hank Sauer (1952), **Ernie Banks** (1958–1959), **Ryne Sandberg** (1984), **Andre Dawson** (1987), and **Sammy Sosa** (1998). **Cy Young Award** winners are **Ferguson Jenkins** (1971), **Bruce Sutter** (1979), Rick Sutcliffe (1984), and **Greg Maddux** (1992). **Rookie of the Year** winners are **Billy Williams** (1961), Ken Hubbs (1962), Jerome Walton (1989), Kerry Wood (1998), and Geovany Soto (2008).

Cubs players who have led the NL in **batting average** are **Ross Barnes** (1876), George Gore (1880), Cap Anson (1881, 1888), **King Kelly** (1884, 1886), Heinie Zimmerman (1912), Phil Cavarretta (1945), Billy Williams (1972), Bill Madlock (1975–1976), Bill Buckner (1980), and Derrek Lee (2005). Leaders in **home runs** are Ned Williamson (1884), Abner Dalrymple (1885), Jimmy Ryan (1888), Walt Wilmot (1890), Frank Schulte (1910–1911), Heinie Zimmerman (1912), Cy Williams (1916), **Hack Wilson** (1926–1928, 1930), Bill Nicholson (1943–1944), Hank Sauer (1952), Ernie Banks (1958, 1960), Dave Kingman (1979), Andre Dawson (1987), Ryne Sandberg (1990), and Sammy Sosa (2000, 2002). Leaders in **runs batted in** are **Deacon White** (1876), Cap Anson (1880–1882, 1884–1886, 1888, 1891), Harry Steinfeldt (1906), Frank Schulte (1911), Heinie Zimmerman (1916, part of season with **New York Giants**), Hack Wilson (1929–1930), Bill Nicholson (1943–1944), Hank Sauer (1952), Ernie Banks (1958–1959), Andre Dawson (1987), and Sammy Sosa (1998, 2001).

Cubs pitchers who have led the NL in **wins** are Al Spalding (1876), Larry Corcoran (1881), **John Clarkson** (1885, 1887), Bill Hutchinson (1890–1892), **Mordecai Brown** (1909), Larry Cheney (1912), Hippo Vaughn (1918), **Grover Alexander** (1920), Charlie Root (1927), Pat Malone (1929–1930), Lon Warneke (1932), Bill Lee (1938), Larry Jackson (1964),

Ferguson Jenkins (1971), Rick Sutcliffe (1987), Greg Maddux (1992), and Carlos Zambrano (2006). **Earned run average (ERA)** leaders are Larry Corcoran (1882), **Clark Griffith** (1898), Jack W. Taylor (1902), Mordecai Brown (1906), Jack Pfiester (1907), King Cole (1910), Hippo Vaughn (1918), Grover Alexander (1919–1920), Lon Warneke (1932), Bill Lee (1938), and Ray Prim (1945). **Strikeouts** leaders are Larry Corcoran (1880), John Clarkson (1885, 1887), Bill Hutchinson (1892), Fred Beebe (1906, part of season with **St. Louis Cardinals**), Orval Overall (1909), Hippo Vaughn (1918–1919), Grover Alexander (1920), Pat Malone (1929), Clay Bryant (1938), Claude Passeau (1939, part of season with **Philadelphia Phillies**), Johnny Schmitz (1946), Sam Jones (1955–1956), Ferguson Jenkins (1969), and Kerry Wood (2003). By leading in wins, ERA, and strikeouts, Hippo Vaughn won the **Triple Crown** for pitchers in 1918. By leading in wins, ERA, and strikeouts, Grover Alexander won the Triple Crown for pitchers in 1920.

Other notable players and managers in Cubs' history include Frank Baumholtz, Glenn Beckert, Guy Bush, Jim Callahan, Starlin Castro, **Kiki Cuyler**, Bill Dahlen, Frank Demaree, Ryan Dempster, Shawon Dunston, **Leo Durocher**, Dick Ellsworth, Don Elston, Woody English, Bill Everitt, **Johnny Evers**, Larry French, Augie Galan, Fred Goldsmith, Mark Grace, Charlie Grimm, Stan Hack, Bill Hands, **Billy Herman**, Ken Holtzman, Rogers Hornsby, Randy Hundley, Randy Jackson, Billy Jurges, Don Kessinger, Johnny Kling, Bill Lange, Carl Lundgren, Carlos Marmol, **Joe McCarthy**, Andy Pafko, Fred Pfeffer, Mark Prior, Aramis Ramirez, Ed Reulbach, Rick Reuschel, Bob Rush, **Ron Santo**, Lee Smith, Alfonso Soriano, Riggs Stephenson, **Joe Tinker**, and Jake Weimer.

CHICAGO FEDERALS. *See* CHICAGO WHALES.

CHICAGO ORPHANS. *See* CHICAGO CUBS.

CHICAGO PIRATES. The Chicago Pirates were a team in the **Players League (PL)** in 1890, the one year of the PL's existence. The team finished in fourth place, with a 75–62 record. Mark Baldwin of the Pirates led the league in **wins**, with 33, and **strikeouts**, with 206. Silver King of the Pirates had the league's lowest **earned run average** (2.69). In addition to Baldwin and King, other notable players on the Pirates were **Hugh Duffy**, Tip O'Neill, and Jimmy Ryan.

CHICAGO WHALES. The Chicago Whales, also called the Chicago Federals or ChiFeds, were a team in the **Federal League (FL)** in 1914 and 1915, the two seasons the FL existed as a **major league**. Chicago finished 1 1/2 games behind the pennant-winning **Indianapolis Hoosiers** in 1914, and then edged the **St. Louis Terriers** by .001 percentage points to win the pennant in 1915. The club played its home games at Weeghman Park, named for owner Charles A. Weeghman. When the FL folded after the 1915 season, Weeghman became owner of the **Chicago Cubs** of the **National League** as part of the settlement. He moved the club into Weeghman Park, which is still in use by the Cubs and is now named **Wrigley Field**. Dutch Zwilling of the Whales led the FL in **home runs** in 1914, with 15, and **runs batted in** in 1915, with 94. Claude Hendrix of the Whales was the league's best **pitcher** in 1914. Hendrix led in **wins**, with 29, and had the lowest **earned run average**, with 1.69. George McConnell of the Whales led the FL with 25 wins in 1915. Other notable players for the Whales included Max Flack, Les Mann, and **Joe Tinker**.

CHICAGO WHITE SOX. The Chicago White Sox are a team in the Central Division of the **American League (AL)**. The White Sox were members of the Western League when that league was renamed the American League in 1900. In 1901, the AL was recognized as a **major league**. The White Sox played their home games at South Side Park from 24 April 1901 to 27 June 1910, and then at **Comiskey Park**, named for owner **Charles Comiskey**, from 1 July 1910 to 30 September 1990. They have played at their current home, **U.S. Cellular Field**, beginning with the 1991 season. Until 2003, U.S. Cellular Field was also called Comiskey Park.

Manager and star **pitcher Clark Griffith** led Chicago to a first-place finish in 1901. The White Sox, known derisively as the "hitless wonders," won another pennant in 1906, under manager Fielder Jones, and then upset their intracity rivals, the **Chicago Cubs**, in the **World Series**. The White Sox won again in 1917, defeating the **New York Giants**, but the team lost the 1919 Series to the underdog **Cincinnati Reds**. In the 1919 Series, eight Chicago players, forever remembered as the "Black Sox," were later charged with deliberately playing to lose the Series. The eight, including star players Eddie Cicotte, Happy Felsch, Chick Gandil, **Joe Jackson**, Buck Weaver, and Lefty Williams, were permanently banned from baseball by **Kenesaw Landis**, the game's new **commissioner**.

The White Sox did not win another pennant until 1959, and the team then lost in the World Series to the **Los Angeles Dodgers**. Eighty-eight years after defeating the Giants in 1917, the White Sox finally won another World Series, a four-game sweep of the **Houston Astros** in 2005. Chicago has also lost two **American League Division Series** and two **American League Championship Series**.

Chicago White Sox who have won the AL's **Most Valuable Player Award** are **Nellie Fox** (1959), Dick Allen (1972), and **Frank Thomas** (1993–1994). **Cy Young Award** winners are **Early Wynn** (1959), LaMarr

Hoyt (1983), and Jack McDowell (1993). **Rookie of the Year** winners are **Luis Aparicio** (1956), Gary Peters (1963), Tommy Agee (1966), Ron Kittle (1983), and Ozzie Guillen (1985).

White Sox players who have led the league in **batting average** are **Luke Appling** (1936, 1943) and Frank Thomas (1997). **Home run** leaders are Braggo Roth (1915, part of season with **Cleveland Indians**), Bill Melton (1971), and Dick Allen (1972, 1974). Dick Allen, in 1972, is the only White Sox player to lead the league in **runs batted in**.

White Sox pitchers who have led the league in **wins** are Doc White (1907), **Ed Walsh** (1908), Eddie Cicotte (1917, 1919), **Ted Lyons** (1925, 1927), Billy Pierce (1957), Early Wynn (1959), Gary Peters (1964), Wilbur Wood (1972–1973), LaMarr Hoyt (1982–1983), and Jack McDowell (1993). **Earned run average** leaders are Doc White (1906), Ed Walsh (1907, 1910), Eddie Cicotte (1917), **Red Faber** (1921–1922), Thornton Lee (1941), Ted Lyons (1942), Joe Haynes (1947), Saul Rogovin (1951, part of season with **Detroit Tigers**), Billy Pierce (1955), Frank Baumann (1960), Gary Peters (1963, 1966), and Joel Horlen (1967). **Strikeouts** leaders are Ed Walsh (1908, 1911), Frank Smith (1909), Billy Pierce (1953), Early Wynn (1958), and Esteban Loaiza (2003).

Other notable players and managers in White Sox history include Nick Altrock, Harold Baines, Floyd Bannister, Zeke Bonura, Clint Brown, Mark Buehrle, Jim Callahan, Chico Carrasquel, **Eddie Collins**, Shano Collins, **George Davis**, Dick Donovan, Richard Dotson, Ray Durham, Jermaine Dye, Jimmy Dykes, Bibb Falk, Alex Fernandez, **Carlton Fisk**, Gavin Floyd, Kid Gleason, **Harry Hooper**, Bobby Jenks, Tommy John, Lance Johnson, Willie Kamm, Dickey Kerr, Paul Konerko, Mike Kreevich, **Tony LaRussa**, Carlos Lee, Chet Lemon, Sherm Lollar, **Al Lopez**, Jerry Manuel, Minnie Minoso, Johnny Mostil, Magglio Ordonez, Frank Owen, Roy Patterson, A. J. Pierzynski, Juan Pizzaro, Carlos Quentin, Rip Radcliff, Alexei Ramirez, Paul Richards, Alex Rios, Pants Rowland, Reb Russell, Chris Sale, **Ray Schalk**, Jim Scott, Earl Sheely, Bobby Thigpen, Tommy Thomas, Mike Tresh, Robin Ventura, Greg Walker, **Hoyt Wilhelm**, and Taft Wright.

CHICAGO WHITE STOCKINGS (NA). The Chicago White Stockings were a team in the National Association (NA) in 1871, the NA's first season, and then again in 1874 and 1875, the NA's final two seasons. Notable players for the White Stockings included Davy Force, Paul Hines, and Levi Meyerle. In 1876, the White Stockings became charter members of the new **National League**.

CHICAGO WHITE STOCKINGS (NL). *See* CHICAGO CUBS; NATIONAL LEAGUE (NL).

CHYLAK, NESTOR, JR. B. 11 May 1922, Olyphant, Pennsylvania. **D.** 17 February 1982, Dunmore, Pennsylvania. Nestor Chylak served as a U.S. Army Ranger (1942–1946), winning a Silver Star and a Purple Heart at the Battle of the Bulge. He joined the **American League (AL)** as an **umpire** in 1954 and remained in that role through the 1978 season. From 1979 through 1981, he served as the assistant supervisor of AL umpires. Chylak umpired in 3,857 **major-league** games, six **All-Star Games**, five **World Series**, and three **American League Championship Series**. The **Veterans Committee** elected him to the **National Baseball Hall of Fame** in 1999.

CINCINNATI KELLY'S KILLERS. *See* CINCINNATI PORKERS.

CINCINNATI OUTLAW REDS. The Cincinnati Outlaw Reds were a team in the **Union Association (UA)** in 1884, the one year of the UA's existence. Cincinnati's 69–36 record was the league's second best. Jim McCormick of the Outlaw Reds had the league's lowest **earned run average** (1.54).

CINCINNATI PORKERS. The Cincinnati Porkers were members of the **American Association (AA)** for part of the 1891 season, the AA's final year of existence. The team, also known as the Cincinnati Kelly's Killers, was managed by **King Kelly**, their **catcher** and best player. The Porkers had a 43–57 record when they were dropped from the league in August. Many of the players, but not Kelly, then joined the AA's newly created **Milwaukee Brewers**.

CINCINNATI RED STOCKINGS (AA). The Cincinnati Red Stockings were charter members of the **American Association (AA)**. They played in the AA from 1882 to 1889 and then joined the **National League** in 1890, changing their name from Red Stockings to Reds. The Red Stockings won the AA's first pennant in 1882 and had winning seasons each year but 1886. Notable players for the Red Stockings included **Bid McPhee**, Tony Mullane, John Reilly, Mike Smith, and Will White.

CINCINNATI RED STOCKINGS (NABBP). The Cincinnati Red Stockings were formed as the Cincinnati Base Ball Club in 1866 and played other members of the **National Association of Base Ball Players (NABBP)** from 1867 to 1870. In 1869, the NABBP allowed professional members, and the Red Stockings are generally recognized as the first all-professional team. They went 57–0 that season. When the NABBP gave way to the **National Association of Professional Base Ball Players** in 1871, the Cincinnati club did not enter the league; however, many of their former players did become part of the National Association's **Boston Red Stockings**. Notable members of the Cinncinnati Red Stockings included Asa Brainard, Andy Leonard, **Cal McVey**, **George Wright**, and **Harry Wright**.

CINCINNATI RED STOCKINGS (NL). In 1876, the Cincinnati Red Stockings (also called Reds) were charter members of the **National League (NL)**. They played for five years in the NL before being dismissed from the league following the 1880 season. The Reds had little success on the field or at the gate. They finished second in 1878, but were also-rans in the other seasons. Notable players for the Red Stockings included **Ross Barnes**, **King Kelly**, **Cal McVey**, **Lip Pike**, **Deacon White**, and Will White.

CINCINNATI REDLEGS. *See* CINCINNATI REDS.

CINCINNATI REDS. The Cincinnati Reds are a team in the Central Division of the **National League (NL)**. They have been a member of the NL since 1890, after having played as the **Cincinnati Red Stockings** in the **American Association** from 1882 to 1889. From 1954 to 1959, the team was known as the Cincinnati Redlegs. The Reds played their home games at two parks known as League Park from 1890 to 1901, at Palace of the Fans from 1902 to 1911, at **Crosley Field** (known as Redland Field, 1912–1933) from 11 April 1912 to 24 June 1970, at **Riverfront Stadium** from 30 June 1970 to 22 September 2002, and at **Great American Ball Park** since 2003.

The Reds won their first NL pennant in 1919, 30 years after joining the league. They defeated the **Chicago White Sox** in the **World Series**, a Series in which eight Chicago players, forever remembered as the "Black Sox," were later charged with deliberately playing to lose. The Reds had second-place finishes in 1922 and 1923, but, after 1919, they were mostly a second-division team before winning back-to-back pennants in 1939 and 1940. They were swept by the **New York Yankees** in the 1939 Series but defeated the **Detroit Tigers** in seven games in 1940. After another long interval, the Reds returned to the World Series in 1961, losing again to the Yankees.

Cincinnati dominated the NL in the decade of the 1970s, as "The Big Red Machine" finished first in their division (then the Western Division) six times. They won four of six **National League Championship Series (NLCS)**, losing in 1973 and 1979, and split four World Series. After losing to the **Baltimore Orioles** in 1970 and the **Oakland Athletics** in 1972, the Reds won the Series from the **Boston Red Sox** in 1975 and the Yankees in 1976. Cincinnati's last world championship was in 1990, an upset sweep of Oakland. They lost in the NLCS in 1995 and the **National League Division Series** in 2010 and 2012.

Cincinnati Reds who have won the NL's **Most Valuable Player Award** are **Ernie Lombardi** (1938), Bucky Walters (1939), Frank McCormick (1940), **Frank Robinson** (1961), **Johnny Bench** (1970, 1972), **Pete Rose** (1973), **Joe Morgan** (1975–1976), George Foster (1977), **Barry Larkin** (1995), and Joey Votto (2010). No Cincinnati **pitcher** has won the **Cy Young Award**. **Rookie of the Year** winners are Frank Robinson (1956), Pete Rose (1963), Tommy Helms (1966), Johnny Bench (1968), Pat Zachry (1976), Chris Sabo (1988), and Scott Williamson (1999).

Reds players who have led the NL in **batting average** are Cy Seymour (1905), Hal Chase (1916), **Edd Roush** (1917, 1919), Bubbles Hargrave (1926), Ernie Lombardi (1938), and Pete Rose (1968–1969, 1973). **Home run** leaders are Bug Holliday (1892), **Sam Crawford** (1901), Fred Odwell (1905), Ted Kluszewski (1954), Johnny Bench (1970, 1972), and George Foster (1977–1978). **Runs batted in** leaders are Cy Seymour (1905), Sherry Magee (1918), Frank McCormick (1939), Ted Kluszewski (1954), Deron Johnson (1965), Johnny Bench (1970, 1972, 1974), George Foster (1976–1978), and Dave Parker (1985).

Reds pitchers who have led the NL in **wins** are **Eppa Rixey** (1922), Dolf Luque (1923), Pete Donohue (1926), Bucky Walters (1939–1940, 1944), Elmer Riddle (1943), Ewell Blackwell (1947), Joey Jay (1961), **Tom Seaver** (1981), Danny Jackson (1988), and Aaron Harang (2006). **Earned run average (ERA)** leaders are Billy Rhines (1890, 1896), Dolf Luque (1923, 1925), Bucky Walters (1939–1940), Elmer Riddle (1941), and Ed Heusser (1944). **Strikeouts** leaders are Noodles Hahn (1899–1901), Bucky Walters (1939), Johnny Vander Meer (1941–1943), Ewell Blackwell (1947), Jose Rijo (1993), and Aaron Harang (2006). By leading in wins, ERA, and strikeouts in 1939, Bucky Walters won the **Triple Crown** for pitchers.

Other notable players and **managers** in Reds' history include **Sparky Anderson**, Bronson Arroyo, Ed Bailey, Dusty Baker, **Jake Beckley**, Gus Bell, Bob Bescher, Jack Billingham, Pedro Borbon, Ted Breitenstein, Rube Bressler, Tom Browning, Jay Bruce, Leo Cardenas, Clay Carroll, Sean Casey, Dave Concepcion, Tommy Corcoran, Hughie Critz, Johnny Cueto, Jake Daubert, Eric Davis, Paul Derringer, Dan Driessen, Adam Dunn, Frank Dwyer, Hod Eller, Bob Ewing, **Buck Ewing**, John Franco, Lonny Frey, Cesar Geronimo, Ival Goodman, Danny Graves, Ken Griffey, **Ken Griffey Jr.**, Heinie Groh, Don Gullett, **Chick Hafey**, Dummy Hoy, **Miller Huggins**, Fred Hutchinson, Arlie Latham, Red Lucas, Jim Maloney, Lee May, **Bill McKechnie**, Roy McMillan, **Bid McPhee**, Mike Mitchell, Pat Moran, Hal Morris, Gary Nolan, Fred Norman, Joe Nuxhall, Ron Oester, Paul O'Neill, Jim O'Toole, **Tony Perez**, Heinie Peitz, Brandon Phillips, Vada Pinson, Wally Post, Bob Purkey, Ken Raffensberger, Reggie Sanders, Mario Soto, Drew Stubbs, Johnny Temple, Fred Toney, Curt Walker, Jake Weimer, and Billy Werber.

CITI FIELD. Citi Field, located in Queens, New York, has been the home field of the **New York Mets** of the **National League** since 2009. Previously, the Mets played at the **Polo Grounds** (1962–1963) and at **Shea Stadium** (1964–2008). Citi Field, which has a seating capacity of approximately 41,800, is scheduled to host the major league **All-Star Game** in 2013.

See also STADIUMS.

CITIZENS BANK PARK. Citizens Bank Park, located in Philadelphia, Pennsylvania, has been the home field of the **Philadelphia Phillies** of the **National League** since 2004. The Phillies previously played their home games at Recreation Park from 1883 to 1886, at Huntingdon Grounds from 1887 to 1894, at the Baker Bowl from 1895 to 30 June 1938, at **Shibe Park** from 4 July 1938 to 1 October 1970 (renamed Connie Mack Stadium in 1953), and at **Veterans Stadium** from 1971 to 2003. Citizens Bank Park has a seating capacity of approximately 43,600.

See also STADIUMS.

CLARKE, FRED CLIFFORD. B. 3 October 1872, Winterset, Iowa. D. 14 August 1960, Winfield, Kansas. On 30 June 1894, Fred Clarke made his **major-league** debut with five **hits** in five **at-bats** for the **Louisville Colonels**. In 1897, at the age of 24, he was named **manager** of the Colonels. He retained his post as **player-manager** for the Colonels and then the **Pittsburgh Pirates** through the 1915 season. Louisville was dropped from the **National League (NL)** for the 1900 season, whereupon owner **Barney Dreyfuss**, who also owned a half interest in the NL Pirates, brought 14 former Louisville players to Pittsburgh with him. Among them were Clarke, **Honus Wagner**, and **Rube Waddell**. Clarke's teams won four pennants, were second five times, and finished in the first division in 14 of his 19 seasons. In 1903, he led the Pirates to their third consecutive pennant, while also batting .351 and leading the NL in **doubles** and **slugging percentage**. In the first modern **World Series**, Pittsburgh lost to the Boston Americans. Six years later, the 1909 Pirates won the Series, defeating the **Detroit Tigers**.

In addition to his managerial duties, Clarke, a 5-foot, 10-inch, 165-pound left-handed hitter, was the team's left fielder. He had a .312 career **batting average**, with 2,678 hits. His 220 **triples** are seventh best all-time. Clarke's career record as a manager was 1,602–1,181. At one point, he held the major-league record for most managerial wins. In 1945, the **Old Timers Committee** elected Clarke to the **National Baseball Hall of Fame**, as a player.

CLARKSON, JOHN GIBSON. B. 1 July 1861, Cambridge, Massachusetts. D. 4 February 1909, Belmont, Massachusetts. John Clarkson was a right-handed **pitcher** in the **National League (NL)** for 12 seasons. After appearing briefly for the **Worcester Ruby Legs** in 1882, Clarkson pitched for the Chicago White Stockings (1884–1887), Boston Beaneaters (1888–1892), and **Cleveland Spiders** (1892–1894). From 1885 through 1892, the 5-foot, 10-inch, 155-pound Clarkson never won fewer than 25 games in a season. His best years were with 1885 White Stockings and 1889 Beaneaters. In 1885, he led the league with 53 **wins**, 68 **complete games**, 10 **shutouts**, 623 **innings pitched**, and 308 **strikeouts**. In 1889, Clarkson captured the pitcher's **Triple Crown** with 49 wins, a 2.73 **earned run average (ERA)**, and 284 strikeouts. Clarkson won 328 games in his career, had a .648 win-loss percentage, and had a 2.81 ERA. He led the NL in wins and strikeouts three times each, and in innings pitched four times. He also hit 24 **home runs** in his career. In 1963, the **Veterans Committee** elected Clarkson to the **National Baseball Hall of Fame**.

CLEANUP HITTER. The cleanup hitter is the player who bats fourth in the **batting order** and is usually the team's best power hitter.

CLEMENS, WILLIAM ROGER. B. 4 August 1962, Dayton, Ohio. Roger Clemens was a **major-league pitcher** for four teams in a career that lasted 24 seasons. During that span, the 6-foot, 4-inch, 205-pound right-hander won an unprecedented seven **Cy Young Award**s. Clemens pitched in the **American League (AL)** for the **Boston Red Sox** (1984–1996), **Toronto Blue Jays** (1997–1998), and **New York Yankees** (1999–2003, 2007). Between his two stints with the Yankees, Clemens pitched in the **National League** for the 2004–2006 **Houston Astros**. His Cy Young Awards came with Boston in 1986, 1987, and 1991; Toronto in 1997 and 1998; New York in 2001; and Houston in 2004.

Clemens was a six-time 20-game winner, an 11-time **All-Star**, and a two-time winner of the **Triple Crown** for pitchers (1997–1998). He was the *Sporting News*'s choice as AL **Pitcher of the Year** five times and the **Major League Player of the Year** in 1986. He led his league in **wins** four times, **earned run average (ERA)** seven times, **shutouts** six times, and **strikeouts** five times. Clemens had a career record of 354–184, with a 3.12 ERA and 46 shutouts. His 4,672 strikeouts are third all-time, behind **Nolan Ryan** and **Randy Johnson**, and his 354 wins are the ninth highest all-time. Clemens retired after the 2007 season, but charges that he used performance-enhancing drugs in the late stages of his career could affect his election to the **National Baseball Hall of Fame**.

CLEMENTE, ROBERTO (WALKER). B. 18 August 1934, Carolina, **Puerto Rico**. D. 31 December 1972, San Juan, Puerto Rico. Roberto Clemente was a four-time **National League (NL)** batting champion who bettered the .300 mark in 13 of his 18 seasons (1955–1972), all with the **Pittsburgh Pirates**. A 5-foot, 11-inch, 175-pound right-handed **batter** and thrower, he had 200 or more **hits** in four seasons and led the NL twice. Clemente was the league's **Most Valuable Player (MVP)** in 1966 and an **All-Star** 12 times. He led the Pirates to a seven-game **World Series** win over the **Baltimore Orioles** in 1971. Clemente, who had batted .310 in Pittsburgh's seven-game Series win over the **New York Yankees** in 1960, batted .414 against the Orioles, with two **home runs** and a .759 **slugging percentage**. He was voted the Series MVP and the winner of the **Babe Ruth Award**.

An outstanding defensive **outfielder**, Clemente won 12 consecutive **Gold Glove Awards**, from 1961 to 1972, his final season. Playing mostly right field, he used his powerful throwing arm to lead NL outfielders in **assists** five times. Clemente had a .317 career **batting average** and 3,000 hits. He reached the 3,000th hit mark on the final day of the 1972 season. On 31 December 1972, Clemente died in a plane crash while flying to **Nicaragua** to bring supplies to earthquake victims. The **Baseball Writers' Association of America** waived the mandatory five-year waiting period to elect Clemente to the **National Baseball Hall of Fame** in 1973. He was the first Latin American elected to the Hall.

CLEVELAND BLUES (AA). The Cleveland Blues were a team that played in the **American Association** in 1887 and 1888. The team won a combined 89 games and lost 174. The two best players for the Blues were Jersey Bakley and Ed McKean. In 1889, the Blues moved to the **National League** and became known as the **Cleveland Spiders**.

CLEVELAND BLUES (AL). *See* CLEVELAND INDIANS.

CLEVELAND BLUES (NL). The Cleveland Blues were a team that played in the **National League** from 1879 through 1884. The Blues were originally called the **Cleveland Forest Citys**, the name used by the Cleveland club in the National Association in 1871 and 1872. Beginning in 1882, they began being called the Cleveland Blues because of their blue uniforms. The team played its home games at Kennard Street Park. The Blues were disbanded after the 1884 season. Notable players for the Blues included Hugh Dailey, Fred Dunlap, Jack Glasscock, and Jim McCormick.

CLEVELAND BRONCHOS. *See* CLEVELAND INDIANS.

CLEVELAND FOREST CITYS. The Cleveland Forest Citys were a charter member of the National Association (NA). They played in the NA in 1871 and 1872, before disbanding after the 1872 season. On 4 May 1871, Cleveland hosted the first-ever NA game, defeating the **Fort Wayne Kekiongas**, 2–0. The two most notable players for the Forest Citys were Ezra Sutton and **Deacon White**. The Cleveland Forest Citys was also the original name of the **Cleveland Blues** when they joined the **National League** in 1879.

CLEVELAND INDIANS. The Cleveland Indians are a team in the Central Division of the **American League (AL)**. The Indians have been members of the AL since 1901, the first year the AL was recognized as a **major league**. The team was called the **Cleveland Blues** in 1901, Cleveland Bronchos in 1902, and Cleveland Naps from 1903 to 1914, in honor of **Nap Lajoie**, their star **second baseman** and **manager** for many of those years. The Indians played their home games at League Park from 1901 through 1946, although many games from the mid-1930s to 1946 were played at **Cleveland Municipal Stadium**. Beginning with the 1947 season, all home games were played at Cleveland Municipal Stadium until the club moved to Jacobs Field in 1994. Jacobs Field was renamed **Progressive Field** in 2008.

The Indians won their first **World Series** in 1920, under **player-manager Tris Speaker**. They defeated the Brooklyn Robins, five games to two, in the best-of-nine-game Series. They did not make another World Series appearance until 1948, when another player-manager, **Lou Boudreau**, led them to a six-game victory over the **Boston Braves**. That was Cleveland's last world championship, as World Series losses followed each of their three subsequent pennants: to the **New York Giants** in 1954, the **Atlanta Braves** in 1995, and the Florida Marlins in 1997. Cleveland also has lost three times in the **American League Division Series** and twice in the **American League Championship Series**.

Cleveland players who have won the AL's **Most Valuable Player Award** are George Burns (1926), Lou Boudreau (1948), and Al Rosen (1953). **Cy Young Award** winners are **Gaylord Perry** (1972), C. C. Sabathia (2007), and Cliff Lee (2008). **Rookie of the Year** winners are Herb Score (1955), Chris Chambliss (1971), Joe Charboneau (1980), and Sandy Alomar Jr. (1990).

Cleveland players who have led the league in **batting average** are Nap Lajoie (1902–1904, 1910), **Elmer Flick** (1905), Tris Speaker (1916), Lew Fonseca (1929), Lou Boudreau (1944), and Bobby Avila (1954). **Home run** leaders are Braggo Roth (1915, part of season with **Chicago White Sox**), Al Rosen (1950, 1953), **Larry Doby** (1952, 1954), Rocky Colavito (1959), and Albert Belle (1995). **Runs batted in** leaders are Nap Lajoie (1904), Hal Trosky (1936), Al Rosen (1952–1953), Larry Doby (1954), Rocky Colavito (1965), Joe Carter (1986), Albert Belle (1993, 1995–1996), and **Manny Ramirez** (1999).

Cleveland **pitchers** who have led the league in **wins** are **Addie Joss** (1907), Jim Bagby (1920), George Uhle (1923, 1926), **Bob Feller** (1939–1941, 1946–1947, 1951), **Bob Lemon** (1950, 1954–1955), **Early Wynn** (1954), Jim Perry (1960), Gaylord Perry (1972), and Cliff Lee (2008). **Earned run average (ERA)** leaders are Earl Moore (1903), Addie Joss (1904, 1908), Vean Gregg (1911), **Stan Coveleski** (1923), Mel Harder (1933), Bob Feller (1940), Gene Bearden (1948), Mike Garcia (1949, 1954), Early Wynn (1950), Sam McDowell (1965), Luis Tiant (1968), Rick Sutcliffe (1982), Kevin Millwood (2005), and Cliff Lee (2008). **Strikeouts** leaders are Stan Coveleski (1920), Bob Feller (1938–1941, 1946–1948), Allie Reynolds (1943), Bob Lemon (1950), Herb Score (1955–1956), Early Wynn (1957), Sam McDowell (1965–1966, 1968–1970), Len Barker (1980–1981), and **Bert Blyleven** (1985, part of season with **Minnesota Twins**). By leading in wins, ERA, and strikeouts in 1940, Bob Feller won the **Triple Crown** for pitchers.

Other notable players and managers in Indians' history include Johnny Allen, **Roberto Alomar**, **Earl Averill**, Carlos Baerga, Harry Bay, Gary Bell, Bill Bernhard, Bill Bradley, Asdrubal Cabrera, Tom Candiotti, Fausto Carmona, Ray Chapman, Shin-Soo Cho, Bartolo Colon, **Dennis Eckersley**, Wes Ferrell, Ray Fosse, Tito Francona, Travis Fryman, **Joe Gordon**, Jack Graney, Steve Gromek, Travis Hafner, Mike Hargrove, Jeff Heath, Jim Hegan, Woody Held, Otto Hess, Johnny Hodapp, Willis Hudlin, **Joe Jackson**, Brook Jacoby, Charlie Jamieson, Ken Keltner, Kenny Lofton, **Al Lopez**, Victor Martinez, Minnie Minoso, Dale Mitchell, Ed Morgan, Guy Morton, Charles Nagy, Steve O'Neill, **Satchel Paige**, Roger Peckinpaugh, Vic Power, Bob Rhoads, **Frank Robinson**, John Romano, **Joe Sewell**, Luke Sewell, Sonny Siebert, Grady Sizemore, Elmer Smith, **Jim Thome**, Andre Thornton, Terry Turner, **Omar Vizquel**, Joe Vosmik, Bill Wambsganss, Eric Wedge, and Bob Wickman.

CLEVELAND INFANTS. The Cleveland Infants were a team in the **Players League (PL)** in 1890, the one year of the PL's existence. The team finished in seventh place but had the league's batting champion in **Pete Browning**, who had a .373 **batting average**. In addition to Browning, other notable players on the Infants were **Ed Delahanty**, Henry Larkin, Cub Stricker, Sy Sutcliffe, and Patsy Tebeau.

CLEVELAND MUNICIPAL STADIUM. Cleveland Municipal Stadium, located in Cleveland, Ohio, was the part-time home of the **Cleveland Indians** of the **American League** from the mid-1930s to 1946, and the full-time home from 1947 until 1993. The Indians played their home games at League Park from 1901 through 1946, although many games from the mid-

1930s to 1946 were played at Cleveland Municipal Stadium. In 1994, the Indians moved to Jacobs Field, which was renamed **Progressive Field** in 2008. Cleveland Municipal Stadium hosted the **major league All-Star Game** in 1935, 1954, 1963, and 1981.

CLEVELAND NAPS. *See* CLEVELAND INDIANS.

CLEVELAND SPIDERS. The Cleveland Spiders were a team in the **National League (NL)** from 1889 to 1899. Playing as the **Cleveland Blues**, the team had played in the **American Association** in 1887 and 1888, before moving to the NL in 1889. The Spiders were also-rans for most of their 11 seasons, but second-place finishes in 1895 and 1896 allowed them to compete for the **Temple Cup**, a seven-game series between the NL's first-place and second-place finishers. In both seasons, they played the first-place **Baltimore Orioles**. The Spiders defeated the Orioles in 1894, but the team lost to them in 1895.

In 1899, the owners of the Cleveland club bought the St. Louis Perfectos, also of the NL, and transferred most of Cleveland's best players to St. Louis. The 1899 Spiders, stripped of their talent, had the worst season in **major-league** history. They won only 20 of their 154 games and had a NL record-losing streak of 24 consecutive games. When the NL contracted from 12 teams to eight in 1900, the Cleveland franchise was one of the four eliminated. Notable players for the Cleveland Spiders included **Jesse Burkett**, Cupid Childs, **John Clarkson**, Nig Cuppy, Ed McKean, Jack O'Connor, Jack Powell, Lou Sockalexis, Patsy Tebeau, **Bobby Wallace**, **Cy Young**, and Chief Zimmer.

COACH. A coach is a team member in uniform appointed by the **manager** to perform such duties as the manager may designate, such as but not limited to acting as a **base coach**. Other coaches, aside from base coaches, may be **bench** coaches, who serve as assistant managers, batting coaches, pitching coaches, infield coaches, and **outfield** coaches.

COBB, TYRUS RAYMOND "TY," "THE GEORGIA PEACH". B. 18 December 1886, Narrows, Georgia. D. 17 July 1961, Atlanta, Georgia. Ty Cobb, a center fielder for the **Detroit Tigers** from 1905 to 1926 and the **Philadelphia Athletics** in 1927 and 1928, played most of his career in the low-scoring **Deadball Era**. Although the 6-foot, 1-inch, 175-pound Cobb hit only 117 **home runs** during his 24 seasons, he is generally judged the best all-around player of the first half of the 20th century. When the fiery, aggressive, win-at-all-costs Cobb retired after the 1928 season, he held 90 **major-league** records. Cobb won his first batting championship as a 20-year-old in

1907, and he went on to lead the **American League (AL)** in batting 10 more times. Only a controversial one percentage point loss to **Nap Lajoie** in 1910 prevented him from winning nine straight titles, from 1907 to 1915. He batted above .400 three times, including a career-high .420 in 1911, when he was the AL's **Most Valuable Player**.

Cobb, who batted left-handed and threw right-handed, won his only home run title, with nine in 1909, the year he won the **Triple Crown**. In addition to his 11 batting championships, he led the AL in **hits** eight times and had more than 200 hits nine times. Cobb was number one in **slugging percentage** eight times, **on-base percentage** seven times, **total bases** six times, **runs** scored five times, **runs batted in** and **triples** four times, and **doubles** and **extra-base hits** three times. A speedy, hard-sliding **base runner**, he led the AL in **stolen bases** in six different seasons, and his total of 96 in 1915 was the modern major-league record until 1962.

Cobb's lifetime **batting average** of .366 is the highest ever, and his 4,189 hits was the major-league record until **Pete Rose** passed it in 1985. He is second best all-time in runs (2,246) and fourth best in stolen bases (897). Cobb served as the Tigers' manager from 1921 to 1926. Detroit finished in the first division in four of those seasons, including a second-place finish in 1923. In 1936, Cobb, **Walter Johnson**, **Christy Mathewson**, **Babe Ruth**, and **Honus Wagner** were the first members elected by the **Baseball Writers' Association of America** to the new **National Baseball Hall of Fame**. Cobb got the most votes.

COCHRANE, GORDON STANLEY "MICKEY," "BLACK MIKE". B. 6 April 1903, Bridgewater, Massachusetts. D. 28 June 1962, Lake Forest, Illinois. Mickey Cochrane was a leader, both as a **catcher** for the **Philadelphia Athletics** (1925–1933) and then as a catcher (1934–1937) and later **manager** of the **Detroit Tigers** (1934–1938). He played in five **World Series**, three with the Athletics in 1929–1931, and two as the **player-manager** of the Tigers in 1934 and 1935. The Tigers purchased Cochrane from Philadelphia in December 1933, and he led them to pennants in his first two seasons.

Cochrane was a 5-foot, 10-inch, 180-pound left-handed hitter, who compiled a .320 **batting average** in his 13 seasons. He was twice voted the **Most Valuable Player** in the **American League (AL)**, in 1928 with Philadelphia, and in 1934, his first year in Detroit. He led AL catchers in games caught five times and **putouts** six times, including every season from 1926 to 1930. On 25 May 1937, Cochrane suffered a severe head injury after being beaned by Bump Hadley of the **New York Yankees**. That ended his playing career, and, in mid-1938, the Tigers replaced him as manager. He later served as

general manager of the Athletics and vice president of the Tigers. In 1947, the **Baseball Writers' Association of America** elected Cochrane to the **National Baseball Hall of Fame**.

COLLEGE BASEBALL. The first known intercollegiate baseball game took place in Pittsfield, Massachusetts, on 1 July 1859, between squads representing Amherst College and Williams College. College baseball is played under the auspices of the National Collegiate Athletic Association (NCAA) or the National Association of Intercollegiate Athletics (NAIA). The NCAA writes the rules of play, while each sanctioning body supervises season-ending tournaments. The final rounds of the NCAA tournaments are known as the College World Series, one for each of the three levels of competition sanctioned by the NCAA. The College World Series for Division I schools is held in Omaha, Nebraska, in June.

The playoff bracket for Division I consists of 64 teams, with four teams playing at each of 16 regional sites in a double-elimination format. The 16 winners advance to the Super Regionals at eight sites, where they play head-to-head in a best-of-three series. The eight winners then advance to the College World Series, a double-elimination tournament, using two separate four-team brackets, to determine the two national finalists. The finalists play a best-of-three series to determine the Division I national champion. The 2012 College World Series winner was the University of Arizona.

The Division II College World Series has been played since 1968. The 2012 winner was **West Chester (Pennsylvania) University**. The Division III College World Series has been played since 1976. The 2012 winner was Marietta (Ohio) College. The NAIA World Series has been played since 1957. The 2012 winner was **Tennessee Wesleyan College**.

COLLINS, EDWARD TROWBRIDGE "EDDIE". B. 2 May 1887, Millerton, New York. D. 25 March 1951, Boston, Massachusetts. Eddie Collins was a 1907 graduate of Columbia University in New York City, where he played quarterback on the football team. In 1908, he took over the **second-base** position for the **Philadelphia Athletics** of the **American League (AL)**. Led by their "$100,000 infield," which consisted of Stuffy McInnis at **first base**, Collins at second, Jack Barry at **shortstop**, and **Frank Baker** at **third base**, the Athletics won AL pennants in 1910, 1911, 1913, and 1914. In three of those years, the A's won the **World Series**, defeating the **Chicago Cubs** in 1910 and the **New York Giants** in 1911 and 1913. Although heavily favored to win again in 1914, they were swept in four games by the **Boston Braves**. Collins was voted the AL's **Most Valuable Player (MVP)** in 1914;

nevertheless, A's **manager Connie Mack**, reacting to the financial losses he suffered that season and fearing he might lose Collins to the new **Federal League**, sold him to the **Chicago White Sox** after the season.

Collins played 12 seasons for the White Sox. He finished second in the MVP race in 1923 and 1924, and was on the world championship team that defeated the Giants in 1917. He was also a member of the 1919 "Black Sox" team that lost the World Series to the **Cincinnati Reds**. Eight Chicago players on that team were later charged with involvement in deliberately losing the Series, but Collins, the team captain, was not among them. After managing the White Sox for part of the 1924 season, and all of 1925 and 1926, he was released and went back to the Athletics as a player and **coach**. Collins played his final four seasons with Philadelphia and then served as the **general manager** of the **Boston Red Sox** until his death in 1951. In his 25-year playing career, the longest in AL history, the 5-foot, 9-inch, 170-pound Collins led the league in **runs** three times and **stolen bases** four times. A left-handed hitter, he batted .300 or better 17 times, accumulated 3,315 **hits**, and had a lifetime **batting average** of .333. Defensively, he holds numerous records for **second basemen**. In 1939, the **Baseball Writers' Association of America** elected Collins to the **National Baseball Hall of Fame**.

COLLINS, JAMES JOSEPH "JIMMY". B. 16 January 1870, Buffalo, New York. D. 6 March 1943, Buffalo, New York. Jimmy Collins was regarded by both **John McGraw** and **Connie Mack** as the best **third baseman** ever. The 5-foot, 9-inch, 178-pound Collins played for the Boston Beaneaters of the **National League (NL)** from 1895 through 1900. (For part of the 1895 season, he was lent to the **Louisville Colonels**.) Collins, a right-handed hitter, batted .346 in 1897 and .328 in 1898, while leading the NL in 1898 in **home runs** (15) and **total bases** (286). The Beaneaters won the pennant in both those seasons.

In 1901, Collins jumped to the Boston Americans of the new **American League (AL)** as a **player-manager**. He continued to be a steady hitter and an excellent and innovative third baseman, playing off the **base** at a time when most others played close to the base. He led AL third basemen in **putouts** five times and **assists** four times. Collins led the Americans (forerunners of the **Boston Red Sox**) to a pennant in 1903 and was the winning **manager** in the first modern **World Series**, when the Americans defeated the NL's **Pittsburgh Pirates**. The Americans won the pennant again in 1904, but the NL winner, the **New York Giants**, refused to play them in the World Series. Collins, who had a career **batting average** of .294, and finished one **hit** short of 2,000, was elected to the **National Baseball Hall of Fame** as a player by the **Old Timers Committee** in 1945.

COLORADO ROCKIES. The Colorado Rockies are a team in the Western Division of the **National League (NL)**. The team, based in Denver, entered the NL with the Florida Marlins in 1993, as part of a two-team NL **expansion**. The Rockies played their home games at Mile High Stadium in 1993 and 1994, before moving to **Coors Field** in 1995.

The Rockies reached the **National League Division Series (NLDS)** in 1995, their first year playing at Coors Field, but the team lost to the **Atlanta Braves**. They also lost in the NLDS to the **Philadelphia Phillies** in 2009. The Rockies won their only NL pennant in 2007, but were swept in four games in the **World Series** by the **Boston Red Sox**.

Larry Walker, in 1997, is the only Colorado Rockies player to win the **Most Valuable Player Award**. No Rockies **pitcher** has won the **Cy Young Award**. Jason Jennings, in 2002, is the Rockies' only **Rookie of the Year** winner.

Rockies players who have led the league in **batting average** are Andres Galarraga (1993), Larry Walker (1998–1999, 2001), Todd Helton (2000), Matt Holiday (2007), and Carlos Gonzalez (2010). Leaders in **home runs** are Dante Bichette (1995), Andres Galarraga (1996), and Larry Walker (1997). Leaders in **runs batted in** are Dante Bichette (1995), Andres Galarraga (1996–1997), Todd Helton (2000), Preston Wilson (2003), Vinny Castilla (2004), and Matt Holiday (2007).

No Rockies pitcher has led the NL in **wins**. No Rockies pitcher has led the NL in **earned run average**. No Rockies pitcher has led the NL in **strikeouts**.

Other notable players and **managers** in Rockies' history include Pedro Astacio, Garrett Atkins, Clint Barmes, Don Baylor, Ellis Burks, Aaron Cook, Jeff Francis, Brian Fuentes, Brad Hawpe, Clint Hurdle, Ubaldo Jiminez, Neifi Perez, Huston Street, Jim Tracy, Troy Tulowitzki, and Eric Young.

COLT STADIUM. *See* HOUSTON ASTROS.

COLUMBIA PARK. *See* PHILADELPHIA ATHLETICS (AL).

COLUMBUS (OHIO) BUCKEYES. *See* COLUMBUS (OHIO) COLTS.

COLUMBUS (OHIO) COLTS. The Columbus Colts, who also played as the Columbus Buckeyes and Columbus Senators, were members of the **American Association (AA)** in 1883 and 1884. Led by **pitchers** Frank Mountain and Ed Morris, Columbus finished in second place in 1884. Nevertheless, financial constraints forced the AA to drop four teams after the 1884 season, and the small-market Colts was one of them.

COLUMBUS (OHIO) SENATORS. *See* COLUMBUS (OHIO) COLTS.

COLUMBUS (OHIO) SOLONS. The Columbus Solons were members of the **American Association (AA)** from 1889 to 1891, the AA's final three seasons. Like the previous Columbus entry in the league, the **Columbus Colts**, the Solons were also sometimes called the Columbus Buckeyes or Columbus Senators. The Solons' best season was 1890, when they finished in second place. Notable players for the Solons included Mark Baldwin, Elton Chamberlain, Jack O'Connor, and Dave Orr.

COMBS, EARLE BRYAN. B. 14 May 1899, Pebworth, Kentucky. D. 21 July 1976, Richmond, Kentucky. Earle Combs's 12-year career with the **New York Yankees** (1924–1935) was shortened by two serious on-field collisions, one in 1934 and one in 1935. In nine full seasons with New York (1925–1933), the speedy left-handed-batting **leadoff** man batted .300 or better every season but one, 1926, when he batted .299. For the first eight of those seasons, he had more than 100 **runs** scored and more than 30 **doubles**. Combs's best season was in 1927, when he had a .356 **batting average** and led the **American League (AL)** with 231 **hits** and 23 **triples**. He had three seasons with more than 200 hits and three seasons in which he led the AL in triples. The 6-foot, 185-pound Combs batted a combined .350 in four **World Series**. Although Combs had a less-than-stellar throwing arm, his great speed helped him twice lead AL center fielders in **putouts**. He finished his career with a .325 batting average. **Joe DiMaggio** replaced Combs in center field in 1936. Combs became a Yankees **coach**, helping teach the rookie DiMaggio the intricacies of playing the **outfield** at **Yankee Stadium**. In 1970, the **Veterans Committee** elected Combs to the **National Baseball Hall of Fame**.

COMERICA PARK. Comerica Park, located in Detroit, Michigan, has been the home of the **Detroit Tigers** of the **American League** since 11 April 2000. Before then, the Tigers played their home games at Bennett Park from 1901 to 1911, and at **Tiger Stadium** from 1912 to 1999. Comerica Park has a seating capacity of approximately 41,200. It was the site of the **major league All-Star Game** in 2005.

See also STADIUMS.

COMISKEY, CHARLES ALBERT "CHARLIE," "THE OLD RO-MAN". B. 15 August 1859, Chicago, Illinois. D. 26 October 1931, Eagle River, Wisconsin. Charlie Comiskey is best remembered as the owner of the **Chicago White Sox** of the **American League (AL)** from 1901, the first year the AL had **major-league** status, until his death in 1931. But earlier, the 6-foot, 180-pound Comiskey had been a right-handed-hitting **first baseman** and successful **manager**. He played for the **St. Louis Browns** of the

American Association (AA) from 1882 to 1889, jumped to the **Chicago Pirates** of the **Players League** in 1890, returned to the Browns in 1891, and finished his playing days with the **Cincinnati Reds** of the **National League (NL)** from 1892 to 1894. Comiskey had a .264 career **batting average** in 1,390 games and led the AA in **putouts** by a first baseman three times.

Comiskey was named **player-manager** of the Browns in 1883, his second season with the club. He filled that role in each season after that, first with St. Louis, then with Chicago and Cincinnati, until his retirement following the 1894 season. His best years were with the Browns, who were the AA's most successful franchise, winning four consecutive pennants from 1885 to 1888. After each pennant-winning season, the Browns played the NL pennant winner in a championship series that was a predecessor to the modern **World Series**. After a tie in 1885, they won in 1886 and lost in 1887–1888.

The Comiskey-owned Chicago White Sox were charter members of the AL. Under Comiskey's ownership, the White Sox opened **Comiskey Park** in 1910. During his 31-year reign, the White Sox won three pennants and the World Series in 1906 and 1917. The team's deliberate loss to the Cincinnati Reds in 1919 has been blamed, in part, on Comiskey's tightfistedness in dealing with his players. In 1939, Comiskey was elected to the **National Baseball Hall of Fame** by the **Old Timers Committee** as a pioneer/executive.

COMISKEY PARK. Comiskey Park, located in Chicago, Illinois, and named for owner **Charles Comiskey**, was the home of the **Chicago White Sox** of the **American League** from 1 July 1910 to 30 September 1990. Before that, the White Sox played their home games at South Side Park from 24 April 1901 to 27 June 1910. In 1991, the White Sox moved to a new park, also called Comiskey Park, until 2003, when the name was changed to **U.S. Cellular Field**. Comiskey Park was also the home field for the **Chicago American Giants** of the **Negro American League** from 1941 to 1952. Comiskey Park hosted the first **major league All-Star Game** in 1933, and again in 1950 and 1983.

See also STADIUMS.

COMMISSIONER OF BASEBALL. The commissioner of baseball is chosen by a vote of the owners of all the **major-league** teams. His role is to oversee the operation of the major leagues and **minor leagues** and to maintain the integrity of the game. He is responsible for hiring and maintaining the **umpiring** crews and negotiating marketing, labor, and television contracts. The first commissioner was **Kenesaw Landis**, who served from 12 November 1920 to 25 November 1944. The current commissioner is **Bud Selig**, who has served since 7 September 1992. Commissioners who served between Landis and Selig were **Happy Chandler** (24 April 1945–15 July 1951), **Ford Frick** (20 September 1951–16 November 1965), Spike Eckert (17 November 1965–20 November 1968), **Bowie Kuhn** (4 February 1969–20 September 1984), Peter Ueberroth (1 October 1984–30 September 1988), Bart Giamatti (1 April 1989–1 September 1989), and Fay Vincent (13 September 1989–7 September 1992).

COMMITTEE ON AFRICAN AMERICAN BASEBALL. The Committee on African American Baseball was a special committee of 12 baseball historians formed to honor contributions to the game by **African Americans**. The committee, which existed in 1975 and 1976, considered almost 100 **Negro League** and pre–Negro League players, **managers**, and executives. In February 2006, the committee elected 17 of those 39 individuals to the **National Baseball Hall of Fame**.

COMPLETE GAMES (CG). A **pitcher** is credited with a complete game if he pitches an entire official game, no matter how many **innings** or whether his team wins or loses. In the early days of Major League Baseball, teams carried few pitchers, and the vast majority of **games started** by pitchers resulted in complete games. Thus, the all-time single-season high is by Will White of the 1879 **Cincinnati Reds** of the **National League (NL)**. White completed all 75 of his games started.

The single-season leader post-1893, when the pitching distance was extended to its current 60 feet, 6 inches, is **Amos Rusie** of the 1893 **New York Giants**. Rusie completed 50 of the 52 games he started. The single-season leader in the **American League (AL)** is **Jack Chesbro** of the 1904 **New York Yankees**, with 48.

The career leader is **Cy Young**, with 749. Young pitched for the **Cleveland Spiders** of the NL (1890–1898), **St. Louis Cardinals** of the NL (1899–1900), Boston Americans of the AL (1901–1908), Cleveland Naps of the AL (1909–1911), and Boston Rustlers of the NL (1911).

CONGRESS STREET GROUNDS. *See* BOSTON BRAVES.

CONLAN, JOHN BERTRAND "JOCKO". B. 6 December 1899, Chicago, Illinois. D. 16 April 1989, Scottsdale, Arizona. Jocko Conlan, a onetime **outfielder** with the **Chicago White Sox** in 1934 and 1935, was an **umpire** in the **National League (NL)** from 1941 through 1965. Conlan was the only NL umpire to wear an outside chest protector. He was also the only umpire in either league to make his **out** calls with his left hand rather than his right.

Conlan umpired in 3,621 **major-league** games, six **All-Star Games**, five **World Series**, and three NL playoffs. The **Veterans Committee** elected him to the **National Baseball Hall of Fame** in 1974.

CONNIE MACK STADIUM. *See* SHIBE PARK.

CONNOLLY, THOMAS HENRY, SR. "TOM". B. 31 December 1870, Manchester, England. D. 28 April 1961, Natick, Massachusetts. Tom Connolly was an **umpire** in the **National League (NL)** from 1898 to 1900. In 1901, **Ban Johnson**, president of the **American League (AL)**, which was in its first year as a **major league**, hired Connolly to umpire in the new league. On 24 April 1901, Connolly was the umpire for the first AL game, a contest between the **Chicago White Sox** and **Cleveland Blues** at **Comiskey Park** in Chicago. He later umpired the first AL games at **Shibe Park** in Philadelphia, **Fenway Park** in Boston, and **Yankee Stadium** in New York. Overall, Connolly umpired in 4,768 major-league games.

Connolly and Hank O'Day, of the NL, were the umpires for the first modern **World Series**, in 1903, between the Boston Americans and **Pittsburgh Pirates**. In all, he umpired in eight World Series. In June 1931, Connolly retired as an active umpire, whereupon AL president **Will Harridge** named him the league's umpire in chief, a position he held until January 1954. In 1953, the **Veterans Committee** selected Connolly and the NL's **Bill Klem** as the first umpires to be elected to the **National Baseball Hall of Fame**.

CONNOR, ROGER. B. 1 July 1857, Waterbury, Connecticut. D. 4 January 1931, Waterbury, Connecticut. Roger Connor, a 6-foot, 3-inch, 220-pound **switch-hitting first baseman**, played 17 seasons in the **National League (NL)** and one (1890) in the **Players' League (PL)**. Connor began his career with the **Troy Trojans** of the NL in 1880, but when the Trojans disbanded after the 1882 season, he moved on to the New York Gothams. He remained with the Gothams, renamed the **New York Giants** in 1885, through the 1889 season. The Giants won pennants in 1888 and 1889 and played the **American Association (AA)** pennant winners in a championship series that was a predecessor to the modern **World Series**. Connor batted a combined .328, as the Giants defeated the **St. Louis Browns** in 1888 and Brooklyn Bridegrooms in 1889.

In 1890, Connor was one of many players who left both the NL and AA to form the PL. Connor's PL team was also called the **New York Giants**, but, when the league folded after one season, Connor rejoined the NL Giants in 1891. He moved to the **Philadelphia Phillies** in 1892 and back to the Giants in 1893. In June 1894, the Giants sent him to the St. Louis Browns, who had joined the NL in 1892. He stayed with the Browns until the end of his playing career, in 1897, briefly **managing** the club in 1896.

Connor's best season was in 1885, when he led the NL with a .371 **batting average**, 169 **hits**, a .435 **on-base percentage**, and 225 **total bases**. He twice led the NL in **triples** and **slugging percentage**, and once in **runs batted in**. Although he led his league in **home runs** only once—his tally of 14 in 1890 was tops in the PL—Connor was the 19th century's most prolific home-run hitter. His career total of 138 stood as the **major-league** record until **Babe Ruth** passed it in 1921. He batted above .300 twelve times and finished with a lifetime batting average of .316. His 233 triples are fifth all-time. In 1976, the **Veterans Committee** elected Connor to the **National Baseball Hall of Fame**.

COOPER, ANDREW LEWIS "ANDY". B. 24 April 1896, Waco, Texas. D. 3 June 1941, Waco, Texas. Andy Cooper was a 6-foot, 2-inch, 220-pound left-handed **pitcher** who spent 19 seasons in the **Negro Leagues**. He pitched for the Detroit Stars of the **Negro National League (NNL)** (1920–1927, 1930), and for the **Kansas City Monarchs** (1928–1929, 1931–1939) in both the NNL and **Negro American League (NAL)**. He later managed the Monarchs to three NAL championships. In 2006, Cooper was elected to the **National Baseball Hall of Fame** in a special election conducted by the **Committee on African American Baseball**.

See also AFRICAN AMERICANS IN BASEBALL.

COORS FIELD. Coors Field, located in Denver, Colorado, is the home field of the **Colorado Rockies** of the **National League**. The **stadium** opened in 1995, replacing Mile High Stadium, where the Rockies played in 1993 and 1994. Because of the thin air in Denver, which is nearly a mile above sea level, balls carry further, which makes Coors Field the most hitter-friendly park in the **major leagues**. Coors Field, which has a seating capacity of approximately 50,400, hosted the major league **All-Star Game** in 1998.

COVELESKI, STANLEY ANTHONY "STAN". B. Stanislaus Kowalewski, 13 July 1889, Shamokin, Pennsylvania. D. 20 March 1984, South Bend, Indiana. **Pitcher** Stan Coveleski was a 5-foot, 11-inch, 166-pound right-hander whose best pitch was the **spitball**. He had a 2–1 record for the 1912 **Philadelphia Athletics**, including a **shutout** in his first **major-league** game. After three-plus years in the **minor leagues**, he returned to the **American League (AL)** with the 1916 **Cleveland Indians**, winning 172 games during the course of the next nine seasons. Coveleski was a 20-game winner for four consecutive seasons (1918–1921). In Cleveland's 1920 **World Series** victory against the Brooklyn Robins, he had three **complete-game** wins and a 0.67 **earned run average (ERA)**. Traded to the **Washington Senators** for the 1925 season, he went 20–5, with a league-leading 2.84 ERA for the pennant-winning Senators. He was 0–2 against the **Pittsburgh Pirates** in the World Series. Coveleski, who retired after going 5–1 for the 1928 **New York Yankees**, finished his career with a record of 215–142 and a 2.89 ERA. He led the AL in ERA and shutouts twice, and in **strikeouts** once. In 1969, the **Veterans Committee** elected him to the **National Baseball Hall of Fame**.

COX, ROBERT JOSEPH "BOBBY". B. 21 May 1941, Tulsa, Oklahoma. Bobby Cox was a 5-foot, 11-inch, 180-pound right-handed-hitting **third baseman** who batted .225 in 220 games for the 1968–1969 **New York Yankees**. He later managed the **Atlanta Braves** from 1978 to 1981, and the **Toronto Blue Jays** from 1982 to 1985, leading the Jays to a first-place finish in the **American League's (AL)** Eastern Division in 1985. He then returned to the Braves as the **general manager** and, in 1990, took over as the manager. From 1991 to 2005, the Braves finished first in their division 14 times, including 11 straight from 1995 to 2005. They won five **National League (NL)** pennants, but the team won only one **World Series**, against the **Cleveland Indians** in 1995.

Cox, who retired after the 2010 season, had a career record of 2,504–2,001 in 29 seasons. Upon his retirement, he had the fourth-highest win total among managers. The always combative Cox was ejected from 159 games, the highest number of ejections all-time. The *Sporting News* gave Cox its **major league Manager of the Year Award** in 1985 and its NL Manager of the Year Award in 1991, 1993, 1999, and 2002–2005. The **Baseball Writers' Association of America** gave him its AL Manager of the Year Award in 1985 and its NL Manager of the Year Award in 1991 and 2004–2005. Cox is sure to be elected to the **National Baseball Hall of Fame** when he becomes eligible.

CRAWFORD, SAMUEL EARL "SAM," "WAHOO SAM". B. 18 April 1880, Wahoo, Nebraska. D. 15 June 1968, Hollywood, California. **Outfielder** Sam Crawford used his speed and power to set the **major-league** record for most career **triples**. While playing four seasons for the **Cincinnati Reds** of the **National League (NL)** (1899–1902) and 15 seasons with the **Detroit Tigers** of the **American League (AL)** (1903–1917), he amassed 309 three-base hits; he led the AL five times and the NL once. The 6-foot, 190-pound Crawford also holds the single-season record for most inside-the-park **home runs**, with 12 for Cincinnati in 1901. The left-handed swinger led the NL in home runs that year, with 16, and he led the AL in home runs in 1908, with seven. Crawford led his league in **runs batted in (RBI)** three times and **total**

bases twice. His .314 **batting average** in 1914, along with his leading the league in triples and RBI, earned him second place to **Eddie Collins** of the **Philadelphia Athletics** in the voting for the **Most Valuable Player Award**. Crawford and his outfield teammate **Ty Cobb** played on three consecutive pennant winners with Detroit (1907–1909), but lost in the **World Series** each time. Crawford retired with a .309 career batting average and 2,961 **hits**. The **Veterans Committee** elected him to the **National Baseball Hall of Fame** in 1957.

CREIGHTON, JAMES "JIM". B. 15 April 1841, Brooklyn, New York. D. 18 October 1862, Brooklyn, New York. **Pitcher** Jim Creighton has been called baseball's first superstar. He began playing as a teenager and played for six years (1857–1862), most famously for the **Brooklyn Excelsiors** (1859–1862). Before Creighton, pitchers had to deliver the ball underhand. Creighton delivered the ball with an unprecedented combination of speed, spin, and command that changed the manner of delivery for all those who followed. A great hitter, as well as a great pitcher, he suffered an internal injury while taking a hard swing at a pitch. After a few days of internal hemorrhaging, he died from his still undiagnosed injury, which was likely the rupture of an organ. He was 21 years old.

CRONIN, JOSEPH EDWARD "JOE". B. 12 October 1906, San Francisco, California. D. 7 September 1984, Barnstable, Massachusetts. Joe Cronin was a major figure in baseball for half a century. For most of his playing career, he was the best **shortstop** in the game. He was also a **manager**, a **general manager**, and the president of the **American League (AL)**. He played his first two seasons with the **Pittsburgh Pirates**, in 1926 and 1927, but didn't reach stardom until he joined the **Washington Senators** in 1928. The right-handed-hitting Cronin batted above .300 in four of his seven seasons with the Senators, including a career-high .346 in 1931. In 1933, Senators owner **Clark Griffith** chose the 26-year-old Cronin as his manager. The Senators won the pennant, but the team lost to the **New York Giants** in the **World Series**.

After the Senators finished seventh in 1934, Cronin was traded to the **Boston Red Sox**, where he was again chosen to manage the team. He remained as a player with Boston until early 1945, and as the manager through 1947. The Red Sox won their only pennant under Cronin in 1946, but the team lost the World Series to the **St. Louis Cardinals**.

The 5-foot, 11-inch, 180-pound Cronin (he grew considerably heavier later in his career) compiled a .301 **batting average**, with 1,424 **runs batted in**. A seven-time **All-Star**, he led AL shortstops three times in **putouts** and **assists** and twice in fielding percentage. He was later the general manager of the Red

Sox (1948–1959) and president of the American League (1959–1973). Cronin was elected to the **National Baseball Hall of Fame** by the **Baseball Writers' Association of America** as a player in 1956.

CROSLEY FIELD. Crosley Field, located in Cincinnati, Ohio, was the home of the **Cincinnati Reds** of the **National League** from 11 April 1912 to 24 June 1970, when they moved to **Riverfront Stadium**. Before moving to Crosley Field, known as Redland Field from 1912 to 1933, the Reds played their home games at two parks known as League Park from 1890 to 1901, and at the Palace of the Fans from 1902 to 1911. Crosley Field hosted the **major league All-Star Game** in 1938 and 1953.

See also STADIUMS.

CUBA. Baseball has been played in Cuba since the 1860s. The first league, the all-white Cuban League, was organized in 1878, consisting of three teams—Almendares, Habana, and Mantanzas. In 1900, the league began admitting blacks, and soon many of the best players from the American **Negro Leagues** were playing on integrated teams in Cuba. In the 1960s, following the revolution in which Fidel Castro seized power, the government abolished all professional sports on the island. Since then, Cuban amateur teams have continued their long domination of international competition, for example, in the **Baseball World Cup**, Intercontinental Cup, Pan-American Games, Central American and Caribbean Games, and World Baseball Challenge.

The most notable players and **managers** born in Cuba include **Esteban Bellan**, Bert Campaneris, Jose Canseco, Jose Cardenal, Leo Cardenas, Aroldis Chapman, Yoenis Cespedes, Mike Cuellar, **Martin Dihigo**, Preston Gomez, Fredi Gonzalez, Livan Hernandez, Orlando Hernandez, Omar Linares, Adolfo Luque, **Jose Mendez**, Minnie Minoso, Tony Oliva, Alejandro Oms, **Rafael Palmeiro**, Camilo Pascual, **Tony Perez**, Pedro Ramos, Cookie Rojas, Diego Segui, Tony Taylor, Luis Tiant, and **Cristobal Torriente**.

CUBS PARK. *See* WRIGLEY FIELD.

CUMMINGS, WILLIAM ARTHUR "CANDY". B. 18 October 1848, Ware, Massachusetts. D. 16 May 1924, Toledo, Ohio. Candy Cummings played for several amateur baseball clubs in the New York City area after the Civil War, including the **Brooklyn Excelsiors** in 1866 and 1867. It was during this time that Cummings allegedly invented the **curveball**. After **Henry Chadwick** named Cummings America's best amateur **pitcher** in 1871, the 5-foot, 9-inch, 120-pound right-hander turned professional. Cummings's **major-league** career lasted six seasons, four in the National Association

(NA) and two in the **National League (NL)**. He was in the NA with the **New York Mutuals** in 1872, **Baltimore Canaries** in 1873, **Philadelphia White Stockings** in 1874, and **Hartford Dark Blues** in 1875. He was with Hartford again in 1876, when that club entered the NL, and he spent his final big-league season, 1877, with the NL's **Cincinnati Reds**.

Cummings led the NA in **shutouts** twice, and, on 9 September 1876, he became the first major-league pitcher to start and win both ends of a **double-header**. In all, Cummings won 124 games and lost just 72 in the NA, including a 33-win season in 1872, and a 35-win season in 1875, but he was an unimpressive 21–22 in the NL. The **Old Timers Committee** elected Cummings to the **National Baseball Hall of Fame** in 1939.

CURVEBALL. The curveball, also known as the "the bender," "the hook," "Uncle Charlie," and "the hammer," is thrown by the **pitcher** in such a way that it breaks sharply downward as it approaches **home plate**. Other curveballs are thrown in such a way that they break down and toward the pitcher's off hand. The curveball was allegedly invented by pitcher **Candy Cummings** in the late 1860s. Pitchers noted for the effectiveness of their curveballs include **Bert Blyleven**, **Mordecai Brown**, **Steve Carlton**, **Bob Feller**, Dwight Gooden, Orel Hershiser, **Sandy Koufax**, Sal Maglie, Camilo Pascual, **Nolan Ryan**, Herb Score, and Virgil Trucks.

CUYLER, HAZEN SHIRLEY "KIKI". B. 30 August 1898, Harrisville, Michigan. D. 11 February 1950, Ann Arbor, Michigan. Kiki Cuyler batted .321 in his 18-year career in the **National League (NL)**, which lasted from 1921 through 1938. Cuyler, a 5-foot, 10-inch, 180-pound right-handed-hitting **outfielder**, played with the **Pittsburgh Pirates** (1921–1927), **Chicago Cubs** (1928–1935), **Cincinnati Reds** (1935–1937), and **Brooklyn Dodgers** (1938). Cuyler led the NL in **stolen bases** four times and batted better than .300 10 times and better than .350 four times. He also led NL right fielders in **fielding percentage** three times. In three **World Series**, against the **Washington Senators** in 1925, **Philadelphia Athletics** in 1929, and **New York Yankees** in 1932, he batted a combined .281 during the course of 16 games. Cuyler's best season was in 1925, when he batted .357 and had a league-leading 26 **triples** and 144 **runs** scored. In 1968, the **Veterans Committee** elected him to the **National Baseball Hall of Fame**.

CY YOUNG AWARD. The Cy Young Award is named for **Cy Young**, baseball's all-time winningest **pitcher**. The award came into existence in 1956, at the urging of Commissioner **Ford Frick**. Originally, voters from the **Baseball Writers' Association of America** chose one winner, covering both **major leagues**. The first winner was Don Newcombe of the **Brooklyn**

Dodgers. Beginning in 1967, the writers chose an **American League (AL)** winner and a **National League (NL)** winner. From 1956 to 1969, each writer voted for just one pitcher. But after the AL vote ended in a tie in 1969, each writer voted for three different pitchers: The first-place vote was worth five points, the second-place vote three points, and the third-place vote one point.

Beginning with the 2010 season, each writer voted for five different pitchers: The first-place vote is worth seven points, the second-place vote four points, the third-place vote three points, the fourth-place vote two points, and the fifth-place vote one point. **Roger Clemens** has won the most Cy Young Awards, with seven, followed by **Randy Johnson**, with five, and **Steve Carlton** and **Greg Maddux**, each with four. The 2012 winners were David Price of the **Tampa Bay Rays** in the AL and R. A. Dickey of the **New York Mets** in the NL.

CYCLE. A player is said to have "hit for the cycle" when he has a **single**, **double**, **triple**, and **home run** in the same game. Making the **hits** in that particular order is known as a "natural cycle." Babe Herman, Bob Meusel, and John Reilly are the only **major-league** players to have three cycles.

CYNERGY FIELD. *See* RIVERFRONT STADIUM.

D

DANDRIDGE, RAYMOND EMMETT, SR. "RAY". B. 31 August 1913, Richmond, Virginia. D. 12 February 1994, Palm Bay, Florida. Ray Dandridge was a 5-foot, 7-inch, 170-pound right-handed **batter** who hit for high average, but with little power. He began his career in 1933 and had his best years with the Newark Eagles of the **Negro National League** (1936–1939, 1942, 1944). An outstanding fielder, Dandridge is considered the best **third baseman** to have played in the **Negro Leagues**. He also played many seasons in the Cuban Winter League and Mexican League, and four years for the Minneapolis Millers, the top farm team of the **New York Giants** of the **National League**. As a member of the Millers in 1950, Dandridge won the Class Triple-A American Association's **Most Valuable Player Award**. In 1987, the **Veterans Committee** elected Dandridge to the **National Baseball Hall of Fame**.

See also AFRICAN AMERICANS IN BASEBALL.

DAVIS, GEORGE STACEY. B. 23 August 1870, Cohoes, New York. D. 17 October 1940, Philadelphia, Pennsylvania. George Davis began his **major-league** career in 1890 as a center fielder for the **Cleveland Spiders** of the **National League (NL)**. In February 1893, Cleveland traded the 5-foot, 9-inch, 180-pound Davis to the **New York Giants** for **Buck Ewing**, the Giants' great **catcher**. Davis, a **switch-hitter**, played **third base** in his first two seasons in New York, but he was primarily a **shortstop** for the rest of his career. Davis batted better than .300 in each of his nine seasons in New York, and he was the NL **runs batted in** leader in 1897, with 135. He also managed the Giants for parts of the 1895 and 1900 seasons and all of 1901. Davis jumped to the **Chicago White Sox** of the new **American League (AL)** in 1902, and he then changed his mind and returned to the Giants for the 1903 season. AL president **Ban Johnson** and White Sox owner **Charles Comiskey** used the courts to keep Davis sidelined for almost the entire season. He played in only four games for the 1903 Giants and then returned to the White Sox in 1904 and remained with them until the end of his career in 1909. Davis was considered an intelligent player and also a "clean" player, when that was not the norm. He accumulated 2,665 **hits** and had a .295 lifetime **batting average**. A superior defensive player, he led his league in **double plays** five times and **total chances** and **fielding percentage** four times. In 1998, the **Veterans Committee** elected Davis to the **National Baseball Hall of Fame**.

DAWSON, ANDRE NOLAN "THE HAWK". B. 10 July 1954, Miami, Florida. Andre Dawson played 21 seasons in the **major leagues**, from 1976 to 1996. He was with the **Montreal Expos** (1976–1986), **Chicago Cubs** (1987–1992), **Boston Red Sox** (1993–1994), and Florida Marlins (1995–1996). The 6-foot, 3-inch, 180-pound Dawson was the **National League (NL) Rookie of the Year** with the Expos in 1977, and the league's **Most Valuable Player** with the Cubs 10 years later. That year, 1987, the right-handed-hitting Dawson led the NL with 49 **home runs**, 137 **runs batted in (RBI)**, and 353 **total bases**. The winner of four **Silver Slugger Award**s, he had a career **batting average** of .279, with 438 home runs, 2,774 **hits**, 1,591 RBI, and 314 **stolen bases**. Playing mostly in right field or center field, Dawson was an outstanding fielder with an excellent arm. He was an eight-time **Gold Glove Award** winner and led NL outfielders in **putouts** three times. An eight-time **All-Star** and winner of the **Hutch Award** in 1994, Dawson was elected by the **Baseball Writers' Association of America** to the **National Baseball Hall of Fame** in 2010.

DAY, LEON. B. 30 October 1916, Alexandria, Virginia. D. 13 March 1995, Baltimore, Maryland. Leon Day was a right-handed **pitcher** for various **Negro League** teams from 1934 to 1950. Day pitched for the **Homestead Grays** and **Baltimore Elite Giants**, but his best years (1936–1939, 1941–1943, 1946) were with the Newark Eagles of the **Negro National League**. The 5-foot, 9-inch, 170-pound Day was an outstanding hitter who often played **second base** or the **outfield** when he was not pitching. During the winters, he played in **Cuba**, **Mexico**, and **Venezuela**. In 1995, the **Veterans Committee** elected Day to the **National Baseball Hall of Fame**.
    See also AFRICAN AMERICANS IN BASEBALL.

D.C. STADIUM. *See* ROBERT F. KENNEDY STADIUM.

DEADBALL ERA. The years from 1901 to 1919 are known as baseball's Deadball Era. The era featured mostly low-scoring games that relied more on **bunts**, **stolen bases**, and strategy than power hitting and **home runs**.

DEAN, JAY HANNA "DIZZY". B. 16 January 1910, Lucas, Arkansas. D. 17 July 1974, Reno, Nevada. Dizzy Dean, the son of farm workers, left school in the fourth grade and, at the age of 16, joined the U.S. Army. In 1929, the **St. Louis Cardinals** signed him and sent him to the **minor leagues.** From 1932, his **rookie** season, to 1936, the 6-foot, 2-inch, 182-pound right-hander won 120 games. He led the **National League (NL)** in **wins** in 1934 (30) and 1935 (28), and he is the last NL **pitcher** to win 30 games in a season. Dean won two games against the **Detroit Tigers** in the 1934 **World Series**, including an 11–0 **shutout** in the seventh and deciding game. Dean was the NL's **Most Valuable Player** that year. In the 1937 **All-Star Game**, a line drive by **Earl Averill** of the **Cleveland Indians** struck Dean's toe, breaking it. Trying to come back too soon, Dean injured his pitching arm.

After the 1937 season, the Cardinals traded Dean to the **Chicago Cubs,** for whom he pitched until 1940, including one losing start in the 1938 World Series, but he was never again as effective as he had been before his injury. He appeared in one game for the Cubs in 1941 and one for the **St. Louis Browns** in 1947, finishing with a career record of 150–83. Despite his poor command of the English language, Dean later became a successful baseball broadcaster on radio and television. In 1953, the **Baseball Writers' Association of America** elected him to the **National Baseball Hall of Fame.**

DEFENSIVE CHANCES. A **fielder's** defensive chances are the sum of his total **putouts**, total **assists**, and total **errors.**

DEFENSIVE INDIFFERENCE. Rule 10.04 of the **major-league** rulebook states the following: The **official scorer** shall not score a **stolen base** when a **base runner** advances solely because of the defensive team's indifference to the runner's advance.

DELAHANTY, EDWARD JAMES "ED". B. 30 October 1867, Cleveland, Ohio. D. 2 July 1903, Niagara Falls, Ontario, Canada. Ed Delahanty's .346 lifetime **batting average** trails only **Rogers Hornsby** among **major league** right-handed **batters.** The 6-foot, 1-inch, 170-pound **outfielder** began his career with the Philadelphia Quakers of the **National League (NL)** in 1888. In 1890, he jumped to the **Cleveland Infants** of the **Players' League (PL).** The PL folded after one season, and, in 1891, Delahanty was back with the Philadelphia team in the NL, now called the **Philadelphia Phillies.** Delahanty was among the game's top hitters during the decade of the 1890s. In 1902, he left the Philadelphia Phillies for the **Washington Senators** of the **American League (AL).** He batted .376 for Washington, while leading the

AL in **doubles, on-base percentage**, and **slugging percentage**. The next year, 1903, Delahanty was batting .333 on 2 July, when he fell to his death from a bridge over Niagara Falls.

Overall, Delahanty batted better than .400 three times, including a NL-leading .410 in 1899, and in four seasons he had 200 or more **hits**. He led his league in doubles and slugging percentage five times, **runs batted in** three times, and **home runs** and on-base percentage twice. On 13 July 1896, he hit four home runs in a game. Delahanty had 455 **stolen bases** as a major leaguer, including a league-high 58 in 1898, the first season the current scoring system for stolen bases was in effect. He was elected to the **National Baseball Hall of Fame** by the **Old Timers Committee** in 1945.

DESIGNATED HITTER (DH). The designated hitter (DH), adopted by the **American League (AL)** in 1973, allows teams to designate a player to bat in place of the **pitcher** each time the pitcher would otherwise come to **home plate**. Rule 6.10 (b) in the Major League Baseball rulebook states the following: "A hitter may be designated to bat for the starting pitcher and all subsequent pitchers in any game without otherwise affecting the status of the pitcher(s) in the game." Since then, most collegiate, amateur, and professional leagues have adopted the rule or some variant of it. The **National League (NL)** and Nippon Professional Baseball's Central League in **Japan** do not have the DH rule; however, the DH rule is used by NL teams when the AL is the home team during **interleague play** and the **World Series**.

DETROIT TIGERS. The Detroit Tigers are a team in the Central Division of the **American League (AL)**. The Tigers have been members of the AL since 1901, the first year the AL was recognized as a **major league**. The Tigers played their home games at Bennett Park from 1901 to 1911; at **Tiger Stadium** from 1912 to 1999; and, since 2000, at **Comerica Park**. Tiger Stadium was previously known as Navin Field (1912–1937) and Briggs Stadium (1938–1960), both names in honor of the team's owner at the time.

Hughie Jennings led the Tigers to pennants in his first three seasons as **manager** (1907–1909), but they lost the **World Series** to the **Chicago Cubs** in 1907 and 1908, and to the **Pittsburgh Pirates** in 1909. Twenty-five years passed before the Tigers made it back to the World Series, but the 1934 club also lost, to the **St. Louis Cardinals**. A year later, the Tigers captured their first world championship by defeating the Cubs in the 1935 Series. Detroit played in two World Series in the 1940s, losing to the **Cincinnati Reds** in 1940, and defeating the Cubs again in 1945. The Tigers have won only four pennants since the end of World War II. They defeated the Cardinals in the

1968 World Series and the **San Diego Padres** in 1984, and the team lost to the Cardinals in 2006 and the **San Francisco Giants** in 2012. In 1972, 1987, and 2011, Detroit lost in the **American League Championship Series**.

Detroit Tigers who have won the AL's **Most Valuable Player Award** are **Ty Cobb** (1911), **Mickey Cochrane** (1934), **Hank Greenberg** (1935, 1940), **Charlie Gehringer** (1937), **Hal Newhouser** (1944–1945), Denny McLain (1968), Willie Hernandez (1984), Justin Verlander (2011), and Miguel Cabrera (2012). **Cy Young Award** winners are Denny McLain (1968–1969), Willie Hernandez (1984), and Justin Verlander (2011). **Rookie of the Year** winners are Harvey Kuenn (1953), Mark Fidrych (1976), Lou Whitaker (1978), and Justin Verlander (2006).

Tigers players who have led the league in **batting average** are Ty Cobb (1907–1909, 1911–1915, 1917–1919), **Harry Heilmann** (1921, 1923, 1925, 1927), **Heinie Manush** (1926), Charlie Gehringer (1937), **George Kell** (1949), **Al Kaline** (1955), Harvey Kuenn (1959), Norm Cash (1961), Magglio Ordonez (2007), and Miguel Cabrera (2011–2012). Leaders in **home runs** are **Sam Crawford** (1908), Ty Cobb (1909), Hank Greenberg (1935, 1938, 1940, 1946), Rudy York (1943), Darrell Evans (1985), Cecil Fielder (1990–1991), and Miguel Cabrera (2008, 2012). Leaders in **runs batted in (RBI)** are Ty Cobb (1907–1909, 1911), Sam Crawford (1910, 1914–1915), Bobby Veach (1915, 1917–1918), Hank Greenberg (1935, 1937, 1940, 1946), Rudy York (1943), Ray Boone (1955), Cecil Fielder (1990–1992), and Miguel Cabrera (2010). By leading the AL in batting average, home runs, and RBI, Ty Cobb won the **Triple Crown** for **batters** in 1909. Miguel Cabrera won the triple crown in 2012.

Tigers **pitchers** who have led the league in **wins** are George Mullin (1909), Tommy Bridges (1936), Dizzy Trout (1943), Hal Newhouser (1944–1946, 1948), Frank Lary (1956), **Jim Bunning** (1957), Earl Wilson (1967), Denny McLain (1968–1969), Mickey Lolich (1971), Jack Morris (1981), Bill Gullickson (1991), and Justin Verlander (2009, 2011). **Earned run average (ERA)** leaders are Ed Siever (1902), Dizzy Trout (1944), Hal Newhouser (1945–1946), Hank Aguirre (1962), Mark Fidrych (1976), and Justin Verlander (2011). **Strikeouts** leaders are Tommy Bridges (1935–1936), Hal Newhouser (1944–1945), Virgil Trucks (1949), Jim Bunning (1959–1960), Mickey Lolich (1971), Jack Morris (1983), and Justin Verlander (2009, 2011–2012). By leading in wins, earned run average, and strikeouts in 1945, Hal Newhouser won the **Triple Crown** for pitchers. By leading in wins, ERA, and strikeouts in 2011, Justin Verlander won the Triple Crown for pitchers.

Other notable players and managers in Tigers' history include **Sparky Anderson**, Elden Auker, Johnny Bassler, Al Benton, Lu Blue, Donie Bush, Tony Clark, Rocky Colavito, Joe Coleman, Harry Coveleski, Hooks Dauss, Bill Donovan, Jean Dubuc, Hoot Evers, Prince Fielder, Bob Fothergill, Pete

Fox, Bill Freehan, Travis Fryman, Kirk Gibson, **Goose Goslin**, Curtis Granderson, Carlos Guillen, Mike Henneman, Bobby Higginson, John Hiller, Willie Horton, Fred Hutchinson, Brad Inge, Todd Jones, Steve Kemp, Ed Killian, Ron Leflore, Chet Lemon, Jim Leyland, Aurelio Lopez, Charlie Maxwell, Dick McAuliffe, Barney McCosky, Don Mossi, Pat Mullin, Bobo Newsom, Jim Northrup, Lance Parrish, Dan Petry, Tony Phillips, Placido Polanco, **Ivan Rodriguez**, Schoolboy Rowe, Mickey Stanley, John Stone, Ed Summers, Frank Tanana, Birdie Tebbetts, Jason Thompson, Alan Trammell, Dick Wakefield, Gee Walker, Vic Wertz, Earl Whitehill, and Ed Willett.

DETROIT WOLVERINES. The Detroit Wolverines were a team in the **National League (NL)** from 1881 to 1888, after which they disbanded. In 1887, the Wolverines won the NL pennant and then won 10 of 15 games from the **St. Louis Browns**, champions of the **American Association**, in a championship series that was a predecessor to the modern **World Series**. Notable players for the Wolverines included Lady Baldwin, Hardy Richardson, Jack Rowe, **Sam Thompson**, and **Deacon White**.

DICKEY, WILLIAM MALCOLM "BILL". B. 6 June 1907, Bastrop, Louisiana. D. 12 November 1993, Little Rock, Arkansas. During his 17 seasons with the **New York Yankees** (1928–1943, 1946), **catcher** Bill Dickey played on eight pennant winners and seven **World Series** champions. He had 37 hits, five **home runs**, and 24 **runs batted in (RBI)** in Series play. An exceptional handler of **pitchers** and a consistent hitter, he was a key ingredient in the Yankees' success during those years.

A 6-foot, 1-inch, 185-pound left-handed hitter, Dickey had a career **batting average** of .313 and slugged 202 home runs. He topped the .300 mark in 10 of his first 11 full seasons, had more than 100 RBI four times, and was selected to the **All-Star** team 11 times. Defensively, Dickey's 100 or more games caught for 13 consecutive seasons is still the **American League (AL)** record. He led AL catchers in **fielding percentage** four times, **putouts** six times, and **assists** three times. Dickey spent 1944 and 1945 in the U. S. Navy before returning to play a final 54 games in 1946. He was also the Yankees' **manager** for 105 games in 1946. The **Baseball Writers' Association of America** elected Dickey to the **National Baseball Hall of Fame** in 1954.

DIHIGO, MARTIN MAGDALENO (LANOS). B. 25 May 1905, Matanzas, **Cuba**. D. 20 May 1971, Cienfuegos, Cuba. Martin Dihigo played every position except **catcher** in his professional career, which lasted from 1922 to 1950. Dihigo played 12 seasons in the **Negro Leagues**, most notably for the Cuban Stars East of the **Eastern Colored League** and the **New York Cu-**

bans of the **Negro National League**. In addition, he spent many years playing in Cuba, **Mexico**, and **Venezuela**. As a right-handed **pitcher**, the six-feet-two, 190-pound Dihigo is reputed to have won more than 250 games. As a **batter**, the **switch-hitting** Dihigo was a steady .300 hitter with exceptional power and outstanding speed. He is a member of the Cuban Hall of Fame and Mexican Hall of Fame, and, in 1977, a special **Negro Leagues Committee** elected him to the **National Baseball Hall of Fame**.

DIMAGGIO, JOSEPH PAUL "JOE," "THE YANKEE CLIPPER". B. Giuseppe Paolo DiMaggio, 25 November 1914, Martinez, California. D. 8 March 1999, Hollywood, Florida. Three years in the U.S. Army during World War II limited Joe DiMaggio's career with the **New York Yankees** to just 13 seasons (1936–1942 and 1946–1951). Speedy and graceful, at 6 feet, 2 inches tall and 193 pounds, he excelled as a center fielder, as well as a hitter. He batted better than .300 in 11 of his 13 seasons, missing only in 1946 (.290), his first year back from the service, and in 1951, his final season (.263).

DiMaggio, an **All-Star** in each of his 13 seasons, played in 10 **World Series** as a Yankee. The Yanks won nine of the Series, with DiMaggio batting .271 with eight **home runs** in 51 games. In 1936, his **rookie** season, the right-handed-hitting DiMaggio led the **American League (AL)** with 15 **triples**. The following year, he had 167 **runs batted in (RBI)** and led the AL in **runs** (151), home runs (46), **slugging percentage** (.673), and **total bases** (418). He was the runner-up to **Charlie Gehringer** of the **Detroit Tigers** in voting for the **Most Valuable Player (MVP) Award**. DiMaggio's .381 **batting average** in 1939 won him his first batting title and his first MVP Award. He was also voted the **Major League Player of the Year** by the *Sporting News*.

DiMaggio repeated as the batting champion in 1940, with a .352 mark, and, in 1941, he won his second MVP Award. He batted .357 and led the AL in RBI and total bases, but DiMaggio's 1941 season is best remembered for his 56 consecutive-game hitting streak. The streak broke **Willie Keeler's** single-season record of 44 and has not been seriously challenged since. The drama surrounding the streak captured the attention of the nation and cemented the DiMaggio legend. And while DiMaggio was never as good after the war as he had been in his early years, he did win a third MVP Award, in 1947, and he led the league in home runs, RBI, and total bases in 1948. DiMaggio, who struck out only 369 times in his **major-league** career, had a lifetime batting average of .325, with 361 home runs and 1,537 RBI. At baseball's 1969 centennial celebration, he was named the game's greatest living player. In 1955, DiMaggio was elected by the **Baseball Writers' Association of America** to the **National Baseball Hall of Fame**.

DISABLED LIST (DL). Major-league teams can remove injured players from their active **roster** by placing them on the disabled list (DL). Doing so allows them to replace the injured player with a healthy one. There are three time frames for the DL, which include the following: 60 days, 15 days, and a seven-day list added in 2011 that is strictly for concussions or other brain-related injuries.

DOBY, LAWRENCE EUGENE "LARRY". B. 13 December 1923, Camden, South Carolina. D. 18 June 2003, Montclair, New Jersey. When Larry Doby made his **major-league** debut for the **Cleveland Indians** on 5 July 1947, he became the first **African American** to play in the **American League (AL)**. Doby, who had played for the Newark Eagles of the **Negro National League (NNL)** in 1942, 1943, 1946, and 1947, went on to a 13-year career in the AL. He had two stints with Cleveland (1947–1955 and 1958), had two with the **Chicago White Sox** (1956–1957 and 1959), and played part of the 1959 season with the **Detroit Tigers**.

The 6-foot, 1-inch, 180-pound Doby batted left-handed and threw right-handed. He was a seven-time **All-Star** whose 32 **home runs** led the AL in both 1952 and 1954. He also led in **slugging percentage** and **runs** in 1952 and in **on-base percentage** in 1950. He had five seasons in which he drove in more than 100 runs, including a league-high 126 in the Indians' pennant-winning season of 1954. **Yogi Berra** of the second-place **New York Yankees** won the **Most Valuable Player Award** that year, with Doby coming in a close second. He had batted .318 in Cleveland's **World Series** win over the **Boston Braves** in 1948, but only .125 as the Indians were swept in four games by the **New York Giants** in 1954. Doby, a **second baseman** in the NNL, twice led AL center fielders in **fielding percentage**. He had a career **batting average** of .283, with 253 home runs. In 1998, Doby was elected by the **Veterans Committee** to the **National Baseball Hall of Fame**.

DODGER STADIUM. Dodger Stadium, located in Los Angeles, California, is the home field of the **Los Angeles Dodgers** of the **National League**. The Dodgers played their first game at Dodger Stadium on 10 April 1962. From 1958, when they relocated from Brooklyn, to 1961, the Dodgers played their home games at the Los Angeles Memorial Coliseum. Dodger Stadium, which has a seating capacity of approximately 56,000, hosted the **major league All-Star Game** in 1980. The Los Angeles Memorial Coliseum hosted the second of the two games played in 1959.

DOERR, ROBERT PERSHING "BOBBY". B. 7 April 1918, Los Angeles, California. From 1937 through 1951— missing only the 1945 season when he was in the military—Bobby Doerr played in 1,865 games for the

Boston Red Sox, 1,852 of them as a **second baseman**. The 5-foot, 11-inch, 175-pound Doerr led **American League** second basemen in **fielding percentage** and **putouts** four times, **double plays** five times, and **assists** three times. Doerr was Boston's team captain in the years after World War II. A right-handed hitter, he had a lifetime **batting average** of .288. At the time of his retirement, Doerr's 223 **home runs** and 1,247 **runs batted in** were among the highest ever for a second baseman. In his one **World Series**, he batted .409 in a seven-game loss to the **St. Louis Cardinals** in 1946. A ninetime **All-Star** selectee, Doerr was elected to the **National Baseball Hall of Fame** by the **Veterans Committee** in 1986.

DOLPHIN STADIUM. *See* SUN LIFE STADIUM.

DOMINICAN REPUBLIC. Professional baseball has been played in the Dominican Republic since the early 1920s. The league currently consists of six teams. Tigres del Licey and Leones de Escogido are located in Santo Domingo, Estrellas Orientales is located in San Pedro de Macoris, Gigantes del Ciabo is located in San Francisco de Macoris, Aguilas del Cibao is located in Santiago, and Azucareros del Este is located in La Romana. Each team plays a 60-game schedule that runs from the end of October to February. The league champion advances to the **Caribbean Series** to play against the champions of **Mexico, Venezuela**, and **Puerto Rico**. The 2012 winner of the Caribbean Series was the Leones de Escogido team, representing the Dominican Republic.

The most notable players and **managers** born in the Dominican Republic include Manny Acta, Felipe Alou, Jesus Alou, Matty Alou, Joaquin Andujar, Pedro Astacio, Erick Aybar, Jose Bautista, George Bell, Adrian Beltre, Pedro Borbon, Melky Cabrera, Robinson Cano, Rico Carty, Luis Castillo, Starlin Castro, Cesar Cedeno, Bartolo Colon, Nelson Cruz, Juan Encarnacion, Julio Franco, Rafael Furcal, Damaso Garcia, Freddy Garcia, Cesar Geronimo, Alfredo Griffin, Pedro Guerrero, Vladimir Guerrero, Julian Javier, Francisco Liriano, **Juan Marichal, Pedro Martinez**, Ramon Martinez, Raul Mondesi, Manny Mota, David Ortiz, Tony Pena, Placido Polanco, **Albert Pujols**, Aramis Ramirez, Hanley Ramirez, Jose Reyes, Juan Samuel, Alfonso Soriano, Rafael Soriano, **Sammy Sosa**, Mario Soto, Frank Taveras, and Miguel Tejada.

DOUBLE PLAY (DP). A double play occurs when a team or an individual **fielder** makes two **outs** during the same continuous playing action. The most common type of double play occurs with a **runner** on **first base** and a ground ball hit to an **infielder**. The player fielding the ball throws to the fielder covering **second base**, who steps on the **base** before the runner from first arrives, to force that runner out, and then throws the ball to the **first baseman** to retire the **batter** for the second out. Other double plays occur most often when after a fly ball is caught, a **base runner** tries unsuccessfully to get back to his base or to advance to the next base, or when a runner is **caught stealing** following a **strikeout**.

DOUBLEHEADER (DH). A doubleheader is two regularly scheduled or rescheduled games played on the same day. There may be single admission charge for both games or a separate charge for each game.

DOUBLES (2B). A double is any batted ball where the **batter** reaches **second base** safely without the benefit of any fielding **errors**. An **umpire** may also award the batter a double when the result of a batted ball is covered by a specific **grounds rule**.

The **major league** single-season leader in doubles is Earl Webb of the 1931 **Boston Red Sox**, with 67. The single-season leader in the **National League** is **Joe Medwick** of the 1936 **St. Louis Cardinals**, with 64. The career leader is **Tris Speaker**, with 792. Speaker played for the Boston Red Sox from 1907 through 1915, **Cleveland Indians** from 1916 through 1926, **Washington Senators** in 1927, and **Philadelphia Athletics** in 1928.

DREYFUSS, BERNHARD "BARNEY". B. 23 February 1865, Freiburg, Germany. D. 5 February 1932, New York, New York. Barney Dreyfuss was a part owner and later sole owner of the **Louisville Colonels** of the **American Association**. He remained the owner when Louisville played in the **National League (NL)** from 1889 to 1899. When the Colonels were dropped from the NL for the 1900 season, Dreyfuss, who had arranged a deal that allowed him to purchase a half interest in the **Pittsburgh Pirates**, brought 14 former Louisville players to Pittsburgh with him. Among them were **Honus Wagner**, **Fred Clarke**, and **Rube Waddell**. A year later he became sole owner of the Pirates.

Dreyfuss was one of the original advocates of a **commissioner's** office in baseball. He helped establish the modern **World Series**, and, in 1909, he built **Forbes Field**, baseball's first modern steel and concrete park. Dreyfuss was the president of the Pirates from 1900 until his death in 1932, during which time Pittsburgh won six pennants and two World Series and finished in third place or better 21 times. He was elected to the **National Baseball Hall of Fame** by the **Veterans Committee** in 2008.

DRYSDALE, DONALD SCOTT "DON". B. 23 July 1936, Van Nuys, California. D. 3 July 1993, Montreal, Canada. Don Drysdale, a sidearming right-hander, was just 20 years old when he won 17 games for the 1957

Brooklyn Dodgers. The next year, the Dodgers moved to Los Angeles. Pitching in the Los Angeles Memorial Coliseum, Drysdale continued to compile double-digit victory totals, but he truly blossomed after the club moved to **Dodger Stadium** in 1962. The 6-foot, 5-inch, 190-pound Drysdale led the **National League (NL)** in **wins**, with 25, **innings pitched**; with 314 1/3; and **strikeouts**, with 232. He won the **Cy Young Award**, and the *Sporting News* named him NL **Pitcher of the Year** and cowinner with teammate Maury Wills as the **Major League Player of the Year**. In 1968, Drysdale ran off a string of 58 consecutive scoreless **innings**, breaking **Walter Johnson's major-league** record. (His record was broken by Orel Hershiser of the Dodgers in 1988.) Notorious for knocking down **batters**, Drysdale led the league in hit batters five times. He was also one of the best-hitting pitchers ever, with 29 **home runs** in his career.

Drysdale appeared in five **World Series**, winning three games and losing three, with a 2.95 **earned run average (ERA)** and one **shutout**. He pitched in eight **All-Star Games**, five as the starter for the NL. Drysdale retired after the 1969 season with a career record of 209–166, an ERA of 2.95, and 49 shutouts. In 1984, the **Baseball Writers' Association of America** elected him to the **National Baseball Hall of Fame**. Drysdale was in Montreal working as a broadcaster for the Dodgers when he died of a heart attack on 3 July 1993.

DUFFY, HUGH. B. 26 November 1866, Cranston, Rhode Island. D. 19 October 1954, Boston, Massachusetts. Hugh Duffy played in four different **major leagues** between 1888 and 1901, and he batted better than .300 in each of them. Duffy, a right-handed-hitting **outfielder**, began his big-league career with the Chicago White Stockings of the **National League (NL)** in 1888–1889. After a year with the **Chicago Pirates** of the **Players' League (PL)** in 1890, and a season with the **Boston Reds** of the **American Association (AA)** in 1891, he returned to the NL in 1892 with the Boston Beaneaters. He had led the PL in **hits** and **runs** in 1890, and the AA in **runs batted in** in 1891. Duffy had his best years with the Beaneater teams of the 1890s, helping lead them to four pennants. In addition to being an outstanding defensive outfielder, Duffy, a diminutive 5 feet, 7 inches tall and 168 pounds, consistently hit for a high average and displayed surprising power. He batted in 100 or more runs for seven consecutive seasons (1893–1899) and led the league in **home runs** in 1894 and 1897.

In 1894, Duffy batted an astronomical .440, the highest **batting average** since the pitching distance was extended to its current 60 feet, 6 inches in 1893. He also led the league in hits, home runs, and **doubles** that season. Duffy left Boston in 1901 and was instrumental in forming the new **American League (AL)**, where he batted. 302 as the **player-manager** of the **Milwaukee Brewers**. He managed in the **minor leagues** the next two seasons, but he then returned to the NL as the manager and an occasional player for the **Philadelphia Phillies** in 1904, 1905, and 1906. He later managed in the AL with the **Chicago White Sox** (1910–1911) and **Boston Red Sox** (1921–1922), as well as in the minors and at Harvard College and Boston University. Duffy had a lifetime batting average of .326 and 106 home runs, a high number at the time. He was elected to the **National Baseball Hall of Fame** by the **Old Timers Committee** in 1945.

DUGOUT. The dugout and **bench** are seating facilities reserved for players, substitutes, and other team members in uniform when they are not actively engaged on the playing field.

DUROCHER, LEO ERNEST "THE LIP". B. 27 July 1905, West Springfield, Massachusetts. D. 7 October 1991, Palm Springs, California. Leo Durocher was a scrappy, aggressive, **umpire**-baiting **shortstop** for the **New York Yankees** (1925, 1928–1929), **Cincinnati Reds** (1930–1933), **St. Louis Cardinals** (1933–1937), and **Brooklyn Dodgers** (1938–1941, 1943, 1945). He later became a scrappy, aggressive, umpire-baiting **manager** for the Dodgers (1939–1946, 1948), **New York Giants** (1948–1955), **Chicago Cubs** (1966–1972), and **Houston Astros** (1972–1973). Better known for his fielding than his batting, the 5-foot, 10-inch, 160-pound right-handed-hitting Durocher had a career **batting average** of .247 in 1,637 games, and he led **National League (NL)** shortstops in **fielding percentage** three times.

Team president **Larry MacPhail** chose his brash shortstop to manage the Dodgers in 1939. In 1941, Durocher led Brooklyn to its first pennant in 21 years, but the Dodgers lost to the Yankees in the **World Series**. The 1946 Dodgers finished in a first-place tie with the Cardinals, but St. Louis won the pennant in the NL's first-ever playoff series. Durocher missed the 1947 season after **Commissioner Happy Chandler** gave him a one-year suspension for "conduct detrimental to baseball." Durocher had led the team during **spring training**, where he helped quell a movement among some Dodgers players to keep **African American Jackie Robinson** off the team.

After returning to Brooklyn in 1948, Durocher left in mid-July to manage the archrival Giants. In 1951, he led the Giants to a pennant after overcoming a 13-game lead the Dodgers had built in August. Another World Series loss to the Yankees followed. The Giants won the pennant again in 1954, and the team then swept the heavily favored **Cleveland Indians** in the Series, but Durocher was fired after the 1955 season. He worked as a broadcaster and **coach** before returning in 1966 to manage the Cubs. Durocher was with the Cubs for seven seasons and then managed the Astros for two seasons. His overall record in 24 seasons as a manager was 2,008–1,709. The *Sporting*

News gave him its **major league Manager of the Year Award** three times, in 1941, 1951, and 1954. Durocher was elected to the **National Baseball Hall of Fame** by the **Veterans Committee** as a manager in 1994.

E

EARNED RUN AVERAGE (ERA). Earned run average (ERA) for **pitchers** is a measure of pitcher effectiveness; a lower ERA suggests a more effective pitcher. ERA is calculated by dividing the **earned runs (ER)** a pitcher has allowed by the number of his **innings pitched (IP)** and multiplying that number by nine (ER/IP*9). Example: A pitcher who has allowed 91 ER in 268 innings has an ERA of 3.06.

The single-season **major-league** leader in ERA is **Tim Keefe** of the 1880 **Troy Trojans** of the **National League (NL)**, at 0.86. The single-season leader since 1893, when the distance from the pitcher's mound to home plate was established at 60 feet, 6 inches, is Hubert "Dutch" Leonard of the 1914 **Boston Red Sox**, at 0.96. The single-season leader in the NL, post-1893, is **Mordecai Brown** of the 1906 **Chicago Cubs**, at 1.04. The career leader is **Ed Walsh**, at 1.82. Walsh pitched for the **Chicago White Sox** from 1904 through 1916, and for the **Boston Braves** in 1917.

EARNED RUNS (ER). An earned run is a **run** that is ruled by the **official scorer** to have resulted exclusively from actions by the batting team and not because of **errors** by the defense.

EASTERN COLORED LEAGUE (ECL). The Eastern Colored League (ECL) existed from 1923 through 1928. The ECL's two most prominent teams were the Hilldale Daisies, of Darby, Pennsylvania, and the Bacharach Giants, of Atlantic City, New Jersey.
See also NEGRO LEAGUES.

EBBETS, CHARLES HERCULES "CHARLIE". B. 29 October 1859, New York, New York. D. 18 April 1925, New York, New York. Charlie Ebbets was an enterprising young architect who designed many New York buildings. He served on the Brooklyn City Council for four years and in the New York State Assembly for one year. In 1883, he went to work for the Brooklyn Bridegrooms of the **National League (NL)**, and, in 1890, he bought a minor interest in the club. Ebbets managed the Bridegrooms briefly and unsuccessfully in 1898, by which time he was the club's president. In 1907, Ebbets became the principal owner, with 60 percent of the shares. He sold half his stock in the club in 1912 to raise money for a new park in Brooklyn, **Ebbets Field**, which formally opened on 9 April 1913. An innovative entrepreneur, Ebbets is credited with proposing a permanent schedule, with fixed dates, for the **World Series**. During Ebbets's tenure with the Brooklyn club, they finished first in the NL in 1889 and 1890 as the Bridegrooms, in 1899 and 1900 as the Brooklyn Superbas, and in 1916 and 1920 as the Brooklyn Robins.

EBBETS FIELD. Ebbets Field, named for owner **Charlie Ebbets**, was located in Brooklyn, New York. It was the home of the **Brooklyn Dodgers** of the **National League** from 9 April 1913 to 24 September 1957. From 1890 to 1912, prior to the opening of Ebbets Field, the Dodgers played their home games at various incarnations of Washington Park. Ebbets Field hosted the **major league All-Star Game** in 1949.

See also STADIUMS.

ECKERSLEY, DENNIS LEE. B. 3 October 1954, Oakland, California. Dennis Eckersley was selected by the **Cleveland Indians** of the **American League (AL)** in the third round of the 1972 **Amateur Draft**. In 1975, the 6-foot, 2-inch, 190-pound right-handed **pitcher** had a 13–7 record and a 2.60 **earned run average** that earned him the **rookie Pitcher of the Year** Award from the *Sporting News*. Eckersley pitched three seasons for the Indians before being traded to the **Boston Red Sox**. He went 20–8 in his first season in Boston, his only 20-win season. The Red Sox traded him to the **Chicago Cubs** in May 1984. Then, in 1987, he was traded to the **Oakland Athletics**. At that point, Eckersley had been in the big leagues for 13 seasons. He had been in 376 games, 359 of which had been starts. He had 151 **wins** and three **saves**. At Oakland, **manager Tony LaRussa** used him initially as a middle-innings relief pitcher, before converting him into his full-time closer. Eckersley led the AL in saves in 1988, with 45, and he then added four more against the Red Sox in the **American League Championship Series**, where he was chosen the Series **Most Valuable Player (MVP)**. He led the AL again in 1992, when he had 51 saves and was voted the AL Pitcher of the Year.

After a successful nine-year career in Oakland, the A's traded Eckersley to the **St. Louis Cardinals** in 1996, where he was reunited with LaRussa. He saved 66 games in two seasons in St. Louis and finished his career with the 1998 Red Sox. Overall, Eckersley won 197 games, had 390 saves, and was voted to the **All-Star** team six times. In 11 postseason Series, he compiled 15 saves in 28 games. With Oakland, in 1992, he was selected as the AL's **Cy Young Award** winner and its MVP. In 2004, the **Baseball Writers' Association of America** elected Eckersley to the **National Baseball Hall of Fame.**

ECKFORD CLUB OF BROOKLYN. *See* BROOKLYN ECKFORDS.

EDISON INTERNATIONAL FIELD OF ANAHEIM. *See* ANGEL STADIUM OF ANAHEIM.

EJECTIONS. **Umpires** have the right to eject players, **managers**, or **coaches** from a game for excessive arguing, throwing at **batters**, fighting, or other hostile or unsportsmanlike conduct. Depending upon the severity of the offense, ejections may be followed by a fine, a suspension, or both. **Bobby Cox**, who was a player for two seasons and a manager for 29 seasons (four with the **Toronto Blue Jays** and 25 with the **Atlanta Braves**) was ejected from 159 games, the most all-time.

ELIZABETH (NEW JERSEY) RESOLUTES. The Elizabeth Resolutes were members of the National Association for one season, 1873, during which they played 23 games and lost 21.

ELYSIAN FIELDS. In 1845, the **Knickerbocker Base Ball Club** of New York began playing intrasquad games at a site in Hoboken, New Jersey, called Elysian Fields. On 19 June 1846, the Knickerbockers played the New York Base Ball Club at Elysian Fields in what is believed to be the first official, prearranged match between two clubs.
See also STADIUMS.

ENRON FIELD. *See* MINUTE MAID PARK.

ERRORS (E). The **official scorer** charges an error against any **fielder** whose misplay of a ball allows a **batter** or a **base runner** to reach one or more additional **bases**, when such an advance should have been prevented given ordinary effort by the fielder.

ESTADIO DE BÉISBOL MONTERREY. Estadio de Béisbol Monterrey, located in Monterrey, **Mexico**, is the home field of the Monterrey Sultans (Sultanes de Monterrey) of the Class AAA Mexican League. It opened in 1990 and holds 27,000 people. It is the largest baseball **stadium** in Mexico and the third largest in Latin America. In 1996, the **San Diego Padres** and **New York Mets** played a three-game series at Estadio de Béisbol Monterrey, the first time a **major-league** game was played in Mexico. It was also the site of an Opening-Day game between the **Colorado Rockies** and **San Diego Padres** on 4 April 1999.

EUROPEAN BASEBALL CHAMPIONSHIP. The European Baseball Championship is the main championship tournament between national baseball teams in Europe. The governing body is the Confederation of European Baseball. **Italy** won the first championship in 1954, and, along with the **Netherlands**, the country has dominated the competition ever since. The tournament is held every other year, in even-numbered years. The most recent European Baseball Championship, held in the Netherlands in September 2012, was won by Italy.

EVANS, WILLIAM GEORGE "BILLY". B. 10 February 1884, Chicago, Illinois. D. 23 January 1956, Miami, Florida. Billy Evans became an **umpire** in the **American League (AL)** in 1906, at the age of 22. The youngest man ever to serve as a **major-league** umpire, he worked 3,319 games. Evans umpired in six **World Series**, including 1909, when he became the youngest man ever to umpire a Series game. Throughout his umpiring career, the former journalist also contributed articles to *Collier's* magazine and the *Sporting News*. After retiring as an umpire, following the 1927 season, Evans was the **general manager** of the **Cleveland Indians** until 1935, and he then spent five years (1936–1940) as the farm director for the **Boston Red Sox**. He was the general manager of the Cleveland Rams of the National Football League in 1941, president of the Southern Association from 1942 to 1946, and back in the AL as general manager of the **Detroit Tigers** from 1947 to 1951. The **Veterans Committee** elected Evans to the **National Baseball Hall of Fame** in 1973.

EVERS, JOHN JOSEPH "JOHNNY". B. 21 July 1881, Troy, New York. D. 28 March 1947, Albany, New York. Johnny Evers played **second base** for the **Chicago Cubs** from 1902 through 1913. The Cubs won four pennants and two **World Series** (1907 and 1908) during that time. Although just 5 feet, nine inches tall, and extremely light at 125 pounds, the left-handed-hitting Evers was a key member of those Cubs teams. He joined with **shortstop Joe Tinker** and **first baseman Frank Chance** to form one of baseball's most memorable **double-play** combinations. Evers's best season offensively was 1912, when he had a career-high .341 **batting average**. In 1914, Chicago traded Evers to the **Boston Braves**, where he played a major role in leading the Braves to the pennant and batted .438 in a four-game upset sweep of the **Philadelphia Athletics** in the World Series. The baseball writers voted him the winner of the **Chalmers Award** as the league's **Most Valuable**

Player. Evers remained with the Braves through mid-1917 and finished the season, his last, with the **Philadelphia Phillies**. He served as a **manager** for the Cubs (1913 and 1921) and **Chicago White Sox** (1924), and he was later employed as a **coach** and **scout**. In 1946, the **Old Timers Committee** elected Evers to the **National Baseball Hall of Fame**.

EWING, WILLIAM "BUCK". B. 17 October 1859, Hoagland, Ohio. D. 20 October 1906, Cincinnati, Ohio. Buck Ewing was baseball's best **catcher** of the 19th century, and the best and most versatile athlete of his era. The 5-foot, 10-inch, 188-pound Ewing played all nine positions during his 18 **major-league** seasons. In addition to his 636 games caught, he played 253 games at **first base**, 235 in the **outfield**, and 127 at **third base**. Ewing began his career with the **Troy Trojans** of the **National League (NL)** in 1880, but when the Trojans disbanded after the 1882 season, he moved to the New York Gothams. He led the NL with 10 **home runs** in 1883 and 20 **triples** in 1884. He remained with the Gothams, renamed the **New York Giants** in 1885, through the 1889 season. The Giants won pennants in 1888 and 1889 and played the **American Association (AA)** pennant winners in a championship series that was a predecessor to the modern **World Series**. Ewing batted a combined .290 in wins over the 1888 **St. Louis Browns** and 1889 Brooklyn Bridegrooms.

Ewing was one of the many players who left the NL and AA in 1890 to form the **Players' League (PL)**. Ewing managed his PL team, also called the **New York Giants**, to a third-place finish, but when the league folded after one season, he rejoined the NL Giants in 1891. In 1893, the Giants traded Ewing to the **Cleveland Spiders** for shortstop **George Davis**. The right-handed-hitting Ewing had his best season that year, batting .344, with 122 **runs batted in** and 47 **stolen bases**. An off year in 1894 caused the Spiders to release him. He signed with the **Cincinnati Reds** as a **player-manager**, played two years, and managed until 1899. He returned to the Giants as a manager for part of the 1900 season. Ewing's .303 career **batting average**, great speed, and outstanding defense led the **Old Timers Committee** to elect him to the **National Baseball Hall of Fame** in 1939.

EXHIBITION STADIUM. *See* STADIUMS; TORONTO BLUE JAYS.

EXPANSION. The number of franchises in the **American League (AL)** remained at eight from 1901, the year the league attained **major-league** status, through 1960. In 1961, the AL expanded to 10 teams by adding the Los Angeles Angels and **Washington Senators**. (The original **Washington Senators** moved to Minnesota that year and became the **Minnesota Twins**. In 1972, the expansion Senators moved to Texas and became the **Texas**

Rangers.) In 1969, the AL expanded to 12 teams by adding the **Kansas City Royals** and Seattle Pilots. (In 1970, the Seattle franchise was moved to Milwaukee and became the **Milwaukee Brewers**.) In 1977, the AL expanded to 14 teams by adding the **Seattle Mariners** and **Toronto Blue Jays**, the AL's first team from **Canada**. In 1998, the AL added the Tampa Bay Devil Rays; however, the move of the Milwaukee Brewers from the AL to the **National League (NL)** kept the total number of AL clubs at 14.

The NL began play in 1876, with franchises in eight cities, including the following: Boston, Chicago, Cincinnati, Hartford, Louisville, New York, Philadelphia, and St. Louis. The league was reduced to six teams in 1877 and 1878, before going back to eight from 1878 to 1891, with various franchises coming and going. After the **American Association** disbanded following the 1891 season, the NL added four teams and was a 12-team league from 1892 through 1899. Before the 1900 season, the league eliminated the franchises in Baltimore, Cleveland, Louisville, and Washington. The NL remained an eight-team league from 1900 through 1961.

In 1962, the NL expanded to 10 teams by adding the Houston Colt .45s and **New York Mets**. In 1969, the NL expanded to 12 teams by adding the **Montreal Expos**, the first team from outside the United States, and **San Diego Padres**. In 1993, the NL expanded to 14 teams by adding the **Colorado Rockies** and Florida Marlins. In 1998, the NL increased its total number of teams to 16, when they added the **Arizona Diamondbacks** and the Milwaukee Brewers switched from the AL to the NL. In 2013, the **Houston Astros** are scheduled to move from the NL to the AL, giving each league 15 teams.

EXPANSION ERA VETERANS COMMITTEE. *See* VETERANS COMMITTEE.

EXPOSITION PARK. *See* PITTSBURGH PIRATES; STADIUMS.

EXTRA-BASE HITS (EBH). Extra-base hits are any **hits** that are not **singles**. They can be **doubles, triples**, or **home runs**. A player's total extra-base hits are the sum of his doubles, triples, and home runs. The **major league** single-season leader in extra-base hits is **Babe Ruth** of the 1921 **New York Yankees**, with 119. The single-season record in the **National League** is 107, held by **Chuck Klein** of the 1930 **Philadelphia Phillies** and **Barry Bonds** of the 2001 **San Francisco Giants**. The career leader is **Hank Aaron**, with 1,477. Aaron played for the **Milwaukee Braves** from 1954 through 1965, **Atlanta Braves** from 1966 through 1974, and **Milwaukee Brewers** in 1975 and 1976.

F

FABER, URBAN CLARENCE "RED". B. 6 September 1888, Cascade, Iowa. D. 25 September 1976, Chicago, Illinois. Red Faber was a right-handed **pitcher** for the **Chicago White Sox** from 1914 through 1933. One of the last pitchers legally allowed to throw the **spitball,** he won 254 games (254–213) for a team that finished in the second division in 15 of his 20 seasons with them. The 6-foot, 2-inch, 180-pound Faber played on two pennant winners—in 1917 and 1919. In 1917, he won three games and had a 2.33 **earned run average (ERA)** in Chicago's **World Series** win against the **New York Giants.** A sore arm prevented him from appearing in the infamous 1919 Series against the **Cincinnati Reds.** Faber won 20 or more games four times, and he led the **American League** in ERA and **complete games** in 1921 and 1922. In 1964, the **Old Timers Committee** elected him to the **National Baseball Hall of Fame.**

FAIR BALL. A fair ball is a batted ball that settles in **fair territory** between **home plate** and **first base**, or between home plate and **third base**, or that is on or over fair territory when bounding to the outfield past first or third base, or that touches first base, **second base**, or third base, or that first falls on fair territory on or beyond first base or third base, or that, while on or over fair territory, touches the person of an **umpire** or player, or that, while over fair territory, passes out of the playing field in flight. A fly shall be judged fair or foul according to the relative position of the ball and the **foul line,** including the foul pole, and not as to whether the fielder is on fair or **foul territory** at the time he touches the ball.

FAIR TERRITORY. Fair territory is that part of the playing field within, and including the **first base** and **third base** lines, from **home plate** to the bottom of the playing field fence, and perpendicularly upward. All **foul lines** are in fair territory.
See also FAIR BALL.

FAIR-FOUL HIT. In baseball's early days, it was legitimate to hit a squib that at first landed fair, and then rolled foul. It was called a fair-foul hit and was scored as a **hit**. The maneuver's invention is credited to **Dickey Pearce,** and its most proficient practitioner was **Ross Barnes**. The maneuver was outlawed after the 1876 season.

FASTBALL. The fastball, which can exceed 100 miles per hour, is the delivery used most often by the vast majority of **pitchers**. It can be a two-seam fastball, in which the pitcher holds the baseball where the seams are the closest together, or a four-seam fastball, in which the pitcher holds the baseball where the seams are furthest apart. Pitchers noted for the speed of their fastballs include **Roger Clemens, Bob Feller, Lefty Grove, Randy Johnson, Walter Johnson, Sandy Koufax, Amos Rusie,** and **Nolan Ryan.**

FEDERAL LEAGUE (FL). The Federal League (FL) existed as a **major league** in 1914 and 1915. The league, which was able to attract only a limited number of star players from the already established **American League (AL)** and **National League (NL)**, consisted of eight teams each season. In 1914, the teams were the **Baltimore Terrapins, Brooklyn Tip-Tops, Buffalo Blues, Chicago Whales, Indianapolis Hoosiers, Kansas City Packers, Pittsburgh Rebels,** and **St. Louis Terriers**. The Hoosiers won the 1914 FL pennant by 1 1/2 games over Chicago; nevertheless, in 1915, the Indianapolis franchise was shifted to Newark, New Jersey, and became the **Newark Peppers**. Chicago won the 1915 pennant by .001 over St. Louis.

Following the 1914 season, FL owners brought an antitrust lawsuit against the AL and NL. Federal judge **Kenesaw Landis** urged the FL to settle peacefully. The FL owners were unable to survive financially, and the league folded after the 1915 season. Notable players who spent time in the FL included Hugh Bedient, **Chief Bender, Mordecai Brown,** Hal Chase, Doc Crandall, Russ Ford, **Eddie Plank,** Jack Quinn, **Edd Roush,** Tom Seaton, and **Joe Tinker**. Benny Kauff was the league's most productive player, winning the batting championship in both seasons.

FELLER, ROBERT WILLIAM ANDREW "BOB," "RAPID ROBERT". B. 3 November 1918, Van Meter, Iowa. D. 15 December 2010, Cleveland, Ohio. Bob Feller began pitching for the **Cleveland Indians** in 1936, when he was just 17 years old and still in high school. On 23 August that year, he struck out 15 **St. Louis Browns** in his first big-league start. The 6-foot, 185-pound right-hander had a legendary **fastball** that he mixed with a superior **curveball**. On 2 October 1938, he set a then record for **strikeouts** in a game when he fanned 18 **Detroit Tigers**.

Before World War II, Feller led the **American League (AL)** in **wins** for three consecutive seasons (1939–1941) and strikeouts for four consecutive seasons (1938–1941). His 27 wins, 2.61 **earned run average**, and 261 strikeouts in 1940 earned him the **Triple Crown** for **pitchers**. When the war came, Feller enlisted in the U.S. Navy, one of the first major leaguers to leave baseball for military service. He missed almost four years at the peak of his career. In 1946, his first full year back, he won 26 games and had 348 strikeouts to again lead the league in those departments. He repeated the feat in 1947.

In his 18 seasons (1936–1941, 1945–1956), Feller led the AL in wins six times, **innings pitched** five times, and strikeouts seven times. The *Sporting News* voted him the **Major League Player of the Year** in 1940 and the AL **Pitcher of the Year** in 1951. He was an eight-time **All-Star**, but in his only **World Series**, in 1948, he lost two games to the **Boston Braves**. Despite the four years missed, Feller won 266 games (266–162), threw 279 **complete games**, and compiled 2,581 strikeouts. He pitched three **no-hitters** and 12 one-hitters. In 1962, the **Baseball Writers' Association of America** elected Feller to the **National Baseball Hall of Fame**.

FENWAY PARK. Fenway Park, located in Boston, Massachusetts, is the home field of the **Boston Red Sox** of the **American League**. Opened on 20 April 1912, it is the oldest **major-league** park still in use. The Red Sox previously played at the Huntington Avenue Baseball Grounds (1901–1911). The **Boston Braves** of the **National League** played several games at Fenway Park in 1913, 1914, 1915, and 1946, including their two home games against the **Philadelphia Athletics** in the 1914 **World Series**. Fenway Park, whose seating capacity is approximately 37,500, hosted the major league **All-Star Game** in 1946, the second game in 1961, and in 1999.

See also STADIUMS.

FERGUSON, ROBERT VAVASOUR "BOB," "DEATH TO FLYING THINGS". B. 31 January 1845, Brooklyn, New York. D. 3 May 1894, Brooklyn, New York. Bob Ferguson was one of the pioneers of early Major League Baseball, serving as a **player**, a **manager**, an **umpire**, and a league president. After playing for Enterprise of Brooklyn in 1865 and the **Brooklyn Atlantics** (1866–1870), Ferguson joined the **New York Mutuals** of the newly formed National Association (NA), baseball's first **major league**, as their **player-manager**. He also served in both capacities with two other NA teams, the Brooklyn Atlantics (1872–1874), and **Hartford Dark Blues** (1875).

Ferguson, who was also the president of the NA from 1872 to 1875, stayed with Hartford after it entered the **National League (NL)** as a charter member in 1876, and was again with the Dark Blues, now called the Brooklyn Hartfords, in 1877. He continued as a player-manager in the NL with the **Chicago White Stockings** (1878), **Troy Trojans** (1879–1882), and Philadelphia Quakers (1883). He then moved to the **American Association (AA)** as the player-manager of the **Pittsburgh Alleghenys** in 1884, and as the manager of the **New York Metropolitans** in 1886 and 1887. In 1888, he became an umpire in the AA and, in 1890, left the AA to umpire in the **Players' League**. As a player, the 5-foot, 9-inch, 149-pound Ferguson played primarily at **second base** and **third base**. Credited with being the major league's first **switch-hitter**, his career **batting average** for 14 big-league seasons was .265. His 16-season managerial record was 417–516.

FERRELL, RICHARD BENJAMIN "RICK". B. 12 October 1905, Durham, North Carolina. D. 27 July 1995, Bloomfield Hills, Michigan. Rick Ferrell was a **catcher** in the **American League (AL)** for 18 seasons, mostly with the **St. Louis Browns** (1929–1933, 1941–1943) and **Washington Senators** (1937–1941, 1944–1945, 1947). Ferrell was with the **Boston Red Sox** from 1933 to 1937. He was an eight-time selectee to the **All-Star** team and caught the entire game in 1933, the first All-Star Game played. Ferrell, a 5-foot, 10-inch, 160-pound right-handed hitter, had a .281 career **batting average**, better than most catchers of his era, and he was outstanding defensively. He had an excellent throwing arm, leading the AL in throwing out potential base stealers four times. He had a great knack for handling **pitchers** who threw the **knuckleball**. Ferrell caught more than 100 games for nine consecutive seasons (1930–1938). His 1,806 games caught stood as an AL record for 40 years. In 1984, the **Veterans Committee** elected him to the **National Baseball Hall of Fame**.

FIELDER. A fielder is defined as any defensive player.
See also FIELDER'S CHOICE (FC); FIELDING PERCENTAGE (FP).

FIELDER'S CHOICE (FC). A fielder's choice is the act of a **fielder** who handles a **fair** grounder and, instead of throwing to **first base** to retire the **batter**, he throws to another **base** in an attempt to put out a preceding runner. The term is also used by **official scorers** (a) to account for the advance of the batter-runner who takes one or more extra bases when the fielder who handles his safe hit attempts to put out a preceding runner; (b) to account for the advance of a runner (other than by **stolen base** or **error**) while a fielder is attempting to put out another runner; and (c) to account for the advance of a runner made solely because of the defensive team's indifference (undefended steal).

FIELDING PERCENTAGE (FP). Fielding percentage is calculated by dividing a **fielder's** total **putouts**, plus his total **assists**, by his total putouts, total assists, and total **errors**. Example: A player with 214 putouts, 423 assists, and 16 errors has a fielding percentage of .975.

FINGERS, ROLAND GLEN "ROLLIE". B. 25 August 1946, Steubenville, Ohio. Rollie Fingers was a right-handed relief **pitcher** who spent 17 seasons in the **major leagues**. The 6-foot, 4-inch, 190-pound Fingers pitched for the **Oakland Athletics** of the **American League (AL)** from 1968 through 1976, the **San Diego Padres** of the **National League (NL)** from 1977 through 1980, and the **Milwaukee Brewers** of the AL in 1981–1982 and 1984–1985. Fingers had been a starting pitcher in the **minor leagues** and early in his big-league career, before **Dick Williams**, his **manager** at Oakland, converted him to a full-time reliever in 1971. Serving in that role, Fingers helped lead Oakland to three consecutive world championships from 1972 to 1974. He appeared in 16 **World Series** games, with a 1.35 **earned run average (ERA)** and six **saves**. He was voted the Series' **Most Valuable Player (MVP)** in 1974.

After signing as a **free agent** with San Diego in December 1976, Fingers led the NL in saves in 1977 and 1978. He was voted the NL's Rolaids Relief Pitcher of the Year in 1977, 1978, and 1980. Traded to Milwaukee following the 1980 season, Fingers was instrumental in the Brewers reaching the playoffs in 1981. He again led the league in saves, which, along with a 1.06 ERA, won him the AL's MVP Award and **Cy Young Award**, along with his fourth Rolaids Relief Pitcher of the Year honors. Overall, Fingers won 114 games, with a 2.90 ERA and 341 saves. He was picked for the **All-Star** team seven times. The **Baseball Writers' Association of America** elected Fingers to the **National Baseball Hall of Fame** in 1992.

FIRST BASE. First base is the first of four stations on a baseball diamond that a **base runner** must safely touch in succession to score a **run** for that player's team.
See also FIRST BASEMAN (1B).

FIRST BASEMAN (1B). The first baseman is the defensive player on the team who fields the area nearest to **first base** and is responsible for the majority of plays made at that **base**. In the numbering system used to record defensive plays, the first baseman is assigned the number 3.

The **major-league** career leader in **games played** by a first baseman is 2,413, by **Eddie Murray** (1977–1997). The major-league career leader in **fielding percentage** (minimum 500 games) is Casey Kotchman (2004–2012 and still active), at .9977.

The single-season leader in **putouts** by a first baseman is Jiggs Donohue of the 1907 **Chicago White Sox**, with 1,846. The **National League** single-season leader is **George Kelly** of the 1920 **New York Giants**, with 1,759. The career leader is **Jake Beckley** (1888–1907), with 23,731.

The single-season leader in **assists** is **Albert Pujols** of the 2009 **St. Louis Cardinals**, with 185. The **American League** single-season leader is Bill Buckner of the 1985 **Boston Red Sox**, with 184. The career leader is Eddie Murray, with 1,865.

FISK, CARLTON ERNEST "PUDGE". B. 26 December 1947, Bellows Falls, Vermont. Carlton Fisk, sometimes called "Pudge," was an **American League (AL) catcher** for 24 seasons, 11 with the **Boston Red Sox** and 13 with the **Chicago White Sox**. Fisk, who briefly attended the University of New Hampshire on a basketball scholarship, was Boston's first pick and fourth overall in the 1967 **Amateur Draft**. After brief trials in 1969 and 1971, he came up to stay in 1972 and was unanimously voted the AL's **Rookie of the Year**. The 6-foot, 3-inch, 200-pound Fisk led the league with nine **triples** that year, a rare feat for a catcher. He is best remembered in Boston for his dramatic game-winning **home run** against the **Cincinnati Reds** in Game Six of the 1975 **World Series**. Television cameras captured Fisk waving for his 12th-inning drive down the left-field line at **Fenway Park** to stay fair. In 1981, Fisk signed as a **free agent** with the White Sox, where he remained until his release in June 1993.

At one point, Fisk, a .269 career hitter, held the **major-league** record for most games caught (2,226) and most home runs by a catcher (351). Fisk's 37 home runs in 1985 set a single-season AL record for a right-handed-hitting catcher. He also set records for most seasons, **putouts**, and **total chances** by a catcher. All those records have since been surpassed. Selected to the **All-Star** team 11 times, Fisk was elected to the **National Baseball Hall of Fame by** the **Baseball Writers' Association of America** in 2000.

FLICK, ELMER HARRISON. B. 11 January 1876, Bedford, Ohio. D. 9 January 1971, Bedford, Ohio. In his first four **major-league** seasons (1898–1901), left-handed-hitting **outfielder** Elmer Flick batted a combined .338 for the **Philadelphia Phillies**. In 1900, he led the **National League** with 110 **runs batted in (RBI)**, while reaching career highs in **batting average** (.367) and **hits** (200). Flick and teammate **Nap Lajoie** left the Phillies in 1902 in an attempt to join the crosstown **Philadelphia Athletics** of the new

American League (AL). The Phillies went to court and got an injunction preventing the two from playing in Philadelphia, so instead they joined the AL's Cleveland Bronchos, forerunner of the **Cleveland Indians.** Flick played just 11 games for the 1902 Athletics.

In 1905, the 5-foot, 9-inch, 168-pound Flick led the AL in batting with a .308 average. Only **Carl Yastrzemski** of the **Boston Red Sox,** who batted .301 in 1968, won a major-league batting title with a lower average. Flick's last productive season was 1907, but he remained with Cleveland through 1910. He finished with a .313 career batting average and led the league in **triples** three times and **stolen bases** twice. In 1963, the **Veterans Committee** elected Flick to the **National Baseball Hall of Fame.**

FLOOD, CURTIS CHARLES "CURT". B. 18 January 1938, Houston, Texas. D. 20 January 1997, Los Angeles, California. Curt Flood began his career playing in eight games for the 1956–1957 **Cincinnati Reds** and ended it with 13 games for the 1971 **Washington Senators.** From 1958 to 1969, the 5-foot, 9-inch, 165-pound Flood was an outstanding center fielder for the **St. Louis Cardinals.** A right-handed **batter,** he had a .293 career **batting average,** seven seasons in which he batted above .300, led the **National League (NL)** with 211 **hits** in 1964, and played on three pennant-winning teams. A seven-time **Gold Glove Award** winner, he led NL **outfielders** in **putouts** four times and **fielding percentage** twice.

Following the 1969 season, the Cardinals traded Flood to the **Philadelphia Phillies** in a multiplayer deal, which included Tim McCarver going to Philadelphia and Dick Allen coming to St. Louis. Flood refused to go to Philadelphia and asked **Commissioner Bowie Kuhn** to declare him a **free agent.** Kuhn denied the request, whereupon Flood filed a suit on 16 January 1970, stating that baseball had violated the nation's antitrust laws. The case went to the Supreme Court, with former Supreme Court Justice Arthur Goldberg serving as Flood's lawyer. The Supreme Court upheld the District Court and Court of Appeals rulings favoring Organized Baseball. Flood sat out the 1970 season, but he signed with the Senators for the 1971 season. He retired in April after playing only 13 games.

FLORIDA MARLINS. *See* MIAMI MARLINS.

FORBES FIELD. Forbes Field was located in Pittsburgh, Pennsylvania. The **Pittsburgh Pirates** of the **National League** played their first game at Forbes Field on 30 June 1909, and their last on 28 June 1970. Before that, they played at Exposition Park from 1887 to 29 June 1909. After leaving Forbes Field, they played at **Three Rivers Stadium** from 16 July 1970 to the end of the 2000 season, and, since 2001, they have played at **PNC Park**. In the 1930s and 1940s, two **Negro National League** teams, the **Homestead Grays** and Washington Homestead Grays, also played home games at Forbes Field. Forbes Field hosted the **major league All-Star Game** in 1944 and the first game in 1959.

See also STADIUMS.

FORCE PLAY (FP). A force play is a play in which a **runner** legally loses his right to occupy **second base** or **third base**, or reach **home plate**, by reason of the **batter** becoming a runner by successfully reaching **first base**.

FORD, EDWARD CHARLES "WHITEY". B. 21 October 1928, New York, New York. Whitey Ford pitched for the **New York Yankees** for 16 seasons (1950, 1953–1967). His 236 **wins** are the most in Yankees' history. A 5-foot, 10-inch, 178-pound left-hander, he led the **American League (AL)** in wins and **winning percentage** three times, and in **earned run average (ERA)**, **shutouts**, and **innings pitched** twice. Ford was a member of the AL **All-Star** team eight times; the *Sporting News*'s choice as AL **Pitcher of the Year** in 1955, 1961, and 1963; and a winner of the **Cy Young Award** in 1961. He was also the winner of the **Babe Ruth Award** and **Most Valuable Player Award** for his pitching in the 1961 **World Series**. Ford appeared in 11 World Series, compiling a 10–8 record and 2.71 ERA. He holds the Series records for most wins and most **strikeouts**. Ford's career record is 236–106. His winning percentage of .690 is the best of any **major-league pitcher** in the 20th century with at least 200 wins. His 2.75 ERA is the second best for a left-handed pitcher with at least 200 wins. He was elected by the **Baseball Writers' Association of America** to the **National Baseball Hall of Fame** in 1974.

FORFEITED GAME. A forfeited game is a game declared ended by the **umpire** in chief in favor of the offended team by the score of 9 to 0, for violation of the rules.

FORT WAYNE (INDIANA) KEKIONGAS. The Fort Wayne Kekiongas were charter members of the National Association (NA), but the team only played in the NA's first season, 1871. The Kekiongas lost to the **Cleveland Forest Citys**, 2–0, in the first-ever NA game. The most notable member of the Kekiongas was **Bobby Mathews**.

FOSTER, ANDREW "RUBE". B. 17 September 1879, Calvert, Texas. D. 9 December 1930, Kankakee, Illinois. Rube Foster was a **pitcher**, a **manager**, and an executive in the **Negro Leagues** from 1902 to 1926. His greatest success came with the **Chicago American Giants** of the **Negro National**

League, a league he almost single-handedly created. Foster, a 6-foot, 200-pound right-hander, pitched for the club from 1911 to 1917. He had taken over as the owner and manager in 1911, and he remained in that capacity through 1926. In 1981, the **Veterans Committee** elected Foster to the **National Baseball Hall of Fame**. He was the first representative from the Negro Leagues elected as a pioneer or executive rather than as a player.

See also AFRICAN AMERICANS IN BASEBALL; FOSTER, WILLIAM HENDRICK "BILL".

FOSTER, WILLIAM HENDRICK "BILL". B. 12 June 1904, Calvert, Texas. D. 16 September 1978, Lorman, Mississippi. Bill Foster was a younger half-brother of **Rube Foster**. The 6-foot, 1-inch, 195-pound Foster is recognized as one of the top left-handed **pitchers** from the **Negro Leagues**. His career lasted from 1923 to 1938, with his best seasons coming with the **Chicago American Giants** of the **Negro National League** from 1923 to 1930. In 1996, the **Veterans Committee** elected Foster to the **National Baseball Hall of Fame**.

See also AFRICAN AMERICANS IN BASEBALL; FOSTER, ANDREW "RUBE".

FOUL BALL. A foul ball is a batted ball that settles on **foul territory** between **home plate** and **first base**, or between home plate and **third base**, or that bounds past first base or third base on or over foul territory, or that first falls on foul territory beyond first base or third base, or that, while on or over foul territory, touches the person of an **umpire** or player, or any object foreign to the natural ground. A fly ball shall be judged **fair** or foul according to the relative position of the ball and the **foul line**, including the foul pole, and not as to whether the **fielder** is on foul or **fair territory** at the time he touches the ball.

FOUL LINES. Foul lines are either of two straight lines in **fair territory** extending from the rear of **home plate** to the outer edge of the playing field. One extends past **first base**, and one extends past **third base**. They indicate the area in which a **fair ball** can be hit.

FOUL STRIKE RULE. Prior to 1901 in the **National League**, and 1903 in the **American League**, **foul balls** were not counted as **strikes**. A **batter** could foul off any number of pitches with no strikes counted against him, the exception being on **bunt** attempts.

FOUL TERRITORY. Foul territory is that part of the playing field outside the **first base** and **third base** lines extended to the fence and perpendicularly upward.

See also FOUL LINES.

FOX, JACOB NELSON "NELLIE". B. 25 December 1927, St. Thomas, Pennsylvania. D. 1 December 1975, Baltimore, Maryland. After 98 games during the course of three seasons with the **Philadelphia Athletics** (1947–1949), Nellie Fox was traded to the **Chicago White Sox**, where he became one of the top **second basemen** in the **American League (AL)**. In 14 seasons with the White Sox, Fox was among the most durable players in the league. Although just 5 feet, 10 inches tall and 160 pounds, he led the AL in **games played**, **plate appearances**, and **at-bats**, five times each. The left-handed-batting Fox also led in **hits** four times and **singles** eight times, and he finished in the top 10 in **triples** 11 times. He was exceptionally difficult to strike out, leading the AL in the ratio of **strikeouts** to at-bats 12 times. Fox is sixth all-time in that department.

In addition, he led AL second basemen in games played eight times; **putouts** for 10 consecutive years, from 1952 to 1961; **fielding percentage** five times; and **assists** five times. Fox was a 12-time **All-Star**, and, in 1959, he won the **Most Valuable Player Award**, helping lead Chicago to its first pennant in 40 years. He batted .375 in a six-game **World Series** loss to the **Los Angeles Dodgers**. Fox spent his final two seasons (1964 and 1965) with Houston of the **National League**. Fox, who had a lifetime **batting average** of .288 and 2,663 hits, was elected to the **National Baseball Hall of Fame** by the **Veterans Committee** in 1997.

FOXX, JAMES EMORY "JIMMIE," "THE BEAST". B. 22 October 1907, Sudlersville, Maryland. D. 21 July 1967, Miami, Florida. Jimmie Foxx was nicknamed "The Beast" for his prodigious strength and power. **Frank Baker**, the manager at Easton (Maryland) in the Eastern Shore League, signed the 16-year-old Foxx in 1924 and then sold him to the **Philadelphia Athletics**. The 6-foot, 195-pound right-handed-hitting Foxx played for **Connie Mack's** Athletics for 11 seasons (1925–1935), originally as a **catcher**, and later as a **first baseman**. In 1932, he led the **American League (AL)** in **home runs** (58), **runs batted in (RBI)** (169), and **runs** (151). The following season, he won the AL's **Triple Crown** by leading the league in **batting average** (.356), home runs (48), and RBI (163). Foxx again led in home runs in 1935, but, after the season, the financially strapped A's traded him to the **Boston Red Sox** for a pair of marginal players and $150,000. In 1938, Foxx again led the AL in batting and RBI. He also had 50 home runs that year, second to **Hank Greenberg's** 58, but he then led the league again in 1939.

Foxx, who also played in the **National League**, for the **Chicago Cubs** in 1942 and 1944 and the **Philadelphia Phillies** in 1945, was the second player after **Babe Ruth** to reach 500 home runs. He finished with 534, at the time the most ever by a right-handed **batter**. Foxx later managed in the **minor leagues**, and, in 1952, he was the manager of the Fort Wayne (Indiana) Daisies of the **All-American Girls Professional Baseball League**. An alcoholic who was unable to hold a job after baseball, Foxx was destitute when he died at the age of 59. During his 20-year big-league career, he was selected to the AL **All-Star** team for nine consecutive seasons (1933–1941) and three times was voted the AL's **Most Valuable Player**, in 1932 and 1933 for Philadelphia, and in 1938 for Boston. He played on three consecutive pennant-winning teams for the Athletics (1929–1931), two of which (1929 and 1930) won the **World Series**. In 1951, the **Baseball Writers' Association of America** elected Foxx to the **National Baseball Hall of Fame**.

FREE AGENT. A free agent is a player whose contract with a team has expired and who is thus eligible to sign with another team. Free agents are classified as either Type A, Type B, or unclassified. Type A free agents are those determined to be in the top 20 percent of all players based on the previous two seasons. Type B free agents are those in the next 20 percent. Unclassified free agents are those remaining.

Teams that lose a Type A free agent, to whom they have offered arbitration, receive the top draft pick from the team that signs the free agent, plus a supplemental draft pick in the upcoming draft, as compensation. Teams losing Type B free agents, to whom they have offered arbitration, receive only a supplemental pick as compensation. Teams that lose unclassified free agents, or who do not offer arbitration to classified free agents, do not receive any compensation.

FRICK, FORD CHRISTOPHER. B. 19 December 1894, Wawaka, Indiana. D. 8 April 1978, Bronxville, New York. Ford Frick was a former sportswriter who served as president of the **National League** from 1934 until he succeeded **Happy Chandler** as **commissioner of baseball** in 1951. He remained commissioner through 1965, overseeing a period of franchise shifts and **expansion**. Frick, who was instrumental in the creation of the **National Baseball Hall of Fame**, was himself elected to the Hall of Fame by the **Veterans Committee** in 1970.

FRISCH, FRANK FRANCIS "FRANKIE," "THE FORDHAM FLASH". B. 9 September 1898, Bronx, New York. D. 12 March 1973, Wilmington, Delaware. Frankie Frisch was fresh out of Fordham University when he made his debut as a 20-year-old infielder with the 1919 **New York Giants**. Tutored by **manager John McGraw,** Frisch was the **second baseman** on four consecutive Giants' pennant winners (1921–1924). He batted better than .300 in every season from 1921 to 1926, and he led the **National League (NL)** in **stolen bases** in 1921, **hits** in 1923, and **runs** scored in 1924. But following the 1926 season, in a trade that involved two of the game's best players, the Giants traded Frisch to the **St. Louis Cardinals** for their great second baseman, **Rogers Hornsby.**

The 5-foot, 11-inch, 165-pound Frisch, a **switch-hitter,** played for the Cardinals through the 1937 season, batting .300 or above seven more times. He led the league in stolen bases twice more, and, in 1931, he was voted the league's **Most Valuable Player.** He was named to manage the Cardinals in mid-1933 and led the famed Gashouse Gang to a **World Series** win in 1934. Frisch, who managed the Cardinals until 1938, later led the **Pittsburgh Pirates** (1940–1946) and **Chicago Cubs** (1949–1951), but he never won another pennant. A member of the first three NL **All-Star** teams, Frisch also took part in eight World Series, four with the Giants and four with the Cardinals, batting .294 in 50 games while setting several Series fielding records for second basemen. His career **batting average** was .316, and he had 2,880 hits and 419 stolen bases. In 1947, the **Baseball Writers' Association of America** elected Frisch to the **National Baseball Hall of Fame.**

FULTON COUNTY STADIUM. Fulton County Stadium, located in Atlanta, Georgia, and also known as Atlanta Stadium, was the home of the **Atlanta Braves** of the **National League** from 1966, the Braves' first season in Atlanta, to 1996. Fulton County Stadium hosted the **major league All-Star Game** in 1972. In 1997, the Braves moved to **Turner Field**, their present home. *See also* STADIUMS.

G

GALVIN, JAMES FRANCIS "JIM," "PUD". B. 25 December 1856, St. Louis, Missouri. D. 7 March 1902, Pittsburgh, Pennsylvania. **Pitcher** Pud Galvin played in four **major leagues** during his 15-year career, including the National Association (NA), **National League (NL)**, **American Association (AA)**, and **Players' League (PL)**. The 5-foot, 8-inch, 190-pound right-hander was known for his **fastball** and **changeup**, as well as for his adeptness at picking off **base runners**. Galvin began his big-league career with the **St. Louis Brown Stockings** of the NA in 1875. His 1.16 **earned run average** led the league, but for the next three seasons he pitched for independent and **minor-league** teams. Galvin returned to the major leagues in 1879, with the **Buffalo Bisons** of the NL. In four and a half seasons with Buffalo, he won 218 games, including back-to-back 46-win seasons in 1883 and 1884. Galvin was sold to the **Pittsburgh Alleghenys** of the AA in July 1885, a team that moved from the AA to the NL in 1887.

After winning 29 games for the Alleghenys in 1889, Galvin jumped to the **Pittsburgh Burghers** of the PL in 1890. When the PL folded, after just one season, Galvin returned to the Pittsburgh club of the NL, now renamed the **Pittsburgh Pirates**. In June 1892, the Pirates traded Galvin to the St. Louis Browns of the NL, where he spent the final few months of his career. Galvin won 365 games and lost 310 in his big-league career. The 310 losses are second only to **Cy Young**. Galvin also trails only Young in **complete games**, with 646, and in **innings pitched**, with 6,003 1/3. The first pitcher to win 300 games, he was elected to the **National Baseball Hall of Fame** by the **Veterans Committee** in 1965.

GAMES FINISHED (GF). A relief **pitcher** is credited with a game finished (GF) if he is the last pitcher to pitch for his team in a game. (A starting pitcher is not credited with a GF for pitching a **complete game**.) The **major league** single-season leader in GF is Mike Marshall of the 1979 **Minnesota Twins**, with 84. Marshall is also the single-season leader in the **National**

League, with 83 for the 1974 **Los Angeles Dodgers**. The career leader is **Mariano Rivera**, with 883. Rivera has spent his entire career (1995–2012) with the **New York Yankees**.

GAMES PLAYED (G). A player is credited with a game played (G) if his name appears in the starting lineup card handed to the **umpire** before the start of the game. A player is also credited with a G if his name is announced into the game in any capacity after the game starts, whether or not he actually plays. Prior to 1907, in the **American League (AL)**, and, prior to 1912, in the **National League (NL)**, substitute players, for example, **pinch hitters** and **pinch runners**, were not always credited with a G.

The **major league** single-season leader in games played is Maury Wills of the 1962 **Los Angeles Dodgers**, with 165. Wills played in all the Dodgers' 162 regularly scheduled games in 1962, and in three additional games in the NL playoff against the **San Francisco Giants**. The AL single-season leader in games played is Cesar Tovar of the 1967 **Minnesota Twins**, with 164. The career leader is **Pete Rose**, with 3,562. Rose played for the **Cincinnati Reds** (1963–1978, 1984–1986), **Philadelphia Phillies** (1979–1983), and **Montreal Expos** (1984).

GAMES STARTED (GS). Games started (GS) is a statistic used for **pitchers**. A pitcher must face the opposing team's first **batter** to be credited with a game started. In the early days of Major League Baseball, teams carried few pitchers, and the vast majority of the starts were made by one pitcher. Thus, the all-time **major league** single-season leader in GS are **Pud Galvin** of the 1883 **Buffalo Bisons** of the **National League (NL)** and Will White of the 1879 **Cincinnati Reds** of the NL, each with 75. The single-season leader post-1893, when the pitching distance was extended to its current 60 feet, 6 inches, is **Amos Rusie** of the 1893 **New York Giants**, with 52. The single-season leader in the **American League (AL)** is **Jack Chesbro** of the 1904 **New York Yankees**, with 51. The career leader is **Cy Young**, with 815. Young pitched for Cleveland of the NL (1890–1898), St. Louis of the NL (1899–1900), Boston of the AL (1901–1908), Cleveland of the AL (1909–1911), and Boston of the NL (1911).

GEHRIG, HENRY LOUIS "LOU," "THE IRON HORSE". B. 19 June 1903, New York, New York. D. 2 June 1941, Bronx, New York. After playing a combined 23 games for the **New York Yankees** in 1923 and 1924, Lou Gehrig took over the **first base** job from Wally Pipp in June 1925. From that point through 1938, the 6-foot, 200-pound Gehrig was one of baseball's most feared hitters, one who ranks near the top in almost every offensive category. Playing in the shadow of first **Babe Ruth** and then **Joe DiMaggio**, the left-handed-hitting Gehrig led the **American League (AL)** in **home runs** and walks three times, **total bases** and **runs** scored four times, **slugging percentage** and **doubles** twice, and **on-base percentage** and **runs batted in (RBI)** five times. His 184 RBI in 1931 is still the AL record.

Gehrig won his only batting title in 1934, with a .363 average, which, combined with his league-leading 49 home runs and 165 RBI, earned him the **Triple Crown**. He was the AL's **Most Valuable Player** in 1927 and 1936, and he finished second in the voting in 1931 and 1932. Gehrig was the AL's starting first baseman in each of the first five **All-Star Games**. A left-handed thrower, he is eighth all-time in **games played** at first base and ninth in **putouts** at the position. In seven **World Series** as a Yankee, six of which they won, he battered **National League** opponents with a .361 **batting average**, 10 home runs, and 35 RBI in 34 games. His career totals include a .340 batting average, 493 home runs, 1,995 RBI, a .447 on-base percentage, and a .632 slugging percentage, third all-time.

Gehrig was the captain of the Yankees from 1935 until he retired eight games into the 1939 season. Amyothropic lateral sclerosis (also known as "Lou Gehrig's disease"), a degenerative nerve disorder that took his life two years later, caused Gehrig to bench himself. His streak of 2,130 consecutive games played, once thought unbreakable, was surpassed by **Cal Ripken** of the **Baltimore Orioles** in 1995. Gehrig was elected to the **National Baseball Hall of Fame** in a special election by the **Baseball Writers' Association of America** in 1939.

GEHRINGER, CHARLES LEONARD "CHARLIE," "THE ME-CHANICAL MAN". B. 11 May 1903, Fowlerville, Michigan. D. 21 January 1993, Bloomfield Hills, Michigan. Charlie Gehringer batted above .300 13 times in his 19 seasons with the **Detroit Tigers** (1924–1942). During that span, he drove in more than 100 **runs** and had more than 200 **hits** seven times each. In 1934, Gehringer batted .356 and finished second in the **Most Valuable Player (MVP)** voting to **Mickey Cochrane**, his teammate and the Tigers' **manager**. Three years later, in 1937, the 5-foot, 11-inch, 180-pound left-handed hitter won the **American League (AL)** batting title with a .371 average, and this time he was voted the league's MVP. The Tigers were pennant winners in 1934 and 1935, and again in 1940. Gehringer batted .379 in the 1934 **World Series** loss to the **St. Louis Cardinals** and .375 in the 1935 win over the **Chicago Cubs**, but he batted only .214 in the 1940 loss to the **Cincinnati Reds**.

Gehringer was the AL's starting **second baseman** in each of the first six **All-Star Games**. He played every inning of those six games, while compiling a .500 **batting average**. Known as "The Mechanical Man" for his steady, unspectacular play at bat and in the field, Gehringer led AL second basemen in **fielding percentage** five times, **assists** seven times, and **putouts** three times. He finished his career with 2,839 hits and a .320 batting average. Gehringer later served as vice president and **general manager** of the Tigers. He was elected to the **National Baseball Hall of Fame** by the **Baseball Writers' Association of America** in 1949.

GENERAL MANAGER (GM). The general manager (GM) of a baseball team hires and fires the **manager** and his coaching staff. He typically controls trades and **free agent** signings and negotiates on behalf of the team during contract negotiations with the players. In earlier times, the GM was often called the business manager and was also responsible for hiring broadcasters and the administration of the ballpark.

GIBSON, JOSHUA "JOSH". B. 21 December 1911, Buena Vista, Georgia. D. 20 January 1947, Pittsburgh, Pennsylvania. Josh Gibson was the greatest **catcher** to play in the **Negro Leagues**. Gibson was a 6-foot, 1-inch, 210-pound right-handed slugger, who played from 1930 to 1946, mostly for the **Homestead Grays** and the **Pittsburgh Crawfords**, both of the **Negro National League**. He teamed with **Buck Leonard** to make the Grays one of the Negro Leagues' most successful teams. In addition to hitting for high averages, he was the Negro Leagues' most prolific **home-run** hitter, despite playing most of his home games in spacious **Forbes Field** in Pittsburgh and **Griffith Stadium** in Washington. In 1972, a special **Negro Leagues Committee** elected Gibson to the **National Baseball Hall of Fame**.

See also AFRICAN AMERICANS IN BASEBALL.

GIBSON, ROBERT "BOB". B. Pack Robert Gibson, 9 November 1935, Omaha, Nebraska. Bob Gibson was a hard-throwing, intimidating right-hander who spent his entire 17-year big-league career with the **St. Louis Cardinals** (1959–1975). The 6-foot, 1-inch, 189-pound Gibson won 20 games or more five times, including a league-leading 23 in 1970. Two years earlier, in 1968, Gibson had one of the all-time great pitching seasons. He went 22–9, while leading the **National League (NL)** with 13 **shutouts** and a 1.12 **earned run average (ERA)**, the lowest in the **major leagues** in 54 years. He won the **Cy Young Award** that year, as he would again in 1970, and he also captured the NL **Most Valuable Player (MVP) Award**. The *Sporting News* named him the NL **Pitcher of the Year** in both 1968 and 1970.

Gibson appeared in three **World Series**, all of which went seven games. The Cardinals won in 1964 against the **New York Yankees** and in 1967 against the **Boston Red Sox**, and the team lost in 1968 against the **Detroit Tigers**. Gibson made a combined nine starts, with a 7–2 record and eight **complete games**. Over 81 **innings**, his ERA was just 1.89. His seven consecutive **wins** and 17 **strikeouts** in a game are World Series records. He won the **Babe Ruth Award** in 1964 and the Series MVP Award in 1964 and 1967. Gibson was a nine-time **All-Star**, and his superior fielding ability earned him nine **Gold Glove Awards**. Gibson's career record was 251–174, with a 2.91 ERA, 56 shutouts, and 3,117 strikeouts. In 1981, the **Baseball Writers' Association of America** elected him to the **National Baseball Hall of Fame**.

GILES, WARREN CRANDALL. B. 28 May 1896, Tiskilwa, Illinois. D. 7 February 1979, Cincinnati, Ohio. From 1937 to 1951, Warren Giles was the **general manager** and later the president of the **Cincinnati Reds**. In September 1951, he succeeded **Ford Frick** as president of the **National League (NL)**. During Giles's tenure as NL president—he served through 1969—the league expanded from eight teams to 12 and had three franchise shifts. The **Boston Braves** relocated to Milwaukee, and the **Brooklyn Dodgers** and **New York Giants** relocated to California, bringing Major League Baseball to the West Coast. Giles was elected to the **National Baseball Hall of Fame** by the **Veterans Committee** in 1979.

GILLICK, LAWRENCE PATRICK DAVID "PAT". B. 22 August 1937, Chico, California. Pat Gillick began his front-office career in 1963 as the assistant farm director for the **Houston Astros**. He moved to the **New York Yankees** in 1974 as their coordinator of player development. He was the **general manager** of the **Toronto Blue Jays** (1978–1994), **Baltimore Orioles** (1996–1998), **Seattle Mariners** (2000–2003), and **Philadelphia Phillies** (2006–2008). Gillick's teams made the postseason 11 times, and his 1992 and 1993 Blue Jays and 2008 Phillies won the **World Series**. He was elected to the **National Baseball Hall of Fame** by the **Veterans Committee** in 2011.

GLAVINE, THOMAS MICHAEL "TOM". B. 25 March 1966, Concord, Massachusetts. Tom Glavine was a left-handed **pitcher** for the **Atlanta Braves** from 1987 to 2002. He spent five seasons with the **New York Mets** (2003–2007) after signing with them as a **free agent**, before returning to Atlanta for a final partial season in 2008. The 6-foot, 175-pound Glavine was a five-time 20-game winner with Atlanta (1991–1993, 1998, 2000), and he led the **National League (NL)** in **wins** in each of those seasons. He also led the league six times in **games started**. Glavine won two **Cy Young Award**s, in 1991 and 1998, and finished second twice and third twice. He was also the *Sporting News*'s choice as the NL **Pitcher of the Year** in 1991 and 2000.

As a member of the successful Braves (and 2006 Mets), Glavine made many postseason appearances. He was 4–3 in nine **National League Division Series**, 6–10 in 10 **National League Championship Series**, and 4–3 in five **World Series**. He was 2–0 in Atlanta's World Series win over the **Cleveland Indians** in 1995, earning him the Series **Most Valuable Player Award** and the **Babe Ruth Award**. A ten-time **All-Star**, Glavine was also a good-hitting pitcher who won four **Silver Slugger Awards**. He had a career record of 305 wins and 203 **losses**, with a 3.54 **earned run average**. Glavine, whose last active season was 2008, is sure to be elected to the **National Baseball Hall of Fame** when he becomes eligible.

GOLD GLOVE AWARD. Officially called the Rawlings Gold Glove Award, the award is given annually to the players at each fielding position judged to have exhibited superior individual fielding performances. The voters are the **managers** and **coaches** in each league, although managers are not permitted to vote for their own players. The Rawlings Company created the award in 1957 to commemorate the best fielding performance at each position. Initially, only one Gold Glove Award per position was awarded to the top fielder at each position in the **major leagues**, but, beginning in 1958, separate awards were given for the **National League** and **American League**.

The players who have won the most Gold Glove Awards for each position through 2012 are: **pitcher, Greg Maddux** (18); **catcher, Ivan Rodriguez** (13); **first base**, Keith Hernandez (11); **second base, Roberto Alomar** (10); **third base, Brooks Robinson** (16); **shortstop, Ozzie Smith** (13); **outfield, Roberto Clemente**; and **Willie Mays** (12).

GOLDEN ERA VETERANS COMMITTEE. *See* VETERANS COMMITTEE.

GOMEZ, VERNON LOUIS "LEFTY". B. 26 November 1908, Rodeo, California. D. 17 February 1989, Greenbrae, California. Lefty Gomez, a fun-loving, gregarious left-hander, pitched for the **New York Yankees** from 1930 to 1942. He was a four-time 20-game winner who led the **American League (AL)** in **wins**, **winning percentage**, and **earned run average (ERA)** twice, and in **strikeouts** and **shutouts** three times. Gomez, a lanky 6 feet, two inches tall and 173 pounds, led the AL in wins, ERA, and strikeouts in both 1934 and 1937 to earn the pitcher's **Triple Crown** in those two seasons. He was a member of the AL team for the first seven **All-Star Games** and the starting and winning **pitcher** in the first game on 6 July 1933. Although a notoriously weak **batter**, he also had the All-Star Game's first **run batted in**. He was a member of five **World Series** champions, compiling a 6–0 Series record. After pitching (and losing) one game for the 1943 **Washington Sena-**

tors, Gomez retired with a 189–102 record and a .649 winning percentage. He was elected by the **Veterans Committee** to the **National Baseball Hall of Fame** in 1972.

GORDON, JOSEPH LOWELL "JOE," "FLASH". B. 18 February 1915, Los Angeles, California. D. 14 April 1978, Sacramento, California. In 1938, Joe Gordon replaced **Tony Lazzeri** at **second base** for the **New York Yankees**. The acrobatic Gordon was part of the Yankees' **American League (AL)** pennant-winning teams in five of the next six seasons, missing only in 1940. In four of those seasons (1938, 1939, 1941, and 1943) the Yankees won the **World Series**. The 5-foot, 10-inch, 180-pound Gordon led the AL three times in **double plays** and four times in **assists**. In addition, the right-handed-hitting Gordon reached double figures in **home runs** in each of his 11 **major-league** seasons. He was the first AL **second baseman** to hit at least 20 home runs in a season, a total he reached seven times. Gordon's 246 career home runs as a second baseman is still the AL record. His best year was 1942, when he batted .322, with 18 home runs, and was voted the league's **Most Valuable Player**.

Gordon missed the 1944 and 1945 seasons serving in the U.S. Army. He had a subpar year in 1946, and, when the season ended, the Yankees traded him to the **Cleveland Indians** for **pitcher** Allie Reynolds. Gordon returned to his old form in 1947 and 1948, playing a major role in the Indians winning the 1948 pennant and World Series. Gordon retired after the 1950 season and became a **minor-league manager** and **scout**, but he returned to the AL in 1958 as the manager of the Indians. He later managed the **Detroit Tigers**, **Kansas City Athletics**, and **Kansas City Royals**. His career record for his five years as a manager was 305–308. In 2009, the **Veterans Committee** elected Gordon to the **National Baseball Hall of Fame**.

GOSLIN, LEON ALLEN "GOOSE". B. 16 October 1900, Salem, New Jersey. D. 15 May 1971, Bridgeton, New Jersey. Goose Goslin played left field for 18 seasons in the **American League (AL)** with the **Washington Senators** (1921–1930, 1933, 1938), **St. Louis Browns** (1930–1932), and **Detroit Tigers** (1934–1937). During his first stint with Washington, the 5-foot,11-inch, 185-pound Goslin led the AL in **triples** in 1923 and 1925, in **runs batted in (RBI)** in 1924, and **batting average** with a .379 mark in 1928. The Senators won pennants in 1924 and 1925. Goslin returned to Washington in 1933, after two and a half fine seasons with the Browns, and the Senators won the pennant again. Traded to Detroit after the 1933 season, he played on the Tigers' pennant-winning teams of 1934 and 1935. In five **World Series**, encompassing 32 games, the left-handed-hitting Goslin batted .287, with seven **home runs** and 19 RBI. Goslin had a career batting average of .316, with 1,609 RBI and 2,735 **hits**. He topped the .300 mark in batting average and the 100 mark in RBI 11 times each. Goslin was elected to the **National Baseball Hall of Fame** by the **Veterans Committee** in 1968.

GOSSAGE, RICHARD MICHAEL "RICH," "GOOSE". B. 5 July 1951, Colorado Springs, Colorado. Rich Gossage was a right-handed relief **pitcher** who spent 22 years in the **major leagues**. The 6-foot, 3-inch, 180-pound Gossage broke in with the **Chicago White Sox** of the **American League (AL)** in 1972 and eventually pitched for nine different teams, five in the AL and four in the **National League (NL)**. His best years were with the **New York Yankees** from 1978 through 1983, and with the **San Diego Padres** from 1984 to 1987. He also pitched for the **Texas Rangers**, **Oakland Athletics**, and **Seattle Mariners** in the AL, and the **Pittsburgh Pirates**, **San Francisco Giants**, and **Chicago Cubs** in the NL.

Gossage, whose best pitch was a **fastball**, led the AL in **saves** three times—with the 1975 White Sox and 1978 and 1980 Yankees—and finished second twice. He was a nine-time member of his league's **All-Star** team and appeared in 1,002 games with a 124–107 won-lost record. Gossage retired with 310 saves, which was then the fourth-highest total all-time. The **Baseball Writers' Association of America** elected him to the **National Baseball Hall of Fame** in 2008.

GRAND SLAM. A **home run** with the **bases** loaded, which gives the **batter** four **runs batted in**, is called a grand slam. The record for the most grand slams in a single season is six, held by Don Mattingly of the 1987 **New York Yankees** and Travis Hafner of the 2006 **Cleveland Indians**. The most grand slams in a season by a **National League** batter is five, by **Ernie Banks** of the 1955 **Chicago Cubs** and **Albert Pujols** of the 2009 **St. Louis Cardinals**. The career leaders are **Lou Gehrig** and **Alex Rodriguez**, each with 23. Gehrig played for the New York Yankees from 1923 through 1939. Rodriguez played for the **Seattle Mariners** (1994–2000), the **Texas Rangers** (2001–2003), and the New York Yankees (2004–2012) and is still active.

GRANT, ULYSSES F. "FRANK". B. 1 August 1865, Pittsfield, Massachusetts. D. 27 May 1937, New York, New York. Frank Grant was a **second baseman** and **shortstop** who played in the **minor leagues** in the 1880s, before blacks were barred from playing in the organized white professional leagues. After 1887, his last minor-league season, the 5-foot, 7 1/2-inch, 155-pound Grant played with **African American** teams before they were formed into organized leagues. Grant, who batted right-handed, is considered the best African American player of the 19th century. In 2006, he was elected to the **National Baseball Hall of Fame** in a special election conducted by the **Committee on African American Baseball**.

GREAT AMERICAN BALL PARK. Great American Ball Park, located in Cincinnati, Ohio, has been the home field of the **Cincinnati Reds** of the **National League** since 31 March 2003. Prior to that, the Reds played at two parks known as League Park from 1890 to 1901, at Palace of the Fans from 1902 to 1911, at **Crosley Field** from 11 April 1912 to 24 June 1970 (known as Redland Field from 1912 to 1933), and at **Riverfront Stadium** from 30 June 1970 to 22 September 2002. Great American Ball Park has a seating capacity of approximately 42,300.

See also STADIUMS.

GREENBERG, HENRY BENJAMIN "HANK". B. 1 January 1911, New York, New York. D. 4 September 1986, Beverly Hills, California. Hank Greenberg, baseball's first star player of Jewish descent, was one of the game's leading sluggers in the 1930s and 1940s. The 6-foot, 3-inch, 210-pound Greenberg played 12 seasons (1930, 1933–1941, and 1945–1946) for the **Detroit Tigers** and a final season (1947) with the **Pittsburgh Pirates**. A right-handed-hitting **first baseman** and sometimes **outfielder**, he missed four and a half seasons in mid-career for military service in World War II. Greenberg was twice voted the **Most Valuable Player** in the **American League (AL)**. He won in 1935, when he led the league with 36 **home runs**, 170 **runs batted in (RBI)**, and 389 **total bases**, and in 1940, when he again led in home runs (41), RBI (150), and total bases (384). He also had a league-high **slugging percentage** of .670 in 1940. Yet, his two greatest slugging accomplishments were his 183 RBI in 1937, second only to **Lou Gehrig's** AL record of 184, and his 58 home runs in 1938, which at the time tied him with **Jimmie Foxx** as the **major leagues'** third-highest home run total ever, trailing only **Babe Ruth's** 60 and 59 home-run seasons.

Greenberg played in four **World Series** for the Tigers. He batted a combined .318, with five home runs, in Series wins against the **Chicago Cubs** in 1935 and 1945, and losses to the **St. Louis Cardinals** in 1934 and **Cincinnati Reds** in 1940. After his playing days, he served as the **general manager** of the **Cleveland Indians** and vice president and part owner of the **Chicago White Sox**. Overall, Greenberg had a .313 career **batting average**, and he led the AL in home runs and RBI four times each. In 1956, the **Baseball Writers' Association of America** elected him to the **National Baseball Hall of Fame**.

GRIFFEY, GEORGE KENNETH, JR. "KEN," "JUNIOR". B. 21 November 1969, Donora, Pennsylvania. Ken Griffey Jr. joined the **Seattle Mariners** as a 19-year-old in 1989. He played for the Mariners through the 1999 season, when he was traded to the **Cincinnati Reds**. In July 2008, the Reds traded Griffey to the **Chicago White Sox**. He left as a **free agent** at the end of 2008 and returned to Seattle for a final two seasons. A center fielder for almost all his career, the 6-foot, 3-inch, 195-pound Griffey was a 13-time **All-Star** and the winner of seven **Silver Slugger Awards** and 10 **Gold Glove Awards**. Griffey, who batted and threw left-handed, led the **American League (AL)** in **home runs** four times, reaching a career-high 56 in 1997 and 1998. He was the AL's **Most Valuable Player** and the **Major League Player of the Year** in 1997, when he also led the league in **runs**, **runs batted in (RBI)**, and **slugging percentage**. Considered by many the best player in the game until injuries slowed him down, he had a .284 career **batting average**, 630 home runs, and 1,836 RBI. Griffey, whose last active season was 2010, is sure to be elected to the **National Baseball Hall of Fame** when he becomes eligible.

GRIFFITH, CLARK CALVIN "THE OLD FOX". B. 20 November 1869, Clear Creek, Missouri. D. 27 October 1955, Washington, District of Columbia. Clark Griffith was a **major league pitcher**, **manager**, and owner for more than 60 years. He began his big-league career in the **American Association** in 1891, with the **St. Louis Browns** and **Boston Reds**. In 1893, the 5-foot, 6-inch, 156-pound right-hander joined the Chicago Colts of the **National League (NL)**, the forerunner of the **Chicago Cubs**. Griffith was a six-time 20-game winner for the Colts (also called the Orphans) before leaving in 1901 to join the **Chicago White Sox** of the new **American League (AL)** as a **player-manager**. Chicago won the AL's first pennant under Griffith, who also contributed a 24–7 record on the mound.

When the New York Highlanders came into existence in 1903, Griffith left Chicago to manage the New York club. After six stormy seasons in New York, he returned to the NL to manage the **Cincinnati Reds** for three seasons (1909–1911). In 1912, AL president **Ban Johnson** lured Griffith back to the AL as manager and part owner of the **Washington Senators**. Griffith managed the Senators through the 1920 season, but he remained the team's principal owner until his death.

As a pitcher, Griffith had a sparkling 237–146 won-lost record and seven 20-win seasons. He led the NL with a 1.88 **earned run average** in 1898, and he led the AL with a .774 **winning percentage** in 1901. His overall record in 20 seasons as a manager was 1,491–1,367, with the one pennant winner in 1901. Under his ownership, the Senators won pennants in 1924, 1925, and 1933, and the **World Series** in 1924. Griffith was elected as a player to the **National Baseball Hall of Fame** by the **Old Timers Committee** in 1946.

GRIFFITH STADIUM. Griffith Stadium, called National Park from 1911 to 1921, and Clark Griffith Park in 1922, was located in Washington, D.C. It was the home of the original **Washington Senators** of the **American League** from 1911 to 1960, and the **expansion** Washington Senators of the AL in 1961. The **Homestead Grays** of the **Negro National League** also played home games at Griffith Stadium in the 1930s and 1940s. The **stadium** hosted the **major league All-Star Game** in 1937 and 1956.

GRIMES, BURLEIGH ARLAND. B. 18 August 1893, Emerald, Wisconsin. D. 6 December 1985, Clear Lake, Wisconsin. Burleigh Grimes was the last **pitcher** legally allowed to throw the **spitball** after the pitch was banned in 1920. He pitched for seven different teams in a **major-league** career that lasted 19 seasons, from 1916 to 1934. The 5-foot, 10-inch, 175-pound right-hander had three tours of duty with the **Pittsburgh Pirates**, two with the **St. Louis Cardinals**, and one each with the Brooklyn Robins, **New York Giants**, **Chicago Cubs**, **Boston Braves**, and **New York Yankees**. Grimes had five 20-win seasons, four with Brooklyn and one with Pittsburgh. He led the **National League (NL)** in **wins** twice, **complete games** four times, and **innings pitched** three times. He pitched for pennant winners in Brooklyn in 1920, St. Louis in 1930 and 1931, and Chicago in 1932, and he had a 3–4 record in the **World Series**. Grimes led NL pitchers in **assists** four times and **putouts** twice. After his playing days were over, he managed the **Brooklyn Dodgers** to a sixth-place finish in 1937, and a seventh-place finish in 1938. In 1964, the **Veterans Committee** elected Grimes to the **National Baseball Hall of Fame**.

GROUNDS RULES. Grounds rules are special rules particular to the unique design of each ballpark, including fences, **dugouts**, bullpens, railings, domes, photographer's wells, and television camera booths. The rules define the way to handle situations in which these objects may interact or interfere with the ball in play or with the players. Professional baseball has a set of "universal ground rules" that apply to all parks; however, individual parks have the latitude to set ground rules above and beyond the universal ground rules, as long as they do not directly contradict one another.

GROVE, ROBERT MOSES "LEFTY". B. 6 March 1900, Lonaconing, Maryland. D. 22 May 1975, Norwalk, Ohio. Lefty Grove is considered by many the greatest left-handed pitcher ever. Possessed of a blazing fastball, he pitched for the Baltimore Orioles of the International League from 1920 to 1924, winning 109 games while losing just 36, and leading the league in **strikeouts** four times.

Orioles owner Jack Dunn sold the six-feet-three, 190-pound Grove to the **Philadelphia Athletics** of the **American League (AL)** in 1925. He won 10 games that year and 13 the next, but from 1927 through 1933, Grove never won fewer than 20 games, leading the American League in **wins** in 1928 (24), 1930 (28), 1931 (31) and 1933 (24). He led the AL in strikeouts in each of his first seven seasons, and was the league-leader in **winning percentage** four times and **earned run average (ERA)** five times during his nine years with the Athletics. In 1931, he won 16 games in a row before dropping a 1–0 decision to the **St. Louis Browns**.

In December 1933, A's **manager** and owner **Connie Mack** traded Grove and two of his other front liners, second baseman Max Bishop and pitcher Rube Walberg, to the **Boston Red Sox** for two second-line players and $125,000.

Grove's record with Philadelphia was 195–79 and he had helped pitch the A's to three consecutive pennants (1929–1931), and two **World Series** championships (1929 and 1930). His Series record was 4-2 with a 1.75 ERA. In his eight seasons with the Red Sox, the notoriously ill-tempered Grove won 105 and lost 62. He led the AL in ERA four more times and in winning percentage once.

Grove won his 300th game in 1941, his final season, to finish with a career record of 300–141. His .680 win-loss percentage is the second highest in AL history. Grove was an AL **All-Star** six times, the AL's **Most Valuable Player** in 1931, and the winner of the pitchers **Triple Crown** in 1930 and 1931. In 1947, the **Baseball Writers' Association of America** elected Grove to the **National Baseball Hall of Fame**.

GWYNN ANTHONY KEITH, SR. "TONY". B. 9 May 1960, Los Angeles, California. Tony Gwynn batted .289 as a **rookie** with the **San Diego Padres** in 1982. Gwynn played the next 19 seasons with the Padres and never again batted below .300. In 1984, the 5-foot, 11-inch, 185-pound Gwynn, who batted and threw left-handed, won his first **National League (NL)** batting championship. He added three straight batting titles from 1987 to 1989, and four straight from 1994 to 1997. Gwynn's eight batting championships tied him with **Honus Wagner** for the most ever in the NL. Gwynn had more than 200 **hits** five times and led the league in hits seven times and **singles** seven times. He won seven **Silver Slugger Awards** and five **Gold Glove Awards** as a right fielder. A 15-time **All-Star**, he was the winner of the **Branch Rickey Award** in 1995, the **Lou Gehrig Memorial Award** in 1998, and the **Roberto Clemente Award** in 1999. Gwynn had a .338 career **batting average** and 3,141 hits. In 2007, he was elected by the **Baseball Writers' Association of America** to the **National Baseball Hall of Fame**.

H

HAFEY, CHARLES JAMES "CHICK". B. 12 February 1903, Berkeley, California. D. 2 July 1973, Calistoga, California. Chick Hafey was a right-handed-hitting **outfielder** for the **St. Louis Cardinals** (1924–1931) and **Cincinnati Reds** (1932–1935, 1937). Hampered by poor vision, he was one of the first **major-league** players to wear glasses while playing. Hafey often had contract disputes with **Branch Rickey**, the **general manager** of the Cardinals. The 6-foot, 185-pound Hafey won the **National League** batting title with a .349 average in 1931, but when he and Rickey could not agree on a salary for 1932, Rickey traded him to Cincinnati. Injuries caused Hafey to miss most of the 1935 season and all of 1936. His comeback attempt in 1937 was unsuccessful. Hafey appeared in four **World Series** for the Cardinals, against the **New York Yankees** in 1926 and 1928, and against the **Philadelphia Athletics** in 1930 and 1931. Despite a lifetime **batting average** of .317, he batted just .205 in 23 Series games. In 1971, the **Veterans Committee** elected Hafey to the **National Baseball Hall of Fame**.

HAINES, JESSE JOSEPH "POP". B. 22 July 1893, Clayton, Ohio. D. 5 August 1978, Dayton, Ohio. Jesse Haines pitched in one game for the 1918 **Cincinnati Reds**. In 1920, he joined the **St. Louis Cardinals**, where he remained until 1937. Haines, a 6-foot, 190-pound right-hander whose best pitches were a **fastball** and a **knuckleball**, was a three-time 20-game winner and twice led the **National League** in **shutouts**. A member of five Cardinals pennant winners, he appeared in four **World Series**, with a 3–1 record, including two victories over the **New York Yankees** in 1926. Haines's career record was 210–158, with a 3.64 **earned run average**. In 1970, the **Veterans Committee** elected him to the **National Baseball Hall of Fame**.

HALL OF FAME. *See* NATIONAL BASEBALL HALL OF FAME (HOF).

HALLADAY, HARRY LEROY "ROY". B. 14 May 1977, Denver, Colorado. Right-handed **pitcher** Roy Halladay was the first-round choice of the **Toronto Blue Jays** in the 1995 **Amateur Draft**. He made his debut in 1998 and pitched for the Blue Jays until he was traded to the **Philadelphia Phillies** following the 2009 season. The 6-foot, 6-inch, 230-pound Halladay has won the **Cy Young Award** twice, in 2003 for Toronto and in 2010 for Philadelphia. Halladay was the *Sporting News*'s choice as his league's **Pitcher of the Year** in both those seasons. He pitched two **no-hitters** in 2010, one a regular-season **perfect game** against the Florida Marlins, and then a no-hitter against the **Cincinnati Reds** in Game One of the **National League Division Series**. An eight time **All-Star**, Halladay has led his league in **complete games** seven times, **innings pitched** and **shutouts** four times, and **wins** twice. At the end of the 2012 season, he had a career record of 199–100, a .666 **winning percentage**, and a 3.31 **earned run average**. Halladay has a strong chance to be elected to the **National Baseball Hall of Fame** when he becomes eligible.

HAMILTON, WILLIAM ROBERT "BILLY," "SLIDING BILLY". B. 15 February 1866, Newark, New Jersey. D. 15 December 1940, Worcester, Massachusetts. Billy Hamilton was a speedy center fielder who played for the **Kansas City Cowboys** of the **American Association** (1888–1889) and the **Philadelphia Phillies** (1890–1895) and Boston Beaneaters (1896–1901) of the **National League (NL)**. The 5-foot, 6-inch, 165-pound Hamilton's 914 career **stolen bases** was the **major-league** record until **Lou Brock** broke it almost 80 years later. From 1889 to 1895, Hamilton led the NL in steals five times. In those years, however, stolen bases were credited to anyone who took an extra **base** on a **hit** or an **error**.

Hamilton, a left-handed **batter**, also led the NL in walks and **on-base percentage** five times and **runs** scored four times. He was the NL's batting champion in 1891 and 1893, yet his best season was 1894, when he batted .403 and led the league in runs, walks, stolen bases, and on-base percentage. Hamilton's 198 runs scored in 1894 remains the major-league record. He topped the .300 mark for 12 consecutive seasons and finished with a lifetime **batting average** of .344, tied with **Ted Williams** for seventh all-time. Hamilton is one of the few players whose career runs scored (1,697) exceeded his **games played** (1,594). He was elected to the **National Baseball Hall of Fame** by the **Veterans Committee** in 1961.

HANK AARON AWARD. The **Hank Aaron** Award is presented annually by Major League Baseball to the player in each league voted the best overall offensive performer. The award was first given in 1999. The **American League (AL)** winner was **Manny Ramirez** of the **Cleveland Indians**. The **National League (NL)** winner was **Sammy Sosa** of the **Chicago Cubs**. Since 2003, the winner has been determined by the combined vote of play-by-play broadcasters and color analysts from each club's radio and television stations (70 percent) and the fans (30 percent). The 2012 winner in the AL was **Miguel Cabrera** of the **Detroit Tigers**. The 2012 winner in the NL was Buster Posey of the **San Francisco Giants**.

HANLON, EDWARD HUGH "NED". B. 22 August 1857, Montville, Connecticut. D. 14 April 1937, Baltimore, Maryland. Ned Hanlon was a highly innovative and successful **manager** in the 1890s and early 1900s. Before that, he had been a left-handed-hitting **outfielder** for 13 **major-league** seasons, 12 in the **National League (NL)**. Hanlon played for the **Cleveland Blues** in 1880, **Detroit Wolverines** from 1881 to 1888, Pittsburgh Alleghenys in 1889, **Pittsburgh Pirates** in 1891, and **Baltimore Orioles** in 1892. He left the NL for the **Players' League** in 1890, joining the **Pittsburgh Burghers** as their **player-manager**. The 5-foot, 9-inch, 170-pound Hanlon, who had a .260 career **batting average**, had been a player-manager with the Alleghenys in 1889. When he returned to the NL Pirates in 1891, he was again a player-manager. In late 1892, he became a player-manager for the Orioles, although it was his last active season, and he played in only 11 games. As the **manager** of the Orioles from 1892 to 1898, he led the club to three NL pennants (1894–1896) and finished second twice.

Hanlon took over the **Brooklyn Dodgers** in 1899, who were renamed the Brooklyn Superbas. (Hanlon's Superbas were a popular vaudeville acrobatic troupe at the time.) The Superbas won pennants in 1899 and 1900. Hanlon remained in Brooklyn through 1905, and he then managed the **Cincinnati Reds** in 1906 and 1907. His 19-year record as a manager was 1,313–1,164. In 1996, the **Veterans Committee** elected Hanlon to the **National Baseball Hall of Fame** as a manager.

HARRIDGE, WILLIAM "WILL". B. 16 October 1883, Chicago, Illinois. D. 9 April 1971, Evanston, Illinois. Will Harridge began his baseball career in 1911, as the secretary to **Ban Johnson**, the president of the **American League (AL)**. In 1931, he succeeded Ernest S. Barnard as AL president and served through 1958. Harridge was elected to the **National Baseball Hall of Fame** by the **Veterans Committee** in 1972.

HARRIS, STANLEY RAYMOND "BUCKY," "BOY WONDER". B. 8 November 1896, Port Jervis, New York. D. 8 November 1977, Bethesda, Maryland. Bucky Harris was a light-hitting **second baseman** for the **Washington Senators** from 1919 to 1928, and for the **Detroit Tigers** in 1929 and 1931. Harris was a 5-foot, 9-inch, 156-pound right-handed hitter with a career **batting average** of .274. He had only nine **home runs** in 1,263 games, but he led the **American League (AL)** in **sacrifice hits** and **hit by pitch** three times each. Defensively, he led AL second basemen in **putouts** four times and **double plays** twice. His 483 putouts in 1922 was a **major-league** record at the time. In 1924, owner **Clark Griffith** appointed the 27-year-old Harris as **manager** of the Senators. When Washington won the pennant, Harris was christened the "Boy Wonder." Washington defeated the **New York Giants** in the **World Series**, as Harris batted .333 and hit two home runs, equaling his career high for a full season. The Senators repeated as pennant winners in 1925, but the team lost the Series to the **Pittsburgh Pirates**, with Harris batting a miniscule .087.

Harris went on to a 29-year managerial career with five teams, including three stints with the Senators (1924–1928, 1935–1942, and 1950–1954). He managed the Tigers twice (1929–1933, and 1955–1956), the **Boston Red Sox** in 1934, the **Philadelphia Phillies** in 1943, and the **New York Yankees** in 1947 and 1948. His teams seldom had winning records, and his only other pennant and World Series championship was with the 1947 Yankees. The *Sporting News* named him its **Manager of the Year** for 1947. Harris's career record as a manager was 2,158–2,219. In 1975, the **Veterans Committee** elected him to the **National Baseball Hall of Fame** as a manager.

HARTFORD DARK BLUES. After playing in the National Association in 1874 and 1875, the Hartford Dark Blues joined the new **National League** in 1876. The next year, owner **Morgan Bulkeley** moved the team to Brooklyn, where they played their home games at the **Union Grounds** and were known as the Brooklyn Hartfords. The club disbanded after the 1877 season. Notable players for Hartford included **Tommy Bond**, **Candy Cummings**, and **Joe Start**.

HARTNETT, CHARLES LEO "GABBY". B. 20 December 1900, Woonsocket, Rhode Island. D. 20 December 1972, Park Ridge, Illinois. **Catcher** Gabby Hartnett played for the **Chicago Cubs** from 1922 to 1940. He had 100 or more games caught 12 times and led **National League (NL)** catchers in **assists** six times and **runners caught stealing** and **putouts** four times. Hartnett, a 6-foot, 1-inch, 195-pound right-handed hitter, was on the NL team for the first six **All-Star Games**. He had his most productive season in 1930, when he batted .339, with 37 **home runs** and 122 **runs batted in (RBI)**. His .344 **batting average** and 91 RBI in 1935 led the Cubs to a pennant and earned Hartnett the NL's **Most Valuable Player Award**.

Hartnett was a **player-manager** for the Cubs from 1938 to 1940, winning the pennant in 1938. In all, he played for four Cubs pennant winners, all of whom lost in the **World Series**. Fired as manager after the 1940 season, he played a final season with the 1941 **New York Giants**. Hartnett had a lifetime batting average of .297, with 236 home runs. Upon his retirement, he held the record for most home runs by a catcher. In 1955, the **Baseball Writers' Association of America** elected Hartnett to the **National Baseball Hall of Fame**.

HARVEY, HAROLD DOUGLAS "DOUG". B. 13 March 1930, South Gate, California. Doug Harvey was an **umpire** in the **National League** from 1962 through 1992. A master of the rule book, he was rated by the **Society for American Baseball Research** as the second-best umpire ever. Only **Bill Klem** was rated higher. Harvey umpired in 4,673 **major-league** games, six **All-Star Games**, five **World Series**, and nine **National League Championship Series**. Harvey, the first major-league umpire with Native American ancestry, was elected to the **National Baseball Hall of Fame** by the **Veterans Committee** in 2009.

HEILMANN, HARRY EDWIN. B. 3 August 1894, San Francisco, California. D. 9 July 1951, Southfield, Michigan. Harry Heilmann played 15 seasons (1914, 1916–1929) for the **Detroit Tigers** before finishing his career with the **Cincinnati Reds** in 1930 and 1932. The 6-foot, 1-inch, 195-pound Heilmann, who batted and threw right-handed, was primarily a right fielder and a sometimes **first baseman**. He had 12 consecutive years of batting above .300 and won four **American League** batting titles with averages above .390: .394 in 1921, .403 in 1923, .393 in 1925, and .398 in 1927. For a good part of his career with Detroit, Heilmann teamed with **Ty Cobb** and Bobby Veach to form one of the game's all-time great **outfield**s; however, the Tigers never won a pennant while he was with them. Heilmann, who was later a Tigers' broadcaster, finished his career with 2,660 **hits**, 1,539 **runs batted in**, and a .342 **batting average**. He was elected to the **National Baseball Hall of Fame** by the **Baseball Writers' Association of America** in 1952. The only right-handed hitters in the Hall of Fame with higher lifetime batting averages are **Ed Delahanty** and **Rogers Hornsby**.

HENDERSON, RICKEY NELSON HENLEY. B. 25 December 1958, Chicago, Illinois. Rickey Henderson is baseball's all-time leader in **runs** scored (2,295) and **stolen bases** (1,406). He is also the leader in most times **caught stealing**, with 335. Henderson, a right-handed-hitting, left-handed-throwing left fielder, accomplished this while playing for nine teams during the course of 25 years, from 1979 to 2003. Henderson played in the **American League (AL)** with the **Oakland Athletics** (1979–1984, 1989–1995, 1998), **New York Yankees** (1985–1989), **Toronto Blue Jays** (1993), Anaheim Angels (1997), **Seattle Mariners** (2000), and **Boston Red**

Sox (2002). He played in the **National League (NL)** for the **San Diego Padres** (1996–1997), **New York Mets** (1999–2000), and **Los Angeles Dodgers** (2003).

The 5-foot, 10-inch, 180-pound Henderson had his best years in the AL, mostly with Oakland and the Yankees. He led the AL in stolen bases from 1980 to 1986 and 12 times overall. His 130 steals in 1982 set a still-existing one-season record. He scored more than 100 runs in 13 seasons and led his league in runs scored five times. He also led in walks four times, and his career total of 2,190 is second all-time. His best single season was with Oakland in 1990, when he batted .325 and led the league in runs, stolen bases, and **on-base percentage**, and he also won the **Most Valuable Player (MVP) Award** that year. Henderson, a 10-time **All-Star**, played in seven league championship series and was the MVP of the 1989 **American League Championship Series**. In three **World Series**, he batted .339 in 14 games. He finished his career with a .279 **batting average**, with 3,055 **hits** and 297 **home runs**. Henderson is the only player to hit a home run in 25 consecutive seasons. In 2009, the **Baseball Writers' Association of America** elected him to the **National Baseball Hall of Fame**.

HERMAN, WILLIAM JENNINGS BRYAN "BILLY". B. 7 July 1909, New Albany, Indiana. D. 5 September 1992, West Palm Beach, Florida. Throughout the 1930s and until he entered the U.S. Navy in 1944, the 5-foot, 11-inch, 180-pound Billy Herman was the **National League's (NL)** premier **second baseman**. He made his debut late in the 1931 season with the **Chicago Cubs**. By the next year, he was the Cubs' regular second baseman, a position he retained until 1941. The right-handed-hitting Herman batted above .300 in seven different full seasons in his career, and he was a member of the NL **All-Star** team for 10 consecutive seasons, 1934 to 1943. His best season was 1935, when he batted .341 for the pennant-winning Cubs, while leading the league with 227 **hits** and 57 **doubles**. On 6 May 1941, he was traded to the **Brooklyn Dodgers** in a deal that proved crucial to Brooklyn winning its first NL pennant in 21 years.

Herman's **batting average** fell from .285 in 1941 to .256 in 1942. The next year, he bounced back with a .330 average, second only to **Stan Musial** of the **St. Louis Cardinals**. After spending the 1944 and 1945 seasons in the military, Herman was traded by the Dodgers to the **Boston Braves** on 15 June 1946. He batted a combined .298 for the two teams, but it was his last full season. Herman retired as a player after 15 games with the **Pittsburgh Pirates** in 1947. He finished his 15-year playing career with 2,345 hits and a .304 batting average. Herman managed the Pirates for part of the 1947 season and the **Boston Red Sox** briefly in 1964, all of 1965, and part of 1966. In 1975, the **Veterans Committee** elected Herman to the **National Baseball Hall of Fame**.

HERZOG, DORREL NORMAN ELVERT "WHITEY". B. 9 November 1931, New Athens, Illinois. Whitey Herzog was a left-handed-hitting **outfielder** in the **American League (AL)** for the **Washington Senators** (1956–1958), **Kansas City Athletics** (1958–1960), **Baltimore Orioles** (1961–1962), and **Detroit Tigers** (1963). The 5-foot, 11-inch, 182-pound Herzog had a career **batting average** of .257 in 634 games. After partial-season stints as the **manager** of the **Texas Rangers** in 1973 and the California Angels in 1974, Herzog was hired to manage the **Kansas City Royals** in 1975. He won three consecutive AL Western Division titles with the Royals (1976–1978), but the team lost to the **New York Yankees** in the **American League Championship Series** each year.

Herzog than managed the **St. Louis Cardinals** from 1980 to 1990, winning **National League (NL)** pennants in 1982, 1985, and 1987, and defeating the **Milwaukee Brewers** in the 1982 **World Series**. His overall managerial record was 1,281–1,125. He later became the **general manager** of the Angels. Herzog won the *Sporting News*'s **Manager of the Year Award** in 1982, and the **Baseball Writers' Association of America's** NL Manager of the Year Award in 1985. He was elected to the **National Baseball Hall of Fame** by the **Veterans Committee** as a manager in 2010.

HILL, JOHN PRESTON "PETE". B. 12 October 1882, Culpepper County, Virginia. D. 19 December 1951, Buffalo, New York. Pete Hill played on various **African American** teams from 1904 to 1925, mostly before the **Negro Leagues** were organized. The 6-foot, 1-inch, 215-pound **outfielder** played for the Philadelphia Giants, Leland Giants, **Chicago American Giants**, and Detroit Stars, among others. A left-handed **batter** and thrower, Hill was a consistent hitter and an outstanding outfielder. In 2006, he was elected to the **National Baseball Hall of Fame** in a special election conducted by the **Committee on African American Baseball**.

HILLTOP PARK. *See* NEW YORK YANKEES.

HINES, PAUL ALOYSIUS. B. 1 March 1855, Virginia. D. 10 July 1935, Hyattsville, Maryland. Paul Hines was a right-handed-hitting center fielder who played in three **major leagues** from 1872 to 1891. Hines played for the **Washington Nationals, Washington Blue Legs,** and Chicago White Stockings in the National Association; the **Chicago White Stockings, Providence Grays, Washington Nationals, Indianapolis Hoosiers,** Pittsburgh Alleghenys, and Boston Beaneaters in the **National League (NL)**; and the **Washington Statesmen** in the **American Association**. The 5-foot, 9-inch, 173-pound Hines led the NL in **batting average** and **total bases** with Providence in

1878 and 1879. Hines also led in **runs batted in** and **home runs** in 1878, making him the first **batter** to win the **Triple Crown**. He retired with a .302 career batting average and 2,133 **hits**, the third-highest total at the time.

HIT-AND-RUN. The hit-and-run describes a play where the **base runner** on **first base** breaks for **second base** as the **pitch** is thrown. Meanwhile, the **batter** tries to hit the ball through the area vacated by the **second baseman** or **shortstop** covering second base on what appears to be a **stolen base** attempt.

HIT BY PITCH (HBP). In 1884, the **American Association (AA)** became the first **major league** to allow a **batter** to take **first base** after being hit by a pitch. The **National League (NL)** followed in 1887. The current rule, 6.08b of the Major League Baseball rulebook, states a batter is awarded first base when he or his equipment (except for his bat) is touched by a pitched ball outside of the **strike zone** and he attempts to avoid it (or had no opportunity to avoid it), and he did not swing at the pitch.

For batters, the major league single-season leader in most times hit by a pitch is **Hughie Jennings** of the 1896 **Baltimore Orioles**, with 51. The single-season leader in the **American League (AL)** is Don Baylor of the 1986 **Boston Red Sox**, with 35. The career leader is Hughie Jennings, with 287. Jennings played for the **Louisville Colonels** of the AA (1891), **Louisville Colonels** of the NL (1892–1893), Baltimore Orioles of the NL (1893–1899), Brooklyn Superbas of the NL (1899–1900, 1903), **Philadelphia Phillies** of the NL (1901–1902), and **Detroit Tigers** of the AL (1907, 1909–1910, 1912, 1918).

For **pitchers**, the major league single-season leader in batters hit prior to 1893, when the pitching distance was extended to its current 60 feet, 6 inches, is Phil Knell of the 1891 **Columbus Solons** of the AA, with 54. The single-season leader after the change in the pitching distance is **Joe McGinnity** of the 1900 Brooklyn Superbas, with 40. The single-season leader in the AL is Chick Fraser of the 1901 **Philadelphia Athletics**, with 32.

The career leader is Gus Weyhing, with 277. Weyhing pitched for the **Philadelphia Athletics** of the AA (1887–1889, 1891), **Brooklyn Wonders** of the **Players' League** (1890), **Philadelphia Phillies** of the NL (1892–1895), **Pittsburgh Pirates** of the NL (1895), Louisville Colonels of the NL (1895–1896), **Washington Senators** of the NL (1898–1899), **St. Louis Cardinals** and Brooklyn Superbas of the NL (1900), Cleveland Blues of the AL (1901), and **Cincinnati Reds** of the NL (1901).

HITS (H). A **batter** is credited with a hit when he reaches **base** safely as the result of his batted ball without the benefit of any fielding **errors**. A hit may be a **single, double, triple,** or **home run.** The **major league** single-season leader in hits is **Ichiro Suzuki** of the 2004 **Seattle Mariners,** with 262. The single-season leaders in the **National League** are Lefty O'Doul of the 1929 **Philadelphia Phillies** and **Bill Terry** of the 1930 **New York Giants,** each with 254. The career leader is **Pete Rose,** with 4,256. Rose played for the **Cincinnati Reds** from 1963 through 1978 and 1984 through 1986, for the Philadelphia Phillies from 1979 through 1983, and for the **Montreal Expos** in 1984.

HITTING STREAK. A hitting streak refers to the number of consecutive official games in which a player gets at least one **hit.** The streak is ended when a player has at least one **plate appearance** and gets no hits. The streak does not end if all official plate appearances result in a **base on balls, hit by pitch, catcher's interference,** or sacrifice **bunt,** but it does end if the player has a **sacrifice fly** and no hit.

Joe DiMaggio of the **New York Yankees** holds the **major league** single-season record with a hit streak of 56 consecutive games in 1941. The **National League** single-season record is 44, held by **Willie Keeler** of the 1897 **Baltimore Orioles** and **Pete Rose** of the 1978 **Cincinnati Reds.**

Joe DiMaggio also holds the **minor-league** record, with 61 consecutive games for the San Francisco Seals of the Pacific Coast League in 1933. (Joe Wilhoit, who played for the Wichita Jobbers of the independent Western League, hit safely in 69 consecutive games in 1919.)

HOME PLATE. Beginning in 1868, home plate was a one-foot square. In 1874, it was rotated so that one point faced the pitcher, making the plate 17 inches wide instead of 12. It became a pentagon following the 1899 season and is now a five-sided slab of whitened rubber, 17 inches square with two of the corners removed so that one edge is 17 inches long, two adjacent sides are 8 1/2 inches, and the remaining two sides are 12 inches and set at an angle to make a point. It is the fourth and final of four stations on a baseball diamond that a **base runner** must safely touch in succession to score a **run** for that player's team.

HOME RUNS (HR). In modern-day baseball, a home run is most often achieved when a **batter** hits a ball that goes over the fence in **fair territory** on the fly, or hits the left-field or right-field foul pole on the fly. A home run can also be achieved inside the park, as it was most often in baseball's early days, by a batter hitting a ball over an **outfielder's** head, or between outfielders, and he is able to circle the **bases** while the ball is in play. The batter is credited with a **hit**, a run scored, and a **run batted in (RBI)**. He also gets credited with RBI for any runner who was on base when he hit the home run.

Before the emergence of **Babe Ruth**, Ned Williamson held the **major-league** record for most home runs in a season. Aided by a home field with favorable dimensions, Williamson had 27 for the 1884 Chicago White Stockings of the **National League**. Ruth broke the record as a member of the 1919 **Boston Red Sox**, with 29. He then broke his own record with 54 in 1920, 59 in 1921, and 60 in 1927, all as a member of the **New York Yankees**. **Roger Maris**, also of the Yankees, set a new record when he hit 61 in 1961. Maris's record was broken by **Mark McGwire**, who had 70 for the 1998 **St. Louis Cardinals**. McGwire's total was then superseded by the current record-holder, **Barry Bonds**, who hit 73 home runs for the 2001 **San Francisco Giants**. Maris still holds the **American League** record.

Roger Connor, with an eventual total of 138, was the career home run leader from 1895 to 1920. Babe Ruth, with an eventual total of 714, was the leader from 1921 to 1973. **Hank Aaron**, with an eventual total of 755, was the leader from 1974 to 2006. Barry Bonds, with 762, is the current career leader. Bonds played for the **Pittsburgh Pirates** from 1986 through 1992, and for the **San Francisco Giants** from 1993 through 2007

The all-time career leader in professional baseball is **Sadaharu Oh**, with 868 home runs. Oh played for the Central League's Yomiuri Giants in **Japan's** Nippon Professional Baseball from 1959 to 1980.

HOME TEAM. The home team is the team at whose park the game is played, or, if the game is played on neutral grounds, the home team shall be designated by mutual agreement. Before 1950, the home team had the option to bat first or last. Since 1950, the home team must bat last.

HOMESTEAD GRAYS. The Homestead Grays played in various **Negro Leagues** but had their greatest success after owner **Cum Posey** entered them in the **Negro National League (NNL)** in 1935. The Grays, who played their home games at **Forbes Field** in Pittsburgh and **Griffith Stadium** in Washington, won eight NNL pennants in the nine years from 1937 to 1945. Among the notable players from the Negro Leagues who played part of their careers with the Grays were **Cool Papa Bell, Oscar Charleston, Martin Dihigo, Bill Foster, Josh Gibson, Judy Johnson, Buck Leonard, Willie Wells, Joe Williams**, and **Jud Wilson**.

HOOPER, HARRY BARTHOLOMEW. B. 24 August 1887, Bell Station, California. D. 18 December 1974, Santa Cruz, California. Harry Hooper was an outstanding right fielder for the **Boston Red Sox** from 1909 to 1920, and

Figure 8.1. **Hank Aaron circling the bases on one of his 755 home runs.** *Credit: National Baseball Hall of Fame Library, Cooperstown, New York.*

for the **Chicago White Sox** from 1921 to 1925. He led **American League** right fielders in **fielding percentage** three times. Hooper, a speedy **leadoff hitter,** is the only man to have played on four Red Sox **World Series** winners—in 1912, 1915, 1916, and 1918. On 13 October 1915, against the **Philadelphia Phillies**, Hooper became the first player to hit two **home runs** in a World Series game. From 1910 to 1915, he teamed with center fielder **Tris Speaker** and left fielder Duffy Lewis to form one of baseball's all-time great **outfields**. The 5-foot, 10-inch, 168-pound Hooper batted left-handed and threw right-handed. He had a career **batting average** of .281, with 160 **triples** and 375 **stolen bases**. Hooper remains Boston's career leader in triples (130) and stolen bases (300). In 1971, the **Veterans Committee** elected him to the **National Baseball Hall of Fame**.

HORNSBY, ROGERS. B. 27 April 1896, Winters, Texas. D. 5 January 1963, Chicago, Illinois. During his 19 years in the **National League (NL)**, Rogers Hornsby was far and away the league's best **batter**. The right-handed-hitting **second baseman** won two **Triple Crowns**, with the **St. Louis Cardinals** in 1922 and 1925, and two **Most Valuable Player Awards**, with the Cardinals in 1925 and the **Chicago Cubs** in 1929. In 1924, he batted .424 for St. Louis, the NL's highest post-1900 single-season **batting average**. The 5-foot, 11-inch, 175-pound Hornsby played for the Cardinals from 1915 through 1926. Then, in a trade that involved two of the game's best players, he was traded to the **New York Giants** for their great second baseman, **Frankie Frisch**. After one year in New York, the Giants traded the often prickly and difficult-to-get-along-with Hornsby to the **Boston Braves**. He won another batting championship in 1928, his one year in Boston, and then was traded to the Chicago Cubs. Hornsby lasted four years with the Cubs, before playing part of the 1933 season back with the Cardinals, and then mostly part-time while he was the **manager** of the 1933 to 1937 **St. Louis Browns**.

Hornsby had his most productive years with the Cardinals. From 1920 to 1925, he won six consecutive batting titles, topping the .400 mark in three of those seasons. He led the NL in **on-base percentage** and **slugging percentage** in each of those six seasons and in total bases in five of them. Hornsby was also a **player-manager** for the Cardinals in 1925 and 1926, winning a **World Series** in 1926. Overall, Hornsby led the league in batting average and total bases seven times, in on-base percentage and slugging percentage nine times, in **runs** scored five times, in **extra-base hits** six times, and in **hits** and **runs batted in** four times. In addition to managing the Cardinals and Browns, he also managed the Boston Braves, Chicago Cubs, and **Cincinnati Reds**. His career batting average was .358, second all-time to only **Ty Cobb**. He had 2,930 hits and a .434 on-base percentage, eighth all-time. In 1942, the **Baseball Writers' Association of America** elected Hornsby to the **National Baseball Hall of Fame**.

HOUSTON ASTROS. The Houston Astros are a team in the Central Division of the **National League (NL)**. They entered the NL as the Houston Colt .45s in 1962—along with the **New York Mets**—as part of the NL's first **expansion** of the 20th century. The two new teams raised the NL's total to 10; it had been at eight since 1900. Houston played its home games at Colt Stadium from 1962 through 1964, before moving into the **Astrodome** in 1965, at which time they changed their name to the Astros. The Astrodome was Major League Baseball's first indoor stadium. In 2000, the Astros opened a new stadium, Enron Field, which is outdoors but has a retractable roof. The stadium was renamed **Minute Maid Park** in 2002.

The Astros lost in the **National League Division Series** in 1981, 1997, 1998, 1999, and 2001, and in the **National League Championship Series** in 1980, 1986, and 2004. They won their only NL pennant in 2005, as the **wild card** team, but the team was swept in four games by the **Chicago White Sox** in the **World Series**. In 2013, the Astros will move to the Western Division of the **American League** so that each league can have 15 teams.

Jeff Bagwell, in 1994, is the only Houston player who has won the **Most Valuable Player Award**. **Cy Young Award** winners are Mike Scott (1986) and **Roger Clemens** (2004). Jeff Bagwell, in 1991, is the Astros' only **Rookie of the Year** winner.

No Astros player has led the league in **batting average** or **home runs**. Leaders in **runs batted in** are Jeff Bagwell (1994) and Lance Berkman (2002).

Astros pitchers who have led the league in **wins** are Joe Niekro (1979), Mike Scott (1989), Mike Hampton (1999), and Roy Oswalt (2004). **Earned run average** leaders are J. R. Richard (1979), **Nolan Ryan** (1981, 1987), Mike Scott (1986), Danny Darwin (1990), Roger Clemens (2005), and Roy Oswalt (2006). **Strikeouts** leaders are J. R. Richard (1978–1979), Mike Scott (1986), and Nolan Ryan (1987–1988).

Other notable players and **managers** in Astros' history include Brad Ausmus, **Craig Biggio**, Enos Cabell, Cesar Cedeno, Jose Cruz, Glenn Davis, Larry Dierker, Bill Doran, Steve Finley, Ken Forsch, Pete Harnisch, Richard Hidalgo, Darryl Kile, Bob Knepper, Carlos Lee, **Joe Morgan**, Hunter Pence, Terry Puhl, Doug Rader, Shane Reynolds, Wandy Rodriguez, Dickie Thon, Bill Virdon, Billy Wagner, Bob Watson, Don Wilson, and Jimmy Wynn.

HOUSTON COLT .45s. *See* HOUSTON ASTROS.

HOYT, WAITE CHARLES. B. 9 September 1899, Brooklyn, New York. D. 25 August 1984, Cincinnati, Ohio. Right-hander Waite Hoyt was just 18 years old when he began his **major-league** career by pitching one game for the **New York Giants** in 1918. Giants **manager John McGraw** was unimpressed, but over the next 20 seasons, the 6-foot, 180-pound Hoyt pitched in the **American League (AL)** for the **Boston Red Sox** (1919–1920), **New York Yankees** (1921–1930), **Detroit Tigers** (1930–1931), and **Philadelphia Athletics** (1931). He then returned to the **National League (NL)** in 1932, splitting the season with the Giants and **Brooklyn Dodgers**. Hoyt also pitched in the NL for the **Pittsburgh Pirates** (1933–1937) before ending his career with the Dodgers in 1937 and 1938.

Aside from 1934, when he went 15–6 for the Pirates, Hoyt's best years were with the Yankees of the 1920s. He had his only two 20-win seasons with the Yankees, 22 in 1927, to lead the AL, and 23 in 1928. Hoyt had a 6–4 record in seven **World Series**, six with New York and one with Philadelphia. He turned in a spectacular performance against the Giants in the 1921 Series. Although he won only two of his three starts, he pitched three **complete games** and allowed no **earned runs**. Hoyt had a career record of 237–182. He later became a broadcaster for the Reds, a job he held from 1942 to 1965. He was elected by the **Veterans Committee** to the **National Baseball Hall of Fame** in 1969.

HUBBARD, ROBERT CALVIN "CAL". B. 31 October 1900, Keytesville, Missouri. D. 17 October 1977, St. Petersburg, Florida. Cal Hubbard was a successful football player for Centenary College in Louisiana and Geneva College in Pennsylvania before entering the National Football League in 1927. For the next 10 seasons, Hubbard was an outstanding tackle for the New York Giants and Green Bay Packers. He joined the **American League (AL)** umpiring staff in 1936 and remained an AL **umpire** through the 1951 season, when an injury to his right eye forced him to retire. During his 16-year career, Hubbard umpired 2,470 **major-league** games, three **All-Star Games**, and in four **World Series**. From 1954 through 1969, he was the assistant supervisor of AL umpires. Hubbard, who had previously been elected to the College Football Hall of Fame and the Professional Football Hall of Fame, was elected by the **Veterans Committee** to the **National Baseball Hall of Fame** in 1976. He is the only person elected to both the professional football and Major League Baseball Halls of Fame.

HUBBELL, CARL OWEN, "KING CARL," "THE MEAL TICKET". B. 22 June 1903, Carthage, Missouri. D. 21 November 1988, Scottsdale, Arizona. Known as "The Meal Ticket" for his dependability, Carl Hubbell pitched for the **New York Giants** for 16 seasons, from 1928 to 1943. The 6-foot, 170-pound left-hander used an exceptional **screwball** to win 253 games (253–154). Hubbell was a 20-game winner for five consecutive seasons (1933–1937), during which time he led the **National League (NL)** in **wins** three times and **earned run average** three times. Hubbell was the NL's **Most**

Valuable Player in 1933 and 1936, and he was selected by the *Sporting News* as the **Major League Player of the Year** in 1936. He won his final 16 decisions in 1936, and his first eight in 1937, for a combined 24-game winning streak, a **major league** two-season record.

Hubbell helped lead the Giants to pennants in 1933, 1936, and 1937. He was 2–0 in the 1933 **World Series** win against the **Washington Senators** and 1–1 in both the 1936 and 1937 losses to the **New York Yankees**. He was chosen to the **All-Star** team nine times. In the 1934 game, he struck out **Babe Ruth, Lou Gehrig, Jimmie Foxx, Al Simmons**, and **Joe Cronin** consecutively, one of baseball's most memorable feats. Hubbell continued to work for the Giants after his retirement as an active player, serving as a **scout** and director of the farm system. In 1947, the **Baseball Writers' Association of America** elected him to the **National Baseball Hall of Fame**.

HUBERT H. HUMPHREY METRODOME. *See* MINNESOTA TWINS.

HUGGINS, MILLER JAMES "HUG". B. 27 March 1878, Cincinnati, Ohio. D. 25 September 1929, New York, New York. Miller Huggins was a **second baseman** with a .265 career **batting average** for 13 seasons in the **National League (NL)**. Huggins, a slightly built 5-foot, 6-inch, 140-pound **switch-hitter**, led the NL in walks four times while playing for the **Cincinnati Reds** (1904–1909) and **St. Louis Cardinals** (1910–1916). Huggins, who had a law degree, served as the **manager** of weak Cardinals teams from 1913 to 1917, compiling a 346–415 record. In 1918, he signed to manage the **New York Yankees**, a team that had yet to win its first pennant. Often disparaged by the press, the fans, and Yankees co-owner Til Huston, Huggins had the full support of the team's other co-owner, **Jacob Ruppert**.

New York acquired **Babe Ruth** in 1920, and although Ruth and some other team members often caused Huggins discipline problems, the Yankees won consecutive pennants in 1921, 1922, and 1923. After losing the **World Series** to the **New York Giants** in 1921 and 1922, they defeated the Giants in 1923 for the team's first world championship. Under Huggins, the Yankees won three consecutive pennants again, from 1926 to 1928, with World Series wins over the **Pittsburgh Pirates** in 1927 and the Cardinals in 1928. Huggins fell ill late in the 1929 season and died on 25 September. The cause of death was determined to be sepsis (blood poisoning.) His won-lost record in 12 years in New York was 1,067–719. Huggins was elected to the **National Baseball Hall of Fame** by the **Veterans Committee** as a manager in 1964.

HULBERT, WILLIAM AMBROSE. B. 23 October 1832, Burlington Flats, New York. D. 10 April 1882, Chicago, Illinois. William Hulbert began his baseball career in 1875 as president of the **Chicago White Stockings** of the National Association (NA). The NA folded after the season, and, in 1876, Hulbert brought the White Stockings into the new **National League,** which he and **Al Spalding** helped found. The next year he became the league president. Until his death in 1882, Hulbert was influential in helping gain respectability for Major League Baseball. The **Veterans Committee** elected him to the **National Baseball Hall of Fame** in 1995.

HUNTER, JAMES AUGUSTUS "JIM," "CATFISH". B. 8 April 1946, Hertford, North Carolina. D. 9 September 1999, Hertford, North Carolina. Catfish Hunter joined the **Kansas City Athletics** as a 19-year-old in 1965. In 1968, owner Charles Finley moved the club to Oakland, where they became the **Oakland Athletics.** In May of that season, Hunter, a 6-foot, 190-pound right-hander, pitched a **perfect game** against the **Minnesota Twins.** By 1971, Oakland had developed into the best team in the **American League (AL),** playing in four **American League Championship Series (ALCS)** and winning three consecutive **World Series** (1972–1974). Hunter was their best pitcher, winning 21, 21, 21, and a league-leading 25 games those four seasons. He led in **winning percentage** in 1972 and 1973, and in **earned run average** in 1974. He won the **Cy Young Award** in 1974 and was also the *Sporting News*'s choice as AL **Pitcher of the Year.**

After a contract dispute with Finley, Hunter became one of the first big-name stars to declare himself a **free agent,** and he signed to play for the **New York Yankees** in 1975. He again led the AL in wins (23) in 1975, but injuries shortened his career. Hunter, who was an eight time **All-Star,** had a combined 4–3 record in the ALCS, and a 5–3 record in six World Series, three with Oakland and three with New York. He had a career record of 224–166, with 42 **shutouts.** He was elected by the **Baseball Writers' Association of America** to the **National Baseball Hall of Fame** in 1987.

HUNTINGDON GROUNDS. *See* PHILADELPHIA PHILLIES.

HUNTINGTON AVENUE BASEBALL GROUNDS. *See* BOSTON RED SOX.

HUTCH AWARD. The Hutch Award is given annually to an active **major-league** player who best exemplifies the fighting spirit and competitive desire of former major-league **pitcher** and **manager** Fred Hutchinson. The award was created in 1965, one year after Hutchinson's death from cancer at the age of 45. The first winner was **Mickey Mantle** of the **New York Yankees**. The 2012 winner was Barry Zito of the **San Francisco Giants**.

I

INDIANAPOLIS BLUES (NL). The Indianapolis Blues were a team in the **National League** in 1878. They finished in fifth place, with a 24–36 record. Attendance was poor, and the club withdrew from the league after the one season. Notable players for the Blues were John Clapp and Orator Shafer.

INDIANAPOLIS HOOSIERS (AA). The Indianapolis Hoosiers, also called the Blues, were members of the **American Association (AA)** in 1884. The Hoosiers finished 12th in the 13-team league, with 29 wins and 78 losses. When the AA cut back to eight teams for the 1885 season, the Indianapolis franchise was dropped.

INDIANAPOLIS HOOSIERS (FL). The Indianapolis Hoosiers were a team in the **Federal League (FL)** in 1914, the first of the two seasons the FL existed as a **major league**. The Hoosiers won the league pennant. They were led by Benny Kauff, who won the batting title (.370); Frank LaPorte, who led in **runs batted in** (107); and **pitcher** Cy Falkenburg, the **strikeouts** leader (236). Other notable players for the Hoosiers included Vin Campbell, **Bill McKechnie**, George Mullin, and Al Scheer. Because the FL wanted to establish itself in the New York metropolitan area, they planned to move the **Kansas City Packers** to Newark, New Jersey, in 1915. But just before the season began, the league chose to move the Indianapolis club instead. The team was renamed the **Newark Peppers**.

INDIANAPOLIS HOOSIERS (NL). The Indianapolis Hoosiers played three seasons in the **National League (NL)** (1887–1889) after taking over the franchise vacated by the **St. Louis Maroons**. The Hoosiers finished eighth in 1887, and seventh in 1888 and 1889. In an attempt to compete with the **Players' League**, the NL arranged to have several of the Hoosiers' best players moved to other franchises for the 1890 season, which led to the team's demise. Notable players for the Hoosiers included Jerry Denny, Jack Glasscock, **Paul Hines**, and **Amos Rusie**.

INFIELD FLY RULE. The purpose of the infield fly rule is to prevent **infielders** from intentionally dropping pop flies to make **double plays** or **triple plays**. An infield fly is a fair fly ball (not including a line drive or an attempted **bunt**) that can be caught by an infielder with ordinary effort, when **first base** and **second base**, or first base, second base, and **third base** are occupied, before two are out. The **pitcher, catcher,** and any **outfielder** who stations himself in the infield on the play shall be considered infielders for the purpose of this rule. When it seems apparent that a batted ball will be an infield fly, the **umpire** shall immediately declare "infield fly" for the benefit of the **base runners**. The ball is alive, and runners may advance at the risk of the ball being caught, or retouch and advance after the ball is touched, the same as on any fly ball. If the fly ball is near the **foul lines**, the umpire must declare "infield fly, if fair." If the ball is not caught and ends up foul (including if it lands fair and then rolls foul), infield fly is cancelled and the play is treated as an ordinary **foul ball**. If the ball lands foul and then rolls fair, infield fly takes effect and the **batter** is out.

INFIELDER (IF). The alignment of the defensive team consists of four infielders—a **first baseman, second baseman, third baseman,** and **shortstop**—who mostly position themselves in the dirt area of the infield diamond. The first baseman plays close to the **first base** bag, the second baseman mostly positions himself between the first base bag and **second base** bag, the third baseman plays close to the **third base** bag, and the shortstop positions himself between the second base bag and third base bag. In the numbering system used to record defensive plays, the first baseman is assigned the number 3, the second baseman is assigned the number 4, the third baseman is assigned the number 5, and the shortstop is assigned the number 6.

INNING. An inning is that portion of a game within which the teams alternate on offense and defense and in which there are three **putouts** for each team. Each team's time at bat is a half inning.

INNINGS PITCHED (IP). Innings pitched (IP) is a statistic used for **pitchers**. A pitcher is credited with one-third of an IP for each **out** he registers. If he gets three outs in an **inning**, that equals one IP. In the early days of Major League Baseball, teams carried few pitchers and the vast majority of IP were attributed to one pitcher. Thus, the all-time single-season leader in IP is Will White of the 1879 **Cincinnati Reds** of the **National League (NL)**, with 680.

The single-season leader post-1893, when the pitching distance was extended to its current 60 feet, 6 inches, is **Amos Rusie** of the 1893 **New York Giants**, with 482. The single-season leader in the **American League (AL)** is

Ed Walsh of the 1908 **Chicago White Sox**, with 464. The career leader is **Cy Young**, with 7,356. Young pitched for Cleveland of the NL (1890–1898), St. Louis of the NL (1899–1900), Boston of the AL (1901–1908), Cleveland of the AL (1909–1911), and Boston of the NL (1911).

INTENTIONAL BASE ON BALLS (IBB). The intentional **base on balls**, or intentional walk, almost always occurs when there is no **base runner** at **first base**. It is done to bypass the current **batter** to face the following batter, whom the defensive team expects a better chance of getting out, to set up a **double play**, or to set up a **force play** at any **base**.

The **major league** single-season leader in receiving intentional walks, which has been an official statistic only since 1955, is **Barry Bonds** of the 2004 **San Francisco Giants**, with 120. The **American League** single-season leaders are **Ted Williams** of the 1957 **Boston Red Sox** and John Olerud of the 1993 **Toronto Blue Jays**, each with 33. Bonds is the career leader, with 688. He played for the **Pittsburgh Pirates** from 1986 through 1992 and the **San Francisco Giants** from 1993 through 2007.

INTERFERENCE. Offensive interference is an act by the team at bat that interferes with, obstructs, impedes, hinders, or confuses any **fielder** attempting to make a play. If the **umpire** declares the **batter** or a **base runner** out for interference, all other runners shall return to the last **base** that was in the judgment of the umpire, legally touched at the time of the interference, unless otherwise provided by these rules. In the event that the batter-runner has not reached first base, all runners shall return to the base last occupied at the time of the pitch.

Defensive interference is an act by a fielder which hinders or prevents a batter from hitting a pitch.

Umpire's interference occurs (a) When an umpire hinders, impedes, or prevents a **catcher's** throw attempting to prevent a **stolen base,** or (b) When a **fair ball** touches an umpire on fair territory before passing a fielder.

Spectator interference occurs when a spectator reaches out of the stands, or goes on the playing field, and touches a live ball. On any interference call, the ball is dead.

INTERLEAGUE PLAY. Interleague play, which began in 1997, describes regular-season games played between a team from the **American League** and a team from the **National League**. All interleague games are counted toward official team and league records.

INTERNATIONAL BASEBALL FEDERATION (IBAF). The International Baseball Federation (IBAF) is the worldwide governing body that oversees, decides, and executes the policy of baseball at the international level. One of its principal responsibilities is to organize, standardize, and sanction international competitions among its 118 national member federations through its various tournaments to determine a world champion and calculate world rankings for both men's and **women's baseball**. The IBAF is the lone entity that can assign the title of "world champion" to any baseball team delegated to represent a nation. The IBAF's headquarters are located in Lausanne, Switzerland.

IRVIN, MONFORD MERRILL "MONTE". B. 25 February 1919, Haleburg, Alabama. Monte Irvin began his professional career in 1938, with the **Newark Eagles** of the **Negro National League**. Irvin played for Newark both before and after World War II, with three years out for service in the U.S. Army. He was a member of the league's **All-Star** team in 1941, and again from 1946 through 1948. The Eagles disbanded in 1948, whereupon Irvin signed to play for the **New York Giants** of the **National League**. On 8 July 1949, Irvin and Hank Thompson were the first two **African Americans** to play for the Giants.

Manager **Leo Durocher** used the 6-foot, 1-inch, 195-pound Irvin primarily as an **outfielder**, with occasional stints as a **first baseman**. Irvin's best season was 1951, when he helped the Giants overcome a 13-game deficit and defeat the **Brooklyn Dodgers** for the pennant. The right-handed-hitting Irvin batted .312, led the league with 121 **runs batted in**, and finished third in the voting for the **Most Valuable Player Award**. He batted .458 in the **World Series** and stole home in Game One. The Giants lost in six games to the **New York Yankees**. In 1952, Irvin broke his ankle in **spring training** and played in only 46 games. He bounced back to bat .329 in 1953. After two more seasons in New York, Irvin played a final season with the **Chicago Cubs** in 1956. After retiring, he worked briefly as a **scout** for the **New York Mets** and, beginning in 1968, spent 17 years doing public relations in the Office of the **Commissioner of Baseball**. In 1973, the **Negro Leagues Committee** elected Irvin to the **National Baseball Hall of Fame**.

ITALY. Baseball was introduced in Italy during the late 19th century. On 27 June 1948, Giuriati Stadium in Milan hosted the first baseball game played by Italians on Italian soil. On 1 November of that same year, Bologna won the first edition of the championship in what would become the Italian Baseball League (Federazione Italiana Baseball). The current league consists of the following eight teams: Fortitudo Baseball Club 1953 Bologna, De Angelis Godo, Montepaschi Baseball Club Orioles Grosseto, Danesi Nettuno, Novara Baseball United, Cariparma Parma Baseball, Telemarket Rimini, and T&A San Marino.

Italy won the first **European Baseball Championship** in 1954, and, along with the **Netherlands**, the country has dominated the competition ever since. The tournament is held every other year, in even-numbered years. Italy won the most recent European Baseball Championship, held in the Netherlands in September 2012. The Italian National team also plays in the **Baseball World Cup** and **World Baseball Classic**. Of the seven **major leaguers** born in Italy, Reno Bertoia, who played 10 seasons in the **American League** (1953–1962), was the most successful.

J

JACK MURPHY STADIUM. *See* SAN DIEGO PADRES.

JACKIE ROBINSON AWARD. *See* ROOKIE OF THE YEAR AWARD.

JACKSON, JOSEPH JEFFERSON "JOE," "SHOELESS JOE". B. 16 July 1887, Pickens County, South Carolina. D. 5 December 1951, Greenville, South Carolina. Joe Jackson is the best known of the eight **Chicago White Sox** players accused of deliberately losing the 1919 **World Series** to the **Cincinnati Reds**. Jackson batted .375 in the Series and was later exonerated by a jury; nevertheless, he was permanently barred from baseball by **Commissioner Kenesaw Landis** following the 1920 season. Jackson, a 6-foot, 1-inch, 200-pound left-handed-hitting **outfielder**, spent 13 seasons (1908–1920) in the **American League (AL)**, two (1908 and 1909) with the **Philadelphia Athletics**, in which he appeared in just 10 games, and then 11 seasons with the **Cleveland Indians** and the White Sox. (The White Sox acquired him from Cleveland in an August 1915 trade.) Between 1910 and 1920, Jackson ranked behind only **Ty Cobb** as the AL's best hitter. His .408 average in 1911 is the highest ever for a **rookie** and the highest ever for a second-place finisher. (Cobb led with .420.) Jackson ended his career with a .356 lifetime **batting average**, the third highest all-time.

JACKSON, REGINALD MARTINEZ "REGGIE," "MR. OCTOBER". B. 18 May 1946, Abington, Pennsylvania. Reggie Jackson was chosen by the **Kansas City Athletics** as the second overall pick in the 1966 **Amateur Draft**. Jackson, an **outfielder**, joined the Athletics for 35 games in 1967. The following season, owner Charles Finley moved the franchise to Oakland. Jackson hit 29 **home runs** in 1968, and he also led the **American League (AL)** in **strikeouts**. It was the first of four consecutive years, and five overall, in which he would lead the AL in strikeouts. In 1969, the 6-foot, 195-pound left-handed **batter** established himself as one of baseball's top power hitters. He slugged 47 home runs, had 118 **runs batted in (RBI)**, tallied a league-leading .608 **slugging percentage**, and scored a league-leading 123

runs. Jackson was a key factor, as Oakland finished first in the AL's Western Division for five consecutive years, from 1971 through 1975, and won three consecutive **World Series**, from 1972 to 1974. In 1973, he won the **Most Valuable Player Award** and was voted **Major League Player of the Year** for leading the AL with 32 home runs, 117 RBI, 99 runs, and a .531 slugging percentage.

Just before the start of the 1976 season, Oakland traded Jackson to the **Baltimore Orioles**. He spent one year in Baltimore, again leading the league in slugging percentage, and then declared for **free agency**. **George Steinbrenner**, owner of the **New York Yankees**, signed Jackson to a lucrative five-year contract. Jackson continued to be a productive player, but his self-aggrandizement caused conflict with **manager** Billy Martin and several Yankees players during his stay in New York. He played in three more World Series with the Yankees, in 1977, 1978, and 1981. In the sixth and deciding game of the 1977 Series against the **Los Angeles Dodgers**, Jackson hit three consecutive home runs on three consecutive pitches. That, along with his .755 slugging percentage and 10 home runs in World Series play, earned him the name "Mr. October." When Jackson's contract expired after the 1981 season, he signed with the California Angels. He spent his final season, 1987, back in Oakland. A 14-time **All-Star**, Jackson ended his career with 2,584 **hits**, including 563 home runs. He also struck out an all-time high 2,597 times. In 1993, he was elected by the **Baseball Writers' Association of America** to the **National Baseball Hall of Fame**.

JACKSON, TRAVIS CALVIN. B. 2 November 1903, Waldo, Arkansas. D. 27 July 1987, Waldo, Arkansas. Travis Jackson played 15 years for the **New York Giants**, beginning with three games in 1922 and going through 1936. For most of his career, he was New York's regular **shortstop**, displaying great range and an outstanding throwing arm. Jackson led **National League** shortstops in **assists** four times, **total chances** three times, and **fielding percentage** and **double plays** twice each. Knee problems forced him to move to **third base** in his final two seasons. For his final five seasons, Jackson was the team captain of the Giants. A right-handed **batter**, the 5-foot, 10-inch, 160-pound Jackson had six seasons of bettering the .300 mark, including a .339 **batting average** in 1930. He played on four pennant winners under **managers John McGraw** and **Bill Terry**, but he hit a meager .149 in four **World Series**. Jackson, who had a .291 lifetime batting average, was elected to the **National Baseball Hall of Fame** by the **Veterans Committee** in 1982.

JACOBS FIELD. *See* PROGRESSIVE FIELD.

JAPAN. Japanese baseball dates to the mid-1870s, when the Shimbashi Athletic Club and Imperial University, among others, began playing the game. In the years before World War II, such **major-league** teams as the **Chicago White Sox** and **New York Giants** (1913) and a team of **All-Stars** (1934) played exhibition games in Japan. It was in the mid-1930s that Nippon Professional Baseball was founded. Nippon Professional Baseball currently consists of two six-team leagues. The Central League has the Chunichi Dragons, located in Nagoya; the Hanshin Tigers, located in Nishinomiya; the Hiroshima Toyo Carp, located in Hiroshima; the Tokyo Yakult Swallows, located in Tokyo; the Yokohama De NA Bay Stars, located in Yokohama; and the Yomiuri Giants, located in Tokyo.

The Pacific League has the Chiba Lotte Marines, located in Chiba City, Chiba; the Fukuoka SoftBank Hawks, located in Fukuoka, Fukuoka; the Hokkaido Nippon-Ham Fighters, located in Sapporo, Hokkaido; the Orix Buffaloes, located in Osaka, Osaka; the Saitama Seibu Lions, located in Tokorozawra, Saitama; and the Tohuku Rakuten Golden Eagles, located in Sendai, Miyagi. The winners from the two leagues compete in the Japan Series.

In 2000, the **Chicago Cubs** and **New York Mets** opened the season by playing two games at the **Tokyo Dome**, the first regular-season major-league games played in Asia. Since then, the **New York Yankees** and Tampa Bay Devil Rays played two games there to open the 2004 season, and the **Boston Red Sox** opened the 2008 season with a game at the Tokyo Dome against the **Oakland Athletics**. The Athletics and **Seattle Mariners** played a two-game series at the Tokyo Dome to open the 2012 season.

In international play, Japan has won the **World Baseball Classic** both times since the tournament was created. They defeated **Cuba** in 2006 and **South Korea** in 2009.

The most notable player in Japanese baseball is **Sadaharu Oh**, who played for the Yomiuri Giants from 1959 to 1980. Oh's 868 career **home runs** are the most ever by a professional player.

Other notable players who have played professionally in Japan include Takehio Bessho, Hideo Fujimoto, Yutaka Fukumoto, Isao Harimoto, Hiromitsu Kadota, Masaichi Kaneda, Sachio Kinugasa, Kazuhiro Kiyohara, Masaaki Koyama, Shigeo Nagashima, Katsuya Nomura, Victor Starffin, Keishi Suzuki, Kazuyoshi Tatsunami, Koji Yamamoto, and Tetsua Yoneda.

Notable Japanese-born players who have played in the major leagues include Yu Darvish, Kosuke Fukudome, Hideki Irabu, Hiroki Kuroda, Hideki Matsui, Kazuo Matsui, Daisuke Matsuzaka, Masanori Murakami (the first Japanese-born major leaguer), Hideo Nomo, Hideki Okajima, **Ichiro Suzuki**, So Taguchi, and Koji Uehara.

JARRY PARK (PARC JARRY). *See* MONTREAL EXPOS.

Figure 10.1.   Japan's Sadaharu Oh is professional baseball's all-time leading home run hitter. *National Baseball Hall of Fame Library, Cooperstown, N.Y.*

JEFFERSON STREET GROUNDS. *See* PHILADELPHIA ATHLETICS (NL).

JENKINS, FERGUSON ARTHUR "FERGIE". B. 13 December 1942, Chatham, Ontario, **Canada**. **Pitcher** Ferguson Jenkins won two games for the **Philadelphia Phillies** as a **rookie** in 1965. The following April, he was traded to the **Chicago Cubs**, where, in 1967, he began a string of six consecutive 20-win seasons, including 24 **wins** in 1971, the best in the **National League (NL)**. But afterward, he won only 14 games in 1973, and the Cubs traded the 6-foot, 5-inch, 205-pound right-hander to the **Texas Rangers**. In Jenkins's first season in Texas, 1974, he led the **American League** with 25 wins. He also led in **complete games**, the fourth time he had led his league in that department, and he was voted Comeback Player of the Year. The Rangers traded Jenkins to the **Boston Red Sox** in November 1975. Two years later, the Red Sox traded him back to the Rangers. He spent four more years in Texas and then signed as a **free agent** and spent his final two seasons, 1982 and 1983, back with the Cubs.

Jenkins won the NL **Cy Young Award** in 1971, along with the *Sporting News*'s NL **Pitcher of the Year** Award. He finished second twice and third twice in Cy Young Award voting. Jenkins's career record was 284–226, with 49 **shutouts**. In 4,500 2/3 **innings pitched**, he had 3,192 **strikeouts** and only 997 walks. Jenkins is the only pitcher to have more than 3,000 strikeouts and fewer than 1,000 walks. In 1991, he was elected by the **Baseball Writers' Association of America** to the **National Baseball Hall of Fame**, the first Canadian-born player so honored.

JENNINGS, HUGH AMBROSE "HUGHIE," "EE-YAH". B. 2 April 1869, Pittston, Pennsylvania. D. 1 February 1928, Scranton, Pennsylvania. Hughie Jennings was the **shortstop** for the famed **Baltimore Orioles** teams of the mid-1890s. After batting .293 as a **rookie** with the **Louisville Colonels** of the **American Association** in 1891, Jennings floundered for the next season and a half with the Louisville club of the **National League (NL)**. He was traded to the NL Orioles in June 1893, where he blossomed under the aggressive, heads-up style of **manager Ned Hanlon**. The right-handed-hitting Jennings batted .359 over six and a half seasons with Baltimore, including a career-high .401 in 1896. Jennings, who stood 5 feet, 8 inches, and weighed 165 pounds, led the league in being **hit by pitch** for five consecutive seasons, from 1894 to 1898. Defensively, he led all NL shortstops in **putouts** four times and **fielding percentage** three times. The Orioles finished in first place from 1894 to 1896, and in second place in 1897 and 1898. They participated in each of the four **Temple Cup** championship series.

In 1899, a syndicate formed that controlled both the Orioles and the Brooklyn Superbas. Jennings played with the Superbas in 1899 and 1900, with the **Philadelphia Phillies** in 1901 and 1902, and a final six games with Brooklyn in 1903. Late in his career, he shifted from shortstop to **first base**. In 1907, Jennings was named to manage the **Detroit Tigers**. He led the Tigers to **American League** pennants in his first three seasons in Detroit, but the team lost each year in the **World Series**. He managed the Tigers through 1920, but he never won another pennant. He later served as a **coach** and occasional fill-in manager with the **New York Giants** under his old Baltimore teammate, **John McGraw**. Jennings batted .312 for his career and is still the all-time leader in hit by pitch, with 287. In 1945, the **Old Timers Committee** elected him to the **National Baseball Hall of Fame** as a player.

JETER, DEREK SANDERSON. B. 26 June 1974, Pequannock, New Jersey. **Shortstop** Derek Jeter was the first-round choice (sixth overall) of the **New York Yankees** in the 1992 **Amateur Draft**. After appearing briefly with the Yankees in 1995, he batted .314 in 1996 and was the **American League (AL) Rookie of the Year**. Overall, the 6-foot, 3-inch, 195-pound right-handed **batter** has hit .300 or higher 12 times, including a career high .349 in 1999. Named team captain in 2003, Jeter is the Yankees' all-time leader in **games played, at-bats, hits, singles,** and **stolen bases**. Jeter is a 13-time **All-Star**. Because of the Yankees' success during his career, he has played on seven **World Series** teams, including five Series winners. His **batting average** in 38 Series games is .321. Jeter was the **Most Valuable Player** and winner of the **Babe Ruth Award** for his outstanding play in the 2000 Series against the **New York Mets**.

Jeter has also won the **Hank Aaron Award** twice (2006, 2009), the **Roberto Clemente Award** (2009), the **Lou Gehrig Memorial Award** (2011), four **Silver Slugger Awards**, and five **Gold Glove Awards**. At the end of the 2012 season, he had played 2,531 games at shortstop, the third highest total ever. His batting average was .313, with 3,304 hits and 1,868 **runs** scored. Still active in 2013, Jeter is sure to be elected to the **National Baseball Hall of Fame** when he becomes eligible.

JOE ROBBIE STADIUM. *See* SUN LIFE STADIUM.

JOHN, THOMAS EDWARD "TOMMY". B. 22 May 1943, Terre Haute, Indiana. Tommy John was a left-handed **pitcher** for six **major-league** teams in a career that lasted 26 seasons. In the **American League**, the 6-foot, 3-inch, 180-pound John pitched for the **Cleveland Indians** (1963–1964), **Chicago White Sox** (1965–1971), **New York Yankees** (1979–1982, 1986–1989), California Angels (1982–1985), and **Oakland Athletics**

(1985). In the **National League,** he was with the **Los Angeles Dodgers** from 1972 to 1974, and again from 1976 to 1978. John missed part of the 1974 season and all of 1975 with torn ligaments in his pitching arm. He underwent the first ligament transplant surgery, now commonly known as "Tommy John surgery," and returned to the Dodgers in 1976. He had a 10–10 record, was voted the Comeback Player of the Year, and earned the **Hutch Award.** In 1977, John won 20 games; he then left after the 1978 season to sign with the Yankees as a **free agent.** He was a 20-game winner twice with New York. John had a 288–231 career record and a 3.34 **earned run average.** He had 46 **shutouts** and led his league in shutouts three times. Yet, despite his outstanding career as a pitcher, Tommy John is best known and most remembered as the first successful recipient of Tommy John surgery.

JOHNSON, BYRON BANCROFT "BAN". B. 5 January 1864, Norwalk, Ohio. D. 28 March 1931, St. Louis, Missouri. Ban Johnson was president of the **minor-league** Western League from 1894 to 1899. In 1900, when the **National League (NL)** was reduced from 12 teams to eight, Johnson moved several of his Western League franchise to NL cities and renamed his league the **American League (AL).** The next year, the AL declared itself a **major league** and started a spirited competition for NL players. The AL proved successful at signing many star players from the NL and forced the older league to declare a truce. In 1903, the AL and NL agreed to play in the first modern **World Series,** a Series won by the AL's Boston Americans.

For the next 20 years, Johnson was the most powerful man in baseball; however, his frequent clashes with **Kenesaw Landis,** who became the **commissioner of baseball** in 1920, greatly diminished his power. The owners mostly sided with Landis, and, after ending up on the losing side of several highly publicized battles, Johnson resigned in July 1927. In 1937, the **Centennial Commission** elected Johnson to the **National Baseball Hall of Fame.**

JOHNSON, RANDALL DAVID "RANDY," "THE BIG UNIT". B. 10 September 1963, Walnut Creek, California. Randy Johnson's size and overpowering **fastball,** coupled with an intimidating manner, made the 6-foot, 10-inch, 225-pound left-hander one of baseball's best **pitchers** ever. In his 22-season career, Johnson pitched in the **National League (NL)** for the **Montreal Expos** (1988–1989), **Arizona Diamondbacks** (1999–2004, 2007–2008), **Houston Astros** (1998), and **San Francisco Giants** (2009). He was also with two **American League (AL)** teams, the **Seattle Mariners** (1989–1998) and **New York Yankees** (2005–2006).

Johnson, a three-time 20-game winner and 10-time **All-Star**, had his best seasons with Seattle and Arizona, going a combined 248–136 with those clubs. He led his league in **winning percentage, earned run average (ERA)**, and **complete games** four times each and **strikeouts** nine times. He topped the 300 mark in strikeouts six times, including five straight seasons from 1998 to 2002. He won the **Cy Young Award** with the Mariners in 1995, and he then added four more Cy Young Awards with the Diamondbacks, winning each year from 1999 to 2002. He was the runner-up for the award three times.

In addition, Johnson was the *Sporting News*'s choice as AL **Pitcher of the Year** in 1995, and he won the pitcher's **Triple Crown** in 2002. His performance in the 2001 **World Series** against the Yankees earned him the **Babe Ruth Award** and the **Most Valuable Player Award** for the Series. He defeated the Yankees three times without a loss and had a 1.04 ERA and 19 strikeouts in 17 1/3 innings. Johnson had a career record of 303–166, with a 3.29 ERA, 37 **shutouts**, and 4,875 strikeouts, second all-time to **Nolan Ryan**. Johnson, whose last active season was 2007, is sure to be elected to the **National Baseball Hall of Fame** when he becomes eligible.

JOHNSON, WALTER PERRY "THE BIG TRAIN". B. 6 November 1887, Humboldt, Kansas. D. 10 December 1946, Washington, D.C. Walter Johnson signed with the **Washington Senators** of the **American League (AL)** in 1907. The 19-year-old Johnson went 5–9 as a **rookie**, 14–14 in 1908, and 13–25 for the lowly Senators in 1909. During the span of the next 10 seasons, however, he won a total of 265 games, winning at least 20 in each season. In all, he had 12 seasons of 20 or more wins, and two seasons, 1912 and 1913, in which he won more than 30 games. His greatest season, and one of the greatest pitching seasons ever, was 1913, when he went 36–7—including a 16-game winning streak—with a 1.14 **earned run average (ERA)** and 11 **shutouts**.

Considered by many to be the best right-handed pitcher ever, the 6-foot, 1-inch, 200-pound Johnson led the AL in **wins** six times. During his 21-year career, all with Washington, he was the league leader in **winning percentage** twice, shutouts seven times, and ERA five times. The fastest pitcher of his era, Johnson led the AL in **strikeouts** 12 times, including eight consecutive seasons between 1912 and 1919. He topped the AL in **innings pitched** five times and **complete games (CG)** six times. Twice Johnson won the AL's **Most Valuable Player Award**, in 1913 (the **Chalmers Award**) and 1924. In both years, and in 1918, he was the winner of the **Triple Crown** for pitchers.

During his career, Johnson won 417 games and pitched 531 CG. Among all **major-league** pitchers, his win and CG totals are second only to **Cy Young** and first among AL pitchers. They are also first among all pitchers who began their careers after the mound was moved to 60 feet, 6 inches in

1893. Johnson had 110 shutouts, still a major-league record, and his 3,509 strikeouts remained the major-league record until it was broken by **Steve Carlton** in 1983.

Johnson pitched for Washington in two **World Series**, in 1924 against the **New York Giants**, and in 1925 against the **Pittsburgh Pirates**. His combined record in the two Series was 3–3, including a win in the seventh and deciding game in 1924. After his playing days were over, Johnson managed the Senators from 1929 to 1932, and the **Cleveland Indians** from June 1933 to August 1935. His highest finish was second place with the 1930 Senators. In 1936, Johnson, **Ty Cobb**, **Christy Mathewson**, **Babe Ruth**, and **Honus Wagner** were the first members elected by the **Baseball Writers' Association of America** to the new **National Baseball Hall of Fame**.

JOHNSON, WILLIAM JULIUS "JUDY". B. 26 October 1899, Snow Hill, Maryland. D. 14 June 1989, Wilmington, Delaware. Judy Johnson was a star **third baseman** in the **Negro Leagues** from 1918 to 1936. Among the teams Johnson played for were the Hilldale Daisies, **Homestead Grays**, and **Pittsburgh Crawfords**. The 5-foot, 11-inch, 150-pound right-handed **batter** was not a **home run** threat, but he often had a high **batting average**. In 1954, Johnson joined the **Philadelphia Phillies** of the **National League** as Major League Baseball's first **African American coach**. In 1975, a special **Negro Leagues Committee** elected him to the **National Baseball Hall of Fame**.

JONES, LARRY WAYNE "CHIPPER". B. 24 April 1972, Deland, Florida. Chipper Jones was selected by the **Atlanta Braves** as the first overall pick in the 1990 **Amateur Draft**. The 6-foot, 4-inch, 210-pound Jones made his debut in September 1993, but an anterior cruciate ligament injury to his knee kept him out of action for the entire 1994 season. Jones returned to stay in 1995, and, aside from 2002 and 2003, when he played left field, he was the Braves' **third baseman** through 2012. The **switch-hitting** Jones topped the .300 mark in 10 seasons and the 100 **runs batted in (RBI)** mark nine times. He was the **National League's (NL) Most Valuable Player** in 1999, and the league's batting champion in 2008, when he hit a career-high .364. A seven-time **All-Star**, he has a combined .288 **batting average** in 11 **National League Division Series**, six **National League Championship Series**, and three **World Series**. Jones has a .303 career **batting average**, with 1,623 RBI and 1,619 **runs** scored. His 468 **home runs** are the most ever by a NL switch-hitter. Jones, who retired after the 2012 season, is sure to be elected to the **National Baseball Hall of Fame** when he becomes eligible.

JOSS, ADRIAN "ADDIE". B. 12 April 1880, Woodland, Wisconsin. D. 14 April 1911, Toledo, Ohio. Addie Joss was only 31 years old when he died of tubercular meningitis in 1911. His career with the Cleveland Naps of the **American League (AL)** lasted just eight and a half seasons, from 1902 to 1910. During that time, the 6-foot, 3-inch, 185-pound right-hander won 160 games and lost only 97. He had 45 **shutouts** and a career **earned run average (ERA)** of 1.89. Only **Ed Walsh**, at 1.82, has a lower career ERA. Joss was a 20-game winner for four consecutive seasons (1905–1908), including an AL best 27 in 1907. He led the league in ERA in 1904 (1.59) and 1908 (1.16), and had two **no-hitters** (one a **perfect game**) and seven one-hitters. Despite his having played fewer than 10 seasons, the minimum for consideration, the **Veterans Committee** elected Joss to the **National Baseball Hall of Fame** in 1978.

K

KALINE, ALBERT WILLIAM "AL". B. 19 December 1934, Baltimore, Maryland. The **Detroit Tigers** signed 18-year-old Al Kaline as an amateur **free agent** in 1953, paying him a bonus of $35,000. Two years later, the 20-year-old right-handed-hitting Kaline became the youngest player ever to win a **major-league** batting championship. He captured the 1955 title with a .340 average, while also leading the league with 200 **hits**. The 6-foot, 1-inch, 175-pound Kaline played 22 seasons for the Tigers, and, although he never reached those totals again, he was a consistent hitter and an excellent defensive right fielder. He was a 15-time **American League All-Star**, winner of 10 **Gold Glove Awards**, and the winner of the **Lou Gehrig Award** in 1968 and the **Roberto Clemente Award** in 1973. His .379 **batting average** in the 1968 **World Series** helped lead the Tigers to a seven-game Series win over the **St. Louis Cardinals**. In 1974, his final season, Kaline became the 12th major leaguer to reach 3,000 hits. He finished his career with 3,007 hits, a .297 batting average, 399 **home runs**, and 1,583 **runs batted in**. After his playing career ended, Kaline, one of the Tigers' greatest and most popular players, stayed on in Detroit as a radio announcer and later in the front office. In 1980, the **Baseball Writers' Association of America** elected him to the **National Baseball Hall of Fame**.

KANSAS CITY ATHLETICS. The Kansas City Athletics came into existence in 1955. The Athletics had played in Philadelphia from 1901 through 1954, but, following the 1954 season, Arnold Johnson purchased the club and moved it to Kansas City. Home games were played at **Municipal Stadium** from 12 April 1955 through 27 September 1967. In their 13 years in Kansas City, under a succession of **managers**, the A's never had a winning record and never finished above sixth place. Johnson died in March 1960, and his heirs sold the team to Charles Finley. In 1968, Finley moved the Athletics to Oakland.

During the Athletics' 13 years in Kansas City, they had no winners of the **Most Valuable Player Award, Cy Young Award**, or **Rookie of the Year Award**. None of their hitters led the league in **batting average, home runs**, or **runs batted in**; none of their **pitchers** led the league in **wins, earned run average**, or **strikeouts**.

Among the players who made their **major-league** debut while the Athletics were in Kansas City were Sal Bando, Bert Campaneris, Ken Harrelson, Dick Howser, **Catfish Hunter, Reggie Jackson**, Hector Lopez, Rick Monday, and Joe Rudi. Other notable players for the Kansas City Athletics included Bob Cerv, Ed Charles, Bud Daley, **Roger Maris**, Vic Power, and Norm Siebern.

KANSAS CITY COWBOYS (AA). The Kansas City Cowboys were a team in the **American Association (AA)** in 1888 and 1889. After finishing eighth and seventh in the eight-team league, the Cowboys left the AA and joined the **minor league** Western Association for the 1890 season. The most notable player for the Cowboys was **Billy Hamilton**, who debuted with the team in 1888.

KANSAS CITY COWBOYS (NL). The Kansas City Cowboys were a team in the **National League (NL)** in 1886. Poor attendance and a dismal seventh-place finish led the NL to expel them after one season.

KANSAS CITY COWBOYS (UA). The Kansas City Cowboys were a team in the **Union Association (UA)** in 1884, the one year of the UA's existence. They joined the league in June and compiled a 16–63 record in their partial season.

KANSAS CITY MONARCHS. The Kansas City Monarchs were the longest-running franchise in the history of the **Negro Leagues**. They were also the most successful, winning 13 league titles. The Monarchs played in the **Negro National League** (1920–1931) and **Negro American League** (1937–1961), and as an independent (1932–1936, 1962–1965). Among the notable players from the Negro Leagues who played part of their careers with the Monarchs were Newt Allen, **Cool Papa Bell, Willard Brown**, Buck O'Neil, **Satchel Paige, Jackie Robinson, Bullet Rogan, Hilton Smith**, and **Turkey Stearnes**. In addition to Paige, Robinson, and Brown, other Monarchs who later played in the **major leagues** were **Ernie Banks**, Elston Howard, and Hank Thompson.

KANSAS CITY PACKERS. The Kansas City Packers were a team in the **Federal League (FL)** in 1914–1915, the two seasons the FL existed as a **major league**. Kansas City finished in sixth place in 1914, and in fourth place in 1915. The FL, wanting to establish itself in the New York metropolitan area, planned to move the Packers to Newark, New Jersey, for the 1915 season, but just before the season began, the league chose to move the **Indianapolis Hoosiers** club instead. Notable players for the Packers included Nick Cullop, Ted Easterly, Duke Kenworthy, and Gene Packard.

KANSAS CITY ROYALS. The Kansas City Royals are a team in the Central Division of the **American League (AL)**. The Royals and Seattle Pilots entered the AL in 1969 as part of a two-team AL expansion. (In 1970, the Seattle franchise was moved to Milwaukee and became the **Milwaukee Brewers**.) The Royals played their home games at **Municipal Stadium** from 1969 through 1972. They played their first game at their current home, **Kauffman Stadium**, on 10 April 1973. Prior to 2 July 1993, Kauffman Stadium was named Royals Stadium.

The Royals have reached the **World Series** twice, losing to the **Philadelphia Phillies** in six games in 1980, and defeating the **St. Louis Cardinals** in seven games in 1985. They also lost in the **American League Division Series** in the split season of 1981, and in the **American League Championship Series** in 1976, 1977, 1978, and 1984.

George Brett, in 1980, is the only member of the Kansas City Royals to win the AL's **Most Valuable Player Award**. **Cy Young Award** winners are Bret Saberhagen (1985, 1989), David Cone (1994), and Zack Greinke (2009). **Rookie of the Year** winners are Lou Piniella (1969), Bob Hamelin (1994), Carlos Beltran (1999), and Angel Berroa (2003).

Royals players who have led the league in **batting average** are George Brett (1976, 1980, 1990) and Willie Wilson (1982). The Royals have had no **home runs** leaders, and Hal McRae, in 1982, is the only Royal to lead in **runs batted in**.

Royals **pitchers** who have led the league in **wins** are Dennis Leonard (1977) and Bret Saberhagen (1989). **Earned run average** leaders are Bret Saberhagen (1989), Kevin Appier (1993), and Zack Greinke (2009). No Royals pitcher has ever led the AL in **strikeouts**.

Other notable **managers** and players in Royals' history include Steve Balboni, Steve Busby, Billy Butler, Johnny Damon, Alex Gordon, Tom Gordon, Mark Gubicza, Larry Gura, **Whitey Herzog**, Eric Hosmer, Dick Howser, Bo Jackson, Charlie Leibrandt, John Mayberry, Jeff Montgomery, Amos Otis, Freddie Patek, Dan Quisenberry, Joe Randa, Joakim Soria, Paul Splittorff, Mike Sweeney, Danny Tartabull, and Frank White.

KAUFFMAN STADIUM. Kauffman Stadium, located in Kansas City, Missouri, is the home field of the **Kansas City Royals** of the **American League**. Royals Stadium, as it was originally named, opened on 10 April 1973. The name was changed to Kauffman Stadium, in honor of the Royals' late owner, on 2 July 1993. The current seating capacity of Kauffman Stadium is approximately 37,900. Royals Stadium hosted the **major league All-Star Game** in 1973. Kauffman Stadium hosted the major league All-Star Game in 2012.

See also STADIUMS.

KEEFE, TIMOTHY JOHN "TIM". B. 1 January 1857, Cambridge, Massachusetts. D. 23 April 1933, Cambridge, Massachusetts. Tim Keefe **pitched** in the **major leagues** from 1880 to 1893. In his **rookie** season, Keefe set the single-season major-league record for lowest **earned run average (ERA)**, with a 0.86 mark for the **Troy Trojans** of the **National League (NL)**. When the Trojans disbanded after the 1882 season, Keefe moved to the **New York Metropolitans** of the **American Association (AA)**. In 1883, the 5-foot, 10-inch, 185-pound right-hander won 41 games for the Metropolitans, and he led the AA with 359 **strikeouts** and 619 **innings pitched**. After winning 37 games in 1884, Keefe moved to the **New York Giants** of the NL, where he won 172 games from 1885 to 1889. Keefe's best season was 1888, when he won the **Triple Crown** for pitchers, leading the NL with 35 **wins**, a 1.74 ERA, and 335 strikeouts. During the 1888 season, he compiled a record 19-game winning streak, and, in a championship series that was a predecessor to the modern **World Series**, he helped lead New York to a six games to four triumph over the **St. Louis Browns** of the AA by winning four games without a loss.

Along with many of his Giants teammates, Keefe left the club in 1890 to become part of the New York Giants team in the **Players' League (PL)**. The PL folded after one season, and Keefe was back with the NL Giants in 1891. After the Giants released him in July, he signed with the **Philadelphia Phillies** in August, where he finished his career. In his 14 seasons, Keefe won 342 games. He led his league twice in wins and strikeouts, and three times in ERA. After his playing career ended, Keefe was an **umpire** in the NL (1894–1896) and a **coach** at Harvard University, Princeton University, and Tufts University. In 1964, the **Veterans Committee** elected him to the **National Baseball Hall of Fame**.

KEELER, WILLIAM HENRY "WILLIE," "WEE WILLIE". B. 3 March 1872, Brooklyn, New York. D. 1 January 1923, Brooklyn, New York. Willie Keeler's ability to "hit 'em where they ain't" allowed him to accumulate 200 **hits** or more for the eight consecutive seasons from 1894 to 1901. Known as "Wee Willie" because of his small stature—he was just 5 feet, 4 inches and 140 pounds—Keeler played 19 seasons in the **major leagues**. He began in the **National League (NL)**, playing briefly with the **New York Giants** in 1892 and 1893, and with the Brooklyn Bridegrooms in 1893. Keeler was traded to the **Baltimore Orioles** in 1894, and both he and the Orioles blossomed. The Orioles won pennants in each of Keeler's first three years in Baltimore. The left-handed-hitting right fielder led the NL in hits and **batting average** in 1897 and 1898. He had a record-setting 44-game hitting streak in 1897, and he reached career highs that season, with 239 hits and a .424 batting average.

In 1899, Keeler was assigned to the Brooklyn Superbas, along with several of his Orioles teammates. Under **manager Ned Hanlon**, the Superbas won pennants in 1899 and 1900. Keeler again led the NL in hits in 1900, and he scored more than 100 **runs** in each season from 1894 to 1901. Prior to the 1903 season, Keeler jumped to the New York Highlanders, who were playing their first season in the **American League**, having replaced the Baltimore franchise. He topped the .300 mark in his first four seasons with New York, but he tailed off the next three before playing a partial final season with the Giants in 1910. Keeler had a .341 career batting average, with 2,932 hits. His 206 **singles** in 1898 stood as a major-league record until **Ichiro Suzuki** of the **Seattle Mariners** had 225 singles in 2004. Keeler's 2,513 singles are still fifth best all-time. In 1939, the **Baseball Writers' Association of America** elected Keeler to the **National Baseball Hall of Fame**.

KELL, GEORGE CLYDE. B. 23 August 1922, Swifton, Arkansas. D. 24 March 2009, Swifton, Arkansas. George Kell was a right-handed-hitting **third baseman** for five different **American League (AL)** teams from 1943 to 1957. Kell played for the **Philadelphia Athletics** (1943–1946), **Detroit Tigers** (1946–1952), **Boston Red Sox** (1952–1954), **Chicago White Sox** (1954–1956), and **Baltimore Orioles** (1956–1957). The 5-foot, 9-inch, 175-pound Kell had his best seasons with the Tigers. He led the AL with a .343 **batting average** in 1949 and led in **hits** and **doubles** in 1950 and 1951. Defensively, he led AL third basemen in **fielding percentage** five times, **games played** and **assists** four times, and **putouts** twice. An **All-Star** for 10 seasons, he finished with a .306 batting average and 2,054 hits. In 1983, Kell was elected to the **National Baseball Hall of Fame** by the **Veterans Committee**.

KELLEY, JOSEPH JAMES "JOE". B. 9 December 1871, Cambridge, Massachusetts. D. 14 August 1943, Baltimore, Maryland. Joe Kelley, a right-handed-hitting **outfielder**, began his big-league career with the Boston Beaneaters in 1891 and ended it with the same team—then known as the Boston Doves—in 1908. Between those two one-year stays in Boston, Kelley played for the **Pittsburgh Pirates** in 1892, the **Baltimore Orioles** from 1892 to 1898, the Brooklyn Superbas from 1899 to 1901, the **Baltimore Orioles** of the **American League** in 1902, and the **Cincinnati Reds** from 1902 to 1906. He was the **player-manager** for the Reds from 1902 to 1905 and the Doves in 1908. His career won-lost record as a **manager** was 338–321.

The 5-foot, 11-inch, 190-pound Kelley was a major contributor to the three pennants won by the Orioles and the two by the Superbas. He batted better than .300 for 11 consecutive seasons, beginning in 1893, his first full season with the **National League (NL)** Orioles, through 1903, with Cincinnati. He scored 100 **runs** or more in six seasons and had 100 or more **runs batted in** five times. Kelley had a career **batting average** of .317 and 443 **stolen bases**, including a NL-high 87 in 1896. The **Veterans Committee** elected Kelley to the **National Baseball Hall of Fame** in 1971.

KELLY, GEORGE LANGE "HIGH POCKETS". B. 10 September 1895, San Francisco, California. D. 13 October 1984, Burlingame, California. George Kelly was a **first baseman** for the **New York Giants** and four other teams in the **National League (NL)** from 1915 to 1932. He missed the 1918 season because of army service during World War I. Kelly was with the Giants from 1915 to 1926, briefly with the **Pittsburgh Pirates** for eight games in 1917, with the **Cincinnati Reds** from 1927 to 1930, the **Chicago Cubs** for part of 1930, and the **Brooklyn Dodgers** in 1932. The 6-foot, 4-inch, 190-pound right-handed-hitting Kelly led the NL with 23 **home runs** in 1921. He had more than 100 **runs batted in (RBI)** five times and led the league with 94 RBI in 1920 and 136 in 1924. He hit better than .300 for six consecutive seasons (1921–1926) and had a lifetime **batting average** of .297. In addition, Kelly was a superior defensive first baseman, establishing then single-season records for **total chances**, **assists**, **putouts**, and **double plays**. Kelly was elected to the **National Baseball Hall of Fame** by the **Veterans Committee** in 1973.

KELLY, MICHAEL JOSEPH "MIKE," "KING". B. 31 December 1857, Troy, New York. D. 8 November 1894, Boston, Massachusetts. Mike Kelly's consistent hitting, daring base running, and sense of showmanship made him not only one of the best players of the 1880s, but also the most popular. He earned the title "King of Baseball," and his sliding abilities had the fans yelling "Slide, Kelly, Slide" when he got on **base**. A right-handed batter and thrower, he was a versatile athlete who played every position on the field, but he was primarily an **outfielder** and a **catcher**. The 5-foot, 10-inch, 170-pound Kelly began his career with the 1878 and 1879 **Cincinnati Reds** of the **National League (NL)**, and he then joined the Chicago White Stockings in 1880. Kelly had his greatest success with **Cap Anson's** White Stockings, helping lead them to five pennants in seven years. Anson credited him with devising the **hit-and-run** play. On 14 February 1887, Chicago sold Kelly to the Boston Beaneaters for $10,000, a record price at that time.

After three seasons with the Beaneaters, and serving as the team's **manager** in 1887, Kelly jumped to the **Boston Reds** of the **Players' League** as a **player-manager** in 1890. The league folded after one season, and Kelly played for three clubs in 1891: the **Cincinnati Porkers** of the **American Association (AA)**, whom he also managed; the **Boston Reds** of the AA; and the Beaneaters of the NL. He played for the Beaneaters again in 1892, and he ended his active career appearing in 20 games for the 1893 **New York Giants**. Kelly, the NL batting champion in 1884 and 1886, had a career **batting average** of .308. He led the league in **on-base percentage** in 1884 and 1886, and in **runs** scored in 1884, 1885, and 1886. Kelly had 50 or more **stolen bases** for five consecutive seasons, although they came at a time when stolen bases were credited to anyone who took an extra base on a **hit** or an **error**. In 1945, the **Old Timers Committee** elected Kelly to the **National Baseball Hall of Fame**.

KEOKUK (IOWA) WESTERNS. The Keokuk Westerns were members of the National Association (NA) in 1875, the NA's final season. They played 13 games and lost 12.

KILLEBREW, HARMON CLAYTON "KILLER". B. 29 June 1936, Payette, Idaho. D. 17 May 2011, Scottsdale, Arizona. Harmon Killebrew began his **major-league** career as an 18-year-old "bonus baby" with the 1954 **Washington Senators**. He spent most of the next five seasons in the **minor leagues**, but, in 1959, his first full season, he hit 42 **home runs** to lead the **American League (AL)**. In 1961, the Senators left Washington and relocated to Minnesota as the **Minnesota Twins**. Killebrew, a muscular 6 feet and 195 pounds, hit 40 or more home runs in each of his first four seasons in Minnesota, and seven times overall as a Twin. During his 22 seasons, including a final unproductive one with the 1975 **Kansas City Royals**, the right-handed-hitting Killebrew led the AL in home runs six times. He also led in **runs batted in (RBI)** three times and had nine seasons in which he had more than 100 RBI. In 1969, Killebrew led in home runs, RBI, **walks**, and **slugging percentage** to earn his only **Most Valuable Player Award**.

A **third baseman** early in his career, who also often played in left field, most of Killbrew's games were as a **first baseman**. He was an 11-time **All-Star** and the winner of the 1971 **Lou Gehrig Memorial Award**. Although he had just a .256 career **batting average**, he hit 573 home runs and drove in

1,584 **runs**. Fifth on the all-time home run list when he retired, Killebrew was elected by the **Baseball Writers' Association of America** to the **National Baseball Hall of Fame** in 1984.

KINER, RALPH MCPHERRAN. B. 27 October 1922, Santa Rita, New Mexico. In 1946, his **rookie** season with the **Pittsburgh Pirates**, Ralph Kiner hit 23 **home runs** to lead the **National League (NL)**. It was the first of seven consecutive seasons that the 6-foot, 2-inch, 195-pound **outfielder** would lead or tie for the NL lead in home runs. No other major leaguer has ever led his league in home runs for seven consecutive seasons, and Kiner is the only one to lead both leagues in home runs for six consecutive seasons (1947–1952). The right-handed-hitting Kiner had 51 home runs in 1947 and 54 in 1949, becoming the first NL player to have two 50-plus home run seasons. He also had his career high in **runs batted in** those two seasons, with 127. Kiner's heroics notwithstanding, the Pirates were perennial also-rans, and, in June 1953, they traded him to the **Chicago Cubs**. He hit a combined 35 home runs that year and 22 for the Cubs in 1954. Following the 1954 season, the Cubs traded him to the **Cleveland Indians**. Kiner hit 18 home runs for Cleveland in 1955 and then retired as an active player with a final home run total of 369. Kiner has been associated with the **New York Mets** broadcasting team since the Mets' first season in 1962. In 1975, the **Baseball Writers' Association of America** elected Kiner to the **National Baseball Hall of Fame**.

KINGDOME. *See* SEATTLE MARINERS.

KLEIN, CHARLES HERBERT "CHUCK". B. 7 October 1904, Indianapolis, Indiana. D. 28 March 1958, Indianapolis, Indiana. Chuck Klein made his **major-league** debut with the **Philadelphia Phillies** in July 1928. He batted .360, with 11 **home runs** in 64 games. During the next five seasons, Klein had one of the greatest stretches of power hitting ever produced. From 1929 to 1933, the 6-foot, 185-pound Klein had a composite **batting average** of .359 and a **slugging percentage** of .636. He averaged 36 home runs, 132 **runs** scored, and 139 **runs batted in (RBI)**. Klein's 107 **extra-base hits** in 1930 is a **National League (NL)** single-season record. (**Barry Bonds** of the **San Francisco Giants** tied the record in 2001.) His 445 **total bases** in 1930 is still the NL record for a left-handed **batter**. On defense, Klein's 44 **assists** from right field in 1930 is the most by any major-league **outfielder** since 1884, when Hugh Nicol of the **American Association's St. Louis Browns** had 48.

In November 1933, the Phillies traded Klein to the **Chicago Cubs**. He was traded back to the Phillies in May 1936. Philadelphia released him in June 1939, whereupon he signed with the **Pittsburgh Pirates**. Klein was given his release at the end of the season, and he returned to the Phillies, where he spent parts of his final five seasons (1940–1944). Klein's accomplishments during his 17-year career include a **Most Valuable Player Award** in 1932, a **Triple Crown** in 1933, and a four-home-run game against Pittsburgh on 10 July 1936. In addition, he led the NL in home runs, total bases, and extra-base hits four times; in runs scored and outfield assists three times; and in RBI twice. In 1980, the **Veterans Committee** elected Klein to the **National Baseball Hall of Fame**.

KLEM, WILLIAM JOSEPH "BILL," "THE OLD ARBITRATOR". B. William Joseph Klimm, 22 February 1874, Rochester, New York. D. 16 September 1951, Miami, Florida. The **Society for American Baseball Research** has rated Bill Klem baseball's best **umpire** ever. "The Old Arbitrator," as Klem was called, umpired 5,370 games in the **National League** from 1905 through 1941, a **major-league** record. He was the last umpire to work exclusively at **home plate**. Klem, who umpired the first major league **All-Star Game** in 1933, holds the record for most **World Series** umpired, with 18. His 239 **ejections** of various **managers**, **players**, and **coaches** are also a major-league record. Klem is credited with raising the dignity, integrity, and working conditions for all umpires, and for such innovations as audible **strike** calls and hand gestures to indicate if a batted ball was **fair** or **foul**. In 1953, the **Veterans Committee** chose Klem and **Tom Connolly** of the **American League** as the first umpires to be elected to the **National Baseball Hall of Fame**.

KNICKERBOCKER BASE BALL CLUB. The Knickerbocker Base Ball Club of New York was the first organized baseball club. The club started playing in Manhattan, New York, in 1842, but it did not formally organize until 1845. Under the leadership of club president and committee chairman **Doc Adams**, the Committee to Revise the Constitution and By-Laws created a set of 20 rules to govern the club. On 19 June 1846, at **Elysian Fields**, in Hoboken, New Jersey, the Knickerbockers played the New York Base Ball Club in what is believed to be first official, prearranged match between two clubs.

KNICKERBOCKER RULES. On 23 September 1845, the **Knickerbocker Base Ball Club** formally organized, approving the following set of 20 rules to govern the club:

1. Members must strictly observe the time agreed upon for exercise, and be punctual in their attendance.
2. When assembled for exercise, the President, or in his absence, the Vice President, shall appoint an **Umpire**, who shall keep the game in a book provided for that purpose, and note all violations of the By-Laws and Rules during the time of exercise.
3. The presiding officer shall designate two members as Captains, who shall retire and make the match to be played, observing at the same time that the players opposite to each other should be as nearly equal as possible, the choice of sides to be then tossed for, and the first in hand to be decided in like manner.
4. The **bases** shall be from "home" to **second base**, 42 paces; from first to **third base**, 42 paces, equidistant.
5. No stump match shall be played on a regular day of exercise.
6. If there should not be a sufficient number of members of the Club present at the time agreed upon to commence exercise, gentlemen not members may be chosen in to make up the match, which shall not be broken up to take in members that may afterward appear; but in all cases, members shall have the preference, when present, at the making of the match.
7. If members appear after the game is commenced, they may be chosen in if mutually agreed upon.
8. The game is to consist of 21 counts, or aces; but at the conclusion an equal number of hands must be played.
9. The ball must be pitched, not thrown, for the bat.
10. A ball knocked out of the field, or outside the range of the first and third base, is foul.
11. Three balls being struck at and missed and the last one caught is a hand-out; if not caught it is considered fair, and the striker bound to run.
12. If a ball be struck, or tipped, and caught, either flying or on the first bound, it is a hand out.
13. A player running the bases shall be out, if the ball is in the hands of an adversary on the base, or the runner is touched with it before he makes his base; it being understood, however, that in no instance is a ball to be thrown at him.
14. A player running who shall prevent an adversary from catching or getting the ball before making his base, is a hand out.
15. Three hands out, all out.
16. Players must take their **strike** in regular turn.
17. All disputes and differences relative to the game are to be decided by the Umpire, from which there is no appeal.
18. No ace or base can be made on a **foul** strike.

19. A runner cannot be put out in making one base, when a **balk** is made on the pitcher.
20. But one base is allowed when a ball bounds out of the field when struck.

KNUCKLEBALL. The knuckleball, or knuckler, is a pitch thrown to minimize the spin of the ball in flight, which produces an unpredictable trajectory as the ball travels from the **pitcher** to **home plate**. The knuckleball is difficult for the **batter** to hit, difficult for the pitcher to control, and difficult for the **catcher** to handle. The knuckleball was originally thrown by gripping the ball with the knuckles instead of the fingers, but later pitchers altered the grip by squeezing the ball with the tips of the pointer and middle fingers, and using the thumb for balance. Pitchers noted for the effectiveness of their knuckleballs include Eddie Cicotte, R. A. Dickey, **Jesse Haines**, Charlie Hough, **Ted Lyons**, Joe Niekro, **Phil Niekro**, Eddie Rommel, Tim Wakefield, **Hoyt Wilhelm**, and Wilbur Wood.

KOUFAX, SANFORD "SANDY". B. Sanford Braun, 30 December 1935, Brooklyn, New York. Sandy Koufax was the most dominant **pitcher** of the 1960s. He entered the **major leagues** as a 19-year-old "bonus baby" with the 1955 **Brooklyn Dodgers**, but he did not become a great pitcher until after the Dodgers moved to Los Angeles in 1958. The 6-foot, 2-inch, 210-pound left-hander showed signs of what was to come in 1961, when he won 18 games and led the **National League (NL)** in **strikeouts**. In 1963, Koufax won the pitcher's **Triple Crown** by leading the NL with 25 **wins**, a 1.88 **earned run average (ERA)**, and 306 **strikeouts**. He also led in **shutouts** (11), earning him both the **Cy Young Award** and the **Most Valuable Player (MVP) Award**. He led again in shutouts in 1964, when his 19–5 record gave him the NL's best **winning percentage** (.792). Koufax won his second and third Triple Crowns in 1965 and 1966, with 26 wins, a 2.04 ERA, and a then-record 382 strikeouts in 1965, and 27 wins, a 1.73 ERA, and 317 strikeouts in 1966. He won the Cy Young Award in both seasons. Koufax appeared in four **World Series** with the Dodgers (1959, 1963, 1965, and 1966), and while his record was just 4–3, his ERA during the span of 57 innings was a miniscule 0.95.

An arthritic elbow ended Koufax's career at the age of 30, following the 1966 season. Overall, he had a 165–87 record, a 2.76 ERA, and 2,396 strikeouts in 2,324 1/3 **innings pitched**. He led the NL in ERA for five consecutive seasons, strikeouts four times, and shutouts and wins three times. He threw **no-hitters** in four consecutive years from 1961 to 1965, including a **perfect game** in 1965. In addition to his three Cy Young Awards and one NL MVP, Koufax earned many other honors from 1963 through 1966. He won the **Babe Ruth Award** in 1963 and 1965, the World Series MVP in 1963 and 1965, the *Sporting News*'s NL **Pitcher of the Year** from 1963 through 1966, the **Major League Player of the Year** in 1963 and 1965, and the **Hutch Award** in 1966. Koufax was elected by the **Baseball Writers' Association of America** to the **National Baseball Hall of Fame** in 1972.

KUHN, BOWIE KENT. B. 28 October 1926, Takoma Park, Maryland. D. 15 March 2007, Jacksonville, Florida. Bowie Kuhn was the **commissioner of baseball** from 1969 to 1984. His tenure included a defense of the **reserve clause** in a court suit brought by **Curt Flood** and the introduction of the **designated hitter** in the **American League (AL)**. He oversaw the playing of night games in the **World Series**, and the splitting of the American League and **National League** into two divisions each, making it necessary to have league championship series. The **Veterans Committee** elected Kuhn to the **National Baseball Hall of Fame** in 2008.

L

LAJOIE, NAPOLEON "NAP," "LARRY". B. 5 September 1874, Woonsocket, Rhode Island. D. 7 February 1959, Daytona Beach, Florida. Nap Lajoie, who played from 1896 through 1916, was the greatest **second baseman** of his era. In his five seasons with the **Philadelphia Phillies** of the **National League (NL)** (1896–1900), he had a combined **batting average** of .345, never falling below .324. In 1901, Lajoie left the NL to join the **Philadelphia Athletics** of the new **American League (AL)**. Lajoie's 1901 season is one of the greatest ever. In addition to winning the AL's **Triple Crown** by leading the league in batting average (.426), **home runs** (14), and **runs batted in (RBI)** (125), he also led in **runs, hits, doubles, on-base percentage, slugging percentage**, and **total bases**. When the NL sued to ban Lajoie from playing in the state of Pennsylvania, AL president **Ban Johnson** arranged to have Lajoie moved to the Cleveland Bronchos. In 1903, the club was renamed the Cleveland Naps in Lajoie's honor. Lajoie played for Cleveland through 1914, before returning to the Philadelphia Athletics for his final two seasons. He also managed the Cleveland club from 1905 to 1909.

At 6 feet, 1 inch and 195 pounds, Lajoie was big for his time, especially for a second baseman. During his years with Cleveland, the right-handed-hitting Lajoie won four more batting championships, including a controversial one in 1910, when he edged **Ty Cobb** on the final day of the season. Overall, he led his league in doubles five times, hits and slugging percentage four times, RBI three times, and on-base percentage twice. He was also the best defensive second baseman of his time, leading in **fielding percentage** seven times, **putouts** five times, and **assists** three times. Lajoie had a career batting average of .338, with 3,242 hits and 1,599 RBI. In 1937, the **Baseball Writers' Association of America** chose Lajoie as the sixth player elected to the **National Baseball Hall of Fame**.

LAKEFRONT PARK. *See* CHICAGO CUBS.

LAND SHARK STADIUM. *See* SUN LIFE STADIUM.

LANDIS, KENESAW MOUNTAIN. B. 20 November 1866, Millville, Ohio. D. 25 November 1944, Chicago, Illinois. Kenesaw Landis was a federal judge who, in 1920, was asked by the **major-league** owners to become the first **commissioner of baseball**. When the owners accepted Landis's request for absolute power, he agreed to take the position. Landis had won favor with the owners in 1915, when he failed to rule on an antitrust suit brought by the **Federal League (FL)** against Organized Baseball. The action preserved the **American League** and **National League**'s monopoly and doomed the FL to extinction after just two seasons. Hired to deal with baseball's most pressing problem, gambling, Landis acted immediately. He banned for life eight **Chicago White Sox** players accused of taking money to deliberately lose the 1919 **World Series** to the **Cincinnati Reds**. He also banned several other players whom he believed had ties to gamblers. A fierce opponent of baseball's farm system, Landis declared nearly 200 **minor-league** players **free agents**. In 1944, the **Old Timers Committee** elected Landis to the **National Baseball Hall of Fame**.

LARKIN, BARRY LOUIS. B. 28 April 1964, Cincinnati, Ohio. Barry Larkin played **shortstop** for the **Cincinnati Reds** for 19 seasons, from 1986 to 2004. He was drafted by the Reds out of the University of Michigan as the fourth overall pick in the 1985 **Amateur Draft**. Larkin, a 6-foot, 185-pound right-handed hitter, compiled a career **batting average** of .295, with 379 **stolen bases**. He was a 12-time **All-Star** and the winner of three **Gold Glove Awards** and nine **Silver Slugger Awards**. Defensively, he twice led **National League (NL)** shortstops in **games played** and **putouts** and led in **assists** and **fielding percentage** once each.

Larkin appeared in one **National League Division Series**, two **National League Championship Series**, and one **World Series**. His overall batting average was .338, including a .353 mark in Cincinnati's World Series sweep of the **Oakland Athletics** in 1990. He won the **Roberto Clemente Award** in 1993 and the **Lou Gehrig Memorial Award** in 1994, and he was the NL's **Most Valuable Player** in 1995. Larkin later became a baseball analyst on television. In 2012, he was elected by the **Baseball Writers' Association of America** to the **National Baseball Hall of Fame**.

LARUSSA, ANTHONY "TONY". B. 4 October 1944, Tampa, Florida. Tony LaRussa was an **infielder**, primarily a **second baseman**, who batted .199 in 132 games in six **major-league** seasons. The 6-foot, 175-pound right-handed-hitting LaRussa played for the **Kansas City Athletics** (1963), **Oakland Athletics** (1968–1971), **Atlanta Braves** (1971), and **Chicago Cubs** (1973). Late in the 1979 season, LaRussa took over as **manager** of the **Chicago White Sox**, a post he held until nearly halfway through the 1986 season. His White Sox finished first in the **American League's (AL)** Western Division in 1983, but the team lost to the **Baltimore Orioles** in the **American League Championship Series**. Three weeks after he was fired by the White Sox, LaRussa was named to manage the Oakland Athletics. He had four first-place Western Division finishes in Oakland, won three consecutive pennants (1988–1990), and defeated the **San Francisco Giants** in the 1989 **World Series**.

LaRussa left the Athletics after the 1995 season and moved to the **National League (NL)** to take over the **St. Louis Cardinals**. He remained with St. Louis from 1996 until his retirement following the 2011 season. LaRussa had seven first-place division finishes with the Cardinals, won three pennants (2004, 2006, 2011), and had World Series wins in 2006 over the **Detroit Tigers** and in 2011 over the **Texas Rangers**. The *Sporting News* gave him its **Manager of the Year Award** in 1983 and its AL Manager of the Year Award in 1988 and 1992. The **Baseball Writers' Association of America** gave him its AL Manager of the Year Award in 1983, 1988, and 1992, and its NL Manager of the Year Award in 2002.

LaRussa is the sixth manager to win pennants in both the AL and NL, the first to win multiple pennants in both leagues, and he is one of only two managers to win the World Series in both leagues. His career record was 2,728–2,365, and his win total trails only **Connie Mack** and **John McGraw**. He joined Mack as only the second manager to have managed more than 5,000 major-league games. LaRussa is sure to be elected to the **National Baseball Hall of Fame** when he becomes eligible.

LASORDA, THOMAS CHARLES "TOM". B. 22 September 1927, Norristown, Pennsylvania. Tom Lasorda, a 5-foot, 10-inch, 175-pound left-handed **pitcher**, never won a **major-league** game. He made four appearances for the **Brooklyn Dodgers** in both 1954 and 1955, without a decision, and he was 0–4 in 1956 for the **Kansas City Athletics**; however, Lasorda was a successful pitcher in the **minor leagues**. In a 14-year career in the minors, which both preceded and followed his big-league career, he won 136 games. He was a **scout** and **manager** in the minors for the **Los Angeles Dodgers** from 1965 to 1972, and a **coach** for the team the next three years. During the final week of the 1976 season, the Dodgers named him their new manager to replace **Walter Alston**, who was retiring. Lasorda managed the Dodgers for the next 20 seasons. Under his leadership, Los Angeles won eight Western Division titles and four pennants, including two in his first two full seasons. In both those years, 1977 and 1978, the Dodgers lost to the **New York Yankees** in the **World Series**. The Dodgers later won two Series titles under Lasorda, against the Yankees in 1981, and against the **Oakland Athletics** in 1988. During his tenure as manager, nine Dodgers won **Rookie of the Year** honors.

Lasorda suffered a heart attack in June 1996, and he officially retired in July. The next year, he became a vice president of the club and continues to be involved with the Dodgers as a goodwill ambassador. The **Baseball Writers' Association of America** gave him its **National League Manager of the Year Award** in 1983 and 1988, and, in 2006, he was the winner of the **Branch Rickey Award**. Overall, Lasorda's managerial record was 1,599–1,439, plus 61 games managed in the postseason. In 1997, the **Veterans Committee** elected him to the **National Baseball Hall of Fame**.

LAZZERI, ANTHONY MICHAEL "TONY". B. 6 December 1903, San Francisco, California. D. 6 August 1946, San Francisco, California. In 1925, Tony Lazzeri batted .355 in 197 games for the Salt Lake City Bees of the Pacific Coast League. In addition, Lazzeri set Pacific Coast League records, with 60 **home runs**, 202 **runs** scored, and 222 **runs batted in (RBI)**. The **New York Yankees** purchased his contract, and, from 1926 to 1937, he was their **second baseman**. Lazzeri, a 5-foot, 11-inch, 170-pound right-handed hitter, batted .300 or better five times and had seven seasons of 100 or more RBI. On 24 May 1936, he drove in 11 runs in a game, a still-standing **American League** record. In that game, he became the first **major-league** player to hit two **grand slams** in one game.

As the Yankees' first Italian-American star, Lazzeri was popular in New York; nevertheless, the Yankees released him after the 1937 season to make way for **rookie** second baseman **Joe Gordon**. Lazzeri played with the **Chicago Cubs** in 1938 and with the **Brooklyn Dodgers** and **New York Giants** in 1939. He had a lifetime **batting average** of .292, with 178 home runs. Lazzeri batted .262 in seven **World Series**, six with the Yankees and one with the Cubs. While his raw numbers were not outstanding, Lazzeri was valued for his clutch hitting, consistency, and leadership. In 1991, the **Veterans Committee** elected him to the **National Baseball Hall of Fame**.

LEADOFF HITTER. The leadoff hitter is the player whose name appears first in the **batting order**. He is his team's first **batter** in the first **inning**. The leadoff hitter, also called the leadoff batter, can also refer to the hitter who bats first in any succeeding inning.

LEAGUE AWARD. *See* MOST VALUABLE PLAYER (MVP) AWARD.

LEAGUE PARK (CINCINNATI). *See* CINCINNATI REDS.

LEAGUE PARK (CLEVELAND). *See* CLEVELAND INDIANS.

LEFT FIELDER. *See* OUTFIELDER (OF).

LEMON, ROBERT GRANVILLE "BOB". B. 22 September 1920, San Bernardino, California. D. 11 January 2000, Long Beach, California. Bob Lemon played briefly as a **third baseman** for the **Cleveland Indians** in 1941 and 1942. Converted to a **pitcher** in 1946, after having served in World War II, Lemon became one of the top hurlers in the **American League (AL).** He was a seven-time 20-game winner and led the AL in **wins** in 1950, 1954, and 1955. The 6-foot, 180-pound right-hander was a workhorse on the mound; he led in **complete games** five times and **innings pitched** four times. Lemon was 2–0 in Cleveland's 1948 **World Series** win over the **Boston Braves**, and 0–2 in their 1954 Series loss to the **New York Giants**. His career record in 15 seasons was 207–128. He was voted to the **All-Star** team for seven consecutive seasons (1948–1954) and was the *Sporting News*'s choice as AL **Pitcher of the Year** in 1948, 1950, and 1954. Lemon was also an excellent **batter** and **fielder**. He had 37 career **home runs** for Cleveland, one short of Wes Ferrell's **major-league** record for pitchers. Defensively, he led AL pitchers in **assists** six times and **putouts** five times.

Lemon later spent all or parts of nine seasons as a **manager** in the AL. He led the **Kansas City Royals** (1970–1972), **Chicago White Sox** (1977–1978), and **New York Yankees** (1978–1979, 1981–1982). He won two pennants and one World Series with the Yankees. In 1976, while Lemon was still active as a manager, the **Baseball Writers' Association of America** elected him to the **National Baseball Hall of Fame** as a player.

LEONARD, WALTER FENNER "BUCK". B. 8 September 1907, Rocky Mount, North Carolina. D. 27 November 1997, Rocky Mount, North Carolina. Buck Leonard, who batted and threw left-handed, played for the Brooklyn Royal Giants in 1933, and then for the **Homestead Grays** of the **Negro National League** from 1934 to 1950. His 17 years with the Grays is the longest term of service with one team in **Negro Leagues** history. The 5-foot, 10-inch, 185-pound Leonard was a smooth-fielding **first baseman** who hit for average and power. He teamed with **Josh Gibson** to make the Grays one of the Negro Leagues' most successful teams. In 1972, a special **Negro Leagues Committee** elected Leonard to the **National Baseball Hall of Fame**.

See also AFRICAN AMERICANS IN BASEBALL.

LINDSTROM, FREDERICK ANTHONY "FREDDIE". B. 21 November 1905, Chicago, Illinois. D. 4 October 1981, Chicago, Illinois. Freddie Lindstrom joined the **New York Giants** in 1924. That year, the 18-year-old Lindstrom played **third base** in all seven games of the **World Series** against the **Washington Senators**. He is still the youngest player ever to appear in the Series. In the bottom of the twelfth **inning** of the final game, a ground ball by Washington's Earl McNeely hit a pebble and got by Lindstrom to drive in the run that gave the Senators the championship. In both 1928 and 1930, he totaled 231 **hits**, leading the league in 1928. The 5-foot, 11-inch, 170-pound Lindstrom remained with the Giants until the end of the 1932 season. Expecting to replace **John McGraw** as **manager**, he was passed over in favor of **Bill Terry** and then traded to the **Pittsburgh Pirates** in a three-team deal that also involved the **Philadelphia Phillies**. He later played for the 1935 **Chicago Cubs** and 1936 **Brooklyn Dodgers**. Lindstrom, a right-handed hitter, had a lifetime **batting average** of .311. His two best seasons were 1928 and 1930. He hit .358 with 14 **home runs** and 107 **runs batted in (RBI)** in 1928, and .379 with 22 home runs and 106 RBI in 1930. Lindstrom, who played both as a **third baseman** and an **outfielder** during his 13-year **National League** career, was elected to the **National Baseball Hall of Fame** by the **Veterans Committee** in 1976.

LITTLE LEAGUE BASEBALL. Little League Baseball and Softball (officially, Little League Baseball, Incorporated) claims to be the largest organized youth sports organization in the world. The Little League was founded as a three-team league by Carl E. Stotz in Williamsport, Pennsylvania, in 1939. The following year, a second league was formed in Williamsport, and from there Little League Baseball grew to become an international organization of nearly 200,000 teams in every U.S. state and more than 80 countries around the world. By 1946, Little League had expanded to 12 leagues, all in Pennsylvania. The first league outside of Pennsylvania was founded in New Jersey, in 1947. That year, the first Little League Baseball World Series was played, in Williamsport. In 1974, Little League rules were revised to allow participation by girls in the baseball program following the result of a lawsuit filed by the National Organization for Women. A Little League softball program for both boys and girls was also created.

According to the Little League Baseball and Softball participation statistics, there are close to three million boys and girls in Little League Baseball worldwide, including 400,000 boys and girls registered in softball. For tournament purposes, Little League Baseball is divided into 16 geographic regions: eight national and eight international. Each summer, Little League operates seven **World Series** tournaments at various locations throughout the United States (Little League softball and Junior League, Senior League, and Big League baseball and softball).

In 1951, leagues were formed in **Canada** and near the Panama Canal, making them the first leagues outside the United States. By 1955, there was a Little League organization in each of the 48 U.S. states. That year, George W. Bush began playing Little League in Midland, Texas. He later became the first Little League graduate to be elected president of the United States.

In 1959, the Little League World Series moved from Williamsport to the newly built Little League Headquarters in South Williamsport. One year later, Little League had grown to 27,400 teams in more than 5,500 leagues, and a team from West Germany was the first European team to play in the Little League World Series. In 1967, a team from **Japan** was the first team from Asia to win the Little League World Series, but two years later another Asian nation, Taiwan, won the first of its 17 Little League World Series titles.

The Little League World Series was expanded from eight to 16 teams in 2001, using these regional configurations. In the United States, the East Region contains the New England and Mid-Atlantic regions. The Central Region contains the Great Lakes and Midwest regions. The South Region contains the Southeast and Southwest regions. And the West Region created a new Northwest Region.

Internationally, all of Canada is one region. The Latin America Region created new regions for the Caribbean and **Mexico**. The Far East Region split into an Asia Region and a Pacific Region. The Europe Region created a new TransAtlantic Region.

In 2010, the World Series tournament was reorganized, eliminating pool play and adopting double-elimination until the bracket winners are determined. Then, in 2011, the World Series officially eliminated the two four-team brackets and put all eight teams in the United States bracket and all eight teams in the International bracket.

Little League Baseball has several baseball divisions for boys and girls, based on age. Tee Ball Baseball is for boys and girls 5 to 6 years of age (with a local option for 7-year-olds and/or 8-year-olds) who want to learn the fundamentals of hitting and fielding. In Tee Ball, players hit a ball off a batting tee. Rules of the game may be varied to accommodate the need for teaching. The primary goals of Tee Ball are to instruct children in the fundamentals of baseball and allow them to experience the value of teamwork.

Minor League Baseball programs for boys and girls may be operated within each division for younger players with less experience. The Minor League may be players ages 7 to 12. Divisions may be established within the Minor League targeting various age groups.

The 9 to 10 Year Old Baseball Division for boys and girls was established as a tournament program in 1994. It gives children in this age range the opportunity to experience tournament competition, up to state level. Players on these teams can be chosen from among Major Division and/or Minor Division teams. The diamond used is a 60-foot diamond, and the pitching distance is 46 feet.

The Little League Baseball Division (sometimes known as the Major Division) is for boys and girls ages 9 to 12. A local league may choose to limit its Major Division to 10-year-olds, 11-year-olds, and 12-year-olds, or 11-year olds to 12-year-olds. The diamond used is a 60-foot diamond, and the pitching distance is 46 feet. The local league has an option to choose a Tournament Team (or "**All-Stars**") of 11-year-olds to 12-year-olds from within this division, and the team may enter the International Tournament.

The Junior League Baseball Division is a program for boys and girls ages 13 to 14, using a conventional 90-foot diamond with a pitching distance of 60 feet, 6 inches. (A modified diamond is available during the regular season.) The local league has an option to choose a Tournament Team (or "All-Stars") of 13-year-olds to 14-year-olds from within this division (and/or from within the Senior League Division), and the team may enter the International Tournament.

The Senior League Baseball Division is for boys and girls 14 to 16 years of age, using a conventional 90-foot diamond with a pitching distance of 60 feet, 6 inches. The local league has an option to choose a Tournament Team (or "All-Stars") of 14-year-olds to 16-year-olds from within this division (and/or from within the Junior League or Big League divisions), and the team may enter the International Tournament.

The Big League Baseball Division is for boys and girls ages 16 to 18, using a conventional 90-foot diamond with a pitching distance of 60 feet, 6 inches. The local league has an option to choose a Tournament Team (or "All-Stars") of 16-year-olds to 18-year-olds from within this division (and/or from within the Senior League Division), and the team may enter the International Tournament.

In all age categories, the culmination of the International Tournament is a World Series, featuring teams from around the world.

Little League introduced the Challenger Division in 1989 to provide opportunities for children with physical and developmental challenges to participate in the Little League program. The Challenger Division utilizes a "buddy system" in which Little Leaguers assist Challenger participants in the areas of batting, running, and fielding. Challenger Division games are typically noncompetitive in nature. As of 2011, nearly 1,000 Little Leagues around the world offered the Challenger Division, providing an opportunity for more than 30,000 children with physical or developmental challenges to participate in the Little League program.

LLOYD, JOHN HENRY "POP". B. 25 April 1884, Palatka, Florida. D. 19 March 1965, Atlantic City, New Jersey. John Henry Lloyd was a left-handed-hitting **shortstop** who played for numerous **Negro Leagues** teams from 1906 to 1932. He played mostly for the Lincoln Giants; **Chicago American Giants**; and Bacharach Giants, whom he also managed. The 5-foot, 11-inch, 180-pound Lloyd often drew comparisons, both offensively and defensively, to **Honus Wagner**, the best shortstop then playing in the **major leagues**. In 1977, a special **Negro Leagues Committee** elected Lloyd to the **National Baseball Hall of Fame**.

LOMBARDI, ERNESTO NATALI "ERNIE". B. 6 April 1908, Oakland, California. D. 26 September 1977, Santa Cruz, California. Ernie Lombardi was big—6 feet, 3 inches tall and 230 pounds—and he was slow, even for a **catcher**; nevertheless, he played 17 seasons for four **National League (NL)** teams. Lombardi spent his **rookie** season, 1931, with the Brooklyn Robins, but he spent the bulk of his career with the **Cincinnati Reds** (1932–1941). He also played for the **Boston Braves** in 1942, and he finished his career with the **New York Giants** (1943–1947). Despite his lack of speed, the right-handed-hitting Lombardi had 10 seasons where he hit better than .300, including a league-leading .342 for the Reds in 1938. He was the NL's **Most Valuable Player** that year. Lombardi won a second batting title with a .330 mark in 1942, his one year with the Braves. He was the first catcher to win two batting championships. Lombardi, a superior handler of **pitchers**, was a member of seven NL **All-Star** teams. He played in the **World Series** for Cincinnati in 1939 and 1940, batting a combined .235 in six games. He had a career **batting average** of .306, with 190 **home runs**. Lombardi was elected to the **National Baseball Hall of Fame** by the **Veterans Committee** in 1986.

LOPEZ, ALFONSO RAMON "AL". B. 20 August 1908, Tampa, Florida. D. 30 October 2005, Tampa, Florida. Al Lopez was a **major-league catcher** for 19 seasons and a major-league **manager** for 17 seasons. Lopez spent 18 seasons in the **National League (NL)**, with the **Brooklyn Dodgers** (1928, 1930–1935), Boston Bees (1936–1940), and **Pittsburgh Pirates** (1940–1946). His final year as a player was 1947, with the **Cleveland Indians** of the **American League (AL)**. The 5-foot, 11-inch, 165-pound right-handed-hitting Lopez played in 1,950 games, with a career **batting average** of .261. Known for his durability, he at one time held the records for most games caught in the major leagues (1,918) and the National League (1,861), and for most years in the NL catching 100 or more games (12). Lopez then became a successful manager in the AL. He had an overall record of 1,410–1,004 with Cleveland (1951–1956) and the **Chicago White Sox** (1957–1965, 1968–1969). His teams won two pennants, but both lost in the **World Series**, the Indians in 1954 to the **New York Giants**, and the White Sox in 1959 to the **Los Angeles Dodgers**. Lopez was elected to the **National Baseball Hall of Fame** by the **Veterans Committee** as a manager in 1977.

LORD BALTIMORE. *See* BALTIMORE CANARIES.

LOS ANGELES ANGELS. *See* LOS ANGELES ANGELS OF ANA-HEIM.

LOS ANGELES ANGELS OF ANAHEIM. The Los Angeles Angels of Anaheim are a team in the Western Division of the **American League (AL)**. They entered the AL as the Los Angeles Angels in 1961— along with the **Washington Senators**—as part of Major League Baseball's first **expansion** of the 20th century. The two new teams raised the AL's total of teams to 10; it had been eight since the league achieved **major-league** status in 1901. On 2 September 1965, the team changed its name to the California Angels; in 1997, it was renamed the Anaheim Angels. The team's name changed again in 2005 to its current name. The Angels played their home games at Los Angeles's Wrigley Field in 1961, before becoming tenants of the **Los Angeles Dodgers** in 1962. The Angels played at **Dodger Stadium**, which they called Chavez Ravine, through the 1965 season. In 1966, they moved into the newly built Anaheim Stadium, renamed Edison International Field of Anaheim in 1998, and **Angel Stadium of Anaheim** in 2004.

The Angels have finished first in the AL West eight times. They lost in the **American League Division Series (ALDS)** in 2004, 2007, and 2008. They won the ALDS in 1979, 1982, 1986, 2005, and 2009, but the team lost each year in the **American League Championship Series (ALCS)**. The Angels were the **wild card** team in 2002, but they won the ALDS and ALCS to capture their only pennant. They then defeated the **San Francisco Giants** in seven games to win the **World Series**.

Angels players who have won the AL's **Most Valuable Player Award** are Don Baylor (1979) and Vladimir Guerrero (2004). **Cy Young Award** winners are Dean Chance (1964) and Bartolo Colon (2005). **Rookie of the Year** winners are Tim Salmon (1993) and Mike Trout (2012).

Alex Johnson, in 1970, is the only Angels player to lead the league in **batting average**. Leaders in **home runs** are Bobby Grich (1981), **Reggie Jackson** (1982), and Troy Glaus (2000). Don Baylor, in 1979, is the Angels only **runs batted in** leader.

Angels pitchers who have led the league in **wins** are Dean Chance (1964), Bartolo Colon (2005), and Jered Weaver (2012). **Earned run average** leaders are Dean Chance (1964), Frank Tanana (1977), and John Lackey (2007). **Strikeouts** leaders are **Nolan Ryan** (1972–1974, 1976–1979), Frank Tanana (1975), and Jered Weaver (2010).

Other notable players and **managers** in Angels history include Jim Abbott, Garret Anderson, Bob Boone, **Rod Carew**, Doug DeCinces, Brian Downing, Jim Edmonds, Darin Erstad, Chone Figgins, Chuck Finley, Jim Fregosi, Dan Haren, Torii Hunter, Wally Joyner, Howie Kendrick, Adam Kennedy, Mark Langston, Gene Mauch, Kirk McCaskill, Andy Messersmith, Donnie Moore,

Kendrys Morales, Mike Napoli, Troy Percival, Gary Pettis, **Albert Pujols**, Bill Rigney, Juan Rivera, Francisco Rodriguez, Ervin Santana, Dick Schofield, Mike Scioscia, Mike Witt, Clyde Wright, and Geoff Zahn.

LOS ANGELES DODGERS. The Los Angeles Dodgers are a team in the Western Division of the **National League (NL)**. The team originated in Brooklyn in 1890, where they played through 1957. In 1958, Major League Baseball came to the West Coast, with the **Brooklyn Dodgers** moving to Los Angeles, and the **New York Giants** moving to San Francisco. The Dodgers played their home games at the Los Angeles Memorial Coliseum from 1958 to 1961. They played their first game at their current home, **Dodger Stadium**, on 10 April 1962.

The Dodgers won the **World Series** in 1959, their second season in Los Angeles, defeating the **Chicago White Sox**. They have subsequently won four more Series, over the **New York Yankees** in 1963, the **Minnesota Twins** in 1965, the Yankees in 1981, and the **Oakland Athletics** in 1988. The Dodgers lost in the Series to the **Baltimore Orioles** in 1966, the Athletics in 1974, and the Yankees in 1977–1978. They have been eliminated in four **National League Division Series** and four **National League Championship Series**.

Los Angeles Dodgers who have won the NL's **Most Valuable Player Award** are Maury Wills (1962), **Sandy Koufax** (1963), Steve Garvey (1974), and Kirk Gibson (1988). **Cy Young Award** winners are **Don Drysdale** (1962), Sandy Koufax (1963, 1965–1966), Mike Marshall (1974), Fernando Valenzuela (1981), Orel Hershiser (1988), Eric Gagne (2003), and Clayton Kershaw (2011). **Rookie of the Year** winners are Frank Howard (1960), Jim Lefebvre (1965), Ted Sizemore (1969), Rick Sutcliffe (1979), Steve Howe (1980), Fernando Valenzuela (1981), Steve Sax (1982), Eric Karros (1992), **Mike Piazza** (1993), Raul Mondesi (1994), Hideo Nomo (1995), and Todd Hollandsworth (1996).

Tommy Davis, in 1962 and 1963, is the only Los Angeles Dodger to lead the league in **batting average**. Leaders in **home runs** are Adrian Beltre (2004) and Matt Kemp (2011). Leaders in **runs batted in** are Tommy Davis (1962) and Matt Kemp (2011).

Los Angeles Dodgers **pitchers** who have led the league in **wins** are Don Drysdale (1962), Sandy Koufax (1963, 1965–1966), Andy Messersmith (1974), Fernando Valenzuela (1986), Orel Hershiser (1988), Derek Lowe (2006), Brad Penny (2006), and Clayton Kershaw (2011). **Earned run average (ERA)** leaders are Sandy Koufax (1962–1966), Don Sutton (1980), Alejandro Pena (1984), Kevin Brown (2000), and Clayton Kershaw (2011–2012). **Strikeouts** leaders are Don Drysdale (1959–1960, 1962), Sandy Koufax (1961, 1963, 1965–1966), Fernando Valenzuela (1981), Hideo Nomo (1995), and Clayton Kershaw (2011). By leading in wins, ERA, and strikeouts in 1963, 1965, and 1966, Sandy Koufax won the **Triple Crown** for pitchers in those three years. By leading in wins, ERA, and strikeouts in 2011, Clayton Kershaw won the Triple Crown for pitchers.

Other notable players and **managers** in Los Angeles Dodgers history include **Walter Alston**, Dusty Baker, Chad Billingsley, Jim Brewer, Bill Buckner, Brett Butler, Ron Cey, Willie Crawford, Willie Davis, Andre Ethier, Ron Fairly, Joe Ferguson, Jim Gilliam, Shawn Green, Pedro Guerrero, Burt Hooton, Tommy John, Jeff Kent, **Tom Lasorda**, James Loney, Davey Lopes, Ramon Martinez, Don Mattingly, Claude Osteen, Wes Parker, Ron Perranoski, Johnny Podres, Doug Rau, John Roseboro, Bill Russell, Mike Scioscia, **Gary Sheffield**, Larry Sherry, Bill Singer, Reggie Smith, **Joe Torre**, Bob Welch, and Steve Yeager.

LOS ANGELES MEMORIAL COLISEUM. *See* LOS ANGELES DODGERS.

LOSING PITCHER (LP). The **official scorer** will credit a loss to the **pitcher** who allows the **run** that gives the opposing team the lead with which the game is won (the go-ahead run, at which point the winning team assumes the lead and stays in the lead for the rest of the game). The pitcher receives the loss, even if this or any other runs are not earned.

If a pitcher leaves the game with his team in the lead or with the score tied, but with the go-ahead run on **base**, and this **runner**subsequently scores the go-ahead run, the pitcher who allowed this runner to reach base is responsible for the loss. A loss will not be awarded to a pitcher when a team loses by **forfeit**.

LOSSES BY PITCHER. In the early days of Major League Baseball, teams carried few **pitchers**, so the vast majority of the losses were awarded to just one pitcher. Thus, the all-time single-season leader in games lost is John Coleman of the 1883 Philadelphia Quakers of the **National League (NL)**, with 48.

The single-season leader post-1893, when the pitching distance was extended to its current 60 feet, 6 inches, is Red Donahue of the 1897 St. Louis Browns of the NL, with 35. The single-season leaders in the **American League (AL)** are John Townsend of the 1904 **Washington Senators** and Bob Groom of the 1909 Senators, each with 26.

The career leader in pitchers' losses is **Cy Young**, with 316. Young pitched for Cleveland of the NL (1890–1898), St. Louis of the NL (1899–1900), Boston of the AL (1901–1908), Cleveland of the AL (1909–1911), and Boston of the NL (1911).

See also LOSING PITCHER (LP).

LOU GEHRIG MEMORIAL AWARD. The Lou Gehrig Memorial Award was established by **Lou Gehrig's** college fraternity, Phi Delta Theta, at Columbia University. The award is presented annually to the Major League Baseball (MLB) player who, both on and off the field, best exemplifies the character of Lou Gehrig. This award is the first and only "officially" sanctioned MLB award given to ballplayers by a fraternity. The first winner was Alvin Dark of the **New York Giants** in 1955. The 2011 winner was **Derek Jeter** of the **New York Yankees**.

LOUISVILLE COLONELS (AA). The Louisville Colonels, who played their first three seasons as the Louisville Eclipse, were members of the **American Association (AA)** from 1882 to 1891, the entire length of the AA's existence. In 1889, Louisville won 27 games and lost 111, becoming the first **major-league** team to lose 100 games in a season. Their 26-game losing streak that season is the major leagues' longest ever. The next year, 1890, the Colonels won the AA pennant. Facing the Brooklyn Bridegrooms of the **National League (NL)** in a championship series that was a predecessor to the modern **World Series**, each team won three games, with one game ending in a tie. When the AA folded following the 1891 season, the Colonels were one of four AA teams taken in by the NL. Notable players for Louisville's AA teams included **Pete Browning**, Hub Collins, Guy Hecker, Tony Mullane, Toad Ramsey, and Chicken Wolf.

LOUISVILLE COLONELS (NL). The Louisville Colonels were a team in the **National League (NL)** from 1892 to 1899. The Colonels had played in the **American Association (AA)** from 1882 to 1891. When the AA folded following the 1891 season, Louisville was one of the four AA franchises that the NL added in their **expansion** from an eight-team league to a 12-team league. The Colonels never finished higher than ninth in their eight NL seasons, and they were last three times. When the NL went back to eight teams in 1900, the Louisville franchise was one of the four eliminated. Louisville's owner, **Barney Dreyfuss**, became the owner of the **Pittsburgh Pirates** and brought 14 former Louisville players to Pittsburgh with him. Among them were **Honus Wagner** and **Fred Clarke**, and pitchers **Rube Waddell** and Deacon Phillippe.

LOUISVILLE ECLIPSE. *See* LOUISVILLE COLONELS (AA).

LOUISVILLE GRAYS. The Louisville Grays were members of the new **National League (NL)** in the league's first two seasons, 1876 and 1877. They played their home games at Louisville Baseball Park. In their first game in the league, on 25 April 1876, the Grays were shut out, 4–0, by **Al Spald-**

ing of the Chicago White Stockings, the first **shutout** ever in the NL. The Grays were leading the league in August 1877, when it was uncovered that several of their players, including ace pitcher Jim Devlin, were being bribed by gamblers to deliberately lose games. As a result, Devlin and four other players were banned for life, and the Grays were not retained by the league in 1878.

LYONS, THEODORE AMAR "TED". B. 28 December 1900, Lake Charles, Louisiana. D. 25 July 1986, Sulphur, Louisiana. Ted Lyons pitched for mostly weak **Chicago White Sox** teams from 1923 to 1942, spent three years in the Marine Corps during World War II, and pitched a final five games for Chicago in 1946. He managed the White Sox from mid-1946 through 1948, compiling a 185–245 record. Lyons, a 5-foot, 11-inch, 200-pound right-hander, won 20 games three times, leading the **American League** in wins in 1925 and 1927. He also led the league twice in **shutouts**, **complete games**, and **innings pitched**. In 1942, at the age of 41 and in his final season before going off to war, he started 20 games and completed them all, with a 14–6 record and a league-best 2.10 **earned run average**. With a career record of 260–230, Lyons was elected by the **Baseball Writers' Association of America** to the **National Baseball Hall of Fame** in 1955.

M

MACK, CORNELIUS ALEXANDER "CONNIE". B. Cornelius Alexander McGillicuddy, 22 December 1862, East Brookfield, Massachusetts. D. 8 February 1956, Philadelphia, Pennsylvania. Connie Mack spent 11 seasons as a **catcher**, 10 in the **National League** for the **Washington Nationals** (1886–1889) and **Pittsburgh Pirates** (1891–1896), and one in the **Players' League** with the 1890 **Buffalo Bisons**. Mack, a 6-foot, 1-inch, 150-pound, right-handed hitter, batted a cumulative .244 in 724 games. In his final three seasons in Pittsburgh, Mack served as the team's **manager**. He then managed the Milwaukee club in the **minor league** Western League from 1897 to 1900. In 1900, league commisioner **Ban Johnson** changed the name of the Western League to the **American League**, and, in 1901, he declared it a **major league**. Mack moved to the newly founded **Philadelphia Athletics** as their manager. He remained in that role—adding ownership of the club in 1937—for half a century before finally stepping down following the 1950 season.

Under Mack, the A's won nine pennants (1902, 1905, 1910–1911, 1913–1914, and 1929–1931) and five **World Series** (1910–1911, 1913, 1929–1930). Among his greatest players were **Frank Baker**, **Chief Bender**, **Mickey Cochrane**, **Eddie Collins**, **Jimmie Foxx**, **Lefty Grove**, **Eddie Plank**, **Al Simmons**, and **Rube Waddell**. **Shibe Park**, where the Athletics had played since 1909, was renamed Connie Mack Stadium in 1953. In his 53 years as a manager, Mack's record was 3,731–3,948. His wins, losses, and total games managed are all major-league records not likely to be broken. In 1937, the **Centennial Commission** elected Mack to the **National Baseball Hall of Fame**.

MACKEY, JAMES RALEIGH "BIZ". B. 27 July 1897, Eagle Pass, Texas. D. 22 September 1965, Los Angeles, California. Biz Mackey was a player and **manager** in various **Negro Leagues** from 1918 to 1950. The 6-foot, 200-pound Mackey was a dangerous **switch-hitter** and an outstanding **catcher**. He is considered second only to **Josh Gibson** as the best catcher in Negro

Leagues history. In 2006, Mackey was elected to the **National Baseball Hall of Fame** in a special election conducted by the **Committee on African American Baseball**.

See also AFRICAN AMERICANS IN BASEBALL.

MACPHAIL, LELAND STANFORD, JR. "LEE". B. 25 October 1917, Nashville, Tennessee. D. 8 November 2012, Delray Beach, Florida. Lee MacPhail is the son of **National Baseball Hall of Fame** executive **Larry MacPhail**. Lee spent many years working in the **New York Yankees'** farm system before becoming **general manager** of the **Baltimore Orioles** in 1959. He served as president of the Orioles from 1960 to 1965, worked in Commissioner William Eckert's office in 1966, and then acted as general manager of the Yankees from 1967 to 1973. In 1974, MacPhail replaced **Joe Cronin** as president of the **American League**. He resigned in 1984 to become president of the Major League Player Relations Committee, representing the owners in negotiations with the Major League Baseball Players' Association. In 1998, the **Veterans Committee** elected MacPhail to the National Baseball Hall of Fame.

MACPHAIL, LELAND STANFORD, SR. "LARRY". B. 3 February 1888, Cass City, Michigan. D. 1 October 1975, Miami, Florida. Larry MacPhail was a volatile, flamboyant, and forward-looking executive for the **Cincinnati Reds**, **Brooklyn Dodgers**, and **New York Yankees**. MacPhail, **general manager** of the Reds from 1933 to 1936, brought night baseball to the **major leagues** in 1935, when he had lights installed at **Crosley Field**. In 1938, he was hired to be the general manager of the Dodgers and rescue a franchise that was failing both financially and on the field. MacPhail cleaned up what had been a decaying **Ebbets Field**, installed lights, bought and traded for star players, and hired **Leo Durocher** as his **manager**. Attendance soared, and, by 1941, the Dodgers were **National League** champions.

MacPhail went into the military after the 1942 season, returning in 1945 as co-owner of the Yankees, with Dan Topping and Del Webb, and also the Yankees general manager. As he had done in Cincinnati and Brooklyn, MacPhail brought night baseball to **Yankee Stadium**. At a victory party after the Yankees won the 1947 **World Series**, MacPhail got into one of his frequent alcohol-induced public brawls, leading to a buyout by his partners. He was elected to the **National Baseball Hall of Fame** by the **Veterans Committee** in 1978.

MADDUX, GREGORY ALAN "GREG". B. 14 April 1966, San Angelo, Texas. Greg Maddux was a right-handed **pitcher** in the **National League (NL)** for 23 seasons. Maddux was with the **Chicago Cubs** (1986–1992,

2004–2006), **Atlanta Braves** (1993–2003), **Los Angeles Dodgers** (2006, 2008), and **San Diego Padres** (2007–2008). The 6-foot, 170-pound right-hander was the NL's premier pitcher of his era, leading the league in **wins** three times, **winning percentage** twice, **earned run average (ERA)** four times, **innings pitched** five times, and **games started** seven times. Maddux won the **Cy Young Award** in 1992, as a Cub, and repeated in each of his first three seasons in Atlanta (1993–1995), becoming the first pitcher to win the Cy Young Award in four consecutive seasons. He was also the *Sporting News*'s choice as NL **Pitcher of the Year** in each of those seasons. In the postseason, he was 5–3 in 11 **National League Division Series**, 4–8 in nine **National League Championship Series**, and 2–3 in three **World Series**.

Maddux, an eight time **All-Star**, was among the best **fielders** at his position, winning 18 **Gold Glove Awards**. He led NL pitchers in **assists** 12 times and **putouts** eight times, and he is the all-time leader among pitchers in putouts and **double plays**. The only **major-league** pitcher with at least 15 wins in 17 consecutive seasons, Maddux had a career record of 355–227, with a 3.16 ERA and 3,371 **strikeouts**. His 355 wins are the eighth highest all-time. Maddux, whose last active season was 2008, is sure to be elected to the **National Baseball Hall of Fame** when he becomes eligible.

MAJOR LEAGUE PLAYER OF THE YEAR. In 1936, the *Sporting News* began presenting an annual Major League Player of the Year Award. It is currently the only major award that is given to a single player in Major League Baseball, rather than to a player in each league. The award goes to the player judged by the *Sporting News*'s baseball experts to have had the most outstanding season. The 2012 winner was **third baseman Miguel Cabrera** of the **Detroit Tigers**.

MAJOR LEAGUES. Two leagues, the **National League (NL)** and the **American League (AL)** , comprise the American **major leagues**. The NL was founded in 1876. The AL was founded in 1900, but it was not recognized as a major league until 1901. Beginning with the 2013 season, the **Houston Astros** will move from the NL's Central Division, which currently has six teams, to the AL's Western Division, which currently has four teams. The move will give each league 15 teams, made up of three five-team divisions.

Other leagues, now extinct, that are recognized as major leagues by most historians are the National Association (1871–1875), **Union Association** (1884), **American Association** (1882–1891), **Players' League** (1890), and **Federal League** (1914–1915).

MANAGER. The manager is a person appointed by the club to be responsible for the team's actions on the field, and for representing the team in communications with the **umpire** and the opposing team. An active player may also be a team's manager. The manager may be in uniform or out, but, if he is not in uniform, he must designate a **coach** or player to conduct any action on the field.

MANAGER OF THE YEAR. The *Sporting News* began presenting a Manager of the Year Award in 1936. The award was to honor the one **major-league manager** who had done the best job of managing in that season. The first winner was **Joe McCarthy** of the pennant-winning **New York Yankees**. In 1986, the *Sporting News* began giving two awards, one for the **American League (AL)** and one for the **National League (NL)**. The 2012 winners were Buck Showalter of the **Baltimore Orioles** in the AL and Davey Johnson of the **Washington Nationals** in the NL.

In 1983, the **Baseball Writers' Association of America** began giving its own Manager of the Year Award to one manager in each league. The first winners were **Tony LaRussa** of the **Chicago White Sox** in the AL and **Tom Lasorda** of the **Los Angeles Dodgers** in the NL. The Baseball Writers' Association of America's 2012 winners were Bob Melvin of the **Oakland Athletics** in the AL and Davey Johnson in the NL.

MANLEY, EFFA L. B. 27 March 1897, Philadelphia, Pennsylvania. D. 16 April 1981, Los Angeles, California. Effa Manley was, along with her husband Abe, the co-owner and business manager of the **Newark Eagles** of the **Negro National League** from 1936 to 1948. Under Manley, the Eagles were one of the most professional organizations in the **Negro Leagues**. She used her position to improve the conditions of all the black players and to push for civil rights legislation for all blacks. In 2006, in a special election conducted by the **Committee on African American Baseball**, Manley became the first woman elected to the **National Baseball Hall of Fame**.

See also AFRICAN AMERICANS IN BASEBALL; WOMEN'S BASEBALL.

MANTLE, MICKEY CHARLES. B. 20 October 1931, Spavinaw, Oklahoma. D. 13 August 1995, Dallas, Texas. Mickey Mantle was the youngest player in the **American League (AL)** when he joined the **New York Yankees** as their right fielder in 1951. When **Joe DiMaggio** retired after the season, Mantle took his place in center field. He remained the Yankees' center fielder through 1966, and then, wracked by leg injuries, he played his final two seasons at **first base**. The 5-foot, 11-inch, 195-pound Mantle combined tremendous power and great speed to become baseball's all-time best

switch-hitter. Famous for his tape-measure **home runs**, he led the AL four times in homers and twice topped the 50-homer mark. He led in **runs** and walks five times each, **slugging percentage** four times, and **on-base percentage, total bases**, and **fielding percentage** for center fielders three times. A free swinger, he also led in **strikouts** five times.

Mantle won his only batting title in 1956. His .353 average, combined with his league-leading 52 home runs and 130 **runs batted in (RBI)** earned him the **Triple Crown**. It also earned him the first of his three **Most Valuable Player Awards**. He won again in 1957 and 1962, and he finished second in 1960, 1961, and 1964. His other awards were **Major League Player of the Year** in 1956 and the **Hutch Award** in 1965. He was a member of the AL **All-Star** team every season from 1952 to 1968, with the exception of 1966.

Mantle appeared in 12 **World Series**, setting records for home runs (18), RBI (40), runs (42), total bases (123), **extra-base hits** (26), walks (43), and strikeouts (54). A physically subpar Mantle batted below .300 in each of his last four seasons, dropping his career **batting average** to .298. He had 536 home runs, 1,509 RBI, and a .557 slugging percentage. His 1,710 career strikeouts were a record at the time. Mantle was elected to the **National Baseball Hall of Fame** by the **Baseball Writers' Association of America** in 1974.

MANUSH, HENRY EMMETT "HEINIE". B. 20 July 1901,Tuscumbia, Alabama. D. 12 May 1971, Sarasota, Florida. Heinie Manush compiled 2,524 **hits** and a .330 **batting average** in his 17-year **major-league** career. The 6-foot, 1-inch, 200-pound Manush was a left-handed **batter** and thrower who played the **outfield**, mostly left field, for six different teams. Most of his success came in his first 14 seasons, playing for the **Detroit Tigers** (1923–1927), **St. Louis Browns** (1928–1930), **Washington Senators** (1930–1935), and **Boston Red Sox** (1936). Manush's best seasons were with Detroit in 1926, when he led the league with a .378 batting average, and with St. Louis in 1928, when he again batted .378, second in the league, but led with 241 hits and 47 **doubles**. He finished second in the voting for the **Most Valuable Player Award** that year.

Playing for Washington in 1933, Manush batted .336, again led in hits, and also led in **triples**. In that year's **World Series**, his only one, he had only two hits in 18 **at-bats** against the **New York Giants**. In 1937, Manush moved to the **Brooklyn Dodgers**, where he played his last full season. He played in just a few games for both the Dodgers and **Pittsburgh Pirates** in 1938, and again for the Pirates in 1939. He was elected to the **National Baseball Hall of Fame** by the **Veterans Committee** in 1964.

MARANVILLE, WALTER JAMES VINCENT "RABBIT". B. 11 November 1891, Springfield, Massachusetts. D. 5 January 1954, New York, New York. Although small in stature, at 5 feet, 5 inches tall and 155 pounds, Rabbit Maranville played 23 seasons in the **National League (NL)**. He had a .258 lifetime **batting average** and 2,605 **hits**. Maranville played 15 years with the **Boston Braves**, from 1912 to 1920 at the start of his career, and from 1929 to 1933 and in 1935, at the end. Between his two stays with the Braves, Maranville played for the **Pittsburgh Pirates** (1921–1924); **Chicago Cubs** (1925), where he served briefly as the **manager**; **Brooklyn Dodgers** (1926); and **St. Louis Cardinals** (1927–1928). Maranville played in two **World Series**, 14 years apart. He was a member of the "miracle" Braves team that swept the **Philadelphia Athletics** in 1914, and the 1928 Cardinals who were swept by the **New York Yankees**. He batted .308 in each Series.

An outstanding defensive player, Maranville was a **shortstop** for his entire career, except for 1924 and 1932–1933, when he moved to **second base**. He led NL shortstops in **fielding percentage** and **assists** three times each and **putouts** six times. He is still the all-time leader in putouts by a shortstop. Maranville was elected to the **National Baseball Hall of Fame** by the **Baseball Writers' Association of America** in 1954.

MARICHAL, JUAN ANTONIO (SANCHEZ). B. 20 October 1937, Laguna Verdi, **Dominican Republic**. Juan Marichal made his debut with the **San Francisco Giants** on 19 July 1960, by pitching a one-hit, 2–0 **shutout** over the **Philadelphia Phillies**. It was the first of 52 shutouts Marichal would have during his 14 seasons with the Giants. He had none with the 1974 **Boston Red Sox** or 1975 **Los Angeles Dodgers**. His most memorable pitching performance was on 2 July 1963, at **Candlestick Park**, when he defeated **Warren Spahn** and the **Milwaukee Braves**, 1–0, in 16 innings. Both **pitchers** threw **complete games**, and the only **run** came on a **home run** by **Willie Mays**.

Marichal was a 6-foot, 185-pound right-hander who had a distinctive high kick before delivering the ball. He won more games during the decade of the 1960s than any other pitcher, including six seasons in which he won 20 or more. Marichal led the **National League** in **wins**, with 25 in 1963, and 26 in 1968. He led in **earned run average (ERA)** in 1969, **winning percentage** in 1966, and shutouts in 1965 and 1969. Marichal had a 2–0 record, with an 0.50 ERA in eight **All-Star Games**, and he was the **Most Valuable Player** of the 1965 game. He finished with 243 wins and 142 losses and an ERA of 2.89. Known for his excellent control, he had 2,303 **strikeouts** and only 709 walks. The **Baseball Writers' Association of America** elected Marichal to the **National Baseball Hall of Fame** in 1983.

MARIS, ROGER EUGENE. B. Roger Eugene Maras, 10 September 1934, Hibbing, Minnesota. D. 14 December 1985, Houston, Texas. Roger Maris was a right fielder for the **Cleveland Indians** (1957–1958), **Kansas City Athletics** (1958–1959), **New York Yankees** (1960–1966), and **St. Louis Cardinals** (1967–1968). The 6-foot, 197-pound left-handed hitter won back-to-back **Most Valuable Player Awards** with the Yankees in 1960 and 1961. He led the **American League (AL)** in **runs batted in** both of those seasons. In 1961, Maris was named the **Major League Player of the Year** when he hit 61 **home runs** to break **Babe Ruth's major-league** record of 60, set in 1927. Several **National League** players have since surpassed Maris's total of 61, but it remains the AL record.

MARLINS PARK. Marlins Park, located in Miami, Florida, is the home field of the **Miami Marlins** of the **National League**. The Marlins played their first game at Marlins Park on 4 April 2012. Previously, when they were known as the Florida Marlins, they played their home games at **Sun Life Stadium**, from 1993, their first season, through 2011. Sun Life Stadium, originally called Joe Robbie Stadium, and built primarily for football, has also been called Pro Player Stadium, Dolphin Stadium, and Land Shark Stadium. Marlins Park, which has a retractable roof, has a current seating capacity of 37,400.

See also STADIUMS.

MARQUARD, RICHARD WILLIAM "RUBE". B. 9 October 1886, Cleveland, Ohio. D. 1 June 1980, Baltimore, Maryland. Rube Marquard was a **pitcher** for the **New York Giants** (1908–1915), Brooklyn Robins (1915–1920), **Cincinnati Reds** (1921), and **Boston Braves** (1922–1925). Marquard was purchased by the Giants from the **minor leagues** in July 1908, for a then-record price of $11,000. The 6-foot, 3-inch, 180-pound left-hander struggled his first three seasons, but he starred for the pennant-winning Giants of 1911 to 1913. He won his first 19 decisions in 1912, tying **Tim Keefe's** record for most consecutive **wins** in a season. His final record was 24–7, with a league-leading .774 **winning percentage** and 237 **strikeouts**. Marquard led the **National League** with 26 wins in 1912, and he added 23 more wins in 1913. In 1915, he pitched a **no-hitter** against Brooklyn.

Marquard appeared in five **World Series**, the three with the 1911 to 1913 Giants, and in 1916 and 1920 with the Robins. He had a 2–5 record and a 3.07 **earned run average (ERA)** in 58 2/3 **innings pitched**. Both wins came in the 1912 Series, which the Giants lost to the **Boston Red Sox**. Marquard, with a career record of 201–177 and a 3.08 ERA, was elected to the **National Baseball Hall of Fame** by the **Veterans Committee** in 1971.

MARTINEZ, PEDRO JAIME. B. 25 October 1971, Manoguayabo, Distrito Nacional, **Dominican Republic.** Pedro Martinez was a right-handed **pitcher** for the **Los Angeles Dodgers** (1992–1993), **Montreal Expos** (1994–1997), **Boston Red Sox** (1998–2004), **New York Mets** (2005–2008), and **Philadelphia Phillies** (2009). The slender 5-foot, 11-inch, 175-pound Martinez was an eight-time **All-Star** who led his league in **earned run average (ERA)** five times (once with Montreal and four times with Boston), and in **winning percentage** and **strikeouts** three times each (all with Boston). Martinez won three **Cy Young Award**s, one with the Expos in 1997, and two with the Red Sox in 1999 and 2000. He was also the *Sporting News*'s choice as his league's **Pitcher of the Year** in those three seasons. He won the **American League Triple Crown** for pitchers in 1999 and was the **Most Valuable Player** in that year's All-Star Game. Martinez had a career record of 219–100, with a .687 winning percentage, a 2.93 ERA, and 3,154 strikeouts. He is sure to be elected to the **National Baseball Hall of Fame** when he becomes eligible.

MASSACHUSETTS GAME. The Massachusetts Game refers to an early form of "base ball" played in New England in the mid-19th century. Although it was recognizably a type of baseball, some features of the Massachusetts Game are very different from modern baseball, which is more closely related to the Massachusetts Game's chief rival, the **New York Game.** The rules of the Massachusetts Game were drawn up in 1858 by the Massachusetts Association of Base Ball Players. The playing field had four **bases,** 60 feet apart. The fourth base was called home, but the "striker" stood midway between fourth and **first base. Fielders** were allowed to put a **runner** out by hitting him with a thrown ball—a practice called "soaking" or "plugging." There was no **foul territory,** and **base runners** were not required to stay within the baselines. **Pitchers** had to deliver the ball overhand, and balls hit in the air had to be caught on the fly, unlike the New York rules, where a catch on one bounce was allowed.

MATHEWS, EDWIN LEE "EDDIE". B. 13 October 1931, Texarkana, Texas. D. 18 February 2001, La Jolla, California. In 1952, his **rookie** year, Eddie Mathews of the **Boston Braves** hit an impressive 25 **home runs**; however, he also led the **National League (NL)** with 115 **strikeouts.** The Braves moved to Milwaukee in 1953, and the 21-year-old **third baseman** led the NL in home runs, with 47, and finished second to Brooklyn's **Roy Campanella** in voting for the **Most Valuable Player Award.** Mathews's 47 home runs was a record for third basemen that lasted until **Mike Schmidt** of the Philadelphia Phillies broke it in 1980. The 6-foot, 1-inch, 190-pound left-handed slugger had double-digit home run totals in the first 16 years of his

17-year career, while hitting 30 or more in nine consecutive seasons. Mathews, who led the NL in home runs again in 1959, teamed up with **Hank Aaron** to give the Braves one of the most formidable lefty–righty home-run duos in the game's history.

Mathews was still with the Braves when they moved again, to Atlanta, in 1966, making him the only man to play for the Boston Braves, **Milwaukee Braves**, and **Atlanta Braves**. He later managed the Atlanta-based Braves from 1972 to 1974. Mathews ended his career with the **Houston Astros** in 1967 and **Detroit Tigers** in 1967 and 1968. It was as a member of the Astros that he became the seventh player to reach 500 home runs. He was a nine-time **All-Star** with the Braves and a four-time leader of the NL in walks. He finished with a .271 **batting average** and 512 home runs. In 1978, he was elected by the **Baseball Writers' Association of America** to the **National Baseball Hall of Fame**.

MATHEWS, ROBERT T. "BOBBY". B. 21 November 1851, Baltimore, Maryland. D. 17 April 1898, Baltimore, Maryland. **Pitcher** Bobby Mathews spent 15 years in three different **major leagues**. He pitched for the **Fort Wayne Kekiongas, Baltimore Canaries**, and **New York Mutuals** in the National Association (NA); the **New York Mutuals, Cincinnati Reds, Providence Grays**, and Boston Red Stockings in the **National League**; and the **Philadelphia Athletics** in the **American Association**. On 4 May 1871, Mathews, pitching for Fort Wayne, threw the first pitch in a NA game. The pitcher, who threw right-handed, stood only 5 feet, 5 inches tall and weighed just 140 pounds. He won 20 or more games eight times and finished with a career record of 297–248. Mathews is thought to be one of the first pitchers to throw both the **spitball** and **curveball**.

MATHEWSON, CHRISTOPHER "CHRISTY," "MATTY". B. 12 August 1880, Factoryville, Pennsylvania. D. 7 October 1925, Saranac Lake, New York. Christy Mathewson was just 19 years old in 1900 when he went 0–3 as a **rookie** with the **New York Giants**. Although Mathewson had originally been the property of the Giants, he had been drafted by the **Cincinnati Reds** in December 1900, and then traded back to New York later that month for **pitcher Amos Rusie**. Mathewson won 34 and lost 34 during the next two seasons, but he blossomed in 1903 under **John McGraw**, who was in his first full season as Giants' **manager**. The 6-foot, 1-inch, 195-pound right-hander won 30 or more games in each of the next three seasons, and he led the **National League (NL)** in **strikeouts** in each one. He won the **Triple Crown** for pitchers in 1905, by leading the league with 31 **wins**, a 1.28 **earned run average (ERA)**, and 201 strikeouts. In the **World Series** that year, he put on the greatest pitching performance in Series history. Mathewson, who led the NL with eight **shutouts** during the season, blanked the **Philadelphia Athletics** three times, as the Giants won in five games. During the next nine seasons, Mathewson never won fewer than 22 games, and, in 1908, he won 37 games, a still-standing NL record. His 1.43 ERA and 259 strikeouts that year gave him his second Triple Crown. Mathewson played in three more World Series, all of which the Giants lost—to Philadelphia in 1911 and 1913, and to the **Boston Red Sox** in 1912. Although his overall Series record is 5–5, his ERA is a miniscule 0.97. Mathewson still holds the Series record for most **complete games** (10) and most shutouts (4).

Mathewson's streak of 20-plus win seasons ended when he went 8–14 in 1915. In July 1916, his friend McGraw traded him to Cincinnati to afford him the opportunity to be a big-league manager. During World War I, Mathewson joined the U.S. Army as a captain. While serving in France in 1918, he was the victim of an accidental gassing during a training exercise, which evidently led to him developing tuberculosis. He spent much of the postwar period at a sanitorium in Saranac Lake, New York, where he died in 1925. Mathewson ended his career with 373 victories, a NL record that was later tied by **Grover Alexander**. He led the league in wins four times and ERA and strikeouts five times. In 1936, the **Baseball Writers' Association of America** elected Mathewson as one of the first five members of the **National Baseball Hall of Fame**.

MAYS, WILLIE HOWARD "THE SAY HEY KID". B. 6 May 1931, Westfield, Alabama. Willie Mays was a teenager when he began playing professional baseball with the Birmingham Black Barons of the **Negro American League** from 1948 to 1950. Signed by the **New York Giants** of the **National League (NL)**, he was called up from the Minneapolis Millers, the Giants' Class Triple-A farm team, in May 1951. His .274 **batting average**, 20 **home runs**, and spectacular play in center field helped New York win the pennant and earned him the NL **Rookie of the Year Award**. Dubbed "The Say Hey Kid" because of the way he greeted everyone, Mays missed most of the 1952 season and all of 1953 because of military service. The 5-foot, 10-inch, 170-pounder returned in 1954 and began displaying the speed, power, and defensive ability that has led many to call him the greatest player ever.

Mays, a right-handed hitter, led the NL in batting average (.345), **slugging percentage** (.667), and **triples** (13) in 1954. The Giants won the pennant, and Mays was voted the NL's **Most Valuable Player (MVP)** and the **Major League Player of the Year**. In 1955, he hit 51 home runs to lead the league—the first of four times he would lead in home runs—while repeating as the leader in triples and slugging percentage. The Giants left New York for San Francisco in 1958, although Mays returned to New York in 1972 for a final two seasons with the **New York Mets**. Playing for the **San Francisco**

Giants, Mays again led in home runs in 1962 and 1964. He won his second MVP Award in 1965, after he hit a career-high 52 home runs, while also leading in slugging percentage and **on-base percentage.**

During his career, Mays led the NL in slugging percentage five times, triples and **total bases** three times, and **runs** and on-base percentage twice. He batted in 100 or more runs 10 times, hit 30 or more home runs 11 times, and scored 100 or more runs in 12 consecutive seasons. In addition, he led the NL in **stolen bases** from 1956 to 1959. Mays won 12 consecutive **Gold Glove Awards,** beginning in 1957, the year the award was introduced. He was the winner of the 1971 **Roberto Clemente Award,** played in a record-tying 24 **All-Star Games,** and was the MVP of the 1963 and 1968 games. Mays had a career batting average of .302, with 3,283 **hits** and 660 home runs. His home run total was third only to **Hank Aaron** and **Babe Ruth** when he retired, but, since **Barry Bonds** passed Aaron for the number one

Figure 13.1.   Willie Mays is greeted at home plate by Monte Irvin and Don Mueller as Brooklyn Dodgers catcher Roy Campanella looks on. *National Baseball Hall of Fame Library, Cooperstown, N.Y.*

spot, Mays is now fourth. Mays scored 2,062 runs (seventh all-time) and had 1,903 runs batted in (10th all-time). He was elected by the **Baseball Writers' Association of America** to the **National Baseball Hall of Fame** in 1979.

MAZEROSKI, WILLIAM STANLEY "BILL". B. 5 September 1936, Wheeling, West Virginia. Bill Mazeroski played **second base** for the **Pittsburgh Pirates** from 1956 to 1972. In those 17 years, the 5-foot, 11-inch, 183-pound right-handed hitter had a .260 **batting average** and never batted higher than the .283 average he had in 1957, his second season. It was, however, Mazeroski's defense that made him a seven-time **All-Star**. He won eight **Gold Glove Awards** and led **National League second basemen** six times in **games played**, nine times in **assists**, five times in **putouts**, and three times in **fielding percentage**. Nevertheless, Mazeroski is best remembered for his **home run** off Ralph Terry of the **New York Yankees** in the 1960 **World Series**. The home run, leading off the home half of the ninth inning of Game Seven, won the Series for Pittsburgh. It was the first-ever Series-ending home run. Mazeroski batted .320 for the Series, with a .640 **slugging percentage**. His heroics earned him the **Babe Ruth Award** and selection as the **Major League Player of the Year**. Mazeroski was elected by the **Veterans Committee** to the **National Baseball Hall of Fame** in 2001.

MCAFEE COLISEUM. *See* O.CO COLISEUM.

MCCARTHY, JOSEPH VINCENT "JOE". B. 21 April 1887, Philadelphia, Pennsylvania. D. 13 January 1978, Buffalo, New York. Joe McCarthy spent 15 years in the **minor leagues** as a player and **manager**. He never reached the **major leagues** as a player, but he did as a manager, where he became one of the most successful managers ever. From 1926 to 1930, McCarthy managed the **Chicago Cubs**. The Cubs won the **National League** pennant in 1929, but the team lost the **World Series** to the **Philadelphia Athletics**. He had his greatest success with the **New York Yankees**, whom he managed from 1931 until midway through the 1946 season. The Yankees won eight **American League** pennants and seven World Series under McCarthy, including four straight Series from 1936 to 1939. McCarthy's Yankees defeated the Cubs in 1932 and 1938, the **New York Giants** in 1936 and 1937, the **Cincinnati Reds** in 1939, the **Brooklyn Dodgers** in 1941, and the **St. Louis Cardinals** in 1943. His lone Series loss with the Yankees came against the Cardinals in 1942. McCarthy also managed the **Boston Red Sox** in 1948, 1949, and part of 1950. His record in 24 years as a big-league manager was 2,125–1,333, a **winning percentage** of .615, and his teams never finished lower than fourth place. In 1936, the *Sporting News* began presenting a **Manager of the Year Award** to honor the major-league manager who had done the best job that season. McCarthy was the first winner, and he won again in 1938 and 1943. He was elected to the **National Baseball Hall of Fame** by the **Veterans Committee** in 1957.

MCCARTHY, THOMAS FRANCIS MICHAEL "TOMMY". B. 24 July 1863, South Boston, Massachusetts. D. 5 August 1922, Boston, Massachusetts. Tommy McCarthy was two weeks short of his 21st birthday when he joined the **Boston Reds** of the **Union Association** in July 1884. A right-handed **batter** and thrower, he had a 0–7 record as a **pitcher** and a .215 **batting average** as an **outfielder**. McCarthy played for the Boston Beaneaters of the **National League (NL)** in 1885, and then for the Philadelphia Quakers of the NL in 1886 and 1887. He played only 66 games in those three seasons, batting a combined .184, while spending much of the time in the **minor leagues**.

The **St. Louis Browns** of the **American Association (AA)** acquired McCarthy in 1888, and it was in the AA that he began to develop his batting ability. Now a full-time outfielder, the 5-foot, 7-inch, 170-pound McCarthy remained with the Browns through 1891, scoring more than 100 **runs** in each of his four seasons in St. Louis. He also became an outstanding base stealer, totaling 93 **stolen bases** in 1888 and a league-leading 83 in 1890. McCarthy returned to the Beaneaters in 1892, before ending his career with the Brooklyn Bridegrooms in 1896. Despite batting .350 in 1890, .346 in 1893, and .349 in 1894, he finished with a lifetime average of just .292. McCarthy was elected to the **National Baseball Hall of Fame** by the **Old Timers Committee** in 1946.

MCCOVEY, WILLIE LEE, "STRETCH". B. 10 January 1938, Mobile, Alabama. Although he played only 52 games for the **San Francisco Giants** in 1959, left-handed-hitting **first baseman** Willie McCovey was named **Rookie of the Year** in the **National League (NL)**. McCovey played 19 seasons for the Giants, from 1959 to 1973, and again from 1977 to 1980. He also played for the **San Diego Padres** from 1974 to 1976, and 11 games for the **Oakland Athletics** in 1976. The 6-foot, 4-inch, 198-pound McCovey was one of the game's most feared sluggers, with 521 **home runs** during his 22-year career. He led the league in home runs and **slugging percentage** three times and **runs batted in (RBI)** twice. Four times he led the NL in receiving intentional walks.

In 1969, McCovey topped the NL in home runs, RBI, slugging percentage, and **on-base percentage**. He was voted the NL **Most Valuable Player (MVP)** and the **Major League Player of the Year**. A six-time **All-Star**, he was also the MVP of the All-Star Game that year. McCovey had a career .270 **batting average** and 1,555 RBI to go along with his 521 home runs. He still holds the NL record for **grand slams** (18) and home runs by a left-handed-hitting first baseman (439). The winner of the **Hutch Award** in 1977, McCovey was elected to the **National Baseball Hall of Fame** by the **Baseball Writers' Association of America** in 1986.

MCGINNITY, JOSEPH JEROME "JOE," "IRON MAN". B. 20 March 1871, Cornwall, Illinois. D. 14 November 1929, Brooklyn, New York. Joe McGinnity was called "Iron Man" because he worked in an iron foundry in the off-season, but the name also described the endurance he displayed as a **pitcher**. McGinnity spent 10 seasons in the **major leagues**. The 5-foot, 11-inch, 206-pound right-hander was already 28 years old when he made his big-league debut with the **Baltimore Orioles** of the **National League (NL)** in 1899. McGinnity had a league-leading 28 **wins** that season, but he was assigned to the Brooklyn Superbas in 1900, after the Orioles were dropped from the league. He again led the NL in wins, with 28, and he also had the highest **winning percentage** (.778). In 1902, McGinnity jumped to the new **Baltimore Orioles** in the new **American League**, but midway through the 1902 season, Orioles **manager John McGraw** left to go back to the NL to manage the **New York Giants**. McGraw took McGinnity and several of Baltimore's best players with him. McGinnity spent the rest of his big-league career, which lasted through 1908, with the Giants.

McGinnity's best season was with the 1904 Giants, when he had 35 wins, with a 1.61 **earned run average (ERA)** and nine **shutouts**, all league bests. During his 10 seasons, McGinnity led the NL in wins five times, and he won more than 20 games eight times, including two seasons in which he won more than 30. He established his "Iron Man" reputation by leading the NL in games pitched six times and **innings pitched** four times. His 434 innings pitched in 1903 remains the NL record. He pitched both ends of five **double-headers** that year. McGinnity's overall record in his abbreviated career was 246–142, with a 2.66 ERA. In 1946, the **Old Timers Committee** elected him to the **National Baseball Hall of Fame**.

MCGOWAN, WILLIAM ALOYSIUS "BILL". B. 18 January 1896, Wilmington, Delaware. D. 9 December 1954, Silver Spring, Maryland. Bill McGowan was an **umpire** in the **American League (AL)** from 1925 through July 1954, when illness forced him to retire. In 1939, he opened the second school for umpires in the country. McGowan umpired in 4,425 **major-league** games; four **All-Star Games**, including the first one in 1933; and eight **World Series**. In 1948, he was the **home plate** umpire in the AL's first-ever playoff game, between the **Boston Red Sox** and **Cleveland Indians**. The **Veterans Committee** elected McGowan to the **National Baseball Hall of Fame** in 1992.

MCGRAW, JOHN JOSEPH "MUGSY". B. 7 April 1873, Truxton, New York. D. 25 February 1934, New Rochelle, New York. John McGraw had an outstanding playing career in the 1890s as the **third baseman** for the famed **Baltimore Orioles** of the **National League (NL)**; however, he is best remembered as the successful **manager** of the **New York Giants** from 1902 to 1932. Both as a player and manager, the undersized McGraw—he was 5 feet, 7 inches tall and 155 pounds—was arrogant, abrasive, and pugnacious. McGraw began his big-league career with the **Baltimore Orioles** of the **American Association (AA)** in 1891. The AA folded after the season, and, in 1892, McGraw joined the Baltimore Orioles of the NL. After the Orioles were eliminated from the NL following the 1899 season, McGraw played for the **St. Louis Cardinals** in 1900. In 1901, he jumped to yet another **Baltimore Orioles** team, this one in the new **American League (AL)**; however, in mid-1902, after repeated clashes with AL president **Ban Johnson**, McGraw went back to the NL as the manager of the Giants.

As a player, the left-handed-hitting McGraw had a .334 **batting average** and led the NL in **on-base percentage** three times and **runs** scored and walks twice. McGraw had managed the NL Orioles in 1899, and the AL Orioles from their inception until he left to take over the moribund Giants. He won his first pennant in 1904, but both he and the Giants' owner, John Brush, refused to meet the Boston Americans, the AL pennant winner, in the **World Series**. The Giants won the pennant again in 1905, and this time they did play in the World Series, defeating the **Philadelphia Athletics**.

McGraw's swaggering, argumentative, win-at-all-costs manner made him hated around the league; nevertheless, he was successful. In his 31 seasons in New York, he won 10 pennants, although only three World Series. He retired in June 1932, turning the reins over to **Bill Terry**, his star **first baseman**. In 1933, when the first **All-Star Game** was played, McGraw was called out of retirement to manage the NL team. In 1937, the **Centennial Commission** elected him to the **National Baseball Hall of Fame** as a manager.

MCGWIRE, MARK DAVID. B. 1 October 1963, Pomona, California. Mark McGwire was a right-handed-hitting **first baseman** for the **Oakland Athletics** (1986–1997) and **St. Louis Cardinals** (1997–2001). McGwire was the **Rookie of the Year** in the **American League (AL)** in 1987, when he led the league in **home runs** and **slugging percentage**. His 49 home runs for Oakland set a new **rookie** record. The 6-foot, 5-inch, 215-pound McGwire led the AL with 52 home runs in 1996. He had 58 more in 1997, the most in the **major leagues**, but his July 31 trade from the AL Athletics to the **National League** Cardinals prevented him from winning the home run title in either league.

In 1998, McGwire and **Sammy Sosa** of the **Chicago Cubs** waged a dramatic, season-long race for the home run championship. McGwire won by hitting 70, setting a major-league record; Sosa finished with 66. In 1999, McGwire had a league-leading 65 home runs and was honored with the **Lou Gehrig Memorial Award**. A 12-time **All-Star** and winner of three **Silver Slugger Awards**, McGwire led his league in home runs and slugging percentage four times. He had a .263 career **batting average**, with 583 home runs and 1,414 **runs batted in**; however, charges that McGwire used performance-enhancing drugs during his career have negatively affected his chances of election to the **National Baseball Hall of Fame**.

MCKECHNIE, WILLIAM BOYD "BILL," "DEACON". B. 7 August 1886, Wilkinsburg, Pennsylvania. D. 29 October 1965, Bradenton, Florida. Bill McKechnie was a **major-league manager** for 25 seasons. Before that, he was a **switch-hitting infielder**, mostly a **third baseman**, for seven teams in three leagues for 11 seasons. The 5-foot, 10-inch, 160-pound McKechnie played mostly in the **National League**, for the **Pittsburgh Pirates** (1907, 1910–1912, 1918, and 1920), **Boston Braves** (one game in 1913), **New York Giants** (1916), and **Cincinnati Reds** (1916–1917). He also played in the **American League**, for the New York Yankees in 1913, and in the **Federal League**, for the **Indianapolis Hoosiers** in 1914, and for the **Newark Peppers** when the Indianapolis team moved to Newark in 1915. He had a .251 career **batting average**, with his .304 average for the Hoosiers by far his best.

McKechnie's first managerial job was as a **player-manager** with the 1915 Peppers. After his playing days were over, he managed the Pirates from 1922 to 1926, the **St. Louis Cardinals** in 1928 and 1929, the Braves from 1930 to 1937, and the Reds from 1938 to 1946. His career won-lost record was 1,896–1,723. He won pennants with the 1925 Pirates, 1928 Cardinals, and 1939 and 1940 Reds. His 1925 Pirates and 1940 Reds also won the **World Series**. McKechnie was the first manager to win a pennant with three different teams, and he was the first to win the World Series with two different teams. The *Sporting News* gave him its **Manager of the Year Award** in 1937 and 1940. McKechnie was elected to the **National Baseball Hall of Fame** by the **Veterans Committee** as a manager in 1962.

MCPHEE, JOHN ALEXANDER "BID". B. 1 November 1859, Massena, New York. D. 3 January 1943, San Diego, California. Bid McPhee played his entire 18-year big-league career as a Cincinnati **second baseman**. McPhee was with the **Cincinnati Red Stockings** of the **American Association (AA)** from 1882 to 1889, and, when the AA team moved to the **National League (NL)**, he was with the NL's **Cincinnati Reds** from 1890 to 1899. In 1901 and 1902, he was **manager** of the Reds. A 5-foot, 8-inch, 152-pound right-handed hitter, McPhee was a capable **leadoff** man who had a .272 career **batting average**. He led the AA in **home runs** (8) in 1886 and **triples** (19) in 1887, and he scored more than 100 **runs** in 10 different seasons and 1,684 for his career. McPhee played his first 14 seasons barehand, although the use of gloves had become common by 1886; nevertheless, he led his league's second basemen in **games played** four times, **fielding percentage** nine times, **double plays** 11 times, **putouts** eight times, and **assists** six times. McPhee was elected to the **National Baseball Hall of Fame** by the **Veterans Committee** in 2000.

MCVEY, CALVIN ALEXANDER "CAL". B. 30 August 1849, Montrose, Iowa. D. 20 August 1926, San Francisco, California. Cal McVey was just 20 years old in 1869, when **player-manager Harry Wright** signed him to play for the **Cincinnati Red Stockings**, baseball's first openly professional team. When Wright joined the **Boston Red Stockings** of the newly formed National Association (NA) in 1871, McVey followed, batting .431 that first year. He played for the Red Stockings in 1871 and 1872, and again in 1874 and 1875. McVey also played for the **Baltimore Canaries** of the NA in 1873, and in the **National League** for the Chicago White Stockings (1876–1877) and **Cincinnati Reds** (1878–1879). McVey, a 5-foot, 9-inch, 170-pound right-handed hitter, who also threw right-handed, played all positions during his career, including **pitcher** and **catcher**. He led the NA in **hits** and **runs batted in (RBI)** twice, and in **slugging percentage**, **runs** scored, and **doubles** once each. McVey, the NA's all-time leader in RBI, had a .346 lifetime **batting average** for his nine **major-league** seasons. He also was the player-manager in Baltimore in 1873 and Cincinnati in 1878 and 1879.

MEDWICK, JOSEPH MICHAEL "JOE," "DUCKY". B. 24 November 1911, Carteret, New Jersey. D. 21 March 1975, St. Petersburg, Florida. Left fielder Joe Medwick was a top **National League (NL)** slugger in the 1930s and early 1940s. Medwick, a 5-foot, 10-inch, 187-pound right-handed hitter, had 11 full seasons in which he batted above .300. In 1934, two years after he made his debut with the **St. Louis Cardinals**, Medwick batted .319 and led the NL with 18 **triples**. He also had the first of six consecutive seasons in which he had 100 or more **runs batted in (RBI)**. The rowdy Cardinals, known as the Gashouse Gang, won the pennant and defeated the **Detroit Tigers** in a seven-game **World Series**. Medwick batted .379 and set off a near riot with an aggressive slide into Tiger's **third baseman** Marv Owen in Game Seven at Detroit.

In 1936, Medwick led the league in **hits** and RBI, and his 64 **doubles** set a still-standing NL single-season record. His 1937 season was even better, as he won the **Triple Crown** with a .374 **batting average**, 31 **home runs**, and 154 RBI. No National Leaguer has won a Triple Crown since. Medwick, the league's **Most Valuable Player** in 1937, also led in doubles, **runs,** hits, **slugging percentage**, and **total bases**. On 7 July 1937, at **Griffith Stadium**, he became the first player to get four hits in an **All-Star Game**. In June 1940, the Cardinals traded Medwick to the **Brooklyn Dodgers**. In the first post-trade series between the teams, at **Ebbets Field**, Cardinals **pitcher** Bob Bowman beaned Medwick, causing another near riot. Medwick recovered from the concussion caused by the blow and remained a solid hitter. He had some good years with Brooklyn, and later with the **New York Giants** and **Boston Braves**, but he was never again the spirited player he had been before the beaning. He played his final two seasons, 1947 and 1948, back with the Cardinals. Medwick, a ten-time All-Star, hit 40 or more doubles for seven consecutive seasons, and he led the NL in RBI for three consecutive seasons (1936–1938). He had a .324 career batting average and 1,383 RBI. The **Baseball Writers' Association of America** elected him to the **National Baseball Hall of Fame** in 1968.

MEMORIAL STADIUM. Memorial Stadium, located in Baltimore, Maryland, was the home of the **Baltimore Orioles** of the **American League** from 1954, the year the **St. Louis Browns** franchise moved to Baltimore, through 1991. In 1992, the team moved to **Oriole Park at Camden Yards**. Memorial Stadium hosted the **major league All-Star Game** in 1958.

See also STADIUMS.

MENDEZ, JOSE DE LA CARIDAD. B. 19 March 1887, Cardenas, Matanzas, **Cuba**. D. 31 October 1928, Havana, Cuba. Jose Mendez was a star **pitcher** in the Cuban Winter League in the early years of the 20th century. The 5-foot, 8-inch, 190-pound right-hander played for various teams in the **Negro Leagues** from 1908 to 1926, including seven seasons (1920–1926) with the **Kansas City Monarchs** of the **Negro National League**. In 1939, Mendez was one of the first players selected for the Cuban Baseball Hall of Fame. In 2006, he was elected to the **National Baseball Hall of Fame** in a special election conducted by the **Committee on African American Baseball**.

METROPOLITAN STADIUM. *See* MINNESOTA TWINS.

MEXICO. Baseball has been played in Mexico since the late 19th century. Professional baseball began with the formation of the Mexican League in 1925. In the mid-1950s, the league became a part of Organized Baseball when they were granted **minor-league** status; however, Mexican League teams are not affiliated with specific **major-league** teams. Mexico currently has two leagues: Liga Mexicana de Beisbol and Liga Mexicana del Pacífico. Liga Mexicana de Beisbol has 14 teams. The Northern Division has Vaqueros Laguna, located in Torreon, Coahuila; Diablos Rojos del Mexico, located in Mexico City; Acereros de Monclova, located in Monclova, Coahuila; Sultanes de Monterrey, located in Monterrey, Nueva Leon; Pericos de Puebla, located in Puebla, Puebla; Broncos de Reynosa, located in Reynosa, Tamaulipas; and Saraperos de Saltille, located in Saltillo, Coahuila.

The Southern Division has Piratas de Campeche, located in Campeche, Campeche; Petroleros de Minatitlan, located in Minatitlan, Veracruz; Guerreros de Oaxaca, located in Oaxaca, Oaxaca; Tigres de Quintana Roo, located in Cancun, Quintana Roo; Olmecas de Tabasco, located in Villahermoso, Tabasco; Rojos del Aguila de Veracruz, located in Veracruz, Veracruz; and Leones de Yucatan, located in Merida, Yucatan.

The Liga Mexicana del Pacific has eight teams: Tomateros de Culiacán, located in Culiacán, Sinaloa; Algodoneros de Guasave, located in Guasave, Sinaloa; Venados de Mazatlán, located in Mazatlán, Sinaloa; Águilas de Mexicali, located in Mexicali, Baja California; Cañeros de Los Mochis, located in Los Mochis, Sinaloa; Naranjeros de Hermosillo, located in Hermosillo, Sonora; Mayos de Navojoa, located in Navajoa, Sonora; and Yaquis de Obregón, located in Ciudad Obregón, Sonora.

Yaquis de Obregón were the Mexican representatives in the 2011 and 2012 **Caribbean Series,** won by the Leones del Escogido team representing the **Dominican Republic.** The 2013 Caribbean Series is scheduled to be played in Hermosillo, Mexico. Mexico is also a member of the **International Baseball Federation** and competes in the **Baseball World Cup.**

In 1996, the **San Diego Padres** and **New York Mets** played a three-game series at **Estadio de Béisbol Monterrey,** the home field of the Monterrey Sultans (Sultanes de Monterrey). It was the first time a major-league game was played in Mexico. Estadio de Béisbol Monterrey was also the site of an Opening Day game between the **Colorado Rockies** and San Diego Padres on 4 April 1999.

Some of the most notable players in Mexican baseball are Angel Castro, Hector Espino, Lucas "El Indio" Juarez, Epitacio "La Mala" Torres, and Jesus Valenzuela. Notable Mexican-born players who played in the major leagues include Juan Acevedo, Alfredo Aceves, Mel Almada, Ruben Amaro, Roberto Avila, Francisco Barrios, Vinny Castilla, Jesse Flores, Yovani Gallardo, Jaime Garcia, Teddy Higuera, Esteban Loaiza, Aurelio Lopez, Jorge Orta, Aurelio Rodriguez, Vincente Romo, Joakim Soria, Alex Trevino, and Fernando Valenzuela.

MIAMI MARLINS. The Miami Marlins are a team in the Eastern Division of the **National League (NL)**. The team, then known as the Florida Marlins, entered the NL with the **Colorado Rockies** in 1993 as part of a two-team **major-league expansion**. The name change from Florida Marlins to Miami Marlins occurred in 2012, when the team moved into its new home, **Marlins Park**. From its entrance into the NL in 1993 through the 2011 season, the Marlins played their home games at **Sun Life Stadium**, previously called Joe Robbie Stadium, Pro Player Stadium, Dolphin Stadium, and Land Shark Stadium. The Marlins have reached the postseason twice, in 1997 and 2003. Both times, they were the **wild card** team, and both times they won the **World Series**. In 1997, they defeated the **Cleveland Indians**, and, in 2003, they defeated the **New York Yankees**.

No member of the Marlins has won a **Most Valuable Player Award** or a **Cy Young Award**. **Rookie of the Year** winners are Dontrelle Willis (2003), Hanley Ramirez (2006), and Chris Coghlan (2009).

Hanley Ramirez, in 2009, is the only Marlins player to lead the NL in **batting average**. No member of the Marlins has led the league in **home runs** or **runs batted in**.

Dontrelle Willis, in 2005, is the only Marlins **pitcher** to lead the NL in **wins**. Leaders in **earned run average** are Kevin Brown (1996) and Josh Johnson (2010). No Marlins pitcher has led the league in **strikeouts**.

Other notable players and **managers** in Marlins' history include Antonio Alfonseca, Josh Beckett, Emilio Bonifacio, Mark Buehrle, A. J. Burnett, Miguel Cabrera, Luis Castillo, Jeff Conine, Ryan Dempster, Juan Encarnacion, Alex Fernandez, Cliff Floyd, Alex Gonzalez, Fredi Gonzalez, Jeremy Hermida, Charles Johnson, Mark Kotsay, Derrek Lee, Al Leiter, Jim Leyland, Mike Lowell, Jack McKeon, Kevin Millar, Logan Morrison, Robb Nen, Rickey Nolasco, Scott Olsen, Carl Pavano, Brad Penny, Juan Pierre, Edgar Renteria, Jose Reyes, Edwin Rodriguez, **Ivan Rodriguez**, Cody Ross, Anibel Sanchez, **Gary Sheffield**, Giancarlo Stanton, Dan Uggla, and Preston Wilson.

MIDDLETOWN (CONNECTICUT) MANSFIELDS. The Middletown Mansfields played in the National Association for part of one season (1872). Their most notable players were Asa Brainard and **Jim O'Rourke**.

MILE HIGH STADIUM. *See* COLORADO ROCKIES; COORS FIELD.

MILLER, MARVIN JULIAN. B. 14 April 1917, Brooklyn, New York. D. 27 November 2012, New York, New York. Marvin Miller was a labor lawyer who headed the Major League Baseball Players Association (MLBPA) from 1966 to 1983. During that time, he led the players through three player strikes and two lockouts, and he was a key figure in the development of **free agency**. Miller was responsible for negotiating the MLBPA's first collective bargaining agreement with the team owners in 1968, and he was able to get arbitration included in the collective bargaining agreement in 1970. Miller considered arbitration, which meant that disputes would be taken to an independent arbitrator to resolve disputes, the baseball union's greatest achievement of the early years.

In 1974, an arbitrator ruled that the owner of the **Oakland Athletics**, Charlie Finley, had failed to make an annuity payment as required by **pitcher Catfish Hunter**'s contract. Because Finley had not met the terms of the contract, Hunter was free to negotiate with any team, making him a free agent. When Hunter signed a lucrative contract with the **New York Yankees**, the players saw the amount of money that could be made when they were free to negotiate with any team. Miller also challenged the **reserve clause** in 1974, and, when arbitrator Peter Seitz ruled in his favor, it effectively eradicated the reserve clause and ushered in the age of free agency.

MILLER PARK. Miller Park, located in Milwaukee, Wisconsin, has been the home field of the **Milwaukee Brewers** of the **National League** since 2001. Prior to moving to Miller Park, the Brewers played at **Milwaukee County Stadium**. Miller Park, which has a retractable roof, has a seating capacity of approximately 41,900. The park hosted the **major league All-Star Game** in 2002.

See also STADIUMS.

MILLS, ABRAHAM GILBERT "A. G.". B. 12 March 1844, New York, New York. D. 26 August 1929, Falmouth, Massachusetts. A. G. Mills served as president of the **National League** in 1883 and 1884. In 1905, Mills and six other men formed a group that came to be known as the Mills Commission. Their purpose was to prove that baseball was strictly an American invention that had no ties to the English game of "rounders." Based on the testimony of one Abner Graves, the report they issued claimed that baseball was invented in 1839 by Abner Doubleday, at Cooperstown, New York, as an improved version of the old game of "town ball." This claim has long been discredited.

MILWAUKEE BRAVES. The Milwaukee Braves were a team in the **National League (NL)** from 1953 to 1965. The shifting of the Braves franchise from Boston to Milwaukee in 1953 was the first relocation of a **major-**

league team since 1903. The Braves played their home games at **Milwaukee County Stadium**. They won back-to-back pennants in 1957 and 1958. Milwaukee defeated the **New York Yankees** in a seven-game **World Series** in 1957, and the team lost to New York in seven games in 1958. In 1966, the Braves moved again, leaving Milwaukee for Atlanta.

Hank Aaron, in 1957, was the only Milwaukee Braves player to win the NL's **Most Valuable Player Award**. **Warren Spahn**, in 1957, was the only Milwaukee Braves **pitcher** to win the **Cy Young Award**. No Milwaukee Braves player won the **Rookie of the Year Award**.

Hank Aaron, in 1956 and 1959, was the only Milwaukee Braves player to lead the NL in **batting average**. **Home run** leaders were **Eddie Mathews** (1953, 1959) and Hank Aaron (1957, 1963). The only Milwaukee Braves player to lead the NL in **runs batted in** was Hank Aaron, in 1957, 1960, and 1963.

Milwaukee Braves pitchers who led the league in **wins** were Warren Spahn (1953, 1957–1961) and Lew Burdette (1959). **Earned run average** leaders were Warren Spahn (1953, 1961) and Lew Burdette (1956). No Milwaukee Braves pitcher led the league in **strikeouts**.

Other notable players and **managers** for the Milwaukee Braves included Joe Adcock, Bill Bruton, Bob Buhl, Rico Carty, Tony Cloninger, Wes Covington, Del Crandall, Charlie Grimm, Fred Haney, Johnny Logan, Don McMahon, Andy Pafko, **Red Schoendienst**, and **Joe Torre**.

MILWAUKEE BREWERS (AA). The Milwaukee Brewers were a team in the **American Association (AA)** for the latter part of the 1891 season, the AA's final year of existence. The Brewers replaced the **Cincinnati Porkers**, who had a 43–57 record when they were dropped from the league in August. The Brewers, who had been leading the **minor league** Western League, won 21 of their 36 AA games.

MILWAUKEE BREWERS (AL). The Milwaukee Brewers were members of the **American League (AL)** in 1901, the first year the AL was recognized as a **major league**. The Brewers finished in last place in 1901, and the team then moved to St. Louis in 1902, becoming the **St. Louis Browns**. In 1954, the Browns moved to Baltimore, becoming the **Baltimore Orioles**. Notable players for Milwaukee in 1901 were John Anderson and **player-manager Hugh Duffy**.

MILWAUKEE BREWERS (AL/NL). In 1969, the **American League (AL)** expanded, creating two new teams: the **Kansas City Royals** and Seattle Pilots. The Seattle franchise was unsuccessful, and the league moved it to Milwaukee in 1970, creating the modern **Milwaukee Brewers**. The Brewers' owner was **Bud Selig**, who later became the **commissioner of baseball**. In 1997, Milwaukee was moved out of the AL and into the Central Division of the **National League (NL)**. The Brewers played in **Milwaukee County Stadium** from 1970 to 2000, before moving to newly constructed **Miller Park** in 2001.

The Brewers have made four postseason appearances. They lost the **American League Division Series** to the **New York Yankees** in 1981, the **National League Division Series** to the **Philadelphia Phillies** in 2008, and the **National League Championship Series** to the **St. Louis Cardinals** in 2011. Milwaukee won its only pennant in 1982, but the team lost to the Cardinals in the **World Series**.

Two players from the AL Milwaukee Brewers won the **Most Valuable Player Award (MVP)**: **Rollie Fingers** in 1981, and **Robin Yount** in 1982 and 1989. One NL Brewer has won the MVP award: Ryan Braun in 2011. Two AL Brewers won the **Cy Young Award**: Rollie Fingers in 1981 and Pete Vuckovich in 1982. No NL Brewer has won the Cy Young Award. One AL Brewer won the **Rookie of the Year Award**, Pat Listach in 1992, and one NL Brewer has won the award, Ryan Braun in 2007.

Neither the AL Brewers nor the NL Brewers have had a leader in **batting average**. **Home run** leaders for the AL Brewers were George Scott (1975), Gorman Thomas (1979, 1982), and Ben Oglivie (1980), and for the NL Brewers, Prince Fielder (2007). **Runs batted in** leaders for the AL Brewers were George Scott (1975) and Cecil Cooper (1980, 1983), and for the NL Brewers, Prince Fielder (2009) and Ryan Braun (2012).

Pete Vuckovich of the AL Brewers led in **wins** in 1981. No NL Brewers **pitcher** has led in wins. Neither the AL Brewers nor the NL Brewers have had an **earned run average** leader. Neither the AL Brewers nor the NL Brewers have had a **strikeouts** leader.

Other notable players and managers in Brewers' history include George Bamberger, Chris Bosio, Jeromy Burnitz, Mike Caldwell, Jeff Cirillo, Yovani Gallardo, Jim Gantner, Phil Garner, Moose Haas, Cory Hart, Teddy Higuera, Geoff Jenkins, Harvey Kuenn, Sixto Lezcano, Mark Loretta, **Paul Molitor**, Don Money, Charlie Moore, Dan Plesac, Buck Rodgers, Ben Sheets, Ted Simmons, Jim Slaton, B. J. Surhoff, Tom Treblehorn, Greg Vaughn, Rickie Weeks, and Bob Wickman.

MILWAUKEE COUNTY STADIUM. Milwaukee County Stadium, located in Milwaukee, Wisconsin, was the home of the **Milwaukee Braves** of the **National League (NL)** from 1953 through 1965. It later became the home of the **expansion Milwaukee Brewers** of the **American League** from 1970 until the team, which had become a member of the NL in 1997, moved to **Miller Park** in 2001. Milwaukee County Stadium hosted the **major league All-Star Game** in 1955 and 1975.

See also STADIUMS.

MILWAUKEE GRAYS (NL). The Milwaukee Grays, also known as the Cream Citys, were a team in the **National League** in 1878. Their record of 15–45 landed them in sixth place in the six-team league. Financial problems caused ownership to dissolve the team after the one season. Notable players for the Grays were **Charlie Bennett**, Abner Dalrymple, and John Peters.

MILWAUKEE GRAYS (UA). The Milwaukee Grays were a team in the **Union Association (UA)** in 1884, the one year of the UA's existence. They joined the league in September as a replacement for the **Wilmington Quick-steps** and won eight of their 12 games.

MINNESOTA TWINS. The Minnesota Twins are a team in the Central Division of the **American League (AL)**. The franchise was a charter member of the AL, entering in 1901 as the **Washington Senators**. The Senators relocated to Minnesota in 1961. The Twins played their home games at Metropolitan Stadium, in Bloomington, Minnesota, from 1961 to 1981, and at the Hubert H. Humphrey Metrodome, in Minneapolis, Minnesota, from 1982 to 2009. They played their first game at their current home, **Target Field**, in Minneapolis, on 12 April 2010. Metropolitan Stadium hosted the **major league All-Star Game** in 1965, and the Metrodome hosted the game in 1985.

The Twins won the AL pennant in 1965, their fifth year of existence, but the team lost the **World Series** in seven games to the **Los Angeles Dodgers**. They finished first in the Western Division in 1969 and 1970, but they were swept in the **American League Championship Series (ALCS)** by the **Baltimore Orioles** in both years. Minnesota has won two World Series, in 1987 against the **St. Louis Cardinals**, and in 1991 against the **Atlanta Braves**. Since then they have lost in the ALCS in 2002, and in the **American League Division Series** in five consecutive appearances (2003, 2004, 2006, 2009, and 2010).

Minnesota Twins who have won the AL's **Most Valuable Player Award** are Zoilo Versalles (1965), **Harmon Killebrew** (1969), **Rod Carew** (1977), Justin Morneau (2006), and Joe Mauer (2009). **Cy Young Award** winners are Jim Perry (1970), Frank Viola (1988), and Johan Santana (2004, 2006). **Rookie of the Year** winners are Tony Oliva (1964), Rod Carew (1967), John Castino (1979), Chuck Knoblauch (1991), and Marty Cordova (1995).

Twins players who have led the league in **batting average** are Tony Oliva (1964–1965, 1971), Rod Carew (1969, 1972–1975, 1977–1978), **Kirby Puckett** (1989), and Joe Mauer (2006, 2008–2009). Harmon Killebrew

(1962–1964, 1967, 1969) is the only member of the Twins to lead the AL in **home runs**. Leaders in **runs batted in** are Harmon Killebrew (1962, 1969, 1971), Larry Hisle (1977), and Kirby Puckett (1994).

Twins **pitchers** who have led the league in **wins** are Mudcat Grant (1965), Jim Kaat (1966), Jim Perry (1970), Dave Goltz (1977), Frank Viola (1988), Scott Erickson (1991), and Johan Santana (2006). **Earned run average (ERA)** leaders are Allan Anderson (1988) and Johan Santana (2004, 2006). **Strikeouts** leaders are Camilo Pascual (1961–1963), **Bert Blyleven** (1985, part of season with **Cleveland Indians**), and Johan Santana (2004–2006). By leading in wins, ERA, and strikeouts in 2006, Johan Santana won the **Triple Crown** for pitchers.

Other notable players and **managers** in Twins' history include Rick Aguilera, Bob Allison, Scott Baker, Earl Battey, Dave Boswell, Tom Brunansky, Michael Cuddyer, Gary Gaetti, Greg Gagne, Ron Gardenhire, Jimmie Hall, Kent Hrbek, Torii Hunter, Jacque Jones, Tom Kelly, Jerry Koosman, Francisco Liriano, Gene Mauch, Sam Mele, Joe Nathan, Ron Perranoski, Brad Radke, Bill Rigney, Rich Rollins, Roy Smalley, Kevin Tapani, Cesar Tovar, and Geoff Zahn.

MINOR LEAGUES. The minor leagues are professional leagues below the level of the **major leagues**. Known colloquially as the "farm system," Minor League Baseball reached its peak participation in 1948, when there were 59 different leagues. Under the current system, Class AAA is the highest minor-league level, followed in descending order of readiness for the major leagues by Class AA, Class A-Advanced, Class A, Class A-Short Season, and Rookie.

Class AAA leagues are the International League, Pacific Coast League, and Mexican League (Liga Mexicana de Beisbol). Unlike all other minor-league teams, Mexican League teams are not affiliated with specific major-league teams.

Class AA leagues are the Eastern League, Southern League, and Texas League. Class A-Advanced leagues are the California League, Carolina League, and Florida State League. Class A leagues are the Midwest League and South Atlantic League. Class A-Short Season leagues are the New York–Penn League and Northwest League. Rookie leagues are the Appalachian League, Arizona League, Dominican Summer League, Gulf Coast League, Pioneer League, and Venezuelan Summer League.

MINUTE MAID PARK. Minute Maid Park, located in Houston, Texas, is the home field of the **Houston Astros** of the **National League**. The park opened in 2000 as Enron Field, but it was renamed Minute Maid Park in

2002. Minute Maid Park, which has a retractable roof, has a seating capacity of approximately 40,900. Minute Maid Park hosted the **major league All-Star Game** in 2004.

See also STADIUMS.

MIZE, JOHN ROBERT "JOHNNY". B. 7 January 1913, Demorest, Georgia. D. 2 June 1993, Demorest, Georgia. Johnny Mize was a hard-hitting **first baseman** for the **St. Louis Cardinals** (1936–1941), **New York Giants** (1942, 1946–1949), and **New York Yankees** (1949–1953). He missed the 1943, 1944, and 1945 seasons while serving in the U.S. Navy. The left-handed-hitting Mize batted above .300 in each of his first nine seasons, including a career-high .349 in 1939, the year he won his only batting title. Mize, who stood 6 feet, 2 inches tall and weighed 215 pounds, led or tied for the **home run** lead twice with the Cardinals and twice with the Giants. His high was 51 for the 1947 Giants, and he hit three homers in a game six times in his career. In each of the three years from 1938 to 1940, he led the **National League (NL)** in **slugging percentage** and **total bases**, and he again led in slugging percentage in 1942, his first season with the Giants.

In August 1949, the Giants sold the 36-year-old Mize to the Yankees, where he played on five consecutive world championship teams. **Casey Stengel**, the Yankees' **manager**, used Mize as a **pinch hitter** and occasional starter to great effect. Mize batted a combined .286 in five **World Series** with the Yankees. In the 1952 Series, he hit .400 and blasted three home runs against the **Brooklyn Dodgers**. His performance earned him the **Babe Ruth Award**. Despite his slowness afoot, Mize, who threw right-handed, was a fine **fielder**. He led NL first basemen in **fielding percentage** four times and **putouts** and **assists** twice. Mize had a career **batting average** of .312, with 359 home runs. The ten-time **All-Star** was elected by the **Veterans Committee** to the **National Baseball Hall of Fame** in 1981.

MOLITOR, PAUL LEO. B. 22 August 1956, Saint Paul, Minnesota. Paul Molitor played 21 seasons in the **American League**, mostly with the **Milwaukee Brewers**. Molitor played for the Brewers from 1978 to 1992. Granted **free agency** in 1993, he signed with the **Toronto Blue Jays**. After three seasons in Toronto, he was a free agent again, and, in 1996, he signed to play his final three seasons with his hometown **Minnesota Twins**. A 6-foot, 185-pound right-handed hitter, Molitor batted better than .300 12 times in his career and had a 39 consecutive-game hitting streak in 1987. He had more than 200 **hits** four times, while leading the league in both hits and **runs** three times each. He was especially effective in the two **World Series** in which he played. He batted .355 for Milwaukee against the **St. Louis Cardinals** in 1982, and .500 for Toronto against the **Philadelphia Phillies** in 1993.

His combined average for the two Series was .418. He was the Series' **Most Valuable Player** and winner of the **Babe Ruth Award** in 1993. Molitor also won the **Hutch Award** in 1987, the **Lou Gehrig Memorial Award** in 1997, and the **Branch Rickey Award** in 1998.

Molitor, a seven-time **All-Star**, was extremely versatile in the field. During his career, he played 791 games at **third base**; 400 games at **second base**; and a total of 304 games at **first base, shortstop**, and center field. In the final years of his career, he was used mostly as a **designated hitter**, winning four **Silver Slugger Awards** at that position. Molitor had a career **batting average** of .306, with 1,782 runs scored, 504 **stolen bases**, 605 **doubles** (tied for 11th all-time), and 3,319 hits (ninth all-time). In 2004, the **Baseball Writers' Association of America** elected him to the **National Baseball Hall of Fame**.

MONTREAL EXPOS. The Montreal Expos entered the **National League (NL)** in 1969 as part of a two-team **expansion** that also added the **San Diego Padres**. The additional two teams raised the NL's total from 10 to 12, which led to the league creating two divisions, each consisting of six teams. The Expos, the first **major-league** team outside the United States, played their home games at Jarry Park from 1969 through 1976, before moving into Olympic Stadium in 1977. Olympic Stadium hosted the major league **All-Star Game** in 1982. The Expos played at Olympic Stadium through the 2004 season, after which the franchise was moved from Montreal to Washington, D.C., and renamed the **Washington Nationals**.

The Expos reached postseason play only once in their 36 years, in 1981, when they lost the **National League Championship Series** in five games to the **Los Angeles Dodgers**. In 1994, the Expos were in first place in the Eastern Division when a players' strike ended the season.

No Montreal player won the NL's **Most Valuable Player Award**. The only winner of the **Cy Young Award** was **Pedro Martinez**, in 1997. **Rookie of the Year** winners were Carl Morton (1970) and **Andre Dawson** (1977).

Expos players who led the NL in **batting average** were Al Oliver (1982) and Tim Raines (1986). No Expos batter ever led the league in **home runs**. **Runs batted in** leaders were Al Oliver (1982) and **Gary Carter** (1984).

Ken Hill, in 1994, was the only Expos **pitcher** to lead the league in **wins**. **Earned run average** leaders were Steve Rogers (1982), Dennis Martinez (1991), and Pedro Martinez (1997). No Expos pitcher ever led the league in **strikeouts**.

Other notable players and **managers** for the Expos included Moises Alou, Tim Burke, Warren Cromartie, Jeff Fassero, Andres Galarraga, Vladimir Guerrero, Bill Gullickson, Livan Hernandez, Charlie Lea, Mike Marshall,

Gene Mauch, Jeff Reardon, Steve Renko, Buck Rodgers, Mel Rojas, Ken Singleton, Bryn Smith, Rusty Staub, Bill Stoneman, Ellis Valentine, Javier Vasquez, Jose Vidro, Larry Walker, Tim Wallach, and **Dick Williams**.

MORGAN, JOE LEONARD. B. 19 September 1943, Bonham, Texas. Joe Morgan was a **major-league second baseman** for the **Houston Astros** (1963–1971, 1980)—they were the Houston Colt .45s in 1963 and 1964— **Cincinnati Reds** (1972–1979), **San Francisco Giants** (1981–1982), **Phila- delphia Phillies** (1983), and **Oakland Athletics** (1984). He is best remem- bered as the **National League's (NL)** premier second baseman for Cincinna- ti's "Big Red Machine" teams of the 1970s. In eight seasons with the Reds, Morgan, a 5-foot, 7-inch, 160-pound left-handed **batter,** led the NL in **on- base percentage** four times and won back-to-back **Most Valuable Player Award**s **(MVP)** and selection as **Major League Player of the Year** in 1975 and 1976.

Morgan played in seven **National League Championship Series**, five with Cincinnati, and four **World Series**, three with Cincinnati. A 10-time **All-Star** and the MVP of the 1972 All-Star Game, he led the NL in walks four times, and his career total of 1,865 is fifth best all-time. He led NL second basemen in **putouts** three times and **fielding percentage** twice, and he won five consecutive **Gold Glove Awards** from 1973 to 1977. Among second basemen, his 2,527 **games played** trails only **Eddie Collins**, and he is third all-time in **assists** and fourth in putouts. Morgan had a career **batting average** of .271, with 268 **home runs.** He scored 1,650 **runs**, and tallied 689 **stolen bases** (11th all-time). Morgan was a baseball broadcaster for many years after his retirement. He was elected by the **Baseball Writers' Associa- tion of America** to the **National Baseball Hall of Fame** in 1990.

MOST VALUABLE PLAYER (MVP) AWARD. The Most Valuable Player (MVP) Award is baseball's most prestigious single-season honor. There have been three different "official" MVP Awards in Major League Baseball. The first was the **Chalmers Award** (1911–1914), given to the one player in each league "who should prove himself as the most important and useful player to his club and to the league at large in point of deportment and value of services rendered."

In 1922, the **American League (AL)** created a new award, known as the League Award, to honor the "baseball player who is of the greatest all- around service to his club." A player could win the award only once. The **National League (NL)** began making a League Award in 1924, but the league allowed for repeat winners. The AL dropped the award after 1928, and the NL dropped it after 1929.

The current award, which is given to one player in each league, was begun in 1931. The winners are chosen by members of the **Baseball Writers' Association of America**. The winner receives a trophy, now called the Kenesaw Mountain Landis Memorial Baseball Award. **Barry Bonds** won the MVP Award a record seven times. There have been nine three-time winners, including **Yogi Berra, Roy Campanella, Joe DiMaggio, Jimmie Foxx, Mickey Mantle, Stan Musial, Albert Pujols, Alex Rodriguez**, and **Mike Schmidt**. The 2012 winners were **third baseman Miguel Cabrera** of the **Detroit Tigers** in the AL, and **catcher** Buster Posey of the **San Francisco Giants** in the NL.

MUNICIPAL STADIUM. Municipal Stadium was located in Kansas City, Missouri. The **Kansas City Athletics** played their home games there from 12 April 1955 through 27 September 1967. The **Kansas City Royals** played their home games there from 8 April 1969 to 4 October 1972. In 1973, the Royals moved to Royals Stadium, later renamed **Kauffman Stadium**. In 1960, Municipal Stadium hosted the second of the two **major league All-Star Games**.
See also STADIUMS.

MURRAY, EDDIE CLARENCE "STEADY EDDIE". B. 24 February 1956, Los Angeles, California. Eddie Murray was a third-round pick by the **Baltimore Orioles** in the 1973 **Amateur Draft**. He was the **American League Rookie of the Year** as a 21-year-old in 1977, and he played with the Orioles through 1988. Murray, who had his best seasons in Baltimore, later played for the **Los Angeles Dodgers** (1989–1991), the **New York Mets** (1992–1993), the **Cleveland Indians** (1994–1996), the Orioles again (1996), and a final season with both the Dodgers and the Anaheim Angels in 1997. Murray was a 6-foot, 2-inch, 190-pound **first baseman**, although he began and ended his career as a **designated hitter**. He led his league only once in **home runs, runs batted in (RBI)**, and **on-base percentage**, all as an Oriole, yet Murray was a consistently productive hitter. He had double-digit home run totals and 75 or more RBI in the first 20 of his 21 seasons. He was an eight-time **All-Star** and the winner of three **Silver Slugger Awards** and three **Gold Glove Awards**.

One of the few players with 3,000 **hits** (3,255) and 500 home runs (504), Murray had a career **batting average** of .287, and his tally of 1,917 RBI is the most ever by a **switch-hitter**. He led his league's first basemen in **games played, fielding percentage, putouts**, and **assists** three times each, and he is the all-time leader among first basemen in games played and assists, and fourth in putouts. Murray was elected by the **Baseball Writers' Association of America** to the **National Baseball Hall of Fame** in 2003.

MUSIAL, STANLEY FRANK "STAN," "STAN THE MAN". B. 21 November 1920, Donora, Pennsylvania. Stan Musial shares the **National League (NL)** record with **Cap Anson** and **Mel Ott** for the most seasons played with one team, 22. Musial played for the **St. Louis Cardinals** from 1941 through 1963, with 1945 out for military service. When he retired, the 6-foot, 175-pound left-handed-hitting **outfielder** and **first baseman** ranked at or near the top of baseball's all-time lists in almost every batting category. He held or shared 17 **major-league** records and 29 NL records. The likeable Musial batted above .300 for 16 consecutive seasons, and 17 overall. His high was .376 in 1948, tops in both leagues. He also led the major league that year in **hits** (230), **doubles** (46), **triples** (18), **total bases** (429), and **slugging percentage** (.702). His 39 **home runs** were one short of the NL lead, denying him the **Triple Crown**. In all, he won seven batting championships and led the NL in hits six times, totaling 200 or more in six seasons.

Musial also led the NL in doubles eight times; **extra-base hits** seven times; total bases, **on-base percentage**, and slugging percentage six times; **games played**, triples, and **runs** scored five times; and **runs batted in (RBI)** twice. He was the NL's **Most Valuable Player** in 1943, 1946, and 1948, and he finished second in 1949, 1950, 1951, and 1957. His other awards include the **Major League Player of the Year** in 1946 and 1951, and the **Lou Gehrig Memorial Award** in 1957. Musial was an **All-Star** for a record 24 seasons, and he holds nine All-Star Game records. The Cardinals won the NL pennant in each of his first four full seasons, but he hit just .256 in 23 **World Series** games. He finished with a career **batting average** of .331 and 3,630 hits, fourth all-time. The incredibly consistent Musial had exactly half of his hits at home and half on the road. He had 475 home runs; 1,951 RBI, sixth all-time; and 725 doubles, third all-time. In 1969, he was elected by the **Baseball Writers' Association of America** to the **National Baseball Hall of Fame**.

N

NATIONAL ASSOCIATION (NA). *See* NATIONAL ASSOCIATION OF PROFESSIONAL BASE BALL PLAYERS (NAPBBP).

NATIONAL ASSOCIATION OF BASE BALL PLAYERS (NABBP). The National Association of Base Ball Players (NABBP), consisting of amateur teams primarily from the northeastern and midwestern United States, was formed in New York City in March 1857. By the spring of 1859, its membership included 50 teams. Among the association's most notable teams were the **Brooklyn Atlantics, Brooklyn Eckfords, Cincinnati Red Stockings,** and **New York Mutuals.** When some clubs began paying their players, thus making them professionals, it led to the demise of the association. The NABBP was replaced in 1871 by the **National Association of Professional Base Ball Players**, more commonly known as the National Association.

NATIONAL ASSOCIATION OF PROFESSIONAL BASE BALL PLAYERS (NAPBBP). The National Association of Professional Base Ball Players (NAPBBP), more commonly known as the National Association (NA), was baseball's first professional league. It was formed in New York on 17 March 1871. Nine teams participated in the NA's first season, 1871, including the **Boston Red Stockings, Chicago White Stockings, Cleveland Forest Citys, Fort Wayne Kekiongas, New York Mutuals, Philadelphia Athletics, Rockford Forest Citys, Troy Haymakers,** and **Washington Olympics.**

During the next four seasons, many additional teams were members of the NA, most for one or two seasons, and one for just six games. Other teams in the NA beyond the original nine included the **Baltimore Canaries, Baltimore Marylands, Brooklyn Atlantics, Brooklyn Eckfords, Elizabeth Resolutes, Hartford Dark Blues, Keokuk Westerns, Middletown Mansfields, New Haven Elm Citys, Philadelphia Centennials, Philadelphia White Stockings, St. Louis Brown Stockings, St. Louis Red Stockings, Washington Blue Legs,** and **Washington Nationals.**

The NA's lack of franchise stability and a central authority, severe financial problems, influence of gamblers, and domination on the field by the Boston Red Stockings led to its demise after the 1875 season. In 1876, **William Hulbert**, president of the Chicago White Stockings, spearheaded the formation of a new league, the **National League (NL)**, to replace the NA. In addition to the White Stockings, the eight-team NL included five other former NA clubs: the Boston Red Stockings, Hartford Dark Blues, New York Mutuals, Philadelphia Athletics, and St. Louis Brown Stockings. The other two charter members of the NL were the **Louisville Grays** and **Cincinnati Red Stockings**.

The Philadelphia Athletics won the NA pennant in 1871, and the Boston Red Stockings won from 1872 to 1875. The most notable players from the NA included **Cap Anson**, **Ross Barnes**, **Candy Cummings**, Jim Devlin, **Pud Galvin**, Andy Leonard, **Bobby Mathews**, **Cal McVey**, Levi Meyerle, **Jim O'Rourke**, **Lip Pike**, **Al Spalding**, **Deacon White**, **George Wright**, and **Harry Wright**.

NATIONAL BASEBALL HALL OF FAME (HOF). The National Baseball Hall of Fame and Museum, located in Cooperstown, New York, opened in June 1939. The museum and library serve as the central point for the study of baseball history and the display of baseball-related artifacts and exhibits. The National Baseball Hall of Fame (HOF) is best known for honoring baseball's most accomplished people. The first honorees, **Ty Cobb**, **Walter Johnson**, **Christy Mathewson**, **Babe Ruth**, and **Honus Wagner**, were selected in 1936, three years before the museum opened.

Players are currently inducted into the HOF through election by either the **Baseball Writers' Association of America (BBWAA)** or the **Veterans Committee**, which now consists of three subcommittees, each of which considers and votes for candidates from a separate era of baseball. Five years after retirement, any player with 10 years of **major-league** experience who passes a screening committee (which removes from consideration players of clearly lesser qualification) is eligible to be elected by BBWAA members with 10 or more years of membership. From a final ballot typically including 25 to 40 candidates, each writer may vote for up to 10 players; until the late 1950s, voters were advised to cast votes for the maximum 10 candidates.

Any player named on 75 percent or more of all ballots cast is elected. A player who is named on fewer than 5 percent of ballots is dropped from future elections. In some instances, the screening committee had restored these names to later ballots, but, in the mid-1990s, dropped players were made permanently ineligible for HOF consideration, even by the Veterans Committee. A 2001 change in the election procedures restored the eligibility of these dropped players; while their names will not appear on future BBWAA ballots, they may be considered by the Veterans Committee. With

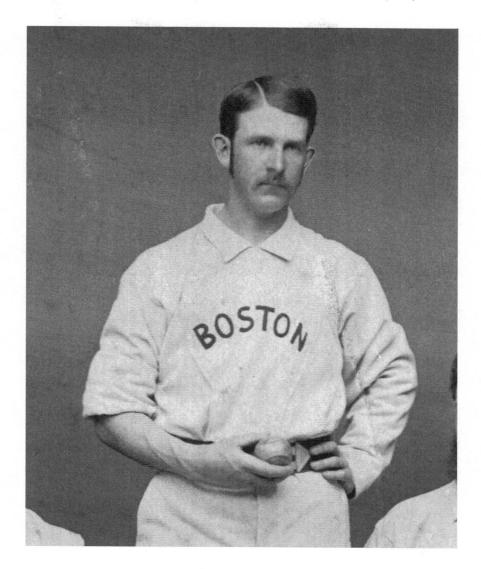

Figure 14.1.   Al Spalding was the star pitcher of the National Association, helped found the National League, and later founded a sporting goods empire.
National Baseball Hall of Fame Library, Cooperstown, N.Y.

the election of **Barry Larkin** and **Ron Santo** in January 2012, 297 individuals have been elected to the HOF, including 207 former major-league players; 19 **managers**; nine **umpires**; 27 pioneers, executives, and organizers; and 35 members of the **Negro Leagues**.

NATIONAL LEAGUE (NL). The National League, officially the National League of Professional Baseball Clubs, is one of two leagues, along with the **American League (AL)**, that comprise the **major leagues**. The National League (NL) was founded in New York City on 2 February 1876, and it replaced the **National Association of Professional Base Ball Players (NAPBBP)**, more commonly known as the National Association (NA). The driving force in the founding of the new league was **William Hulbert**, president of the NA's **Chicago White Stockings**. The first president of the NL was **Morgan Bulkeley**, president of the NA's **Hartford Dark Blues**. Chicago (the present-day **Chicago Cubs**) and Hartford, which folded after the 1877 season, were two of of the NL's eight charter members for the 1876 season.

The other charter members were the **Philadelphia Athletics** (expelled after one season), **Boston Red Stockings** (the present-day **Atlanta Braves**), **Cincinnati Red Stockings** (expelled after the 1880 season), **Louisville Grays** (folded after the 1877 season), **New York Mutuals** (expelled after one season), and **St. Louis Brown Stockings** (folded after the 1877 season).

Between 1878 and 1891, the following teams joined and played at least one season in the NL: the **Indianapolis Blues** (1878), **Milwaukee Grays** (1878), **Providence Grays** (1878–1885), **Buffalo Bisons** (1879–1885), **Cleveland Blues** (1879–1884), **Syracuse Stars** (1879), **Troy Trojans** (1879–1882), **Worcester Ruby Legs** (1880–1882), **Detroit Wolverines** (1881–1888), New York Gothams (joined in 1883 and are the present-day **San Francisco Giants**), Philadelphia Quakers (joined in 1883 and are the present-day **Philadelphia Phillies**), **St. Louis Maroons** (joined in 1885 and became the **Indianapolis Hoosiers** in 1887 and folded after the 1889 season), **Kansas City Cowboys** (1886), **Washington Nationals** (1886–1889), Pittsburgh Alleghenys (joined in 1887 and are the present-day **Pittsburgh Pirates**), **Cleveland Spiders** (1889–1899), **Cincinnati Reds** (joined in 1890 and are still in the league), Brooklyn Bridegrooms (joined in 1890 and are the present-day **Los Angeles Dodgers**), **Baltimore Orioles** (1892–1899), **Louisville Colonels** (1892–1899), St. Louis Browns (joined in 1892 and are the present-day **St. Louis Cardinals**), and **Washington Senators** (1892–1899).

By 1900, the NL had eight teams, located in Boston, Brooklyn, Chicago, Cincinnati, New York, Philadelphia, Pittsburgh, and St. Louis. It remained that way until 1953, when the **Boston Braves** moved to Milwaukee and became the **Milwaukee Braves**. In 1958, the NL added the West Coast to the major-league roster, when the **Brooklyn Dodgers** moved to Los Angeles and became the Los Angeles Dodgers, and the **New York Giants** moved to San Francisco and became the San Francisco Giants. In 1966, the Milwaukee Braves moved to Atlanta and became the Atlanta Braves.

In 1962, the league expanded, adding two new teams, the Houston Colt .45s (now the **Houston Astros**) and **New York Mets**. In 1969, the NL expanded from 10 teams to 12, adding the **Montreal Expos** (the first major-league team from outside the United States) and **San Diego Padres**. Two more teams, the **Colorado Rockies** and Florida Marlins (now the **Miami Marlins**) were added in 1993. The present total of 16 teams was achieved in 1998, with the addition of the **Arizona Diamondbacks** and the transfer of the **Milwaukee Brewers** from the AL to the NL. In 2005, the league moved the Montreal Expos to Washington, where they became the Washington Nationals.

The NL is made up of three divisions. The Eastern Division has the Atlanta Braves, Miami Marlins, New York Mets, Philadelphia Phillies, and Washington Nationals. The Central Division has the Chicago Cubs, Cincinnati Reds, Houston Astros, Milwaukee Brewers, Pittsburgh Pirates, and St. Louis Cardinals. The Western Division has the Arizona Diamondbacks, Colorado Rockies, Los Angeles Dodgers, San Diego Padres, and San Francisco Giants. In 2013, the Houston Astros will move to the Western Division of the AL so that each league can have 15 teams.

Morgan Bulkeley, the NL's original president, served only one year, 1876. He was succeeded by William Hulbert (1877–1882), Arthur Soden (1882), Abraham G. Mills (1883–1884), Nicholas Young (1885–1902), Harry C. Pulliam (1903–1909), John Heydler (1909), Thomas J. Lynch (1910–1913), John K. Tener (1913–1918), John Heydler (1918–1934), **Ford Frick** (1934–1951), **Warren Giles** (1951–1969), Charles Feeney (1970–1986), Bart Giamatti (1986–1989), Bill White (1989–1994), and Leonard Coleman (1994–1999). The office of league president was abolished after the 1999 season.

NATIONAL LEAGUE CHAMPIONSHIP SERIES (NLCS). The National League Championship Series (NLCS) is now the second round of the postseason playoffs in the **National League (NL)**. The NLCS began in 1969, when the league expanded to 12 teams and split into an Eastern Division and a Western Division. The winners of each division played a best-of-five series to determine who would advance to the **World Series**. In 1985, the format changed from a best-of-five to a best-of-seven. In 1994, the league was restructured into an Eastern Division, a Central Division, and a Western Division. Beginning in 1995, the three division winners and a **wild-card** team advanced to a new first round of playoffs called the **National League Division Series (NLDS)**. The two NLDS winners advance to the NLCS, with the winner of the best-of-seven NLCS going on to represent the NL in the World Series.

NATIONAL LEAGUE DIVISION SERIES (NLDS). The National League Division Series (NLDS) was first played in 1995, one year after the 14-team **National League (AL)** was restructured into an Eastern Division, a Central Division, and a Western Division. From 1995–2011, the NLDS consisted of two best-of-five series, featuring the winners of the three divisions plus a **wild-card** team, the second-place team with the best record. Beginning with the 2012 season, the wild card team is the winner of a "play-in" game between the two non-division winners with the best record. That team will become the fourth qualifier for the NLDS. The two NLDS winners then advance to the **National League Championship Series (NLCS)**, with the NLCS winner going on to represent the NL in the **World Series**. A NLDS was played during the strike-season of 1981, matching the pre-strike leaders and the post-strike leaders in each division.

NATIONALS PARK. Nationals Park, located in Washington, D.C., has been the home field of the **Washington Nationals** of the **National League** since 2008. The Nationals previously played at **Robert F. Kennedy Stadium** from 2005 through 2007. Nationals Park has a seating capacity of approximately 42,300. It has yet to host the **major league All-Star Game**.
See also STADIUMS.

NAVIN FIELD. *See* TIGER STADIUM.

NEGRO AMERICAN LEAGUE (NAL). The Negro American League (NAL) began play in 1937, and the league remained fairly viable through 1957, although the beginning of integration in the **major leagues** in the late 1940s and early 1950s made the NAL much less attractive to black fans. Among the NAL's most prominent teams were the Birmingham Black Barons, Cleveland Buckeyes, Indianapolis Clowns, **Kansas City Monarchs**, and Memphis Red Sox.
See also NEGRO LEAGUES.

NEGRO LEAGUES. The Negro Leagues were formed after black players were barred from playing in the **major leagues**. The Negro Leagues existed roughly from 1885 until the 1950s, when the integration of the major leagues made them much less attractive to black fans. There were numerous leagues formed during these years, but most were poorly administered. Three leagues that did have success and produced many outstanding players were the **Eastern Colored League**, **Negro American League**, and **Negro National League**.

NEGRO LEAGUES COMMITTEE. The Negro Leagues Committee was a special committee formed in 1971 to recognize the players in the **Negro Leagues** who were deserving of election to the **National Baseball Hall of Fame (HOF)**. The committee elected one or two players per year for seven years. Beginning in 1978, the **Veterans Committee** became responsible for the election of Negro Leaguers to the HOF.

NEGRO NATIONAL LEAGUE (NNL). The Negro National League (NNL) had two incarnations. In the first, from 1920 through 1931, the league championship was won each year by one of three teams: the **Chicago American Giants** (1920–1922, 1926–1927), **Kansas City Monarchs** (1923–1925, 1929), and **St. Louis Stars** (1930–1931). The economic depression caused the league to cease operations in 1932, but it returned in 1933 and lasted through 1948, when the integration of the **major leagues** made a league for black players no longer necessary. The **Homestead Grays** were far and away the dominant team in the new NNL, winning championships in 1937, 1938, 1940, 1941, 1942, 1943, 1944, 1945, and 1948. Among the league's other prominent teams were the **Baltimore Elite Giants, Pittsburgh Crawfords, Philadelphia Stars, New York Cubans**, and **Newark Eagles**.

See also NEGRO LEAGUES.

NETHERLANDS. Baseball was introduced to Holland in 1911, although it was not until 1922 that the first professional league was formed. The Koninklijke Nederlandse Baseball en **Softball** Bond is the national governing body for baseball in the Netherlands. The teams in the league, currently known as the Honkball Hoofdklasse, include AdoLakers; Almere Magpies; Corenden Kinheim; DOOR Neptunus; Konica Minolta Pioniers; LAmsterdam; Mr. Cocker HCAW; and Sparta/Feyenoord. Teams play roughly a 40-game regular season, from about June to mid-September. The top four teams make the playoffs, where they compete in a best-of-five semifinals, followed by a best-of-five Holland Series. Each team also has one minor league team that plays a 37-game season.

The Netherlands National Baseball Team is consistently ranked in the top 10 of the **International Baseball Federation's** world rankings and has won the **European Baseball Championship** 20 times. The 2012 European Baseball Championship, held in the Netherlands in September 2012, was won by Italy. The Netherlands was the first European team to win since Great Britain won the first Baseball World Cup in 1938.

The Kingdom of the Netherlands also includes Aruba and Curacao.The most notable **major league** player born in Holland is **Bert Blyleven**. The most notable player born in Curacao is Andruw Jones. The most notable player born in Aruba is Sidney Ponson.

NETWORK ASSOCIATES COLISEUM. *See* O.CO COLISEUM.

NEW HAVEN ELM CITYS. The New Haven Elm Citys were members of the National Association (NA) in 1875, the NA's final season. They lost 40 of their 47 games played.

NEW YORK CUBANS. The New York Cubans played in the **Negro Leagues** from 1935 to 1950. In 1947, the Cubans were the champions of the **Negro National League**. The team was made up of **African Americans** and Latin Americans. Among the notable players from the Negro Leagues who played part of their careers with the Cubans were Perucho Cepeda, **Martin Dihigo**, Minnie Minoso, and Luis Tiant Sr.

NEW YORK GAME. The New York Game refers to an early form of "base ball" played in the mid-19th century in New York City, Brooklyn, and nearby areas. There were four **bases**, usually posts set in the ground, although shallow holes were used in less formal play. The layout was asymmetrical. The **batter**, called the "striker," was stationed about 36 feet to the right of the fourth post; he had to run, at an angle, 45 feet to the first post, then 60 feet to second, 72 feet to third, and another 72 feet to fourth, or home.

There were usually 11 players per team, but the number could range from eight to 15, depending on how many happened to be available. The thrower had to toss the ball underhanded, and the batter had to try to make it to **first base** after hitting the ball, no matter where it went. Because the entire field was in play, there were two **catchers** stationed well behind the hitter.

The ball used in the New York Game was made of loose shavings of rubber wrapped in yarn and covered with leather, usually horsehide. It was larger and considerably softer than the ball used in the rival **Massachusetts Game**. Generally, a team was given three **outs** per **inning**, and the game ended when one team scored 100 **runs**. Sometimes, however, the "one out, all out" rule was used. Later, the name "New York Game" was also applied to the version of baseball developed by the **Knickerbocker Base Ball Club**.

NEW YORK GIANTS (NL). The New York Giants, known as the New York Gothams in 1883 and 1884, entered the **National League (NL)** in 1883. Almost half of the original Gotham players were members of the recently disbanded **Troy Trojans** of the NL. The Giants played their home games at various incarnations of the **Polo Grounds**, including the last incarnation, from 28 June 1911 to 29 September 1957. (From 1912 to 1919, the park was alternately known as Brush Stadium, in honor of owner John Brush.)

The Giants won back-to-back NL pennants in 1888 and 1889 and then played the **American Association** pennant winner in a championship series that was a predecessor to the modern **World Series**. In 1888, the Giants defeated the St. Louis Browns, and, in 1889, they defeated the Brooklyn Bridegrooms.

John McGraw, the Giants' **manager** from 1902 to 1932, led them to 10 pennants, but the team had a 3–6 record in nine World Series. (McGraw and Brush declined to play in a World Series against the Boston Americans in 1904 because of their refusal to recognize the new **American League** as a **major league**.) Giants World Series victories under McGraw were against the **Philadelphia Athletics** (1905) and **New York Yankees** (1921–1922). Their Series losses were to the Athletics (1911, 1913), **Boston Red Sox** (1912), **Chicago White Sox** (1917), Yankees (1923), and **Washington Senators** (1924). Later Giants teams won the 1933 World Series against the Senators and the 1954 Series against the **Cleveland Indians**. They also lost three times, all to the Yankees, in 1936, 1937, and 1951. In 1958, owner Horace Stoneham moved the Giants to San Francisco.

New York Giants who won the NL's **Most Valuable Player Award** were Larry Doyle (1912), **Carl Hubbell** (1933, 1936), and **Willie Mays** (1954). No New York Giants **pitcher** won the **Cy Young Award**. Willie Mays, in 1951, was the only winner of the **Rookie of the Year Award**.

New York Giants players who led the NL in **batting average** were **Roger Connor** (1885), Jack Glasscock (1890), Larry Doyle (1915), **Bill Terry** (1930), and Willie Mays (1954). **Home run** leaders were **Buck Ewing** (1883), Mike Tiernan (1890–1891), Bill Joyce (1896, part of season with **Washington Senators**), Red Murray (1909), Dave Robertson (1916–1917), **George Kelly** (1921), **Mel Ott** (1932, 1934, 1936–1938, 1942), **Johnny Mize** (1947–1948), and Willie Mays (1955). **Runs batted in** leaders were Roger Connor (1889), **George Davis** (1897), Sam Mertes (1903), Bill Dahlen (1904), Heinie Zimmerman (1916–1917, part of 1916 season with **Chicago Cubs**), George Kelly (1920, 1924), Irish Meusel (1923), Mel Ott (1934), Johnny Mize (1942, 1947), and **Monte Irvin** (1951).

New York Giants pitchers who led the NL in **wins** were **Tim Keefe** (1886, 1888), **Amos Rusie** (1894), **Joe McGinnity** (1903–1904, 1906), **Christy Mathewson** (1905, 1907–1908, 1910), **Rube Marquard** (1912), Jesse Barnes (1919), Larry Benton (1928), Carl Hubbell (1933, 1936–1937), Larry Jansen (1951), and Sal Maglie (1951). **Earned run average (ERA)** leaders were Tim Keefe (1885, 1888), John Ewing (1891), Amos Rusie (1894, 1897), Joe McGinnity (1904), Christy Mathewson (1905, 1908–1909, 1911, and 1913), Jeff Tesreau (1912), Fred Anderson (1917), Phil Douglas (1922), Bill Walker (1929, 1931), Carl Hubbell (1933–1934, 1936), Dave Koslo (1949), Sal Maglie (1950), **Hoyt Wilhelm** (1952), and Johnny Antonelli (1954). **Strikeouts** leaders were Tim Keefe (1888), Amos Rusie (1890–1891, 1893–1895), Cy Seymour (1897–1898), Christy Mathewson (1903–1905, 1907–1908), Rube Marquard (1911), Carl Hubbell (1937), and Bill Voiselle (1944). By leading in wins, ERA, and strikeouts in 1894, Amos Rusie won the **Triple Crown** for pitchers. By leading in wins, ERA, and strikeouts in 1905 and 1908, Christy Mathewson won the Triple Crown for pitchers in both those years.

Other notable players and **managers** for the New York Giants included Ace Adams, Red Ames, **Dave Bancroft**, Virgil Barnes, Dick Bartell, Jack Bentley, Rube Benton, **Roger Bresnahan**, George Burns, Walker Cooper, Doc Crandall, Harry Danning, Alvin Dark, Art Devlin, Mike Donlin, **Leo Durocher**, Freddie Fitzsimmons, Art Fletcher, **Frankie Frisch**, Jim Hearn, **Travis Jackson**, **Fred Lindstrom**, Whitey Lockman, Gus Mancuso, Willard Marshall, Jouett Meekin, Cliff Melton, Fred Merkle, Chief Meyers, Jo-Jo Moore, Don Mueller, Jim Mutrie, Art Nehf, **Jim O'Rourke**, Pol Perritt, Hal Schumacher, Fred Snodgrass, Eddie Stanky, Dummy Taylor, Bobby Thomson, George Van Haltren, **John Montgomery Ward**, **Mickey Welch**, Wes Westrum, Hooks Wiltse, and **Ross Youngs**.

NEW YORK GIANTS (PL). The New York Giants were a team in the **Players' League (PL)** in 1890, the one year of the PL's existence. Led by **catcher Buck Ewing,** who also served as **player-manager,** the team mostly consisted of members of the 1889 **New York Giants** of the **National League.** Despite the presence of stars like Ewing, **Jim O'Rourke**, and **Roger Connor,** who led the PL in **home runs,** with 14, the Giants finished third. Other notable players on the Giants of the PL were George Gore, **Tim Keefe**, and Hank O'Day.

NEW YORK GOTHAMS. *See* NEW YORK GIANTS (NL); TROY (NEW YORK) TROJANS.

NEW YORK HIGHLANDERS. *See* NEW YORK YANKEES.

NEW YORK METROPOLITANS. The New York Metropolitans were a team in the **American Association (AA)** from 1883 to 1887. In 1884, they won the AA pennant, but the team lost to the **Providence Grays** of the **National League (NL),** three games to none in the first championship series between the AA and NL. These postseason games were a predecessor to the modern **World Series**. Notable players for the Metropolitans included Dude Esterbrook, **Tim Keefe**, Jack Lynch, and Dave Orr.

NEW YORK METS. The New York Mets are a team in the Eastern Division of the **National League (NL)**. They entered the NL along with the Houston Colt .45s (now the **Houston Astros**) in 1962 as part of the NL's first **expansion** of the 20th century. The two new teams raised the NL's total of teams to 10; it had been eight since 1900. There had been no NL team in New York City since 1958, when the **Brooklyn Dodgers** moved to Los Angeles and the **New York Giants** moved to San Francisco. The Mets played their home games at the **Polo Grounds**, the former home of the Giants, in 1962 and 1963, before moving to **Shea Stadium** in Queens, New York, in 1964. In 2009, the Mets opened a new stadium, **Citi Field**, which is next to the site of the demolished Shea Stadium.

The Mets have won four NL pennants and two **World Series**. They won the 1969 Series over the **Baltimore Orioles** in five games and the 1986 Series over the **Boston Red Sox** in seven games. In 1973, they lost the Series to the **Oakland Athletics** in seven games, and, in 2000, they lost to the **New York Yankees** in five games. The Mets have lost in the **National League Championship Series** three times, in 1988, 1999, and 2006.

No New York Mets player has won the NL's **Most Valuable Player Award**. **Cy Young Award** winners are **Tom Seaver** (1969, 1973, 1975), Dwight Gooden (1985), and R. A. Dickey (2012). **Rookie of the Year** winners are Tom Seaver (1967), Jon Matlack (1972), Darryl Strawberry (1983), and Dwight Gooden (1984).

Jose Reyes, in 2011, is the only Mets player to lead the league in **batting average**. **Home run** leaders are Dave Kingman (1982), Darryl Strawberry (1988), and Howard Johnson (1991). Howard Johnson, in 1991, is the only Mets player to lead the league in **runs batted in**.

New York Mets **pitchers** who have led the NL in **wins** are Tom Seaver (1969, 1975) and Dwight Gooden (1985). **Earned run average (ERA)** leaders are Tom Seaver (1970–1971, 1973), Craig Swan (1978), Dwight Gooden (1985), and Johan Santana (2008). **Strikeouts** leaders are Tom Seaver (1970–1971, 1973, 1975–1976), Dwight Gooden (1984–1985), David Cone (1990–1991), and R. A. Dickey (2012). By leading in wins, ERA, and strikeouts in 1985, Dwight Gooden won the **Triple Crown** for pitchers.

Other notable players and **managers** for the Mets include Edgar Alfonzo, Wally Backman, Carlos Beltran, **Yogi Berra**, **Gary Carter**, Ron Darling, Ike Davis, Lenny Dykstra, Pedro Feliciano, Sid Fernandez, John Franco, Bud Harrelson, Keith Hernandez, Gil Hodges, Davey Johnson, Cleon Jones, Jerry

Koosman, Ed Kranepool, Al Leiter, Jon Matlack, Lee Mazzilli, Tug McGraw, Bob Ojeda, Jesse Orosco, **Mike Piazza**, Rusty Staub, John Stearns, **Casey Stengel**, Bobby Valentine, Mookie Wilson, and David Wright.

NEW YORK MUTUALS (NA). The New York Mutuals, a team in existence since 1857, joined the National Association (NA) in 1871, and the team remained in the NA throughout its five-year existence. Notable players for the Mutuals included **Candy Cummings**, **Bobby Mathews**, and **Joe Start**. In 1876, the Mutuals became a charter member of the new **National League**, but they were expelled from the league after one season for failing to complete their schedule.

NEW YORK MUTUALS (NL). The New York Mutuals left the National Association (NA) after the NA disbanded following the 1875 season. In 1876, the Mutuals were a charter member of the new **National League (NL)**, where they finished sixth in the eight-team league. The Mutuals were expelled from the NL after the season for failing to complete their schedule.

NEW YORK YANKEES. The New York Yankees are a team in the Eastern Division of the **American League (AL)**. The team originated as the **Baltimore Orioles** in 1901, the first year the AL was recognized as a **major league**. After the 1902 season, the franchise was moved to New York and renamed the New York Highlanders, and eventually the **New York Yankees**. The Highlanders played their home games at Hilltop Park from the time of their arrival in 1903 through the 1912 season. They were tenants of the **New York Giants** of the **National League (NL)** at the **Polo Grounds** from 1913 to 1922, before moving into their new park, **Yankee Stadium (I)**, in 1923. When Yankee Stadium was closed for renovations, in 1974 and 1975, the Yankees were again the tenants of a NL team, playing at **Shea Stadium**, the home of the **New York Mets**. They played in the refurbished Yankee Stadium (I) from 1976 through 2008. In 2009, the Yankees moved into their current home, **Yankee Stadium (II)**.

The Yankees finished as high as second place three times in their first 18 seasons, but they were mostly also-rans. Then, in 1920, new owners **Jacob Ruppert** and Til Huston purchased **Babe Ruth** from the **Boston Red Sox**, and the Yankees went on to become the most successful baseball team ever. Through 2011, the Yankees had won 40 pennants and 27 world championships, far exceeding the number won by any other team. Their **World Series** triumphs have come against the New York Giants (1923, 1936–1937, 1951), **Pittsburgh Pirates** (1927), **St. Louis Cardinals** (1928, 1943), **Chicago Cubs** (1932, 1938), **Cincinnati Reds** (1939, 1961), **Brooklyn Dodgers** (1941, 1947, 1949, 1952–1953, 1956), **Philadelphia Phillies** (1950, 2009),

Milwaukee Braves (1958), San Francisco Giants (1962), Los Angeles Dodgers (1977–1978), Atlanta Braves (1996, 1999), San Diego Padres (1998), and New York Mets (2000).

New York's World Series losses were to the New York Giants (1921–1922), St. Louis Cardinals (1926, 1942, 1964), Brooklyn Dodgers (1955), Milwaukee Braves (1957), Pittsburgh Pirates (1960), Los Angeles Dodgers (1963, 1981), Cincinnati Reds (1976), Arizona Diamondbacks (2001), and Florida Marlins (2003). A frequent playoff participant, the Yankees have lost in the American League Division Series seven times and the American League Championship Series in 1980, 2004, 2010, and 2012.

New York Yankees who have won the AL's Most Valuable Player Award are Babe Ruth (1923), Lou Gehrig (1927, 1936), Joe DiMaggio (1939, 1941, 1947), Joe Gordon (1942), Spud Chandler (1943), Phil Rizzuto (1950), Yogi Berra (1951, 1954–1955), Mickey Mantle (1956–1957, 1962), Roger Maris (1960–1961), Elston Howard (1963), Thurman Munson (1976), Don Mattingly (1985), and Alex Rodriguez (2005, 2007). Cy Young Award winners are Bob Turley (1958), Whitey Ford (1961), Sparky Lyle (1977), Ron Guidry (1978), and Roger Clemens (2001). Rookie of the Year winners are Gil McDougald (1951), Bob Grim (1954), Tony Kubek (1957), Tom Tresh (1962), Stan Bahnsen (1968), Thurman Munson (1970), Dave Righetti (1981), and Derek Jeter (1996).

Yankees players who have led the AL in batting average are Babe Ruth (1924), Lou Gehrig (1934), Joe DiMaggio (1939–1940), George Stirnweiss (1945), Mickey Mantle (1956), Don Mattingly (1984), Paul O'Neill (1994), and Bernie Williams (1998). Leaders in home runs are Wally Pipp (1916–1917), Babe Ruth (1920–1921, 1923–1924, 1926–1931), Bob Meusel (1925), Lou Gehrig (1931, 1934, 1936), Joe DiMaggio (1937, 1948), Nick Etten (1944), Mickey Mantle (1955–1956, 1958, 1960), Roger Maris (1961), Graig Nettles (1976), Reggie Jackson (1980), Alex Rodriguez (2005, 2007), and Mark Teixeira (2009). Leaders in runs batted in (RBI) are Babe Ruth (1920–1921, 1923, 1926, and 1928), Bob Meusel (1925), Lou Gehrig (1927–1928, 1930–1931, 1934), Joe DiMaggio (1941, 1948), Nick Etten (1945), Mickey Mantle (1956), Roger Maris (1960–1961), Don Mattingly (1985), Alex Rodriguez (2007), Mark Teixeira (2009), and Curtis Granderson (2011). By leading the AL in batting average, home runs, and RBI, Lou Gehrig won the Triple Crown for batters in 1934. By leading the AL in batting average, home runs, and RBI, Mickey Mantle won the Triple Crown for batters in 1956.

Yankees pitchers who have led the AL in wins are Jack Chesbro (1904), Al Orth (1906), Carl Mays (1921), Waite Hoyt (1927), George Pipgras (1928), Lefty Gomez (1934, 1937), Red Ruffing (1938), Spud Chandler (1943), Whitey Ford (1955, 1961, 1963), Bob Turley (1958), Ralph Terry (1962), Catfish Hunter (1975), Ron Guidry (1978, 1985), Jimmy Key

(1994), Andy Pettitte (1996), David Cone (1998), Chien-Ming Wang (2006), and C. C. Sabathia (2009–2010). **Earned run average (ERA)** leaders are Bob Shawkey (1920), Wilcy Moore (1927), Lefty Gomez (1934, 1937), Spud Chandler (1943), Allie Reynolds (1952), Ed Lopat (1953), Whitey Ford (1956, 1958), Bobby Shantz (1957), Ron Guidry (1978–1979), Rudy May (1980), and Dave Righetti (1981). **Strikeouts** leaders are Red Ruffing (1932), Lefty Gomez (1933–1934, 1937), Vic Raschi (1951), Allie Reynolds (1952), and Al Downing (1964). By leading in wins, ERA, and strikeouts in 1934 and 1937, Lefty Gomez won the Triple Crown for pitchers in both those years.

Other notable players and **managers** for the Yankees include Johnny Allen, **Frank Baker**, Hank Bauer, **Wade Boggs**, Hank Borowy, Jim Bouton, Clete Boyer, Joe Bush, Ray Caldwell, Robinson Cano, Chris Chambliss, Ben Chapman, Hal Chase, **Earle Combs**, Frank Crosetti, **Bill Dickey**, Joe Dugan, Ryne Duren, Ed Figueroa, Russ Ford, Jason Giambi, Joe Girardi, **Goose Gossage**, **Rickey Henderson**, Tommy Henrich, Ralph Houk, **Miller Hug-**

Figure 14.2. The 1939 New York Yankees swept the Cincinnati Reds in the World Series and are thought by many to be baseball's best team ever. *National Baseball Hall of Fame Library, Cooperstown, N.Y.*

gins, **Tommy John**, Charlie Keller, Mark Koenig, Don Larsen, **Tony Lazze-ri**, Billy Martin, Tino Martinez, Hideki Matsui, **Joe McCarthy**, Bobby Murcer, Johnny Murphy, Mike Mussina, Joe Page, Roger Peckinpaugh, **Herb Pennock**, Joe Pepitone, Fritz Peterson, Lou Piniella, Jorge Posada, Willie Randolph, Bobby Richardson, **Mariano Rivera**, Red Rolfe, Wally Schang, George Selkirk, Bill Skowron, **Casey Stengel**, Mel Stottlemyre, **Joe Torre**, David Wells, Roy White, **Dave Winfield**, and Gene Woodling.

NEWARK (NEW JERSEY) EAGLES. The Newark Eagles played in the **Negro National League (NNL)** from 1936 to 1948. The Eagles, owned by **Effa Manley**, the first woman to own a professional sports team, were the NNL champions in 1946. Among the notable players who spent part of their careers with the Eagles were **Leon Day**, **Ray Dandridge**, **Larry Doby**, **Monte Irvin**, **Biz Mackey**, Don Newcombe, and **Willie Wells**.

NEWARK (NEW JERSEY) PEPPERS. The Newark Peppers were a team in the **Federal League (FL)** in 1915, the second of the two seasons the FL existed as a **major league**. The Peppers had relocated from Indianapolis, replacing the **Indianapolis Hoosiers**, winners of the league pennant in 1914. The shift was made because the FL wanted to establish itself in the New York metropolitan area. They had planned to move the **Kansas City Packers** to Newark, but just before the season started they chose to move the Indianapolis club instead. Having lost their star player, Benny Kauff, to the **Brooklyn Tip-Tops**, the Peppers slipped to fifth place. Notable players for the Peppers included Vin Campbell; **Bill McKechnie**; Earl Moseley, who led the league in **earned run average**; **Edd Roush**; and Ed Reulbach.

NEWHOUSER, HAROLD "HAL," "PRINCE HAL". B. 20 May 1921, Detroit, Michigan. D. 10 November 1998, Detroit, Michigan. Hal Newhouser was 18 years old when he signed with the hometown **Detroit Tigers** in 1939. During the next four seasons (1940–1943), the slender 6-foot, 2-inch, 180-pound left-handed **pitcher** won 34 games and lost 51. His career took off in 1944, and, during the final two years of World War II, he was baseball's best pitcher. Newhouser's record in 1944 was 29–9, with a 2.22 **earned run average (ERA)**, and, in 1945, it was 25–9, with a 1.81 ERA. In both seasons, he led the league in **wins**, and, in 1945, he was the ERA leader. By also leading the **American League (AL)** with 212 **strikeouts** in 1945, Newhous-er earned the **Triple Crown** for pitchers. Newhouser was the AL's **Most Valuable Player** and **Pitcher of the Year** in both 1944 and 1945. He was the **Major League Player of the Year** in 1945, capping the season by winning two games in Detroit's seven-game **World Series** victory over the **Chicago Cubs**.

Some critics claimed that Newhouser's success had come against the lesser competition of the war years, but, in 1946, "Prince Hal" led the AL in wins (26) for a third consecutive season, and in ERA (1.94) for a second consecutive season. Newhouser had a fourth 20-plus win season (21–12) in 1948. He also pitched in four **All-Star Games**, with a 2.53 ERA in 10 2/3 **innings**. Released by the Tigers in July 1953, Newhouser signed with the **Cleveland Indians** in 1954, where he had his last productive season. Pitching almost exclusively in relief, he went 7–2, with a 2.51 ERA, for the pennant-winning Indians. Newhouser retired after just two games in 1955, concluding his career with 207 wins and 150 losses. He was elected to the **National Baseball Hall of Fame** by the **Veterans Committee** in 1992.

NICARAGUA. Baseball has been played in Nicaragua since the 19th century, and it is the country's national game. Professional baseball has come and gone, with the current league dating back to 2004. The Nicaraguan Professional Baseball League (La Liga Nicaragüense de Beisbol Profesional) has four teams: the Indios del Boer, Tigres del Chinandega, Leones de Leon, and Orientales de Granada. Nicaraguan teams compete in the **Baseball World Cup**, Pan-American Games, Central American Games, Central American and Caribbean Games, and **World Baseball Classic**.

Dennis Martinez, a **major-league pitcher** from 1976 to 1998, is the most notable player born in Nicaragua. Other notable Nicaraguan-born major leaguers were Marvin Benard, David Green, Vicente Padilla, and Albert Williams. Two who starred in the early years of baseball in Nicaragua were Stanley Cayasso and Jose Angel "Chino" Melendez.

NICHOLS, CHARLES AUGUSTUS "KID". B. 14 September 1869, Madison, Wisconsin. D. 11 April 1953, Kansas City, Missouri. Kid Nichols was a 20-year-old **rookie pitcher** for the 1891 Boston Beaneaters when he won 27 games and led the **National League (NL)** in **shutouts**. He followed by winning 30 or more games in seven of the next eight seasons (he won "only" 26 in 1895), while leading the NL in **wins** in 1896, 1897, and 1898. Nichols won more games than any other pitcher during the 1890s, and Boston won five NL championships during his 12 years with them. Nichols became part-owner and **manager** of a **minor-league** club in Kansas City, for whom he pitched in 1902 and 1903. He returned to the NL in 1904 as a **player-manager** for the **St. Louis Cardinals**. He won 21 games in 1904, but he was fired as manager in mid-1905 and finished his career with the 1905 and 1906 **Philadelphia Phillies**. Nichols, a 5-foot, 10-inch, 175-pound right-hander, is the youngest pitcher to win 300 games. He won 361 (361–208), seventh best all-time. His 532 **complete games** (in 562 **games started**) is fourth best. In 1949, the **Old Timers Committee** elected Nichols to the **National Baseball Hall of Fame**.

NIEKRO, PHILIP HENRY "PHIL". B. 1 April 1939, Blaine, Ohio. Phil Niekro was the most successful **knuckleball pitcher** in **major-league** history. He won 318 games, and his 121 **wins** after the age of 40 is a major-league record. Combined with brother Joe's 221 wins, the Niekro brothers' 539 victories are the most ever by two brothers. Phil made his debut with the **Milwaukee Braves** in 1964, but he did not become a regular starter until 1966, after the Braves relocated to Atlanta. In 1967, his 1.87 **earned run average** led the **National League (NL)**. He also led the league in **wild pitches**, with 19. Because of the difficulty many **catchers** have with handling a knuckleball, Niekro led the league in wild pitches three times and had 226 in his career. The 6-foot, 1-inch, 180-pound right-hander was a workhorse. He led the NL in **innings pitched** four times, with more than 300 **innings** each time. He also led four times in both **games started** and **complete games**. Pitching for mostly mediocre teams in Atlanta, Niekro led the league in **losses** for four consecutive seasons (1977–1980). His 1979 record was 21–20, the third and final time he was a 20-game winner. His .810 **winning percentage** (17–4) in 1982 was tops in the NL. Also a strong **fielder**, he won five **Gold Glove Awards** in his career.

In 1984, Niekro signed as a **free agent** with the **New York Yankees**. He was a 16-game winner for the Yanks in 1984 and 1985, and he then signed as a free agent with the **Cleveland Indians** in 1986. In his final season, 1987, Niekro pitched for Cleveland and the **Toronto Blue Jays**, before making one final start for the Braves. Niekro, 16th all-time in career wins and 11th in career **strikeouts**, was elected to the **National Baseball Hall of Fame** by the **Baseball Writers' Association of America** in 1997.

NIPPON PROFESSIONAL BASEBALL. *See* JAPAN.

NO-HITTER. An official no-hit game occurs when a **pitcher** (or pitchers) allows no **hits** during the entire course of a game, which consists of at least nine **innings**. In a no-hit game, a **batter** may reach **base** via a walk, an **error**, a **hit by pitch**, a **passed ball** or **wild pitch** on strike three, or **catcher's interference**.

There have been 279 no-hitters in the **major leagues** through the 2012 season, including 23 that were **perfect games**, one in which the pitcher (or pitchers) allows no runners to reach base at all.

The first **major league** no-hitter was thrown by Joe Borden of the **Philadelphia White Stockings** of the National Association on 28 July 1875. The first **National League (NL)** no-hitter was thrown by George Bradley of the **St. Louis Brown Stockings** on 15 July 1876. The first no-hitter at the modern pitching distance of 60 feet, 6 inches was thrown by Bill Hawke of the **Baltimore Orioles** of the NL on 16 August 1893. The first **American League** no-hitter was thrown by Jim Callahan of the **Chicago White Sox** on 20 September 1902.

There have been two postseason no-hitters. On 8 October 1956, in Game Five of the **World Series**, Don Larsen of the **New York Yankees** pitched a perfect game against the **Brooklyn Dodgers**. On 6 October 2010, in Game One of the **National League Division Series**, **Roy Halladay** of the **Philadelphia Phillies** pitched a no-hitter against the **Cincinnati Reds**. **Nolan Ryan** holds the record for the most no-hitters, with seven.

OAKLAND ATHLETICS. The Oakland Athletics are a team in the Western Division of the **American League (AL)**. They were the **Philadelphia Athletics** when they joined the AL as a charter member in 1901. The Athletics moved to Kansas City and became the **Kansas City Athletics** in 1955, and the team moved to Oakland in 1968. The team has played its home games at what was originally called the Oakland-Alameda County Coliseum since 7 April 1968. The Oakland-Alameda County Coliseum has also been called the Network Associates Coliseum, McAfee Coliseum, and Overstock.com Coliseum. It is currently called **O.co Coliseum**.

Owned by the colorful Charles Finley, Oakland finished in first place in the AL's Western Division for five consecutive years from 1971 through 1975. They lost the **American League Championship Series (ALCS)** in 1971 and 1975, but the A's won three consecutive **World Series** from 1972 to 1974. They defeated the **Cincinnati Reds** in 1972, **New York Mets** in 1973, and **Los Angeles Dodgers** in 1974. Oakland also lost the ALCS in 1981, 1992, 2006, and 2012. The A's lost four consecutive **American League Division Series** from 2000 through 2003. Under **manager Tony LaRussa**, the A's won consecutive pennants in 1988, 1989, and 1990. They won the 1989 World Series in a sweep of the **San Francisco Giants**, but they lost in five games to the Los Angeles Dodgers in 1988 and in four games to the Cincinnati Reds in 1990.

Seven Oakland Athletics have won the AL's **Most Valuable Player Award,** including Vida Blue (1971), **Reggie Jackson** (1973), Jose Canseco (1988), **Rickey Henderson** (1990), **Dennis Eckersley** (1992), Jason Giambi (2000), and Miguel Tejada (2002). **Cy Young Award** winners are Vida Blue (1971), **Catfish Hunter** (1974), Bob Welch (1990), Dennis Eckersley (1992), and Barry Zito (2002). **Rookie of the Year** winners are Jose Canseco (1986), **Mark McGwire** (1987), Walt Weiss (1988), Ben Grieve (1998), Bobby Crosby (2004), Huston Street (2005), and Andrew Bailey (2009).

No Oakland player has led the AL in **batting average**. Leaders in **home runs** are Reggie Jackson (1973, 1975), Tony Armas (1981), Mark McGwire (1987, 1996), and Jose Canseco (1988, 1991). Leaders in **runs batted in** are Reggie Jackson (1973) and Jose Canseco (1988).

Oakland **pitchers** who have led the league in **wins** are Catfish Hunter (1974–1975), Steve McCatty (1981), Dave Stewart (1987), Bob Welch (1990), Tim Hudson (2000), Mark Mulder (2001), and Barry Zito (2002). **Earned run average** leaders are Diego Segui (1970), Vida Blue (1971), Catfish Hunter (1974), and Steve Ontiveros (1994). No Oakland pitcher has led the AL in **strikeouts**.

Other notable players and managers in Oakland history include Sal Bando, Trevor Cahill, Bert Campaneris, Eric Chavez, Alvin Dark, Mark Ellis, **Rollie Fingers**, Dan Haren, Ken Holtzman, Art Howe, Matt Keough, Rick Langford, Carney Lansford, Billy Martin, Bill North, Tony Phillips, Joe Rudi, Terry Steinbach, Kurt Suzuki, Gene Tenace, and **Dick Williams**.

OAKLAND-ALAMEDA COUNTY COLISEUM. *See* O.CO COLISEUM.

OBSTRUCTION. Obstruction occurs when a play is being made on an obstructed **base runner**, or if the **batter** is obstructed before he touches **first base**. The ball is dead, and all **runners** shall advance to the **bases** they would have reached, in the **umpire's** judgment, if there had been no obstruction. The obstructed runner is awarded at least one base beyond the base he had last legally touched before the obstruction. Any preceding runners, forced to advance by the award of bases as the penalty for obstruction, advance without liability to be put **out**.

Obstruction can also occur when no play is being made on the obstructed runner. In that case, the play shall proceed until no further action is possible. The umpire shall then impose such penalties, if any, as in his judgment will nullify the act of obstruction.

O.CO COLISEUM. The O.co Coliseum, located in Oakland, California, has been the home field of the **Oakland Athletics** of the **American League** since 7 April 1968. Originally called the Oakland-Alameda County Coliseum, it has also been called the Network Associates Coliseum, McAfee Coliseum, and Overstock.com Coliseum. The park, whose current seating capacity is approximately 35,000, hosted the **major league All-Star Game** in 1987.

See also STADIUMS.

OFFENSIVE INTERFERENCE. Offensive **interference** is an act by the team at bat that interferes with, **obstructs**, impedes, hinders, or confuses any **fielder** attempting to make a play. If the **umpire** declares the **batter** or a **base runner** out for interference, all other **runners** must return to the last **base** that was in the judgment of the umpire, legally touched at the time of the interference.

OFFICIAL GAME. An official game is one that has progressed beyond the point at which it can be considered complete if necessary. The fifth **inning** is used as the threshold for an official game. If the visiting team is leading, or the game is tied, the end of the fifth inning marks this point. If the home team (which bats last) is already ahead and theoretically would not need its half of the fifth inning, then 4 1/2 innings is considered an official game. The game is also considered official if the home team scores to take the lead in the bottom of the fifth inning, since the game would end immediately if the same thing happened in the ninth inning.

Any game that has reached this point may be stopped and shortened as needed, with the result being final, and all records and statistics counted. A game that has not reached this point before being stopped is either considered a **suspended game** (to be continued at a later date from the point of stoppage), or is simply canceled and replayed from the start. In either case, no statistics are counted until the game becomes official.

OFFICIAL SCORER. The league presidents appoint an official scorer for each game. The official scorer sits in the press box and has sole authority to make all decisions involving judgment, such as whether a **batter's** advance to **first base** is the result of a **hit** or an **error**. He must make all decisions concerning judgment calls within 24 hours after a game has been officially concluded. The official scorer is not permitted to make a scoring decision that is in conflict with the scoring rules.

After each game, the scorer prepares a report listing the date of the game, where it was played, the names of the competing clubs and the **umpires**, the full score of the game, and all records of individual players compiled according to the system specified in the Official Scoring Rules. He sends the report to the league office within 36 hours after the game ends.

OH, SADAHARU. B. 20 May 1940, Sumida, Tokyo, **Japan**. Sadaharu Oh is professional baseball's all-time career leader in **home runs**. Oh was a 5-foot, 11-inch, 175-pound **first baseman** who batted and threw left-handed. He spent his entire career, from 1959 to 1980, playing for the Central League's Yomiuri Giants in Japan's Nippon Professional Baseball. From

1984 to 1988, he was also the team's **manager**. Oh later managed the Fukuoka Daiei/Fukuoka SoftBank Hawks (from 1995 to 2008) and the Japanese national team in the first **World Baseball Classic**.

Oh led the Central League in home runs 15 times, 13 consecutively, and he finished his career with 868 home runs. He was a five-time batting champion and twice a winner of the **Triple Crown**, and his 55 home runs in 1964 is the Central League record. He was the league's **Most Valuable Player** in nine seasons. His career **batting average** was .301, with 2,786 **hits** and 2,170 **runs batted in**.

OLD TIMERS COMMITTEE. The Old Timers Committee consisted of a small group of high-ranking **major-league** executives and, later, veteran sportswriters, that existed from 1939 through 1949. They were charged with electing 19th-century players, **managers**, and executives to the **National Baseball Hall of Fame**. Voting sporadically over an 11-year period, they elected nearly 30 individuals before disbanding, leading to the formation of the **Veterans Committee** in 1953.

OLYMPIC GAMES. Baseball at the Summer Olympics had its unofficial debut at the 1904 Summer Games, and it had a long history as an exhibition/demonstration sport in the Olympics. At the 1992 games, in Barcelona, Spain, the International Olympic Committee (IOC) granted the sport medal status. Olympic baseball is governed by the **International Baseball Federation (IBAF)**. The event was last played in the 2008 Olympics in Beijing, China, with South Korea taking the gold.

At the IOC meeting on 7 July 2005, baseball and **softball** were voted out of the 2012 Summer Olympics in London, England, The elimination excised 16 teams and more than 300 athletes from the 2012 Olympics. It was officially decided in August 2009, at the IOC Board meeting in Berlin, Germany, that baseball would also not be included in the 2016 Summer Olympics. On 1 April 2011, the IBAF and the International Softball Federation announced that they were preparing a joint proposal to revive play of both sports at the 2020 Summer Olympics.

OLYMPIC STADIUM (STADE OLYMPIQUE). *See* MONTREAL EXPOS.

O'MALLEY, WALTER FRANCIS. B. 9 September 1903, Bronx, New York. D. 9 August 1979, Rochester, Minnesota. Walter O'Malley joined the **Brooklyn Dodgers** as the team's attorney in 1941. He later became part-owner, and, in 1950, he gained control of the team by buying out another coowner, **Branch Rickey**. In 1958, O'Malley moved the Dodgers to Los

Angeles. At the same time, **New York Giants'** owner Horace Stoneham moved his club to San Francisco, thereby bringing Major League Baseball to the West Coast. Using "sweetheart" real estate deals, O'Malley built a magnificent **Dodger Stadium**, which opened in 1962. After moving to California, the Dodgers set attendance records and won the **World Series** in 1959, 1963, and 1965. During his years in Los Angeles, O'Malley was baseball's most influential owner. He remained as chairman of the board of the Dodgers until his death. O'Malley was elected to the **National Baseball Hall of Fame** by the **Veterans Committee** in 2008.

ON-BASE PERCENTAGE (OBP). On-base percentage (OBP) is calculated by dividing the sum of a **batter's hits (H)**, **bases on balls (BB)**, and **hit by pitch (HBP)** by his **at-bats (AB)**, BB, HBP, and **sacrifice flies (SF)**. Example: A player with 116 hits, 48 bases on balls, four hit by pitch, 427 at-bats, and four sacrifice flies (116 + 48 + 4 / 427 + 48 + 4 + 4) has an OBP of .348.

The **major league** single-season leader in OBP is **Barry Bonds** of the 2004 **San Francisco Giants**, with .609. The **American League** single-season leader is **Ted Williams** of the 1941 **Boston Red Sox**, with .553. The career leader is also Williams, at .482. Williams played his entire career with the Red Sox, from 1939 through 1942, and from 1946 through 1960.

ON-BASE PLUS SLUGGING (OPS). On-base plus slugging (OPS) is a relatively new statistic that measures power plus the ability to get on base. It is the sum of a **batter's on-base percentage (OBP)** plus his **slugging percentage (SLG)**. Example: A batter with a .398 OBP and a .621 SLG would have an OPS of 1.019.

The **major league** single-season leader in OPS is **Barry Bonds** of the 2004 **San Francisco Giants**, with 1.422. The **American League** single-season leader is **Babe Ruth** of the 1920 **New York Yankees**, with 1.379. Ruth is also the career leader, with 1.164. Ruth played for the **Boston Red Sox** from 1914 through 1919, for the New York Yankees from 1920 through 1934, and for the **Boston Braves** in 1935.

ORIOLE PARK AT CAMDEN YARDS. Oriole Park at Camden Yards, commonly known as Camden Yards, is located in Baltimore, Maryland, and it has been the home of the **Baltimore Orioles** since 1992. Before that, the Orioles played in **Memorial Stadium** from 1954 through 1991. Camden Yards, the first of a new style of park that integrated the city landscape into its design, has a seating capacity of approximately 46,000. It hosted the **major league All-Star Game** in 1993.

See also STADIUMS.

Figure 15.1. Orioles Park at Camden Yards, opened in Baltimore in 1992, began a period of clubs building new parks, collectively known as "retro-classic ballparks." *National Baseball Hall of Fame Library, Cooperstown, N.Y.*

O'ROURKE, JAMES HENRY "JIM," "ORATOR JIM". B. 1 September 1850, Bridgeport, Connecticut. D. 8 January 1919, Bridgeport, Connecticut. Right-handed-batting Jim O'Rourke was primarily an **outfielder**, but he played all positions during his 23 years in three **major leagues**. O'Rourke played for the **Middletown Mansfields** (1872) and **Boston Red Stockings** (1873–1875) in the National Association; the Boston Red Stockings (1876–1878, 1880), **Providence Grays** (1879), **Buffalo Bisons** (1881–1884), **New York Giants** (1885–1889, 1891–1892, 1904), and **Washington Senators** (1893) in the **National League (NL)**; and the **New York Giants** (1890) in the **Players' League** .

Being a graduate of Yale Law School earned him the name "Orator Jim." The 5-foot, 8-inch, 185-pound O'Rourke played from 1872 through 1893, plus a one-game token appearance with the 1904 Giants. His appearance in that game, at the age of 54, made O'Rourke the oldest player ever to appear in a NL game. O'Rourke was one of the game's biggest stars during its infancy. That, along with his .310 lifetime **batting average** and 2,639 **hits**, led the **Old Timers Committee** to elect him to the **National Baseball Hall of Fame** in 1945.

OTT, MELVIN THOMAS "MEL". B. 2 March 1909, Gretna, Louisiana. D. 21 November 1958, New Orleans, Louisiana. Mel Ott shares the **National League (NL)** record with **Cap Anson** and **Stan Musial** for the most seasons played with one team, 22. Ott played for the **New York Giants** from 1926 through 1947. Only 17 years of age when he played his first big-league game, Ott spent most of his first two seasons on the bench being tutored by **John McGraw**, his **manager**. He became the Giants' right fielder in 1928, and he batted .322 with 18 **home runs**. Despite his relatively small stature— 5 feet, 9 inches tall and 170 pounds—Ott became one of the greatest home-run hitters of his era. A left-handed **batter** who lifted his right leg before swinging, he led the NL in home runs six times. He also led in walks six times and **on-base percentage** four times. In his team's 1933 **World Series** win against the **Washington Senators**, Ott led the Giants with a .389 **batting average** and two home runs. In the 1936 and 1937 Series, both losses to the **New York Yankees**, he batted .304 and .200, respectively, and homered in each Series.

Ott was the first National Leaguer to reach 500 home runs. When he retired, his total of 511 trailed only **Babe Ruth** and **Jimmie Foxx**. Ott was especially dangerous in his home park, the **Polo Grounds**, where the distance directly down the right-field line was just short of 260 feet. His percentage of home runs hit at home is the greatest among those who have hit 500 or more home runs. In 1942, Ott, an 11-time **All-Star**, became a **player-manager**, succeeding **Bill Terry**. He led the Giants to a third-place finish, but he eventually proved too "easygoing" to be a successful **manager**. In July 1948, he was replaced by **Leo Durocher**, who had been managing the rival **Brooklyn Dodgers**. Ott managed the Oakland Oaks of the Pacific Coast League in 1951 and 1952, and he was later a broadcaster for the **Detroit Tigers**. In November 1958, Ott was in a head-on collision in Louisiana and later died from complications resulting from the accident. In 1951, the **Baseball Writers' Association of America** elected him to the **National Baseball Hall of Fame**.

OUTFIELDER (OF). The alignment of the defensive team consists of three outfielders—a left fielder, a center fielder, and a right fielder—who position themselves in the grassy area behind the infield, usually closer to the fences or stands than they are to the diamond. The left fielder mostly positions himself in the outfield area behind the left side of the diamond, the center fielder in the outfield area behind the middle of the diamond, and the right fielder in the outfield area behind the right side of the diamond. In the numbering system used to record defensive plays, the left fielder is assigned the number 7, the center fielder is assigned the number 8, and the right fielder is assigned the number 9.

The **major-league** career leader in **games played** by an outfielder is 2,934 by **Ty Cobb**, who played for the **Detroit Tigers** (1905–1926) and **Philadelphia Athletics** (1927–1928). The major-league career leader in **fielding percentage** by an outfielder (minimum 500 games) is Jacoby Ellsbury (2007–2011 and still active), with a percentage of .9984.

The single-season leader in **putouts** by an outfielder is Taylor Douthit of the 1928 **St. Louis Cardinals**, with 547. The **American League (AL)** single-season leader is Chet Lemon of the 1977 **Chicago White Sox**, with 512. The career leader is **Willie Mays**, with 7,095. Mays played for the **New York Giants** (1951–1952, 1954–1957), **San Francisco Giants** (1958–1972), and **New York Mets** (1972–1973).

The single-season leader in **assists** by an outfielder is Orator Shafer of the 1879 **Chicago White Stockings** of the **National League (NL)**, with 50. The "modern" (post–1893) NL leader is **Chuck Klein** of the 1930 **Philadelphia Phillies**, with 44. The AL single-season leader is **Tris Speaker**, who had 35 with the **Boston Red Sox** in 1909 and 1912. The career leader is Speaker, with 449. Speaker played for the Boston Red Sox (1907–1915), **Cleveland Indians** (1916–1926), **Washington Senators** (1927), and Philadelphia Athletics (1928).

OUTS (O). An out is an event that puts an end to a **batter's** turn at the plate or to a **base runner's** presence on the **bases**. Once three outs have been recorded, the half-**inning** is over, and the fielding team becomes the batting team, and vice-versa.

The single-season leader in outs made is Omar Moreno of the 1980 **Pittsburgh Pirates**, with 560. The **American League** single-season leader is Horace Clarke of the 1970 **New York Yankees**, with 542. The career leader is **Pete Rose**, with 10,328. Rose played for the **Cincinnati Reds** (1963–1978, 1984–1986), **Philadelphia Phillies** (1979–1983), and **Montreal Expos** (1984).

OVERSTOCK.COM COLISEUM. *See* O.CO COLISEUM.

P

PAC BELL PARK. *See* AT&T PARK.

PAIGE, LEROY ROBERT "SATCHEL". B. 7 July 1906, Mobile, Alabama. D. 8 June 1982, Kansas City, Missouri. Satchel Paige was the greatest and most celebrated **pitcher** in the **Negro Leagues**. The 6-foot, 3-inch, 180-pound right-hander pitched for several teams, most notably the Birmingham Black Barons (1927–1930), **Pittsburgh Crawfords** (1932–1934, 1936), and **Kansas City Monarchs** (1935, 1939–1947). He also spent many off-seasons barnstorming against white teams, led by such **major-league** stars as **Dizzy Dean** and **Bob Feller**. The general consensus was that Paige was as good a pitcher as any in the majors. Paige finally got to the big leagues in July 1948, when the **Cleveland Indians** purchased his contract. At the age of 42, he was the oldest player ever to make a big-league debut. He spent two seasons in Cleveland (1948–1949), was with the **St. Louis Browns** (1951–1953), and made a publicity stunt one-game appearance for the **Kansas City Athletics** in 1965. Overall, Paige's major-league record was 28–31. In 1971, a special **Negro Leagues Committee** elected him to the **National Baseball Hall of Fame**.
See also AFRICAN AMERICANS IN BASEBALL.

PALACE OF THE FANS. *See* CINCINNATI REDS.

PALMEIRO, RAFAEL (CORRALES). B. 24 September 1964, Havana, **Cuba**. Rafael Palmeiro was the first-round pick of the **Chicago Cubs** in the 1985 **Amateur Draft**. The 6-foot, 180-pound Palmeiro played for the Cubs from 1986 to 1988, and he then did two stints with both the **Texas Rangers** (1989–1993, 1999–2003) and **Baltimore Orioles** (1994–1998, 2004–2005). After being used primarily as an **outfielder** by the Cubs, the left-handed-hitting and throwing Palmeiro played most of his career as a **first baseman**. He led **American League** first basemen in **games played** five times, **assists** six times, and **putouts** three times. Palmeiro batted better than .300 in six seasons, including a career-high .324 for the 1999 Rangers, when he was

Figure 16.1. **Satchel Paige on the mound for the Kansas City Monarchs.** *National Baseball Hall of Fame Library, Cooperstown, N.Y.*

voted the **Major League Player of the Year**. He was a four-time **All-Star** and the winner of three **Gold Glove Awards** and two **Silver Slugger Awards**. Palmeiro had a .288 career **batting average**, with 569 **home runs** and 3,020 **hits**. Yet, despite his having more than 500 home runs and 3,000 hits, charges that Palmeiro used performance-enhancing drugs during his career have negatively affected his chances of election to the **National Baseball Hall of Fame**.

PALMER, JAMES ALVIN "JIM". B. 15 October 1945, New York, New York. Jim Palmer was a **pitcher** for the **Baltimore Orioles** for 19 seasons (1965–1967, 1969–1984). His 268 **wins** are the most in Orioles' history. Palmer, a 6-foot, 3-inch, 190-pound right-hander, won 20 or more games eight times. He led the **American League (AL)** in wins three times; **innings pitched** four times; and **earned run average (ERA)**, **shutouts**, and won-lost percentage twice each. Palmer had a 4–1 record with a 1.96 ERA in six **American League Championship Series**, and a 4–2 record with a 3.20 ERA in six **World Series**. His victories against the **Los Angeles Dodgers** in 1966, **Cincinnati Reds** in 1970, **Pittsburgh Pirates** in 1971, and **Philadelphia Phillies** in 1983 make him the only pitcher to win World Series games in three different decades. Palmer was a six-time **All-Star**; the winner of four **Gold Glove Awards**; and a three-time winner of the **Cy Young Award**, in 1973, 1975, and 1976. He was also the *Sporting News*'s choice as AL **Pitcher of the Year** in those three seasons. Palmer, who later became a baseball broadcaster for the Orioles, had a career record of 268–152, a 2.86 ERA, and 53 shutouts. He was elected by the **Baseball Writers' Association of America** to the **National Baseball Hall of Fame** in 1990.

PANAMA. Baseball has been played in Panama since the late 19th century. In 1945, the Professional Baseball League of Panama was organized, and Panama became one of the four key national groups that formed the important **Caribbean Series**, whose first event was played in Havana, **Cuba**, in 1949. Panama hosted the Caribbean World Series in 1952, 1956 and 1960, but, by 1972, professional baseball had disappeared. A brief revival in 1999 and 2000 was a failure. The Panama national baseball team currently competes in the **Baseball World Cup**. The most recent Baseball World Cup, won by the **Netherlands**, was held in Panama in 2011, and it included 16 teams from four continents. Panama also competes in the **World Baseball Classic**.

Notable early-day players in Panama included Andrés "Alambre" Alonso, Frank "Bin-Bin" Austin, Pablo Bernard Marco A. Cobos, León Kellman, Fernando Alberto "Mamavila" Osorio, and Clyde Paris. Notable Panamanian-born players who played in the **major leagues** include Juan Berenguer, **Rod Carew**, Bruce Chen, Roberto Kelly, Carlos Lee, Hector Lopez, Ramiro Mendoza, Omar Moreno, Ben Oglivie, Adolfo Phillips, **Mariano Rivera**, Ruben Rivera, Humberto Robinson, Carlos Ruiz, Manny Sanguillen, and Rennie Stennett.

PASSED BALL (PB). The **official scorer** will charge the **catcher** with a passed ball (PB) if a pitch gets away from the catcher that the scorer believes could have been handled with ordinary effort. A passed ball may only be scored if one or more **runners** advance. The **major league** single-season leader in allowing passed balls prior to 1893, when the pitching distance was extended to its current 60 feet, 6 inches, is Rudy Kemmler of the 1883 **Columbus Colts** of the **American Association**, with 114. The single-season leader after the change in the pitching distance is Marty Bergen of the 1898 Boston Beaneaters, with 38. The single-season leader in the **American League** is Geno Petralli of the 1987 **Texas Rangers**, with 35. The career leader, with 763, is Charles "Pop" Snyder, who played in the National Association, National League, American Association, and **Players' League** (1873–1879, 1881–1891).

PEARCE, RICHARD J. "DICKEY". B. 29 February 1836, Brooklyn, New York. D. 18 September 1908, Wareham, Massachusetts. Dickey Pearce is credited with creating the **shortstop** position as we know it today. Until the 1850s, this position was more that of a short fielder, similar to the position now used in **softball**. Pearce turned it from the infield position with the least responsibility into the one with the most. He also is credited with introducing the **fair-foul hit**, a squib that hit fair at first, and then rolled foul and was counted as a **hit**. The 5-foot, 3-inch, 161-pound Pearce was already 35 years old when the National Association (NA) was formed in 1871; nevertheless, he played in all five years of the NA's existence, with the **New York Mutuals** in 1871 and 1872, the **Brooklyn Atlantics** in 1873 and 1874, and the **St. Louis Brown Stockings** in 1875. He played briefly with the Brown Stockings in the **National League (NL)** in 1876 and 1877. The right-handed-hitting Pearce batted a combined .251 in his seven **major-league** seasons. He later was an **umpire** in the NL for several seasons.

PENNOCK, HERBERT JEFFERIS "HERB". B. 10 February 1894, Kennett Square, Pennsylvania. D. 30 January 1948, New York, New York. Herb Pennock joined the **Philadelphia Athletics** as an 18-year-old in 1912, beginning a 22-season career as a **pitcher** in the **American League (AL)**. In addition to the Athletics (1912–1915), the 6-foot, 160-pound left-hander was with the **Boston Red Sox** (1915–1917, 1919–1922, 1934) and **New York Yankees** (1923–1933). His career record was 241–162, but with the Yankees it was 162–90. Pennock had his only two 20-win seasons with the Yankees, and he had two more in which he won 19 games. Steady but unspectacular, he led the AL with a .760 **winning percentage** in 1923 and five **shutouts** in 1928. Defensively, he led AL pitchers in **fielding percentage** three times. In five **World Series**, four with New York, he had a 5–0 record and a 1.95

earned run average in 55 1/3 **innings pitched**. He was later the farm director for the Red Sox and, from 1944 to 1948, the **general manager** of the **Philadelphia Phillies**. The **Baseball Writers' Association of America** elected Pennock to the **National Baseball Hall of Fame** in 1948.

PEREZ, ATANASIO (RIGAL) "TONY". B. 14 May 1942, Camaguey, Camaguey, **Cuba**. Tony Perez played 23 seasons in the **major leagues**, from 1964 to 1986. The **Cincinnati Reds** was Perez's first team (1964–1976), as well as his last (1984–1986). He also played for the **Montreal Expos** (1977–1979), **Boston Red Sox** (1980–1982), and **Philadelphia Phillies** (1983). He is best remembered as the slugging **first baseman** for Cincinnati's "Big Red Machine" teams of the mid-1970s. In the five seasons from 1967 to 1971, the Reds played Perez at **third base**. A 6-foot, 2-inch, 175-pound right-handed hitter, Perez had six seasons of 100 or more **runs batted in (RBI)** for the Reds, and seven overall. He also had eight seasons of 20 or more **home runs** for the Reds. He appeared in seven **All-Star Games** and was the game's **Most Valuable Player** in his first, in 1967, when his 15th-inning home run off **Catfish Hunter** gave the **National League** a 2–1 victory.

Perez played in six **National League Championship Series**, five with Cincinnati and one with Philadelphia, and five **World Series**, all but 1983 with Cincinnati. Perez had a .279 career **batting average**, with 379 home runs and 1,652 RBI. He served briefly as a **manager** for the Reds, in 1993, and for the Florida Marlins for most of the 2001 season. He currently works in the **Miami Marlins** front office. Winner of the **Lou Gehrig Memorial Award** in 1980, Perez was elected by the **Baseball Writers' Association of America** to the **National Baseball Hall of Fame** in 2000.

PERFECT GAME. A perfect game occurs when a **pitcher** (or pitchers) allows no **base runners** during the entire course of a game, which consists of at least nine **innings**. That is, no **batter** may reach **base** via a **hit**, a walk, an **error**, a **hit by pitch**, a **passed ball** or **wild pitch** on strike three, or **catcher's interference**.

There were 23 perfect games pitched in the **major leagues** through the 2012 season. The first perfect game was thrown by Lee Richmond of the **Worcester Ruby Legs** of the **National League (NL)** on 12 June 1880. The first perfect game at the modern pitching distance of 60 feet, 6 inches, and the first in the **American League**, was thrown by **Cy Young** of the Boston Americans on 5 May 1904. The first perfect game at the modern pitching distance in the NL was by **Jim Bunning** of the **Philadelphia Phillies** in the first game of a **doubleheader** on 21 June 1964. There has been one **World**

Series perfect game. It was pitched by Don Larsen of the **New York Yankees** against the **Brooklyn Dodgers** on 8 October 1956, in Game Five of the Series.

PERRY, GAYLORD JACKSON. B. 15 September 1938, Williamston, North Carolina. Gaylord Perry pitched for eight teams in a **major-league** career that lasted 22 seasons. In the **National League**, Perry was with the **San Francisco Giants** (1962–1971), **San Diego Padres** (1978–1979), and **Atlanta Braves** (1981). In the **American League**, he was with the **Cleveland Indians** (1972–1975), **Texas Rangers** (1975–1977, 1980), **New York Yankees** (1980), **Seattle Mariners** (1982–1983), and **Kansas City Royals** (1983). Perry won 20 or more games five times. He led his league in wins three times, with the Giants in 1970, the Indians in 1972, and the Padres in 1978. Perry won the **Cy Young Award** with Cleveland in 1972, and with San Diego in 1978, making him the first **pitcher** to win the award in each league. The 6-foot, 4-inch, 205-pound right-hander had a career record of 314–265, with 3,534 **strikeouts**, number eight all-time. His 5,350 **innings pitched** is exceeded by only five other pitchers. Perry was elected by the **Baseball Writers' Association of America** to the **National Baseball Hall of Fame** in 1991.

PETCO PARK. Petco Park, located in San Diego, California, has been the home of the **San Diego Padres** of the **National League** since the start of the 2004 season. Prior to that, the Padres played at Qualcomm Stadium, previously called San Diego Stadium and Jack Murphy Stadium. Petco Park, which has a seating capacity of approximately 42,700, has never hosted the **major league All-Star Game**.
See also STADIUMS.

PHILADELPHIA ATHLETICS (AA). The Philadelphia Athletics were a team in the **American Association (AA)** from 1882 to 1891, the entire length of the AA's 10-year existence. In 1883, Philadelphia captured the AA pennant, but in each of the other nine seasons they finished at least 10 games out of first place. The Athletics were disbanded after the 1890 season, but they were replaced in 1891 by the Philadelphia Quakers of the **Players' League**, which had folded after one season. The Quakers took the Athletics' name. Notable players for Philadelphia's AA team included Al Atkinson, Henry Larkin, Denny Lyons, **Bobby Mathews**, **Wilbert Robinson**, Ed Seward, **Harry Stovey**, and Gus Weyhing.

PHILADELPHIA ATHLETICS (AL). The Philadelphia Athletics were a team in the **American League (AL)** from 1901, the first year the AL was recognized as a **major league**, through 1954. Home games were played at Columbia Park from 12 April 1901 to 3 October 1908, and at **Shibe Park**, renamed Connie Mack Stadium in 1953, from 12 April 1909 to 19 September 1954.

The Athletics, also known as the A's, were originally owned by Benjamin Shibe. Ownership remained in the Shibe family until 1937, when **Connie Mack**, the A's **manager** from 1901 through 1950, took control. Under Mack's leadership, the Athletics won pennants in 1905, 1910, 1911, 1913, 1914, 1929, 1930, and 1931. They were **World Series** champions five times, defeating the **Chicago Cubs** in 1910 and 1929, the **New York Giants** in 1911 and 1913, and the **St. Louis Cardinals** in 1930. Following the 1954 season, the Athletics team was sold to Arnold Johnson, who moved the franchise to Kansas City, where they became the **Kansas City Athletics**.

Philadelphia Athletics who won the AL's **Most Valuable Player Award** were **Eddie Collins** (1914), **Mickey Cochrane** (1928), **Lefty Grove** (1931), **Jimmie Foxx** (1932–1933), and Bobby Shantz (1952). The **Cy Young Award** came into existence in 1956, after the A's had left for Kansas City. Harry Byrd, in 1952, was the team's only **Rookie of the Year** winner.

Philadelphia Athletics players who led the AL in **batting average** were **Nap Lajoie** (1901), **Al Simmons** (1930–1931), Jimmie Foxx (1933), and Ferris Fain (1951–1952). Leaders in **home runs** were Nap Lajoie (1901), Socks Seybold (1902), Harry Davis (1904–1907), **Frank Baker** (1911–1914), Tillie Walker (1918), Jimmie Foxx (1932–1933, 1935), and Gus Zernial (1951). Leaders in **runs batted in (RBI)** were Nap Lajoie (1901), Harry Davis (1905–1906), Frank Baker (1912–1913), Al Simmons (1929), Jimmie Foxx (1932–1933), and Gus Zernial (1951). By leading the AL in batting average, home runs, and RBI, Nap Lajoie won the **Triple Crown** for **batters** in 1901. By leading the AL in batting average, home runs, and RBI, Jimmie Foxx won the Triple Crown for batters in 1933.

Philadelphia Athletics **pitchers** who led the AL in **wins** were **Rube Waddell** (1905), Jack Coombs (1910–1911), Eddie Rommel (1922, 1925), Lefty Grove (1928, 1930–1931, 1933), George Earnshaw (1929), and Bobby Shantz (1952). **Earned run average (ERA)** leaders were Rube Waddell (1905), Harry Krause (1909), and Lefty Grove (1926, 1929–1932). **Strikeouts** leaders were Rube Waddell (1902–1907) and Lefty Grove (1925–1931). By leading in wins, ERA, and strikeouts in 1905, Rube Waddell won the Triple Crown for pitchers. By leading in wins, ERA, and strikeouts in 1930 and 1931, Lefty Grove won the Triple Crown for pitchers in both those years.

Other notable players for the Philadelphia Athletics included **Chief Bender**, Max Bishop, Lou Brissie, Sam Chapman, Doc Cramer, Jimmy Dykes, Pinky Higgins, Bob Johnson, Eddie Joost, Alex Kellner, Hank Majeski, Phil Marchildon, Barney McCosky, Bing Miller, Wally Moses, **Eddie Plank**, Buddy Rosar, Amos Strunk, Pete Suder, and Elmer Valo.

PHILADELPHIA ATHLETICS (NA). The Philadelphia Athletics were a team in the National Association (NA) from 1871 to 1875, the NA's entire existence. They were the NA champions in 1871, the only season in which the Boston Red Stockings did not finish first. Notable players for the Athletics included **Cap Anson**, Wes Fisler, Dick McBride, Levi Meyerle, and Wes Sutton. In 1876, the Athletics became charter members of the new **National League**.

PHILADELPHIA ATHLETICS (NL). The Philadelphia Athletics had been members of the **National Association (NA)** from 1871 through 1875, the NA's entire existence. In 1876, they became a charter member of the **National League (NL)**. On 22 April 1876, the Athletics hosted the **Boston Red Stockings** at the Jefferson Street Grounds in the NL's first-ever game. Financial problems caused the club to fold after just one season. Philadelphia's best players in 1876 were Dave Eggler, George Hall, Levi Myerle, and Ezra Sutton.

PHILADELPHIA CENTENNIALS. The Philadelphia Centennials were members of the National Association (NA) in 1875, the NA's final season. They played 14 games and lost 12.

PHILADELPHIA KEYSTONES. The Philadelphia Keystones were a team in the **Union Association (UA)** in 1884, the one year of the UA's existence. They had a record of 21–46 when they were disbanded in early August and replaced by the **Wilmington Quicksteps**.

PHILADELPHIA PHILLIES. The Philadelphia Phillies are a team in the Eastern Division of the **National League (NL)**. Philadelphia entered the NL in 1883, replacing the **Worcester Ruby Legs** in the league. The team has played its home games at **Citizens Bank Park** since 12 April 2004. The Phillies, previously called the Philadelphia Quakers from 1883 to 1889, played their home games at Recreation Park from 1883 to 1886, at Huntingdon Grounds from 1887 to 1894, at the Baker Bowl from 1895 to 30 June 1938, at **Shibe Park** from 4 July 1938 to 1 October 1970, and at **Veterans Stadium** from 1971 to 2003. Shibe Park was renamed Connie Mack Stadium in 1953.

Philadelphia did not win its first pennant until 1915, and the team then lost in the **World Series** to the **Boston Red Sox**. A dreadful 35-year pennant drought followed, with the Phillies usually finishing at or near the bottom of the NL standings. A pennant won on the last day of the 1950 season was followed by a four-game World Series loss to the **New York Yankees**. The Phillies lost three consecutive **National League Championship Series (NLCS)** (1976–1978), before defeating the **Kansas City Royals** in 1980 for their first world championship. In four subsequent World Series, they have lost to the **Baltimore Orioles** (1983), **Toronto Blue Jays** (1993), and Yankees (2009), and they defeated the **Tampa Bay Rays** (2008). Philadelphia has also lost three **National League Division Series** (1981, 2007, 2011), and another NLCS in 2010.

Philadelphia Phillies who have won the NL's **Most Valuable Player Award** are **Chuck Klein** (1932), Jim Konstanty (1950), **Mike Schmidt** (1980–1981, 1986), Ryan Howard (2006), and Jimmy Rollins (2007). **Cy Young Award** winners are **Steve Carlton** (1972, 1977, 1980, 1982), John Denny (1983), Steve Bedrosian (1987), and **Roy Halladay** (2010). **Rookie of the Year** winners are Jack Sanford (1957), Dick Allen (1964), Scott Rolen (1997), and Ryan Howard (2005).

Phillies players who have led the NL in **batting average** are **Billy Hamilton** (1891, 1893), **Ed Delahanty** (1899), Sherry Magee (1910), Lefty O'Doul (1929), Chuck Klein (1933), Harry Walker (1947, part of season with **St. Louis Cardinals**), and **Richie Ashburn** (1955, 1958). **Home run** leaders are **Sam Thompson** (1889, 1895), Ed Delahanty (1893, 1896), Gavy Cravath (1913–1915, 1917–1919), Cy Williams (1920, 1923, 1927), Chuck Klein (1929, 1931–1933), Mike Schmidt (1974–1976, 1980–1981, 1983–1984, 1986), **Jim Thome** (2003), and Ryan Howard (2006, 2008). **Runs batted in (RBI)** leaders are Sam Thompson (1894–1895), Ed Delahanty (1893, 1896, 1899), **Nap Lajoie** (1898), **Elmer Flick** (1900), Sherry Magee (1907, 1910, 1914), Gavy Cravath (1913, 1915), Chuck Klein (1931, 1933), Don Hurst (1932), Del Ennis (1950), Greg Luzinski (1975), Mike Schmidt (1980–1981, 1984, 1986), Darren Daulton (1992), and Ryan Howard (2006, 2008–2009). By leading the NL in batting average, home runs, and RBI, Chuck Klein won the **Triple Crown** for **batters** in 1933.

Phillies **pitchers** who have led the NL in **wins** are **Grover Alexander** (1911, 1914–1917), Tom Seaton (1913), Jumbo Elliott (1931), **Robin Roberts** (1952–1955), Steve Carlton (1972, 1977, 1980, 1982), John Denny (1983), and Roy Halladay (2010). **Earned run average (ERA)** leaders are Dan Casey (1887), Grover Alexander (1915–1916), and Steve Carlton (1972). **Strikeouts** leaders are Earl Moore (1910), Grover Alexander (1912, 1914–1917), Tom Seaton (1913), Kirby Higbe (1940), Robin Roberts (1953–1954), Jack Sanford (1957), **Jim Bunning** (1967), Steve Carlton (1972, 1974, 1980, 1982–1983), and Curt Schilling (1997–1998). By leading in wins, ERA, and strikeouts in 1915 and 1916, Grover Alexander won the Triple Crown for pitchers in both those years. By leading in wins, ERA, and strikeouts, Steve Carlton won the Triple Crown for pitchers in 1972.

Other notable players and **managers** in Phillies' history include Bobby Abreu, Bob Boone, Larry Bowa, Pat Burrell, Johnny Callison, Dolph Camilli, Kid Carsey, Spud Davis, Bill Duggleby, Lenny Dykstra, Charlie Ferguson, Kid Gleason, Tony Gonzalez, Dallas Green, Cole Hamels, Granny Hamner, Von Hayes, Willie Jones, John Kruk, Fred Luderus, Garry Maddox, Charlie Manuel, Gene Mauch, Erskine Mayer, Tug McGraw, Irish Meusel, George McQuillan, Pat Moran, Al Orth, Danny Ozark, Placido Polanco, Ron Reed, **Eppa Rixey**, **Pete Rose**, Carlos Ruiz, Juan Samuel, Eddie Sawyer, Andy Seminick, Chris Short, Curt Simmons, Dick Sisler, Tully Sparks, Jack B. Taylor, Tony Taylor, Roy Thomas, Chase Utley, Eddie Waitkus, Jayson Werth, Pinky Whitney, and **Harry Wright**.

PHILADELPHIA QUAKERS (NL). *See* PHILADELPHIA PHILLIES.

PHILADELPHIA QUAKERS (PL). The Philadelphia Quakers were a team in the **Players' League (PL)** in 1890, the one year of the PL's existence. The team finished in fifth place, with a 68–63 record. In 1891, the Quakers replaced the disbanded **Philadelphia Athletics** of the **American Association** and took the Athletics' name. Notable players on the Quakers were Charlie Buffinton, Phil Knell, and Billy Shindle.

PHILADELPHIA STARS. The Philadelphia Stars played in the **Negro National League (NNL)** from 1934 to 1948, and in the **Negro American League** from 1949 to 1952. The Stars were the NNL champions in 1934. Among the notable players from the **Negro Leagues** who played part of their careers with the Stars were **Oscar Charleston**, **Biz Mackey**, **Satchel Paige**, **Turkey Stearnes**, and **Jud Wilson**.

PHILADELPHIA WHITE STOCKINGS. The Philadelphia White Stockings, also known as the Philadelphia Whites, were members of the National Association (NA) in the NA's final three seasons, from 1873 through 1875. Notable players for the White Stockings included Bill Craver, **Candy Cummings**, Levi Meyerle, and George Zettlein.

PHILADELPHIA WHITES. *See* PHILADELPHIA WHITE STOCKINGS.

PIAZZA, MICHAEL JOSEPH "MIKE". B. 4 September 1968, Norristown, Pennsylvania. Mike Piazza was a slugging **catcher** who spent most of his 16-year **major-league** career in the **National League (NL)** with the **Los Angeles Dodgers** (1992–1998) and **New York Mets** (1998–2005). Piazza also played briefly for the Florida Marlins in 1998. He spent his final two seasons with the **San Diego Padres**, in 2006, and as a **designated hitter** with the **Oakland Athletics** of the **American League**, in 2007. The 6-foot, 3-inch, 200-pound Piazza was the NL **Rookie of the Year** in 1991, and he was twice the runner-up for the **Most Valuable Player (MVP) Award**. He was selected for the **All-Star** team 12 times and voted the MVP of the 1996 game. Piazza played in five **National League Division Series**, two **National League Championship Series**, and one **World Series**, batting a combined .242, with six **home runs**.

Piazza twice led NL catchers in games caught and **assists**, and four times he led in **putouts**. Yet, he was never considered a strong defensive catcher, leading in **errors** four times and **passed balls** twice. His relatively weak throwing arm caused him to allow the most **stolen bases** in the league 10 times. The 1,400 stolen bases he allowed in his career is the seventh most all-time. As a **batter**, however, the right-handed-hitting Piazza is arguably the best offensive catcher ever. He won 10 consecutive **Silver Slugger Awards** and had a .308 career **batting average**, with 2,127 **hits** and 427 home runs. He hit 396 of those home runs as a catcher, far and away the most by any catcher. Piazza is likely to be elected to the **National Baseball Hall of Fame** when he becomes eligible.

PIKE, LIPMAN EMANUEL "LIP". B. 25 May 1845, New York, New York. D. 10 October 1893, Brooklyn, New York. Lip Pike is thought to be baseball's first Jewish player and among its first professional players. Beginning in 1865, he played for several amateur teams, including the **Brooklyn Atlantics**. He entered the National Association (NA), baseball's first **major league**, with the 1871 **Troy Haymakers**. During the next four years in the NA, four years in the **National League** (1876–1878, 1881), and one final game for the **New York Metropolitans** of the **American Association** in 1887, Pike played for nine different teams, with a career **batting average** of .322. The 5-foot, 8-inch, 158-pound speedster played all the infield positions, but mostly **second base**. A left-handed **batter**, he led the NA in **home runs** in each of its first three seasons, with four for Troy in 1871, and seven and four, respectively, for the **Baltimore Canaries** in 1872 and 1873. Pike's total of 16 home runs was the most hit by a NA player. He won a fourth home run title when he had four for the NL's **Cincinnati Reds** in 1877.

PINCH HITTER (PH). A pinch hitter (PH) is a **batter** used as a substitute for another batter. A PH comes into the game only when the batter whose turn he is taking is due to bat. At that time, he is "announced into the game"; the batter he replaced is out of the game permanently. When the PH's team takes the field the next half **inning**, the pinch hitter can either take the defensive position of the player for whom he pinch hit, take another position on the field, or be replaced by a defensive substitute.

PINCH RUNNER (PR). A pinch runner (PR) is a substitute used for a **runner** who is already on **base**. A PR can be used at any base and, in certain situations, can even enter a game between bases when a player who is entitled to advance to a base without ability to be put **out** is unable to proceed to that base because of injury. When a pinch runner is used, the player for whom he runs is out of the game permanently. The following half-**inning**, the pinch runner may replace the player he substituted on defense as well, or move to another defensive position, or be replaced by a defensive substitute.

PITCHER (P). The pitcher begins each play by throwing the ball from the **pitcher's mound** toward the **catcher** in an attempt to retire the **batter**. In the numbering system used to record defensive plays, the pitcher is assigned the number 1.

The **major-league** career leader in games pitched is Jesse Orosco (1979, 1981–2003), with 1,252. The single-season leader in **putouts** is Dave Foutz of the 1886 **St. Louis Browns** of the **American Association (AA)**, with 57. The single-season leader post-1893, when the pitching distance was extended to its current 60 feet, 6 inches, is Mike Boddicker of the 1984 **Baltimore Orioles**, with 49. The **National League (NL)** single-season leader, post-1893, is Ted Breitenstein of the 1895 St. Louis Browns (now the **St. Louis Cardinals**), with 46. The career leader is **Greg Maddux** (1986–2008), with 546. Maddux pitched for the **Chicago Cubs** (1986–1992, 2004–2006), **Atlanta Braves** (1993–2003), **Los Angeles Dodgers** (2006, 2008), and **San Diego Padres** (2007–2008).

The single-season leader in **assists** is **Ed Walsh** of the 1907 **Chicago White Sox**, with 227. The NL single-season leader is **John Clarkson** of the 1885 Chicago White Stockings (now the **Chicago Cubs**), with 174. The post-1893 leader in the NL is **Cy Young** of the 1896 **Cleveland Spiders**, with 145. The career leader is Cy Young, with 2,014. Young pitched for Cleveland of the NL (1890–1898), St. Louis of the NL (1899–1900), Boston of the **American League (AL)** (1901–1908), Cleveland of the AL (1909–1911), and Boston of the NL (1911).

PITCHER OF THE YEAR. The Pitcher of the Year Award was established by the *Sporting News* in 1944. The award is given annually to the **pitcher** in the **American League (AL)** and the pitcher in the **National League (NL)** judged by the *Sporting News*'s baseball experts as having had the most outstanding season. No awards were given in 1946 or 1947. The 2012 co-winners in the AL were Justin Verlander of the **Detroit Tigers** and David Price of the **Tampa Bay Rays**. The NL winner was R. A. Dickey of the **New York Mets**.

PITCHER'S MOUND. The pitcher's mound is where the **pitcher** stands when delivering a pitch. It is located equidistant between **first base** and **third base**, and 60 feet, 6 inches from **home plate**. When Major League Baseball began in 1871, the pitcher was compelled to pitch from within a "box" whose front edge was 45 feet from the "point" of home plate. Although he had to release the ball before crossing the line, he also had to start his delivery from within the box. In an attempt to increase batting, the front edge of the pitcher's box was moved back 5 feet in 1881, to 50 feet from home plate.

The size of the box was altered throughout the years. Pitchers were allowed to throw overhand starting in 1884. In 1887, the box was set at 4 feet wide and 5 1/2 feet deep, with the front edge still 50 feet from home plate; however, the pitcher was compelled to deliver the ball with his back foot at the 55 1/2-foot line of the box. In 1893, the box was replaced by the pitcher's plate. Exactly 5 feet was added to the point that the pitcher had to toe, resulting in the current pitching distance of 60 feet, 6 inches.

PITTSBURGH ALLEGHENYS (AA). The Pittsburgh Alleghenys were charter members of the **American Association (AA)** in 1882. They played in the AA from 1882 to 1886. The Alleghenys' best season was 1886, when they finished in second place. In 1887, they jumped to the **National League (NL)**, becoming the first AA team to move to the NL. Notable players for Pittsburgh's AA team included Tom Brown, **Pud Galvin**, Ed Morris, and Ed Swartwood.

See also PITTSBURGH PIRATES.

PITTSBURGH ALLEGHENYS (NL). *See* PITTSBURGH PIRATES.

PITTSBURGH BURGHERS. The Pittsburgh Burghers were a team in the **Players' League (PL)** in 1890, the one year of the PL's existence. The Burghers finished in sixth place, with a 60–68 record. Notable players on the Burghers were **Jake Beckley** and Fred Carroll.

PITTSBURGH CRAWFORDS. The Pittsburgh Crawfords played in the **Negro National League (NNL)** from 1933 to 1938. The Crawfords were the NNL champions in 1935 and 1936. Among the notable players from the **Negro Leagues** who played part of their careers with the Crawfords were **James Bell, Oscar Charleston, Josh Gibson, Judy Johnson, Satchel Paige**, and Ted Radcliffe.

PITTSBURGH PIRATES. The Pittsburgh Pirates are a team in the Central Division of the **National League (NL)**. They have been a member of the NL since entering the league in 1887 as the Pittsburgh Alleghenys. The Alleghenys, who had played in the **American Association (AA)** from 1882 to 1886, were the first AA team to move to the NL. The Alleghenys were renamed the Pirates in 1891. The team played its home games at Exposition Park from 1887 to 29 June 1909, at **Forbes Field** from 30 June 1909 to 28 June 1970, at **Three Rivers Stadium** from 16 July 1970 to the end of the 2000 season, and at **PNC Park** since 2001.

Barney Dreyfuss, who owned the **Louisville Colonels** of the NL, was nevertheless allowed to purchase a half interest in the Pirates. When the Colonels were dropped from the NL for the 1900 season, Dreyfuss, soon to become the sole owner of the Pirates, brought 14 former Louisville players to Pittsburgh with him. Among them were **Honus Wagner, Fred Clarke**, and **Rube Waddell**.

The Pirates, who had been mostly a second-division team, finished second under **manager** Clarke in 1900, and the team then won the next three NL pennants. They played in the first modern **World Series** in 1903, losing to the Boston Americans. The Pirates played in six subsequent World Series, winning five. They defeated the **Detroit Tigers** in 1909, the **Washington Senators** in 1925, the **New York Yankees** in 1960, and the **Baltimore Orioles** in 1971 and 1979. Their only other loss was to the Yankees in 1927. Pittsburgh has appeared in nine **National League Championship Series**, winning only in 1971 and 1979.

Pittsburgh Pirates who have won the NL's **Most Valuable Player Award** are **Paul Waner** (1927), Dick Groat (1960), **Roberto Clemente** (1966), Dave Parker (1978), **Willie Stargell** (1979), and **Barry Bonds** (1990, 1992). **Cy Young Award** winners are Vern Law (1960) and Doug Drabek (1990). Jason Bay, in 2004, is the only Pirate who has been voted **Rookie of the Year**.

Pittsburgh Pirates players who have led the NL in **batting average** are Honus Wagner (1900, 1903–1904, 1906–1909, 1911), Ginger Beaumont (1902), Paul Waner (1927, 1934, 1936), **Arky Vaughan** (1935), Debs Garms (1940), Dick Groat (1960), Roberto Clemente (1961, 1964–1965, 1967), Matty Alou (1966), Dave Parker (1977–1978), Bill Madlock (1981, 1983), and Freddy Sanchez (2006). **Home run** leaders are Tommy Leach (1902),

Ralph Kiner (1946–1952), and Willie Stargell (1971, 1973). **Runs batted in** leaders are Honus Wagner (1901–1902, 1908–1909, 1912), Jim Nealon (1906), Chief Wilson (1911), Paul Waner (1927), Ralph Kiner (1949), and Willie Stargell (1973).

Pittsburgh Pirates **pitchers** who have led the NL in **wins** are Frank Killen (1893, 1896), **Jack Chesbro** (1902), Wilbur Cooper (1921), Ray Kremer (1926, 1930), Lee Meadows (1926), **Burleigh Grimes** (1928), Heinie Meine (1931), Rip Sewell (1943), Bob Friend (1958), Doug Drabek (1990), and John Smiley (1991). **Earned run average** leaders are Rube Waddell (1900), Jesse Tannehill (1901), Sam Leever (1903), Ray Kremer (1926–1927), Cy Blanton (1935), Bob Friend (1955), and John Candelaria (1977). **Strikeouts** leaders are Preacher Roe (1945) and Bob Veale (1964).

Other notable players and managers in Pirates' history include Babe Adams, Steve Blass, **Jake Beckley**, Howie Camnitz, John Candelaria, **Max Carey**, **Kiki Cuyler**, Roy Face, George Gibson, Brian Giles, Dave Giusti, Charlie Grimm, Jason Kendall, Lefty Leifield, Jim Leyland, Nick Maddox, **Bill Mazeroski**, Andrew McCutchen, **Bill McKechnie**, Al Oliver, Deacon Phillippe, Rick Rhoden, Jake Stenzel, Gus Suhr, Chuck Tanner, Kent Tekulve, **Pie Traynor**, Andy Van Slyke, Bill Virdon, Neil Walker, **Lloyd Waner**, **Vic Willis**, and Emil Yde.

PITTSBURGH REBELS. The Pittsburgh Rebels, also called the Pittsburgh Stogies, were a team in the **Federal League (FL)** in 1914 and 1915, the two seasons the FL existed as a **major league**. After finishing in seventh place in 1914, the Rebels finished third in 1915, just half a game behind the pennant-winning **Chicago Whales**. Notable players for the Rebels included Frank Allen, Hugh Bradley, Howie Camnitz, Elmer Knetzer, Ed Konetchy, Ed Lennox, and Rebel Oakes.

PITTSBURGH STOGIES (FL). *See* PITTSBURGH REBELS.

PITTSBURGH STOGIES (UA). The Pittsburgh Stogies were a team in the **Union Association (UA)** in 1884, the one year of the UA's existence. They replaced the disbanded **Chicago Browns** in August and won seven of their 18 games.

PLANK, EDWARD STEWART "EDDIE". B. 31 August 1875, Gettysburg, Pennsylvania. D. 24 February 1926, Gettysburg, Pennsylvania. **Pitcher** Eddie Plank joined the **Philadelphia Athletics** of the **American League (AL)** in 1901, the first year the AL was recognized as a **major league**. Led by **manager Connie Mack**, the Athletics played in five **World Series** during Plank's 14 seasons in Philadelphia, and Plank pitched in four of them. Facing the **New York Giants** in 1905, 1911, and 1913, and the **Boston Braves** in 1914, he won two and lost five, despite a stellar 1.32 **earned run average (ERA)**. Plank, a 5-foot, 11-inch, 175-pound left-hander, was a 20-game winner seven times for Philadelphia; nevertheless, Mack released him as part of a general purge after the 1914 season. Plank joined the **St. Louis Terriers** of the **Federal League (FL)**, for whom he won 21 games and posted an ERA of 2.08, second best in the FL. The FL disbanded in 1916, and he went back to the AL, joining the **St. Louis Browns**. After going 21–21 in two seasons with the Browns, Plank was traded to the **New York Yankees** in January 1918, but instead he chose to retire. Plank finished his major-league career with a record of 326–194 and a 2.35 ERA. His 69 **shutouts** are the most ever by a left-hander and the fifth highest overall. In addition, he was the first left-hander to win 300 games, and his 305 **wins** in the AL are the most by a left-hander in the league. In 1946, the **Old Timers Committee** elected Plank to the **National Baseball Hall of Fame**.

PLATE APPEARANCES (PA). Total plate appearances (PA) are calculated by adding **at-bats (AB)** + **bases on balls (BB)** + **hit by pitch (HBP)** + **sacrifice flies (SF)** + **sacrifice hits (SH)** + **catcher interferences (CI)**. The **major league** single-season leader in plate appearances is Jimmy Rollins of the 2007 **Philadelphia Phillies** of the **National League**, with 778. The **American League** leader is **Ichiro Suzuki** of the 2004 **Seattle Mariners**, with 762. The career leader is **Pete Rose**, with 15,890. Rose played for the **Cincinnati Reds** (1963–1978, 1984–1986), Philadelphia Phillies (1979–1983), and **Montreal Expos** (1984).

PLAYER-MANAGER. A player-manager is someone who serves as both a team's **manager** and as an active player on that team's **roster**. Player-managers were far more common in the early days of baseball. There has not been a full-time player-manager in the **major leagues** since **Pete Rose** of the 1984, 1985, and 1986 **Cincinnati Reds**. **National Baseball Hall of Fame** players who served as player-managers include **Cap Anson, Lou Boudreau, Fred Clarke, Ty Cobb, Mickey Cochrane, Joe Cronin, Frank Robinson,** and **Tris Speaker**.

PLAYERS' LEAGUE (PL). The Players' League (PL) (officially the Players' National League of Professional Base Ball Clubs) existed as a **major league** for one season, 1890. The league was an outgrowth of the Brotherhood of Professional Base-Ball Players, baseball's first players' union. The brotherhood objected to the establishment of a **reserve clause** and a fixed salary structure by team owners. Unable to get these strictures changed, leader **John Montgomery Ward**, of the **New York Giants** of the **National League (NL)**, led many of the NL's best players out of the league and formed the new PL.

The PL consisted of eight teams, including the **Boston Reds, Brooklyn Wonders, Buffalo Bisons, Chicago Pirates, Cleveland Infants**, New York Giants, **Philadelphia Athletics**, and **Pittsburgh Burghers**. Attendance was good in most cities, but several teams were underfunded, and uncertainty about the future caused the league to fold after one season. Meanwhile, the **American Association (AA)**, the third major league, disbanded following the 1891 season, leaving only the NL standing in 1892. With the total number of major-league teams (and players) significantly reduced, the NL owners had much greater bargaining power against the players.

Boston won the PL pennant with an 81–48 record. Cleveland's **Pete Browning** led the league with a .373 **batting average**; New York's **Roger Connor** led in **home runs**, with 14; and Boston's Hardy Richardson led in **runs batted in**, with 146. For **pitchers**, Chicago's Mark Baldwin led in **wins**, with 33, and in **strikeouts**, with 206; Chicago's Silver King had the lowest **earned run average**, at 2.69.

PNC PARK. PNC Park, located in Pittsburgh, Pennsylvania, has been the home field of the **Pittsburgh Pirates** of the **National League** since 9 April 2001. Prior to that, the Pirates played at Exposition Park from 1887 to 29 June 1909, **Forbes Field** from 30 June 1909 to 28 June 1970, and **Three Rivers Stadium** from 16 July 1970 to the end of the 2000 season. PNC Park has a seating capacity of approximately 38,400. It was the site of the **major league All-Star Game** in 2006.

See also STADIUMS.

POLO GROUNDS. Three earlier parks called the Polo Grounds were the home of the **New York Metropolitans** of the **American Association** and the **New York Giants** (called the New York Gothams in 1882–1883) of the **National League (NL)**. The fourth Polo Grounds was the home of the **New York Giants** of the **Players' League** in 1890, and the NL Giants from 22 April 1891 to 13 April 1911. After it was mostly destroyed by a fire, it reopened as the fifth Polo Grounds on 28 June 1911, and the park remained the home of the NL Giants until 29 September 1957. Known alternately as Brush Stadium from 1912 to 1919, in honor of owner John Brush, the Polo Grounds was also the home of the **New York Yankees** of the **American League** from 1913 to 1922, and the **New York Mets** of the NL in 1962 and 1963. The Polo Grounds hosted the **major league All-Star Game** in 1934 and 1942.

See also STADIUMS.

POMPEZ, ALEJANDRO "ALEX". B. 14 May 1890, Key West, Florida. D. 14 March 1974, New York, New York. Alex Pompez was the owner of the Cuban Stars of the **Eastern Colored League** from 1922 to 1929, and the **New York Cubans** of the **Negro National League** from 1930 to 1950. Pompez served on the **Negro Leagues Committee**, a special committee formed in 1971 to give players from the **Negro Leagues** the same **National Baseball Hall of Fame** treatment as **major leaguers**. In 2006, he himself was elected to the National Baseball Hall of Fame in a special election conducted by the **Committee on African American Baseball**.

POSEY, CUMBERLAND WILLIS POSEY, JR. "CUM". B. 20 June 1890, Homestead, Pennsylvania. D. 28 March 1946, Pittsburgh, Pennsylvania. Cum Posey was an **outfielder**, **manager**, and later the owner of the **Homestead Grays** of the **Negro National League (NNL)** for 35 years. In the nine seasons from 1937 to 1945, the Grays won eight NNL pennants. In 2006, Posey was elected to the **National Baseball Hall of Fame** in a special election conducted by the **Committee on African American Baseball**.
See also AFRICAN AMERICANS IN BASEBALL.

PREINTEGRATION ERA VETERANS COMMITTEE. *See* VETE-RANS COMMITTEE.

PRO PLAYER STADIUM. *See* SUN LIFE STADIUM.

PROGRESSIVE FIELD. Progressive Field, located in Cleveland, Ohio, has been the home field of the **Cleveland Indians** of the **American League** since 1994. The park's original name was Jacobs Field, before it was changed to Progressive Field in 2008. Prior to 1994, the Indians played their home games at League Park from 1901 through 1946, although many games from the mid-1930s to 1946 were played at **Cleveland Municipal Stadium**. Beginning with the 1947 season through 1993, all home games were played at Cleveland Municipal Stadium. Progressive Field has a seating capacity of approximately 43,400. While still known as Jacobs Field, the park played host to the **major league All-Star Game** in 1997.
See also STADIUMS.

PROVIDENCE GRAYS. The Providence Grays were a team in the **National League** from 1878 to 1885. They were one of the most successful teams in the league, winning pennants in 1879 and 1884, and finishing second three times, third twice, and fourth once. The 1884 Grays had an 84–28 record and won the pennant by 10 1/2 games. **Pitcher Charlie Radbourn** had 59 of those 84 victories. The Grays then played a three-game postseason series against the **New York Metropolitans** of the **American Association** and won all three games. In 1885, Providence had its only losing season, and, plagued by poor attendance, the team left the league. The Grays were responsible for several innovations in baseball. They were the first team to install turnstiles, wear a uniform color other than white, and have wire mesh screens to protect fans from **foul balls** hit into the stands. Aside from Radbourn, other notable players for the Grays included **Paul Hines**, **Jim O'Rourke**, **Joe Start**, **John Montgomery Ward**, and Tom York.

PUCKETT, KIRBY. B. 14 March 1960, Chicago, Illinois. D. 6 March 2006, Phoenix, Arizona. Kirby Puckett was the first choice (third overall) of the **Minnesota Twins** in the 1982 **Amateur Draft**. Puckett played for the Twins from 1984 to 1995, when eye problems ended his career prematurely. In those 12 seasons, the right-handed-hitting center fielder batted above .300 eight times, including .339 in 1989, the highest in the **American League (AL)**. His best year, however, was in 1988, when he had career highs in **batting average** (.356) and **hits** (234). The compactly built Puckett—he was 5 feet, 8 inches tall and 178 pounds—led the AL in hits four times and topped the 200 mark five times. He also led in **total bases** in 1988 and 1992, and **runs batted in** in 1994. He played in ten consecutive **All-Star Games** (1986–1995) and was voted the game's **Most Valuable Player (MVP)** in 1993.

Puckett helped lead the Twins to two **World Series** victories, against the **St. Louis Cardinals** in 1987, and the **Atlanta Braves** in 1991. His .429 batting average in the 1991 **American League Championship Series** earned him the Series MVP Award. Puckett was also the winner of the **Branch Rickey Award** in 1993 and the **Roberto Clemente Award** in 1996. He had a .318 career batting average and earned six **Silver Slugger Awards** and six **Gold Glove Awards**. In 2001, the **Baseball Writers' Association of America** elected Puckett to the **National Baseball Hall of Fame**.

PUERTO RICO. The first organized baseball game was played in Puerto Rico between the Borinquen team and the Almendares team on 11 January 1898. The semipro Liga de Béisbol Profesional de Puerto Rico was transformed into the commonwealth's first professional league in 1941. Teams that played in the league at one time or another were Lobos de Arecibo, Metropolitanos de San Juan, Atenienses de Manati,Venerables y Brujos de Guayama, Vaqueros de Bayamón, Tiburones de Aguadilla, Piratas Kofresi de Ponce, Grises de Humacao, Cangrejeros de Santurce, and Senadores de San Juan.

In 2008, the league's name was changed to the Puerto Rico Baseball League, consisting of four teams. Criollos de Caguas is located in Caguas; Gigantes de Carolina is located in Carolina; Indios de Mayaguez is located in Mayaguez; and Leones de Ponce is located in Ponce. The league champion advances to the **Caribbean Series** to play against the champions of the **Dominican Republic, Mexico**, and **Venezuela**. The representative from Puerto Rico in the 2012 Caribbean Series was Indios de Mayaguez. The winner was the Leones de Escogido team representing the Dominican Republic.

The most notable players from the Puerto Rican leagues were Carlos Bernier, Pedro "Perucho" Cepeda (the father of **Orlando Cepeda**), Francisco "Pancho" Coimbre, Luis "Canena" Marquez, Emilio "Millito" Navarro, Luis "Jibarito" Olmo, and Tomas "Planchardon" Quiñones. The first Puerto Rican to play in the big leagues was Hi Bithorn, a **pitcher** for the **Chicago Cubs** in 1942, 1943, and 1946, and for the **Chicago White Sox** in 1947. On 1 April 2001, the **Toronto Blue Jays** and **Texas Rangers** played their Opening-Day game at Hi Bithorn Stadium in San Juan, Puerto Rico.

Other notable **major-league** players and **managers** born in Puerto Rico include **Roberto Alomar**, Sandy Alomar, Luis Arroyo, Carlos Baerga, Carlos Beltran, Juan Beniquez, Tony Bernazard, Ivan Calderon, Orlando Cepeda, **Roberto Clemente**, Alex Cora, Joey Cora, Wil Cordero, Hector Cruz, Jose Cruz, Jose Luis Cruz, Ivan de Jesus, Carlos Delgado, Ed Figueroa, Ruben Gomez, Juan Gonzalez, Jose Guzman, Jose Hernandez, Ramon Hernandez, Roberto Hernandez, Willie Hernandez, Sixto Lezcano, Felipe Lopez, Javy Lopez, Mike Lowell, Candy Maldonado, Felix Mantilla, Orlando Merced, Felix Millan, Bengie Molina, Jose Molina, Yadier Molina, Willie Montanez, Jerry Morales, Jaime Navarro, Juan Nieves, Jose Oquendo, Jose Pagan, Joel Pineiro, Juan Pizzaro, Jorge Posada, Vic Power, Edwin Rodriguez (the first Puerto Rican–born manager), **Ivan Rodriguez**, Jonathan Sanchez, Rey Sanchez, Benito Santiago, Ruben Sierra, Danny Tartabull, Jose Valentin, Javier Vasquez, Jose Vidro, and Bernie Williams.

PUJOLS, JOSE ALBERTO "ALBERT". B. 16 January 1980, Santo Domingo, **Dominican Republic**. Albert Pujols played for the **St. Louis Cardinals** from 2001 to 2011. In December 2011, he left the Cardinals and the **National League (NL)** and signed as a **free agent** with the Los Angeles Angels of the **American League**. Initially used by the Cardinals as an **outfielder** and a **third baseman**, the 6-foot, 3-inch, 230-pound Pujols became a full-time **first baseman** in 2004. Pujols was the NL **Rookie of the Year** in 2001, when he had a .329 **batting average**, 37 **home runs**, and 130 **runs batted in (RBI)**. In each of the next nine seasons, he topped the .300 mark in batting, while hitting more than 30 home runs and driving in more than 100 **runs**. In 2011, his average was .299, and his RBI total 99, but he hit 37 home runs. He set the **major-league** record for most seasons with 100 or more RBI from the start of a career, with 10, and the most seasons with 30 or more home runs from the start of a career, with 12. That record was still active going into the 2013 season.

The right-handed-hitting Pujols was the NL batting champion in 2003 (.359), and he has led the league in runs scored five times, **total bases** and intentional walks four times, **slugging percentage** three times, and RBI once. He is a nine-time **All-Star** and three-time winner of the NL's **Most Valuable Player (MVP) Award**, in 2005, 2008, and 2009. Pujols's other awards include the **Hank Aaron Award**, in 2003 and 2009, the **Roberto Clemente Award** in 2008, and the **Lou Gehrig Memorial Award** in 2009. He was voted the **Major League Player of the Year** in 2003, 2008, and 2009. Pujols has a combined .330 batting average, with 18 home runs and 52 RBI in seven **National League Division Series**, five **National League Championship Series (NLCS)**, and three **World Series**, and he was the MVP of the 2004 NLCS. He has won six **Silver Slugger Awards** and two **Gold Glove Awards** at **first base**. Going into the 2013 season, Pujols had a .325 batting average for his 12 seasons, with 475 home runs and 1,434 RBI. He is sure to be elected to the **National Baseball Hall of Fame** when he becomes eligible.

PUTOUTS (PO). A putout is recorded by a **fielder** each time he takes an action that causes the **batter** or **base runner** to be put **out**. Most often, these actions are catching a fly ball, line drive, or third **strike** before it touches the ground. A putout can also be made by touching a **base** while in possession of the ball to record a force out or retire the batter at **first base**, or tagging a **runner** with the ball, or with a hand or glove holding the ball, while the runner is not safely touching a base.

Q

QUALCOMM STADIUM. *See* SAN DIEGO PADRES.

RADBOURN, CHARLES GARDNER "CHARLIE," "OLD HOSS". B. 11 December 1854, Rochester, New York. D. 5 February 1897, Bloomington, Illinois. Charlie Radbourn holds the **major-league** record for most **wins** by a **pitcher** in a season prior to 1893, when the pitching distance was extended to its current 60 feet, 6 inches. In 1884, Radbourn won 59 games (59–12) for the **Providence Grays** of the **National League (NL)**. The 5-foot, 9-inch, 168-pound right-hander won the pitchers **Triple Crown** that year, as he also led in **earned run average** (1.38) and **strikeouts** (441). Additionally, he led in **winning percentage**, **complete games**, and **innings pitched**. (Radbourn had also led the NL in wins in 1883, with 48.) Providence rode Radbourn's heroic efforts to the NL championship in 1884. The Grays then defeated the **New York Metropolitans** of the **American Association**, three games to none, in the championship series that was a predecessor to the modern **World Series**. Radbourn won all three games for the Grays.

Radbourn pitched for Providence from 1881 to 1885, and also in the NL for the Boston Beaneaters (1886–1889) and **Cincinnati Reds** (1891). In 1890, he was one of the many players who jumped to the **Players' League (PL)**, where he helped the **Boston Reds** win the PL pennant. Radbourn had a career record of 309–194 in his 11 seasons. He won 20 or more games nine times, while finishing 488 of the 502 games he started. In 1939, the **Old Timers Committee** elected Radbourn to the **National Baseball Hall of Fame**.

RAIN CHECK. A baseball game becomes official if the trailing team has batted in at least five **innings**. If rain, bad weather, or other unforeseen circumstances causes the game to be halted before that point, the paying customers are given a rain check good for use in a future game. The 1888 **Detroit Wolverines** of the **National League** are credited with being the first team to use rain checks.

RAMIREZ, MANUEL ARISTIDES (ONELCIDA) "MANNY". B. 30 May 1972, Santo Domingo, **Dominican Republic**. Manny Ramirez was a right-handed-hitting **outfielder** for the **Cleveland Indians** (1993–2000), **Boston Red Sox** (2001–2008), **Los Angeles Dodgers** (2008–2010), **Chicago White Sox** (2010), and **Tampa Bay Rays** (2011). Rather than serve a 50-game suspension for drug use, Ramirez retired after playing only five games for the Rays. While below average defensively, the 6-foot, 225-pound Ramirez was one of the most productive hitters of his era, leading the **American League** in **slugging percentage** and **on-base percentage** three times. He batted .300 or better 11 times and won a batting championship in 2002. He hit 30 or more **home runs** and drove in more than 100 **runs** 12 times each. A 12-time **All-Star**, he won nine **Silver Slugger Awards** and was twice the winner of the **Hank Aaron Award** (1999, 2004). His .412 **batting average** in the 2004 **World Series** earned him the Series **Most Valuable Player Award**. Ramirez had a .312 career batting average, 555 home runs, and 1,831 **runs batted in**; however, his suspension for using performance-enhancing drugs could affect Ramirez's chances for election to the **National Baseball Hall of Fame**.

RANGERS BALLPARK IN ARLINGTON. Rangers Ballpark in Arlington, located in Arlington, Texas, is the home field of the **Texas Rangers** of the **American League**. The Rangers previously played at Arlington Stadium from 1972 to 1993. Rangers Ballpark in Arlington, or The Ballpark in Arlington, as it was originally called, opened on 11 April 1994. From 2004 to 2006, it was called Ameriquest Field in Arlington. The current seating capacity of Rangers Ballpark in Arlington is approximately 48,200. In 1995, the park hosted the **major league All-Star Game**.

See also STADIUMS.

RECREATION PARK. *See* PHILADELPHIA PHILLIES.

REDLAND FIELD. *See* CROSLEY FIELD.

REESE, HAROLD HENRY "PEE WEE," "THE LITTLE COLONEL". B. 23 July 1918, Ekron, Kentucky. D. 14 August 1999, Louisville, Kentucky. Pee Wee Reese was the **shortstop** for the **Brooklyn Dodgers** from 1940, his **rookie** season, until 1957. He missed the 1943, 1944, and 1945 seasons while serving in the U.S. Navy during World War II, and he was a part-time player in 1958, the first year the Dodgers were in Los Angeles. Reese is credited with helping ease **Jackie Robinson's** acceptance as the **major league's** first **African American** player in the 20th century. A ten-time **All-Star**, Reese was a 5-foot, 10-inch, 160-pound right-handed hitter who had a lifetime **batting average** of .269. He led **National League** shortstops in **games played** three times and **putouts** four times. Reese, the Dodgers' team captain in the 1950s, was the winner of the **Lou Gehrig Memorial Award** in 1956. He had a combined .272 batting average while playing shortstop in each game of the seven **World Series** the Dodgers played against the **New York Yankees**. He remains the franchise leader in **runs** scored and walks and is second in **at-bats**. A longtime broadcaster after he retired, Reese was elected by the **Veterans Committee** to the **National Baseball Hall of Fame** in 1984.

RESERVE CLAUSE. The reserve clause was a clause in a player's contract that bound him to a single team for what was essentially forever, even if the individual contract he signed covered only one season. A player had no freedom to change teams unless he was given his unconditional release. The clause was successfully challenged in 1975, in a case involving **pitchers** Dave McNally and Andy Messersmith, who played the season without a signed contract. Arbitrator Peter Seitz ruled that since the owners had written the contract, it was their responsibility to spell out its terms exactly. Because the reserve clause did not explicitly state that it would be applied to the season played without a signed contract, Seitz accepted the players' interpretation that the clause only extended for one season and not in perpetuity. The owners challenged Seitz's ruling in court, but it was upheld, ending more than 80 years of the reserve system; however, today's young players may still be bound for up to 12 years (six in the **minor leagues** and six in the **major leagues**) before they have **free-agent** rights.

RICE, EDGAR CHARLES "SAM". B. 20 February 1890, Morocco, Indiana. D. 13 October 1974, Rossmoor, Maryland. Sam Rice played right field for the **Washington Senators** from 1915 to 1933, and he then played a final season, at the age of 44, for the 1934 **Cleveland Indians**. Rice's first full season was 1917, when he was already 27 years old. He was in the military in 1918 and played only seven games. The 5-foot, 9-inch, 150-pound left-handed **batter** had only 34 **home runs** in his career, but he had six seasons with 200 or more **hits** and one with 199. He scored more than 100 **runs** five times. Rice also led the **American League** in hits in 1924 and 1926; **triples**, with 18, in 1923; and **stolen bases**, with 63, in 1920. Rice batted a combined .302 in three **World Series**, including .364 in 33 **at-bats** in 1925. His career **batting average** was .322, and his 2,987 hits are the most by anyone who did not reach 3,000. Rice was elected by the **Veterans Committee** to the **National Baseball Hall of Fame** in 1963.

RICE, JAMES EDWARD "JIM". B. 8 March 1953, Anderson, South Carolina. Jim Rice made his debut with the **Boston Red Sox** in August 1974. In 1975, his first full season, he batted .309, with 22 **home runs** and 102 **runs batted in (RBI)**. He finished second to his teammate, Fred Lynn, in **Rookie of the Year** voting. Rice continued as a fixture with the Red Sox through 1989, playing left field in all but the final season and a half, when he was often used as the **designated hitter**. During that time, the 6-foot, 2-inch, 200-pound Rice became one of the most feared **batters** in the **American League (AL)**. The right-handed slugger led the league in **total bases** four times, home runs three times, and **slugging percentage** and RBI twice. He also batted better than .300 seven times.

Rice's greatest season was 1978, when he led the AL in home runs (46), **hits** (213), **triples** (15), RBI (139), and slugging percentage (.600), and he had a whopping 406 total bases. He won the AL **Most Valuable Player (MVP) Award**, one of six seasons in which he finished in the top five in MVP voting. Rice was an eight-time **All-Star** and a two-time winner of the **Silver Slugger Award**. In his only **World Series** appearance, he batted .333 in a seven-game loss to the **New York Mets** in 1986. He finished with a .298 career **batting average**, 382 home runs, and 1,451 RBI. The **Baseball Writers' Association of America** elected Rice to the **National Baseball Hall of Fame** in 2009.

RICHMOND VIRGINIAS. The Richmond Virginias were a team in the **American Association** for the latter part of the 1884 season. The Virginias replaced the **Washington Nationals**, who had a 12–51 record when they disbanded on 3 August 1884. Richmond, the first **major-league** team from the Old Confederacy, came from the Eastern League to replace Washington. The Virginias compiled a 12–30 record and then returned to the Eastern League in 1885.

RICKEY, WESLEY BRANCH. B. 20 December 1881, Flat, Ohio. D. 9 December 1965, Columbia, Missouri. Branch Rickey was a part-time **catcher** for three seasons with the **St. Louis Browns** (1905–1906, 1914) and one season with the **New York Yankees** (1907). A 5-foot, 9-inch, 175-pound left-handed hitter, he batted .239 in 120 career games. Rickey was also a **manager**, leading the Browns from the tail end of 1913 to 1915, and the **St. Louis Cardinals** from 1919 to 1925. His overall managerial record was a mediocre 597–644; however, it was as an executive, with the Browns, Cardinals, **Brooklyn Dodgers**, and briefly the **Pittsburgh Pirates**, that Rickey made his greatest contributions, especially with the Cardinals and Dodgers. He was with the Cardinals from 1919 to 1942, during which time he developed a farm system that had the Cardinals controlling up to 33 **minor-league** teams. The players developed on these teams produced six **National League** pennants and four **World Series** winners.

In 1943, Rickey joined the Dodgers as their **general manager**, president, and part owner. The many young players he signed during World War II were the core of the great Brooklyn teams of the 1950s. Rickey's most significant contribution was the selection and signing of **Jackie Robinson** in 1945. Two years later, Robinson became the first **African American** to play in Organized Baseball in the 20th century. As one of baseball's most brilliant and influential leaders, Rickey was elected to the **National Baseball Hall of Fame** by the **Veterans Committee** as a pioneer/executive in 1967.

RIGHT FIELDER (RF). *See* OUTFIELDER (OF).

RIPKEN, CALVIN EDWIN JR. "CAL". B. 24 August 1960, Havre de Grace, Maryland. Cal Ripken played for the **Baltimore Orioles** from 1981 to 2001. Although once thought too big, at 6 feet, 4 inches tall and 200 pounds, to be a **shortstop**, he played there through 1996, before moving to **third base** for his final five seasons. In 1982, Ripken was the **Rookie of the Year** in the **American League (AL)**. A year later, he batted .318 and led the league in **runs** scored, **hits**, and **doubles**, and was the league's **Most Valuable Player (MVP)** and the **Major League Player of the Year**. Ripken repeated as MVP and Major League Player of the Year in 1991, with a .323 **batting average**, 34 **home runs**, 114 **runs batted in (RBI)**, and a league-high 368 **total bases**. Ripken is best known for breaking **Lou Gehrig's** 2,130 consecutive **games played** streak, a record once thought unbreakable. The streak began on 30 May 1982, with game number 2,131 coming on 6 September 1995. It eventually reached 2,632 before Ripken voluntarily ended it by sitting out the game of 20 September 1998. Not only had he played each game during that stretch, he went several seasons where he played each **inning** of every game.

Ripken was an **All-Star** for 19 consecutive seasons and the All-Star Game MVP in 1991 and 2001. He was awarded eight **Silver Slugger Awards** and two **Gold Glove Awards**, and, in 1992, he won both the **Lou Gehrig Memorial Award** and **Roberto Clemente Award**. He led AL shortstops in games played 12 times, **assists** seven times, **putouts** six times, and **fielding percentage** four times. The right-handed-hitting Ripken batted a combined .336 in two **American League Division Series**, three **American League Championship Series**, and one **World Series**. Overall, he had a .276 career batting average, with 3,184 hits, 603 doubles, and 431 home runs. The 350 **double plays** he batted into are a **major-league** record that reflects his long career and slowness afoot. After his retirement, Ripken became active in youth baseball, building a complex in Aberdeen, Maryland, and sponsoring youth leagues. In 2007, he was elected by the **Baseball Writers' Association of America** to the **National Baseball Hall of Fame**.

RIVERA, MARIANO "MO". B. 29 November 1969, Panama City, **Panama**. Through the 2012 season, Mariano Rivera had accumulated more **saves** (608) than any other **pitcher** in **major-league** history. Rivera began his career with the **New York Yankees** in 1995, and he was still active with the Yankees in 2012, though a knee injusry caused him to miss most of the season. Since taking over as the team's closer in 1997, Rivera has saved 30 games or more in each season through 2011, leading the **American League (AL)** three times. He has also led the AL in **games finished** twice, and his 892 games finished are also a major-league record. Rivera appeared in 96 postseason games through 2011, encompassing 16 **American League Division Series**, nine **American League Championship Series (ALCS)**, and seven **World Series**. His record in the postseason has cemented his reputation as the greatest relief pitcher ever. He is 8–1, with a .070 **earned run average (ERA)**, 78 games finished, and 42 saves. He was the **Most Valuable Player (MVP)** and winner of the **Babe Ruth Award** for his one **win** and two saves against the **Atlanta Braves** in the 1999 World Series. He was also the MVP of the 2003 ALCS, when he saved two Yankees' wins against the **Boston Red Sox**.

The 6-foot, 2-inch, 195-pound right-hander has been selected to the **All-Star** team 12 times, and he was voted the AL's Rolaids Relief Pitcher of the Year five times. Through the 2012 season, Rivera had appeared in 1,042 games as a pitcher, ninth all-time. Along with his 608 saves, he has 76 wins (76–58) and a 2.21 ERA. Rivera is sure to be elected to the **National Baseball Hall of Fame** when he becomes eligible.

RIVERFRONT STADIUM. Riverfront Stadium, located in Cincinnati, Ohio, was the home of the **Cincinnati Reds** of the **National League** from from 30 June 1970, when they moved from **Crosley Field**, to 22 September 2002. From 9 September 1996 through 2002, Riverfront Stadium was known as Cinergy Field. Since 2003, the Reds have played their home games at **Great American Ball Park**. Riverfront Stadium hosted the **major league All-Star Game** in 1970 and 1988.

See also STADIUMS.

RIXEY, EPPA. B. 3 May 1891, Culpeper, Virginia. D. 28 February 1963, Terrace Park, Ohio. **Pitcher** Eppa Rixey joined the **Philadelphia Phillies** in 1912, straight from the University of Virginia, completely bypassing the **minor leagues**. The 6-foot, 5-inch, 210-pound left-hander pitched eight seasons for the Phillies (1912–1917, 1919–1920) and 13 seasons for the **Cincinnati Reds** (1921–1933). Rixey's best season was with the 1922 Reds, when he had 25 **wins** to lead the **National League (NL)**. It was the second of his four 20-win seasons. Defensively, he led NL pitchers in **fielding percentage** four times. He made only one **World Series** appearance, losing to the **Boston Red Sox** in 1915 as a member of the Phillies. Playing for mostly weak teams, Rixey had a career won-lost record of 266–251, with a 3.15 **earned run average**. In 1963, he was elected by the **Veterans Committee** to the **National Baseball Hall of Fame**.

RIZZUTO, PHILIP FRANCIS "PHIL," "SCOOTER". B. 25 September 1917, Brooklyn, New York. D. 13 August 2007, West Orange, New Jersey. Phil Rizzuto was an excellent-fielding **shortstop** for the **New York Yankees** for 13 seasons, from 1941 to 1956. (He missed 1943–1945 for World War II service in the U.S. Navy.) Rizzuto was just 5 feet, 6 inches and 150 pounds, but he was the glue of the Yankees' infield until his skills began to fade in 1954. He was an **All-Star** five times, but his greatest season by far was in 1950. That year, the right-handed-hitting Rizzuto had a career-high **batting average** of .324 and a career-high 200 **hits**, and he was voted the **Most Valuable Player (MVP)** in the **American League (AL)** and the **Major League Player of the Year**. (He had finished second to **Ted Williams** in the MVP voting the year before.) Rizzuto, an exceptionally good bunter, had a career batting average of .273. In addition to often getting **bunt** hits, he led the AL in **sacrifice hits** each season from 1949 to 1952. Rizzuto appeared in nine **World Series**, winning the **Babe Ruth Memorial Award** for his play in the 1951 Series against the **New York Giants**. After his retirement, he spent four decades as a Yankees broadcaster. Rizzuto was elected by the **Veterans Committee** to the **National Baseball Hall of Fame** in 1994.

ROBERT F. KENNEDY STADIUM. Robert F. Kennedy Stadium, located in Washington, D.C., was the home of the **expansion Washington Senators** of the **American League** from 1962 until the team left to become the **Texas Rangers** in 1972. In the Senators' first year of existence, 1961, they played their home games in **Griffith Stadium**. Originally called D.C. Stadium, the park was renamed for the slain Senator Robert F. Kennedy in 1969. From 2005 through 2007, Robert F. Kennedy Stadium (RFK Stadium, as it was more commonly called) was the home of the **Washington Nationals** of the **National League**, the relocated **Montreal Expos**. In 2008, the Nationals moved to **Nationals Park**. RFK Stadium hosted two **major league All-Star Games**, the second of the two games played in 1962—when it was still called D. C. Stadium—and again in 1969.
  See also STADIUMS.

ROBERTO CLEMENTE AWARD. The Roberto Clemente Award is given annually to the **major-league** player who "best exemplifies the game of baseball, sportsmanship, community involvement, and the individual's contribution to his team." Originally known as the Commissioner's Award, it has been presented by Major League Baseball since 1971. In 1973, the award was renamed in honor of **Roberto Clemente**. The change followed the **Pittsburgh Pirates' outfielder's** death in a plane crash while delivering supplies to victims of an earthquake in **Nicaragua**.

During the season, one player is selected from each of the 30 teams, with the winner announced at the **World Series**. Voting is done by baseball fans and members of the media. Since 2007, Chevrolet has donated money and a Chevrolet vehicle to the national winner's charity of choice, and additional money is donated to the Roberto Clemente Sports City, a nonprofit organization in Carolina, Puerto Rico, designed to provide recreational sports activities for children. Chevrolet also donates money to the charity of choice of each of the 30 club selections. The first winner of the award was **Willie Mays** of the **San Francisco Giants**. The 2012 winner was Clayton Kershaw of the **Los Angeles Dodgers**. No one has received the award more than once.

ROBERTS, ROBIN EVAN. B. 30 September 1926, Springfield, Illinois. D. 6 May 2010, Temple Terrace, Florida. Robin Roberts was a **pitcher** for the **Philadelphia Phillies** from 1948 through 1961. He later pitched for the **Baltimore Orioles** from 1962 to 1965, the **Houston Astros** in 1965 and 1966, and the **Chicago Cubs** in 1966. But it was with the Phillies in the 1950s that Roberts established himself as the **National League's (NL)** most dominant right-hander of the decade. The 6-foot, 190-pound Roberts had six consecutive 20-**win** seasons (1950–1955), the last four of which he was the NL's top winner. He also led in **games started** in each of those six seasons and led for five consecutive seasons in **complete games** (1952–1956) and **innings pitched** (1951–1955). Roberts was a seven-time **All-Star** and the NL's starting pitcher in five of the games. In 1952, when he went 28–7, he was selected by the *Sporting News* as the **Major League Player of the Year** and NL **Pitcher of the Year**. He won the NL Pitcher of the Year Award again in 1955. In 1962, he earned the **Lou Gehrig Memorial Award**. Roberts had a career record of 286–245, with 45 **shutouts**. The **Baseball Writers' Association of America** elected him to the **National Baseball Hall of Fame** in 1976.

ROBINSON, BROOKS CALBERT. B. 18 May 1937, Little Rock, Arkansas. Brooks Robinson was a **third baseman** for the **Baltimore Orioles** for 23 seasons, from 1955 to 1977. He and **Carl Yastrzemski** of the **Boston Red Sox** share the **major-league** record for most seasons played with one team.

The 6-foot, 1-inch, 180-pound Robinson had no peer as a defensive third baseman. In addition to winning 16 consecutive **Gold Glove Awards** from 1960 to 1975, he led **American League (AL)** third basemen in **games played** and **assists** eight times and **putouts** three times. He is the major-league leader in all three categories among third basemen. Robinson, who batted right-handed, was the AL's **Most Valuable Player (MVP)** in 1964, when he batted .317 and had a league-leading 118 **runs batted in**. He batted .348 in 18 **American League Championship Series** games and .263 in 21 **World Series** games. He was the winner of the MVP Award and **Babe Ruth Award** for his play in the 1970 World Series against the **Cincinnati Reds**. He batted .429 in the Series and made several spectacular plays at **third base**. Robinson was a 15-time **All-Star** and won the MVP Award for the 1966 game. He was the winner of the **Roberto Clemente Award** in 1972, and he finished his career with a lifetime **batting average** of .267, with 2,848 **hits**. In 1983, the **Baseball Writers' Association of America** elected Robinson to the **National Baseball Hall of Fame**.

ROBINSON, FRANK. B. 31 August 1935, Beaumont, Texas. Frank Robinson was the **National League (NL) Rookie of the Year** for the **Cincinnati Reds** in 1956. He played 10 seasons for the Reds, compiling a .303 **batting average** with 324 **home runs**. The right-handed-hitting Robinson led the NL in **runs** scored in 1956 and 1962, **doubles** and **on-base percentage** in 1962, and **slugging percentage** in 1960, 1961, and 1962. In 1961, he led the Reds to a pennant and earned the NL **Most Valuable Player (MVP) Award**. The Reds management eventually soured on the 6-foot, 1-inch, 183-pound slugger and traded him to the **Baltimore Orioles** following the 1965 season. In Robinson's first season in Baltimore, he won the **Triple Crown** by leading the **American League (AL)** in batting average, home runs, and **runs batted in (RBI)**. He also led in runs, on-base percentage, and slugging percentage. The Orioles won the pennant and the **World Series**, and Robinson was voted **Major League Player of the Year** and won his second MVP Award. He is the only player to win the award in the AL and NL. He was also the Series MVP and winner of the **Babe Ruth Award**.

Robinson batted an even .300, with 179 home runs, in his six seasons with Baltimore. He later played for the **Los Angeles Dodgers** (1972), California Angels (1973–1974), and **Cleveland Indians** (1974–1976). He was a 12-time **All-Star** and winner of the MVP Award for the 1971 game. Robinson played in five World Series, one with Cincinnati and four with Baltimore. He had a .294 career batting average, with 586 home runs, 2,943 **hits**, 1,829 runs, and 1,812 RBI. In 1975, he was named **manager** of the Indians, becoming the first **African American** manager in the **major leagues**. Robinson managed for 17 years, leading Cleveland from 1975 to 1977; the **San Francisco Giants** from 1981 to 1984; the Orioles from 1988 to 1991; and the

Montreal Expos from 2002 to 2006, by which time they had relocated to become the **Washington Nationals**. With Baltimore in 1989, Robinson was named AL **Manager of the Year** by both the **Baseball Writers' Association of America** and the *Sporting News*. His career record as a manager was 1,065–1,176. Robinson, who later worked in the commissioner's office, was elected by the Baseball Writers' Association of America to the **National Baseball Hall of Fame** in 1982.

ROBINSON, JACK ROOSEVELT "JACKIE". B. 31 January 1919, Cairo, Georgia. D. 24 October 1972, Stamford, Connecticut. Jackie Robinson was a 28-year-old **rookie** when he joined the **Brooklyn Dodgers** in 1947. The year before, as the first **African American** to play in Organized Baseball in the 20th century, he had been the International League's **Most Valuable Player (MVP)** as a member of the Montreal Royals. Robinson, a right-handed **batter**, was an immediate sensation in the **National League (NL)**, using his **bunting** ability and great speed and daring on the **bases** to upset opposition **fielders** like no player had since **Ty Cobb**. He overcame the harsh opposition of many fans, opponents, and even some teammates to bat .297, lead the league with 29 **stolen bases**, and win **Rookie of the Year** honors. The 5-foot, 11-inch, 190 pound Robinson played **first base** in 1947, but he moved to **second base** the next year. He also played **third base** and left field later in his career. Robinson batted above .300 from 1949 through 1954. He was the NL's MVP in 1949, when he led the league with a .342 **batting average** and 37 stolen bases, while totaling 203 **hits** and driving in 124 **runs**. Robinson was a six time **All-Star** who played in six **World Series**, all against the **New York Yankees**. The Dodgers lost five of those Series, but the team won their first and only world championship in Brooklyn in 1955. Robinson batted a combined .234, but he had 21 walks and six stolen bases, including a steal of home in Game One in 1955.

The Dodgers traded Robinson to the **New York Giants** following the 1956 season, but he chose to retire instead. He spent the rest of his life as a businessman and an advocate for civil rights for African Americans. In 1987, the Rookie of the Year Award was renamed the **Jackie Robinson Award**, and, in 1997, Robinson's number 42 was permanently retired by all **major-league** teams. Robinson, who finished his career with a .311 batting average, was elected by the **Baseball Writers' Association of America** to the **National Baseball Hall of Fame** in 1962.

ROBINSON, WILBERT "UNCLE ROBBIE". B. 29 June 1864, Bolton, Massachusetts. D. 8 August 1934, Atlanta, Georgia. Wilbert Robinson was a **major-league catcher** for 17 years and a major-league **manager** for 19. Robinson, a rotund 5-foot, 8-inch, 215-pound right-handed hitter, played in

Figure 18.1. Jackie Robinson, cap flying, roars into third base. *National Baseball Hall of Fame Library, Cooperstown, N.Y.*

the **American Association (AA)** for the **Philadelphia Athletics** (1886–1890) and **Baltimore Orioles** (1890–1891); in the **National League (NL)** for the **Baltimore Orioles** (1892–1899) and **St. Louis Cardinals** (1900); and in the **American League (AL)** for the **Baltimore Orioles** (1901–1902). Robinson had his most productive years with the successful NL Orioles, a team managed by **Ned Hanlon** that included such stars as **Willie Keeler, Hughie Jennings, Joe Kelley,** and Robinson's close friend **John McGraw.** His best season was 1894, when he batted .353 and had 98 **runs batted in.** His overall career **batting average** was .273 in 1,371 games.

Robinson began his managerial career with the AL Orioles in 1902, which was also his last year as an active player. He signed on as a **coach** for the **New York Giants** under manager McGraw in 1911, but he left after a bitter dispute between the two men following the 1913 **World Series.** In 1914, he became the manager of the Brooklyn Superbas, who soon came to be called the Brooklyn Robins in his honor. Robinson managed in Brooklyn through 1931, and, while he won only two pennants, he became Brooklyn's most beloved manager ever. His 1916 and 1920 pennant-winners both lost in the World Series, in 1916 to the **Boston Red Sox,** and in 1920 to the **Cleveland Indians.** In only one other season, 1924, did the Robins seriously challenge for the pennant. Robinson, who served as president of the club from 1926 to

1929, had a lifetime 1,399–1,398 record as manager. He was elected to the **National Baseball Hall of Fame** by the **Old Timers Committee** as a manager in 1945.

ROBISON FIELD. *See* ST. LOUIS CARDINALS.

ROCHESTER HOP BITTERS. The Rochester Hop Bitters were a team in the **American Association** in 1890. They finished in fifth place, with a 63–63 record, and then moved to the **minor-league** Eastern Association in 1891. Rochester's most notable players were Sandy Griffin and Deacon McGuire.

ROCKFORD (ILLINOIS) FOREST CITYS. The Rockford Forest Citys were charter members of the National Association (NA), but they only played in the NA's first season, 1871. Rockford, whose only notable player was 19-year-old **Cap Anson**, finished ninth in the nine-team league.

RODRIGUEZ, ALEXANDER EMMANUEL "ALEX," "A-ROD". B. 27 July 1975, New York, New York. **Shortstop** Alex Rodriguez, a high school sensation from Miami, Florida, was chosen by the **Seattle Mariners** as the first pick in the 1993 **Amateur Draft**. He joined the Mariners in 1994; in 1996, his first full season, the 20-year-old Rodriguez led the **American League (AL)** in batting (.358), **total bases** (379) **runs** scored (141), and **doubles** (54). In one of the closest votes ever for the league's **Most Valuable Player (MVP)**, he finished second to Juan Gonzalez of the **Texas Rangers**, 290–287. He was, however, selected by the *Sporting News* as the **Major League Player of the Year**. The right-handed-hitting Rodriguez batted .300 or better in three of the next four seasons with the Mariners before declaring himself a **free agent** for the 2001 season. He then signed a 10-year, $252 million contract with the Texas Rangers, at the time the most lucrative contract in baseball history. Rodriguez had three outstanding seasons in Texas (2001–2003), leading the AL in **home runs** each season (52, 57, 47, respectively), runs and total bases twice, and **slugging percentage** and **runs batted in (RBI)** once. He was again the Major League Player of the Year and MVP runner-up in 2002, before winning his first MVP Award in 2003.

The following spring, Texas traded Rodriguez to the **New York Yankees**. Rodriguez had won the **Gold Glove Award** for shortstops the last two seasons, but the Yankees already had **Derek Jeter** at shortstop, so the 6-foot, 3-inch, 225-pound Rodriguez was moved to **third base**. In his nine seasons in New York (2004–2012), Rodriguez has won two more home run titles (2005, 2007), two more MVP Awards, (2005, 2007), and his third Major League Player of the Year award (2007). He has batted .263, with 13 home runs, in a combined 18 postseason series as a member of the Mariners and Yankees: 11 **American League Division Series**, six **American League Championship Series**, and one **World Series**. Rodriguez is a 14-time **All-Star** and the winner of 10 **Silver Slugger Awards**—seven at shortstop and three at third base. He has hit 30 home runs or more 14 times and led the league five times. He has also had 100 or more RBI 14 times, including 13 straight seasons from 1998 to 2010. He has won the **Hank Aaron Award** four times and the **Babe Ruth Award**. Through the 2012 season, Rodriguez has a .300 career **batting average**, 2,901 **hits**, 1,898 runs, 647 home runs, and 1,950 RBI. He is fifth all-time in home runs, 10th in runs, and seventh in RBI. Still active in 2013, he will end his career higher on several of those lists. The brief use of performance-enhancing drugs in the latter stages of his career is not likely to affect Rodriguez's eventual election to the **National Baseball Hall of Fame**.

RODRIGUEZ, IVAN (TORRES) "PUDGE". B. 27 November 1971, Manati, **Puerto Rico**. **Catcher** Ivan Rodriguez was just 19 years old when he began his **major-league** career with the **Texas Rangers** in 1991. He played for the Rangers (1991–2002, 2009), Florida Marlins (2003), **Detroit Tigers** (2004–2008), **New York Yankees** (2008), **Houston Astros** (2009), and **Washington Nationals** (2010–2011). During his 21-year career, especially the first 15 years, the 5-foot, 9-inch, 205-pound right-handed-hitting Rodriguez was a steady hitter who won seven **Silver Slugger Awards**. He is a 14-time **All-Star** and was the **Most Valuable Player (MVP)** in the **American League** in 1999, when he batted .332, with 35 **home runs** and 113 **runs batted in (RBI)**. Rodriguez was the MVP of the 2003 **National League Championship Series** while with Florida. He had a career **batting average** of .296, with 2,844 **hits**, 311 home runs, and 1,332 RBIs. Rodriguez, the winner of 13 **Gold Glove Awards**, led his league in games caught five times, and his career total of 2,427 is the all-time record. He also holds the major-league record for most **putouts** by a catcher (14,864). Despite hints of performance-enhancing drug use late in his career, Rodriguez is likely to be elected to the **National Baseball Hall of Fame** when he becomes eligible.

ROGAN, CHARLES WILBER "BULLET," "BULLET JOE". B. 28 July 1893, Oklahoma City, Oklahoma. D. 4 March 1967, Kansas City, Missouri. Bullet Rogan, also known as "Bullet Joe," was a **pitcher** for the **Kansas City Monarchs** from 1920 to 1938 in both the **Negro National League (NNL)** and **Negro American League**. Rogan, a right-hander, was one of the winningest pitchers to play in the **Negro Leagues**. When he was not pitching, the 5-foot, 7-inch, 160-pound Rogan played the **outfield**. In 1922, Rogan led the NNL with 16 **home runs**. In 1998, a special **Negro Leagues Committee** elected him to the **National Baseball Hall of Fame**.

See also AFRICAN AMERICANS IN BASEBALL.

ROGERS CENTRE. The Rogers Centre, located in Toronto, Ontario, is the home field of the **Toronto Blue Jays** of the **American League**. The **stadium** was called SkyDome when it opened in 1989, and the facility boasted the world's first fully retractable roof. The name was changed to the Rogers Centre in 2004. Prior to the opening of SkyDome, the Blue Jays played their home games at Exhibition Stadium from 7 April 1977 to 28 May 1989. The current seating capacity of the Rogers Centre is approximately 49,300. The Rogers Centre was still called SkyDome when it hosted the **major league All-Star Game** in 1991.

ROOKIE. Eligibility requirements for determining who was a rookie were first set forth in 1957. A player could not have accumulated more than 75 **at-bats**, tallied greater than 45 **innings pitched**, or been on a **major-league roster** between 15 May and 1 September of any previous season. Shortly thereafter, the guidelines were changed to 90 at-bats, 45 innings pitched, or 45 days on a major-league roster before September 1. Revised eligibility requirements for determining who was a rookie were set forth in 1971. A rookie was formally defined as a player with less than 130 at-bats, 50 innings pitched, or 45 days on a major-league roster.

ROOKIE OF THE YEAR AWARD. The Rookie of the Year Award, or Jackie Robinson Award, its official title since 1987, is given to the individual player from each league that had the best overall season during his first year of eligibility. In 1947 and 1948, only one winner was selected from the two **major leagues**. From 1949 onward, two players have been selected each year, one coming from the **American League (AL)** and one from the **National League (NL)**. Since 1980, the members of the **Baseball Writers' Association of America** have named three **rookies** on their ballots. A first-place vote equals five points, second place equals three points, and third place gets one point. Those points are totaled, and the winner is announced at the completion of the season. The 2012 Rookies of the Year were **outfielder** Bryce Harper of the **Washington Nationals** in the NL, and outfielder Mike Trout of the **Los Angeles Angels** in the AL.

ROSE, PETER EDWARD, SR. "PETE," "CHARLIE HUSTLE". B. 14 April 1941, Cincinnati, Ohio. Pete Rose played 24 seasons in the **National League (NL)**, primarily with the **Cincinnati Reds** (1963–1978, 1984–1986). He also played for the **Philadelphia Phillies** (1979–1983) and **Montreal Expos** for part of the 1984 season. Rose, a 5-foot, 11-inch, 192-pound **switch-hitter**, was nicknamed "Charlie Hustle" for his reckless, all-out style of play. Extremely versatile, he played more than 500 games at five different positions, including **first base, second base, third base**, left field, and right field. He was a 17-time **All-Star** at the five different positions and won two **Gold Glove Awards** as an **outfielder** and a **Silver Slugger Award** as a first baseman. After winning the **Rookie of the Year Award** in 1963, Rose went on to have one of the most prolific careers in big-league history. He won three batting championships and had more than 200 **hits** in 10 seasons, while leading the league in hits seven times and **doubles** five times. He played in six **World Series**, four with the Reds and two with the Phillies.

Rose was the NL **Most Valuable Player (MVP)** in 1973. His other honors include the 1968 **Hutch Award**, 1969 **Lou Gehrig Memorial Award**, 1975 World Series MVP Award, and 1976 **Roberto Clemente Award**. He served as **manager** of the Reds for all or part of six seasons (1984–1989), and he was the **player-manager** in 1984, 1985, and 1986. Rose finished his active career with a .303 **batting average** and 4,256 hits, surpassing **Ty Cobbs** long-standing **major-league** record for career hits. He is also the all-time leader in **singles** (3,215), **games played** (3,562), **plate appearances** (15,861), and **at-bats** (14,053). His 746 doubles are second only to **Tris Speaker**. He is sixth in **runs** scored and seventh in **total bases**. Yet, despite his numerous and stellar accomplishments as a player, revelations that Rose bet on baseball while he was manager of the Reds led to **Commissioner of Baseball** Bart Giamatti barring him from the game forever, thus making him ineligible for election to the **National Baseball Hall of Fame**.

ROSTER. In baseball, the term roster refers to the number of players controlled by a team. **Major-league** teams have two rosters, a 25-man roster, also called the active roster, and a 40-man roster, also called the expanded roster. The 25-man roster consists of those 25 players who are playing for the major-league team. These players are generally the only ones who dress in uniform and are the only ones who may take the field in a game at any time.

The expanded roster is composed of the 40 players in a major-league club's organization who are signed to a major-league contract. These are the players who are able to be called up to the 25-man roster at any given time. All players on the active roster are also on the expanded roster. Also on the 40-man roster are any players on the 15-day **disabled list (DL)** and **minor-league** players who are signed to a major-league contract but are on an "optional assignment" to the minors.

Players who were on the 40-man roster but are placed on the 60-day DL are taken off the 40-man roster until the time on the DL is completed. The same applies to players who are suspended. Because players on the 60-day DL are taken off the 40-man roster with no risk of losing the player, teams often transfer injured players from the 15-day DL to the 60-day DL so that they can add another player to the 40-man roster without having to designate a player for assignment. Designating for assignment is the removal of a player from the 40-man roster, whereby the team has 10 days to trade, release, or send the player to the minors.

ROUSH, EDD J. B. 8 May 1893, Oakland City, Indiana. D. 21 March 1988, Bradenton, Florida. After playing nine games for the **Chicago White Sox** at the end of 1913, Edd Roush jumped to the **Indianapolis Hoosiers** of the **Federal League (FL)** in 1914. Roush, a left-handed **batter** and thrower, batted .325 for the Hoosiers. In 1915, the Hoosiers moved to New Jersey to become the **Newark Peppers**. Roush batted .298 for Newark, but the FL folded following the 1915 season, and Roush was acquired by the **New York Giants**. Roush was batting only .188 in July 1916, leading **manager John McGraw** to trade him to the **Cincinnati Reds**.

The 5-foot, 11-inch, 170-pound Roush had little power, but he was a consistent hitter who won batting titles in 1917 and 1919. He batted a disappointing .214 in Cincinnati's win over the Chicago White Sox in the 1919 **World Series**. The Giants got Roush back in 1927 in a trade for **George Kelly**. Roush played three seasons for the Giants, but he sat out the 1930 campaign over a salary dispute. A salary dispute had also caused him to miss most of the 1922 season. He played his final season in 1931, back in Cincinnati. Roush, whose 48-ounce bat was the heaviest in baseball at the time, was one of the most difficult batters to **strike out**. He had a .323 **batting average** for his 18 **major-league** seasons, and he is tied for 15th place on the all-time **triples** list, with 182. An outstanding center fielder with a powerful throwing arm, many considered him the defensive equal of **Tris Speaker**. In 1962, the **Veterans Committee** elected Roush to the **National Baseball Hall of Fame**.

ROYALS STADIUM. *See* KAUFFMAN STADIUM.

RUFFING, CHARLES HERBERT "RED". B. 3 May 1905, Granville, Illinois. D. 17 February 1986, Mayfield Heights, Ohio. On 6 May 1930, Red Ruffing was traded from the **Boston Red Sox** to the **New York Yankees**, where he went from one of the least successful **pitchers** in the **American League** to one of the most successful. Ruffing, who debuted with Boston in 1924, had a 39–96 record at the time of the trade. He pitched for the Yankees through 1946—minus 1943 and 1944, when he was in the military—going 231–124. (He was 3–5 in a final season with the 1947 **Chicago White Sox**.) Ruffing, a 6-foot, 1-inch, 205-pound right-hander, had four straight 20-win seasons for the pennant-winning Yankees of 1936, 1937, 1938, and 1939. In all, he pitched in seven **World Series** for New York, making 10 starts, with a 7–2 record and 2.63 **earned run average**. Ruffing was one of the best-hitting pitchers ever. He had a career **batting average** of .269, with 521 **hits** and 36

home runs. He had a combined career record of 273–225 and was a member of six **All-Star** teams. He was elected by the **Baseball Writers' Association of America** to the **National Baseball Hall of Fame** in 1967.

RULE 5 DRAFT. The Rule 5 Draft aims to prevent **major-league** teams from stockpiling young players on their **minor league** affiliate teams when other teams would be willing to have them play in the majors. The draft occurs each year in December, at the annual winter meeting of **general managers**. The selection order of the teams is based on each team's record from the prior regular season, with each round starting with the team with the worst record and proceeding in order to the team with the best record.

Any player selected in the Rule 5 is immediately added to his new team's 40-man **roster**. Teams who do not have an available roster spot may not participate in the Rule 5 Draft. Selected players must be kept on the selecting team's 25-man major-league roster for the entire season after the draft; he may not be optioned or designated to the minors. To be eligible for the Rule 5 Draft, a player must not be on his major-league organization's 40-man roster. He must also have been signed at the age of 19 or older and been in the organization for four years, or signed at the age of 18 or younger and been in the organization for five years.

RUNNER. A runner, sometimes called a **base runner**, is an offensive player who is advancing toward, touching, or returning to any **base**.

RUNS (R). Teams score runs when one of their players safely touches **first base, second base, third base**, and then **home plate** before the opponents record a third **out**. The team with the most runs scored wins the game. The **major league** single-season leader for most runs scored by an individual player is **Billy Hamilton** of the 1894 **Philadelphia Phillies**, with 198. The **American League** single-season leader is **Babe Ruth** of the 1921 **New York Yankees**, with 177. The career leader is **Rickey Henderson**, with 2,295. Henderson played for the **Oakland Athletics** (1979–1984, 1989–1995, 1998), **New York Yankees** (1985–1988), **Toronto Blue Jays** (1993), **San Diego Padres** (1996–1997, 2001), Anaheim Angels (1997), **New York Mets** (1999–2000), **Seattle Mariners** (2000), **Boston Red Sox** (2002), and **Los Angeles Dodgers** (2003).

RUNS BATTED IN (RBI). Runs batted in (RBI) did not become an official statistic until 1920, but researchers have filled in the gaps for prior years. Rule 10.04 of the **major-league** rulebook states: (a) The **official scorer** shall credit the **batter** with a run batted in for every **run** that scores: (1) unaided by an **error** and as part of a play begun by the batter's safe **hit** (including the batter's **home run**), **sacrifice hit, sacrifice fly**, infield **out** or **fielder's choice**; (2) by reason of the batter becoming a **runner** with the **bases** full (because of a walk), an award of **first base** for being **hit by a pitch**, or for **interference** or **obstruction**); or (3) when, before two are out, an error is made on a play on which a runner from **third base** ordinarily would score.

(b) The official scorer shall not credit a run batted in (1) when the batter grounds into a force **double play** or a reverse-force double play; or (2) when a **fielder** is charged with an error because the fielder muffs a throw at first base that would have completed a force double play.

(c) The official scorer's judgment must determine whether a run batted in shall be credited for a run that scores when a fielder holds the ball or throws to a wrong base. Ordinarily, if the runner keeps going, the official scorer should credit a run batted in; if the runner stops and takes off again when the runner notices the misplay, the official scorer should credit the run as scored on a fielder's choice.

The major league single-season leader in RBI is Hack Wilson of the 1930 **Chicago Cubs**, with 191. The **American League (AL)** single-season leader is **Lou Gehrig** of the 1931 **New York Yankees**, with 184. The career leader is **Hank Aaron**, with 2,297. Aaron played in the **National League** for the **Milwaukee Braves** from 1954 through 1965, and for the **Atlanta Braves** from 1966 through 1974. He finished his career with the **Milwaukee Brewers** of the AL in 1975 and 1976.

RUPPERT, JACOB, JR. "JAKE," "COLONEL". B. 5 August 1867, New York, New York. D. 13 January 1939, New York, New York, Jacob Ruppert's father founded the Ruppert Brewery in New York City in 1867. Jacob Jr. began working at the brewery at the age of 19, became the general superintendent at the age of 23, and was named president when his father died in 1915. Under his presidency, the Ruppert Brewery grew to be the most successful brewery in the United States, with Ruppert the most influential brewer. Ruppert earned the title "Colonel" while serving with the Seventh Regiment of the New York National Guard. He served on the staff of New York governor David Hill and later served four terms in the U.S. House of Representatives as a Democrat.

In 1915, Ruppert and Tillinghast L'Hommedieu Huston purchased the **New York Yankees**, a team that had never won a pennant, for $450,000. In 1918, they hired **Miller Huggins** as their **manager** and, in 1920, named **Ed Barrow** their **general manager**. In January 1920, Ruppert and Huston shocked the baseball world when they purchased **Babe Ruth**, the game's emerging star, from the **Boston Red Sox**. Led by Ruth and other stars that Ruppert, Huston, and Barrow brought to New York, the Yankees won three consecutive pennants in 1921, 1922, and 1923. They played the **New York Giants** in the **World Series** each year, losing the first two and winning in 1923.

Ruth was not only the best player in the game, he was the most popular, and the Yankees were now outdrawing the Giants, their **Polo Grounds** landlord. Giants manager **John McGraw** evicted his tenants, which led Ruppert and Huston to build **Yankee Stadium** in the Bronx, the biggest, most magnificent ballpark yet built. The park opened in 1923, the year of the Yankees' first championship. One year earlier, Ruppert and Huston had a falling out, and Ruppert bought out his partner to become sole owner of the Yankees. Under managers Miller Huggins and **Joe McCarthy**, the Yankees won nine pennants and seven World Series while Ruppert was the owner.

RUSIE, AMOS WILSON, "THE HOOSIER THUNDERBOLT". B. 30 May 1871, Mooresville, Indiana. D. 6 December 1942, Seattle, Washington. **Connie Mack**, the **manager** of the **Philadelphia Athletics** who had a 64-year career in baseball, once said that **pitcher** Amos Rusie had the best **fastball** he had ever seen. Rusie's great speed was a contributing factor in the decision to extended the pitching distance to its current 60 feet, 6 inches in 1893. In that first year at the new distance, Rusie had 50 **complete games**, a post-1893 **National League (NL)** record. Rusie began his NL career with a modest 12–10 record for the 1889 **Indianapolis Hoosiers**. The Indianapolis franchise folded after the season, and Rusie was shifted to the **New York Giants**. The 6-foot, 1-inch, 200-pound right-hander pitched for the Giants through the 1898 season, although he sat out 1896 because of a salary dispute. During that time, Rusie won 20 or more games in eight seasons and 30 or more in four. He led the NL in **shutouts** four times and **earned run average** twice. On 31 July 1891, he pitched the first **no-hitter** in Giants' history. In 1894, he led the NL with 36 wins and added two more as the Giants defeated the **Baltimore Orioles** to win the **Temple Cup**. A sore arm caused Rusie to miss the 1899 and 1900 seasons. In December 1900, the Giants traded him to the **Cincinnati Reds** for **Christy Mathewson**, who had yet to pitch in the **major leagues**. After three games with the Reds, Rusie's career was over. He finished with a record of 246–174 and was elected to the **National Baseball Hall of Fame** by the **Veterans Committee** in 1977.

RUTH, GEORGE HERMAN "BABE," "THE SULTAN OF SWAT". B. 6 February 1895, Baltimore, Maryland. D. 16 August 1948, New York, New York. Babe Ruth began his career in 1914 as a left-handed **pitcher** for the **Boston Red Sox**. By 1918, he was the best left-hander in baseball, with a record of 67–34, including 23 **wins** in 1916 and 24 in 1917. In 1916, he led the **American League (AL)** with a 1.75 **earned run average (ERA)** and nine **shutouts**. He had a 3–0 record, with an 0.87 ERA, in the **World Series** of 1916 and 1918, including a then-record streak of 29 2/3 consecutive scoreless **innings**. Ruth had already demonstrated that he could hit, and, in 1918, **Ed Barrow**, the **manager** of the Red Sox, started playing him in the outfield when he was not pitching. Ruth responded by leading the league in **home runs** (11) and **slugging percentage** (.555). The next year, he became a full-time **outfielder**, and the transformation from a great pitcher to the greatest slugger ever had begun. Ruth hit 29 home runs in 1919, to establish a new **major-league** record. In addition to again leading the league slugging percentage, he led in **runs batted in (RBI)**, **runs** scored, **on-base percentage**, and **total bases**.

In January 1920, Red Sox owner Harry Frazee sold Ruth to the **New York Yankees**. It was the most notorious transfer of a player in sports history, one that affected the fortunes of the two teams for decades to come. The Yankees won seven pennants with Ruth, while the once-dominant Red Sox went a quarter of a century before winning another pennant. Ruth became the biggest name in baseball and one of the biggest celebrities in the world during his 15 years with the Yankees, the idol of millions and especially beloved by children. He almost single-handedly changed baseball from a low-scoring pitchers' game to a free-swinging game that featured the long ball.

In his first year in New York, Ruth broke his own record of 29 home runs in a season, with an astounding 54. The next year, he hit 59 to break it again, and, in 1927, he hit 60, a record that stood until **Roger Maris** hit 61 in 1961. In several seasons, Ruth had more home runs than some entire teams. In addition to the record-breaking home run totals he had in 1920 and 1921, his RBI totals were 137 and 171, respectively; his on-base percentages were .532 and .512, respectively; and his slugging percentages were an astounding .847 and .846, respectively. Aside from injury-shortened seasons in 1922 and 1925, Ruth led the AL in home runs from 1918 to 1931. He led in slugging percentage a total of 13 times, walks 11 times, on-base percentage 10 times, runs scored eight times, and RBI and total bases six times each. Once he became a full-time outfielder, he batted below .300 only twice. His career high was .393 in 1923, but his .378 average the following year gave him his only batting championship. After he batted only .288 with 22 home runs in 1934, the Yankees released the 39-year-old Ruth. He signed with the **Boston Braves** for the 1935 season in hopes of becoming their **manager**, but when that didn't happen, he retired after playing just 28 games.

Ruth played in 10 World Series—three with the Red Sox and seven with the Yankees— compiling a .326 **batting average** with a then-record 15 home runs. His regular-season career batting average was .342, and his total of 714 home runs was a record that lasted until **Hank Aaron** broke it in 1974. Ruth had 2,873 hits, 2,174 runs (tied for fourth with Aaron), 2,213 RBI

Figure 18.2.   Babe Ruth, who stole 123 bases during his career, leads off first base. *National Baseball Hall of Fame Library, Cooperstown, N.Y.*

(second to Aaron), 2,062 walks (third all-time), and a still-record .690 slugging percentage. His pitching record was 94–46, with a 2.28 ERA. In 1936, Ruth, **Ty Cobb, Walter Johnson, Christy Mathewson,** and **Honus Wagner** were the first members elected by the **Baseball Writers' Association of America** to the new **National Baseball Hall of Fame.**

RYAN, LYNN NOLAN. B. 31 January 1947, Refugio, Texas. **Pitcher** Nolan Ryan holds the record for most seasons as a **major leaguer,** with 27. He spent 14 years in the **National League (NL),** with the **New York Mets** (1966, 1968–1971) and **Houston Astros** (1980–1988), and 13 years in the **American League (AL),** with the California Angels (1972–1979) and **Texas Rangers** (1989–1993). The 6-foot, 2-inch, 170-pound right-hander used a blazing **fastball** and sharp-breaking **curveball** to record 5,714 **strikeouts,** by far the most in major-league history. Intimidating and fiercely competitive, he led his league in strikeouts in 11 seasons and, in six of those seasons, topped the 300 mark. He is the only pitcher to strike out more than 300 **batters** in three consecutive seasons (1972–1974). His 383 strikeouts with the 1973 Angels is also a major-league record.

Often wild, Ryan also holds the career record for allowing the most walks, 2,795. He led his league in that category eight times and in **wild pitches** six times. Ryan pitched a record seven **no-hitters**, and he also had 12 one-hitters. The eight-time **All-Star** was was the *Sporting News*'s choice as the AL **Pitcher of the Year** in 1977. Ryan, who was 46 years old in his last season, had been the AL's oldest player in each of his final four seasons. His record in the AL was 189–160, and 135–132 in the NL, for a combined 324–292. His 61 **shutouts** ties him with **Tom Seaver** for seventh all-time, and only four other pitchers had more **innings pitched** than his 5,386. Ryan, who is currently part owner and president of the Texas Rangers, was elected by the **Baseball Writers' Association of America** to the **National Baseball Hall of Fame** in 1999.

S

SACRIFICE FLY (SF). A sacrifice fly (SF) is a fly ball **out** that scores a **base runner**, most often from **third base**. The **batter** is charged with a **plate appearance**, but not with an **at-bat**, and is credited with a **run batted in**. The rule existed for certain years prior to 1954, but it has been in place permanently and tracked statistically only since then.

The **major league** single-season leader in SF since 1954 is Gil Hodges of the 1954 **Brooklyn Dodgers**, with 19. The single-season leader in the **American League** is Bobby Bonilla of the 1996 **Baltimore Orioles**, with 17. The career leader from 1954 forward is **Eddie Murray**, with 128. Murray played for the Baltimore Orioles (1977–1988, 1996), **Los Angeles Dodgers** (1989–1991, 1997), **New York Mets** (1992–1993), **Cleveland Indians** (1994–1996), and Anaheim Angels (1997).

SACRIFICE HIT (SH). The scoring rule in effect since 1940 states that sacrifice hits (SH) are awarded only on **bunts** that advance a **runner** and result in an **out**, or would have resulted in an out but for an **error** or unsuccessful **fielder's choice**. Because the rules on exactly what constituted a SH hit varied considerably during the early days of baseball, SH totals from that era cannot be compared directly with modern SH totals.

The **major league** single-season leader in SH is Ray Chapman of the 1917 **Cleveland Indians**, with 67. The single-season leader in the **National League** is Jimmy Sheckard of the 1909 **Chicago Cubs**, with 46. The career leader is **Eddie Collins**, with 512. Collins played for the **Philadelphia Athletics** (1906–1914, 1927–1930) and **Chicago White Sox** (1915–1926).

SAFE. "Safe" is a declaration made by the **umpire**, vocally and with a hand signal of arms spread, that a **runner** is entitled to the **base** for which he was trying.

SAFECO FIELD. Safeco Field, located in Seattle, Washington, is the home field of the **Seattle Mariners** of the **American League**. The **stadium**, which has a retractable roof, opened on 15 July 1999, replacing the totally enclosed

Kingdome as the home park of the Mariners. The current seating capacity of Safeco Field is approximately 47,900. The Kingdome hosted the **major league All-Star Game** in 1979, and Safeco Field was the host in 2001.

SAN DIEGO PADRES. The San Diego Padres are a team in the Western Division of the **National League**. The Padres entered the National League (NL) in 1969 as part of a two-team **expansion** that also added the **Montreal Expos**. The additional two teams raised the NL's total from 10 teams to 12, which led to the league creating two divisions, each consisting of six teams. The Padres played their home games at what was eventually called Qualcomm Stadium from 1969 through 2003, before moving into **Petco Park** in 2004. Qualcomm Stadium had previously been called San Diego Stadium and Jack Murphy Stadium. San Diego Stadium hosted the **major league All-Star Game** in 1978, and Jack Murphy Stadium hosted the game in 1992.

The Padres have reached postseason play five times. They made it to the **World Series** twice, losing in five games to the **Detroit Tigers** in 1984, and in four games to the **New York Yankees** in 1998. In 1996, 2005, and 2006, the Padres lost in the **National League Division Series**.

Ken Caminiti, in 1996, is the only San Diego Padres player to win the **Most Valuable Player Award**. **Cy Young Award** winners are Randy Jones (1976), **Gaylord Perry** (1978), Mark Davis (1989), and Jake Peavy (2007). **Rookie of the Year Award** winners are Butch Metzger (1976) and Benito Santiago (1987).

Padres players who have led the league in **batting average** are **Tony Gwynn** (1984, 1987–1989, 1994–1997) and **Gary Sheffield** (1992). Fred McGriff, in 1992, is the only member of the Padres to lead the NL in **home runs**. **Runs batted in** leaders are **Dave Winfield** (1979) and Chase Headley (2012).

Padres **pitchers** who have led the leagues in **wins** are Randy Jones (1976), Gaylord Perry (1978), and Jake Peavy (2007). **Earned run average (ERA)** leaders are Randy Jones (1975) and Jake Peavy (2004, 2007). **Strikeouts** leaders are Andy Benes (1994) and Jake Peavy (2005, 2007). By leading in wins, ERA, and strikeouts in 2007, Jake Peavy won the **Triple Crown** for pitchers.

Other notable players and **managers** in Padres' history include **Roberto Alomar**, Steve Arlin, Andy Ashby, Heath Bell, Bruce Bochy, Nate Colbert, Dave Dravecky, Steve Finley, Steve Garvey, Cito Gaston, Brian Giles, Adrian Gonzalez, **Goose Gossage**, Joey Hamilton, Andy Hawkins, Trevor Hoffman, Bruce Hurst, Wally Joyner, Terry Kennedy, Ryan Klesko, Mark Loretta, Phil Nevin, Gene Richards, Eric Show, Gary Templeton, Ed Whitson, and **Dick Williams**.

SAN DIEGO STADIUM. *See* SAN DIEGO PADRES.

SAN FRANCISCO GIANTS. The San Francisco Giants are a team in the Western Division of the **National League (NL).** The team originated in New York in 1883, where they played through 1957. In 1958, Major League Baseball came to the West Coast, when the **New York Giants** moved to San Francisco, and the **Brooklyn Dodgers** moved to Los Angeles. The Giants played their home games at Seals Stadium in 1958 and 1959, and at **Candlestick Park** from 1960 through 1999. They played their first game at their current home, **AT&T Park,** on 11 April 2000. AT&T Park was known as Pac Bell Park from 2000 to 2003, and SBC Park from 2004 to 2006.

The Giants have played in five **World Series** since moving to San Francisco. They lost to the **New York Yankees** in 1962, the **Oakland Athletics** in 1989, and the Anaheim Angels in 2002, but defeated the **Texas Rangers** in 2010 and the **Detroit Tigers** in 2012. They have lost in the **National League Division Series** three times and **National League Championship Series** twice.

San Francisco Giants who have won the NL's **Most Valuable Player Award** are **Willie Mays** (1965), **Willie McCovey** (1969), Kevin Mitchell (1989), **Barry Bonds** (1993, 2001–2004), Jeff Kent (2000), and Buster Posey (2012). **Cy Young Award** winners are Mike McCormick (1967) and Tim Lincecum (2008–2009). **Rookie of the Year Award** winners are **Orlando Cepeda** (1958), Willie McCovey (1959), Gary Matthews (1973), John Montefusco (1975), and Buster Posey (2010).

Barry Bonds (2002 and 2004) and Buster Posey (2012) are the only San Francisco Giants to lead the NL in **batting average.** Leaders in **home runs** are Willie Mays (1962, 1964–1965), Willie McCovey (1963, 1968–1969), Kevin Mitchell (1989), Barry Bonds (1993, 2001), and Matt Williams (1994). Leaders in **runs batted in** are Orlando Cepeda (1961), Willie McCovey (1968–1969), Will Clark (1988), Kevin Mitchell (1989), Matt Williams (1990), and Barry Bonds (1993).

San Francisco Giants **pitchers** who have led the NL in **wins** are Sam Jones (1959), **Juan Marichal** (1963, 1968), Mike McCormick (1967), **Gaylord Perry** (1970), Ron Bryant (1973), and John Burkett (1993). **Earned run average** leaders are Stu Miller (1958), Sam Jones (1959), Mike McCormick (1960), Juan Marichal (1969), Atlee Hammaker (1983), Scott Garrelts (1989), Bill Swift (1992), and Jason Schmidt (2003). Tim Lincecum, in 2008, 2009, and 2010, is the only San Francisco Giants pitcher to lead the NL in **strikeouts.**

Other notable players and **managers** in San Francisco Giants' history include Felipe Alou, Jesus Alou, Dusty Baker, Jim Barr, Rod Beck, Vida Blue, Bruce Bochy, Bob Bolin, Bobby Bonds, Madison Bumgarner, Brett Butler, Matt Cain, Jack Clark, Roger Craig, Jim Davenport, Chili Davis, Ray

Durham, Darrell Evans, Tito Fuentes, Ed Halicki, Tom Haller, Jim Ray Hart, Gary Lavelle, Jeffrey Leonard, Greg Minton, Robb Nen, **Frank Robinson**, Kirk Rueter, Freddy Sanchez, Pablo Sandoval, Jack Sanford, J. T. Snow, Robby Thompson, and Brian Wilson.

SANDBERG, RYNE DEE. B. 18 September 1959, Spokane, Washington. After playing in 13 games with the **Philadelphia Phillies** in 1981, Ryne Sandberg was traded to the **Chicago Cubs**. Sandberg played **third base** as a **rookie** in 1982, but the Cubs switched him to **second base** the following season. He played second base for the Cubs until retiring in June 1994, but, after sitting out the 1995 season, he returned in 1996 for a final two years. The right-handed-hitting Sandberg scored 100 or more **runs** seven times and led the **National League (NL)** in runs scored three times. He was the NL's **Most Valuable Player** and the **Major League Player of the Year** in 1984, when he batted .314 and led the league in runs and **triples**. In 1990, the 6-foot, 1-inch, 175-pound Sandberg slugged a league-leading 40 **home runs** to become the first **second baseman** to lead the NL in home runs since **Rogers Hornsby**.

Sandberg played in two **National League Championship Series**, batting .368 against the **San Diego Padres** in 1984 and .400 against the **San Francisco Giants** in 1989. He was an **All- Star** for 10 consecutive seasons and won seven **Silver Slugger Awards** and nine consecutive **Gold Glove Awards**. Sandberg had a .285 career **batting average**, with 282 home runs and 344 **stolen bases**. He led NL second basemen in **assists** seven times and **fielding percentage** and **games played** three times. At one point, Sandberg held the **major-league** record for most consecutive errorless games by a second baseman, with 123. The **Baseball Writers' Association of America** elected him to the **National Baseball Hall of Fame** in 2005.

SANTO, RONALD EDWARD "RON". B. 25 February 1940, Seattle, Washington. D. 2 December 2010, Scottsdale, Arizona. Ron Santo was a right-handed-hitting **third baseman** for the **Chicago Cubs** from 1960 to 1973. He played a final season for the **Chicago White Sox** in 1974. Diagnosed with type 1 diabetes at the age of 18, he kept it secret until 1971. The 6-foot, 190-pound Santo was a nine-time **All-Star** who finished with a career **batting average** of .277 and 342 **home runs**. An exceptionally gifted defensive player, he won five **Gold Glove Awards** and led **National League (NL)** third basemen seven times each in **games played, putouts**, and **assists**. Santo holds the **major-league** record by a third baseman for most games in a season (164 in 1965) and most seasons leading the league in **total chances** (9). He is tied for the most seasons leading the league in **double plays** by a third baseman, with six. Santo also holds the NL record by a third baseman for most seasons leading the league in games played (7) and most consecutive games played (364). He is tied for most seasons leading the league in putouts (7) and most seasons leading the league in assists (7). Santo, the winner of the **Lou Gehrig Memorial Award** in 1973, was elected by the **Veterans Committee** to the **National Baseball Hall of Fame** in 2011.

SANTOP, LUIS. B. 17 January 1890, Tyler, Texas. D. 6 January 1942, Philadelphia, Pennsylvania. Luis Santop was a **catcher** in the **Negro Leagues** from 1909 to 1926. He played for the Philadelphia Giants, the New York Lincoln Giants, the Brooklyn Royal Giants, and the Hilldale Daisies. The six-feet-four, 240-pound left-handed slugger is rated behind only **Josh Gibson** and **Biz Mackey** among Negro League catchers. In 2006 Santop was elected to the **National Baseball Hall of Fame** in a special election conducted by the **Committee on African-American Baseball.**

SAVES (SV). A **pitcher** is credited with a save (SV) if he is the finishing pitcher in a game won by his team and is not the **winning pitcher.** He must satisfy prescribed criteria as to the lead his team had when he entered the game and/or to the number of **innings** he pitched. The **major league** single-season leader in SV is Francisco Rodriguez of the 2008 Los Angeles Angels, with 62. The single-season leaders in the **National League** are **John Smoltz** of the 2002 **Atlanta Braves** and Eric Gagne of the 2003 **Los Angeles Dodgers**, each with 55. The career leader is **Mariano Rivera**, who had 608 through the 2012 season. Rivera spent his entire career (1995–2012 and still active in 2013) with the **New York Yankees.**

SBC PARK. *See* AT&T PARK.

SCHALK, RAYMOND WILLIAM "RAY". B. 12 August 1892, Harvel, Illinois. D. 19 May 1970, Chicago, Illinois. Ray Schalk was a **catcher** for the **Chicago White Sox** from 1912 through 1928. He finished his career with five **games played** for the 1929 **New York Giants.** The 5-foot, 9-inch, 165-pound Schalk led **American League (AL)** catchers in games caught seven times, **fielding percentage** five times, and **putouts** nine times. He is the **major-league** leader in most seasons leading his league in putouts. Among catchers, his eight seasons of leading his league in **total chances** has been tied by **Yogi Berra** and **Gary Carter**, but never exceeded. Schalk is also the AL's all-time leader in **assists** by a catcher, with 1,811. He participated in 217 **double plays**, which remains the major-league record for catchers. Schalk is credited with being the first catcher to back up **infielders'** throws to **first base** and **outfielders'** throws to **third base.**

Offensively, the right-handed-hitting Schalk was much less impressive. He hit only 11 **home runs**, and his .253 career **batting average** is the lowest of all nonpitchers in the **National Baseball Hall of Fame (HOF)**. He did, however, bat .286 in 14 **World Series** games, including a .304 mark in the 1919 Series. Schalk was one of the "clean" Chicago players in that Series, while eight other members of the White Sox were accused of deliberately losing to the **Cincinnati Reds**. Schalk was the White Sox **manager** in 1927 and 1928, compiling a 102–125 record. In 1955, the **Veterans Committee** elected him to the HOF.

SCHMIDT, MICHAEL JACK "MIKE". B. 27 September 1949, Dayton, Ohio. Mike Schmidt played his entire 18-year career as the **third baseman** for the **Philadelphia Phillies**. Schmidt began with a partial season in 1972, and he ended with a partial season in 1989. In 1973, his **rookie** season, he batted just .196 and struck out 136 times. He did, however, show signs of what was to come by hitting 18 **home runs**. And while the 6-foot, 2-inch, 195-pound right-handed slugger led the **National League (NL)** in **strikeouts** the next three seasons, he also led in home runs. Schmidt led the league in home runs five more times on the way to his career total of 548, which was sixth on the all-time list when he retired. Schmidt led the NL in **slugging percentage** five times, **runs batted in (RBI)** and in walks four times, and **on-base percentage** three times. He was also an excellent **fielder**, leading NL third basemen in **assists** seven times and earning ten **Gold Glove Awards**. A 12-time **All-Star**, Schmidt won six **Silver Slugger Awards** and was voted the **Most Valuable Player (MVP)** in the NL in 1980, 1981, and 1986. He was also the MVP of the 1980 **World Series** and the winner of the 1983 **Lou Gehrig Memorial Award**. Schmidt had a .267 career **batting average** and 1,595 RBI. His 48 home runs in 1980 are the most ever by a NL third baseman. In 1995, Schmidt was elected by the **Baseball Writers' Association of America** to the **National Baseball Hall of Fame**.

SCHOENDIENST, ALBERT FRED "AL," "RED". B. 2 February 1923, Germantown, Illinois. Red Schoendienst was a **switch-hitting**, fine-fielding **second baseman** for the **St. Louis Cardinals** (1945–1956, 1961–1963), **New York Giants** (1956–1957), and **Milwaukee Braves** (1957–1960). Schoendienst missed almost the entire 1959 season after contracting tuberculosis and having a lung removed. He was an **outfielder** in 1945, when he led the **National League (NL)** in **stolen bases** as a **rookie**. In 1946, the Cardinals moved the 6-foot, 170-pounder to **second base**, and he remained there the rest of his career. Schoendienst, a ten-time **All-Star**, had a .269 **batting average** in three **World Series**, one with St. Louis and two with Milwaukee. He was a defensive standout throughout his career, leading NL second basemen in **fielding percentage** seven times and **putouts** and **assists** three times each. His career batting average was .289, with 2,449 **hits**. Schoendienst **managed** the Cardinals from 1965 to 1976, and briefly in 1980 and 1990. His teams won pennants in 1967 and 1968 and the World Series in 1967. His managerial record was 1,041–955. In 1989, the **Veterans Committee** elected Schoendienst to the **National Baseball Hall of Fame** as a player.

SCOUT. Some scouts are primarily interested in the selection of younger players who may require further development by the acquiring team, while others concentrate on players who are already polished professionals whose rights may soon be available, either through **free agency** or trading, and who are seen as filling a team's specific need at a certain position. Other scouts, often called advance scouts, watch the teams that their team is going to play to research their opponents' players and tactics and help determine strategy.

SCREWBALL. A screwball is a pitch that is thrown so as to break in the opposite direction of a **curveball**. When thrown by a right-handed **pitcher**, a screwball breaks from left to right from the point of view of the pitcher; the pitch therefore moves down and in on a right-handed **batter** and down and away from a left-handed batter. When thrown by a left-handed pitcher, a screwball breaks from right to left, moving down and in on a left-handed batter and down and away from a right-handed batter. The most renowned user of the screwball was **Carl Hubbell**, who pitched for the **New York Giants** from 1928 to 1943.

SEALS STADIUM. *See* SAN FRANCISCO GIANTS.

SEATTLE MARINERS. The Seattle Mariners are a team in the Western Division of the **American League (AL)**. Seattle entered the AL in 1977, along with the **Toronto Blue Jays** as part of a two-team AL **expansion**. The Mariners played their home games at the Kingdome, a domed **stadium**, from 6 April 1977 to 27 June 1999. They played their first game at their current home, **Safeco Field**, on 15 July 1999. The Mariners reached the postseason four times, but, despite a then-record-setting total of 116 **wins** in 2001, they have never advanced to the **World Series**. They were defeated in the **American League Division Series** by the **Baltimore Orioles** in 1997, and in the **American League Championship Series** by the **Cleveland Indians** in 1995 and the **New York Yankees** in 2000 and 2001.

Two Mariners have won the **Most Valuable Player Award**: **Ken Griffey Jr.** (1997) and **Ichiro Suzuki** (2001). **Cy Young Award** winners are **Randy Johnson** (1995) and Felix Hernandez (2010). **Rookie of the Year Award** winners are Alvin Davis (1984), Kazuhiro Sasaki (2000), and Ichiro Suzuki (2001).

Seattle Mariners players who have led the league in **batting average** are Edgar Martinez (1992, 1995), **Alex Rodriguez** (1996), and Ichiro Suzuki (2001, 2004). Ken Griffey Jr. (1994, 1997–1999) is the Mariners' only **home run** leader. **Runs batted in** leaders are Ken Griffey Jr. (1997), Edgar Martinez (2000), and Bret Boone (2001).

Felix Hernandez, in 2009, is the only Mariners pitcher to lead the league in **wins**. **Earned run average** leaders are Randy Johnson (1995), Freddy Garcia (2001), and Felix Hernandez (2010). **Strikeouts** leaders are Floyd Bannister (1982), Mark Langston (1984, 1986–1987), and Randy Johnson (1992–1995).

Other notable players and **managers** in Mariners' history include Bruce Bochte, Phil Bradley, Jay Buhner, Raul Ibanez, Jose Lopez, Mike Moore, Jamie Moyer, Jeff Nelson, John Olerud, Tom Paciorek, Joel Pineiro, Lou Piniella, Harold Reynolds, Aaron Sele, and Dan Wilson.

SEATTLE PILOTS. *See* MILWAUKEE BREWERS (AL/NL).

SEAVER, GEORGE THOMAS "TOM," "TOM TERRIFIC". B. 17 November 1944, Fresno, California. Tom Seaver had 16 **wins** in each of his first two seasons with the **New York Mets** (1967–1968). Then, in 1969, Seaver won a **National League (NL)**–leading 25 games (25–7) to help lead the formerly lowly Mets to their first pennant, followed by an upset win over the **Baltimore Orioles** in the **World Series**. Seaver, a 6-foot, 1-inch, 195-pound right-hander, led the league in wins again in 1975; **earned run average (ERA)** in 1970, 1971, and 1973; and **strikeouts** in 1970, 1971, 1973, 1975, and 1976. Seaver was the most popular player in team history and the face of the franchise. By June 1977, he had 189 wins for the Mets, approximately one-quarter of their total during his time with the team, but the club inexplicably traded him to the **Cincinnati Reds**. He was with the Reds through 1982, leading the NL in wins (1981), **winning percentage** (1981), and **shutouts** (1979), and pitching a **no-hitter** (1978) while there. He came back to the Mets for the 1983 season and then ended his career in the **American League** with the **Chicago White Sox** (1984–1986) and **Boston Red Sox** (1986).

Seaver was a 12-time **All-Star**; the **Rookie of the Year** in 1967; and a three-time winner of the **Cy Young Award**, in 1969, 1973, and 1975. He was also the *Sporting News*'s choice as NL **Pitcher of the Year** in 1969 and

1975. He had a career record of 311–205, with a 2.86 ERA and 3,640 strike-outs. His 61 career shutouts ties him with **Nolan Ryan** for seventh highest all-time. Seaver, who later became a broadcaster, was elected by the **Baseball Writers' Association of America** to the **National Baseball Hall of Fame** in 1992.

SECOND BASE. Second base is the second of four stations on a baseball diamond that a **base runner** must safely touch in succession to score a **run** for that player's team.

SECOND BASEMAN (2B). The second baseman is the defensive player on the team who fields the area between **first base** and **second base**. In the numbering system used to record defensive plays, the second baseman is assigned the number 4.

The **major-league** career leader in **games played** by a second baseman is **Eddie Collins**, with 2,650. Collins played for the **Philadelphia Athletics** (1906–1914, 1927–1930) and **Chicago White Sox** (1915–1926). The major-league career leader in **fielding percentage** (minimum 500 games) through 2012 is Placido Polanco (1998–2011 and still active in 2013), at .9927.

The single-season leader in **putouts** is **Bid McPhee** of the 1886 **Cincinnati Red Stockings** of the **American Association**, with 529. The **American League (AL)** single-season leader in putouts is Bobby Grich of the 1974 **Baltimore Orioles**, with 484. The **National League (NL)** single-season leader is **Billy Herman** of the 1933 **Chicago Cubs**, with 466. Bid McPhee is the career leader, with 6,552.

The single-season leader in **assists** is **Frankie Frisch** of the 1927 **St. Louis Cardinals** of the NL, with 641. The AL single-season leader is Oscar Melillo of the 1930 **St. Louis Browns**, with 572. The career leader is Eddie Collins, with 7,630.

SELEE, FRANK GIBSON. B. 26 October 1859, Amherst, New Hampshire. D. 5 July 1909, Denver, Colorado. Frank Selee was one of the first **managers** who had not previously been a star player. Known for his ability to judge talent, Selee led the Boston Beaneaters from 1890 to 1901, and the **Chicago Cubs** from 1902 to 1905. The Beaneaters won **National League** pennants in 1891, 1892, 1893, 1897, and 1898. The 1892 and 1898 teams were the first to **win** more than 100 games in a season. Selee's record with Boston was 1,004–649, and with Chicago it was 280–213, giving him an overall mark of 1,284–862 and a **winning percentage** of .598. In 1999, the **Veterans Committee** elected Selee to the **National Baseball Hall of Fame**.

SELIG, ALLAN HUBER "BUD". B. 30 July 1934, Milwaukee, Wisconsin. Bud Selig became the interim **commissioner of baseball** in September 1992, upon the resignation of the previous commissioner, Fay Vincent. Selig has been the permanent commissioner since 1998. Before that, he was the owner of the **Milwaukee Brewers**. Selig's reign as commissioner has brought **expansion**, labor peace, and several new ballparks to baseball. It also has brought expanded playoffs by the addition of **wild-card** teams, realignment, and **interleague play**.

SEWELL, JOSEPH WHEELER "JOE". B. 9 October 1898, Titus, Alabama. D. 6 March 1990, Tuscaloosa, Alabama. **Shortstop** Joe Sewell, a graduate of the University of Alabama, was 21 years old when he joined the **Cleveland Indians** in September 1920. He was called up to replace Ray Chapman, who had died a month earlier after being hit in the head by a pitch from Carl Mays, a **pitcher** for the **New York Yankees**. Chapman's death is Major League Baseball's only on-field fatality. Sewell continued as the Indians' shortstop for the next 10 years. After he was released in January 1931, he signed as a **free agent** with the Yankees and played another three seasons. Cleveland had moved him to **third base** in 1929, the same position he played in New York.

Sewell, a left-handed hitter who stood only 5 feet, 6 inches and weighed 155 pounds, struck out only 114 times in 7,132 **at-bats** in his career, while leading the **American League (AL)** in at-bats per **strikeout** nine times. In 1932, he struck out only three times, the fewest ever by a **major-league** batter in a full season. Sewell batted just .174 for the Indians in the 1920 **World Series** against the Brooklyn Robins, but he hit .333 for the Yankees in the 1932 Series against the **Chicago Cubs**. Sewell had a career **batting average** of .312, and, as a shortstop, he led the AL in **putouts** and **assists** four times and **fielding percentage** three times. In 1977, the **Veterans Committee** elected him to the **National Baseball Hall of Fame**.

SHEA STADIUM. Shea Stadium was located in the Flushing Meadows section of Queens, New York. The **New York Mets** of the **National League (NL)** played their first official game at Shea Stadium on 17 April 1964, and their last on 28 September 2008. Before moving to Shea Stadium, the Mets played at the **Polo Grounds** (1962–1963). Since 2009, they have played at **Citi Field**, which is next to the site where Shea Stadium formerly stood. In 1974 and 1975, the **New York Yankees** of the **American League** also played their home games at Shea Stadium while renovations were being made to **Yankee Stadium (I)**. Shea Stadium hosted the **major league All-Star Game** in 1964.

SHEFFIELD, GARY ANTONIAN. B. 18 November 1968, Tampa, Florida. Gary Sheffield spent 22 seasons in the **major leagues**, 13 in the **National League (NL)** and nine in the **American League (AL)**. Sheffield began his career with the AL **Milwaukee Brewers** (1988–1991). He also played in the AL for the **New York Yankees** (2004–2006) and **Detroit Tigers** (2007–2008). He played in the NL for the **San Diego Padres** (1992–1993), Florida Marlins (1993–1998), **Los Angeles Dodgers** (1998–2001), **Atlanta Braves** (2002–2003), and **New York Mets** (2009). Primarily a **third baseman** in his first five seasons, Sheffield spent most of his career as a right fielder. The 5-foot, 11-inch, 190-pound right-handed hitter had his best season with the 1992 Padres. He led the NL in batting and **total bases** and was voted the **Major League Player of the Year**. A nine-time **All-Star** and winner of five **Silver Slugger Awards**, Sheffield batted better than .300 nine times. He had a .292 career **batting average**, with 509 **home runs**, 2,689 **hits**, and 1,676 **runs batted in**. Suspicion that Sheffield, who retired after the 2009 season, used performance-enhancing drugs during his career could affect his chances of election to the **National Baseball Hall of Fame**.

SHIBE PARK. Shibe Park, renamed Connie Mack Stadium in 1953, was located in Philadelphia, Pennsylvania. It was the home of the **Philadelphia Athletics** of the **American League** from 12 April 1909 to 19 September 1954. Before that, from 26 April 1901 to 3 October 1908, the Athletics played their home games at Columbia Park. In 1955, the A's were moved to Kansas City, where they became the **Kansas City Athletics**. Shibe Park was also the home of the **Philadelphia Phillies** of the **National League** from 4 July 1938 to 1 October 1970. In 1971, the Phillies moved to **Veterans Stadium**. Shibe Park hosted the **major league All-Star Game** in 1943 and 1952.

See also STADIUMS.

SHORTSTOP (SS). The shortstop is the defensive player on the team who fields the area between **second base** and **third base**. In the numbering system used to record defensive plays, the shortstop is assigned the number 6.

Through 2011, the **major-league** career leader in **games played** by a shortstop is **Omar Vizquel**, with 2,699. Vizquel has played from 1989 through 2011 and is still active in 2012. The major-league career leader in **fielding percentage** through 2011 (minimum 500 games) is Troy Tulowitzki, at .9865. Tulowitzki has played from 2006 through 2011 and is still active in 2012.

The single-season leaders in **putouts** by a shortstop are **Hughie Jennings** of the 1895 **Baltimore Orioles** of the **National League**, and Donie Bush of the 1914 **Detroit Tigers** of the **American League (AL)**, each with 425. The career leader is **Rabbit Maranville**, with 5,139. Maranville played for the **Boston Braves** (1912–1920, 1929–1933, 1935), **Pittsburgh Pirates** (1921–1924), **Chicago Cubs** (1925), Brooklyn Robins (1926), and **St. Louis Cardinals** (1927–1928).

Through 2012, the **major-league** career leader in **games played** by a shortstop is **Omar Vizquel**, with 2,709. Vizquel played from 1989 through 2012. The major-league career leader in **fielding percentage** through 2012 (minimum 500 games) is Troy Tulowitzki, at .9851. Tulowitzki has played from 2006 through 2012 and is still active in 2013.

SHUTOUTS (SHO). A team is credited with a shutout (SHO) when they prevent the opposing team from scoring a **run**. If the winning team uses only one **pitcher**, that pitcher is credited with a SHO. The **major league** single-season leader in SHO by a pitcher post-1893, when the pitching distance was extended to its current 60 feet, 6 inches, is **Grover Alexander** of the 1916 **Philadelphia Phillies** of the **National League (NL)**, with 16. (George Bradley of the NL's 1876 **St. Louis Brown Stockings** also had 16 SHO.) The single-season leader in the **American League** is Jack Coombs of the 1910 **Philadelphia Athletics**, with 13. The career leader is **Walter Johnson**, with 110. Johnson pitched for the **Washington Senators** from 1907 through 1927.

Figure 19.1.   Shortstop Cal Ripken of the Baltimore Orioles sets himself to field a batted ball. *National Baseball Hall of Fame Library, Cooperstown, N.Y.*

SILVER SLUGGER AWARD. The Silver Slugger Award was instituted in 1980 by the Hillerich & Bradsby Company, of Louisville, Kentucky. The specially designed Silver Slugger Award is a silver-plated, 3-foot-tall, bat-shaped trophy that bears the engraved name of the winner and his Silver Slugger teammates. It is awarded annually to the best offensive player at each position in both the **American League (AL)** and **National League (NL)**, as determined by the league's **managers** and **coaches**. Managers and coaches are not permitted to vote for players on their own team. The award is presented to **outfielders** irrespective of their specific position. In addition, only NL **pitchers** receive a Silver Slugger Award. In the AL, the award goes to a **designated hitter**. The players who have won the most Silver Slugger Awards through 2012 are **Barry Bonds** (12), **Mike Piazza** (10), **Alex Rodriguez** (10), **Barry Larkin** (9), **Wade Boggs** (8), and **Ryne Sandberg** (7).

SIMMONS, ALOYSIUS HARRY "AL," "BUCKETFOOT AL". B. Aloys Szymanski, 22 May 1902, Milwaukee, Wisconsin. D. 26 May 1956, Milwaukee, Wisconsin. Al Simmons played for seven different teams during his 20-year **major-league** career, but his best years were with the **Philadelphia Athletics** from 1924 through 1932. The 5-foot, 11-inch, 190-pound **outfielder** compiled **batting averages** above .300 each season with the Athletics, and above .350 in six of those seasons. His .381 average in 1930 and his .390 mark in 1931 earned Simmons back-to-back **American League (AL)** batting titles. He also finished second twice. The Athletics won three consecutive AL pennants (1929–1931) and **World Series** titles in 1929 and 1930. Simmons batted .300, .364, and .333 in the three Series. After Philadelphia finished second in 1932, **manager Connie Mack**, in the process of unloading his star players, sold Simmons to the **Chicago White Sox**. Simmons had two strong seasons in Chicago, but he fell off in 1935. He rebounded in 1936, after being sold to the **Detroit Tigers**, but he spent the rest of his career bouncing around to various teams, including two more stays with the Athletics. In his last seven seasons, Simmons also played for the **Washington Senators, Boston Red Sox, Boston Braves**, and **Cincinnati Reds**.

Simmons, a right-handed hitter, was called "Bucketfoot Al" for his unusual batting stance, in which he pointed his left foot down the **third base** line. Simmons batted above .300 in each his first 11 seasons and 13 times overall. He led the AL in **hits** twice and had 200 hits or more in a season six times. Simmons finished his career with a .334 batting average, 307 **home runs**, and 2,927 hits. At the time of his retirement, his 1,827 **runs batted in** placed him in the top five all-time. In 1953, the **Baseball Writers' Association of America** elected Simmons to the **National Baseball Hall of Fame**.

SINGLES (1B). A single is any batted ball where the **batter** reaches **first base** safely without the benefit of any fielding **errors**. A batter is also credited with a single when his batted ball hits a **base runner**. The **runner** is out, and the batter is awarded first base.

The **major league** single-season leader in singles is **Ichiro Suzuki** of the 2004 **Seattle Mariners**, with 225. The single-season leader in the **National League** is **Willie Keeler** of the 1898 **Baltimore Orioles**, with 206. The career leader is **Pete Rose**, with 3,215. Rose played for the **Cincinnati Reds** (1963–1978, 1984–1986), **Philadelphia Phillies** (1979–1983), and **Montreal Expos** (1984).

SISLER, GEORGE HAROLD. B. 24 March 1893, Manchester, Ohio. D. 26 March 1973, Richmond Heights, Missouri. George Sisler, a former star left-handed **pitcher** for the University of Michigan, joined the **St. Louis Browns** in 1915. The Browns' **manager**, **Branch Rickey**, Sisler's coach at Michigan, soon moved the 5-foot, 11-inch, 170-pound left-handed hitter to **first base**. Sisler played for the Browns from 1915 to 1922, and from 1924 to 1927. He missed the 1923 season with a severe sinus infection. Sisler also played for the **Washington Senators** in 1928, and the **Boston Braves** in 1928, 1929, and 1930. Aside from 1915, his **rookie** season, and 1926, Sisler batted above .300 each year he played. He twice batted over .400, leading the **American League (AL)** with a .407 **batting average** in 1920 and a .420 average in 1922. He led the AL in **hits** twice and had more than 200 six times, and his 257 hits in 1920 stood as a **major-league** record until **Ichiro Suzuki** of the **Seattle Mariners** topped it in 2004.

Sisler's best season was 1922, when he led the AL in batting average, hits, **runs**, **stolen bases**, and **triples**. He had a 41-game hitting streak and was voted the AL's **Most Valuable Player**. He led the league in stolen bases four times, triples twice, and **assists** by a **first baseman** seven times. Sisler was the Browns' **player-manager** for the three seasons, 1924, 1925, and 1926, finishing fourth, third, and seventh, respectively. He ended his career with a total of 2,812 hits and a .340 batting average. In 1939, the **Baseball Writers' Association of America** elected him to the **National Baseball Hall of Fame**.

SKYDOME. *See* TORONTO BLUE JAYS.

SLAUGHTER, ENOS BRADSHER "COUNTRY". B. 27 April 1916, Roxboro, North Carolina. D. 12 August 2002, Durham, North Carolina. Enos Slaughter was a left-handed-hitting right fielder who spent the first 13 years of his 19-year **major-league** career with the **St. Louis Cardinals**. Slaughter was a Cardinal from 1938 to 1953, although he missed the 1943, 1944, and

1945 seasons while serving in the military. Known for his hustle and aggressive style of play, he was an **All-Star** in 10 of those seasons and batted .300 or better in eight. Slaughter, who threw right-handed, led his league's right fielders in **fielding percentage** four times, **putouts** three times, and **assists** twice.

In 1942, the 5-foot, 9-inch, 180-pound Slaughter led the **National League** in **hits**, **triples**, **extra-base hits**, and **total bases**, and he finished a close second to teammate Mort Cooper in the voting for the **Most Valuable Player Award**. He played on two **World Series** champions as a Cardinal, in 1942 and 1946, and is best remembered for his race from **first base** to score the winning run in Game Seven of the 1946 Series against the **Boston Red Sox**. Slaughter was traded to the **New York Yankees** in 1954, and he played with them through 1959, with a brief stay in parts of 1955 and 1956 with the **Kansas City Athletics** and, in 1959, with the **Milwaukee Braves**. He got to play in three more World Series with the Yankees, in 1956, 1957, and 1958. In the 1956 series, against the **Brooklyn Dodgers**, he batted .350 and drove in four **runs**. Slaughter, who had a career **batting average** of .300, was elected by the **Veterans Committee** to the **National Baseball Hall of Fame** in 1985.

SLUGGING PERCENTAGE (SLG). Slugging percentage (SLG) is calculated by dividing a **batter's total bases** by his total **at-bats**. The formula is **singles + doubles*2 + triples*3 + home runs*4**, divided by total at-bats. Example: A player with 111 singles, 30 doubles, three triples, 23 home runs, and 576 at-bats has a SLG of .472.

The **major league** single-season leader in SLG is **Barry Bonds** of the 2001 **San Francisco Giants**, at .863. The **American League** single-season leader is **Babe Ruth** of the 1920 **New York Yankees**, at .847. Ruth is also the career leader, at .690. Ruth played for the **Boston Red Sox** from 1914 through 1919, the **New York Yankees** from 1920 through 1934, and the **Boston Braves** in 1935.

SMITH, HILTON LEE. B. 27 February 1912, Giddings, Texas. D. 18 November 1983, Kansas City, Missouri. Hilton Smith was a standout **pitcher** for the **Kansas City Monarchs** in the **Negro American League** from 1936 to 1948. Although the 6-foot, 2-inch, 180-pound right-hander was one of the Monarchs' most successful pitchers, he never earned the recognition given to his more ostentatious teammate, **Satchel Paige**. Recognition finally came in 2001, when a special **Negro Leagues Committee** elected Smith to the **National Baseball Hall of Fame**.

See also AFRICAN AMERICANS IN BASEBALL.

SMITH, OSBORNE EARL "OZZIE". B. 26 December 1954, Mobile, Alabama. Ozzie Smith played **shortstop** in the **National League (NL)** for 19 seasons, with the **San Diego Padres** (1978–1981) and **St. Louis Cardinals** (1982–1996). Smith, a 5-foot, 11-inch, 150-pound **switch-hitter**, was a 15-time **All-Star**. He had a career **batting average** of .262 and 580 **stolen bases**. On defense, Smith was both spectacular and efficient. He won 13 consecutive **Gold Glove Awards** (1980–1992), while leading NL shortstops in both **fielding percentage** and **assists** eight times. He is the all-time career leader in assists by a shortstop and fourth all-time in **games played** at the position. Smith was the **Most Valuable Player** of the 1985 **National League Championship Series**, and he was the winner of the **Lou Gehrig Memorial Award** in 1989, **Branch Rickey Award** in 1994, and **Roberto Clemente Award** in 1995. He was elected by the **Baseball Writers' Association of America** to the **National Baseball Hall of Fame** in 2002.

SMOLTZ, JOHN ANDREW. B. 15 May 1967, Detroit, Michigan. John Smoltz was a **pitcher** for the **Atlanta Braves** from 1988 to 1999, and from 2001 to 2008. He missed the 2000 season with an arm injury, and he pitched a final season, in 2009, with the **Boston Red Sox** and **St. Louis Cardinals**. The 6-foot, 3-inch, 210-pound right-hander was a starter for his first 12 seasons, during which time he twice led the **National League (NL)** in **winning percentage**, **innings pitched**, and **strikeouts**. In 1996, Smoltz led the NL with 24 **wins**, a .750 winning percentage, and 276 strikeouts, earning him the **Cy Young Award** and selection as the *Sporting News*'s NL **Pitcher of the Year**. When he came back from his injury in 2001, the Braves made Smoltz their closer. The next year, he led the NL with 55 **saves** and was the NL's Rolaids Relief Pitcher of the Year. Returned to a starting role in 2005, he tied for the NL high in wins, with 16.

Smoltz was an eight time **All-Star** and compiled a spectacular 15–4 record for Atlanta in the postseason. He was 7–0 in 11 **National League Division Series**, 6–2 in nine **National League Championship Series (NLCS)**, and 2–2 in five **World Series**. Smoltz was the **Most Valuable Player** of the 1992 NLCS, and he was the recipient of the **Lou Gehrig Memorial Award** and **Roberto Clemente Award** in 2005, and the **Branch Rickey Award** in 2007. He had a career record of 213–155, with a 3.33 **earned run average**, 3,084 strikeouts, and 154 saves. He is the only **major-league** pitcher to have had more than 200 wins and 150 saves. Smoltz, whose last active season was 2009, is sure to be elected to the **National Baseball Hall of Fame** when he becomes eligible.

SNIDER, EDWIN DONALD "DUKE". B. 19 September 1926, Los Angeles, California. D. 27 February 2011, Escondido, California. Duke Snider is the Dodgers' all-time leader in **home runs, runs batted in (RBI),** and **extra-base hits.** The 6-foot, 179-pound center fielder played for the Dodgers in Brooklyn from 1947 to 1957, and in Los Angeles from 1958 to 1962. He also played for the **New York Mets** in 1963 and the **San Francisco Giants** in 1964. Snider, who batted left-handed and threw right-handed, led the **major leagues** in home runs and RBI during the decade of the 1950s. He topped the 40 home run mark for the five seasons from 1953 to 1957, including 43 in 1956, the high in the **National League (NL).** As a **Brooklyn Dodger,** he led the NL in **hits** in 1950; **runs** scored, extra-base hits, and RBI in 1955, **on-base percentage** and walks in 1956; and **slugging percentage** in 1953 and 1956.

Snider was an outstanding defensive center fielder, who possessed great range and an outstanding throwing arm. He was an eight-time **All-Star** and was voted the **Major League Player of the Year** for 1955. Snider played in six **World Series.** Five were with Brooklyn, all against the **New York Yankees,** and one with Los Angeles, against the **Chicago White Sox** in 1959. He batted a combined .286, with 11 home runs and 26 RBI in 36 games. In both the 1952 and 1955 Series, he hit four home runs to tie the record for the most home runs in one World Series. Snider had a .295 lifetime **batting average,** including a career-high .341 in 1954. He hit 407 home runs, while both driving in and scoring more than 100 runs six times each. After he retired, he worked as a batting **coach, scout, minor-league manager,** and broadcaster. In 1980, the **Baseball Writers' Association of America** elected Snider to the **National Baseball Hall of Fame.**

SOCIETY FOR AMERICAN BASEBALL RESEARCH (SABR). The Society for American Baseball Research (SABR) had its beginnings in Cooperstown, New York, in August 1971, when L. Robert (Bob) Davids gathered 15 other baseball researchers at the **National Baseball Hall of Fame** to form the organization. SABR's original purpose was to band together baseball historians, statisticians, and researchers. Today, SABR membership totals more than 6,000 worldwide, including many Major League Baseball and Minor League Baseball officials, broadcasters, and writers, as well as numerous former players. The membership primarily consists of "just plain fans."

SABR members have a variety of interests. There are more than two dozen research committees devoted to the study of a specific area related to the game, from baseball and the arts, to statistical analysis, to the **Negro Leagues,** to women in baseball, and many others. Ernie Harwell, the late **Detroit Tigers'** broadcaster, once said that, "SABR is the Phi Beta Kappa of baseball, providing scholarship [that] the sport has long needed."

SOFTBALL. Softball originated in Chicago, Illinois, in the late 19th century as an indoor alternative to baseball. Within a couple years of its creation, the game moved outdoors and established formal rules. While most early softball players were men, the cultural forces that excluded women from baseball decided that softball was an acceptable game for women to play.

Today, softball has become a popular variation of baseball, with males and females of all ages playing the game. It operates according to the same basic rules as baseball: three **strikes** is an out; four balls is a walk; each team gets three outs per **inning**; a player scores a **run** by returning to **home plate**; and there are nine players per team, a **pitcher**, a **catcher**, four **infielders**, and three **outfielders**. There are variations to this defensive set-up, particularly among the numerous senior leagues, where a team will often have five in-fielders and/or four outfielders.

Softball pitchers stand much closer to the **batter** than baseball pitchers, 40 to 43 feet away, rather than 60 feet, 6 inches. They use a larger ball and throw it underhand, either with a windmill motion or in an arc that cannot exceed 12 feet. A softball infield is dirt rather than grass. Distances vary according to age and sex, but outfield fences are much closer, 220 to 250 feet, and the **bases** are 45 to 65 feet apart rather than 90.

The national governing body for softball is the Amateur Softball Association of America (ASA). Established in 1933, the ASA supervises numerous national tournaments for all ages players of both genders. They are also the governing body for the collegiate girls World Series, won in 2012 by the University of Alabama. The International Softball Federation is the governing body for international softball.

SOSA, SAMUEL PERALTA "SAMMY". B. 12 November 1968, San Pedro de Macoris, **Dominican Republic**. Sammy Sosa began his career with the **Texas Rangers** of the **American League (AL)** in 1989, and he ended it with the Rangers in 2007. The right-handed-hitting **outfielder** also played in the AL for the **Chicago White Sox** (1989–1991) and **Baltimore Orioles** (2005). but his best years were with the **Chicago Cubs** of the **National League (NL)** from 1992 to 2004. The 6-foot, 165-pound Sosa hit 545 **home runs** in his 13 years with the Cubs. He led the NL in home runs in 2000 and 2002, and in three other years—1998, 1999, and 2001—he hit more than 60 home runs. He is the only **major leaguer** to have three seasons of 60 or more home runs. His career high was 66 in 1998. In a dramatic race for the home run title that year, he was beaten by **Mark McGwire** of the **St. Louis Cardinals**, who hit 70 to set a new major-league record. Nevertheless, Sosa, who led in **runs** scored, **total bases**, and **runs batted in (RBI)** in 1998, was chosen the **Major League Player of the Year** and the NL's **Most Valuable Player**. He also won the **Roberto Clemente Award** in 1998 and the **Hank Aaron Award** in 1999. Overall, Sosa led the league in runs scored and total bases three times, and in RBI twice. He was a seven-time **All-Star** and a six-time winner of the **Silver Slugger Award**. He had a .273 career **batting average**, with 609 home runs and 1,667 RBI; however, charges that Sosa used performance-enhancing drugs during his career could affect his chances of election to the **National Baseball Hall of Fame**.

SOUTH END GROUNDS. *See* BOSTON BRAVES.

SOUTH KOREA. The Korea Baseball Organization (KBO) is the governing body for the professional leagues of baseball in South Korea. KBO was founded in 1981 and has been governing two leagues, Korea Professional Baseball and Futures League (since 1982). KBO is one of two major baseball governing bodies; the other is the Korea Baseball Association, which is the governing body for the amateur baseball competitions. KBO is a member of the **International Baseball Federation (IBAF)**, and the group is responsible for the national baseball team for the **World Baseball Classic (WBC)**.

Teams in the KBO include the Doosan Bears, Hanwha Eagles, KIA Tigers, LG Twins, Lotte Giants, NC Dinos, Nexen Heroes, Samsung Lions, and SK Wyverns. South Korea lost to **Japan** in the finals of the 2009 WBC. Notable South Korean-born players who played in the **major leagues** include Hee-Seop Choi, Shin-Soo Choo, Byung-Hyun Kim, Sun-Woo Kim, Chan Ho Park, and Jae Weong Seo.

SOUTH SIDE PARK. *See* CHICAGO CUBS; CHICAGO WHITE SOX.

SOUTHWORTH, WILLIAM HAROLD "BILLY". B. 9 March 1893, Harvard, Nebraska. D. 15 November 1969, Columbus, Ohio. Billy Southworth, a 5-foot, 9-inch, 170-pound left-handed-hitting **outfielder**, played in the **major leagues** for 13 seasons. After two seasons with the **Cleveland Indians** of the **American League** in 1913 and 1915, Southworth spent the rest of his career as a **player** and **manager** in the **National League**, with an overall career **batting average** of .297. He played for the **Pittsburgh Pirates** (1918–1920), **Boston Braves** (1921–1923), **New York Giants** (1924–1926), and **St. Louis Cardinals** (1926–1927, 1929). Southworth then went on to manage two of his former teams, the Cardinals (1929, 1940–1945) and Braves (1946–1951). He won three consecutive pennants with the Cardinals, defeating the **New York Yankees** in the **World Series** of 1942, losing to the Yankees in 1943, and defeating the **St. Louis Browns** in 1944. The *Sporting News* gave him its **Manager of the Year Award** in 1941 and 1942. Southworth won a fourth pennant, with the Braves, in 1948, but the team lost in the

World Series to Cleveland. Southworth's overall record as a manager was 620–346. He was elected to the **National Baseball Hall of Fame** by the **Veterans Committee** in 2008, as a manager.

SPAHN, WARREN EDWARD. B. 23 April 1921, Buffalo, New York. D. 24 November 2003, Broken Arrow, Oklahoma. Left-handed **pitcher** Warren Spahn appeared in four games for the **Boston Braves** in 1942. He spent the next three years in the U.S. Army, where he fought in Europe, earning a Bronze Star and a Purple Heart. Spahn returned to the Braves in 1946, remaining with the organization as they shifted to Milwaukee in 1953, and through the 1964 season. He played a final season at the age of 44, in 1965, split between the **New York Mets** and **San Francisco Giants**. Employing a high kick and a smooth motion, the 6-foot, 172-pound Spahn had 13 seasons in which he won 20 or more games for the Braves. He led the **National League (NL)** in **wins** eight times, including five consecutive seasons from 1957 to 1961. He led in **strikeouts** and **shutouts** four times and **earned run average** three times, in three different decades. A workhorse on the mound, he led the NL in **complete games** in nine seasons, including seven straight, and in **innings pitched** in four seasons.

Spahn threw two **no-hitters**, was named to the NL **All-Star** team in 14 different seasons, won the **Cy Young Award** in 1957 and the **Lou Gehrig Memorial Award** in 1961, and was named the *Sporting News*'s NL **Pitcher of the Year** four times. He appeared in three **World Series** (1948, 1957, 1958), winning four and losing three. Spahn's 363 victories (363–245) are the most by a left-hander. One of the best-hitting pitchers, his 36 **home runs** are the most by a NL pitcher. Spahn was elected by the **Baseball Writers' Association of America** to the **National Baseball Hall of Fame** in 1973.

SPALDING, ALBERT GOODWILL "AL". B. 2 September 1850, Byron, Illinois. D. 9 September 1915, San Diego, California. Al Spalding of the **Boston Red Stockings** was the premier **pitcher** in the five-year existence of the National Association (NA). Spalding led the NA in **wins** in each season, as the Red Stockings won four pennants (1872–1875). When the NA folded, Spalding and **William Hulbert** organized the new **National League (NL)**, with Spalding joining the Chicago White Stockings as a pitcher and the **manager**. In 1876, the 6-foot, 1-inch 170-pound right-hander's league-leading 47 wins led Chicago to the new league's first pennant. Spalding's career won-lost record as a pitcher was 252–65; his .795 **winning percentage** is the highest by a **major-league** pitcher.

Spalding managed the team again in 1877, but he then turned his efforts to business. He served as president of the Chicago club from 1882 to 1891, and he began publishing baseball guides and rule books. He launched a sporting goods company that bore his name and became the biggest purveyor of sporting goods in the country. All the while, Spalding was baseball's great ambassador, promoting the game both nationally and internationally. He wrote one of the first books describing the history of baseball and, in 1908, was behind a commission that promulgated the myth that baseball had been invented by Abner Doubleday in Cooperstown, New York, in 1839. In 1939, Spalding was elected by the **Old Timers Committee** to the **National Baseball Hall of Fame** as a pioneer/executive.

SPEAKER, TRISTRAM E. "TRIS," "THE GREY EAGLE". B. 4 April 1888, Hubbard, Texas. D. 8 December 1958, Lake Whitney, Texas. Tris Speaker's .345 lifetime **batting average** is the sixth highest in the **major leagues.** Speaker, a left-handed **batter** and thrower, played 22 seasons in the **American League (AL);** he was with the **Boston Red Sox** from 1907 to 1915 and the **Cleveland Indians** from 1916 to 1926, and he then spent single seasons with the 1927 **Washington Senators** and the 1928 **Philadelphia Athletics.** The 5-foot, 11-inch, 193-pound Speaker led the AL in **doubles** seven times, and his lifetime total of 792 is still the major-league record. He also led the AL in **on-base percentage** four times and **hits** twice. His best year with the Red Sox was 1912, when he batted .383 and led the league in doubles (53), **home runs** (10), and on-base percentage (.464), and he won the **Chalmers Award** as the league's **Most Valuable Player.** From 1910 to 1915, Speaker, who played center field, teamed with left fielder Duffy Lewis and right fielder **Harry Hooper** to form one of baseball's all-time great outfields. In his 22 seasons, Speaker was credited with 449 outfield **assists,** another major-league record that still stands.

In April 1916, Boston traded Speaker to the **Cleveland Indians**. That season, he led the league in batting (.386), hits (211), doubles (41), on-base percentage (.470), and **slugging percentage** (.502). Speaker was a **player-manager** for the Indians from 1919 to 1926, compiling a 617–520 record. In 1920, he led Cleveland to its first pennant ever and a win over the Brooklyn Robins in the **World Series**. Following the 1926 season, AL president **Ban Johnson** persuaded Speaker to resign as Cleveland's **manager** because of rumors of an alleged fixed game. Speaker, who had also played in the 1912 and 1915 World Series with Boston, had a combined Series average of .306. His 3,514 career hits are fifth all-time, but his hit total was second only to **Ty Cobb** when he retired; his 222 **triples** are sixth all-time. In 1937, Speaker was elected by the **Baseball Writers' Association of America** to the **National Baseball Hall of Fame**.

SPITBALL. A spitball, or spitter, is a pitch in which the **pitcher** applies saliva to the ball to make it move sideways as it approaches **home plate**. The term is sometimes applied loosely to pitches in which the ball is treated with other foreign substances, such as Vaseline. The spitball rose to prominence in the early 1900s and was widely used into the 1910s. The spitball, and all other pitches involving doctoring the ball, was banned before the 1920 season. Seventeen recognized spitball pitchers, including future Hall of Famers **Red Faber** and **Stan Coveleski**, were allowed to continue throwing the pitch for the remainder of their careers. Another future Hall of Famer, **Burleigh Grimes**, who pitched as late as 1934, was the last of the legal spitball pitchers in the **major leagues**. Many pitchers since have been accused of throwing spitballs illegally, and a few were either caught or admitted to doing so after retiring.

SPORTING NEWS. The *Sporting News* was founded by Alfred H. Spink in 1886. Based in St. Louis, Missouri, it became the dominant U.S. publication covering baseball—so much so that it acquired the nickname "The Bible of Baseball." With the demise of other sporting weeklies, including the *New York Clipper* and *Sporting Life*, the *Sporting News* became the only national baseball newspaper by World War I. It is currently owned by American City Business Journals, based in Charlotte, North Carolina, and baseball is just one of seven sports it covers.

With the change in ownership, the company ceased most of its book publishing efforts. The 2006 *Baseball Guide*, a *Sporting News* annual in one form or another since the 1920s, was its last. The 2007 *Baseball Register*, an annual since the early 1940s, was its last. The 2007 *Baseball Record Book* was only available online, as a download. None of these guides were published in 2008. Among the annual awards the *Sporting News* has presented throughtout the years are the **Most Valuable Player Award**, **Major League Player of the Year**, **Pitcher of the Year**, and **Manager of the Year**.

SPORTSMAN'S PARK. There were four parks named Sportsman's Park, all located in St. Louis, Missouri. Sportsman's Park (I) was the home of the **St. Louis Brown Stockings** of the National Association (1875) and the St. Louis Brown Stockings of the **National League (NL)** (1876–1877). Sportsman's Park (II) was the home of the **St. Louis Browns** of the **American Association** (1882–1891) and the St. Louis Browns of the NL (1892). Sportsman's Park (III) was the home of the St. Louis Browns of the **American League (AL)** (1902–1908). Sportsman's Park (IV) was the home of the **St. Louis Browns** of the AL (1909–1953) and the **St. Louis Cardinals** of the NL from 1 July 1920 to 8 May 1966. In 1954, the park was renamed

Busch Stadium in honor of new Cardinals' owner August Busch. Sportsman's Park (IV) hosted the **major league All-Star Game** in 1940 and 1948, and Busch Stadium hosted the game in 1957.

See also STADIUMS.

SPRING TRAINING. Spring training is a series of practices and exhibition games preceding the start of the regular season. The practice of holding spring training began in the late 19th century and was soon adopted by all **major-league** teams. **Pitchers** and **catchers** are traditionally the first players to report to spring training, because pitchers benefit from a longer training period. A week or two later, the position players arrive. Spring training allows new players to try out for **roster** and position spots and gives existing team players practice time prior to competitive play. Spring training typically lasts about six weeks, starting in mid-February and running until just before Opening Day of the regular season. At one time, teams broke camp early and played a series of games in **minor-league** cities on their way north. In the early days of baseball, spring training was held in various states, but it is now held only in Florida, which has 15 teams in what is informally known as the Grapefruit League, and in Arizona, which also has 15 teams in what is informally known as the Cactus League.

SQUEEZE PLAY. Squeeze play is a term to designate a play when a team, with a **runner** on **third base**, attempts to score that runner by means of a **bunt**.

ST. LOUIS BROWN STOCKINGS (AA). *See* ST. LOUIS BROWNS (AA).

ST. LOUIS BROWN STOCKINGS (NA). The St. Louis Brown Stockings were a team in the National Association (NA) in 1875, the NA's final season. They won 39 games and lost 29.

ST. LOUIS BROWN STOCKINGS (NL). The St. Louis Brown Stockings played in the National Association (NA) in 1875. In 1876, after the NA disbanded, the Brown Stockings joined the new **National League**. They played their home games at Grand Avenue Grounds, later renamed **Sportsman's Park**. The Brown Stockings played just two seasons in the NL. Notable players for this short-lived franchise included George Bradley, **Dickey Pearce**, and **Lip Pike**.

ST. LOUIS BROWNS (AA). The St. Louis Browns, who played as the St. Louis Brown Stockings in 1882, were members of the **American Association (AA)** for all 10 years of the AA's existence (1882–1891). They were the league's most successful franchise, winning four consecutive pennants (1885–1888) and finishing second three times under **player-manager Charles Comiskey**. After each pennant-winning season, the Browns played the **National League (NL)** pennant winner in a championship series that was a predecessor to the modern **World Series**. In 1885, they won three games, lost three, and tied one against the Chicago White Stockings. In 1886, they defeated the White Stockings, four games to two. In 1887, they lost to the **Detroit Wolverines**, 10 games to five, and, in 1888, they lost to the **New York Giants**, six games to four. In 1892, after the AA had disbanded, the Browns joined the NL, eventually becoming the present-day **St. Louis Cardinals**. Notable players for the AA Browns included Bob Caruthers, Elton Chamberlain, Dave Foutz, Silver King, Arlie Latham, **Tommy McCarthy**, Jumbo McGinnis, Tony Mullane, Tip O'Neill, and Jack Stivetts.

ST. LOUIS BROWNS (AL). The St. Louis Browns were members of the **American League (AL)** from 1902 to 1953. The franchise originated as the **Milwaukee Brewers** in 1901, the first year the AL was recognized as a **major league**. The Brewers moved to St. Louis in 1902, where they were renamed the St. Louis Browns. The Browns remained in St. Louis until 1954, when they were moved to Baltimore and became the **Baltimore Orioles**. The Browns played their home games at **Sportsman's Park** (III) from 1902 to 1908, and at a rebuilt Sportsman's Park (IV) from 1909 to 1953.

The Browns finished second in 1902, their first year in St. Louis, but they were most often a second-division team. They had another second-place finish in 1922, and the team won their only pennant in 1944. They lost in six games to the **St. Louis Cardinals** in the **World Series**, in which all six games were played at Sportsman's Park (IV). The Cardinals had been successful for several decades, while the Browns had been mostly dreadful, and their attendance matched their performance. Despite the inventiveness and innovation of **Bill Veeck**, who owned the club from July 1951 through the 1953 season, attendance failed to improve and the club was sold to new owners in Baltimore.

The only St. Louis Browns player to win the **Most Valuable Player Award** was **George Sisler**, in 1922. The **Cy Young Award** came into existence in 1956, after the Browns had left for Baltimore. Roy Sievers, in 1949, was the team's only winner of the **Rookie of the Year Award**.

St. Louis Browns players who led the AL in **batting average** were George Stone (1906) and George Sisler (1920, 1922). Leaders in **home runs** were Ken Williams (1922) and Vern Stephens (1945). Leaders in **runs batted in** were Del Pratt (1916), Ken Williams (1922), and Vern Stephens (1944).

Urban Shocker, in 1921, was the only Browns **pitcher** to lead the league in **wins**. No Browns pitcher led the league in **earned run average**. Urban Shocker, in 1922, was the only Browns pitcher to lead the league in **strikeouts**.

Other notable players and **managers** for the St. Louis Browns included Elden Auker, Jimmy Austin, Beau Bell, George Blaeholder, Mark Christman, Harlond Clift, Dixie Davis, Bob Dillinger, **Rick Ferrell**, Lee Fohl, Ned Garver, **Goose Goslin**, Sam Gray, **Rogers Hornsby**, Harry Howell, Baby Doll Jacobson, Walt Judnich, Jack Kramer, Chet Laabs, **Heinie Manush**, Jimmy McAleer, George McQuinn, Bob Muncrief, **Satchel Paige**, Barney Pelty, Nelson Potter, Jack Powell, Harry Rice, **Branch Rickey**, Luke Sewell, Burt Shotton, Lefty Stewart, Jack Tobin, Elam Vangilder, **Bobby Wallace**, Carl Weilman, and Sam West.

ST. LOUIS BROWNS (NL). *See* ST. LOUIS CARDINALS.

ST. LOUIS CARDINALS. The St. Louis Cardinals are a team in the Central Division of the **National League (NL)**. They have been a member of the NL since 1892, after having played as the **St. Louis Browns** during the 10 years of the **American Association's (AA)** existence, from 1882 to 1891. In 1892, after the AA disbanded, the Browns joined the NL. They kept the name Browns through 1898, played as the St. Louis Perfectos in 1899, and have been the Cardinals since 1900. The team played its home games at **Sportsman's Park (II)** in 1892, at Robison Field from 27 April 1893 to 6 June 1920, and at Sportsman's Park (IV) from 1 July 1920 to 8 May 1966. In 1954, Sportsman's Park (IV) was renamed Busch Stadium in honor of the team's new owner, August Busch. **Busch Stadium (II)** was the Cardinals' home from 12 May 1966 to 19 October 2005. Their current home, **Busch Stadium (III)**, opened on 10 April 2006.

St. Louis had won four pennants in the AA, but it took until 1914 for them to reach as high as third place in the NL. They won their first NL pennant in 1926 and went on to be one of the league's most successful clubs. The Cardinals have played in 18 **World Series**, winning 11 of them, the most of any NL team. Their Series wins came against the **New York Yankees** (1926, 1942, 1964), **Philadelphia Athletics** (1931), **Detroit Tigers** (1934, 2006), **St. Louis Browns** (1944), **Boston Red Sox** (1946, 1967), **Milwaukee Brewers** (1982), and **Texas Rangers** (2011). The Cardinals' seven Series losses were to the Yankees (1928, 1943), Athletics (1930), Tigers (1968), **Kansas City Royals** (1985), **Minnesota Twins** (1987), and Red Sox (2004). St. Louis was eliminated in the **National League Division Series** twice and the **National League Championship Series** four times. In 2012, the Cardinals defeated the **Atlanta Braves** in the National League's first **wild card** "play-in" game. The team then defeated the **Washington Nationals** in the **National League Division Series**, but lost to the **San Francisco Giants** in the **National League Championship Series**.

St. Louis Cardinals who have won the NL's **Most Valuable Player Award** are **Rogers Hornsby** (1925), Bob O'Farrell (1926), **Jim Bottomley** (1928), **Frankie Frisch** (1931), **Dizzy Dean** (1934), **Joe Medwick** (1937), Mort Cooper (1942), **Stan Musial** (1943, 1946, 1948), Marty Marion (1944), Ken Boyer (1964), **Orlando Cepeda** (1967), **Bob Gibson** (1968), **Joe Torre** (1971), Keith Hernandez (1979), Willie McGee (1985), and **Albert Pujols** (2005, 2008–2009). **Cy Young Award** winners are Bob Gibson (1968, 1970) and Chris Carpenter (2005). **Rookie of the Year Award** winners are Wally Moon (1954), Bill Virdon (1955), Bake McBride (1974), Vince Coleman (1985), and Albert Pujols (2001).

Cardinals players who have led the league in **batting average** are **Jesse Burkett** (1901), Rogers Hornsby (1920–1925), **Chick Hafey** (1931), Joe Medwick (1937), **Johnny Mize** (1939), Stan Musial (1943, 1946, 1948, 1950–1952, and 1957), Joe Torre (1971), Keith Hernandez (1979), Willie McGee (1985, 1990), and Albert Pujols (2003). Leaders in **home runs** are Rogers Hornsby (1922, 1925), Jim Bottomley (1928), Ripper Collins (1934), Joe Medwick (1937), Johnny Mize (1939–1940), **Mark McGwire** (1998–1999), and Albert Pujols (2009–2010). Leaders in **runs batted in (RBI)** are Rogers Hornsby (1920–1922, 1925), Jim Bottomley (1926, 1928), Joe Medwick (1936–1938), Johnny Mize (1940), **Enos Slaughter** (1946), Stan Musial (1948, 1956), Ken Boyer (1964), Orlando Cepeda (1967), Joe Torre (1971), Mark McGwire (1999), and Albert Pujols (2010). In 1922 and 1925, Rogers Hornsby led the NL in batting average, home runs, and RBI to win the **Triple Crown** for **batters** both years. By leading the NL in batting average, home runs, and RBI, Joe Medwick won the Triple Crown for batters in 1937.

Cardinals **pitchers** who have led the league in **wins** are Flint Rhem (1926), Bill Hallahan (1931), Dizzy Dean (1934–1935), Mort Cooper (1942–1943), Red Barrett (1945, part of season with **Boston Braves**), Howie Pollet (1946), Ernie Broglio (1960), Bob Gibson (1970), Joaquin Andujar (1984), Matt Morris (2001), and Adam Wainwright (2009). **Earned run average** leaders are Ted Breitenstein (1893), Bill Doak (1914, 1921), Mort Cooper (1942), Max Lanier (1943), Howie Pollet (1946), Harry Brecheen (1948), Bob Gibson (1968), John Denny (1976), Joe Magrane (1988), and Chris Carpenter (2009). **Strikeouts** leaders are Fred Beebe (1906, part of season with **Chicago Cubs**), Bill Hallahan (1930–1931), Dizzy Dean (1932–1935), Harry Brecheen (1948), Sam Jones (1958), Bob Gibson (1968), and Jose DeLeon (1989).

Other notable players and **managers** in Cardinals' history include **Grover Alexander**, Ray Blades, Al Brazle, **Lou Brock**, **Steve Carlton**, Walker Cooper, Joe Cunningham, **Leo Durocher**, Eddie Dyer, Jim Edmonds, **Curt Flood**, Bob Forsch, David Freese, **Jesse Haines**, Tom Herr, **Whitey Herzog**, Matt Holliday, **Miller Huggins**, Jason Isringhausen, Larry Jackson, Julian Javier, Whitey Kurowski, Ray Lankford, **Tony LaRussa**, Pepper Martin, Tim McCarver, Lindy McDaniel, Yadier Molina, Terry Moore, Ken Oberkfell, **Branch Rickey**, Scott Rolen, Slim Sallee, **Red Schoendienst**, Mike Shannon, Bill Sherdel, Ted Simmons, Lee Smith, **Ozzie Smith**, **Billy Southworth**, Gabby Street, **Bruce Sutter**, Garry Templeton, Lon Warneke, Bill White, and Todd Worrell.

ST. LOUIS MAROONS (NL). When the **Union Association (UA)** folded after one season (1884), the St. Louis Maroons, who had run away with the UA pennant, joined the **National League (NL)**. The Maroons played in the NL in 1885 and 1886, finishing eighth and sixth, respectively. In 1887, the team was sold and replaced in the league by the **Indianapolis Hoosiers**. Notable players for the Maroons included Jack Glasscock and Alex McKinnon.

ST. LOUIS MAROONS (UA). The St. Louis Maroons were a team in the **Union Association (UA)** in 1884, the one year of the UA's existence. St. Louis dominated the league with a pennant-winning record of 94–10. Fred Dunlap of the Maroons led the league with a .412 **batting average** and 13 **home runs**.

ST. LOUIS PERFECTOS. *See* ST. LOUIS CARDINALS.

ST. LOUIS RED STOCKINGS. The St. Louis Red Stockings were members of the National Association (NA) in 1875, the NA's final season. They played 19 games and won only four.

ST. LOUIS STARS. The St. Louis Stars were a team in the **Negro National League (NNL)** from 1922 through 1931. The Stars were the NNL champions in 1928. Among the notable players from the **Negro Leagues** who played part of their careers with the Stars were **James Bell**, **Mule Suttles**, and **Willie Wells**.

ST. LOUIS TERRIERS. The St. Louis Terriers were a team in the **Federal League (FL)** in 1914 and 1915, the two seasons the FL existed as a **major league**. After finishing in last place in 1914, the Terriers finished second in 1915, .001 percentage points behind the **Chicago Whales**. **Pitcher** Dave

Davenport led the FL in **strikeouts** in 1915, with 229. Other notable players for the Terriers included Al Bridwell, **Mordecai Brown**—who also served as **manager** in 1914—Doc Crandall, Bob Groom, Fielder Jones, Ward Miller, **Eddie Plank**, and Jack Tobin.

ST. PAUL (MINNESOTA) SAINTS. The St. Paul Saints were a team in the **Union Association (UA)** in 1884, the one year of the UA's existence. After they finished their season in the **minor league** Northwestern League, the Saints joined the UA and lost six of eight games, all on the road. St. Paul's franchise was the shortest lived in **major-league** history.

STADIUMS. Baseball was originally played in open fields or public parks. The genesis of modern baseball is most often connected with **Elysian Fields** in Hoboken, New Jersey, where games started being played around the mid-1840s. The name "Field" or "Park" was typically attached to the names of the early ballparks. With the beginnings of professional baseball, the ball field became part of a complex, including fixed spectator seating areas and an enclosure to restrict access to paying customers. The **Union Grounds**, located in Brooklyn, New York, opened in 1862. It was the first baseball park enclosed entirely by a fence, thereby allowing the owner to charge admission, and permitting only paying customers to watch the games. As baseball spread and professional leagues were formed, ballparks were built either near the city center or in working-class neighborhoods.

The first **major-league** ballparks, built in the late 19th and early 20th centuries, were wooden structures, usually with one tier of seating. These included Bennett Park in Detroit, Columbia Park in Philadelphia, Exposition Park in Pittsburgh, the Huntington Avenue Baseball Grounds in Boston, the **Polo Grounds** in New York, and West Side Park in Chicago.

The building of what have now come to be known as "classic ballparks" began in 1909, with the opening of **Shibe Park** in Philadelphia and **Forbes Field** in Pittsburgh. These new parks were built of concrete and steel. Most had two-tiered grandstands, and most were built to fit the constraints of actual city blocks, resulting in asymmetrical outfield dimensions. Ballparks that opened between 1909 and 1923 included **Braves Field** and **Fenway Park** in Boston, **Comiskey Park** and **Wrigley Field** in Chicago, **Ebbets Field** in Brooklyn, **Griffith Stadium** in Washington, D.C., and League Park in Cleveland. In 1923, **Yankee Stadium** in New York opened, the biggest park yet built and the first to feature three tiers of seating.

From the 1960s through the 1980s, teams built mostly multipurpose stadiums. These facilities were usually circular structures made entirely of bare, reinforced concrete, and they were built to hold baseball, as well as football, soccer, and other sports. Among the multipurpose stadiums built in those years were Atlanta–**Fulton County Stadium**, **Busch Stadium** in St. Louis, **Riverfront Stadium** in Cincinnati, **Three Rivers Stadium** in Pittsburgh, and Qualcomm Stadium in San Diego.

In 1965, the **Houston Astros** opened the **Astrodome**, baseball's first completely covered indoor park. Others followed, including the Kingdome in Seattle, Olympic Stadium in Montreal, and **Tropicana Field** in St. Petersburg. **Rogers Centre** in Toronto was the first park with a retractable roof, one that could be closed in inclement weather. Other parks with retractable roofs are **Chase Field** in Phoenix, **Marlins Park** in Miami, **Miller Park** in Milwaukee, **Minute Maid Park** in Houston, and **Safeco Field** in Seattle.

When **Oriole Park at Camden Yards** opened in Baltimore, in 1992, it began a period of clubs building new parks, collectively known as "retro-classic ballparks." These parks evoked the era of the classic parks, with the use of green seats, bricks, stone, and green-painted exposed steel, but they included all the luxuries of the newer parks, including luxury boxes. **AT&T Park** in San Francisco, **Citi Field** in New York, **Comerica Park** in Detroit, **Coors Field** in Denver, and **PNC Park** in Pittsburgh are a few examples of the new retro-classic parks.

The early wooden structure parks had limited seating capacities—as low as 5,000 for the South End Grounds in Boston—and they were financed by the teams' owners. Philadelphia's Columbia Park cost $40,000 to construct and held 9,500 spectators, and New York's Hilltop Park cost $75,000 to erect and held 16,000 fans.

Seating capacities increased to the 30,000 to 45,000 range for most of the classic ballparks, while private financing continued to be the source of revenue for building these parks. The cost of these bigger steel and concrete structures grew accordingly. For example, Redland Field in Cincinnati cost $225,000; Shibe Park, $450,000; Braves Field, $500,000; Ebbets Field, $750,000; and Forbes Field a whopping $1,000,000.

Beginning with the era of the multipurpose stadiums, seating capacities increased, but in the era of the retro-classic ballparks, they dropped back. Los Angeles Memorial Coliseum, where the **Los Angeles Dodgers** played from 1958 through 1961, was by far the biggest, setting major-league attendance records in a park that seated more than 90,000. Recently built parks like **Target Field**, home of the **Minnesota Twins**; **Progressive Field**, home of the **Cleveland Indians**; and **Great American Ball Park**, home of the **Cincinnati Reds** all have seating capacities in the low 40,000s. **Marlins Park**, home of the **Miami Marlins**, and PNC Park, home of the **Pittsburgh Pirates**, seat less than 40,000.

The price of building the new baseball-only stadiums has risen dramatically in recent years. The new Yankee Stadium, which opened in 2009, was built at a cost of $1.6 billion. It has become almost impossible for these new parks to be financed entirely, or even in part, without the help of local

Figure 19.2.   Fans exiting Brooklyn's Ebbets Field. Opened in 1913, it is now regarded as one of baseball's "classic ballparks." *National Baseball Hall of Fame Library, Cooperstown, N.Y.*

governments through taxes on their constituents. Club owners put pressure on these local governments by threatening to relocate their teams, thus robbing their present cities of the revenue generated and prestige attached to having a major-league team. Two recent examples are in Minneapolis, where Target Field opened in 2010, at a cost of $522 million, and in Miami, where Marlins Park opened in 2011, at a cost of $515 million.

STARGELL, WILVER DORNEL "WILLIE," "POPS". B. 6 March 1940, Earlsboro, Oklahoma. D. 9 April 2001, Wilmington, North Carolina. Willie Stargell was a left-handed slugger and team leader for the **Pittsburgh Pirates** from 1962 to 1982. Stargell, who also threw left-handed, played left field through 1974, before switching to **first base** in 1975. The 6-foot, 2-inch, 188-pound Stargell had 15 seasons with 20 or more **home runs** and five seasons with 100 or more **runs batted in (RBI)**. He twice led the **National League (NL)** in home runs, with 48 in 1971, and 44 in 1973. Stargell also led the NL in RBI, **doubles**, and **on-base percentage** in 1973, and he finished second in the voting for the **Most Valuable Player (MVP) Award**. He had also finished second in 1971, but he was the co-winner (with Keith Hernandez of the **St. Louis Cardinals**) in 1979, when he led the Pirates to the pennant. In addition, he was voted the **Major League Player of the Year**. In the **World Series** against the **Baltimore Orioles**, Stargell batted .400, with three home runs, and he was voted Series MVP and winner of the **Babe Ruth Award**. He had also been voted the MVP of the **National League Championship Series**.

A seven-time **All-Star**, Stargell was the winner of **Roberto Clemente Award** and **Lou Gehrig Memorial Award** in 1974, and the **Hutch Award** in 1978. He had a career **batting average** of .282, with 475 home runs and 1,540 RBI. A free swinger, he struck out 1,936 times. The **Baseball Writers' Association of America** elected Stargell to the **National Baseball Hall of Fame** in 1988.

START, JOSEPH "JOE," "OLD RELIABLE". B. 14 October 1842, New York, New York. D. 27 March 1927, Providence, Rhode Island. Joe Start was already 28 years old in 1871, when he joined the **New York Mutuals** of the newly formed National Association (NA), baseball's first **major league**. Start, a **first baseman** who had previously played for Enterprise of Brooklyn (1860–1861) and the **Brooklyn Atlantics** (1862–1870), was with the Mutuals through 1876, the season they entered the **National League (NL)** as a charter member. He also played in the NL with the Brooklyn Hartfords (1877), Chicago White Stockings (1878), **Providence Grays** (1879–1885), and **Washington Nationals** (1886). For the last nine seasons of his career (1878–1886), he was the oldest player in the NL. The 5-foot, 9-inch, 165-pound Start batted .299, with 1,417 **hits**, and he finished in the top four in **batting average** in his league three times. He led NA first basemen in **assists** twice and NL first basemen in **putouts** four times.

STEARNES, NORMAN THOMAS "TURKEY". B. 8 May 1901, Nashville, Tennessee. D. 4 September 1979, Detroit, Michigan. Turkey Stearnes was a speedy, left-handed-hitting center fielder who played in the **Negro Leagues** from 1921 to 1940. Stearnes played for many teams, but his best years were with the Detroit Stars of the **Negro National League**. The 6-foot, 180-pound Stearnes's combination of speed, a high **batting average**, and **home run** power has led some experts to call him the greatest player ever in the Negro Leagues. In 2000, a special **Negro Leagues Committee** elected Stearnes to the **National Baseball Hall of Fame**.

See also AFRICAN AMERICANS IN BASEBALL.

STEINBRENNER, GEORGE MICHAEL III, "THE BOSS". B. 4 July 1930, Rocky River, Ohio. D. 13 July 2010, Tampa, Florida. George Steinbrenner was the major owner of the **New York Yankees** from 1973 until his death in 2010, the longest ownership tenure in team history. Steinbrenner was a blustery, hands-on owner who capriciously hired and fired **managers** and often castigated his players for seemingly minor mistakes. He was, however, generous and often quietly helped out those in need, especially former employees. Steinbrenner took over a team that was in decline and rebuilt it by spending money to facilitate trades and sign **free agents**. Many of the players he brought to New York were failures, but others, like **Catfish Hunter**, **Reggie Jackson**, **Dave Winfield**, **Roger Clemens**, and **Alex Rodriguez**, helped the Yankees win 11 pennants and seven **World Series** during his ownership of the team. Steinbrenner's crowning achievement was building a magnificent new **Yankee Stadium**, which opened in 2009.

STENGEL, CHARLES DILLON "CASEY," "THE OLD PERFESSOR". B. 30 July 1890, Kansas City, Missouri. D. 29 September 1975, Glendale, California. Before he became a successful **manager** for the **New York Yankees**, Casey Stengel had been an unsuccessful manager for the **Brooklyn Dodgers** and **Boston Braves**. And before that, he had been a **National League (NL) outfielder** for 14 seasons (1912–1925) with Brooklyn, the **Pittsburgh Pirates**, the **Philadelphia Phillies**, the **New York Giants**, and the Braves. Stengel, a 5-foot, 11-inch, 175-pound left-handed hitter and thrower, had a .284 career **batting average**. He did particularly well in the three **World Series** in which he appeared. With Brooklyn, he batted .364 against the **Boston Red Sox** in 1916, and, with the Giants, he batted .400 and .417, respectively, against the Yankees in 1922 and 1923. In 12 World Series games, he batted .393, with a .469 **on-base percentage**, a .607 **slugging percentage**, and two **home runs**. Both home runs were in the 1923 Series and were game winners for the Giants.

Stengel managed the Dodgers from 1934 to 1936, and the Braves from 1938 to 1943 (they were the Boston Bees in 1938–1940). In those nine years, his teams had a combined record of 581–742, and they only twice finished as high as fifth place. Given his poor managerial record and reputation as a clown, Stengel's selection to lead the stately Yankees in 1949 surprised the baseball world, but the Yankees won the pennant and the World Series that year and repeated in each of the next four years, giving the team and Stengel an unprecedented five consecutive world championships. The streak ended in 1954, but, from 1955 to 1960, the Yankees won five more pennants and two more World Series. Stengel was fired following the Yankees' 1960 World Series loss to Pittsburgh, despite having won 10 pennants and seven world championships in 12 years and being given the **Manager of the Year Award** by the *Sporting News* in 1949, 1953, and 1958. When the **New York**

Mets joined the NL as an **expansion** team in 1962, Stengel was their first manager, a position in which he remained until mid-1965. Under the new 10-team setup, the Mets finished 10th each season; however, for his unprecedented and unequaled managerial success with the Yankees, Stengel was elected to the **National Baseball Hall of Fame** by the **Veterans Committee** in 1966.

STOLEN BASES (SB). A **base runner** is credited with a stolen base (SB) when he takes possession of the next **base** safely while the **pitcher** is throwing to the **batter**. A SB is not credited if the team in the field is charged with **defensive indifference**. Before 1898, SBs were credited to anyone who took an extra base on a **hit** or an **error**. Because of the lack of uniformity as to what constituted a stolen base prior to 1898, we can only make meaningful comparisons in this category beginning with that year.

The pre-1898 **major league** single-season leader in stolen bases is Hugh Nicol of the 1887 **Cincinnati Red Stockings** of the **American Association**, with 138. The post-1898 single-season leader is **Rickey Henderson** of the 1982 **Oakland Athletics**, with 130. The post-1898 single-season leader in the **National League** is **Lou Brock** of the 1974 **St. Louis Cardinals**, with 118. The career leader is Rickey Henderson, with 1,406. Henderson played for the Oakland Athletics (1979–1984, 1989–1995, 1998), **New York Yankees** (1985–1989), **Toronto Blue Jays** (1993), **San Diego Padres** (1996–1997, 2001), Anaheim Angels (1997), **New York Mets** (1999–2000), **Seattle Mariners** (2000), **Boston Red Sox** (2002), and **Los Angeles Dodgers** (2003).

STOVEY, HARRY DUFFIELD. B. Harry Duffield Stowe, 20 December 1856, Philadelphia, Pennsylvania. D. 20 September 1937, New Bedford, Massachusetts. Harry Stovey was a speedy slugging **outfielder–first baseman** who began his career in the **National League (NL)** in 1880, and ended it there 14 years later. The 5-foot, 11-inch, 175-pound Stovey played in the NL for the **Worcester Ruby Legs** (1880–1882), Boston Beaneaters (1891–1892), **Baltimore Orioles** (1892–1893), and Brooklyn Bridegrooms (1893). Between his two tours of duty in the NL, he played in both the American Association with the **Philadelphia Athletics** from 1883 to 1889, and in the **Players' League** with the **Boston Reds** in 1890. Stovey was a **player-manager** for Worcester briefly in 1881, and for a full season for Philadelphia in 1885. The right-handed-hitting Stovey led his league in **home runs** and **extra-base hits** five times, **triples** and **runs** scored four times, and **slugging percentage** and **total bases** three times. When Stovey retired in 1893, he was the all-time leader in home runs, with 122, and he remained third on the list as late as 1920.

STRIKE (K). The **home plate umpire** will call a strike (K) on the **batter** when a pitch is struck at by the batter and missed; if any part of the ball passes through any part of the **strike zone**, even if it is not struck at; if it is fouled by the batter when he has less than two Ks; if it is **bunted** foul; if it touches the batter as he strikes at it; if it touches the batter in flight in the strike zone; or if it becomes a foul tip. Prior to 1901, **foul balls** were not counted as Ks. That year, the **National League** ruled that foul balls with less than two Ks on the batter would count as Ks. The **American League** adopted the same rule in 1903.

STRIKE ZONE. The strike zone defines the area of **home plate** through which a pitch must pass for it to count as a **strike** when the **batter** does not swing. The strike zone has undergone various revisions throughout the years. The most recent, in 1987, defines it as a "horizontal line at the midpoint between the top of the shoulder and the top of the uniform pants," and, at the lower level, a "line at the top of the knees."

STRIKEOUTS (SO). A strikeout (SO) occurs when a **batter** receives three **strikes** during an **at-bat**. For batters, the **major league** single-season leader in SOs is Mark Reynolds of the 2009 **Arizona Diamondbacks**, with 223. The single-season leader in the **American League** is Adam Dunn of the 2012 **Chicago White Sox**, with 222. The career leader is **Reggie Jackson**, with 2,597. Jackson played for the **Kansas City Athletics** (1967), Oakland Athletics (1968–1975, 1987), **Baltimore Orioles** (1976), **New York Yankees** (1977–1981), and California Angels (1982–1986).

For **pitchers**, the major league single-season leader in SOs prior to 1893, when the pitching distance was extended to its current 60 feet, 6 inches, is Matt Kilroy of the 1886 Baltimore Orioles of the **American Association**, with 513. The single-season leader after the change in the pitching distance is **Nolan Ryan** of the 1973 California Angels, with 383. The single-season leader in the **National League** is **Sandy Koufax** of the 1965 **Los Angeles Dodgers**, with 382. The career leader is Nolan Ryan with 5,714. Ryan pitched for the **New York Mets** (1966, 1968–1971), California Angels (1972–1979), **Houston Astros** (1980–1988), and **Texas Rangers** (1989–1993).

SUN LIFE STADIUM. Sun Life Stadium, located in suburban Miami, Florida, was the home of the Florida Marlins of the **National League** from their first season, 1993, through 2011. Originally called Joe Robbie Stadium, and built primarily for football, Sun Life Stadium has also been called Pro Player Stadium, Dolphin Stadium, and Land Shark Stadium.

SUSPENDED GAME. A suspended game occurs when a game has to be stopped before it can be completed. When a game is suspended, the remainder of the game is to be completed at a later date. A game may be suspended for any of the following reasons: a curfew imposed by law; a predetermined time limit; artificial light failure or other mechanical problems that impact the game; darkness, in certain circumstances; weather, in certain circumstances; or a regulation game called with the score tied.

See also OFFICIAL GAME.

SUTTER, HOWARD BRUCE. B. 8 January 1953, Lancaster, Pennsylvania. Bruce Sutter was the best relief **pitcher** in the **National League (NL)** from the mid-1970s through the mid-1980s. The 6-foot, 2-inch, 190-pound right-hander began his career with the **Chicago Cubs** in 1976. In five seasons with the Cubs, Sutter saved 133 games, while leading the league in **saves** in 1979 and 1980. The Cubs traded him to the **St. Louis Cardinals** after the 1980 season, whereupon he led the league in saves three times in his four years in St. Louis (1981, 1982, 1984). Sutter signed as a **free agent** with the **Atlanta Braves** in 1985, with whom he spent his final three seasons. An elbow injury in 1985 caused him to miss the 1987 season and helped shorten his career. Sutter, whose best pitch was a splitter, was a six-time member of the NL **All-Star** team. He was the game's **winning pitcher** in 1978 and 1979, and he earned saves in 1980 and 1981. He won the **Cy Young Award** in 1979 and the **Babe Ruth Award** in 1982, and he was the NL's Rolaids Relief Pitcher of the Year four times. Overall, Sutter had a 68–71 won-lost record, with 300 saves. He was elected by the **Baseball Writers' Association of America** to the **National Baseball Hall of Fame (HOF)** in 2006. Sutter was the first pitcher elected to the HOF who never started a game in his **major-league** career.

SUTTLES, GEORGE "MULE". B. 31 March 1900, Brockton, Louisiana. D. 9 July 1966, Newark, New Jersey. Mule Suttles spent 23 seasons playing for various teams in the **Negro Leagues**, most notably in the **Negro National League** with the Birmingham Black Barons, **St. Louis Stars**, **Chicago American Giants**, and **Newark Eagles**. Suttles, a **first baseman**, was a right-handed **batter** who stood 6 feet, 3 inches and weighed 215 pounds. He is reputed to have hit the most **home runs** in the Negro Leagues. In 2006, Suttles was elected to the **National Baseball Hall of Fame** in a special election conducted by the **Committee on African American Baseball**.

See also AFRICAN AMERICANS IN BASEBALL.

SUTTON, DONALD HOWARD "DON". B. 2 April 1945, Clio, Alabama. Don Sutton was a **major-league pitcher** for 23 seasons. A 6-foot, 1-inch, 185-pound right-hander, Sutton won 257 games in the **National League (NL)** and 67 in the **American League (AL)**. He pitched for the **Los Angeles Dodgers** (1966–1980, 1988) and **Houston Astros** (1981–1982) in the NL, and the **Milwaukee Brewers** (1982–1984), **Oakland Athletics** (1985), and California Angels (1985–1987) in the AL. His best seasons were with the Dodgers, for whom he won 233 games.

Consistency was Sutton's hallmark. He was a 20-game winner only once, but he had double-digit **win** totals in 21 of his 23 seasons. He never led the league in **strikeouts**, but he struck out more than 100 **batters** in each of his first 21 seasons. His record in the **National League Championship Series** was 3–1, in the **American League Championship Series**, 1–0, and in three **World Series**, 2–3. Sutton is one of 24 major-league pitchers to have won 300 or more games. His lifetime record was 324–256. He had a 3.26 **earned run average**, 58 **shutouts**, and 3,574 strikeouts. Sutton, who later became a baseball broadcaster, was elected by the **Baseball Writers' Association of America** to the **National Baseball Hall of Fame** in 1998.

SUZUKI, ICHIRO. B. 22 October 1973, Kasugai, **Japan**. Ichiro Suzuki had already played nine years for the Orix Blue Wave in Japan's Pacific League when he joined the **Seattle Mariners** in 2001. Suzuki was the first Japanese-born everyday position player in the **major leagues**. The 27-year-old left-handed-hitting Suzuki had a sensational **rookie** season. He led the **American League** in batting, with a .350 average; in **hits**, with a rookie record 242; and in **stolen bases**, with 56. He won both the **Rookie of the Year Award** and the **Most Valuable Player Award**. The 5-foot, 11-inch, 170-pound Suzuki went on to have nine more similar seasons. Between 2001 and 2010, he had more than 200 hits in each season, leading the league seven times. His 262 hits in 2004 broke **George Sisler's** single-season record of 257 that had stood since 1920. Suzuki also batted above .300 in each of those 10 seasons, including a career high .372 in 2004, when he won his second batting championship. In addition, he led the league in **singles** in each of his first 10 seasons, and he has four of the 10 highest one-season single totals, including a record 225 in 2004.

In his amazing first 10 seasons, Suzuki set major-league records for most seasons with 200 or more hits, most consecutive seasons with 200 or more hits, most consecutive seasons with 200 or more hits from the start of a career, most seasons leading the league in singles, most consecutive seasons leading the league in singles from the start of a career, and most consecutive seasons with 150 or more singles. Suzuki was an **All-Star** in each of his first 10 seasons, during which time he won three **Silver Slugger Awards**. Primarily a right fielder, Suzuki is a superior defensive player, with one of the best throwing arms in the game. He won **Gold Glove Awards** in each of his first 10 seasons. Suzuki had his first subpar season in 2011, and was traded to the New York Yankees in July 2012. Through 12 seasons, he has a career **batting average** of .322 and has accumulated 2,606 hits. He is certain to be elected to the **National Baseball Hall of Fame** when he becomes eligible.

SWITCH–HITTER (SH). A switch-hitter (SH) is a **batter** who regularly bats both left-handed and right-handed. Most batters hit better against opposite-handed **pitcher**s than against same-handed pitchers. Right-handed batters tend to hit better against left-handed pitchers than against right-handed pitchers, and left-handed batters do better against right-handed pitchers than left-handed pitchers. Baseball's best switch-hitters include **Roberto Alomar**, Lance Berkman, **Max Carey**, **George Davis**, **Frankie Frisch**, **Chipper Jones**, **Mickey Mantle**, **Eddie Murray**, Tim Raines, **Pete Rose**, **Red Schoendienst**, Ted Simmons, and **Omar Vizquel**.

SYRACUSE STARS (AA). The Syracuse Stars were a team in the **American Association** in 1890. They finished in seventh place, with a 55–72 record, and disbanded after the season. Syracuse's most notable player was Cupid Childs.

SYRACUSE STARS (NL). After two years as a **minor-league** team, the Syracuse Stars joined the **National League** in 1879. They finished in seventh place, with a 22–48 record. The club disbanded with two weeks left in the season. Syracuse's best players were Mike Dorgan, Jack Farrell, and Harry McCormick.

T

TAG. A tag is the action of a **fielder** in touching a **base** with any part of his body while holding the ball securely and firmly in his hand or glove, or touching a **runner** with the ball, or with his hand or glove holding the ball, while holding the ball securely and firmly in his hand or glove.

TAMPA BAY DEVIL RAYS. *See* TAMPA BAY RAYS.

TAMPA BAY RAYS. The Tampa Bay Rays are a team in the Eastern Division of the **American League (AL)**. The Rays entered the AL in 1998 as part of a two-team **major-league expansion**, with the **Arizona Diamondbacks** joining the **National League**. Originally called the Tampa Bay Devil Rays, the name was changed to Tampa Bay Rays in November 2007. The team has always played its home games at **Tropicana Field**, an indoor stadium located in St. Petersburg, Florida.

Tampa Bay finished fifth in the five-team Eastern Division in nine of its first 10 seasons. In the other, 2004, they finished fourth. Then, in 2008, after the name change, the Rays won the division title and advanced to the **World Series**, losing in five games to the **Philadelphia Phillies**. In 2010 and 2011, the Rays won the division title, but the team lost in both years to the **Texas Rangers** in the **American League Division Series**.

No Tampa Bay player has won the **Most Valuable Player Award**. David Price (2012) is the only **Cy Young Award** winner. They have had two **Rookie of the Year Award** winners: Evan Longoria in 2008 and Jeremy Hellickson in 2011.

The Rays have had no leaders in **batting average** or **runs batted in** and only one **home run** leader, Carlos Pena, in 2009.

David Price (2012) is the only Rays **pitcher** to lead the AL in **wins**. David Price (2012) is the only Rays pitcher to lead the league in **earned run average**. Scott Kazmir (2007) is the only Rays pitcher to lead the league in **strikeouts**.

Other notable players and **managers** in Rays' history include Rocco Baldelli, Jason Bartlett, Carl Crawford, Matt Garza, Jeremy Hellickson, Aubrey Huff, Julio Lugo, Joe Maddon, Fred McGriff, Matt Moore, Jeff Niemann, Lou Piniella, James Shields, B. J. Upton, Randy Winn, and Ben Zobrist.

TARGET FIELD. Target Field, located in Minneapolis, Minnesota, has been the home field of the **Minnesota Twins** of the **American League** since 2010. Prior to that, the Twins played at Metropolitan Stadium, in Bloomington, Minnesota, from 1961 to 1981, and at the Hubert H. Humphrey Metrodome, in Minneapolis, Minnesota, from 1982 to 2009. The seating capacity of Target Field is approximately 39,500. Target Field has yet to host the **major league All-Star Game**.

See also STADIUMS.

TAYLOR, BENJAMIN HARRISON "BEN". B. 1 July 1888, Anderson, South Carolina. D. 24 January 1953, Baltimore, Maryland. Ben Taylor was a **first baseman** and **manager** in the **Negro Leagues** from 1908 to 1929. His best years were with the Indianapolis ABCs (1914–1918, 1920–1922). The 6-foot, 1-inch, 190-pound Taylor, who batted and threw left-handed, was a steady .300 hitter and an outstanding defensive player. In 2006, he was elected to the **National Baseball Hall of Fame** in a special election conducted by the **Committee on African American Baseball**.

See also AFRICAN AMERICANS IN BASEBALL.

TEMPLE CUP. From 1892 through 1900, there was only one **major league**, the **National League**. In 1894, William Chase Temple, a millionaire businessman and part owner of the **Pittsburgh Pirates**, sponsored a postseason championship series between the NL's first- and second-place finishers. The winner of the seven-game series, known as the Temple Cup Series or World's Championship Series, would receive the Temple Cup trophy.

Four Temple Cup series were played, all of which involved the **Baltimore Orioles**. In 1894, the second-place **New York Giants** defeated the first-place Orioles, four games to none; in 1895, the second-place **Cleveland Spiders** defeated the first-place Orioles, four games to one; in 1896, the first-place Orioles defeated second-place Cleveland, four games to none; and, in 1897, the second-place Orioles defeated the first-place Boston Beaneaters, four games to one.

TERRY, WILLIAM HAROLD "BILL". B. 30 October 1898, Atlanta, Georgia. D. 9 January 1989, Jacksonville, Florida. Bill Terry joined the **New York Giants** in September 1923. He became the Giants' full-time **first baseman** in 1925, and he remained so through the 1935 season. Beginning in

1927, Terry had a streak of 10 consecutive seasons in which he batted better than .300, and six consecutive seasons in which he topped 100 **runs batted in** and 100 **runs** scored. The 6-foot, 1-inch, 200-pound left-handed hitter had his greatest season in 1930. Terry batted .401—the last player in the **National League (NL)** to reach the .400 mark—and his 254 **hits** tied the single-season NL record set by Lefty O'Doul a year earlier. That record still stands. When **John McGraw** resigned as the Giants' **manager** in June 1932, he named Terry to succeed him. Terry led New York to pennants in 1933 and 1936 as a **player-manager**, and in 1937 strictly as a manager. The Giants defeated the **Washington Senators** in the 1933 **World Series**, but the team lost to the **New York Yankees** in 1936 and 1937. Terry batted .429 against Washington and .295 overall in World Series play. When the Giants failed to contend for the next four seasons (1938–1941), Terry was fired and replaced by another Giants' star, **Mel Ott**. Terry finished his career with a **batting average** that rounded to .3412, good for 15th place all-time. In 1954, the **Baseball Writers' Association of America** elected him to the **National Baseball Hall of Fame**.

TEXAS RANGERS. The Texas Rangers are a team in the Western Division of the **American League (AL)**. The franchise joined the AL in 1961 as the expansion **Washington Senators** and then relocated to Texas in 1972. The Rangers played their home games at Arlington Stadium from 1972 through 1993. They played their first game at their current home, **Rangers Ballpark in Arlington**, on 11 April 1994. Previous names for the park were The Ballpark in Arlington and Ameriquest Field in Arlington.

The Rangers failed to reach the postseason until 1996, the franchise's 25th season in the league, when they lost to the **New York Yankees** in the **American League Division Series (ALDS)**. They reached the ALDS again in 1998 and 1999 and were swept by the Yankees in both years. In 2010, the Rangers won their first AL pennant, but the team lost in the **World Series** to the **San Francisco Giants**. They won the pennant again in 2011, but they lost in a seven-game World Series to the **St. Louis Cardinals**. In 2012, Texas lost to the **Baltimore Orioles** in the American League's first **wild card** "play-in" game.

Texas Rangers who have won the AL's **Most Valuable Player Award** are Jeff Burroughs (1974), Juan Gonzalez (1996, 1998), **Ivan Rodriguez** (1999), **Alex Rodriguez** (2003), and Josh Hamilton (2010). No Texas **pitcher** has won the **Cy Young Award**. **Rookie of the Year** winners are Mike Hargrove (1974) and Neftali Feliz (2010).

Rangers players who have led the league in **batting average** are Julio Franco (1991), Michael Young (2005), and Josh Hamilton (2010). Leaders in **home runs** are Juan Gonzalez (1992–1993) and Alex Rodriguez

(2001–2003). Leaders in **runs batted in** are Jeff Burroughs (1974), Ruben Sierra (1989), Juan Gonzalez (1998), Alex Rodriguez (2002), and Josh Hamilton (2008).

Rangers **pitchers** who have led the league in **wins** are **Ferguson Jenkins** (1974), Kevin Brown (1992), and Rick Helling (1998). Rick Honeycutt (1983) is the only Rangers pitcher to lead the AL in **earned run average**. **Nolan Ryan**, in 1988 and 1989, is the only Rangers pitcher to lead the AL in **strikeouts**.

Other notable players and **managers** in Rangers' history include Elvis Andrus, Buddy Bell, Adrian Beltre, Nelson Cruz, Jose Guzman, Toby Harrah, Derek Holland, Charlie Hough, Frank Howard, Ian Kinsler, Mitch Moreland, Mike Napoli, Johnny Oates, Pete O'Brien, **Rafael Palmeiro**, Kenny Rogers, Jeff Russell, Buck Showalter, Jim Sundberg, Bobby Valentine, Ron Washington, John Wetteland, C. J. Wilson, Bobby Witt, and Richie Zisk.

THE BALLPARK IN ARLINGTON. *See* RANGERS BALLPARK IN ARLINGTON.

THIRD BASE. Third base is the third of four stations on a baseball diamond that a **base runner** must safely touch in succession to score a **run** for that player's team.

THIRD BASEMAN (3B). The third baseman is the defensive player on the team who fields the area nearest **third base** and is responsible for the majority of plays made at that **base**. In the numbering system used to record defensive plays, the third baseman is assigned the number 5.

The **major-league** career leader in **games played** by a third baseman is **Brooks Robinson**, with 2,870. The major-league career leader in **fielding percentage** (minimum 500 games) through 2012 is Placido Polanco (active in 2013), at .9826.

The single-season leader in **putouts** by a third baseman is Denny Lyons of the 1887 **Philadelphia Athletics** of the **American Association**, with 255. The **National League (NL)** single-season leaders in putouts are Jimmy Williams of the 1899 **Pittsburgh Pirates** and **Jimmy Collins** of the 1900 Boston Beaneaters, each with 251. The **American League** single-season leader is Willie Kamm of the 1928 **Chicago White Sox**, with 243. The career leader is Brooks Robinson, with 2,697. Robinson played his entire career (1955–1977) with the **Baltimore Orioles**.

The single-season leader in **assists** by a third baseman is Graig Nettles of the 1971 **Cleveland Indians**, with 412. The NL single-season leader is **Mike Schmidt** of the 1974 **Philadelphia Phillies**, with 404. The career leader is Brooks Robinson, with 6,205.

THOMAS, FRANK EDWARD, "THE BIG HURT". B. 27 May 1968, Columbus, Georgia. Frank Thomas was a 6-foot, 5-inch, 240-pound **first baseman** and **designated hitter (DH)** for the **Chicago White Sox** from 1990 to 2005. Thomas finished his career with the **Oakland Athletics** (2006, 2008) and **Toronto Blue Jays** (2007–2008). The right-handed-hitting Thomas was among the most feared sluggers in the **American League (AL)**. He scored more than 100 **runs** nine times, had more than 100 **runs batted in (RBI)** 11 times, and led the AL in walks and **on-base percentage** four times each. Thomas had nine full seasons in which he batted above .300, including a career-high .353 in 1994. That season, he led the league in runs, walks, on-base percentage, and **slugging percentage** to capture his second consecutive **Most Valuable Player (MVP) Award**. In addition to his MVP Award he won in 1993, he was also voted the **Major League Player of the Year**. Thomas, who won four **Silver Slugger Awards**, two as a first baseman and two as a DH, had a career **batting average** of .301 for his 19 **major-league** seasons. He hit 521 **home runs**, drove in 1,704 RBI, and scored 1,494 runs. Thomas's last active season was 2008. He is sure to be elected to the **National Baseball Hall of Fame** when he becomes eligible.

THOME, JAMES HOWARD "JIM". B. 27 August 1970, Peoria, Illinois. In 2011, Jim Thome became the eighth **major-league** player to reach the 600 **home run** mark. The 6-foot, 4-inch, 250-pound Thome began his big-league career in September 1991, with the **Cleveland Indians**. He played for Cleveland through the 2002 season and then signed as a **free agent** with the **Philadelphia Phillies**, where he played through the 2005 season. Thome has also been with the **Chicago White Sox** (2006–2009), **Los Angeles Dodgers** (2009), and **Minnesota Twins** (2010–2011). He was back in Cleveland late in the 2011 season. He split the 2012 season between the Phillies and the **Baltimore Orioles**.

Thome was a **third baseman** in his first six seasons, but he has been a **first baseman** or **designated hitter** since 1997. He has hit 20 or more home runs 16 times, including a **National League**–leading 47 in 2003 and a career high 52 with the 2002 Indians. He has driven in 100 or more **runs** nine times and also drawn 100 or more walks nine times. A free swinger, the left-handed-hitting Thome led his league in **strikeouts** three times, and his career total of 2,548 (through 2012) is second all-time to **Reggie Jackson**. Through 2012, Thome had a .276 **batting average**; 612 home runs; 1,699 **runs batted in**; 2,328 **hits**; and 1,747 walks, seventh all-time. He was the winner of the **Roberto Clemente Award** in 2002 and **Lou Gehrig Memorial Award** in 2004. Thome is likely to be elected to the **National Baseball Hall of Fame** when he becomes eligible.

THOMPSON, SAMUEL LUTHER "SAM". B. 5 March 1860, Danville, Indiana. D. 7 November 1922, Detroit, Michigan. Sam Thompson was an **outfielder** in the **National League (NL)** for the **Detroit Wolverines** from 1885 to 1888, and for the **Philadelphia Phillies** from 1889 to 1898. In 1906, at the age of 46, Thompson played a final eight games for the **Detroit Tigers** of the **American League**. A 6-foot, 2-inch, 207 pounder who batted and threw left-handed, Thompson was one of the top sluggers of the late 19th century. With Detroit in 1887, he led the NL in **batting average** (.372), **hits** (203), **triples** (23), **runs batted in (RBI)** (166), **slugging percentage** (.565), and **total bases** (308). Thompson batted .362, with two **home runs**, as the Wolverines won 10 of 15 games from the **St. Louis Browns**, champions of the **American Association**, in that year's championship series, which was a predecessor to the modern **World Series**. Thompson had .415 and .392 batting averages, respectively, for the Phillies in 1894 and 1895, while leading the league in RBI and slugging percentage in both seasons. He led the NL in both hits and RBI three times and home runs and **doubles** twice. In addition to being an excellent fielder with a fine throwing arm, Thompson compiled a career batting average of .331. He was elected to the **National Baseball Hall of Fame** by the **Veterans Committee** in 1974.

THREE RIVERS STADIUM. Three Rivers Stadium, located in Pittsburgh, Pennsylvania, was the home of the **Pittsburgh Pirates** of the **National League** from 16 July 1970 to the end of the 2000 season. In 2001, the team moved to its present home, **PNC Park**. Three Rivers Stadium hosted the **major league All-Star Game** in 1974 and 1994.
See also STADIUMS.

TIGER STADIUM. Tiger Stadium, located in Detroit, Michigan, was the home of the **Detroit Tigers** of the **American League** from 20 April 1912 to 27 September 1999. In 2001, the team moved to **Comerica Park**. Tiger Stadium was called Navin Field from its opening in 1912 through 1937, and Briggs Stadium from 1938 to 1960. Both names were in honor of the team's owner at the time. Briggs Stadium hosted the **major league All-Star Game** in 1941 and 1951. Tiger Stadium hosted the game in 1971.

TINKER, JOSEPH BERT "JOE". B. 27 July 1880, Muscotah, Kansas. D. 27 July 1948, Orlando, Florida. Joe Tinker was a **shortstop** for the **Chicago Cubs**, where he teamed with **second baseman Johnny Evers** and **first baseman Frank Chance** to form one of baseball's most memorable **double-play** combinations. Tinker, a 5-foot, 9-inch, 175-pound right-handed **batter**, played for the Cubs from 1902 through 1912. The Cubs won four **National League (NL)** pennants and two **World Series** (1907 and 1908) during that time. Following the 1912 season, Chicago traded Tinker to the **Cincinnati Reds**. He batted .317 for the Reds in 1913, his career-high **batting average**, while serving as the team's **player-manager**. The following year, he left the Reds to become the player-manager for the 1914 and 1915 **Chicago Whales** of the **Federal League**. When the league folded after the 1915 season, he returned to the Cubs as their **manager** in 1916. It was his final season in the **major leagues**, although he later owned and managed clubs in the **minor leagues**. Tinker's career batting average was just .262, but he led NL short-stops in **fielding percentage** five times, **putouts** twice, and **assists** three times. In 1946, the **Old Timers Committee** elected Tinker to the **National Baseball Hall of Fame**.

TOKYO DOME. The Tokyo Dome, located in Tokyo, **Japan**, is the home field of the Yomiuri Giants, a team in the Central League of Nippon Profes-sional Baseball. The Tokyo Dome opened on 17 March 1988, and the facility has a capacity seating of 42,000 for baseball. In 2002, the **Chicago Cubs** and **New York Mets** opened the **major-league** season by playing two games at the Tokyo Dome, the first regular-season major-league games played in Asia. Since then, the **New York Yankees** and Tampa Bay Devil Rays played two games there to open the 2004 season, and the **Boston Red Sox** and **Oakland Athletics** opened the 2008 season with a game at the Tokyo Dome. The Athletics and **Seattle Mariners** played a two-game series at the Tokyo Dome to open the 2012 season.

TOLEDO BLUE STOCKINGS. The Toledo Blue Stockings were a team in the **American Association** in 1884. They finished eighth in a 13-team league, with a record of 46–58, and disbanded after the season. Toledo's **roster** included **Fleetwood Walker** and his brother, Welday Walker, the only acknowledged **African American** players in the **major leagues** prior to **Jackie Robinson**.

TOLEDO MAUMEES. The Toledo Maumees were a team in the **American Association** in 1890. They finished fourth in the nine-team league, with a record of 68–64. The Maumees' most notable player was Ed Swartwood.

TORONTO BLUE JAYS. The Toronto Blue Jays are a team in the Eastern Division of the **American League (AL)**. Toronto, the first AL team located in **Canada**, entered the league with the **Seattle Mariners** in 1977 as part of a two-team AL **expansion**. The Blue Jays played their home games at Exhibition Stadium from 7 April 1977 to 28 May 1989. They played their first game at SkyDome, a **stadium** that had the world's first fully retractable roof, on 5 June 1989. In 2004, the name SkyDome was changed to **Rogers Centre**.

In 1992, the Blue Jays defeated the **Atlanta Braves** in six games to become the first Canadian team to win the **World Series**. They won again the next year, defeating the **Philadelphia Phillies** in six games. Toronto had previously lost in the **American League Championship Series** three times, to the **Kansas City Royals** in 1985, the **Oakland Athletics** in 1989, and the **Minnesota Twins** in 1991. All three of those teams went on to win the World Series.

The only Toronto Blue Jay to win the **Most Valuable Player Award** was George Bell in 1987. **Cy Young Award** winners are Pat Hentgen (1996), **Roger Clemens** (1997–1998), and **Roy Halladay** (2003). **Rookie of the Year** winners are Alfredo Griffin (1979) and Eric Hinske (2002).

John Olerud, in 1993, is the only Blue Jays player to lead the league in **batting average**. Leaders in **home runs** are Jesse Barfield (1986), Fred McGriff (1989), and Jose Bautista (2010–2011). Leaders in **runs batted in** are George Bell (1987) and Carlos Delgado (2003).

Blue Jays **pitchers** who have led the league in **wins** are Jack Morris (1992), Roger Clemens (1997–1998), David Wells (2000), and Roy Halladay (2003). **Earned run average (ERA)** leaders are Dave Stieb (1985), Jimmy Key (1987), Juan Guzman (1996), and Roger Clemens (1997–1998). **Strikeouts** leaders are Roger Clemens (1997–1998) and A. J. Burnett (2008). By leading in wins, ERA, and strikeouts in 1997 and 1998, Roger Clemens won the **Triple Crown** for pitchers in both years.

Other notable players and **managers** in Blue Jays' history include **Roberto Alomar**, Pat Borders, Jim Clancy, **Bobby Cox**, Tony Fernandez, Damaso Garcia, Cito Gaston, Shawn Green, Kelly Gruber, Tom Henke, Aaron Hill, Manny Lee, Lloyd Moseby, Rance Mulliniks, Alex Rios, Ricky Romero, Shannon Stewart, Todd Stottlemyre, Willie Upshaw, Duane Ward, Vernon Wells, Devon White, and Ernie Whitt.

TORRE, JOSEPH PAUL "JOE". B. 18 July 1940, Brooklyn, New York. Joe Torre spent 18 seasons as a player in the **National League (NL)**, followed by 29 seasons as a **manager** in both the National League and the **American League (AL)**. Originally a **catcher**, the 6-foot, 2-inch, 212-pound Torre spent the latter half of his playing career as a **third baseman** and **first baseman**. Torre played for the **Milwaukee Braves** (1960–1965), **Atlanta Braves** (1966–1968), **St. Louis Cardinals** (1969–1974), and **New York Mets** (1975–1977). The right-handed-hitting Torre, a nine-time **All-Star**, had his greatest season with the 1971 Cardinals. He led the NL with a .363 **batting average**, 230 **hits**, 137 **runs batted in**, and 352 **total bases**, all of which were individual career highs. Torre was voted the NL's **Most Valu-**

able **Player**, the **Major League Player of the Year**, and the winner of the **Hutch Award**. He finished his playing career with a .297 batting average, 2,342 hits, and 252 **home runs**.

Torre managed the Mets from 1977 to 1981, and the Braves from 1982 to 1984. After serving as a broadcaster for the California Angels, he returned to managing with the Cardinals, from 1990 to 1995. In 1996, he was the surprise choice to manage the **New York Yankees**. Torre had unprecedented success in his 12 years with New York, winning 1,173 games and compiling a .605 **winning percentage**. He led the Yankees to 10 first-place finishes and two seconds in the AL's Eastern Division. The Yankees won six pennants and four **World Series**, but Torre was let go after the club finished second in 2007. He moved to the **Los Angeles Dodgers**, where he won the NL's Western Division title in 2008 and 2009. Torre retired after the 2010 season with an overall managerial record of 2,326–1,997. The **Baseball Writers' Association of America** gave him its AL **Manager of the Year Award** in 1996 and 1998, and the *Sporting News* gave him its AL **Manager of the Year Award** in 1998. Torre is likely to be elected to the **National Baseball Hall of Fame** when he becomes eligible.

TORRIENTE, CRISTOBAL "THE CUBAN BABE RUTH". B. 16 November 1893, Cienfuegos, **Cuba**. D. 11 April 1938, New York, New York. Cristobal Torriente played in the **Negro National League** for the **Chicago American Giants** (1920–1925), **Kansas City Monarchs** (1926), and Detroit Stars (1927–1928). Torriente was a left-handed-hitting and throwing **outfielder** and occasional **pitcher**. For years, he also starred in Cuban baseball, where he was called "The Cuban **Babe Ruth**." The 5-foot, 9-inch, 190-pound Torriente is recognized as the greatest Cuban position player during the first half of the 20th century. In 1939, he was one of the first players selected for the Cuban Baseball Hall of Fame. In 2006, Torriente was elected to the **National Baseball Hall of Fame** in a special election conducted by the **Committee on African American Baseball**.

TOTAL BASES (TB). The formula for total bases (TB) is **singles + doubles*2 + triples*3 + home runs*4**. Example: A player with 100 singles, 25 doubles, 10 triples, and 20 home runs has 260 TB.

The **major league** single-season leader in total bases is **Babe Ruth** of the 1921 **New York Yankees**, with 457. The single-season leader in the **National League** is **Rogers Hornsby** of the 1922 **St. Louis Cardinals**, with 450. The career leader is **Hank Aaron**, with 6,856. Aaron played for the **Milwaukee Braves** (1954–1965), **Atlanta Braves** (1966–1974), and **Milwaukee Brewers** (1975–1976).

TOTAL CHANCES (TC). Total chances are the sum of a **fielder's put-outs**, **assists**, and **errors**.

TRAYNOR, HAROLD JOSEPH "PIE". B. 11 November 1898, Framing-ham, Massachusetts. D. 16 March 1972, Pittsburgh, Pennsylvania. Pie Trayn-or was a playing member of the **Pittsburgh Pirates** for 17 seasons (1920–1935, 1937), their regular **third baseman** from 1922 through 1934, and their **manager** from mid-1934 through 1939. He had a winning record in four of his six seasons as manager, but his highest finish was second place in 1938. The right-handed-hitting Traynor, who stood 6 feet and weighed 170 pounds, batted .300 or better 10 times. He had 100 or more **runs batted in** seven times, while never exceeding 28 **strikeouts** in any one season. His 19 **triples** led the **National League (NL)** in 1923, but it was the only time he led the league in any offensive category. Defensively, Traynor led NL third basemen in **putouts** seven times and **assists** three times. Traynor ended his playing career with a .320 **batting average** and 2,416 **hits**. In 1948, the **Baseball Writers' Association of America** elected him to the **National Baseball Hall of Fame**.

TRIPLE CROWN (BATTERS). For a **batter** to win the Triple Crown in a season, he must lead his league in **batting average**, **home runs**, and **runs batted in**. **National League** batters who have won the Triple Crown are **Paul Hines** of the **Providence Grays** (1878), **Rogers Hornsby** of the **St. Louis Cardinals** (1922, 1925), **Chuck Klein** of the **Philadelphia Phillies** (1933), and **Joe Medwick** of the St. Louis Cardinals (1937). **American League** batters who have won the Triple Crown are **Nap Lajoie** of the **Philadelphia Athletics** (1901), **Ty Cobb** of the **Detroit Tigers** (1909), **Jim-mie Foxx** of the Philadelphia Athletics (1933), **Lou Gehrig** of the **New York Yankees** (1934), **Ted Williams** of the **Boston Red Sox** (1942, 1947), **Mickey Mantle** of the New York Yankees (1956), **Frank Robinson** of the **Baltimore Orioles** (1966), **Carl Yastrzemski** of the Boston Red Sox (1967), and **Miguel Cabrera** of the Detroit Tigers (2012). The only **American Asso-ciation** batter to win a Triple Crown was Tip O'Neill of the 1887 **St. Louis Browns**.

TRIPLE CROWN (PITCHERS). For a **pitcher** to win the Triple Crown in a season, he must lead his league in **wins**, **earned run average**, and **strike-outs**. **National League** pitchers who have won the Triple Crown are **Tommy Bond** of the Boston Red Stockings (1877), **Charlie Radbourn** of the **Provi-dence Grays** (1884), **Tim Keefe** of the **New York Giants** (1888), **John Clarkson** of the Boston Beaneaters (1889), **Amos Rusie** of the New York Giants (1894), **Christy Mathewson** of the New York Giants (1905, 1908),

Grover Alexander of the **Philadelphia Phillies** (1915, 1916) and **Chicago Cubs** (1920), Hippo Vaughn of the Chicago Cubs (1918), **Dazzy Vance** of the Brooklyn Robins (1924), Bucky Walters of the **Cincinnati Reds** (1939), **Sandy Koufax** of the **Los Angeles Dodgers** (1963, 1965, 1966), **Steve Carlton** of the Philadelphia Phillies (1972), Dwight Gooden of the **New York Mets** (1985), **Randy Johnson** of the **Arizona Diamondbacks** (2002), Jake Peavy of the **San Diego Padres** (2007), and Clayton Kershaw of the Los Angeles Dodgers (2011).

American League pitchers who have won the Triple Crown are **Cy Young** of the Boston Americans (1901), **Rube Waddell** of the **Philadelphia Athletics** (1905), **Walter Johnson** of the **Washington Senators** (1913, 1918, 1924), **Lefty Grove** of the Philadelphia Athletics (1930, 1931), **Lefty Gomez** of the **New York Yankees** (1934, 1937), **Bob Feller** of the **Cleveland Indians** (1940), **Hal Newhouser** of the **Detroit Tigers** (1945), **Roger Clemens** of the **Toronto Blue Jays** (1997, 1998), **Pedro Martinez** of the **Boston Red Sox** (1999), Johan Santana of the **Minnesota Twins** (2006), and Justin Verlander of the Detroit Tigers (2011). The only **American Association** pitcher to win the Triple Crown was Guy Hecker of the 1884 **Louisville Colonels**.

TRIPLE PLAY. A triple play is a play by the defense in which three offensive players are put out as a result of continuous action, providing that there is no **error** between **putouts**.

TRIPLES (3B). A triple is any batted ball where the **batter** reaches **third base** safely without the benefit of any fielding **errors**. The **major league** single-season leader in triples is Owen Wilson of the 1912 **Pittsburgh Pirates**, with 36. The single-season leaders in the **American League** are **Sam Crawford** of the 1914 **Detroit Tigers** and **Joe Jackson** of the 1912 **Cleveland Indians**, with 26. The career leader is Sam Crawford, with 309. Crawford played for the **Cincinnati Reds** (1899–1902) and Detroit Tigers (1903–1917).

TROPICANA FIELD. Tropicana Field, located in St. Petersburg, Florida, is the home field of the **Tampa Bay Rays** of the **American League**. It is a domed **stadium** with artificial turf. The Rays played their first official game there on 31 March 1998. The approximate current seating capacity of Tropicana Field is 34,100. Tropicana Field has never hosted the **major league All-Star Game**.

Figure 20.1.   Lefty Grove of the Philadelphia Athletics won the American League Triple Crown for pitchers in 1930 and 1931. *National Baseball Hall of Fame Library, Cooperstown, N.Y.*

TROY (NEW YORK) HAYMAKERS. The Troy Haymakers were charter members of the National Association (NA). They played in the NA in 1871, but the team disbanded midway through the 1872 season. The two most notable players for the Haymakers were Davy Force and **Lip Pike**.

TROY (NEW YORK) TROJANS. The Troy Trojans, sometimes referred to by their National Association name, **Troy Haymakers**, were a team in the **National League (NL)** from 1879 to 1882. The Trojans were disbanded after the 1882 season. In 1883, the New York Gothams, later the **New York Giants** and then the **San Francisco Giants**, took Troy's place in the NL. Nearly half of the original Gotham players were members of the recently disbanded Trojans. Notable players for the Trojans included **Dan Brouthers**, **Roger Connor**, **Buck Ewing**, **Tim Keefe**, and **Mickey Welch**.

TURNER FIELD. Turner Field, located in Atlanta, Georgia, has been the home of the **Atlanta Braves** of the **National League** since 4 April 1997. Prior to that, the Braves played at **Fulton County Stadium** from 1966 to 1996. Turner Field, which has a seating capacity of approximately 49,500, hosted the **major league All-Star Game** in 2000.
    See also STADIUMS.

TWENTY-THIRD STREET GROUNDS. *See* CHICAGO CUBS.

UMPIRES. The major duties of a baseball umpire are enforcing the rules of the game and the **grounds rules** particular to the park where the game is being played. Umpires are also responsible for the calling of **balls** and **strikes**, making **safe** or **out** calls, and enforcing discipline. One umpire was deemed sufficient to handle a game from baseball's beginnings until the early years of the 20th century. Throughout the years, that number has gradually increased, especially at the **major-league** level, to two, then three, and now umpiring crews most commonly consist of four umpires—one at **home plate** and one at each of the three **bases**. The umpires rotate their positions from one game to the next, moving in a clockwise fashion. The home plate umpire goes to **third base**, the third base umpire to **second base**, and the second base umpire to **first base**.

The home plate umpire is the umpire in chief for that game and has responsibility for the start and end of the game, delays, substitutions, and just about everything else pertaining to the conduct of the game. Each umpiring crew also has a crew chief, usually the senior member of the crew. The crew chief serves as a liaison between the league office and the crew and has a supervisory role over other members of the crew. Two umpires were added to the crew for the 1947 **World Series**, one stationed down the left-field **foul line**, and one stationed down the right-field foul line. Six-man umpire crews are now standard for all League Division Series, League Championship Series, World Series, and **All-Star Games**.

Nine major-league umpires have been elected to the **National Baseball Hall of Fame**, including **Al Barlick, Nestor Chylak, Jocko Conlan, Tom Connolly, Billy Evans, Doug Harvey, Cal Hubbard, Bill Klem**, and **Bill McGowan**. Other prominent umpires, some of whom are still active, include Larry Barnett, Joe Brinkman, Derryl Cousins, Jerry Crawford, Bill Dinneen, Mike Emslie, Bruce Froemming, Larry McCoy, Ed Montague, Mike Reilly, Cy Rigler, Harry Wendestedt, and Joe West.

Figure 21.1.   Bill Klem umpired a major-league-record 5,370 games in the National League, He was the last umpire to work exclusively at home plate. *National Baseball Hall of Fame Library, Cooperstown, N.Y.*

UNION ASSOCIATION (UA). The Union Association (UA) existed as a **major league** for one season, 1884, although many historians question its major-league status. Franchise instability, the overall quality of the players, and the dominance of one team, the **St. Louis Maroons**, caused the league to disband after the one season. Twelve other teams played all or part of the 1884 season in the UA, including the **Altoona Mountain Citys, Baltimore Monumentals, Boston Reds, Chicago Browns, Cincinnati Outlaw Reds, Kansas City Cowboys, Milwaukee Grays, Philadelphia Keystones, Pittsburgh Stogies, St. Paul Saints, Washington Nationals**, and **Wilmington Quicksteps**.

Fred Dunlap of the St. Louis Maroons led the league with a .412 **batting average** and 13 **home runs**. Bill Sweeney of the Baltimore Monumentals led UA **pitchers** in **wins** (40); Jim McCormick of the Cincinnati Outlaw Reds had the lowest **earned run average** (1.54), and Hugh Dailey, who pitched for the Chicago Browns, Pittsburgh Stogies, and Washington Nationals, led in **strikeouts** (483).

UNION GROUNDS (BROOKLYN). The Union Grounds, located in Brooklyn, New York, opened in 1862. It was the first baseball park entirely enclosed by a fence, thereby allowing proprietor William Cammeyer to charge admission, permitting only paying customers to watch the games. During its early years, the Union Grounds was the home field for several clubs, including the **Brooklyn Eckfords**, the 1862 and 1863 champions of the **National Association of Base Ball Players**, a group of amateur teams primarily from the Northeast and Midwest.

After the formation of the first professional league, the National Association (NA), the Union Grounds was home to the **New York Mutuals** from 1871 to 1875, (also in 1876, the only year the Mutuals were members of the new **National League [NL]**), the Brooklyn Eckfords of the NA in 1872, and the **Brooklyn Atlantics** of the NA from 1873 to 1875. It also served as home field for the Brooklyn Hartfords during the 1877 NL season. The final **major-league** game played at the Union Grounds was on 26 July 1878, when the **Providence Grays** defeated the **Milwaukee Grays**, 4–1.

See also STADIUMS.

U.S. CELLULAR FIELD. U.S. Cellular Field, located in Chicago, Illinois, has been the home field of the **Chicago White Sox** of the **American League** since 18 April 1991. From its opening through the 2002 season, the park was called **Comiskey Park**, like its predecessor. The White Sox played in the original Comiskey Park from 1 July 1910 to 30 September 1990, and before that at South Side Park from 24 April 1901 to 27 June 1910. U.S. Cellular Field, which has a seating capacity of approximately 40,600, was the site of the **major league All-Star Game** in 2003.

V

VANCE, CHARLES ARTHUR "DAZZY". B. 4 March 1891, Orient, Iowa. D. 16 February 1961, Homosassa Springs, Florida. In 1915, Dazzy Vance pitched in one game for the **Pittsburgh Pirates** and eight games for the **New York Yankees**. Vance spent the next five years in the **minor leagues**, with the exception of two games with the Yankees in 1918. In 1922, everything changed for the 6-foot, 2-inch, 200-pound right-hander, when at the advanced age of 31, he joined the Brooklyn Robins. Vance used his blazing fastball to lead the **National League (NL)** in **strikeouts** in each of his first seven seasons with the Robins. Overall, during 12 seasons in Brooklyn, he won 20 or more games three times, and he led the NL in **wins** twice, **earned average (ERA)** three times, and **shutouts** four times. In 1924, Vance led the NL in wins (28), ERA (2.16), and strikeouts (262) to win the **Triple Crown** for **pitchers** and selection as the NL's **Most Valuable Player**. He beat out **Rogers Hornsby**, who batted .424 for the **St. Louis Cardinals**. Brooklyn traded Vance to St. Louis in 1933. He spent 1933 and part of 1934 with the Cardinals, and also part of 1934 with the **Cincinnati Reds**, before a final season back in Brooklyn in 1935. Vance had a career won-lost record of 197–140, with a 3.24 ERA and 2,045 strikeouts. In 1955, he was elected by the **Baseball Writers' Association of America** to the **National Baseball Hall of Fame**.

VAUGHAN, JOSEPH FLOYD "ARKY". B. 9 March 1912, Clifty, Arkansas. D. 30 August 1952, Eagleville, California. Arky Vaughan was a hard-hitting **shortstop** for the **Pittsburgh Pirates** from 1932 through 1941. Shaky in the field at first, he later led **National League (NL)** shortstops in several fielding categories. The 5-foot, 10-inch, 170-pound left-handed hitter batted .300 or better in each of his 10 seasons in Pittsburgh. His highest **batting average** was his league-leading .385 in 1935. Vaughn also led the NL that year with 97 walks, a .491 **on-base percentage**, and a .607 **slugging percentage**. In his career, he led the NL in **triples**, walks, on-base percentage, and **runs** three times each.

On 12 December 1941, the Pirates traded Vaughan to the **Brooklyn Dodgers** for four players. He was the Dodgers' **third baseman** in 1942, but he moved back to shortstop in 1943 when the Dodgers lost **Pee Wee Reese** to the military. Vaughan clashed with Brooklyn **manager Leo Durocher** before a 1943 game against the Pirates, which led to a near mutiny by the Brooklyn team. His retirement at the end of the season may have been related to that incident, because he stayed out of baseball for three seasons. Vaughan returned to the Dodgers in 1947 and played in his only **World Series**, a losing effort against the **New York Yankees**. He retired after the 1948 season. Vaughan played in seven **All-Star Games**, batting a combined .364. In 1941, he became the first player from either league to hit two **home runs** in an All-Star Game. Vaughan was on a fishing trip when he drowned in August 1952, at the age of 40. He was elected to the **National Baseball Hall of Fame** by the **Veterans Committee** in 1985.

VEECK, WILLIAM LOUIS, JR. "BILL". B. 9 February 1914, Chicago, Illinois. D. 2 January 1986, Chicago, Illinois. Bill Veeck was the flamboyant and innovative owner of three **American League (AL)** teams. Veeck owned the **Cleveland Indians** from 1946 to 1949, during which time he signed **Larry Doby**, the AL's first **African American** player, and **Satchel Paige**, the legendary **Negro Leagues pitcher**. In 1948, the Indians won their first **World Series** since 1920. Veeck purchased the hapless **St. Louis Browns** in July 1951, and he owned them through the 1953 season. It was with the Browns, on 29 August 1951, that Veeck had a midget named Eddie Gaedel bat in a game.

In 1959, Veeck was part of a group that purchased the **Chicago White Sox**. The team won its first pennant since 1919 that season, and, as with Cleveland when Veeck owned them, the club set attendance records. Veeck sold his shares of the White Sox in 1961, but he returned as the team's sole owner in 1975. He sold out in 1981 and retired from baseball. Best remembered for his many fan-friendly schemes, Veeck was elected by the **Veterans Committee** to the **National Baseball Hall of Fame** in 1991.

VENEZUELA. The Venezuelan Professional Baseball League (Liga Venezolana de Béisbol Profesional) began play in 1946. The current Liga Venezolana de Béisbol Profesional consists of eight teams, playing a 63-game schedule. The teams are Águilas del Zulia, located in Maracaibo; Bravos de Margarita, located in Porlamar; Cardenales de Lara, located in Barquisimeto; Caribes de Anzoátegui, located in Puerto La Cruz; Leones del Caracas, located in Caracas; Navegantes del Magallanes, located in Valencia; Tiburones de la Guaira, located in La Guaira; and Tigres de Aragua, located in Maracay.

The Venezuelan champion moves on to the **Caribbean Series** to face the champions of the baseball leagues of the **Dominican Republic, Puerto Rico,** and **Mexico**. Venezuela has won the Caribbean Series seven times, most recently by the Tigres de Aragua in 2009. Tigres de Aragua was also the Venezuelan representative in the 2011 and 2012 Caribbean Series, won by the Leones del Escogido team representing the Dominican Republic.

Venezuela's best players prior to the start of the Liga Venezolana de Béisbol Profesional include Hall of Famer **Luis Aparicio**'s father, Luis Aparicio "El Grande"; Daniel "Chino" Canonico; Ramon "Dumbo" Fernandez; Luis "Camaleon" Garcia; and Vidal Lopez. The most notable **major-league** players and **managers** born in Venezuela include Bobby Abreu, Edgardo Alfonzo, Wilson Alvarez, Elvis Andrus, Luis Aparicio, Tony Armas, Rafael Betancourt, Henry Blanco, Asdrubal Cabrera, **Miguel Cabrera**, Miguel Cairo, Alex Carrasquel (the first Venezuelan-born major leaguer), Chico Carrasquel, Roger Cedeno, Endy Chavez, Dave Concepcion, Vic Davalillo, Bo Diaz, Kelvim Escobar, Andres Galarraga, Carlos Garcia, Freddy Garcia, Alex Gonzalez, Carlos Guillen, Ozzie Guillen (the first Venezuelan-born manager), Franklin Gutierrez, Felix Hernandez, Ramon Hernandez, Richard Hidalgo, Omar Infante, Cesar Izturis, Maicer Izturis, Jorge Julio, Jose Lopez, Victor Martinez, Miguel Montero, Melvin Mora, Dioner Navarro, Magglio Ordonez, Gerardo Parra, Eddie Perez, Martin Prado, Juan Rivera, Francisco Rodriguez, Luis Salazar, Anibal Sanchez, Pablo Sandoval, Johan Santana, Marco Scutaro, Luis Sojo, Yorvit Torrealba, Cesar Tovar, Manny Trillo, Ugueth Urbina, **Omar Vizquel**, Carlos Zambrano, and Victor Zambrano.

VETERANS COMMITTEE. The Veterans Committee has existed to elect individuals to the **National Baseball Hall of Fame** since 1953. Throughout the years, both the makeup of the committee and its voting procedures have changed several times. Candidates are currently classified by the era in which they made their greatest contributions, as follows: Pre-Integration Era Veterans Committee (1871–1946), Golden Era Veterans Committee (1947–1972), and Expansion Era Veterans Committee (1973 and later). Candidates from each era are considered every third year, starting with the Expansion Era in the 2011 election, followed by the Golden Era, and then by the Pre-Integration Era. Voting is done by a committee of players, executives, and members of the media. One has to be named on 75 percent of ballots to earn Hall of Fame honors.

VETERANS STADIUM. Veterans Stadium, located in Philadelphia, Pennsylvania, was the home of the **Philadelphia Phillies** of the **National League** from 10 April 1971 to 28 September 2003. In 2004, the Phillies moved to **Citizens Bank Park**. Veterans Stadium hosted the **major league All-Star Game** in 1976 and 1996.

VIZQUEL, OMAR ENRIQUE (GONZALEZ). B. 24 April 1967, Caracas, **Venezuela**. At his retirement following the 2012 season, Omar Vizquel held the all-time **major-league** record for most **games played** at **shortstop** (2,709). Vizquel is also second all-time among shortstops in **fielding percentage**, third all-time in **assists**, and 11th all-time in **putouts**. The 5-foot, 9-inch, 180-pound **switch-hitter** began his big-league career with the 1989 **Seattle Mariners**. In addition to his five years in Seattle (1989–1993), Vizquel has played for the **Cleveland Indians** (1994–2004), **San Francisco Giants** (2005–2008), **Texas Rangers** (2009), **Chicago White Sox** (2010–2011), and **Toronto Blue Jays**. Vizquel has a .272 **batting average**, with 2,877 **hits** in his 24 seasons. He was an **All-Star** only three times, but he has won 11 **Gold Glove Awards** and led his league in fielding percentage six times. He also won the **Hutch Award** in 1996. His defensive prowess makes Vizquel a likely candidate to be elected to the **National Baseball Hall of Fame** when he becomes eligible.

WADDELL, GEORGE EDWARD "RUBE". B. 13 October 1876, Bradford, Pennsylvania. D. 1 April 1914, San Antonio, Texas. Left-handed **pitcher** Rube Waddell made his **major-league** debut with the 1897 **Louisville Colonels** of the **National League**. In 1900, the Louisville club was one of four dropped by the league. Colonels' owner **Barney Dreyfuss**, who also owned a half interest in the **Pittsburgh Pirates**, had **Fred Clarke**, Louisville's **manager**, and several of the Colonels' best players, including Waddell and **Honus Wagner**, transferred to Pittsburgh. Waddell had a mediocre 8–13 record in 1900, but he led the league with a 2.37 **earned run average (ERA)**. Then, early in the 1901 season, Pittsburgh traded him to the Chicago Orphans (forerunner of the **Chicago Cubs**). In late June 1902, Waddell joined the **Philadelphia Athletics** of the **American League (AL)**, for whom he had 24 **wins** (24–7), and a league-leading 210 **strikeouts**. It was the first of six consecutive seasons in which Waddell would lead the AL in strikeouts. His 349 strikeouts in 1904 was the post-1893 major-league record until **Sandy Koufax** of the **Los Angeles Dodgers** had 382 strikeouts in 1965.

Three more 20-win seasons followed (1903–1905), including a league-high 27 wins in 1905. That year, the 6-foot, 1-inch, 196-pound Waddell also led in ERA (1.48) and strikeouts (287) to earn the pitchers **Triple Crown**, despite missing the last four weeks of the season with an injured shoulder. Waddell also missed the **World Series**, a five-game loss to the **New York Giants**. In February 1908, the Athletics sold Waddell to the **St. Louis Browns**, where the erratic pitcher spent his final three seasons. Waddell won 193 games in his career, with a 2.16 ERA, 11th best all-time, and 50 **shutouts**, the fourth-highest total by a left-hander. Yet, his carefree attitude, lack of discipline, alcoholism, and possible developmental disorders prevented him from being an even greater pitcher. In 1946, the **Old Timers Committee** elected Waddell to the **National Baseball Hall of Fame**.

WADSWORTH, LEWIS F. B. 1825. D. 1908. Lewis Wadsworth was a **first baseman** for the Gotham and **Knickerbocker Base Ball Clubs** in the 1850s. Wadsworth attended the first Base Ball Convention, held in New

York City, in 1857. At a meeting of the Committee on Rules and Regulations, Wadsworth is credited with establishing the number of players per side at nine, and nine as the number of **innings** required to complete a game.

WAGNER, JOHN PETER "HONUS," "THE FLYING DUTCHMAN". B. 24 February 1874, Chartiers, Pennsylvania. D. 6 December 1955, Carnegie, Pennsylvania. Honus Wagner played for the **Louisville Colonels** of the **National League (NL)** from 1897 to 1899. When Louisville was dropped from the NL for the 1900 season, owner **Barney Dreyfuss**, who also owned a half interest in the **Pittsburgh Pirates**, had **Fred Clarke**, Louisville's **manager**, and several of the Colonels' best players, including Wagner and **Rube Waddell**, transferred to Pittsburgh. Wagner had played **first base**, **third base**, and left field with the Colonels, and in his first year in Pittsburgh before being installed as the permanent **shortstop**. He remained with the Pirates through the 1917 season, earning recognition as the greatest NL player of the **Deadball Era** and the greatest shortstop ever. Wagner, a barrel-chested, 5-foot, 11-inch, 200-pound right-handed hitter, led the league in batting eight times, a NL record later tied by **Tony Gwynn**. Wagner also led the NL in **slugging percentage** and **total bases** six times, **on-base percentage** four times, **stolen bases** five times, **runs batted in** five times, **triples** three times, **extra-base hits** and **doubles** seven times, and **hits** and **runs** scored twice.

Wagner played in two **World Series**, against the Boston Americans in 1903, in the first ever modern Series, and against the **Detroit Tigers** in 1909. He batted just .222 in the loss to Boston, but he redeemed himself in the 1909 win against Detroit. He batted .333, with six stolen bases, while completely outshining Tigers star **Ty Cobb**, the best player in the **American League**. Wagner batted .300 or better for 15 consecutive seasons, from 1899 to 1913. After four sub-.300 years, he retired following the 1917 season, at the age of 43. His lifetime **batting average** was .328, with 3,420 hits, seventh all-time. He had 1,739 runs scored, 1,733 runs driven in, 643 doubles (9th all-time), 252 triples (third all-time), and 723 stolen bases (10th all-time). In 1936, Wagner, Cobb, **Walter Johnson**, **Christy Mathewson**, and **Babe Ruth** were the first members elected by the **Baseball Writers' Association of America** to the new **National Baseball Hall of Fame**.

WALKER, MOSES FLEETWOOD "FLEET". B. 7 October 1856, Mount Pleasant, Ohio. D. 11 May 1924, Cleveland, Ohio. Fleet Walker was long thought to be the first **African American** to play in the **major leagues**; however, recent research by the **Society for American Baseball Research** suggests that William Edward White, who played in one game for the 1879 **Providence Grays** of the **National League**, may actually have been the first

African American to play in a big-league game. Walker, a 159-pound right-handed-hitting **catcher**, batted .263 in 42 games for the 1884 **Toledo Blue Stockings** of the **American Association**, Walker's only big-league season, as a cabal of other owners and players demanded that he and his brother, Weldy Walker, be removed from the league. No African Americans played Major League Baseball again until **Jackie Robinson** joined the **Brooklyn Dodgers** in 1947.

WALKS. *See* BASES ON BALLS (BB).

WALLACE, RHODERICK JOHN "BOBBY". B. 4 November 1873, Pittsburgh, Pennsylvania. D. 3 November 1960, Torrance, California. During the course of his 25-year **major-league** career, Bobby Wallace played in the **National League** for the **Cleveland Spiders** (1894–1898) and **St. Louis Cardinals** (1899–1901, 1917–1918), and most famously in the **American League (AL)** for the **St. Louis Browns** (1902–1916). The Spiders used the 5-foot, 8-inch, 170-pound Wallace, who batted and threw right-handed, as a **pitcher** in his first three seasons. He won 24 games and lost 22, but he blossomed after being moved to **third base** in 1897, reaching career highs in **batting average** (.335) and **runs batted in** (112). Wallace was assigned to St. Louis (called the Perfectos) in 1899 and converted to **shortstop**, a position he mostly played for the rest of his career. He jumped to the Browns in 1902, where he was the best shortstop in the AL during the early 20th century, leading in **fielding percentage** four times and **assists** three times. Wallace, who batted .268 in his career, was an unsuccessful **manager** for a season and a half with the 1911 and 1912 Browns, and in 25 games with the 1937 **Cincinnati Reds**. In 1953, the **Veterans Committee** elected him to the **National Baseball Hall of Fame.**

WALSH, EDWARD AUGUSTINE "ED". B. 14 May 1881, Plains, Pennsylvania. D. 26 May 1959, Pompano Beach, Florida. Ed Walsh was a right-handed **pitcher** for the **Chicago White Sox** from 1904 to 1916, plus four games with the 1917 **Boston Braves**. In 1908, the 6-foot, 1-inch, 193-pound Walsh had one of the greatest seasons ever by a pitcher. He led the **American League (AL)** in **wins** (40), **winning percentage** (.727), **complete games** (42), and **strikeouts** (269). His 464 **innings pitched** remains the AL record. In the seven seasons between 1906 and 1912, Walsh led the AL in **earned run average (ERA)** and complete games twice, **shutouts** three times, and innings pitched four times. He was 2–0, with a 0.60 ERA, in the White Sox's 1906 **World Series** win over the **Chicago Cubs**. A sprained arm suffered at **spring training** in 1913 ended Walsh's effectiveness. During his final five seasons, he won only 13 games. Walsh, whose best pitch was a

spitball, had a career record of 195–126, and his career ERA of 1.82 is the lowest ever in the **major leagues**. He was elected to the **National Baseball Hall of Fame** by the **Old Timers Committee** in 1946.

WANER, LLOYD JAMES "LITTLE POISON". B. 16 March 1906, Harrah, Oklahoma. D. 22 July 1982, Oklahoma City, Oklahoma. Lloyd Waner joined his brother **Paul Waner** as a member of the **Pittsburgh Pirates** in 1927. Lloyd, a left-handed-hitting center fielder, batted .355 as a **rookie**, while leading the league with 133 **runs** scored. He batted .400 in the **World Series**, but the Pirates were swept by the **New York Yankees**. Slightly taller than his brother, Lloyd was 5 feet, nine inches tall, but he weighed only 150 pounds. While a speedier **base runner**, he was not as good a hitter as Paul; nevertheless, he exceeded the 200-**hit** mark four times, including his first three seasons, and batted better than .300 nine times. After leaving the Pirates in 1941, Waner played for the **Boston Braves**, **Cincinnati Reds**, **Philadelphia Phillies**, and **Brooklyn Dodgers** before ending his career with the Pirates in 1944 and 1945. Lloyd Waner led the **National League** in **singles** four times, fewest **strikeouts** per **at-bat** five times, and **putouts** by an **outfielder** four times. He had a lifetime **batting average** of .316, with 2,459 hits. In 1967, the **Veterans Committee** elected Waner to the **National Baseball Hall of Fame**.

WANER, PAUL GLEE "BIG POISON". B. 16 April 1903, Harrah, Oklahoma. D. 29 August 1965, Sarasota, Florida. Paul Waner, a left-handed-hitting right fielder, was among the **National League's (NL)** most consistent hitters while playing for the **Pittsburgh Pirates** from 1926 through 1940. Primarily a **singles** hitter, the 5-foot, 8-inch, 153-pound Waner batted .300 or better 13 times, including his first 12 seasons. He had 200 **hits** or more eight times and won three batting championships. He later played for the **Brooklyn Dodgers** (1941, 1943–1944), the **Boston Braves** (1941–1942), and briefly for the **New York Yankees** in 1944 and 1945. Waner's best season was with the Pirates' pennant winners of 1927, the year in which his brother, **Lloyd Waner**, joined the team as its center fielder. Paul Waner led the NL that season with a .380 **batting average**, 237 hits, 131 **runs batted in**, 342 **total bases**, and 18 **triples**, and he won the **Most Valuable Player Award**. He batted .333 in the **World Series**, but the Pirates were swept by the Yankees. Waner finished his 20-year career with a .333 batting average, 3,152 hits, 605 **doubles**, 191 triples, 1,627 **runs**, and an **on-base percentage** of .404. He was elected to the **National Baseball Hall of Fame** by the **Baseball Writers' Association of America** in 1952.

WARD, JOHN MONTGOMERY "MONTE". B. 3 March 1860, Belle-fonte, Pennsylvania. D. 4 March 1925, Augusta, Georgia. Monte Ward was a **pitcher** for his first seven **major-league** seasons and a **shortstop** for his final 10. Ward spent his entire career (1878–1894) in the **National League (NL),** except for 1890, when he joined the **Players' League (PL),** a league created at his urging. The 5-foot, 9-inch, 165-pound Ward, who threw right-handed and batted left-handed, pitched for the **Providence Grays** from 1878 to 1882, and for the New York Gothams in 1883 and 1884. Ward won 22 games and led the NL with a 1.51 **earned run average (ERA)** as a **rookie.** The following year, 1879, he had his best season as a pitcher. Ward led the league in **wins** (47), **winning percentage** (.712), and **strikeouts** (239) to lead the Grays to the pennant. In 1880, he won 39 games and led the league with eight **shutouts.** Ward joined the Gothams in 1883 (renamed the **New York Giants** in 1885), but, after two seasons, a nagging sore arm caused him to evolve into a full-time shortstop. Ward's career record as a pitcher was 164–103, with a 2.10 ERA. On 17 June 1880, he pitched the major leagues' second **perfect game.** Ward played for the Giants through 1889, but he left to become the **player-manager** of the **Brooklyn Wonders** of the PL in 1890.

The PL was an outgrowth of the Brotherhood of Professional Base-Ball Players, baseball's first players' union. Led by Ward, who had a law degree, the brotherhood objected to the ownership's establishment of a **reserve clause** and a fixed salary structure. Unable to get these strictures changed, Ward led many of the NL's best players out of the league and into the PL. The league folded after one season, and Ward returned to the NL as a player-manager for the Brooklyn Bridegrooms in 1891 and 1892, and for the Giants in 1893 and 1894. In 1894, the second-place Giants defeated the first-place **Baltimore Orioles,** four games to none, to win the **Temple Cup.** Ward had a .275 career **batting average,** led his league's shortstops in **putouts** four times, and had a 412–320 record as a **manager.** In 1964, the **Veterans Committee** elected him to the **National Baseball Hall of Fame** as a player.

WASHINGTON BLUE LEGS. The Washington Blue Legs were members of the National Association for one season, 1873. They played 39 games and lost 31.

WASHINGTON NATIONALS (AA). The Washington Nationals were a team in the **American Association** for the first part of the 1884 season. The club had a 12–51 record when they disbanded on 3 August and were replaced by the **Richmond Virginias.**

WASHINGTON NATIONALS (NA). In 1872, the Washington Nationals played 11 games in the National Association (NA), lost all 11, and folded. In 1875, the NA's final season, another club called the Washington Nationals lost 23 of the 28 games they played.

WASHINGTON NATIONALS (NL) 1886–1889. The Washington Nationals, also called the Senators, were a team in the **National League** from 1886 to 1889. The Nationals finished seventh once and eighth three times in the eight-team league. After the 1889 season, the league's owners expelled the franchise and replaced it with the **Cincinnati Reds**. Notable players for the 1886, 1887, 1888, and 1889 Nationals included **Paul Hines**, Dummy Hoy, **Connie Mack**, and Jim Whitney.

WASHINGTON NATIONALS (NL) 2005–. The Washington Nationals are a team in the Eastern Division of the **National League**. The Nationals came into existence in 2005, as a result of the relocation of the **Montreal Expos** to Washington, D.C. The team played its home games at **Robert F. Kennedy Stadium** from 2005 through 2007, before moving to the new **Nationals Park** in 2008. The Nationals had their first winning season in 2012, but the team lost to the **St. Louis Cardinals** in the **National League Division Series (NLDS).**

The Washington Nationals have had no winners of the **Most Valuable Player Award** or **Cy Young Award**. Bryce Harper (2012) is their only **Rookie of the Year Award** winner. No Nationals player has led the league in **batting average**, **home runs**, or **runs batted in**. Gio Gonzalez (2012) is the only Nationals **pitcher** to lead the league in **wins**. No Nationals pitcher has led the league in **earned run average** or **strikeouts**.

The Nationals' most notable players and **managers** include Matt Capps, Tyler Clippard, Chad Cordero, Ian Desmond, Adam Dunn, Christian Guzman, Livan Hernandez, Edwin Jackson, Davey Johnson, Nick Johnson, John Lannan, Adam LaRoche, Michael Morse, **Ivan Rodriguez**, Alfonso Soriano, Drew Storen, Stephen Strasburg, Jayson Werth, Jordan Zimmerman, and Ryan Zimmerman.

WASHINGTON NATIONALS (UA). The Washington Nationals were a team in the **Union Association (UA)** in 1884, the one year of the UA's existence. Washington finished with a 47–65 record.

WASHINGTON OLYMPICS. The Washington Olympics were charter members of the National Association (NA). They played in the NA in 1871 and 1872, and the team then disbanded after the 1872 season. Notable players for the Olympics included Doug Allison, Davy Force, and Andy Leonard.

WASHINGTON PARK. *See* BROOKLYN DODGERS.

WASHINGTON SENATORS (AL) 1901–1960. The Washington Senators were a team in the **American League (AL)** from 1901, the first year the AL was recognized as a **major league**, through 1960. Home games were played at American League Park (I) from 1901 to 1903, American League Park (II) from 1904 to 1910, and **Griffith Stadium** from 1911 to 1960. **Clark Griffith**, for whom the **stadium** was named, was the team's **manager** from 1912 to 1920, and its principal owner beginning in 1912 until his death in 1955.

The Senators, or Nationals as they were sometimes called, were usually a second-division team, and they won only three pennants in their 60 years of existence. They won their first pennant in 1924 and defeated the **New York Giants** in the **World Series** to win their only championship. They lost in the Series to the **Pittsburgh Pirates** in 1925, and to the Giants in 1933. Following the 1960 season, owner Calvin Griffith, Clark Griffith's nephew, moved the franchise to Minnesota, where they were renamed the **Minnesota Twins**.

Washington Senators who won the **Most Valuable Player Award** were **Walter Johnson** (1913, 1924) and Roger Peckinpaugh (1925). The Senators had no **Cy Young Award** winners. **Rookie of the Year** winners were Albie Pearson (1958) and Bob Allison (1959).

Senators players who led the league in **batting average** were **Goose Goslin** (1928), Buddy Myer (1935), and Mickey Vernon (1946, 1953). **Home run** leaders were Roy Sievers (1957) and **Harmon Killebrew** (1959). **Runs batted in** leaders were Goose Goslin (1924) and Roy Sievers (1957).

Senators **pitchers** who led the league in **wins** were Walter Johnson (1913–1916, 1918, 1924), Alvin Crowder (1932–1933), and Bob Porterfield (1953). **Earned run average (ERA)** leaders were Walter Johnson (1912–1913, 1918–1919, 1924), **Stan Coveleski** (1925), and Garland Braxton (1928). **Strikeouts** leaders were Walter Johnson (1910, 1912–1919, 1921, 1923–1924) and Bobo Newsom (1942). By leading the league in wins, ERA, and strikeouts in 1913, 1918, and 1924, Walter Johnson won the **Triple Crown** for pitchers in each of those three seasons.

Other notable players and **managers** for the Washington Senators included Ossie Bluege, George Case, **Joe Cronin**, **Ed Delahanty**, **Bucky Harris**, Sid Hudson, Tom Hughes, Joe Judge, Joe Kuhel, Emil "Dutch" Leonard,

Buddy Lewis, **Heinie Manush**, Firpo Marberry, Clyde Milan, Camilo Pascual, Case Patten, Pedro Ramos, **Sam Rice**, Jim Shaw, Stan Spence, John Stone, Cecil Travis, Monte Weaver, **Early Wynn**, and Eddie Yost.

WASHINGTON SENATORS (AL) 1961–1971. The Washington Senators entered the **American League (AL)** in 1961 as part of a two-team **expansion** that also added the Los Angeles Angels. The AL's first expansion of the 20th century raised the total number of teams in the league to 10; it had been eight since the AL achieved **major-league** status in 1901. The former Washington team in the AL, who were also called the Senators and had played in Washington from 1901 to 1960, was relocating to become the **Minnesota Twins** that same year, 1961.

The new Senators played their home games in **Griffith Stadium** in 1961, where the departing Senators had played since 1911. In 1962, they moved into the new D.C. Stadium, renamed **Robert F. Kennedy Stadium** (more commonly called RFK Stadium) in 1969. In 11 years of existence, the expansion Senators had only one winning season, in 1969, under **manager Ted Williams**. In 1972, the team was sold and left Washington to become the **Texas Rangers**.

No member of the Washington Senators won a **Most Valuable Player Award**, **Cy Young Award**, or **Rookie of the Year Award**. The Senators had no leaders in **batting average**, but Frank Howard was the **home run** leader in 1968 and 1970, and the **runs batted in** leader in 1970. No Senators **pitcher** led the league in **wins** or **strikeouts**, but Dick Donovan, in 1961, and Dick Bosman, in 1969, led in **earned run average**.

Other notable players and managers for the expansion Washington Senators included Eddie Brinkman, Paul Casanova, Joe Coleman, Casey Cox, Bennie Daniels, Mike Epstein, Chuck Hinton, Gil Hodges, Darold Knowles, Don Lock, Ken McMullen, Phil Ortega, Camilo Pascual, Pete Richert, Aurelio Rodriguez, Del Unser, and Mickey Vernon.

WASHINGTON SENATORS (NL). The Washington Senators, sometimes called the Nationals, were a team in the **National League (NL)** from 1892 to 1899. The team had played in the **American Association (AA)** as the **Washington Statesmen** in 1891. When the NL expanded from eight teams to 12 in 1892, they added four teams from the AA, including Washington. The Statesmen were a last-place team in the AA in 1891, and they were mostly at or near the bottom of the NL during their eight-year existence as the Senators. When the NL went back to eight teams in 1900, the Washington franchise was one of the four eliminated. Despite their lowly finishes, the Senators had many outstanding players. Among them were Tom Brown, Gene

DeMontreville, Duke Farrell, Buck Freeman, Dummy Hoy, Bill Joyce, Frank Killen, Deacon McGuire, Win Mercer, **Jim O'Rourke**, Kip Selbach, and Tommy Tucker.

WASHINGTON STATESMEN. The Washington Statesmen were a team in the **American Association (AA)** in 1891. Despite their last-place finish, when the AA disbanded after the season, Washington was one of four AA teams added to the **National League** for the 1892 season, where they were renamed the **Washington Senators**.

WEAVER, EARL SIDNEY. B. 14 August 1930, St. Louis, Missouri. Earl Weaver spent 14 years as a player and 11 years a **manager** in the minor **leagues**. In mid-1968, the **Baltimore Orioles** chose Weaver to succeed Hank Bauer as their manager. Weaver remained with the Orioles through the 1982 season and then returned in mid-1985, but he stayed only through 1986. His career record as a big-league manager was 1,480–1,060. Weaver won consecutive **American League** pennants in 1969, 1970, and 1971, and again in 1979. His 1970 team defeated the **Cincinnati Reds** in the **World Series**. Weaver's Orioles suffered World Series losses to the **New York Mets** in 1969 and the **Pittsburgh Pirates** in 1971 and 1979. The *Sporting News* gave Weaver its **Manager of the Year Award** twice, in 1977 and 1979. The **Veterans Committee** elected him to the **National Baseball Hall of Fame** in 1996.

WEEGHMAN PARK. *See* WRIGLEY FIELD.

WEISS, GEORGE MARTIN. B. 23 June 1895, New Haven, Connecticut. D. 13 August 1973, Greenwich, Connecticut. George Weiss was the director of **minor-league** teams for the **New York Yankees** from 1932 to 1947. During that time, the Yankees won nine **American League (AL)** pennants and eight **World Series**. He was promoted to **general manager** in 1948, holding that position through 1960. In his 13-year tenure as general manager, the Yankees won 10 more AL pennants and seven more World Series. Weiss was a four-time winner of the *Sporting News*'s Major League Executive of the Year Award (1950–1952, 1960). After he was let go by the Yankees, Weiss served as president and general manager of the **New York Mets** from the time of their creation in 1961 to 1966, and as an advisor until 1971. He was elected to the **National Baseball Hall of Fame** by the **Veterans Committee** in 1971.

WELCH, MICHAEL FRANCIS "MICKEY". B. Michael Walsh, 4 July 1859, Brooklyn, New York. D. 30 July 1941, Concord, New Hampshire. Mickey Welch used a **curveball** and **screwball** to win 307 games in the **National League** from 1880 to 1892. The 5-foot, 8-inch, 160-pound right-hander was 34–30, with 574 **innings pitched**, in his **rookie** season with the **Troy Trojans**. When the Trojans disbanded after the 1882 season, Welch moved to the New York Gothams, who, in 1885, changed their name to the **New York Giants**. Welch won 44 games and lost 11 in 1885, for a league-leading **winning percentage** of .800. He also had a 39-win season in 1884 and a 33-win season in 1886. His career record was 307–210, with a 2.71 **earned run average** and 41 **shutouts**. Welch, the third **pitcher** to reach 300 **wins**, was elected to the **National Baseball Hall of Fame** by the **Veterans Committee** in 1973.

WELLS, WILLIE JAMES. B. 10 August 1908, Austin, Texas. D. 22 January 1989, Austin, Texas. Willie Wells played **shortstop** in the **Negro Leagues** from 1924 to 1948. Wells played for the **St. Louis Stars, Chicago American Giants, Newark Eagles**, and several other teams. An outstanding defensive player with great speed, the 5-foot, 9-inch, 170-pound right-handed **batter** had a consistently high **batting average**. Wells, who is considered second only to **John Henry Lloyd** among Negro League shortstops, played for years in **Mexico** and the Cuban League, where he won two **Most Valuable Player Awards**. In 1997, a special **Negro Leagues Committee** elected Wells to the **National Baseball Hall of Fame**.

See also AFRICAN AMERICANS IN BASEBALL.

WEST SIDE PARK. *See* CHICAGO CUBS.

WHEAT, ZACHARIAH DAVIS "ZACK". B. 23 May 1888, Hamilton, Missouri. D. 11 March 1972, Sedalia, Missouri. More than 85 years after he played his last game for the **Brooklyn Dodgers**, Zach Wheat still holds the Brooklyn/Los Angeles franchise record for most **games played, at-bats, hits, doubles, triples**, and **total bases**. Wheat, a left fielder, played for the Dodgers from 1909 through 1926. The team was also called the Brooklyn Superbas and Brooklyn Robins during his time there. He played a final season, 1927, with the **Philadelphia Athletics**.

A 5-foot, 10-inch, 170-pound left-handed line-drive hitter, Wheat batted .300 or better 13 times, and he had more than 200 hits three times. He led the **National League** in **slugging percentage** and total bases for Brooklyn's 1916 pennant winners. Wheat was also the club's leading hitter when they won again in 1920. Brooklyn lost in the **World Series** both times, to the

Boston Red Sox in 1916, and to the Cleveland Indians in 1920. Wheat finished his career with a .317 batting average and 2,884 hits. In 1959, the Veterans Committee elected him to the National Baseball Hall of Fame.

WHEATON, WILLIAM RUFUS. B. 7 May 1814, New York, New York. D. 11 September 1888, San Francisco, California. William Wheaton wrote the first set of baseball rules for the Gotham Baseball Club of New York City in 1837. Eight years later, in 1845, he was on the Committee on By-laws for the Knickerbocker Base Ball Club, of which he was a founding member.

WHITE, JAMES LAURIE "DEACON". B. 7 December 1847, Caton, New York. D. 7 July 1939, Aurora, Illinois. Deacon White played in three different major leagues between 1871 and 1890, including the National Association (NA) from 1871 to 1875, the National League (NL) from 1876 to 1889, and the Players' League (PL) in 1890. The 5-foot, 11-inch, 175-pound left-handed hitter was primarily a catcher during the early part of his career, and a third baseman in the latter part. On 4 May 1871, White, playing for the Cleveland Forest Citys, was the first-ever batter in a major-league game. His double off Bobby Mathews of the Fort Wayne Kekiongas was Major League Baseball's first hit. White was with Cleveland again in 1872, and he was then with the Boston Red Stockings from 1873 to 1875. He joined the Chicago White Stockings of the NL in 1876, the NL's first year of existence. White later played for the Boston Red Stockings team in the NL and four subsequent NL teams, including the Cincinnati Reds, Buffalo Bisons, Detroit Wolverines, and Pittsburgh Alleghenys. He spent his final season, 1890, with the Buffalo Bisons of the PL. White played on six pennant-winning teams during his 20 seasons. He won batting championships in both the NA (.367 in 1875) and NL (.387 in 1877), and he had a career batting average of .312.

WHITE, KING SOLOMON "SOL". B. 12 June 1868, Bellaire, Ohio. D. 26 August 1955, Central Islip, New York. Sol White was one of the pioneers of black baseball as a player, a manager, and an executive for teams in the Negro Leagues from 1887 to 1926. The 5-foot, 9-inch, 170-pound White, a right-handed-hitting infielder, also played five seasons with teams in integrated minor leagues. In 1907, he authored *Sol White's Official Base Ball Guide*, a critical piece of African American baseball history, and he later spent many years as a sportswriter. In 2006, White was elected to the National Baseball Hall of Fame in a special election conducted by the Committee on African American Baseball.

See also AFRICAN AMERICANS IN BASEBALL.

WILD CARD. In 1994, the two **major leagues** changed from two divisions to three. Under the new format, in addition to the three division champions in each league, the second-place finisher with the best record would also make the playoffs. In the best-of-five first round of both the **American League Division Series** and **National League Division Series**, the wild-card winner played the team with the best record in the league, providing that the team came from another division. If the team with the best record in the league came from the same division as the wild-card team, the wild-card team would play the division winner with the second-best record. Because of the players' strike in 1994, the wild-card format did not go into effect until 1995. Beginning with the 2012 season, the wild-card team was the winner of a "play-in" game between the two non-division winners with the best record.

WILD PITCH (WP). The **official scorer** will charge the **pitcher** with a wild pitch (WP) when he delivers a pitch too high, too low, or too wide of **home plate** for the **catcher** to handle it with ordinary effort. A WP may only be scored if one or more **base runners** advance. The WP was added as a statistical category in 1883. It was scored as an **error** for the pitcher until 1889. The WP is part of the calculation used for measuring **earned runs**.

The **major league** single-season leader in throwing WPs prior to 1893, when the pitching distance was extended to its current 60 feet, 6 inches, is Mark Baldwin of the 1889 **Columbus Solons** of the **American Association**, with 83. The single-season leader after the change in the pitching distance is Leon "Red" Ames of the 1905 **New York Giants**, with 30. The single-season leader in the **American League** is Juan Guzman of the 1993 **Toronto Blue Jays**, with 26.

The career leader is Tony Mullane, who spent the majority of his career in the pre-1893 era. Mullane, who threw 343 WPs, pitched in the **National League** and American Associaton from 1881 through 1894, except for 1885. The post-1893 career leader is **Nolan Ryan**, with 277. Ryan pitched for the **New York Mets** (1966, 1968–1971), California Angels (1972–1979), **Houston Astros** (1980–1988), and **Texas Rangers** (1989–1993).

WILHELM, JAMES HOYT. B. 26 July 1922, Huntersville, North Carolina. D. 23 August 2002, Sarasota, Florida. World War II veteran Hoyt Wilhelm made his **major-league** debut with the 1952 **New York Giants** at the advanced age of 29. Appearing in a league-leading 71 games, all in relief, he had a 15–3 record and topped the **National League (NL)** with a 2.43 **earned run average (ERA)** and an .833 **winning percentage**. Wilhelm was the first **rookie** to lead the NL in both ERA and winning percentage. He also hit a **home run** in his first **at-bat**, the only home run in his 21-year career. Wilhelm finished second in the voting for **Rookie of the Year** and fourth in the

Most Valuable Player Award race. Primarily a relief pitcher, Wilhelm pitched in 1,070 games, a record at the time, and only 52 were as a starter. An extremely effective knuckleball allowed the 6-foot, 190-pound right-hander to continue pitching until the age of 49.

In addition to the Giants (1952–1956), Wilhelm pitched for the St. Louis Cardinals (1957), Cleveland Indians (1957–1958), Baltimore Orioles (1958–1962), Chicago White Sox (1963–1968), California Angels (1969), Atlanta Braves (1969–1971), and Los Angeles Dodgers (1971–1972). In each of his final eight seasons, he was the oldest player in his league. Wilhelm made 43 of his 52 career starts under manager Paul Richards at Baltimore. In 1958, he pitched a no-hitter against the New York Yankees, and, in 1959, he won 15 games and led the American League with a 2.19 ERA. He had a career record of 143–122, a 2.52 ERA, and 227 retroactively computed saves. In 1985, the Baseball Writers' Association of America chose Wilhelm as the first relief pitcher to be enshrined in the National Baseball Hall of Fame.

WILKINSON, J. LESLIE "J. L". B. 14 May 1878, Algona, Iowa. D. 21 August 1964, Kansas City, Missouri. J. L. Wilkinson was the owner of the Kansas City Monarchs from 1920 to 1948. The Monarchs, who produced more stars than any other team in the Negro Leagues, played in both the Negro National League and Negro American League. Wilkinson is sometimes credited with introducing the lighting systems that made night games possible in baseball. In 2006, Wilkinson was elected to the National Baseball Hall of Fame in a special election conducted by the Committee on African American Baseball.

See also AFRICAN AMERICANS IN BASEBALL.

WILLIAMS, BILLY LEO. B. 15 June 1938, Whistler, Alabama. Left fielder Billy Williams played for the Chicago Cubs from 1959 to 1974. In 1961, his first full season, he was the National League (NL) Rookie of the Year. Williams, who was 6 feet, 1 inch tall and 175 pounds, with a picture-perfect left-handed swing, had 14 seasons with 20 or more home runs, five seasons with 100 or more runs scored, and three seasons with 200 or more hits. His top home run season was 1970, when he hit 42. Williams was named the Major League Player of the Year in 1972, after leading the NL with a .333 batting average, a .606 slugging average, and 348 total bases. It was the third time he had led the league in total bases. Williams led the NL in games played five times, while compiling a streak of 1,117 consecutive games played, a league record that has since been broken. He finished his career with the 1975 and 1976 Oakland Athletics. Williams had a lifetime batting average of .290, with 2,711 hits, 426 home runs, and 1,475 **runs batted in**. The **Baseball Writers' Association of America** elected him to the **National Baseball Hall of Fame** in 1987.

WILLIAMS, JOSEPH "JOE," "SMOKEY JOE". B. 6 April 1885, Seguin, Texas. D. 25 February 1951, New York, New York. Joe Williams was the best **pitcher** in the **Negro Leagues** during the early years of the 20th century. According to several Negro Leagues historians, the 6-foot, 4-inch, 200-pound right-hander, with his legendary **fastball**, was an even better pitcher than **Satchel Paige**. Williams's best seasons were with the New York Lincoln Giants (1911–1923) and **Homestead Grays** (1925–1932). In 1999, a special **Negro Leagues Committee** elected him to the **National Baseball Hall of Fame**.

See also AFRICAN AMERICANS IN BASEBALL.

WILLIAMS, RICHARD HIRSCHFELD "DICK". B. 7 May 1929, St. Louis, Missouri. D. 7 July 2011, Las Vegas, Nevada. Dick Williams played **first base**, **third base**, and the **outfield** for 13 **major-league** seasons. Williams was a 6-foot, 190-pound right-handed **batter** who played in the **National League (NL)** for the **Brooklyn Dodgers** (1951–1954, 1956), and in the **American League (AL)** for the **Baltimore Orioles** (1956–1958, 1961–1962), **Cleveland Indians** (1957), **Kansas City Athletics** (1959–1960), and **Boston Red Sox** (1963–1964). He had a career **batting average** of .260 in 1,023 games. Williams then went on to be a major-league **manager** for 21 seasons. In the AL, he managed the Red Sox (1967–1969), **Oakland Athletics** (1971–1973), California Angels (1974–1976), and **Seattle Mariners** (1986–1988), and, in the NL, he managed the **Montreal Expos** (1977–1981) and **San Diego Padres** (1982–1985). His teams won four pennants: Boston in 1967, Oakland in 1972 and 1973, and San Diego in 1984. His Oakland teams defeated the **Cincinnati Reds** (1972) and **New York Mets** (1973) in the **World Series**. Williams, to whom the *Sporting News* gave its **Manager of the Year Award** in 1967, had a 1,571–1,451 career record. He was elected to the **National Baseball Hall of Fame** by the **Veterans Committee** as a manager in 2008.

WILLIAMS, THEODORE SAMUEL "TED". B. 30 August 1918, San Diego, California. D. 5 July 2002, Inverness, Florida. Ted Williams is recognized as baseball's best pure hitter. Blessed with exceptional vision, he had a career **on-base percentage (OBP)** of .482, the highest of any major leaguer. Williams played for the **Boston Red Sox** from 1939 to 1960, but he lost close to five seasons serving as a U.S. Marine fighter pilot during World War II and the Korean War. Williams, who stood 6 feet, 3 inches tall and weighed

205 pounds, played right field as a **rookie** in 1939, but left field for the rest of his career. He batted .327 as a rookie, with 31 **home runs**, while leading the **American League (AL)** with 145 **runs batted in (RBI)** and 344 **total bases**. He followed with a .344 **batting average** in 1940, and he led the league in **runs** and OBP. In 1941, the left-handed-hitting Williams batted .406; he is the last **major-league** player to top the .400 mark. He repeated as batting champion in 1942, and also led the league in home runs and RBI, to earn the **Triple Crown**.

Williams missed the next three seasons while he was in the military, but he returned to bat .342 in 1946 and win another Triple Crown in 1947. Oddly, Williams finished second in the **Most Valuable Player (MVP) Award** voting in both of his Triple Crown years, but he was chosen as the MVP in 1946 and 1949. In all, he finished in the top four in the MVP voting in nine different seasons. He was the *Sporting News*'s choice as the **Major League Player of the Year** five times, in 1941, 1942, 1947, 1949, and 1957. Williams batted just .200 in his one **World Series**, a 1946 loss to the **St. Louis Cardinals**. An **All-Star** 17 times, his two-out game-winning home run in the 1941 All-Star Game was the most dramatic hit in All-Star history. In the 1946 game, he went 4-for-4 and hit two more home runs.

Williams led AL **outfielders** in **games played** four times, but he was mostly an indifferent **fielder**. As a hitter, however, he led the AL in numerous categories numerous times, including batting average (6), runs (6), home runs (4), RBI (4), total bases (6), **extra-base hits** (5), walks (8), OBP (12), and **slugging percentage** (9). Williams had a lifetime batting average of .344 (tied for seventh best with **Billy Hamilton**), 2,654 **hits**, 521 home runs (which trailed only **Babe Ruth** and **Jimmie Foxx** when he retired), and a slugging percentage of .634 (second only to Ruth). He later managed the **Washington Senators** from 1969 to 1971, and he continued to manage the club in 1972, when they became the **Texas Rangers**. His record for the four seasons was 273–364. In 1966, Williams was elected by the **Baseball Writers' Association of America** to the **National Baseball Hall of Fame**.

WILLIS, VICTOR GAZAWAY "VIC". B. 12 April 1876, Cecil County, Maryland. D. 3 August 1947, Elkton, Maryland. Right-handed **pitcher** Vic Willis won 25 games as a **rookie** for the 1898 Boston Beaneaters. The next year, he won 27 and led the **National League (NL)** with a 2.50 **earned run average (ERA)** and five **shutouts**. His 45 **complete games** in 1902 are the most in the NL since 1900. The 6-foot, 2-inch, 185-pound Willis had two more 20-win seasons before Boston traded him to the **Pittsburgh Pirates** in December 1905. After having led the NL in losses with the Beaneaters in 1904 and 1905, Willis was a 20-game winner in each of his four seasons in Pittsburgh. He was 0–1 gainst the **Detroit Tigers** in the 1909 **World Series**, won by Pittsburgh. Willis pitched a final season in 1910 for the **St. Louis**

Figure 23.1.   Ted Williams exhibiting one of baseball's classic swings. *National Baseball Hall of Fame Library, Cooperstown, N.Y.*

Cardinals, who had purchased him in February of that year. Willis had a career record of 249–205, with a 2.63 ERA and 50 shutouts. In 1995, the **Veterans Committee** elected him to the **National Baseball Hall of Fame**.

WILMINGTON (DELAWARE) QUICKSTEPS. The Wilmington Quicksteps were a team in the **Union Association (UA)** in 1884, the one year of the UA's existence. They joined the league on 18 August as a replacement for the **Philadelphia Keystones**, but, after winning only two of their 18 games, they were replaced in September by the **Milwaukee Grays**.

WILSON, ERNEST JUDSON "JUD". B. 28 February 1897, Remington, Virginia. D. 24 June 1963, Washington, D.C. Jud Wilson was a **first baseman**, **third baseman**, and **manager** in the **Negro Leagues** from 1922 to 1945. He served primarily with the Baltimore Black Sox of the **Eastern Colored League** and **Philadelphia Stars** and **Homestead Grays** of the **Negro National League**. A left-handed **batter** who consistently hit for a high average, the 5-foot, 8-inch, 195-pound Wilson also played for several years in the Cuban Winter League. In 2006, Wilson was elected to the **National Baseball Hall of Fame** in a special election conducted by the **Committee on African American Baseball**.

See also AFRICAN AMERICANS IN BASEBALL.

WILSON, LEWIS ROBERT "HACK". B. 26 April 1900, Ellwood City, Pennsylvania. D. 23 November 1948, Baltimore, Maryland. Hack Wilson was a slugging center fielder for the **Chicago Cubs** from 1926 to 1931. Before his years in Chicago, Wilson played for the **New York Giants** (1923–1925); after leaving the Cubs, he played for the **Brooklyn Dodgers** (1932–1934) and **Philadelphia Phillies** (1934). As a member of the Cubs, the 5-foot, 6-inch, 190-pound right-handed **batter** led the **National League (NL)** in **home runs** four times, including hitting 56 in 1930, a NL record. That record stood until **Mark McGwire** of the **St. Louis Cardinals** broke it in 1998. Wilson led the NL in **runs batted in (RBI)** twice and had 100 or more RBI in six seasons, and his 191 RBI in 1930 remains the **major-league** record. He also led the league in **strikeouts** five times. In his 12-season career, Wilson had a .307 **batting average**, with 244 home runs. In 1979, the **Veterans Committee** elected him to the **National Baseball Hall of Fame**.

WINFIELD, DAVID MARK "DAVE". B. 3 October 1951, Saint Paul, Minnesota. Dave Winfield, who stood at 6 feet, 6 inches and weighed 220 pounds, went directly from the University of Minnesota to the **major leagues**, where he played for six teams during the span of 22 seasons (1973–1995). (Winfield spent the 1989 season on the **disabled list**.) The right-handed-hitting **outfielder** was the fourth overall pick of the **San Diego Padres** in the 1973 **Amateur Draft**. He played eight seasons for the Padres and led the **National League** in **runs batted in (RBI)** and **total bases** in 1979. In 1981, Winfield signed as a **free agent** with the **New York Yankees**, where he had 100 or more RBI for five consecutive seasons (1982–1986) and batted a career-high .340 in 1984. His eight and a half tumultous years in New York, marked by feuds with Yankees' owner **George Steinbrenner**, ended in May 1990, when he was traded to the California Angels. Steinbrenner had openly criticized Winfield for his .045 **batting average** in the Yankees' 1981 **World Series** loss to the **Los Angeles Dodgers**.

Winfield later signed as a free agent with three more **American League** clubs, including the **Toronto Blue Jays** in 1992, the **Minnesota Twins** in 1993, and the **Cleveland Indians** in 1995. Winfield was a 12-time **All-Star** and the winner of six **Silver Slugger Awards** and seven **Gold Glove Awards**. As a member of the Blue Jays, he won the **Babe Ruth Award** as the **Most Valuable Player** of the 1992 World Series; he also won the **Roberto Clemente Award** that same year. Winfield is a member of the 3,000-**hit** club, finishing with a total of 3,110. He had a .283 career **batting average**, with 465 **home runs** and 1,833 RBI. In 2001, he was elected by the **Baseball Writers' Association of America** to the **National Baseball Hall of Fame**.

WINNING PERCENTAGE. Winning percentage (or win-loss percentage) can refer to a team or a **pitcher**. Winning percentage for a team is defined as the number of its **wins** divided by the number of its wins plus the number of its losses. Example: A team with 87 wins and 75 losses has a winning percentage of .537.

Winning percentage for a pitcher is defined as the number of his wins> divided by the number of his wins plus the number of his losses. Example: A pitcher with 17 wins and 10 losses has a win-loss percentage of .630.

The **major league** single-season leader in winning percentage among pitchers with at least 15 decisions is Roy Face of the 1959 **Pittsburgh Pirates**, at .947 (18–1). The single-season leader in the **American League** is Johnny Allen of the 1937 **Cleveland Indians**, at .938 (15–1).

The career leader in winning percentage among pitchers with at least 100 decisions is **Al Spalding**, at .795. Spalding pitched for the **Boston Red Stockings** of the National Association (1871–1875) and the Chicago White Stockings of the **National League** (1876–1877). The career leader post-1893, when the pitching distance was extended to its current 60 feet, 6 inches, is Spud Chandler, at .717. Chandler pitched for the **New York Yankees** from 1937 to 1947.

WINNING PITCHER (WP). For each game, the **official scorer** will award a **win** to one **pitcher** on the winning team. Only one pitcher for each game can receive a win. The winning pitcher (WP) is defined as the pitcher who last pitched prior to the half **inning** when the winning team took the lead for the last time. There are two exceptions to this rule. The more common exception is that a starting pitcher must complete five innings to earn a win (four innings for a game that lasted five innings on defense). If the starting pitcher fails to meet the innings requirement, the official scorer awards the win to the relief pitcher, who, in his judgment, was the most effective. The second exception applies only to a relief pitcher who makes a "brief appearance" and is himself later relieved. If in the official scorer's judgment the relief pitcher was "ineffective," the win is awarded to the succeeding relief pitcher, who, in the official scorer's judgment, was most effective. A win will not be awarded to a pitcher when a team wins by **forfeit**.

WINS (BY PITCHER). In the early days of Major League Baseball, teams carried few **pitchers**, and the vast majority of wins were awarded to one pitcher. Thus, the **major league** all-time single-season leader in games won is **Charlie Radbourn** of the 1884 **Providence Grays** of the **National League**, with 59.

The single-season leader post-1893, when the pitching distance was extended to its current 60 feet, 6 inches, is **Jack Chesbro** of the 1904 **New York Yankees**, with 41. The post-1893 single-season leader in the NL is **Christy Mathewson** of the 1908 **New York Giants**, with 37.

The career leader is **Cy Young**, with 511. Young pitched for the **Cleveland Spiders** of the **National League (NL)** (1890–1898), the **St. Louis Cardinals** (1899–1900) (they were the Perfectos in 1899), the Boston Americans (later the **Boston Red Sox**) of the **American League (AL)** (1901–1908), the Cleveland Naps of the AL (1909–1911), and the Boston Rustlers of the NL (1911).

See also WINNING PITCHER (WP).

WINS ABOVE REPLACEMENT (WAR). Wins above replacement (WAR) is a relatively recent analytical tool used to measure a player's value. It is a single number calculated to represent the number of wins the player added to the team above what an average or replacement player would add.

The **major league** single-season leader in WAR among position players is **Babe Ruth** of the 1923 **New York Yankees**, with 13.7. The **National League (NL)** single-season leader is **Rogers Hornsby** of the 1924 **St. Louis Cardinals**, with 12.0. Babe Ruth is also the career leader, with 159.2. Ruth played for the **Boston Red Sox** (1914–1919), **New York Yankees** (1920–1934), and **Boston Braves** (1935).

The all-time single-season leader in WAR among pitchers is **Pud Galvin** of the 1884 **Buffalo Bisons** of the NL, with 19.9. The single-season leader post-1893, when the pitching distance was extended to its current 60 feet, 6 inches, is is **Walter Johnson** of the 1913 **Washington Senators**, with 14.3. The single-season leader in the NL is **Amos Rusie** of the 1894 **New York Giants**, with 13.8. The career leader is **Cy Young**, with 162.3. Young pitched for the **Cleveland Spiders** of the NL (1890–1898), the **St. Louis Cardinals** (1899–1900) (they were the Perfectos in 1899), the Boston Americans (later the **Boston Red Sox**) of the **American League (AL)** (1901–1908), the Cleveland Naps of the AL (1909–1911), and the Boston Rustlers of the NL (1911).

WOMEN'S BASEBALL. Organized women's baseball, once almost nonexistent, is currently played in the United States, Australia, **Japan**, Taiwan, **Cuba**, Hong Kong, **Canada**, the **Netherlands**, India, **South Korea**, Vene-

zuela, Argentina, **Puerto Rico**, Colombia, Brazil, the **Dominican Republic**, and Pakistan. The strongest and most organized leagues are in the United States, Australia, Japan, Taiwan, Cuba, Hong Kong, and Canada. The other countries listed, however, do have national governing bodies that support baseball programs for girls and women.

Organized international competition in women's baseball began with the 2001 Women's World Series, played in Toronto. Women's World Series events were held in 2002 in the United States, in 2003 in Australia, and in 2004 in Japan. The Women's World Series is now defunct, but it paved the way for the official Women's Baseball World Cup competitions.

The Women's Baseball World Cup is a tournament sanctioned by the **International Baseball Federation (IBAF)** in which national teams from around the world compete. The tournament has been held four times. The United States won the first two Women's Baseball World Cups, in 2004 and 2006, and Japan won the last two, in 2008 and 2010. Teams from 11 countries competed in the 2010 tournament. The 2012 Women's Baseball World Cup will be held in Edmonton, Canada.

The history of baseball for girls and women in the United States was one of mostly exclusion. Previous generations' notions of gender and femininity kept many girls and women out of the sport in the 19th and early 20th centuries. In 1929, the American Legion officially barred girls from its baseball leagues, as did **Little League Baseball** from its founding in 1939. Whether by law or custom, girls were not allowed to play on high school or college teams for boys and men, or to field teams of their own.

That all changed when Congress passed Title IX of the Education Amendments of 1972. The purpose of Title IX was to end sex discrimination across all educational programs, but it is best known for its effect on interscholastic sports. However, the effects of Title IX influenced nonscholastic programs as well. In 1974, Little League rules were revised to allow participation by girls in the baseball program. As of 2012, there are a number of girls playing high school baseball, and even a few playing at the college level.

No woman has ever actually played at the **major-league** level, but three— Toni Stone, Connie Morgan, and Mamie "Peanuts" Johnson— played in the **Negro Leagues** in the 1950s. **Effa Manley**, owner of the **Newark Eagles** of the **Negro National League**, is the only woman elected to the **National Baseball Hall of Fame (HOF)**. Several other American women have played pioneering roles in professional baseball. In 1898, Lizzie Arlington became the first woman to sign a professional baseball contract while pitching for the Reading Coal Heavers of the Atlantic League. In 1904, Amanda Clement was the first woman to be paid to **umpire** a baseball game; she umpired professionally for six years after that. Helene Britton was the first woman to own a major-league team. She owned the **St. Louis Cardinals** from 1911 to 1916. In 1946, Edith Houghton became the first woman to **scout** for a major-league team.

In 1969, Bernice Gera became the first woman to sign a professional umpire contract. In 1976, Christine Wren umpired in the Class A Northwest League, and, from 1977 to 1983, Pam Postema umpired at each level of Minor League Baseball, beginning in the Rookie Gulf Coast League and moving up to the Triple A Pacific Coast League. In 1988 and 1999, **Commissioner of Baseball** Bart Giamatti invited Postema to umpire **spring training** games and the HOF game. In 1989, Julie Croteau became the first woman to play collegiate men's varsity baseball, when she played **first base** for St. Mary's College of Maryland, a Division III school.

Left-handed **pitcher** Ila Borders was the first woman to win a collegiate baseball scholarship and the first woman to pitch and win a complete collegiate baseball game (1995). Three years later, Borders became the first woman to win a men's professional game while pitching for the Duluth Dukes, an independent **minor-league** team.

The most well-known example of women playing baseball in the United States is the **All-American Girls Professional Baseball League**, which existed from 1943 to 1954, although its rules were a hybrid of baseball and **softball**.

WORCESTER (MASSACHUSETTS) RUBY LEGS. The Worcester Ruby Legs, also called the Brown Stockings, were a team in the **National League** from 1880 to 1882. They finished fifth in the eight-team league in 1880, and eighth in 1881 and 1882. In December 1882, the team sold its franchise rights, but not its players, to a Philadelphia group. **Pitcher** Lee Richmond of Worcester threw the first **perfect game** in the **major leagues** against the **Cleveland Blues** on 12 June 1880. Other notable players for the Ruby Legs were Buttercup Dixon, Pete Hotaling, and **Harry Stovey**.

WORLD BASEBALL CLASSIC. The World Baseball Classic is an international baseball tournament sanctioned by the **International Baseball Federation** and created by Major League Baseball and other professional baseball leagues and their players' associations around the world. The tournament is the first of its kind to allow national baseball teams to use professional players from the **major leagues**. **Japan** has won the **World Baseball Classic** both times since the tournament was created. They defeated **Cuba** in 2006 and **South Korea** in 2009. The next World Baseball Classic is scheduled to be played in San Francisco, California, in 2013.

WORLD SERIES. Beginning in 1884 and continuing through 1890, the champion of the **American Association (AA)** met the champion of the **National League (NL)** in an early version of the World Series. These early Series were less organized than the modern version, with as few as three games played, and as many as 15. The Series of 1885 and 1890 ending in disputed ties. The NL won four of these Series, while the AA won only one, in 1886, when the **St. Louis Browns** defeated the Chicago White Stockings.

The modern World Series, which determines the champions of Major League Baseball, is played between the pennant winners from the National League and **American League (AL)**. The first modern World Series, in 1903, was a best-of-nine, in which the Boston Americans of the AL defeated the **Pittsburgh Pirates** of the NL. There was no Series in 1904, because **manager John McGraw** and owner John Brush of the NL's pennant-winning **New York Giants** refused to play against the AL winner, Boston. In 1905, the Giants agreed to play the AL's **Philadelphia Athletics**, and the World Series has been played every year since then, except for 1994, when it was canceled because of a players' strike. Aside from 1903, and 1919 to 1921, when it was a best-of-nine, the Series has always been a best-of-seven.

The AL has won 62 of the 108 World Series played through 2012. The **New York Yankees** have played in the most World Series (40) and won the most times (27). Among NL teams, the **San Francisco Giants** (formerly the **New York Giants**) have played in the most Series (19), with the Cardinals winning the most times (11). The Giants were the winners of the 2012 Series, sweeping the **Detroit Tigers** in four games.

WRIGHT, GEORGE. B. 28 January 1847, New York, New York. D. 21 August 1937, Boston, Massachusetts. George Wright batted .633 and hit 49 **home runs** as the **shortstop** for the undefeated and openly professional **Cincinnati Red Stockings** in 1869. When the National Association (NA) was formed in 1871, Wright was the first player hired by the **Boston Red Stockings**, managed by his brother, **Harry Wright**. George Wright was instrumental in Boston's winning four pennants (1872–1875) in the NA's five-year existence. In 1876, the Red Stockings became charter members of the new **National League (NL)**.

On 22 April 1876, Wright, a right-handed hitter, was the first **batter** in NL history. He played for Boston from 1876 to 1878, and again in 1880 and 1881. Wright also played for the **Providence Grays** in 1879 and 1882. As **player-manager** of the Grays in 1879, he led them to the NL pennant. Wright had a .350 **batting average** for his five years in the NA and a .301 average overall. He is the NA's all-time leader in **triples** and number two in **hits** and **runs** scored. The 5-foot, 9-inch, 150-pound Wright led his league's shortstops in **putouts** five times and **assists** four times. In 1937, he was elected to the **National Baseball Hall of Fame** by the **Centennial Commission** as a pioneer/executive.

WRIGHT, WILLIAM HENRY "HARRY". B. 10 January 1835, Sheffield, England. D. 3 October 1895, Atlantic City, New Jersey. Harry Wright was the organizer, **manager**, and center fielder for the **Cincinnati Red Stockings**, who, in 1869, became an openly professional team. When the National Association (NA) was formed in 1871, Wright was hired to manage the **Boston Red Stockings**. He brought many of his best players from Cincinnati with him, including his younger brother, **George Wright**. Harry Wright managed the Red Stockings to four pennants (1872–1875) in the NA's five-year existence, and he added two more, in 1877 and 1878, after the Red Stockings became charter members of the new **National League**. He managed the Red Stockings through 1881, the **Providence Grays** in 1882 and 1883, and the Philadelphia Quakers (renamed the **Philadelphia Phillies** in 1890) from 1884 to 1893. Wright, a 5-foot, 9-inch, 157-pound right-handed hitter, had a .276 **batting average** in 180 **games played**, all but two in the NA. His 23-year managerial record was 1,225–885, with six pennants won. Wright was elected to the **National Baseball Hall of Fame** by the **Veterans Committee** as a pioneer/executive in 1953.

WRIGLEY FIELD. Wrigley Field, located in Chicago, Illinois, is the home field of the **Chicago Cubs** of the **National League (NL)**. Called Weeghman Park from its opening in 1914 until 1918, it served as the home of the **Chicago Whales** of the **Federal League (FL)** in 1914 and 1915. The Cubs played their first game there on 20 April 1916. Wrigley Field is the oldest NL park still in use, and it is the only one to have been used by a FL team. Known as Cubs' Park from 1919 to 1926, it acquired its current name, Wrigley Field, in 1927, in honor of new owner William Wrigley. The Cubs had previously played at the Twenty-Third Street Grounds (1876–1877), Lakefront Park (1878–1884), and West Side Park (1885–1915). They also played some home games at South Side Park in 1891, 1892, 1893, and 1897. Wrigley Field, whose seating capacity is approximately 41,200, hosted the **major league All-Star Game** in 1947, the second game in 1962, and in 1990.
See also STADIUMS.

WYNN, EARLY. B. 6 January 1920, Hartford, Alabama. D. 4 April 1999, Venice, Florida. Early Wynn, a 6-foot, 190-pound right-handed **pitcher**, spent 23 seasons in the **American League (AL)**. Wynn, whose career spanned four decades, pitched for the **Washington Senators** (1939,

1941–1944, 1946–1948), **Cleveland Indians** (1949–1957, 1963), and **Chicago White Sox** (1958–1962). Wynn won 20 or more games five times, leading the league in **wins** in 1954 and 1959, and **earned run average** in 1950. He led the league in **games started** five times and **innings pitched** three times.

In 1959, at the age of 39, Wynn won the **Cy Young Award** in recognition of his 22 wins as the ace of the staff for the pennant-winning White Sox. He was also chosen by the *Sporting News* as the **Major League Player of the Year** and the AL **Pitcher of the Year**. Wynn split two decisions against the **Los Angeles Dodgers** in the 1959 **World Series**. Earlier, Wynn had appeared in the 1954 World Series as a member of the Indians, going 0–1 against the **New York Giants**. Wynn returned to the Indians in 1963, where he picked up his 300th and final win (300–244). The seven-time **All-Star** was an above-average **batter**, and he was often used as a **pinch hitter**. He had 365 **hits** and 17 **home runs** in his career. In 1972, the **Baseball Writers' Association of America** elected Wynn to the **National Baseball Hall of Fame**.

Y

YANKEE STADIUM (I). Yankee Stadium (I), located in the Bronx, New York, was the home of the **New York Yankees** of the **American League (AL)** from 1923 to 1973, and then again from 1976 through 2008. In 2009, the Yankees moved into their current home, **Yankee Stadium (II)**. Yankee Stadium (I) was closed for renovations in 1974 and 1975, during which time the Yankees played at **Shea Stadium**, the home of the **New York Mets** of the **National League (NL)**. Before moving to Yankee Stadium in 1923, the Yankees played their home games at Hilltop Park from the time of their arrival in the AL in 1903 through the 1912 season, and at the **Polo Grounds**, as tenants of the **New York Giants** of the NL, from 1913 to 1922. Yankee Stadium (I) hosted the **major-league All-Star Game** in 1939, 1977, and 2008.

See also STADIUMS.

YANKEE STADIUM (II). Yankee Stadium (II), located in the Bronx, New York, has been the home of the **New York Yankees** of the **American League** since 2009. Prior to that, the Yankees played their home games at Hilltop Park from 1903 through 1912, the **Polo Grounds** from 1913 to 1922, **Yankee Stadium (I)** from 1923 to 1973 and 1976 to 2008, and **Shea Stadium** in 1974 and 1975. Yankee Stadium (II) has a seating capacity of approximately 50,300.

YASTRZEMSKI, CARL MICHAEL, "YAZ". B. 22 August 1939, Southampton, New York. In 1961, Carl Yastrzemski succeeded **Ted Williams** as the left fielder for the **Boston Red Sox**. He remained with Boston as their left fielder and later as a **designated hitter** for 23 seasons, tying **Brooks Robinson** of the **Baltimore Orioles** for the **major-league** record for most seasons played with one team. During his career, Yastrzemski, a 5-foot, 11-inch, 175-pound left-handed hitter, won three batting championships (1963, 1967, and 1968). He also led the league in **on-base percentage** five times; **slugging percentage**, **runs** scored, and **doubles** three times; and in **hits** twice. Although he led the league in **home runs** only once, with 44 in 1967, he also led that year in **batting average** and **runs batted in (RBI)**. That gave Yastrzemski the **Triple Crown** and earned him the **American League's Most Valuable Player (MVP) Award** and recognition as the **Major League Player of the Year**. He also won the **Hutch Award** in 1967.

Yastrzemski won seven **Gold Glove Awards** as an **outfielder**, was selected to the **All-Star** team 18 times, and was the game's MVP in 1970. He batted .352 in two seven-game **World Series** losses, to the **St. Louis Cardinals** in 1967, and to the **Cincinnati Reds** in 1975. Yastrzemski, whose 3,308 **games played** is second only to **Pete Rose**, had a .285 career batting average, with 452 home runs and 1,844 RBI. All-time, he is sixth in walks and eighth in hits and doubles. In 1989, the **Baseball Writers' Association of America** elected Yastrzemski to the **National Baseball Hall of Fame**.

YAWKEY, THOMAS AUSTIN "TOM". B. Thomas Austin, 21 February 1903, Detroit, Michigan. D. 9 July 1976, Boston, Massachusetts. Tom Yawkey was born Thomas Austin, but, when his father died, he was adopted by his uncle, Bill Yawkey, and took his uncle's last name. Born into great wealth, Yawkey was only 30 when he purchased the **Boston Red Sox** in 1933. He was the team's sole owner for 44 years. During that time, the Red Sox had five **general managers** and 17 **managers**, but the team won only three pennants—in 1946, 1967, and 1975. Boston lost the **World Series** in seven games in each of those years, in 1946 and 1967 to the **St. Louis Cardinals**, and in 1975 to the **Cincinnati Reds**. When Yawkey died in 1976, his wife, Jean Yawkey, inherited the team. Among the many notable players Tom Yawkey brought to Boston were **Joe Cronin**, Dom DiMaggio, **Bobby Doerr**, **Jimmie Foxx**, **Lefty Grove**, George Kell, Mel Parnell, Johnny Pesky, **Jim Rice**, Vern Stephens, **Ted Williams**, and **Carl Yastrzemski**. In 1980, the **Veterans Committee** elected Yawkey to the **National Baseball Hall of Fame**.

YOMIURI GIANTS. *See* JAPAN.

YOUNG, DENTON TRUE "CY". B. 29 March 1867, Gilmore, Ohio. D. 4 November 1955, Newcomerstown, Ohio. Cy Young's 22-year **major-league** career was split almost evenly between the **National League (NL)** and **American League (AL)**. He was with the **Cleveland Spiders** (1890–1898), **St. Louis Cardinals** (1899–1900)—they were the Perfectos in 1899—and the Boston Rustlers (1911) in the NL, and the Boston Americans (1901–1908)—they were the **Boston Red Sox** in 1908—and Cleveland Naps (1909–1911) in the AL. In 1901, the AL's first major-league season, Young, pitching for Boston, won the **Triple Crown** for **pitchers**, with 33 **wins**, a 1.62 **earned run average**, and 158 **strikeouts**. In 1903, he won two games in

Boston's victory against the **Pittsburgh Pirates** in the first modern **World Series**. Young had 20 or more wins 15 times and 30 or more wins five times. The 6-foot, 2-inch, 210-pound right-hander led his league in wins five times and **shutouts** seven times. Young is the all-time leader in the following pitching categories: wins (511), **losses** (316), **games started** (815), **complete games** (749), and **innings pitched** (7,356). He is fourth all-time in shutouts, with 76. Beginning in 1967, the best pitcher in each league (there was just one award encompassing both leagues from 1956 through 1966) is honored with the **Cy Young Award**, named in his honor. In 1937, Young was elected by the **Baseball Writers' Association of America** to the **National Baseball Hall of Fame**.

YOUNGS, ROSS MIDDLEBROOK, "PEP". B. Royce Middlebrook Youngs, 10 April 1897, Shiner, Texas. D. 22 October 1927, San Antonio, Texas. Ross Youngs was just 30 years old when he died from Bright's disease in 1927. He had been the right fielder for the **New York Giants** from 1917, when he appeared in seven games, to August 1926, when he became too ill to play. The 5-foot, 8-inch, 162-pound Youngs batted above .300 in seven of his eight full seasons. He led the **National League (NL)** in **doubles** in 1919 and **runs** scored in 1923. Youngs, a member of four consecutive Giants pennant winners (1921–1924), batted .286 with 26 hits in 26 **World Series** games. A left-handed batter and right-handed thrower, he was a speedy defender with a strong throwing arm who led NL right fielders in **assists** five times. Youngs, who had a lifetime **batting average** of .322, was elected to the **National Baseball Hall of Fame** by the **Veterans Committee** in 1972.

YOUNT, ROBIN R. B. 16 September 1955, Danville, Illinois. Robin Yount debuted with the **Milwaukee Brewers** of the **American League (AL)** as an 18-year-old **shortstop** in 1974. He spent his entire 20-year career with the Brewers, switching to center field in 1985 because of an injured shoulder. Yount batted .300 or better six times, but his best season was 1982, when he led the Brewers to the AL pennant. The 6-foot, 165-pound right-handed-hitting shortstop batted a career high .331 and led the AL with 210 **hits**, 46 **doubles**, 367 **total bases**, and a .578 **slugging percentage**. He was voted the AL's **Most Valuable Player (MVP)** and the **Major League Player of the Year**. Yount batted .414 in the **World Series**, but Milwaukee lost to the **St. Louis Cardinals** in seven games.

In 1989, Yount won his second MVP Award, this time as a center fielder. He also won a **Gold Glove Award** and two **Silver Slugger Awards** as a shortstop. As a center fielder, Yount led in **fielding percentage** three times, in addition to winning a third Silver Slugger Award. He had a .285 career

batting average, with 3,142 hits and 1,406 **runs batted in**. In 1999, the **Baseball Writers' Association of America** elected Yount to the **National Baseball Hall of Fame**.

Appendix A: World Series Results

1903 Boston (AL) 5, Pittsburgh (NL) 3
1904 not held
1905 New York (NL) 4, Philadelphia (AL) 1
1906 Chicago (AL) 4, Chicago (NL) 2
1907 Chicago (NL) 4, Detroit (AL) 0 (one tie)
1908 Chicago (NL) 4, Detroit (AL) 1
1909 Pittsburgh (NL) 4, Detroit (AL) 3
1910 Philadelphia (AL) 4, Chicago (NL) 1
1911 Philadelphia (AL) 4, New York (NL) 2
1912 Boston (AL) 4, New York (NL) 3 (one tie)
1913 Philadelphia (AL) 4, New York (NL) 1
1914 Boston (NL) 4, Philadelphia (AL) 0
1915 Boston (AL) 4, Philadelphia (NL) 1
1916 Boston (AL) 4, Brooklyn (NL) 1
1917 Chicago (AL) 4, New York (NL) 2
1918 Boston (AL) 4, Chicago (NL) 2
1919 Cincinnati (NL) 5, Chicago (AL) 3
1920 Cleveland (AL) 5, Brooklyn (NL) 2
1921 New York (NL) 5, New York (AL) 3
1922 New York (NL) 4, New York (AL) 0 (one tie)
1923 New York (AL) 4, New York (NL) 2
1924 Washington (AL) 4, New York (NL) 3
1925 Pittsburgh (NL) 4, Washington (AL) 3
1926 St. Louis (NL) 4, New York (AL) 3
1927 New York (AL) 4, Pittsburgh (NL) 0
1928 New York (AL) 4, St. Louis (NL) 0
1929 Philadelphia (AL) 4, Chicago (NL) 1
1930 Philadelphia (AL) 4, St. Louis (NL) 2
1931 St. Louis (NL) 4, Philadelphia (AL) 3
1932 New York (AL) 4, Chicago (NL) 0
1933 New York (NL) 4, Washington (AL) 1
1934 St. Louis (NL) 4, Detroit (AL) 3
1935 Detroit (AL) 4, Chicago (NL) 2
1936 New York 4 (AL), New York (NL) 2
1937 New York (AL) 4, New York (NL) 1
1938 New York (AL) 4, Chicago (NL) 0
1939 New York (AL) 4, Cincinnati (NL) 0

1940 Cincinnati (NL) 4, Detroit (AL) 3
1941 New York (AL) 4, Brooklyn (NL) 1
1942 St. Louis (NL) 4, New York (AL) 1
1943 New York (AL) 4, St. Louis (NL) 1
1944 St. Louis (NL) 4, St. Louis (AL) 2
1945 Detroit (AL) 4, Chicago (NL) 3
1946 St. Louis (NL) 4, Boston (AL) 3
1947 New York (AL) 4, Brooklyn (NL) 3
1948 Cleveland (AL) 4, Boston (NL) 2
1949 New York (AL) 4, Brooklyn (NL) 1
1950 New York (AL) 4, Philadelphia (NL) 0
1951 New York (AL) 4, New York (NL) 2
1952 New York (AL) 4, Brooklyn (NL) 3
1953 New York (AL) 4, Brooklyn (NL) 2
1954 New York (NL) 4, Cleveland (AL) 0
1955 Brooklyn (NL) 4, New York (AL) 3
1956 New York (AL) 4, Brooklyn (NL) 3
1957 Milwaukee (NL) 4, New York (AL) 3
1958 New York (AL) 4, Milwaukee (NL) 3
1959 Los Angeles (NL) 4, Chicago (AL) 3
1960 Pittsburgh (NL) 4, New York (AL) 3
1961 New York (AL) 4, Cincinnati (NL) 1
1962 New York (AL) 4, San Francisco (NL) 3
1963 Los Angeles (NL) 4, New York (AL) 0
1964 St. Louis (NL) 4, New York (AL) 3
1965 Los Angeles (NL) 4, Minnesota (AL) 3
1966 Baltimore (AL) 4, Los Angeles (NL) 0
1967 St. Louis (NL) 4, Boston (AL) 3
1968 Detroit (AL) 4, St. Louis (NL) 3
1969 New York (NL) 4, Baltimore (AL) 1
1970 Baltimore (AL) 4, Cincinnati (NL) 1
1971 Pittsburgh (NL) 4, Baltimore (AL) 3
1972 Oakland (AL) 4, Cincinnati (NL) 3
1973 Oakland (AL) 4, New York (NL) 3
1974 Oakland (AL) 4, Los Angeles (NL) 1
1975 Cincinnati (NL) 4, Boston (AL) 3
1976 Cincinnati (NL) 4, New York (AL) 0
1977 New York (AL) 4, Los Angeles (NL) 2
1978 New York (AL) 4, Los Angeles (NL) 2
1979 Pittsburgh (NL) 4, Baltimore (AL) 3
1980 Philadelphia (NL) 4, Kansas City (AL) 2
1981 Los Angeles (NL) 4, New York (AL) 2
1982 St. Louis (NL) 4, Milwaukee (AL) 3

1983 Baltimore (AL) 4, Philadelphia (NL) 1
1984 Detroit (AL) 4, San Diego (NL) 1
1985 Kansas City (AL) 4, St. Louis (NL) 3
1986 New York (NL) 4, Boston (AL) 3
1987 Minnesota (AL) 4, St. Louis (NL) 3
1988 Los Angeles (NL) 4, Oakland (AL) 1
1989 Oakland (AL) 4, San Francisco (NL) 0
1990 Cincinnati (NL) 4, Oakland (AL) 0
1991 Minnesota (AL) 4, Atlanta (NL) 3
1992 Toronto (AL) 4, Atlanta (NL) 2
1993 Toronto (AL) 4, Philadelphia (NL) 2
1994 not held
1995 Atlanta (NL) 4, Cleveland (AL) 2
1996 New York (AL) 4, Atlanta (NL) 2
1997 Florida (NL) 4, Cleveland (AL) 3
1998 New York (AL) 4, San Diego (NL) 0
1999 New York (AL) 4, Atlanta (NL) 0
2000 New York (AL) 4, New York (NL) 1
2001 Arizona (NL) 4, New York (AL) 3
2002 Anaheim (AL) 4, San Francisco (NL) 3
2003 Florida (NL) 4, New York (AL) 2
2004 Boston (AL) 4, St. Louis (NL) 0
2005 Chicago (AL) 4, Houston (NL) 0
2006 St. Louis (NL) 4, Detroit (AL) 1
2007 Boston (AL) 4, Colorado (NL) 0
2008 Philadelphia (NL) 4, Tampa Bay (AL) 1
2009 New York (AL) 4, Philadelphia (NL) 2
2010 San Francisco (NL) 4, Texas (AL) 1
2011 St. Louis (NL) 4, Texas (AL) 3
2012 San Francisco (NL) 4, Detroit (AL) 0

Appendix B: Career Leaders in Games Played

1. Pete Rose 3,562
2. Carl Yastrzemski 3,308
3. Hank Aaron 3,298
4. Rickey Henderson 3,081
5. Ty Cobb 3,034
6. Eddie Murray 3,026
6. Stan Musial 3,026
8. Cal Ripken 3,001
9. Willie Mays 2,992
10. Barry Bonds 2,986
11. Dave Winfield 2,973
12. Omar Vizquel 2,968
13. Rusty Staub 2,951
14. Brooks Robinson 2,896
15. Robin Yount 2,856
16. Craig Biggio 2,850
17. Al Kaline 2,834
18. Rafael Palmeiro 2,831
19. Harold Baines 2,830
20. Eddie Collins 2,826
21. Reggie Jackson 2,820
22. Frank Robinson 2,808
23. Honus Wagner 2,794
24. Tris Speaker 2,789
25. Tony Perez 2,777
26. Mel Ott 2,730
27. George Brett 2,707
28. Graig Nettles 2,700

Appendix C: Career Leaders in Batting Average (Minimum 3,000 Plate Appearances

1. Ty Cobb .3664
2. Rogers Hornsby .3585
3. Joe Jackson .3558
4. Lefty O'Doul .3493
5. Ed Delahanty .3458
6. Tris Speaker .3447
7. Billy Hamilton .3444
7. Ted Williams .3444
9. Dan Brouthers .3421
9. Babe Ruth .3421
11. Dave Orr .3420
12. Harry Heilmann .3416
13. Pete Browning .3415
14. Willie Keeler .3413
15. Bill Terry .3412
16. Lou Gehrig .3401
16. George Sisler .3401
18. Jesse Burkett .3382
18. Tony Gwynn .3382
20. Nap Lajoie .3381
21. Jake Stenzel .3378
22. Riggs Stephenson .3361
23. Al Simmons .3342
24. Cap Anson .3341
25. John McGraw .3336
26. Eddie Collins .3332
26. Paul Waner .3332
28. Mike Donlin .3326
29. Sam Thompson .3314
30. Stan Musial .3308

Appendix D: Players with 500 Home Runs

1. Barry Bonds 762
2. Hank Aaron 755
3. Babe Ruth 714
4. Willie Mays 660
5. Alex Rodriguez 647*
6. Jim Thome 612
7. Ken Griffey Jr. 630
8. Sammy Sosa 609
9. Frank Robinson 586
10. Mark McGwire 583
11. Harmon Killebrew 573
12. Rafael Palmeiro 569
13. Reggie Jackson 563
14. Manny Ramirez 555
15. Mike Schmidt 548
16. Mickey Mantle 536
17. Jimmie Foxx 534
18. Willie McCovey 521
18. Frank Thomas 521
18. Ted Williams 521
21. Ernie Banks 512
21. Eddie Mathews 512
23. Mel Ott 511
24. Gary Sheffield 509
25. Eddie Murray 504
* Active in 2012.

Appendix E: Career Leaders in Runs Batted In

1. Hank Aaron 2,297
2. Babe Ruth 2,213
3. Cap Anson 2,075
4. Barry Bonds 1,996
5. Lou Gehrig 1,995
6. Stan Musial 1,951
7. Alex Rodriguez 1,950*
8. Ty Cobb 1,938
9. Jimmie Foxx 1,922
10. Eddie Murray 1,917
11. Willie Mays 1,903
12. Mel Ott 1,860
13. Carl Yastrzemski 1,844
14. Ted Williams 1,839
15. Ken Griffey Jr. 1,836
16. Rafael Palmeiro 1,835
17. Dave Winfield 1,833
18. Manny Ramirez 1,831
19. Al Simmons 1,827
20. Frank Robinson 1,812
21. Honus Wagner 1,733
22. Frank Thomas 1,704
23. Reggie Jackson 1,702
24. Jim Thome 1,669*
25. Cal Ripken 1,695
* Active in 2012.

Appendix F: Career Leaders in Runs Scored

1. Rickey Henderson 2,295
2. Ty Cobb 2,246
3. Barry Bonds 2,227
4. Hank Aaron 2,174
4. Babe Ruth 2,174
6. Pete Rose 2,165
7. Willie Mays 2,062
8. Cap Anson 1,999
9. Stan Musial 1,949
10. Alex Rodriguez 1,898*
11. Lou Gehrig 1,888
12. Tris Speaker 1,882
13. Derek Jeter 1,769*
14. Mel Ott 1,859
15. Craig Biggio 1,844
16. Frank Robinson 1,829
17. Eddie Collins 1,821
18. Carl Yastrzemski 1,816
19. Ted Williams 1,798
20. Paul Molitor 1,782
21. Charlie Gehringer 1,774
22. Jimmie Foxx 1,751
23. Honus Wagner 1,739
24. Jim O'Rourke 1,729
25. Jesse Burkett 1,720
26. Willie Keeler 1,719
* Active in 2012.

Appendix G: Players with 3,000 Hits

1. Pete Rose 4,256
2. Ty Cobb 4,189
3. Hank Aaron 3,771
4. Stan Musial 3,630
5. Tris Speaker 3,514
6. Cap Anson 3,435
7. Honus Wagner 3,420
8. Carl Yastrzemski 3,419
9. Paul Molitor 3,319
10. Eddie Collins 3,315
11. Derek Jeter 3,304*
12. Willie Mays 3,283
13. Eddie Murray 3,255
14. Nap Lajoie 3,242
15. Cal Ripken 3,184
16. George Brett 3,154
17. Paul Waner 3,152
18. Robin Yount 3,142
19. Tony Gwynn 3,141
20. Dave Winfield 3,110
21. Craig Biggio 3,060
22. Rickey Henderson 3,055
23. Rod Carew 3,053
24. Lou Brock 3,023
25. Rafael Palmeiro 3,020
26. Wade Boggs 3,010
27. Al Kaline 3,007
28. Roberto Clemente 3,000
* Active in 2012.

Appendix H: Career Leaders in Games Pitched

1. Jesse Orosco 1,252
2. Mike Stanton 1,178
3. John Franco 1,119
4. Dennis Eckersley 1,071
5. Hoyt Wilhelm 1,070
6. Dan Plesac 1,064
7. Mike Timlin 1,058
8. Mariano Rivera 1,051*
9. Kent Tekulve 1,050
10. Trevor Hoffman 1,035
11. Jose Mesa 1,022
11. Lee Smith 1,022
13. Roberto Hernandez 1,010
14. Michael Jackson 1,005
15. Rich Gossage 1,002
16. Lindy McDaniel 987
17. Todd Jones 982
18. David Weathers 964
19. Rollie Fingers 944
20. Gene Garber 931
21. Eddie Guardado 908
22. Cy Young 906
23. Arthur Rhodes 900
* Active in 2012.

Appendix I: Pitchers with 300 Games Won

1. Cy Young 511
2. Walter Johnson 417
3. Grover Alexander 373
3. Christy Mathewson 373
5. Pud Galvin 365
6. Warren Spahn 363
7. Kid Nichols 361
8. Greg Maddux 355
9. Roger Clemens 354
10. Tim Keefe 342
11. Steve Carlton 329
12. John Clarkson 328
13. Eddie Plank 326
14. Nolan Ryan 324
14. Don Sutton 324
16. Phil Niekro 318
17. Gaylord Perry 314
18. Tom Seaver 311
19. Charlie Radbourn 309
20. Mickey Welch 307
21. Tom Glavine 305
22. Randy Johnson 303
23. Lefty Grove 300
23. Early Wynn 300

Appendix J: Career Leaders in Earned Run Average (Minimum 1,000 Innings Pitched)

1. Ed Walsh 1.816
2. Addie Joss 1.887
3. Jim Devlin 1.896
4. Jack Pfiester 2.024
5. Joe Wood 2.033
6. Mordecai Brown 2.057
7. Monte Ward 2.099
8. Christy Mathewson 2.133
8. Al Spalding 2.133
10. Tommy Bond 2.138
11. Rube Waddell 2.161
12. Walter Johnson 2.167
13. Mariano Rivera 2.214*
14. Jake Weimer 2.231
15. Orval Overall 2.233
16. Will White 2.276
17. Babe Ruth 2.277
18. Ed Reulbach 2.284
19. Jim Scott 2.298
* Active in 2012.

Appendix K: Career Leaders in Strikeouts

1. Nolan Ryan 5,714
2. Randy Johnson 4,875
3. Roger Clemens 4,672
4. Steve Carlton 4,136
5. Bert Blyleven 3,701
6. Tom Seaver 3,640
7. Don Sutton 3,574
8. Gaylord Perry 3,534
9. Walter Johnson 3,509
10. Greg Maddux 3,371
11. Phil Niekro 3,342
12. Ferguson Jenkins 3,192
13. Pedro Martinez 3,154
14. Bob Gibson 3,117
15. Curt Schilling 3,116
16. John Smoltz 3,084
17. Jim Bunning 2,855
18. Mickey Lolich 2,832
19. Mike Mussina 2,813
20. Cy Young 2,803
21. Frank Tanana 2,773
22. David Cone 2,668
23. Chuck Finley 2,610
24. Tom Glavine 2,607
25. Warren Spahn 2,583
26. Bob Feller 2,581
27. Tim Keefe 2,564
28. Jerry Koosman 2,556
29. Javier Vasquez 2,536
30. Christy Mathewson 2,507

Appendix L: College World Series Winners

1947 University of California
1948 University of Southern California
1949 University of Texas
1950 University of Texas
1951 University of Oklahoma
1952 Holy Cross College
1953 University of Michigan
1954 University of Missouri
1955 Wake Forest University
1956 University of Minnesota
1957 University of California
1958 University of Southern California
1959 Oklahoma State University
1960 University of Minnesota
1961 University of Southern California
1962 University of Michigan
1963 University of Southern California
1964 University of Minnesota
1965 Arizona State University
1966 Ohio State University
1967 Arizona State University
1968 University of Southern California
1969 Arizona State University
1970 University of Southern California
1971 University of Southern California
1972 University of Southern California
1973 University of Southern California
1974 University of Southern California
1975 University of Texas
1976 University of Arizona
1977 Arizona State University
1978 University of Southern California
1979 California State University, Fullerton
1980 University of Arizona
1981 Arizona State University
1982 University of Miami
1983 University of Texas

1984 California State University, Fullerton
1985 University of Miami
1986 University of Arizona
1987 Stanford University
1988 Stanford University
1989 Wichita State University
1990 University of Georgia
1991 Louisiana State University
1992 Pepperdine University
1993 Louisiana State University
1994 University of Oklahoma
1995 California State University, Fullerton
1996 Louisiana State University
1997 Louisiana State University
1998 University of Southern California
1999 University of Miami
2000 Louisiana State University
2001 University of Miami
2002 University of Texas
2003 Rice University
2004 California State University, Fullerton
2005 University of Texas
2006 Oregon State University
2007 Oregon State University
2008 California State University, Fresno
2009 Louisiana State University
2010 University of South Carolina
2011 University of South Carolina
2012 University of Arizona

Bibliography

CONTENTS

I. INTRODUCTION

More books have been written about baseball than any other sport, so it would be impossible to include them all. Baseball books likely began with *Beadle's Dime Base-Ball Player*, one of a large number of "dime books" published in the 19th century. Edited by Henry Chadwick, it is recognized as the earliest set of baseball guides, having been published from 1860 to 1881. With the advent of professional leagues in the 1870s, books about the national game, its teams, and its star players began appearing. Beginning in the 20th century, the flourishing of the game has been matched by a flourishing industry of baseball publications. Each year, dozens of new titles appear covering every aspect of baseball.

The greatest portion of this volume is dedicated to the American major leagues, and the number of entries in the bibliography reflects that measure. The major-league section is devoted to books on general history; the various leagues recognized as major leagues; teams; individual and groups of seasons; biographies of players, managers, executives, and so forth; ballparks, broadcasting; the business aspects of baseball; the Hall of Fame; the World Series; and the growing field of analysis and sabermetrics. A miscellaneous section includes such topics as encyclopedias and record books, the All-Star Game, and expansion, amongst others. The bibliography continues with selections on the minor leagues, the Negro Leagues, women's baseball, college baseball, and other countries where baseball is prominent.

Many books cover the history of baseball. The following are recommended for their coverage of the entire history of the game or one specific era: *Our Game: An American Baseball History*, by Charles C. Alexander; *Baseball before We Knew It: A Search for the Roots of the Game*, by David Block; *The Baseball Chronology*, by James Charlton; *The Fix Is In: A History of Baseball Gambling and Game-Fixing Scandals*, by Daniel E. Ginsburg; *Koppett's Concise History of Major League Baseball*, by Leonard Koppett; *A. G. Spalding and The Rise of Baseball*, by Peter Levine; *A Game of Inches: The Stories behind the Innovations That Shaped Baseball*, by Peter Morris; *Baseball: A History of America's Game*, by Benjamin Rader; *Baseball's First Inning: A History of the National Pastime through the Civil War*, by William J. Ryczek; *Baseball: The Early Years* and *Baseball: The Golden Age*, by Harold and Dorothy Seymour; *Baseball: America's National Game, 1839–1915*, by A. G. Spalding; *Baseball in the Garden of Eden: The Secret History of the Early Game*, by John Thorn; and *America through Baseball*, by David Q. Voigt.

Some of the most informative books written about the individual major leagues are *The Beer and Whiskey League*, by David Nemec; *The American League Story*, by Lee Allen; *The Federal League of Base Ball Clubs: The*

History of an Outlaw Major League, 1914–1915, by Robert Peyton Wiggins; *The League That Lasted: 1876 and the Founding of the National League of Professional Base Ball Clubs*, by Neil W. MacDonald; and *The Players League: History, Clubs, Ballplayers, and Statistics*, by Ed Koszarek.

More books have been written about the New York Yankees than any other team, but just about every team, including those now extinct, has had a book written about it. So too have books been written dealing with groups of teams, for example, *The Ball Clubs*, by Donald Dewey and Nicholas Acocella; *Paths to Glory: How Great Baseball Teams Got That Way*, by Mark L. Armour and Daniel R. Levitt; and *Baseball Dynasties: The Greatest Teams of All Time*, by Rob Neyer and Eddie Epstein.

Two of the most comprehensive of the Yankees books are Marty Appel's *Pinstripe Empire: The New York Yankees from before the Babe to after the Boss*, and Harvey Frommer's *A Yankee Century: A Celebration of the First Hundred Years of Baseball's Greatest Team*. Other informative team books include *Red Sox Century: One Hundred Years of Red Sox Baseball*, by Glenn Stout and Richard A. Johnson; *The Chicago White Sox*, by Warren Brown; *The Cleveland Indians*, by Franklin A. Lewis; *The New York Mets*, by Jack Lang and Peter Simon; *Mound City Memories: Baseball in St. Louis*, by Bob Tiemann; *Bums: An Oral History of the Brooklyn Dodgers*, by Peter Golenbock; *The Giants of the Polo Grounds*, by Noel Hynd; and *The Athletics of Philadelphia: Connie Mack's White Elephants, 1901–1954*, by David M. Jordan.

Among the many books listed that cover individual seasons are *Mack, McGraw, and the 1913 Baseball Season*, by Richard Adler; *1947: When All Hell Broke Loose in Baseball*, by Red Barber; *1939, Baseball's Pivotal Year*, by Talmage Boston; *Baseball's Greatest Season: 1924*, by Reed Browning; *Baseball in '41*, by Robert W. Creamer; *A Game of Brawl: The Orioles, the Beaneaters, and the Battle for the 1897 Pennant*, by Bill Felber; *The Dizziest Season: The Gashouse Gang Chases the Pennant*, by G. H. Fleming; *Ball Four*, by Jim Bouton; *October 1964* and *Summer of '49*, by David Halberstam; *Crazy '08: How a Cast of Cranks, Rogues, Boneheads, and Magnates Created the Greatest Year in Baseball History*, by Cait Murphy; *The Echoing Green: The Untold Story of Bobby Thomson, Ralph Branca, and the Shot Heard round the World*, by Joshua Prager; and *1921: The Yankees, the Giants, and the Battle for Baseball Supremacy in New York*, by Lyle Spatz and Steve Steinberg.

A look at the bibliography will reveal that nearly every famous person associated with baseball, and many who are not so famous, have had their biographies written. The following are just a few: *The Last Hero: A Life of Henry Aaron*, by Howard Bryant; *Chief Bender's Burden: The Silent Struggle of a Baseball Star*, by Tom Swift; *Babe: The Legend Comes to Life*, by Robert W. Creamer; *Clemente: The Passion and Grace of Baseball's Last*

Hero, by David Maraniss; *Ty Cobb*, by Charles C. Alexander; *Joe Cronin: A Life in Baseball*, by Mark Armour; *Joe DiMaggio: The Hero's Life*, by Richard Ben Cramer; *The Best Pitcher in Baseball: The Life of Rube Foster, Negro League Giant*, by Robert C. Cottrell; *Luckiest Man: The Life and Death of Lou Gehrig*, by Jonathan Eig; *Harry Hooper: An American Baseball Life*, by Paul J. Zingg; *Shoeless: The Life and Times of Joe Jackson*, by David Fleitz; *Walter Johnson: Baseball's Big Train*, by Henry W. Thomas; *Sandy Koufax: A Lefty's Legacy*, by Jane Leavy; *Matty: An American Hero*, by Ray Robinson; *Stan Musial: An American Life*, by George Vecsey; *Satchel: The Life and Times of an American Legend*, by Larry Tye; *Fifty-Nine in '84: Old Hoss Radbourn, Barehanded Baseball, and the Greatest Season a Pitcher Ever Had*, by Edward Achorn; *Jackie Robinson: A Biography*, by Arnold Rampersad; *The Sizzler: George Sisler, Baseball's Forgotten Great*, by Rick Huhn; and *Ted Williams: The Biography of an American Hero*, by Leigh Montville. Two recommended group biographies are *The Boys of Summer*, by Roger Kahn, and *The Glory of Their Times: The Story of the Early Days of Baseball Told by the Men Who Played It*, by Lawrence S. Ritter.

Books about the other major-league subcategories are also plentiful. The following are just two representative books in each. STADIUMS: *The Greatest Ballpark Ever: Ebbets Field and the Story of the Brooklyn Dodgers*, by Robert McGee, and *Fenway 1912: The Birth of a Ballpark, a Championship Season, and Fenway's Remarkable First Year*, by Glenn Stout. BROADCASTING: *Broadcasting Baseball: A History of the National Pastime on Radio and Television*, by Eldon L. Ham, and *The Storytellers from Mel Allen to Bob Costas: Sixty Years of Baseball Tales from the Broadcast Booth*, by Curt Smith. BUSINESS OF BASEBALL: *Moneyball: The Art of Winning an Unfair Game*, by Michael Lewis, and *Lords of the Realm: The Real History of Baseball*, by John Helyar. HALL OF FAME: *The Road to Cooperstown: A Critical History of Baseball's Hall of Fame Selection Process*, by James F. Vail, and *The Politics of Glory*, by Bill James. WORLD SERIES: *Eight Men Out: The Black Sox and the 1919 World Series*, by Eliot Asinof, and *The History of the World Series*, by Gene Schoor. ANALYSIS AND SABERMETRICS: *The Hidden Game of Baseball*, by John Thorn and Pete Palmer, and *The Numbers Game: Baseball's Lifelong Fascination with Statistics*, by Alan Schwarz. Some recommended books in the MISCELLANEOUS category are *All Bat, No Glove: A History of the Designated Hitter*, by G. Richard McKelvey; *Doubleheaders: A Major League History*, by Charlie Bevis; *Major League Baseball Expansions and Relocations: A History, 1876–2008*, by Frank P. Jozsa Jr.; *Baseball's Greatest Quotations*, by Paul Dickson; *Encyclopedia of Major League Baseball Team Histories: American League* and *Encyclopedia of Major League Baseball Team Histories: National*

League, edited by Peter O. Bjarkman; *The Elias Book of Baseball Records, 2012*, edited by Seymour Siwoff; and *The ESPN Baseball Encyclopedia, 5th Edition*, edited by Gary Gillette and Pete Palmer.

The many different minor leagues, as well as various minor league histories and seasons, are also well represented in the literature. Three of the most comprehensive are *Small-Town Heroes: Images of Minor League Baseball*, by Hank Davis; *The Encyclopedia of Minor League Baseball, 3rd Edition*, by Lloyd Johnson and Miles Wolff; and *The Greatest Minor League: A History of the Pacific Coast League, 1903–1957*, by Dennis Snelling.

Literature dealing with the Negro Leagues has increased greatly in the last few decades, covering every aspect of baseball in the Negro Leagues. General histories include *The Negro Leagues Chronology: Events in Organized Black Baseball, 1920–1948*, by Christopher Hauser; *The Complete Book of Baseball's Negro Leagues: The Other Half of Baseball History*, by John Holway; *Out of the Shadows: African American Baseball from the Cuban Giants to Jackie Robinson*, edited by Bill Kirwin; and *Negro League Baseball: The Rise and Ruin of a Black Institution*, by Neil Lanctot.

Among the Negro Leagues team histories are *The Pittsburgh Crawfords*, by Jim Bankes; *Black Barons of Birmingham: The South's Greatest Negro League Team and Its Players*, by Larry Powell; and *Satchel Paige and Company: Essays on the Kansas City Monarchs, Their Greatest Star, and the Negro Leagues*, edited by Leslie A. Heaphy.

Some of the books covering women and baseball are *No Girls in the Clubhouse: The Exclusion of Women from Baseball*, by Marilyn Cohen; *The Origins and History of the All-American Girls Professional Baseball League*, by Merrie A. Fidler; and *Encyclopedia of Women and Baseball*, edited by Leslie A. Heaphy and Mel Anthony May. *Nine College Nines: A Closeup View of Campus Baseball Programs Today*, by Gregory J. Tully, affords insight into baseball played at the college level.

Baseball without Borders: The International Pastime, edited by George Gmelch, is a good general history of baseball played outside the United States. Some other books related to specific countries or continents are *Taking in a Game: A History of Baseball in Asia*, by Joseph A. Reaves; *Banzai Babe Ruth: Baseball Espionage and Assassination during the 1934 Tour of Japan*, by Robert K. Fitts; *Baseball in Europe: A Country by Country History*, by Josh Chetwynd; *Baseball with a Latin Beat: A History of the Latin American Game*, by Peter O. Bjarkman; *The Pride of Havana: A History of Cuban Baseball*, by Roberto González Echevarría; and *The Tropic of Baseball: Baseball in the Dominican Republic*, by Rob Ruck.

Finally, I have excluded baseball fiction from the bibliography, but the following are some of the best of that genre: *You Know Me Al*, by Ring Lardner; *The Natural*, by Bernard Malamud; *The Universal Baseball Association, Inc., J. Henry Waugh, Proprietor*, by Robert Coover; *The Southpaw* and *Bang the Drum Slowly*, by Mark Harris; *Seasons Past*, by Damon Rice; *The Greatest Slump of All Time*, by David Carkeet; *The Celebrant*, by Eric Rolfe Greenberg; *If I Never Get Back*, by Darryl Brock; and *Shoeless Joe* and *The Iowa Baseball Confederacy*, by W. P. Kinsella.

II. MAJOR LEAGUES

A. General History

Alexander, Charles C. *Breaking the Slump: Baseball in the Depression Era*. New York: Columbia University Press, 2002.

———. *Our Game: An American Baseball History*. New York: Henry Holt, 1991.

Allen, Lee. *100 Years of Baseball*. New York: Bartholomew House, 1950.

Benson, John, and Tony Blengino. *Baseball's Top 100: The Best Individual Seasons of All Time*. Wilton, Conn.: Diamond Library, 1995.

Block, David. *Baseball before We Knew It: A Search for the Roots of the Game*. Lincoln: University of Nebraska Press, 2005.

Charlton, James. *The Baseball Chronology*. New York: Macmillan, 1991.

Costello, James, and Michael Santa Maria. *In the Shadow of the Diamond: Hard Times in the National Pastime*. Dubuque, Iowa: Elysian Fields, 1992.

Crepeau, Richard C. *Baseball: America's Diamond Mind, 1919–1941*. Lincoln: University of Nebraska Press, 2000.

Curran, William. *Big Sticks: The Batting Revolution of the Twenties*. New York: William Morrow, 1990.

———. *Mitts: A Celebration of the Art of Fielding*. New York: William Morrow, 1985.

———. *Strikeout: A Celebration of the Art of Pitching*. New York: Crown, 1995.

Daley, Arthur. *Inside Baseball: A Half Century of the National Pastime*. New York: Grosset & Dunlap, 1950.

Dickson, Paul. *Baseball's Greatest Quotations*. New York: Edward Burlingame, 1991.

———. *The Dickson Baseball Dictionary: The Revised, Expanded, and Now Definitive Work on the Language of Baseball*, 3rd ed. New York: W. W. Norton, 2009.

Dittmar, Joseph J. *The 100 Greatest Baseball Games of the 20th Century Ranked*. Jefferson, N.C.: McFarland, 2000.

———. *Baseball Records Registry: The Best and Worst Single-Day Performances and the Stories behind Them*. Jefferson, N.C.: McFarland, 1997.

Durso, Joseph. *Baseball and the American Dream*. St. Louis, Mo.: Sporting News, 1986.

Einstein, Charles, ed. *The Baseball Reader*. New York: Lippincott & Crowell, 1980.

———. *Willie's Time: A Memoir of Another America*. New York: Berkley Books, 1980.

Gallen, David, ed. *The Baseball Chronicles*. Edison, N.J.: Galahad Books, 1991.

Ginsburg, Daniel E. *The Fix Is In: A History of Baseball Gambling and Game-Fixing Scandals*. Jefferson, N.C.: McFarland, 1995.

Goldstein, Richard. *Spartan Seasons: How Baseball Survived the Second World War*. New York: Macmillan, 1980.

Honig, Donald. *Baseball America*. New York: Macmillan, 1985.

Koppett, Leonard. *Koppett's Concise History of Major League Baseball*. Philadelphia, Pa.: Temple University Press, 1998.

———. *The New Thinking Man's Guide to Baseball*. New York: Simon & Schuster, 1991.

Levine, Peter. *A. G. Spalding and the Rise of Baseball*. New York: Oxford University Press, 1985.

Lieb, Frederick G. *Baseball as I Have Known It*. Lincoln: University of Nebraska Press, 1996.

———. *The Baseball Story*. New York: Putnam, 1950.

Lynch, Michael T., Jr. *Harry Frazee, Ban Johnson, and the Feud That Nearly Destroyed the American League*. Jefferson, N.C.: McFarland, 2008.

Malone, Paul. *Dry Wells: A Century of No-Hitters*. Forest Lake, Minn.: Paul Malone, 1999.

Marshall, William. *Baseball's Pivotal Era, 1945–1951*. Lexington: University Press of Kentucky, 1999.

McCabe, Neal, and Constance McCabe. *Baseball's Golden Age: The Photographs of Charles M. Conlon*. New York: Harry N. Abrams, 1993.

Mills, Dorothy Jane. *A Woman's Work: Writing Baseball History with Harold Seymour*. Jefferson, N.C.: McFarland, 2004.

Moesche, Carl R. *Day-by-Day in Baseball History*. Jefferson, N.C.: McFarland, 2000.

Morris, Peter. *A Game of Inches: The Stories behind the Innovations That Shaped Baseball: Volume 1: The Game on the Field*. Chicago: Ivan R. Dee, 2006.

———. *A Game of Inches: The Stories behind the Innovations That Shaped Baseball: Volume 2: The Game behind the Scenes*. Chicago: Ivan R. Dee, 2006.

Morris, Peter, William J. Ryczek, Jan Finkel, Leonard Levin, and Richard Malatzky, eds. *Base Ball Pioneers, 1850–1870: The Clubs and Players Who Spread the Sport Nationwide*. Jefferson, N.C.: McFarland, 2012.

Nathanson, Mitchell. *A People's History of Baseball*. Champaign: University of Illinois Press, 2012.

Nemec, David. *The Rules of Baseball: An Anecdotal Look at the Rules of Baseball and How They Came to Be*. New York: Lyons & Burford, 1994.

Oakley, J. Ronald. *Baseball's Last Golden Age, 1946–1960: The National Pastime in a Time Of Glory and Change*. Jefferson, N.C.: McFarland, 1994.

Okkonen, Marc. *Baseball Uniforms of the 20th Century*. New York: Sterling, 1991.

Okrent, Daniel, and Harris Lewine, eds. *The Ultimate Baseball Book*. Boston: Houghton Mifflin, 1979.

Rader, Benjamin. *Baseball: A History of America's Game*. Urbana: University of Illinois Press, 1992.

Riess, Steven A. *City Games: The Evolution of American Urban Society and the Rise of Sports*. Urbana: University of Illinois Press, 1991.

———. *Touching Base: Professional Baseball and American Culture in the Progressive Era*, Rev. ed. Urbana: University of Illinois Press, 1999.

Ryczek, William J. *Baseball's First Inning*: *A History of the National Pastime through the Civil War*. Jefferson, N.C.: McFarland, 2009.

———. *When Johnny Came Sliding Home*: *The Post-Civil War Baseball Boom, 1865–1870*. Jefferson, N.C.: McFarland, 1998.

Seymour, Harold. *Baseball: The Early Years*. New York: Oxford University Press, 1960.

———. *Baseball: The Golden Age*. New York: Oxford University Press, 1971.

Shiffert, John. *Baseball in Philadelphia: A History of the Early Game, 1831–1900*. Jefferson, N.C.: McFarland, 2006.

Smith, Robert. *Baseball*. New York: Simon & Schuster, 1947.

———. *Baseball in the Afternoon: Tales from a Bygone Era*. New York: Simon & Schuster, 1993.

Solomon, Burt. *The Baseball Timeline*. New York: Dorling Kindersley, 2001.

Sowell, Mike. *July 2, 1903: The Mysterious Death of Hall-of-Famer Big Ed Delahanty*. New York: Macmillan, 1992.

Spalding, A. G. *Baseball: America's National Game, 1839–1915*. New York: American Sports, 1911.

Spink, Alfred H. *The National Game*, 2nd ed. Carbondale: Southern Illinois University Press, 2000.

Sullivan, Dean A., ed. *Early Innings: A Documentary History of Baseball, 1825–1908*. Lincoln: University of Nebraska Press, 1997.

———, ed. *Final Innings: A Documentary History of Baseball, 1972–2008*. Lincoln: University of Nebraska Press, 2010.

————, ed. *Late Innings: A Documentary History of Baseball, 1945–1972.* Lincoln: University of Nebraska Press, 2002.

————, ed. *Middle Innings: A Documentary History of Baseball, 1900–1948.* Lincoln: University of Nebraska Press, 1998.

Surdam, David George. *Wins, Losses, and Empty Seats: How Baseball Outlasted the Great Depression.* Lincoln: University of Nebraska Press, 2011.

Terry, James L. *Long before the Dodgers: Baseball in Brooklyn, 1855–1884.* Jefferson, N.C.: McFarland, 2002.

Thorn, John. *Baseball in the Garden of Eden: The Secret History of the Early Game.* New York: Simon & Schuster, 2011.

Tygiel, Jules. *Extra Bases: Reflections on Jackie Robinson, Race, and Baseball History.* Lincoln: University of Nebraska Press, 2002.

Voigt, David Q. *America through Baseball.* Chicago: Nelson-Hall, 1976.

Ward, Geoffrey C., and Ken Burns. *Baseball: An Illustrated History.* New York: Alfred A. Knopf, 1994.

White, G. Edward. *Creating the National Pastime: Baseball Transforms Itself, 1903–1953.* Princeton, N.J.: Princeton University Press, 1996.

Worth, Richard. *Baseball Team Names: A Dictionary of the Major, Minor, and Negro Leagues, 1869–2011.* Jefferson, N.C.: McFarland, 2012.

Zoss, Joel, and John Bowman. *Diamonds in the Rough: The Untold History of Baseball.* Lincoln: University of Nebraska Press, 2004.

B. Leagues

Pietrusza, David. *Major Leagues: 18 Professional Baseball Organizations, 1871 to Present.* Jefferson, N.C.: McFarland, 1991.

1. American Association

Achorn, Edward: The Summer of Beer and Whiskey: How Brewers, Barkeeps, Rowdies, Immigrants and a Wild Pennant Fight Made Baseball America's Game. New York: PublicAffairs Books, 2013.

Nemec, David. *The Beer and Whiskey League.* New York: Lyons & Burford, 1995.

2. American League

Allen, Lee. *The American League Story.* New York: Hill & Wang, 1965.

Fitzgerald, Ed, ed. *The Book of Major League Baseball Clubs: The American League.* New York: A. S. Barnes, 1955.

Wilbert, Warren N. *The Arrival of the American League: Ban Johnson and the 1901 Challenge to National League Monopoly.* Jefferson, N.C.: McFarland, 2007.

3. Federal League

Wiggins, Robert Peyton. *The Federal League of Base Ball Clubs: The History of an Outlaw Major League, 1914–1915.* Jefferson, N.C.: McFarland, 2009.
Levitt, Daniel R. The Battle that Forged Modern Baseball: The Federal League Challenge and Its Legacy. Lanham, MD: Ivan R. Dee, 2012.

4. National Association

Batesel, Paul. *Players and Teams of the National Association, 1871–1875.* Jefferson, N.C.: McFarland, 2012.
Ryczek, William J. *Blackguards and Red Stockings*: *A History of Baseball's National Association, 1871–1875.* Jefferson, N.C.: McFarland, 1992.

5. National Association of Base Ball Players

Wright, Marshall D. *The National Association of Base Ball Players, 1857–1870.* Jefferson, N.C.: McFarland, 2000.

6. National League

Allen, Lee. *The National League Story.* New York: Hill & Wang, 1961.
Fitzgerald, Ed, ed. *The Book of Major League Baseball Clubs: The National League.* New York: Grosset & Dunlap, 1952.
MacDonald, Neil W. *The League That Lasted*: *1876 and the Founding of the National League of Professional Base Ball Clubs.* Jefferson, N.C.: McFarland, 2006.
Melville, Tom. *Early Baseball and the Rise of the National League.* Jefferson, N.C.: McFarland, 2001.
Tiemann, Robert L. "The National League in 1893." *Baseball Research Journal,* 22 (1993), 38–41.

7. Players League

Koszarek, Ed. *The Players League: History, Clubs, Ballplayers, and Statistics.* Jefferson, N.C.: McFarland, 2006.

C. Teams

1. General and Multicity

Armour, Mark L., and Daniel R. Levitt. *Paths to Glory: How Great Baseball Teams Got That Way.* Dulles, Va.: Brassey's, 2003.

Bready, James, H. *Baseball in Baltimore: The First 100 Years.* Baltimore, Md.: Johns Hopkins University Press, 1998.

Cohen, Stanley. *Dodgers: The First 100 Years.* New York: Birch Lane Press, 1990.

Dewey, Donald, and Nicholas Acocella. *The Ball Clubs.* New York: Harper-Collins, 1996.

Frommer, Harvey. *Big Apple Baseball: An Illustrated History from the Boroughs to the Ballparks.* Dallas, Tex.: Taylor Press, 1995.

———. *New York City Baseball.* New York: Macmillan, 1980.

Goldblatt, Andrew. *The Giants and the Dodgers: Four Cities, Two Teams, One Rivalry.* Jefferson, N.C.: McFarland, 2003.

Helpingstine, Dan. *The Cubs and the White Sox: A Baseball Rivalry, 1900 to the Present.* Jefferson, N.C.: McFarland, 2010.

Kahn, Roger. *The Era, 1947–1957: When the Yankees, the Giants, and the Dodgers Ruled the World.* New York: Ticknor & Fields, 1993.

Linn, Ed. *The Great Rivalry: The Yankees and the Red Sox, 1901–1990.* New York: Ticknor & Fields, 1991.

Neyer, Rob, and Eddie Epstein. *Baseball Dynasties: The Greatest Teams of All Time.* New York: W. W. Norton, 2000.

Pietrusza, Davis. *Major Leagues: The Formation, Sometimes Absorption, and Mostly Inevitable Demise of 18 Professional Baseball Organizations, 1871 to Present.* Jefferson, N.C.: McFarland, 1991.

Robinson, George, and Charles Salzberg. *On a Clear Day They Could See Seventh Place: Baseball's Worst Teams.* Lincoln: University of Nebraska Press, 2010.

Snider, Duke, with Phil Pepe. *Few and Chosen: Defining Dodger Greatness across the Eras.* Chicago: Triumph Books, 2006.

Stout, Glenn, and Richard A. Johnson. *The Dodgers: 120 Years of Dodgers Baseball.* Boston: Houghton Mifflin, 2004.

Wilbert, Warren N. *A Cunning Kind of Play: The Cubs–Giants Rivalry, 1876–1932.* Jefferson, N.C.: McFarland, 2002.

2. Selected Current Teams

a. Baltimore Orioles   Bready, James H. *The Home Team: Our Orioles 25th Anniversary Edition*. Self-published, 1979.

Macht, Norman L. *Rex Barney's Orioles Memories, 1969–1994*. Woodbury, Conn.: Goodwood Press, 1994.

b. Boston Red Sox   Hubbard, Donald. *The Red Sox before the Babe: Boston's Early Days in the American League, 1901–1914*. Jefferson, N.C.: McFarland, 2009.

Lieb, Frederick G. *The Boston Red Sox*. New York: Putnam, 1947.

McNeil, William F. *Red Sox Roll Call: 200 Memorable Players, 1901–2011*. Jefferson, N.C.: McFarland, 2012.

Nowlin, Bill, and David Vincent. *The Ultimate Red Sox Home Run Guide*. Burlington, Mass.: Rounder Books, 2009.

Pahigian, Joshua R. *The Red Sox in the Playoffs: A Postseason History, 1903–2005*. Jefferson, N.C.: McFarland, 2006.

Stout, Glenn, and Richard A. Johnson. *Red Sox Century: One Hundred Years of Red Sox Baseball*. Boston: Houghton Mifflin, 2000.

c. Chicago Cubs   Roberts, Randy, and Carson Cunningham. *Before the Curse: The Chicago Cubs' Glory Years, 1870–1945*. Champaign: University of Illinois Press, 2012.

Wood, Gerald C., and Andrew Hazucha, eds. *Northsiders: Essays on the History and Culture of the Chicago Cubs*. Jefferson, N.C.: McFarland, 2008.

d. Chicago White Sox   Brown, Warren. *The Chicago White Sox*. New York: Putnam, 1952.

Lindberg, Richard. *Who's on 3rd? The Chicago White Sox Story*. South Bend, Ind.: Icarus, 1983.

Nathan, Daniel A. *Saying It's So: A Cultural History of the Black Sox Scandal*. Urbana: University of Illinois Press, 2005.

e. Cincinnati Reds   Allen, Lee. *The Cincinnati Reds*. New York: Putnam, 1948.

f. Cleveland Indians   Lewis, Franklin A. *The Cleveland Indians*. New York: Putnam, 1949.

Schneider, Russell. *Tribe Memories: The First Century*. Hinkley, Ohio: Moonlight Press, 2000.

g. Detroit Tigers   Harrigan, Patrick. *The Detroit Tigers: Club and Community, 1945–95*. Toronto: University of Toronto Press, 1997.

Lieb, Frederick G. *The Detroit Tigers*. New York: Putnam, 1946.

h. New York Mets   Brand, Dana. *Mets Fan*. Jefferson, N.C.: McFarland, 2007.

Lang, Jack, and Peter Simon. *The New York Mets*. New York: Henry Holt, 1986.

Ryczek, William J. *The Amazin' Mets, 1962–1969*. Jefferson, N.C.: McFarland, 2008.

Silverman, Matthew. *Best Mets: Fifty Years of Highs and Lows from New York's Most Agonizingly Amazin' Team*. Boulder, Colo.: Taylor Press, 2012.

i. New York Yankees Anderson, Dave, Murray Chass, Robert W. Creamer, and Harold Rosenthal. *The Yankees: Four Fabulous Eras of Baseball's Most Famous Team*. New York: Random House, 1979.

Appel, Marty. *Pinstripe Empire: The New York Yankees from before the Babe to after the Boss*. New York: Bloomsbury, 2012.

Chadwick, Bruce, and David Spindel. *The Bronx Bombers*. New York: Abbeville Press, 1991.

Cohen, Robert W. *The Lean Years of the Yankees, 1965–1975*. Jefferson, N.C.: McFarland, 2004.

Freedman, Lew. *DiMaggio's Yankees: A History of the 1936–1944 Dynasty*. Jefferson, N.C.: McFarland, 2011.

Frommer, Harvey. *A Yankee Century: A Celebration of the First Hundred Years of Baseball's Greatest Team*. New York: Berkley Books, 2002.

Gallagher, Mark. *The Yankee Encyclopedia*. Champaign, Ill.: Sagamore, 1996.

Golenbock, Peter. *Dynasty: The New York Yankees, 1949–1964*. New York: Prentice Hall, 1975.

Graham, Frank. *The New York Yankees: An Informal History*. New York: Putnam, 1943.

Henrich, Tommy, with Bill Gilbert. *Five O'Clock Lightning: Ruth, Gehrig, DiMaggio, Mantle, and the Glory Years of the NY Yankees*. New York: Birch Lane Press, 1992.

Istorico, Ray. *Greatness in Waiting: An Illustrated History of the Early New York Yankees, 1903–1919*. Jefferson, N.C.: McFarland, 2008.

Kelley, Brent. *They Too Wore Pinstripes: Interviews with 20 Glory-Days New York Yankees*. Jefferson, N.C.: McFarland, 1998.

Meany, Tom. *The Yankee Story*. New York: E. P. Dutton, 1960.

Reisler, Jim. *Before They Were the Bombers: The New York Yankees' Early Years, 1903–1915*. Jefferson, N.C.: McFarland, 2002.

Spatz, Lyle. *New York Yankee Openers: An Opening Day History of Baseball's Most Famous Team, 1903–1996*. Jefferson, N.C.: McFarland, 1997.

———. *Yankees Coming, Yankees Going: New York Yankee Player Transactions, 1903 through 1999*. Jefferson, N.C.: McFarland, 2000.

Stout, Glenn, and Richard A. Johnson. *Yankees Century: One Hundred Years of New York Yankees Baseball*. Boston: Houghton Mifflin, 2002.

Sullivan, George, and John Powers. *Yankees: An Illustrated History*. Englewood Cliffs, N.J.: Prentice Hall, 1982.

Sullivan, Neil. *The Diamond in the Bronx*. New York: Oxford University Press, 2001.

Surdam, David G. *The Postwar Yankees: Baseball's Golden Age Revisited*. Lincoln: University of Nebraska Press, 2008.

Tan, Cecilia. *The 50 Greatest Yankee Games*. Hoboken, N.J.: John Wiley, 2005.

Tullius, John. *I'd Rather Be a Yankee: An Oral History of America's Most Beloved and Most Hated Baseball Team*. New York: Macmillan, 1986.

j. Oakland Athletics   Markusen, Bruce. *Baseball's Last Dynasty: Charlie Finley's Oakland A's*. Dallas, Tex.: Masters Press, 1998.

k. Philadelphia Phillies   Lieb, Frederick, and Stan Baumgartner. *The Philadelphia Phillies*. New York: Putnam, 1953.

l. Pittsburgh Pirates   Adomites, Paul, and Dennis DeValera. *Baseball in Pittsburgh: An Anthology of New, Unusual, Challenging, and Amazing Facts about the Greatest Game as Played in the Steel City*. Lincoln: University of Nebraska Press, 1995.

Lieb, Frederick. *The Pittsburgh Pirates*. New York: Putnam, 1948.

m. St. Louis Cardinals   Broeg, Bob, and Jerry Vickery. *The St. Louis Cardinals Encyclopedia*. Chicago: Contemporary Books, 1998.

Freese, Mel R. *The St. Louis Cardinals in the 1940s*. Jefferson, N.C.: McFarland, 2007.

Lieb, Frederick. *The St. Louis Cardinals*. New York: Putnam, 1944.

Tiemann, Bob. *Mound City Memories: Baseball in St. Louis*. Lincoln: University of Nebraska Press, 2007.

3. Extinct Teams

a. Baltimore Orioles   Lieb, Frederick. *The Baltimore Orioles*. New York: Putnam, 1955.

Solomon, Burt. *Where They Ain't: The Fabled Life and Untimely Death of the Original Baltimore Orioles, the Team That Gave Rise to Modern Baseball*. New York: Free Press, 1999.

b. Boston Braves   Fuchs, Robert S., and Wayne Soini. *Judge Fuchs and the Boston Braves, 1923–1935*. Jefferson, N.C.: McFarland, 1998.

c. Brooklyn Dodgers   Golenbock, Peter. *Bums: An Oral History of the Brooklyn Dodgers*. New York: G. P. Putnam's Sons, 1984.

Graham, Frank. *The Brooklyn Dodgers*. New York: Putnam, 1945.

Honig, Donald. *The Brooklyn Dodgers: An Illustrated Tribute*. New York: St. Martin's Press, 1981.

Kahn, Roger. *The Boys of Summer*. New York: Harper & Row, 1971.

Marzano, Rudy. *The Brooklyn Dodgers in the 1940s: How Robinson, MacPhail, Reiser, and Rickey Changed Baseball*. Jefferson, N.C.: McFarland, 2005.

————. *The Last Years of the Brooklyn Dodgers: A History, 1950–1957*. Jefferson, N.C.: McFarland, 2008.

McNeil, William F. *The Dodger Encyclopedia*. Champaign, Ill.: Sports Publishing, 1997.

Mele, Andrew Paul. *A Brooklyn Dodgers Reader*. Jefferson, N.C.: McFarland, 2005.

Prince, Carl E. *Brooklyn's Dodgers: The Bums, the Borough, and the Best of Baseball, 1947–1957*. New York: Oxford University Press, 1996.

Tiemann, Robert L. *Dodger Classics*. St. Louis, Mo.: Baseball Histories, 1983.

Wolpin, Stewart. *Bums No More! The Championship Season of the 1955 Brooklyn Dodgers*. New York: Harkavy Press/St. Martin's Press, 1995.

d. Cincinnati Red Stockings   Ellard, Harry. *Baseball in Cincinnati: A History*. Jefferson, N.C.: McFarland, 2004.

Guschov, Steven D. *The Red Stockings of Cincinnati: Base Ball's First All-Professional Team and Its Historic 1869 and 1870 Seasons*. Jefferson, N.C.: McFarland, 1998.

e. Louisville Grays   Cook, William A. *The Louisville Grays Scandal of 1877: The Taint of Gambling at the Dawn of the National League*. Jefferson, N.C.: McFarland, 2005.

f. New York Giants   Graham, Frank. *The New York Giants: An Informal History*. New York: Putnam, 1952.

Hardy, James D., Jr. *The New York Giants Base Ball Club: The Growth of a Team and a Sport, 1870 to 1900*. Jefferson, N.C.: McFarland, 1996.

Hynd, Noel. *The Giants of the Polo Grounds*. New York: Doubleday, 1988.

Stein, Fred. *Under Coogan's Bluff: A Fan's Recollections of the New Giants under Terry and Ott*. Self-published, 1979.

Thornley, Stew. *Land of the Giants: New York's Polo Grounds*. Philadelphia, Pa.: Temple University Press, 2000.

Williams, Peter. *When the Giants Were Giants: Bill Terry and the Golden Age of New York Baseball*. Chapel Hill, N.C.: Algonquin Books, 1994.

g. Philadelphia Athletics   Jordan, David M. *The Athletics of Philadelphia: Connie Mack's White Elephants, 1901–1954*. Jefferson, N.C.: McFarland, 1999.

h. Seattle Pilots   Hogan, Kenneth. *The 1969 Seattle Pilots: Major League Baseball's One-Year Team*. Jefferson, N.C.: McFarland, 2007.

i. St. Louis Browns   Mead, William B. *Even the Browns: The Zany, True Story of Baseball in the Early Forties*. Chicago: Contemporary Books, 1978.

j. Washington Senators   Beale, Morris Allison. *The Washington Senators*. Charlottesville: University of Virginia Press, 1947.

Deveaux, Tom. *The Washington Senators, 1901–1971*. Jefferson, N.C.: McFarland, 2001.

Povich, Shirley. *The Washington Senators*. New York: Putnam, 1954.

D. Seasons

Adelman, Tom. *Black and Blue: The Golden Arm, the Robinson Boys, and the 1966 World Series That Stunned America*. New York: Little, Brown, 2006.

Adler, Richard. *Mack, McGraw, and the 1913 Baseball Season*. Jefferson, N.C.: McFarland, 2008.

Alexander, Charles C. *Turbulent Seasons: Baseball in 1890–1891*. Dallas, Tex.: Southern Methodist University Press, 2011.

Anderson, Dave. *Pennant Races: Baseball at Its Best*. New York: Doubleday, 1994.

Anderson, David W. *More Than Merkle: A History of the Best and Most Exciting Baseball Season in Human History*. Lincoln: University of Nebraska Press, 2000.

Armour, Mark, and Malcolm Allen, eds. *Pitching, Defense, and Three-Run Homers: The 1970 Baltimore Orioles*. Lincoln: University of Nebraska Press, 2012.

Asinof, Eliot. *Eight Men Out*. New York: Holt, Rinehart and Winston, 1963.

Barber, Red. *1947: When All Hell Broke Loose in Baseball*. Garden City, N.Y.: Doubleday, 1982.

Boren, Stephen D., and Thomas Boren. "The 1942 Pennant Race." *National Pastime*, 15 (1995), 133–35.

Boston, Talmage. *1939, Baseball's Pivotal Year*. Fort Worth, Tex.: Summit Group, 1994.

Bouton, Jim. *Ball Four*. New York: Macmillan, 1970.

Browning, Reed. *Baseball's Greatest Season: 1924*. Amherst: University of Massachusetts Press, 2003.

Caillault, Jean-Pierre. *A Tale of Four Cities*: *Nineteenth-Century Baseball's Most Exciting Season, 1889, in Contemporary Accounts*. Jefferson, N.C.: McFarland, 2003.

Cook, William A. *The Summer of '64: A Pennant Lost*. Jefferson, N.C.: McFarland, 2002.

Cottrell, Robert C. *Blackball, the Black Sox, and the Babe: Baseball's Crucial 1920 Season*. Jefferson, N.C.: McFarland, 2002.

Creamer, Robert W. *Baseball in '41*. New York: Penguin Group. 1991.

DiMaggio, Dom, with Bill Gilbert. *Real Grass, Real Heroes: Baseball's Historic 1941 Season*. New York: Zebra Books, 1990.

Doutrich, Paul E. *The Cardinals and the Yankees, 1926: A Classic Season and St. Louis in Seven*. Jefferson, N.C.: McFarland, 2002.

Endsley, Brian M. *Bums No More: The 1959 Los Angeles Dodgers, World Champions of Baseball*. Jefferson, N.C.: McFarland, 2009.

Felber, Bill. *A Game of Brawl: The Orioles, the Beaneaters, and the Battle for the 1897 Pennant*. Lincoln: University of Nebraska Press, 2007.

———. *Under Pallor, Under Shadow: The 1920 American League Pennant Race That Rattled and Rebuilt Baseball*. Lincoln: University of Nebraska Press, 2011.

Feldmann, Doug. *Dizzy and the Gashouse Gang: The 1934 St. Louis Cardinals and Depression-Era Baseball*. Jefferson, N.C.: McFarland, 2000.

———. *El Birdos: The 1967 and 1968 St. Louis Cardinals*. Jefferson, N.C.: McFarland, 2007.

———. *Fleeter Than Birds: The 1985 St. Louis Cardinals and Small Ball's Last Hurrah*. Jefferson, N.C.: McFarland, 2002.

———. *Miracle Collapse: The 1969 Chicago Cubs*. Lincoln: University of Nebraska Press, 2009.

———. *September Streak: The 1935 Chicago Cubs Chase the Pennant*. Jefferson, N.C.: McFarland, 2003.

Fleming, G. H. *The Dizziest Season: The Gashouse Gang Chases the Pennant*. New York: William Morrow, 1984.

Halberstam, David. *October 1964*. New York: Villard Books, 1994.

———. *Summer of '49*. New York: William Morrow, 1989.

Jennison, Christopher. *Wait 'til Next Year: The Yankees, Dodgers, and Giants, 1947–1957*. New York: W. W. Norton, 1974.

Kashatus, William C. *Connie Mack's '29 Triumph: The Rise and Fall of the Philadelphia Athletics Dynasty*. Jefferson, N.C.: McFarland, 1999.

Kubek, Tony, and Terry Pluto. *Sixty-One: The Team, The Record, The Men*. New York: Macmillan, 1987.

Leavengood, Ted. *The 2005 Washington Nationals: Major League Baseball Returns to the Capital*. Jefferson, N.C.: McFarland, 2006.

———. *Ted Williams and the 1969 Washington Senators: The Last Winning Season*. Jefferson, N.C.: McFarland, 2009.

Marzano, Rudy. *New York Baseball in 1951: The Dodgers, the Giants, the Yankees, and the Telescope*. Jefferson, N.C.: McFarland, 2011.

Masters, Todd. *The 1972 Detroit Tigers: Billy Martin and the Half-Game Champs*. Jefferson, N.C.: McFarland, 2010.

Mayer, Ronald A. *The 1923 New York Yankees: A History of Their First World Championship Season*. Jefferson, N.C.: McFarland, 2010.

McNeil, William F. *Miracle in Chavez Ravine: The Los Angeles Dodgers in 1988*. Jefferson, N.C.: McFarland, 2008.

Morgan, Bruce. *Steve Carlton and the 1972 Phillies*. Jefferson, N.C.: McFarland, 2012.

Mosedale, John. *The Greatest of All: The 1927 New York Yankees*. New York: Dial, 1974.

Mulligan, Brian. *The 1940 Cincinnati Reds: A World Championship and Baseball's Only In-Season Suicide.* Jefferson, N.C.: McFarland, 2005.

Murnau, Thad. *An Indian Summer: The 1957 Milwaukee Braves, Champions of Baseball.* Jefferson, N.C.: McFarland, 2007.

Murphy, Cait. *Crazy '08: How a Cast of Cranks, Rogues, Boneheads, and Magnates Created the Greatest Year in Baseball History.* New York: HarperCollins, 2007.

Nathanson, Mitchell. *The Fall of the 1977 Phillies: How a Baseball Team's Collapse Sank a City's Spirit.* Jefferson, N.C.: McFarland, 2008.

Nowlin, Bill, and Dan Desrochers, eds. *The 1967 Impossible Dream Red Sox: Pandemonium on the Field.* Burlington, Mass.: Rounder Books, 2007.

Nowlin, Bill, and Cecilia Tan, eds. *'75: The Red Sox Team That Saved Baseball.* Cambridge, Mass.: Rounder Books, 2005.

Pepe, Phil. *1961*: The Inside Story of the Maris-Mantle Home Run Chase.* Chicago: Triumph Books, 2011.

Prager, Joshua. *The Echoing Green: The Untold Story of Bobby Thomson, Ralph Branca, and the Shot Heard round the World.* New York: Pantheon Books, 2006.

Ranier, Bill, and David Finoli. *When the Bucs Won It All: The 1979 World Champion Pittsburgh Pirates.* Jefferson, N.C.: McFarland, 2005.

Rogers, C. Paul. *The Whiz Kids and the 1950 Pennant.* Philadelphia, Pa.: Temple University Press, 1996.

Rossi, John P. *The 1964 Phillies: The Story of Baseball's Most Memorable Collapse.* Jefferson, N.C.: McFarland, 2005.

Sarnoff, Gary A. *The Wrecking Crew of '33: The Washington Senators' Last Pennant.* Jefferson, N.C.: McFarland, 2009.

Seidel, Michael. *Streak: Joe DiMaggio and the Summer of '41.* New York: McGraw-Hill, 1988.

Shafer, Ronald G. *When the Dodgers Were Bridegrooms: Gunner McGunnigle and Brooklyn's Back-to-Back Pennants of 1889 and 1890.* Jefferson, N.C.: McFarland, 2011.

Smith, Burge Cameron. *The 1945 Detroit Tigers: Nine Old Men and One Young Left Arm Win It All.* Jefferson, N.C.: McFarland, 2010.

Sowell, Mike. *The Pitch That Killed: Carl Mays, Ray Chapman, and the Pennant Race of 1920.* New York: Macmillan, 1989.

Spatz, Lyle, ed. *The Team That Forever Changed Baseball and America: The 1947 Brooklyn Dodgers.* Lincoln: University of Nebraska Press, 2012.

Spatz, Lyle, and Steve Steinberg. *1921: The Yankees, the Giants, and the Battle for Baseball Supremacy in New York.* Lincoln: University of Nebraska Press, 2010.

Waldo, Ronald T. *The Battling Bucs of 1925: How the Pittsburgh Pirates Pulled Off the Greatest Comeback in World Series History.* Jefferson, N.C.: McFarland, 2012.

Webster, Gary. *Tris Speaker and the 1920 Indians: Tragedy to Glory.* Jefferson, N.C.: McFarland, 2012.

Wendel, Tim. *Summer of '68: The Season That Changed Baseball—and America—Forever.* Cambridge, Mass.: Da Capo Press, 2012.

Wilbert, Warren N., and William C. Hageman. *The 1917 White Sox: The World Championship Season.* Jefferson, N.C.: McFarland, 2004.

Wilson, Doug. *Fred Hutchinson and the 1964 Cincinnati Reds.* Jefferson, N.C.: McFarland, 2010.

Zardetto, Ray. *'30: Major League Baseball's Year of the Batter.* Jefferson, N.C.: McFarland, 2008.

Zinn, Paul G., and John G. Zinn. *The Major League Pennant Races of 1916: "The Most Maddening Baseball Melee in History."* Jefferson, N.C.: McFarland, 2009.

Zminda, Don, ed. *Go-Go to Glory: The 1959 Chicago White Sox.* Chicago: Acta Sports, 2009.

Zolecki, Todd, and James Salisbury. *The Rotation: A Season with the Phillies and One of the Greatest Pitching Staffs Ever Assembled.* Philadelphia, Pa.: Running Press, 2012.

E. Biographies

1. Selected Collections, Duos, and Trios

Baldassaro, Lawrence. "Before Joe D: Early Italian Americans in the Major Leagues." In Lawrence Baldassaro and Richard A. Johnson, eds., *The American Game: Baseball and Ethnicity*, 92–115. Carbondale: Southern Illinois University Press, 2002.

———. *Beyond DiMaggio: Italian Americans in Baseball.* Lincoln: University of Nebraska Press, 2011.

Batesel, Paul. *Major League Baseball Players of 1884.* Jefferson, N.C.: McFarland, 2011.

———. *Major League Baseball Players of 1916.* Jefferson, N.C.: McFarland, 2007.

Bogen, Gil. *Tinker, Evers, and Chance: A Triple Biography.* Jefferson, N.C.: McFarland, 2003.

Boxerman, Buton A., and Benita W. Boxerman. *Jews in Baseball: Entering the American Mainstream, 1871–1948.* Jefferson, N.C.: McFarland, 2007.

———. *Jews in Baseball: The Post-Greenberg Years, 1949–2008.* Jefferson, N.C.: McFarland, 2010.

Carmichael, John P., ed. *My Greatest Day in Baseball*. New York: A. S. Barnes, 1945.

Cleve, Craig Allen. *Hardball on the Home Front: Major League Replacement Players of World War II*. Jefferson, N.C.: McFarland, 2004.

Deford, Frank. *The Old Ball Game*. New York: Atlantic Monthly Press, 2005.

Dewey, Donald, and Nicholas Acocella. *The Biographical History of Baseball*. New York: Carroll and Graf, 1995.

Dragseth, P. J. *Major League Scouts: A Biographical Dictionary*. Jefferson, N.C.: McFarland, 2011.

Ephross, Peter, with Martin Abramowitz. *Jewish Major Leaguers in Their Own Words: Oral Histories of 23 Players*. Jefferson, N.C.: McFarland, 2012.

Fleitz, David L. *The Irish in Baseball: An Early History*. Jefferson, N.C.: McFarland, 2009.

Frommer, Harvey. *Rickey and Robinson*. New York: Macmillan, 1982.

Gerlach, Larry. *The Men in Blue: Conversations with Umpires*. Lincoln, Nebr.: Bison Books, 1994.

Gittleman, Sol. *Reynolds, Raschi, and Lopat: New York's Big Three and the Great Yankee Dynasty of 1949–1953*. Jefferson, N.C.: McFarland, 2007.

Grayson, Harry. *They Played the Game*. New York: A. S. Barnes, 1944.

Green, Paul. *Forgotten Fields*. Waupaca, Wisc.: Parker Publications, 1984.

Halberstam, David. *The Teammates: A Portrait of a Friendship*. New York: Hyperion Books, 2003.

Honig, Donald. *Baseball When the Grass Was Real*. Lincoln, Nebr.: Bison Books, 1993.

———. *The Man in the Dugout: Fifteen Big-League Managers Speak Their Minds*. Lincoln, Nebr.: Bison Books, 1995.

Hubbard, Donald. *The Heavenly Twins of Boston Baseball: A Dual Biography of Hugh Duffy and Tommy McCarthy*. Jefferson, N.C.: McFarland, 2008.

Ivor-Campbell, Frederick, Robert L. Tiemann, and Mark Rucker, eds. *Baseball's First Stars*. Lincoln: University of Nebraska Press, 1996.

Jones, David, ed. *Deadball Stars of the American League*. Washington, D.C.: Potomac Books, 2006.

Joyner, Ronnie. *Hardball Legends and Journeymen and Short-Timers: 333 Illustrated Baseball Biographies*. Jefferson, N.C.: McFarland, 2012.

Kiersch, Edward. *Where Have You Gone, Vince DiMaggio?* New York: Bantam Books, 1983.

Kiser, Brett. *Baseball's War Roster: A Biographical Dictionary of Major and Negro League Players Who Served, 1861 to the Present*. Jefferson, N.C.: McFarland, 2012.

Langford, Walter M. *Legends of Baseball: An Oral History of the Game's Golden Age.* South Bend, Ind.: Diamond Communications, 1987.

Lee, Bill. *The Baseball Necrology : The Post-Baseball Lives and Deaths of More Than 7,600 Major League Players and Others.* Jefferson, N.C.: McFarland, 2009.

Linkugel, Wil A., and Edward J. Pappas. *They Tasted Glory: Among the Missing at the Baseball Hall of Fame.* Jefferson, N.C.: McFarland, 1998.

Marazzi, Rich, and Len Fiorito. *Baseball Players of the 1950s: A Biographical Dictionary of All 1,560 Major Leaguers.* Jefferson, N.C.: McFarland, 2010.

McKelvey, G. Richard. *The MacPhails: Baseball's First Family of the Front Office.* Jefferson, N.C.: McFarland, 2000.

Moffi, Larry. *The Conscience of the Game: Baseball's Commissioners from Landis to Selig.* Lincoln: University of Nebraska Press, 2006.

Murdock, Eugene C. *Baseball between the Wars: Memories of the Game by the Men Who Played It.* Westport, Conn.: Meckler Publishing, 1992.

———. *Baseball Players and Their Times: Oral Histories of the Game, 1920–1940.* Westport, Conn.: Meckler Publishing, 1991.

Nemec, David, ed. *Major League Baseball Profiles, 1871–1900, Volume 1: The Ballplayers Who Built the Game.* Lincoln: University of Nebraska Press, 2011.

———, ed. *Major League Baseball Profiles, 1871–1900, Volume 2: The Hall of Famers and Memorable Personalities Who Shaped the Game.* Lincoln: University of Nebraska Press, 2011.

———, ed. *The Rank and File of 19th-Century Major League Baseball: Biographies of 1,084 Players, Owners, Managers, and Umpires.* Jefferson, N.C.: McFarland, 2012.

Parker, Clifton Blue. *Big and Little Poison: Paul and Lloyd Waner, Baseball Brothers.* Jefferson, N.C.: McFarland, 2003.

Peary, Danny, ed. *Cult Baseball Players: The Greats, the Flakes, the Weird, and the Wonderful.* New York: Simon & Schuster, 1990.

Pease, Neal. "Diamonds out of the Coal Mines: Slavic Americans in Baseball." In Lawrence Baldassaro and Richard A. Johnson, eds., *The American Game: Baseball and Ethnicity,* 142–61. Carbondale: Southern Illinois University Press, 2002.

Pietrusza, David, Matthew Silverman, and Michael Gershman, eds. *Baseball: The Biographical Encyclopedia.* Kingston, N.Y.: Total Sports Illustrated, 2000.

Porter, David L., ed. *Biographical Dictionary of American Sports: Baseball,* Rev. and exp. ed. Westport, Conn: Greenwood Press, 2000.

Powers-Beck, Jeffrey. *The American Indian Integration of Baseball.* Lincoln: University of Nebraska Press, 2004.

Reston, James, Jr. *Collision at Home Plate: The Lives of Pete Rose and Bart Giamatti.* New York: Harper Perennial, 1992.

Ritter, Lawrence S. *The Glory of Their Times: The Story of the Early Days of Baseball Told by the Men Who Played It.* New York: William Morrow, 1984.

Rosen, Charley. *The Emerald Diamond: How the Irish Transformed America's Greatest Pastime.* New York: HarperCollins, 2012.

Shatzkin, Mike, ed. *The Ballplayers.* New York: William Morrow, 1990.

Simon, Tom, ed. *Deadball Stars of the National League.* Washington, D.C.: Brassey's, 2004.

Skipper, James K., Jr. *Baseball Nicknames: A Dictionary of Origins and Meanings.* Jefferson, N.C.: McFarland, 1992.

Skipper, John C. *A Biographical Dictionary of the Baseball Hall of Fame,* 2nd ed. Jefferson, N.C.: McFarland, 2008.

———. *A Biographical Dictionary of Major League Baseball Managers.* Jefferson, N.C.: McFarland, 2011.

Stein, Fred. *And the Skipper Bats Cleanup: A History of the Baseball Player-Manager, with 42 Biographies of Men Who Filled the Dual Role.* Jefferson, N.C.: McFarland, 2002.

Thompson, Dick. *The Ferrell Brothers of Baseball.* Jefferson, N.C.: McFarland, 2005.

Tiemann, Robert L., and Mark Rucker, eds. *Nineteenth-Century Stars.* Kansas City, Mo.: Society for American Baseball Research,1989.

Wiggins, Robert Peyton. *The Deacon and the Schoolmaster: Phillippe and Leever, Pittsburgh's Great Turn-of-the-Century Pitchers.* Jefferson, N.C.: McFarland, 2011.

2. Selected Individual Players

a. Hank Aaron   Aaron, Hank. *I Had a Hammer.* New York: HarperCollins, 1991.

Bryant, Howard. *The Last Hero: A Life of Henry Aaron.* New York: Pantheon Books, 2010.

Stanton, Tom. *Hank Aaron and the Home Run That Changed America.* New York: HarperCollins, 2004.

b. Grover Alexander   Kavanagh, Jack. *Ol' Pete: The Grover Cleveland Alexander Story.* South Bend, Ind.: Diamond Communications, 1996.

Skipper, John C. *Wicked Curve: The Life and Troubled Times of Grover Cleveland Alexander.* Jefferson, N.C.: McFarland, 2006.

c. Cap Anson   Anson, Adrian C. *A Ball Player's Career.* Chicago: Era Publishing, 1900.

Fleitz, David L. *Cap Anson: The Grand Old Man of Baseball.* Jefferson, N.C.: McFarland, 2005.

d. Richie Ashburn   Mowday, Bruce, and Jim Donaway. *Richie Ashburn: Why the Hall Not? The Amazing Journey to Cooperstown.* Fort Lee, N.J.: Barricade Books, 2011.

e. Frank Baker   Sparks, Barry. *Frank "Home Run" Baker: Hall of Famer and World Series Hero.* Jefferson, N.C.: McFarland, 2006.

f. Johnny Bench   Bench, Johnny. *Catch Every Ball: How to Handle Life's Pitches.* Wilmington, Ohio: Orange Frazer Press, 2008.

g. Chief Bender   Swift, Tom. *Chief Bender's Burden: The Silent Struggle of a Baseball Star.* Lincoln: University of Nebraska Press, 2008.

Wiggins, Robert Peyton. *Chief Bender: A Baseball Biography.* Jefferson, N.C.: McFarland, 2010.

h. Yogi Berra   Barra, Allan. *Yogi Berra: Eternal Yankee.* New York: W. W. Norton, 2009.

Berra, Yogi, and Dave Kaplan. *Ten Rings: My Championship Seasons.* New York: HarperCollins, 2003.

DeVito, Carlo. *Yogi: The Life and Times of an American Original.* Chicago: Triumph Books, 2008.

i. Barry Bonds   Bloom, John. *Barry Bonds: A Biography.* Westport, Conn.: Greenwood Press, 2004.

Pearlman, Jeff. *Love Me, Hate Me: Barry Bonds and the Making of an Antihero.* New York: HarperCollins, 2006.

j. George Brett   Bannon, Joe, Jr., ed. *George Brett: A Royal Hero.* Kansas City, Mo.: Sports Publishing, 1999.

k. Mordecai Brown   Thomson, Cindy, and Scott Brown. *Three Finger: The Mordecai Brown Story.* Lincoln: University of Nebraska Press, 2006.

l. Jim Bunning   Dolson, Frank. *Jim Bunning: Baseball and Beyond.* Philadelphia, Pa.: Temple University Press, 1998.

m. Roy Campanella   Campanella, Roy. *It's Good to Be Alive.* Lincoln: University of Nebraska Press, 1995.

Lanctot, Neil. *Campy: The Two Lives of Roy Campanella.* New York: Simon & Schuster, 2011.

n. Gary Carter   Carter, Gary. *Still a Kid at Heart: My Life in Baseball and Beyond.* Chicago: Triumph Books, 2008.

o. Fred Clarke   Waldo, Ronald T. *Fred Clarke: A Biography of the Baseball Hall of Fame Player-Manager.* Jefferson, N.C.: McFarland, 2011.

p. Roger Clemens   Pearlman, Jeff. *The Rocket That Fell to Earth: Roger Clemens and the Rage for Baseball Immortality.* New York: HarperCollins, 2009.

q. Roberto Clemente   Maraniss, David. *Clemente: The Passion and Grace of Baseball's Last Hero.* New York: Simon & Schuster, 2006.

r. Ty Cobb   Alexander, Charles C. *Ty Cobb.* New York: Oxford University Press, 1984.

McCallum, John D. *Ty Cobb.* New York: Praeger, 1975.

Okkonen, Marc. *The Ty Cobb Scrapbook*. New York: Sterling Publishing, 2001.

Stump, Al. *Cobb, a Biography: The Life and Times of the Meanest Man Who Ever Played Baseball*. Chapel Hill, N.C.: Algonquin Books, 1994.

s. Mickey Cochrane   Bevis, Charlie. *Mickey Cochrane: The Life of a Baseball Hall of Fame Catcher*. Jefferson, N.C.: McFarland, 1998.

t. Eddie Collins   Huhn, Rick. *Eddie Collins: A Baseball Biography*. Jefferson, N.C.: McFarland, 2008.

u. Roger Conno   Kerr, Roy. *Roger Connor: Home Run King of 19th-Century Baseball*. Jefferson, N.C.: McFarland, 2011.

v. Joe Cronin   Armour, Mark. *Joe Cronin: A Life in Baseball*. Lincoln: University of Nebraska Press, 2010.

w. Kiki Cuyler   Waldo, Ronald T. *Hazen "Kiki" Cuyler: A Baseball Biography*. Jefferson, N.C.: McFarland, 2012.

x. Andre Dawson   Dawson, Andre, with Tom Bird. *Hawk*. Grand Rapids, Mich.: Zondervan Publishing, 1994.

y. Ed Delahanty   Casway, Jerrold. *Ed Delahanty in the Emerald Age of Baseball*. South Bend, Ind.: University Press of Notre Dame, 2004.

z. Joe DiMaggio   Allen, Maury. *Where Have You Gone, Joe DiMaggio? The Story of America's Last Hero*. New York: E. P. Dutton, 1975.

Cramer, Richard Ben. *Joe DiMaggio: The Hero's Life*. New York: Simon & Schuster, 2001.

Moore, Jack B. *Joe DiMaggio: Baseball's Yankee Clipper*. New York: Praeger, 1986.

aa. Larry Doby   Moore, Joseph Thomas. *Pride against Prejudice: The Biography of Larry Doby*. Westport, Conn.: Greenwood Press, 1988.

bb. Johnny Evers   Evers, John J., and Hugh S. Fullerton. *Touching Second*. Jefferson, N.C.: McFarland, 2005.

cc. Buck Ewing   Kerr, Roy. *Buck Ewing: A Baseball Biography*. Jefferson, N.C.: McFarland, 2012.

dd. Red Faber   Cooper, Brian E. *Red Faber: A Biography of the Hall of Fame Spitball Pitcher*. Jefferson, N.C.: McFarland, 2007.

ee. Bob Feller   Feller, Bob, and Bill Gilbert. *Now Pitching, Bob Feller*. New York: Harper Perennial, 1990.

Feller, Bob, with Burton Rocks. *Bob Feller's Little Blue Book of Baseball Wisdom*. Chicago: Triumph Books, 2009.

ff. Rick Ferrell   Ferrell, Kerrie, with William M. Anderson. *Rick Ferrell, Knuckleball Catcher: A Hall of Famer's Life behind the Plate and in the Front Office*. Jefferson, N.C.: McFarland, 2010.

gg. Curt Flood   Snyder, Brad. *A Well-Paid Slave: Curt Flood's Fight for Free Agency in Professional Sports*. New York: Penguin Books, 2006.

hh. Whitey Ford   Coverdale, Miles, Jr. *Whitey Ford: A Biography*. Jefferson, N.C.: McFarland, 2006.

ii. Rube Foster   Cottrell, Robert C. *The Best Pitcher in Baseball: The Life of Rube Foster, Negro League Giant.* New York: New York University Press, 2001.

Lester, Larry. *Rube Foster in His Time: On the Field and in the Papers with Black Baseball's Greatest Visionary.* Jefferson, N.C.: McFarland, 2012.

jj. Nellie Fox   Gough, David, and Jim Bard. *Little Nel: The Nellie Fox Story.* New York: D. L. Megbec Publishing, 2000.

kk. Jimmie Foxx   Gorman, Bob. *Double X: The Story of Jimmie Foxx, Baseball's Forgotten Slugger.* Camden, N.J.: Holy Name Society, 1990.

Harrison, Daniel W. *Jimmie Foxx: The Life and Times of a Baseball Hall of Famer, 1907–1967.* Jefferson, N.C.: McFarland, 2004.

Millikin, Mark. *Jimmie Foxx: The Pride of Sudlersville.* Lanham, Md.: Scarecrow Press, 1998.

ll. Lou Gehrig   Eig, Jonathan. *Luckiest Man: The Life and Death of Lou Gehrig.* New York: Simon & Schuster, 2005.

Graham, Frank. *Lou Gehrig: A Quiet Hero.* New York: Putnam, 1942.

Robinson, Ray. *Iron Horse: Lou Gehrig in His Time.* New York: W. W. Norton, 1990.

mm. Charlie Gehringer   Skipper, John C. *Charlie Gehringer: A Biography of the Hall of Fame Tigers Second Baseman.* Jefferson, N.C.: McFarland, 2008.

nn. Bob Gibson   Gibson, Bob, with Lonnie Wheeler. *Stranger to the Game.* New York: Viking Press, 1994.

oo. Josh Gibson   Brashler, William. *Josh Gibson: A Life in the Negro Leagues.* New York: Harper & Row, 1978.

pp. Lefty Gomez   Gomez, Vernona, and Lawrence Goldstone. *Lefty: An American Odyssey.* New York: Ballantine Books, 2012.

qq. Hank Greenberg   Greenberg, Hank, edited by Ira Berkow. *Hank Greenberg: The Story of My Life.* New York: Times Books, 1989.

rr. Clark Griffith   Leavengood, Ted. *Clark Griffith: The Old Fox of Washington Baseball.* Jefferson, N.C.: McFarland, 2011.

ss. Lefty Grove   Kaplan, Jim. *Lefty Grove: American Original.* Cleveland, Ohio: Society for American Baseball Research, 2000.

tt. Billy Hamilton   Kerr, Roy. *Sliding Billy Hamilton: The Life and Times of Baseball's First Great Leadoff Hitter.* Jefferson, N.C.: McFarland, 2010.

uu. Gabby Hartnett   McNeill, William F. *Gabby Hartnett: The Life and Times of the Cubs' Greatest Catcher.* Jefferson, N.C.: McFarland, 2004.

vv. Harry Hooper   Zingg, Paul J. *Harry Hooper: An American Baseball Life.* Urbana: University of Illinois Press, 1993.

ww. Rogers Hornsby   Alexander, Charles. *Rogers Hornsby: A Biography.* New York: Henry Holt, 1995.

xx. Waite Hoyt   Cook, William A. *Waite Hoyt: A Biography of the Yankees' Schoolboy Wonder*. Jefferson, N.C.: McFarland, 2004.

yy. Carl Hubbell   Blaisdell, Lowell L. *Carl Hubbell: A Biography of the Screwball King*. Jefferson, N.C.: McFarland, 2011.

zz. Joe Jackson   Fleitz, David. *Shoeless: The Life and Times of Joe Jackson*. Jefferson, N.C.: McFarland, 2001.

Gropman, Donald. *Say It Ain't So, Joe: The True Story of Shoeless Joe Jackson*. New York: Lynx Books, 1988.

aaa. Reggie Jackson   Perry, Dayn. *Reggie Jackson LP: The Life and Thunderous Career of Baseball's Mr. October*. New York: HarperCollins, 2010.

bbb. Ferguson Jenkins   Turcotte, Dorothy. *The Game Is Easy, Life Is Hard: The Story of Ferguson Jenkins Jr*. Grimsby, Ontario, Canada: Fergie Jenkins Foundation, 2002.

ccc. Hughie Jennings   Smiles, Jack. *"Ee-Yah": The Life and Times of Hughie Jennings, Baseball Hall of Famer*. Jefferson, N.C.: McFarland, 2008.

ddd. Derek Jeter   O'Connor, Ian. *The Captain: The Journey of Derek Jeter*. New York: Houghton Mifflin Harcourt, 2011.

eee. Randy Johnson   Johnson, Randy, and Jim Rosenthal. *Randy Johnson's Power Pitching: The Big Unit's Secrets to Domination, Intimidation, and Winning*. New York: Three Rivers Press, 2003.

fff. Walter Johnson   Thomas, Henry W. *Walter Johnson: Baseball's Big Train*. Washington, D.C.: Phenom Press, 1995.

ggg. Addie Joss   Longert, Scott. *Addie Joss: King of the Pitchers*. Cleveland, Ohio: Society for American Baseball Research, 1998.

hhh. Al Kaline   Butler, Hal. *Al Kaline and the Detroit Tigers*. Chicago: Henry Regnery, 1973.

Hirshberg, Albert. *The Al Kaline Story*. New York: Julian Messner, 1964.

iii. George Kell   Kell, George, and Dan Ewald. *Hello Everybody, I'm George Kell*. Champaign, Ill.: Sports Publishing. 1998.

jjj. King Kelly   Appel, Marty. *Slide, Kelly, Slide: The Wild Life and Times of Mike "King" Kelly, Baseball's First Superstar*. Lanham, Md.: Scarecrow Press, 1996.

kkk. Ralph Kiner   Kiner, Ralph, with Danny Peary. *Baseball Forever*. Chicago: Triumph Books, 2004.

lll. Sandy Koufax   Leavy, Jane. *Sandy Koufax: A Lefty's Legacy*. New York: HarperCollins, 2002.

mmm. Tony Lazzeri   Votano, Paul. *Tony Lazzeri: A Baseball Biography*. Jefferson, N.C.: McFarland, 2005.

nnn. Buck Leonard   Leonard, Buck, with James A. Riley. *Buck Leonard: The Black Lou Gehrig*. New York: Carroll and Graf, 1995.

ooo. John Henry Lloyd   Singletary, Wes. *The Right Time: John Henry "Pop" Lloyd and Black Baseball*. Jefferson, N.C.: McFarland, 2011.

ppp. Mickey Mantle   Castro, Tony. *Mickey Mantle: America's Prodigal Son*. Dulles, Va.: Brassey's, 2002.

Hall, John G. *Mickey Mantle: Before the Glory*. Leawood, Kans.: Leatherwood Press, 2005.

Leavey, Jane. *The Last Boy: Mickey Mantle and the End of America's Childhood*. New York: Harper, 2010.

Mantle, Mickey, with Herb Gluck. *The Mick: An American Hero, the Legend and the Glory*. New York: Doubleday, 1985.

Swearingen, Randall. *A Great Teammate: The Legend of Mickey Mantle*. Champaign, Ill.: Sports Publishing, 2007.

qqq. Rabbit Maranville   Maranville, Walter "Rabbit." *Run, Rabbit, Run*. Cleveland, Ohio: Society for American Baseball Research, 1991.

rrr. Juan Marichal   Marichal, Juan, and Lew Freedman. *Juan Marichal: My Journey from the Dominican Republic to Cooperstown*. Minneapolis, Minn.: MVP Books, 2011.

sss. Roger Maris   Allen, Maury. *Roger Maris*. New York: Donald I. Fine, 1986.

ttt. Rube Marquard   Mansch, Larry D. *Rube Marquard: The Life and Times of a Baseball Hall of Famer*. Jefferson, N.C.: McFarland, 1998.

uuu. Eddie Mathews   Mathews, Eddie, and Bob Buege. *Eddie Mathews and the National Pastime*. Milwaukee, Wisc.: Douglas American Sports Publications, 1994.

vvv. Christy Mathewson   Hartley, Michael. *Christy Mathewson: A Biography*. Jefferson, N.C.: McFarland, 2004.

Mayer, Robert A. *Christy Mathewson: A Game-by-Game Profile of a Legendary Pitcher*. Jefferson, N.C.: McFarland, 1993.

Robinson, Ray. *Matty: An American Hero*. New York: Oxford University Press, 1993.

www. Willie Mays   Hirsch, James S. *Willie Mays: The Life, the Legend*. New York: Scribner, 2010.

Mays, Willie, as told to Charles Einstein. *Willie Mays: My Life In and Out of Baseball*. Boston: E. P. Dutton, 1966.

Mays, Willie, with Lou Sahadi. *Say Hey: The Autobiography of Willie Mays*. New York: Simon & Schuster, 1988.

xxx. Joe McGinnity   Doxie, Dan. *Iron Man McGinnity: A Baseball Biography*. Jefferson, N.C.: McFarland, 2009.

yyy. Mark McGwire   McGwire, Jay. *Mark and Me: Mark McGwire and the Truth behind Baseball's Worst-Kept Secret*. Chicago: Triumph Books, 2010.

Rains, Rob. *Mark McGwire: Home Run Hero*. New York: St. Martin's Press, 1998.

zzz. Stan Musial   Giglio, James N. *Musial: From Stash to Stan the Man*. Columbia: University of Missouri Press, 2001.

Lansche, Jerry. *Stan the Man Musial: Born to Be a Ballplayer*. Dallas, Tex.: Taylor Publishing, 1994.

Robinson, Ray. *Stan Musial: Baseball's Durable "Man."* New York: G. P. Putnam's Sons, 1963.

Vecsey, George. *Stan Musial: An American Life*. New York: Ballantine Books, 2011.

aaaa. Hal Newhouser   Jordan, David M. *A Tiger in His Time*. South Bend, Ind.: Diamond Communications, 1990.

bbbb. Sadaharu Oh   Oh, Sadaharu, and David Falkner. *A Zen Way of Baseball*. New York: Times Books, 1984.

cccc. Jim O'Rourke   Roer, Mike. *Orator O'Rourke: The Life of a Baseball Radical*. Jefferson, N.C.: McFarland, 2006.

dddd. Mel Ott   Stein, Fred. *Mel Ott: The Little Giant of Baseball*. Jefferson, N.C.: McFarland, 1999.

eeee. Satchel Paige   Paige, Leroy "Satchel," and David Lipman. *Maybe I'll Pitch Forever*. Lincoln: University of Nebraska Press, 1993.

Tye, Larry. *Satchel: The Life and Times of an American Legend*. New York: Random House, 2009.

ffff. Gaylord Perry   Perry, Gaylord, and Bob Sudyk. *Me and the Spitter*. Boston: Dutton, 1974.

gggg. Lip Pike   Michelson, Richard. *Lipman Pike: America's First Home Run King*. Ann Arbor, Mich.: Sleeping Bear Press, 2011.

hhhh. Kirby Puckett   Puckett, Kirby. *I Love This Game! My Life and Baseball*. New York: HarperCollins, 1993.

iiii. Albert Pujols   Ellsworth, Tim, and Scott Lamb. *Pujols: More Than the Game*. Nashville, Tenn.: Thomas Nelson, 2011.

jjjj. Hoss Radbourn   Achorn, Edward. *Fifty-Nine in '84: Old Hoss Radbourn, Barehanded Baseball, and the Greatest Season a Pitcher Ever Had*. New York: HarperCollins, 2010.

kkkk. Manny Ramirez   Rhodes, Jean, and Shawn Boburg. *Becoming Manny: Inside the Life of Baseball's Most Enigmatic Slugger*. New York: Scribner, 2009.

llll. Sam Rice   Carroll, Jeff. *Sam Rice: A Biography of the Washington Senators Hall of Famer*. Jefferson, N.C.: McFarland, 2008.

mmmm. Cal Ripken   Ripken, Cal, and Mike Bryan. *The Only Way I Know*. New York: Viking Press, 1996.

Ripken, Cal, and Donald Phillips. *Get in the Game*. New York: Gotham Books, 2007.

Rosenfeld, Harvey. *Iron Man: The Cal Ripken Story*. New York: St. Martin's Press, 1995.

nnnn. Mariano Rivera   Rosen, Charley. *Bullpen Diaries: Mariano Rivera, Bronx Dreams, Pinstripe Legends, and the Future of the New York Yankees*. New York: HarperCollins, 2011.

oooo. Phil Rizzuto   DeVito, Carlo. *Scooter: The Biography of Phil Rizzuto*. Chicago: Triumph Books, 2010.

pppp. Robin Roberts   Roberts, Robin, and C. Paul Rogers. *My Life in Baseball*. Chicago: Triumph Books, 2003.

qqqq. Frank Robinson   Schneider, Russ. *Frank Robinson: The Making of a Manager*. New York: Coward, McCann & Gheogegan, 1976.

rrrr. Jackie Robinson   Dorinson, Joseph, and Joram Warmund, eds. *Jackie Robinson: Race, Sports, and the American Dream*. Armonk, N.Y.: M. E. Sharpe, 1998.

Eig, Jonathan. *Opening Day: The Story of Jackie Robinson's First Season*. New York: Simon & Schuster, 2007.

Falkner, David. *Great Time Coming: The Life of Jackie Robinson, from Baseball to Birmingham*. New York: Simon & Schuster, 1995.

Lamb, Chris. *Blackout: The Untold Story of Jackie Robinson's First Spring Training*. Lincoln: University of Nebraska Press, 2006.

Rampersad, Arnold. *Jackie Robinson: A Biography*. New York: Ballantine Books, 1997.

Robinson, Jackie. *Baseball Has Done It*. Philadelphia, Pa.: Lippincott, 1964.

Robinson, Jackie, as told to Alfred Duckett. *I Never Had It Made*. New York: G. P. Putnam's Sons, 1972.

Simon, Scott. *Jackie Robinson and the Integration of Baseball*. Hoboken, N.J.: John Wiley & Sons, 2002.

Stevens, Ed. *The Other Side of the Jackie Robinson Story*. Mustang, Okla.: Tate Publishing & Enterprises, 2009.

Tygiel, Jules. *Baseball's Great Experiment: Jackie Robinson and His Legacy*. New York: Vintage Books, 1984.

ssss. Alex Rodriguez   Roberts, Selena. *A-Rod: The Many Lives of Alex Rodriguez*. New York: HarperCollins, 2009.

Stewart, Wayne. *Alex Rodriguez: A Biography*. Westport, Conn.: Greenwood Press, 2007.

tttt. Bullet Rogan   Dixon, Phil S. *Wilber "Bullet" Rogan and the Kansas City Monarchs*. Jefferson, N.C.: McFarland, 2010.

uuuu. Pete Rose   Cook, William A. *Pete Rose: Baseball's All-Time Hit King*. Jefferson, N.C.: McFarland, 2004.

Sokolove, Michael Y. *Hustle: The Myth, Life, and Lies of Pete Rose*. New York: Simon & Schuster, 1990.

Towle, Mike. *Pete Rose: Baseball's Charlie Hustle*. Nashville, Tenn.: Cumberland House, 2003.

vvvv. Edd Roush   Stinson, Mitchell Conrad. *Edd Roush: A Biography of the Cincinnati Reds Star*. Jefferson, N.C.: McFarland, 2010.

wwww. Babe Ruth   Creamer, Robert W. *Babe: The Legend Comes to Life*. New York: Penguin Books, 1974.

Jenkinson, Bill. *The Year Babe Ruth Hit 104 Home Runs*. New York: Carroll and Graf, 2007.

Keane, Robert N., ed. *Babe Ruth at 100: Baseball and the "Sultan of Swat."* New York: AMS Press, 2008.

Meany, Tom. *Babe Ruth: The Big Moments of the Big Fellow*. New York: A. S. Barnes, 1947.

Montville, Leigh. *The Big Bam: The Life and Times of Babe Ruth*. New York: Doubleday, 2006.

Reisler, Jim. *Babe Ruth: Launching the Legend*. New York: McGraw-Hill, 2004.

Ruth, Babe, as told to Bob Considine. *The Babe Ruth Story*. New York: E. P. Dutton, 1948.

Smelser, Marshall. *The Life That Ruth Built: A Biography*. New York: Quadrangle Books, 1975.

Smith, Robert. *Babe Ruth's America*. New York: Thomas Y. Crowell, 1974.

Sobol, Ken. *Babe Ruth and the American Dream*. New York: Ballantine Books, 1974.

Wagenheim, Kal. *Babe Ruth: His Life and Legend*. New York: Henry Holt, 1974.

xxxx. Nolan Ryan Ryan, Nolan, with Harvey Frommer. *Throwing Heat*. New York: Doubleday, 1988.

yyyy. Ron Santo Santo, Ron, with Randy Minkoff. *Ron Santo: For the Love of Ivy*. Chicago: Bonus Books, 1993.

zzzz. Ray Schalk Cooper, Brian E. *Ray Schalk: A Baseball Biography*. Jefferson, N.C.: McFarland, 2009.

aaaaa. Mike Schmidt Kashatus, William C. *Mike Schmidt: Philadelphia's Hall of Fame Third Baseman*. Jefferson, N.C.: McFarland, 2000.

Maaddi, Rob. *Mike Schmidt: The Phillies' Legendary Slugger*. Chicago: Triumph Books, 2010.

bbbbb. Red Schoendienst Schoendienst, Red, and Rob Rains. *Red: A Baseball Life*. Champaign, Ill.: Sports Publishing, 1998.

ccccc. Tom Seaver Schoor, Gene. *Seaver*. Chicago: Contemporary Books, 1986.

Travers, Steven. *The Last Icon: Tom Seaver and His Times*. Lanham, Md.: Rowman & Littlefield, 2011.

ddddd. Al Simmons Parker, Clifton Blue. *Bucketfoot Al: The Baseball Life of Al Simmons*. Jefferson, N.C.: McFarland, 2011.

eeeee. George Sisler Huhn, Rick. *The Sizzler: George Sisler, Baseball's Forgotten Great*. Columbia: University of Missouri Press, 2004.

fffff. Enos Slaughter Slaughter, Enos, with Kevin Reid. *Country Hardball*. Greensboro, N.C.: Tudor Publishers, 1991.

ggggg. Ozzie Smith Smith, Ozzie, and Rob Rains. *Ozzie Smith: The Road to Cooperstown*. Champaign, Ill.: Sports Publishing, 2002.

hhhhh. Duke Snider Snider, Duke, with Bill Gilbert. *The Duke of Flatbush*. New York: Zebra Books, 1988.

iiiii. Tris Speaker Alexander, Charles C. *Spoke: A Biography of Tris Speaker*. Dallas, Tex.: Southern Methodist University Press, 2007.

Gay, Timothy M. *Tris Speaker: The Rough-and-Tumble Life of a Baseball Legend*. Lincoln: University of Nebraska Press, 2005.

jjjjj. Willie Stargell Stargell, Willie, and Tom Bird. *Willie Stargell: An Autobiography*. New York: HarperCollins, 1984.

kkkkk. Ichiro Suzuki Komatsu, Narumi. *Ichiro on Ichiro: Conversations with Narumi Komatsu*. Seattle, Wash.: Sasquatch Books, 2004.

lllll. Pie Traynor Forr, James, and David Proctor. *Pie Traynor: A Baseball Biography*. Jefferson, N.C.: McFarland, 2010.

mmmmm. Dazzy Vance Skipper, John C. *Dazzy Vance: A Biography of the Brooklyn Dodger Hall of Famer*. Jefferson, N.C.: McFarland, 2007.

nnnnn. Rube Waddell Levy, Alan H. *Rube Waddell: The Zany, Brilliant Life of a Strikeout Artist*. Jefferson, N.C.: McFarland, 2000.

ooooo. Honus Wagner DeValeria, Dennis, and Jeanne Burke DeValeria. *Honus Wagner: A Biography*. Pittsburgh, Pa.: University of Pittsburgh Press, 1998.

Hittner, Arthur D. *Honus Wagner: The Life of Baseball's "Flying Dutchman."* Jefferson, N.C.: McFarland, 1996.

ppppp. Fleet Walker Zang, David. *Fleet Walker's Divided Heart*. Lincoln: University of Nebraska Press, 1995.

qqqqq. Ed Walsh Smiles, Jack. *Big Ed Walsh: The Life and Times of a Spitballing Hall of Famer*. Jefferson, N.C.: McFarland, 2008.

rrrrr. John Montgomery Ward DiSalvatore, Bryan. *A Clever Base-Ballist: The Life and Times of John Montgomery Ward*. New York: Random House, 1999.

Stevens, David. *Baseball's Radical for All Seasons: A Biography of John Montgomery Ward*. Lanham, Md.: Scarecrow Press, 1998.

sssss. Billy Williams Williams, Billy, with Fred Mitchell. *Billy Williams: My Sweet-Swinging Lifetime with the Cubs*. Chicago: Triumph Books, 2008.

ttttt. Ted Williams Linn, Ed. *Hitter: The Life and Turmoil of Ted Williams*. New York: Harcourt, Brace, 1994.

Montville, Leigh. *Ted Williams: The Biography of an American Hero*. New York: Doubleday, 2004.

Williams, Ted, as told to John Underwood. *My Turn at Bat: The Story of My Life*. New York: Pocket Books, 1970.

uuuuu. Hack Wilson Parker, Clifton Blue. *Fouled Away: The Baseball Tragedy of Hack Wilson*. Jefferson, N.C.: McFarland, 2000.

vvvvv. Dave Winfield Schoor, Gene. *Dave Winfield: The 23 Million Dollar Man*. Briarcliff Manor, N.Y.: Stein and Day, 1982.

Winfield, David, with Michael Levin. *Dropping the Ball: Baseball's Troubles and How We Can and Must Solve Them*. New York: Scribner, 1987.

Winfield, Dave, with Tom Parker. *Winfield: A Player's Life*. New York: W. W. Norton, 1988.

wwwww. Carl Yastrzemski   Yastrzemski, Carl, and Gerald Eskenazi. *Yaz: Baseball, the Wall, and Me*. New York: Doubleday, 1990.

Yastrzemski, Carl, with Al Hirshberg. *Yaz*. New York: Viking Press, 1968.

xxxxx. Cy Young   Browning, Reed. *Cy Young: A Baseball Life*. Amherst: University of Massachusetts Press, 2003.

3. Selected Individual Managers

a. Walt Alston   Alston, Walter, and Jack Tobin. *A Year at a Time*. Waco, Tex.: Word Books, 1976.

b. Leo Durocher   Durocher, Leo, with Ed Linn. *Nice Guys Finish Last*. New York: Simon & Schuster, 1975.

c. Bucky Harris   Smiles, Jack. *Bucky Harris: A Biography of Baseball's Boy Wonder*. Jefferson, N.C.: McFarland, 2011.

d. Al Lopez   Singletary, Wes. *Al Lopez: The Life of Baseball's El Senor*. Jefferson, N.C.: McFarland, 1999.

e. Connie Mack   Lieb, Frederick G. *Connie Mack: Grand Old Man of Baseball*. New York: Putnam, 1945.

Macht, Norman L. *Connie Mack: The Turbulent and Triumphant Years, 1915–1931*. Lincoln: University of Nebraska Press, 2012.

———. *Connie Mack and the Early Years of Baseball*. Lincoln: University of Nebraska Press, 2007.

f. Joe McCarthy   Levy, Alan H. *Joe McCarthy: Architect of the Yankee Dynasty*. Jefferson, N.C.: McFarland, 2005.

g. John McGraw   Alexander, Charles C. *John McGraw*. New York: Viking Press, 1988.

Graham, Frank. *McGraw of the Giants: An Informal Biography*. New York: Putnam, 1944.

McGraw, John J. *My Thirty Years in Baseball*. Lincoln, Nebr.: Bison Books, 1995.

McGraw, Mrs. John J., and Arthur Mann, ed. *The Real McGraw*. New York: David McKay, 1953.

h. Wilbert Robinson   Kavanagh, Jack, and Norman Macht. *Uncle Robbie*. Cleveland, Ohio: Society for American Baseball Research, 1999.

i. Casey Stengel   Allen, Maury. *You Could Look It Up: The Life of Casey Stengel*. New York: Times Books, 1979.

Bak, Richard. *Casey Stengel: A Splendid Baseball Life*. Dallas, Tex.: Taylor Publishing, 1997.

Creamer, Robert W. *Stengel: His Life and Times.* New York: Simon & Schuster, 1984.

j. Earl Weaver   Weaver, Earl, and Berry Stainback. *It's What You Learn after You Know It All That Counts: The Autobiography of Earl Weaver.* Garden City, N.Y.: Doubleday, 1982.

4. Other Selected Individuals

a. Ed Barrow   Barrow, Edward G., with James M. Kahn. *My Fifty Years in Baseball.* New York: Coward-McCann, 1951.

Levitt, Dan. *Ed Barrow: The Bulldog Who Built the Yankees' First Dynasty.* Lincoln: University of Nebraska Press, 2008.

b. Alexander Cartwright   Nucciarone, Monica. *Alexander Cartwright: The Life behind the Baseball Legend.* Lincoln: University of Nebraska Press, 2009.

c. Henry Chadwick   Schiff, Andrew J. *"The Father of Baseball": A Biography of Henry Chadwick.* Jefferson, N.C.: McFarland, 2008.

d. Happy Chandler   Chandler, Happy. *Heroes, Plain Folks, and Skunks.* Chicago: Bonus Books, 1989.

e. Charles Comiskey   Axelson, G. W. *"Commy": The Life Story of Charles A. Comiskey.* Jefferson, N.C.: McFarland, 2003.

f. Ford Frick   Frick, Ford. *Games, Asterisks, and People: Memoirs of a Lucky Fan.* New York: Crown Books, 1973.

g. Ban Johnson   Murdock, Eugene C. *Ban Johnson: Czar of Baseball.* Westport, Conn.: Greenwood Press, 1982.

h. Bowie Kuhn   Kuhn, Bowie. *Hardball: The Education of a Baseball Commissioner.* New York: McGraw-Hill, 1997.

i. Kenesaw Landis   Pietrusza, David. *Judge and Jury: The Life and Times of Judge Kenesaw Mountain Landis.* South Bend, Ind.: Diamond Communications, 1998.

Spink, J. G. Taylor. *Judge Landis and 25 Years of Baseball.* New York: Thomas Crowell, 1947.

j. Bill McGowan   Luke, Bob. *Dean of Umpires: A Biography of Bill McGowan, 1896–1954.* Jefferson, N.C.: McFarland, 2005.

k. Walter O'Malley   D'Antonio, Michael. *Forever Blue: The True Story of Walter O'Malley, Baseball's Most Controversial Owner, and the Dodgers of Brooklyn and Los Angeles.* New York: Riverhead Books, 2009.

l. Branch Rickey   Lowenfish, Lee. *Branch Rickey: Baseball's Ferocious Gentleman.* Lincoln: University of Nebraska Press, 2007.

O'Toole, Andrew. *Branch Rickey in Pittsburgh: Baseball's Trailblazing General Manager for the Pirates, 1950–1955.* Jefferson, N.C.: McFarland, 2000.

Polner, Murray. *Branch Rickey: A Biography*, Rev. ed. Jefferson, N.C.: McFarland, 2007.

m. Bill Veeck   Dickson, Paul. *Bill Veeck: Baseball's Greatest Maverick*. New York: Walker Publishing, 2012.

Eskenazi, Gerald. *Bill Veeck: A Baseball Legend*. New York: McGraw-Hill, 1988.

Veeck, Bill, with Ed Linn. *The Hustler's Handbook*. New York: Fireside Books, 1965.

———. *Veeck as in Wreck*. New York: Signet, 1962.

n. Harry Wright   Devine, Christopher. *Harry Wright: The Father of Professional Base Ball*. Jefferson, N.C.: McFarland, 2003.

F. Stadiums and Ballparks

Benson, Michael. *Ballparks of North America: A Comprehensive Historical Encyclopedia of Baseball Grounds, Yards, and Stadiums, 1845 to 1988.* Jefferson, N.C.: McFarland, 2009.

Cicotello, David, and Angelo J. Louisa, eds. *Forbes Field: Essays and Memories of the Pirates' Historic Ballpark, 1909–1971*. Jefferson, N.C.: McFarland, 2007.

Gershman, Michael. *Diamonds: The Evolution of the Ballpark*. Boston: Houghton Mifflin, 1993.

Kuklick, Bruce. *To Every Thing a Season: Shibe Park and Urban Philadelphia, 1909–1976*. Princeton, N.J.: Princeton University Press, 1991.

Lowry, Philip J. *Green Cathedrals: The Ultimate Celebration of Major League and Negro League Ballparks*. New York: Walker, 2006.

McGee, Robert. *The Greatest Ballpark Ever: Ebbets Field and the Story of the Brooklyn Dodgers*. New Brunswick, N.J.: Rivergate Books, 2005.

Nowlin, Bill, and Cecilia Tan, eds. *The Fenway Project*. Cambridge, Mass.: Rounder Books, 2004.

Powers, John, and Ron Driscoll. *Fenway Park: A Salute to the Coolest, Cruelest, Longest-Running Major League Baseball Stadium in America*. Philadelphia, Pa.: Running Press, 2012.

Reidenbaugh, Lowell. *Take Me Out to the Ballpark*. St. Louis, Mo.: Sporting News, 1983.

Ritter, Lawrence S. *Lost Ballparks: A Celebration of Baseball's Legendary Fields*. New York: Viking Press, 1992.

Robinson, Ray, and Christopher Jennison. *Yankee Stadium: 75 Years of Drama, Glamour, and Glory*. New York: Penguin Studio, 1998.

Sarnoff, Gary. "War at Griffith Stadium." *National Pastime*, 29 (2009), 73–76.

Selter, Ronald M. *Ballparks of the Deadball Era: A Comprehensive Study of Their Dimensions, Configurations, and Effects on Batting, 1901–1919.* Jefferson, N.C.: McFarland, 2012.

Stout, Glenn. *Fenway 1912: The Birth of a Ballpark, a Championship Season, and Fenway's Remarkable First Year.* Boston: Houghton Mifflin Harcourt, 2011.

G. Broadcasting

Castle, George. *Baseball and the Media: How Fans Lose in Today's Coverage of the Game.* Lincoln: University of Nebraska Press, 2007.

Halberstam, David. *Sports on New York Radio: A Play-by-Play History.* Chicago: Masters Press, 1999.

Ham, Eldon L. *Broadcasting Baseball: A History of the National Pastime on Radio and Television.* Jefferson, N.C.: McFarland, 2011.

Silvia, Tony. *Baseball over the Air: The National Pastime on the Radio and in the Imagination.* Jefferson, N.C.: McFarland, 2007.

———. *Fathers and Sons in Baseball Broadcasting: The Carays, Brennamans, Bucks, and Kalases.* Jefferson, N.C.: McFarland, 2009.

Smith, Curt. *The Storytellers from Mel Allen to Bob Costas: Sixty Years of Baseball Tales from the Broadcast Booth.* New York: Macmillan, 1995.

———. *Voices of the Game: The First Full-Scale Overview of Baseball Broadcasting, 1921 to the Present.* South Bend, Ind.: Diamond Communications, 1987.

Walker, James R., and Robert V. Bellamy Jr. *Center Field Shot: A History of Baseball on Television.* Lincoln: University of Nebraska Press, 2008.

H. The Business of Baseball

Cox, Ronald W., with Daniel Skidmore-Hess. *Free Agency and Competitive Balance in Baseball.* Jefferson, N.C.: McFarland, 2006.

Fetter, Henry D. *Taking on the Yankees: Winning and Losing in the Business of Baseball, 1903–2003.* New York: W. W. Norton, 2003.

Gelzheiser, Robert P. *Labor and Capital in 19th-Century Baseball.* Jefferson, N.C.: McFarland, 2006.

Gorman, Lou. *My Life in the Front Offices of Baseball.* Jefferson, N.C.: McFarland, 2008.

Gould, William B., IV. *Bargaining with Baseball: Labor Relations in an Age of Prosperous Turmoil.* Jefferson, N.C.: McFarland, 2011.

Helyar, John. *Lords of the Realm: The Real History of Baseball.* New York: Ballantine Books, 1994.

Jozsa, Frank P., Jr. *Baseball Inc.: The National Pastime as Big Business.* Jefferson, N.C.: McFarland, 2006.

Knorr, Charles P. *The End of Baseball as We Knew It: The Players Union, 1960–81.* Champaign: University of Illinois Press, 2002.

Lewis, Michael. *Moneyball: The Art of Winning an Unfair Game.* New York: W. W. Norton, 2003.

Lowenfish, Lee, with Tony Lupien. *The Imperfect Diamond: A History of Baseball's Labor Wars.* New York: De Capo Press, 1991.

McKelvey, G. Richard. *For It's One, Two, Three, Four Strikes You're Out at the Owners' Ball Game: Players versus Management in Baseball.* Jefferson, N.C.: McFarland, 2004.

Miller, James Edward. *The Baseball Business: Pursuing Pennants and Profits in Baltimore.* Chapel Hill: University of North Carolina Press, 1990.

Miller, Marvin. *A Whole Different Ballgame: The Sport and Business of Baseball.* New York: Carol Publishing Group, 1991.

Powers, Albert Theodore. *The Business of Baseball.* Jefferson, N.C.: McFarland, 2003.

Zimbalist, Andrew. *Baseball Billions: A Probing Look inside the Big Business of Our National Pastime.* New York: Basic Books, 1992.

I. The Hall of Fame

Astor, Gerald. *The Baseball Hall of Fame 50th Anniversary Book.* New York: Prentice Hall, 1988.

Chafets, Zev. *Cooperstown Confidential: Heros, Rogues, and the Inside Story of the Baseball Hall of Fame.* New York: Bloomsbury, 2009.

Connor, Anthony J. *Baseball for the Love of It: Hall of Famers Tell It Like It Was.* New York: Macmillan, 1982.

Corcoran, Dennis. *Induction Day at Cooperstown: A History of the Baseball Hall of Fame Ceremony.* Jefferson, N.C.: McFarland, 2011.

James, Bill. *The Politics of Glory.* New York: Macmillan, 1994.

McConnell, John. *Cooperstown by the Numbers: An Analysis of Baseball Hall of Fame Elections.* Jefferson, N.C.: McFarland, 2010.

Mullen, Maureen. *"Yogi Was Up with a Guy on Third . . .": Hall of Famers Recall Their Favorite Baseball Games Ever.* Chicago: Triumph Books, 2009.

Shalin, Mike, and Neil Shalin. *Out by a Step: The 100 Best Players Not in the Baseball Hall of Fame.* Lanham, Md.: Diamond Communications, 2002.

Skipper, John. *A Biographical Dictionary of the Baseball Hall of Fame.* Jefferson, N.C.: McFarland, 2000.

Vail, James F. *The Road to Cooperstown: A Critical History of Baseball's Hall of Fame Selection Process.* Jefferson, N.C.: McFarland, 2001.

J. The World Series

Asinof, Eliot. *Eight Men Out: The Black Sox and the 1919 World Series*. New York: Holt, Rinehart and Winston, 1963.

Cantor, George. *World Series Fact Book*. Detroit, Mich.: Visible Ink Press, 1996.

Carney, Gene. *Burying the Black Sox: How Baseball's Cover-Up of the 1919 World Series Fix Almost Succeeded*. Washington, D.C.: Potomac Books, 2006.

Cook, William A. *The 1919 World Series: What Really Happened?* Jefferson, N.C.: McFarland, 2001.

Dabilis, Andy, and Nick Tsiotos. *The 1903 World Series: The Boston Americans, the Pittsburgh Pirates, and the "First Championship of the United States."* Jefferson, N.C.: McFarland, 2004.

Dellinger, Susan. *Red Legs and Black Sox: Edd Roush and the Untold Story of the 1919 World Series*. Cincinnati, Ohio: Emmis Books, 2006.

Finoli, David, and Bill Ranier. *When Cobb Met Wagner: The Seven-Game World Series of 1909*. Jefferson, N.C.: McFarland, 2005.

Gies, Joseph, and Robert H. Shoemaker. *Stars of the Series: A Complete History of the World Series*. New York: Thomas Y. Crowell, 1965.

Hano, Arnold. *A Day in the Bleachers*. New York: Crowell, 1955.

Lieb, Frederick G. *The Story of the World Series*. New York: Putnam, 1949.

Rubinstein, Bruce A. *Chicago in the World Series, 1903–2005: The Cubs and White Sox in Championship Play*. Jefferson, N.C.: McFarland, 2006.

Schoor, Gene. *The History of the World Series*. New York: William Morrow, 1990.

Stark, Benton. *The Year They Called Off the World Series: A True Story*. Garden City Park, N.Y.: Avery Publishing Group, 1991.

Wilbert, Warren N. *The Greatest World Series Games: Baseball Historians Choose 26 Classics*. Jefferson, N.C.: McFarland, 2012.

K. Analysis and Sabermetrics

Costa, Gabriel B., Michael R. Huber, and John T. Saccoman. *Practicing Sabermetrics: Putting the Science of Baseball Statistics to Work*. Jefferson, N.C.: McFarland, 2009.

———. *Understanding Sabermetrics: An Introduction to the Science of Baseball Statistics*. Jefferson, N.C.: McFarland, 2008.

Darby, William. *Deconstructing Major League Baseball, 1991–2004: How Statistics Illuminate Individual and Team Performances*. Jefferson, N.C.: McFarland, 2006.

Faber, Charles F. *Baseball Ratings: The All-Time Best Players at Each Position, 1876 to the Present*, 3rd ed. Jefferson, N.C.: McFarland, 2008.

Grimble, Stephen M. *Setting the Record Straight: Baseball's Greatest Batters*. Wilmington, Del.: Cedar Tree Books, 1998.

Jaffe, Chris. *Evaluating Baseball's Managers: A History and Analysis of Performance in the Major Leagues, 1876–2008*. Jefferson, N.C.: McFarland, 2010.

James, Bill. *The Bill James Historical Baseball Abstract*. New York: Villard Books, 1986.

————. *The New Bill James Historical Baseball Abstract*. New York: Free Press, 2001.

James, Bill, and Rob Neyer. *The Neyer/James Guide to Pitchers*. New York: Fireside Books, 2004.

Kaufman, Alan S., and James C. Kaufman. *The Worst Baseball Pitchers of All Time: Bad Luck, Bad Arms, Bad Teams, and Just Plain Bad*. New York: Citadel Press, 1995.

Runquist, Willie. *Baseball by the Numbers: How Statistics Are Collected, What They Mean, and How They Reveal the Game*. Jefferson, N.C.: McFarland, 1995.

Schwarz, Alan. *The Numbers Game: Baseball's Lifelong Fascination with Statistics*. New York: St. Martin's Press, 2004.

Thorn, John, and Pete Palmer, with David Reuther. *The Hidden Game of Baseball*. New York: Doubleday, 1984.

Wright, Craig R., and Tom House. *The Diamond Appraised*. New York: Simon & Schuster, 1989.

L. Miscellaneous

1. All-Star Game

Eckhouse, Morris, ed. *All-Star Baseball in Cleveland*. Lincoln: University of Nebraska Press, 1997.

Freedman, Lew. *The Day All the Stars Came Out: Major League Baseball's First All-Star Game, 1933*. Jefferson, N.C.: McFarland, 2010.

Vincent, David, Lyle Spatz, and David W. Smith. *The Midsummer Classic: The Complete History of Baseball's All-Star Game*. Lincoln: University of Nebraska Press, 2001.

2. Awards

Fleitz, David L. *Silver Bats and Automobiles: The Hotly Competitive, Sometimes Ignoble Pursuit of the Major League Batting Championship.* Jefferson, N.C.: McFarland, 2011.

Spatz, Lyle. "Retroactive Cy Young Awards." *Baseball Research Journal,* 17 (1988), 65–70.

———. "SABR Picks 1900–1948 Rookies of the Year." *Baseball Research Journal,* 15 (1986), 2–4.

3. Designated Hitter

McKelvey, G. Richard. *All Bat, No Glove: A History of the Designated Hitter.* Jefferson, N.C.: McFarland, 2004.

4. Doubleheaders

Bevis, Charlie. *Doubleheaders: A Major League History.* Jefferson, N.C.: McFarland, 2011.

5. Expansion

Jozsa, Frank P., Jr. *Major League Baseball Expansions and Relocations: A History, 1876–2008.* Jefferson, N.C.: McFarland, 2010.

6. Home Runs

McNeill, William F. *The Single-Season Home Run Kings: Ruth, Maris, McGwire, Sosa, and Bonds,* 2nd ed. Jefferson, N.C.: McFarland, 2003.

Ribowsky, Mark. *The Complete History of the Home Run.* New York: Citadel Press, 2003.

Vincent, David. *Home Run: The Definitive History of Baseball's Ultimate Weapon.* Washington, D.C.: Potomac Books, 2007.

7. Quotations

Dickson, Paul. *Baseball's Greatest Quotations.* New York: Edward Burlingame Books, 1991.

———. *The New Dickson Baseball Dictionary.* New York: Harcourt, Brace, 1999.

Nathan, David H. *The McFarland Baseball Quotations Dictionaries*, 3rd ed. Jefferson, N.C.: McFarland, 2011.

8. Spring Training

Falkner, David. *The Short Season: The Hard Work and High Times of Baseball in the Spring*. New York: Penguin Books, 1987.

Nowlin, Bill. *The Great Red Sox Spring Training Tour of 1911: Sixty-Three Games, Coast to Coast*. Jefferson, N.C.: McFarland, 2010.

Pahigian, Joshua R. *Spring Training Handbook: A Comprehensive Guide to the Ballparks of the Grapefruit and Cactus Leagues*. Jefferson, N.C.: McFarland, 2005.

9. Encyclopedias

The Baseball Encyclopedia: The Complete and Official Records of Major League Baseball. New York: Macmillan, 1969.

Bjarkman, Peter O., ed. *Encyclopedia of Major League Baseball Team Histories: American League*. Westport, Conn.: Meckler Publishing, 1991.

———. *Encyclopedia of Major League Baseball Team Histories: National League*. Westport, Conn.: Meckler Publishing, 1991.

Gillette, Gary, and Pete Palmer, eds. *The ESPN Baseball Encyclopedia*, 5th ed. New York: Sterling, 2008.

Light, Jonathan Fraser. *The Cultural Encyclopedia of Baseball*, 2nd ed. Jefferson, N.C.: McFarland, 2005.

McConnell, Bob, and David Vincent, eds. *SABR Presents the Home Run Encyclopedia: The Who, What, and Where of Every Home Run Hit since 1876*. New York: Macmillan, 1996.

Neft, David S., Richard M. Cohen, and Michael L. Neft. *The Sports Encyclopedia: Baseball 2005*, 25th ed. New York: St. Martin's Press, 2005.

Nemec, David. *The Great Book of Baseball Knowledge*. Chicago: Masters Press, 1999.

———. *The Great Encyclopedia of 19th-Century Major League Baseball*. New York: Donald I. Fine Books, 1997.

Rielly, Edward J. *Baseball: An Encyclopedia of Popular Culture*. Lincoln: University of Nebraska Press, 2007.

Thorn, John, Phil Birnbaum, Bill Deane, et al., eds. *Total Baseball*, 8th ed. Wilmington, Del.: Sports Media Publishing, 2004.

10. Record Books and Guides

Gietschier, Steve, ed. *The 2005 Complete Baseball Record Book*. St. Louis, Mo.: Sporting News, 2005.

Gillette, Gary, and Pete Palmer, eds. *The Emerald Guide to Baseball, 2012*. Phoenix, Ariz.: Society for American Baseball Research, 2012.

Lanigan, Ernest J. *The Baseball Cyclopedia*. New York: Baseball Magazine, 1922.

Moreland, George L. *Balldom: The Britannica of Baseball*. New York: Balldom Publishing, 1914.

Reach Baseball Guides, 1883–1939.

Reichler, Joseph L. *The Great All-Time Baseball Record Book*. New York: Macmillan, 1981.

Richter, Francis C. *Richter's History and Records of Base Ball: The American Nation's Chief Sport*. Jefferson, N.C.: McFarland, 2005.

Siwoff, Seymour, ed. *The Elias Book of Baseball Records, 2012*. New York: Elias Sports Bureau, 2012.

Spalding Baseball Guides, 1883–1939.

Spatz, Lyle, ed. *The SABR Baseball List and Record Book*. New York: Scribner, 2007.

Sporting News Official Baseball Guides, 1886–2005.

III. MINOR LEAGUES

Beverage, Richard. *The Los Angeles Angels of the Pacific Coast League: A History, 1903–1957*. Jefferson, N.C.: McFarland, 2011.

Bevis, Charlie. *The New England League: A Baseball History: 1885–1949*. Jefferson, N.C.: McFarland, 2008.

Davids, L. Robert, ed. *Minor League Baseball Stars*. Cleveland, Ohio: Society for American Baseball Research, 1984.

———, ed. *Minor League Baseball Stars*, Vol. II. Cleveland, Ohio: Society for American Baseball Research, 1985.

———, ed. *Minor League Baseball Stars*, Vol. III. Cleveland, Ohio: Society for American Baseball Research, 1992.

Davis, Hank. *Small-Town Heroes: Images of Minor League Baseball*. Lincoln: University of Nebraska Press, 2003.

Fenster, Kenneth R. "The 1954 Dixie Series." *Baseball in the Peach State* (2010), 82–92.

Hoie, Bob, and Carlos Bauer, comps. *The Historical Register*. San Diego, Calif.: Baseball Press Books, 1999.

Johnson, Lloyd, and Miles Wolff, eds. *The Encyclopedia of Minor League Baseball*, 3rd ed. Durham, N.C.: Baseball America, 2007.

Madden, W. C., and Patrick J. Stewart. *The Western League: A Baseball History, 1885 through 1999*. Jefferson, N.C.: McFarland, 2002.

Mayer, Ronald A. *The 1937 Newark Bears: A Baseball Legend*. East Hanover, N.J.: Vintage Press, 1980.

Pietrusza, David. *Baseball's Canadian-American League: A History of Its Inception, Franchises, Participants, Locales, Statistics, Demise, and Legacy, 1936–1951*. Jefferson, N.C.: McFarland, 1990.

Podoll, Brian A. *The Minor League Milwaukee Brewers, 1859–1952*. Jefferson, N.C.: McFarland, 2003.

Raley, Dan. *Pitchers of Beer: The Story of the Seattle Rainiers*. Lincoln: University of Nebraska Press, 2011.

Selko, Jamie. *Minor League All-Star Teams, 1922–1962: Rosters, Statistics, and Commentary*. Jefferson, N.C.: McFarland, 2007.

Simpson, John A. *"The Greatest Game Ever Played in Dixie": The Nashville Vols, Their 1908 Season, and the Championship Game*. Jefferson, N.C.: McFarland, 2007.

Snelling, Dennis. *The Greatest Minor League: A History of the Pacific Coast League, 1903–1957*. Jefferson, N.C.: McFarland, 2012.

———. *The Pacific Coast League: A Statistical History, 1903–1957*. Jefferson, N.C.: McFarland, 1995.

Stott, John C. *Minor Leagues, Major Boom: Local Professional Baseball Revitalized*. Jefferson, N.C.: McFarland, 2004.

Sumner, Benjamin Barrett. *Minor League Baseball Standings: All North American Leagues, through 1999*. Jefferson, N.C.: McFarland, 2000.

Wright, Marshall D. *The Eastern League in Baseball: A Statistical History, 1923–2005.* Jefferson, N.C.: McFarland, 2007.

———. *The International League: Year-by-Year Statistics, 1884–1953*. Jefferson, N.C.: McFarland, 1998.

———. *The South Atlantic League, 1904–1963: A Year-by-Year Statistical History*. Jefferson, N.C.: McFarland, 2009.

———. *The Southern Association in Baseball, 1885–1961*. Jefferson, N.C.: McFarland, 2002.

———. *The Texas League in Baseball, 1888–1958*. Jefferson, N.C.: McFarland, 2004.

IV. NEGRO LEAGUES

Bankes, Jim. *The Pittsburgh Crawfords*. Jefferson, N.C.: McFarland, 2001.

Brunson, James E., III. *The Early Image of Black Baseball: Race and Representation in the Popular Press, 1871–1890*. Jefferson, N.C.: McFarland, 2009.

Clark, Dick, and Larry Lester, eds. *The Negro Leagues Book*. Lincoln: University of Nebraska Press, 1994.

Debono, Paul. *The Chicago American Giants*. Jefferson, N.C.: McFarland, 2001.

———. *The Indianapolis ABCs: History of a Premier Team in the Negro Leagues*. Jefferson, N.C.: McFarland, 2007.

Hauser, Christopher. *The Negro Leagues Chronology: Events in Organized Black Baseball, 1920–1948*. Jefferson, N.C.: McFarland, 2006.

Heaphy, Leslie A., ed. *Black Baseball and Chicago: Essays on the Players, Teams, and Games of the Negro Leagues' Most Important City*. Jefferson, N.C.: McFarland, 2006.

———. *The Negro Leagues, Aesop, and the Imprint of Medieval Thought, 1869–1960*. Jefferson, N.C.: McFarland, 2003.

———, ed. *Satchel Paige and Company: Essays on the Kansas City Monarchs, Their Greatest Star, and the Negro Leagues*. Jefferson, N.C.: McFarland, 2007.

Holway, John. *Blackball Stars*. New York: Carroll and Graf, 1992.

———. *The Complete Book of Baseball's Negro Leagues: The Other Half of Baseball History*. Fern Park, Fla.: Hastings House, 2001.

Kelley, Brent. *"I Will Never Forget": Interviews with 39 Former Negro League Players*. Jefferson, N.C.: McFarland, 2003.

———. *The Negro Leagues Revisited: Conversations with 66 More Baseball Heroes*. Jefferson, N.C.: McFarland, 2000.

———. *Voices from the Negro Leagues Revisited: Conversations with 52 Baseball Standouts of the Period, 1924–1960*. Jefferson, N.C.: McFarland, 1998.

Kirwin, Bill, ed. *Out of the Shadows: African American Baseball from the Cuban Giants to Jackie Robinson*. Lincoln: University of Nebraska Press, 2005.

Lanctot, Neil. *Negro League Baseball: The Rise and Ruin of a Black Institution*. Philadelphia: University of Pennsylvania Press, 2004.

Lester, Larry. *Baseball's First Colored World Series: The 1924 Meeting of the Hilldale Giants and Kansas City Monarchs*. Jefferson, N.C.: McFarland, 2006.

———. *Black Baseball's National Showcase: The East-West All-Star Game, 1933–1953*. Lincoln: University of Nebraska Press, 2002.

McNeill, William F. *Black Baseball Out of Season: Pay for Play Outside of the Negro Leagues*. Jefferson, N.C.: McFarland, 2007.

———. *Cool Papas and Double Duties: The All-Time Greats of the Negro Leagues*. Jefferson, N.C.: McFarland, 2001.

Peterson, Robert. *Only the Ball Was White: A History of Legendary Black Players and All-Black Professional Teams*. Englewood Cliffs, N.J.: Prentice Hall, 1970.

Powell, Larry. *Black Barons of Birmingham: The South's Greatest Negro League Team and Its Players*. Jefferson, N.C.: McFarland, 2009.

Reisler, Jim. *Black Writers/Black Baseball: An Anthology of Articles from Black Sportswriters Who Covered the Negro Leagues*, Rev. ed. Jefferson, N.C.: McFarland, 2007.

Riley, James A. *Of Monarchs and Black Barons: Essays on Baseball's Negro Leagues*. Jefferson, N.C.: McFarland, 2012.

Rogosin, Donn. *Invisble Men: Life in Baseball's Negro Leagues*. New York: Atheneum, 1983.

White, Sol. *Sol White's History of Colored Baseball with Other Documents on the Early Black Game, 1886–1936*. Lincoln: University of Nebraska Press, 1995.

V. WOMEN'S BASEBALL

Brown, Patricia I. *A League of My Own: Memoir of a Pitcher for the All-American Girls Professional Baseball League*. Jefferson, N.C.: McFarland, 2003.

Cohen, Marilyn. *No Girls in the Clubhouse: The Exclusion of Women from Baseball*. Jefferson, N.C.: McFarland, 2009.

Fidler, Merrie A. *The Origins and History of the All-American Girls Professional Baseball League*. Jefferson, N.C.: McFarland, 2006.

Heaphy, Leslie A., and Mel Anthony May, eds. *Encyclopedia of Women and Baseball*. Jefferson, N.C.: McFarland, 2006.

Madden, W. C. *The All-American Girls Professional Baseball League Record Book: Comprehensive Hitting, Fielding, and Pitching Statistics*. Jefferson, N.C.: McFarland, 2000.

———. *The Women of the All-American Girls Professional Baseball League: A Biographical Dictionary*. Jefferson, N.C.: McFarland, 2005.

Sargent, Jim, and Robert M. Gorman. *The South Bend Blue Sox: A History of the All-American Girls Professional Baseball League Team and Its Players, 1943–1954*. Jefferson, N.C.: McFarland, 2012.

Trombe, Carolyn M. *Dotte Wilson Collins: Strikeout Queen of the All-American Girls Professional Baseball League*. Jefferson, N.C.: McFarland, 2005.

VI. COLLEGE BASEBALL

Madden, W. C., and Patrick J. Stewart. *The College World Series: A Baseball History, 1947–2003.* Jefferson, N.C.: McFarland, 2004.

Tully, Gregory J. *Nine College Nines: A Closeup View of Campus Baseball Programs Today.* Jefferson, N.C.: McFarland, 2009.

VII. BASEBALL IN OTHER COUNTRIES

A. General

Gmelch, George, ed. *Baseball without Borders: The International Pastime.* Lincoln: University of Nebraska Press, 2006.

B. Asia

Franks, Joel S. *Asian Pacific Americans and Baseball: A History.* Jefferson, N.C.: McFarland, 2008.

Reaves, Joseph A. *Taking in a Game: A History of Baseball in Asia.* Lincoln: University of Nebraska Press, 2012.

C. Australia

Clark, Joe. *A History of Australian Baseball: Time and Game.* Lincoln: University of Nebraska Press, 2003.

D. Canada

Swanton, Barry, and Jay-Dell Mah. *Black Baseball Players in Canada: A Biographical Dictionary, 1881–1960.* Jefferson, N.C.: McFarland, 2009.

E. Cuba

Bjarkman, Peter O. *A History of Cuban Baseball, 1864–2006.* Jefferson, N.C.: McFarland, 2007.

Echevarría, Roberto González. *The Pride of Havana: A History of Cuban Baseball.* New York: Oxford University Press, 1999.

Figuredo, Jorge S. *Cuban Baseball: A Statistical History, 1878–1961.* Jefferson, N.C.: McFarland, 2003.

————. *Who's Who in Cuban Baseball: A Statistical History, 1878–1961*. Jefferson, N.C.: McFarland, 2003.

Nieto, Severo. *Early U.S. Blackball Teams in Cuba: Box Scores, Rosters, and Statistics from the Files of Cuba's Foremost Baseball Researcher*. Jefferson, N.C.: McFarland, 2008.

F. Dominican Republic

Ruck, Rob. *The Tropic of Baseball: Baseball in the Dominican Republic*. Lincoln: University of Nebraska Press, 1999.

G. Europe

Chetwynd, Josh. *Baseball in Europe: A Country by Country History*. Jefferson, N.C.: McFarland, 2008.

Chetwynd, Josh, and Brian A. Belton. *British Baseball and the West Ham Club: History of a 1930s Professional Team in East London*. Jefferson, N.C.: McFarland, 2007.

H. Israel

Pribble, Aaron. *Pitching in the Promised Land: A Story of the First and Only Season in the Israel Baseball League*. Lincoln: University of Nebraska Press, 2011.

I. Japan

Fitts, Robert K. *Banzai Babe Ruth: Baseball Espionage and Assassination during the 1934 Tour of Japan*. Lincoln: University of Nebraska Press, 2012.

————. *Wally Yonamine: The Man Who Changed Japanese Baseball*. Lincoln: University of Nebraska Press, 2007.

Guthrie-Shimizu, Sayuri. *Transpacific Field of Dreams: How Baseball Linked the United States and Japan in Peace and War*. Chapel Hill: University of North Carolina Press, 2012.

"A Japanese Baseball Invasion on the Way," *Literary Digest*, May 7, 1921, 48–51.

Johnson, Daniel E. *Japanese Baseball: A Statistical Handbook*. Jefferson, N.C.: McFarland, 2006.

Spatz, Michael M. "Diamond Democracy: Baseball and the Relationship between the United States and Japan." Senior thesis, University of Kansas, Lawrence, Kansas, May 2010.

Staples, Bill, Jr. *Kenichi Zenimura, Japanese American Baseball Pioneer*. Jefferson, N.C.: McFarland, 2011.

J. Latin America

Bjarkman, Peter O. *Baseball with a Latin Beat: A History of the Latin American Game*. Jefferson, N.C.: McFarland, 1994.

Burgos, Adrian, Jr. *Playing America's Game: Baseball, Latinos, and the Color Line*. Berkeley: University of California Press, 2007.

Hernandez, Lou. *The Rise of the Latin American Baseball Leagues, 1947–1961: Cuba, the Dominican Republic, Mexico, Nicaragua, Panama, Puerto Rico, and Venezuela*. Jefferson, N.C.: McFarland, 2011.

Wilson, Nick C. *Early Latino Ballplayers in the United States: Major, Minor, and Negro Leagues, 1901–1949*. Jefferson, N.C.: McFarland, 2005.

K. Mexico

Cisneros, Pedro Treto. *The Mexican League/La Liga Mexicana: Comprehensive Player Statistics, 1937–2001, Bilingual Edition/Estadisticas Comprensivas de los Jugadores, 1937–2001 edicion bilingue*. Jefferson, N.C.: McFarland, 2002.

McKelvey, G. Richard. *Mexican Raiders in the Major Leagues: The Pasquel Brothers vs. Organized Baseball, 1946*. Jefferson, N.C.: McFarland, 2006.

Virtue, John. *South of the Color Barrier: How Jorge Pasquel and the Mexican League Pushed Baseball toward Racial Integration*. Jefferson, N.C.: McFarland, 2008.

L. Puerto Rico

Van Hyning, Thomas E. *Puerto Rico's Winter League: A History of Major League Baseball's Launching Pad*. Jefferson, N.C.: McFarland, 1995.

———. *The Santurce Crabbers: Sixty Seasons of Puerto Rican Winter League Baseball*. Jefferson, N.C.: McFarland, 1999.

M. Taiwan

Yu, Junwei. *Playing in Isolation: A History of Baseball in Taiwan*. Lincoln: University of Nebraska Press, 2007.

N. Venezuela

Jamail, Milton H. *Venezuelan Bust, Baseball Boom: Andrés Reiner and Scouting on the New Frontier*. Lincoln: University of Nebraska Press, 2008.

VIII. SELECTED WEBSITES

baseball-almanac.com
baseball-reference.com
baseballinwartime.com
baseballlibrary.com
deadballera.com
findagrave.com
genealogybank.com
retrosheet.com
sabr.org

About the Author

Lyle Spatz is the author of *New York Yankee Openers: An Opening Day History of Baseball's Most Famous Team, 1903–1996*; *Yankees Coming, Yankees Going: New York Yankee Player Transactions, 1903–1999*; *Bad Bill Dahlen: The Rollicking Life and Times of an Early Baseball Star*; and *Dixie Walker: A Life in Baseball*. He is co-author of *The Midsummer Classic: The Complete History of Baseball's All-Star Game* and *1921: The Yankees, the Giants, and the Battle for Baseball Supremacy in New York*. He is former chief editor of *The Baseball Records Update: 1993, The SABR Baseball List and Record Book*, and *The Team That Forever Changed Baseball and America: The 1947 Brooklyn Dodgers*, and is chief editor of *Bridging Two Dynasties: The 1947 New York Yankees*, scheduled to be published in 2013.

Spatz has also contributed chapters to *The Dictionary of Literary Biography: Sportswriters*; *The Biographical Dictionary of American Sports: Baseball*; *Jackie Robinson: Race, Sports, and the American Dream*; *Baseball and the "Sultan of Swat": Babe Ruth at 100*; *Deadball Stars of the American League*; *Deadball Stars of the National League*; *Baseball's First Stars*; *The Perfect Game*; *Major League Baseball Profiles: 1871–1900*; *American Sports: An Encyclopedia of the Figures, Fans, and Phenomena That Shape Our Culture*; and *Inventing Baseball*.

His articles have appeared in the *New York Times*, the *Washington Post*, *Total Baseball*, *Baseball Weekly*, *Baseball Digest*, the *National Pastime*, the *Baseball Research Journal*, and the *Baltimore Orioles Official Game Program*. In addition, Spatz has presented papers at the Babe Ruth Conference at Hofstra University and the Jackie Robinson Conference at Long Island University. Since moving to Florida in 2002, he has lectured on baseball history to Elderhostel groups and various civic organizations around the state.

A member of the Society for American Baseball Research (SABR) since 1973, Spatz serves as the chairman of SABR's Baseball Records Committee, a post he has held since 1991. In 2000, SABR presented him with the L. Robert Davids Award, its most prestigious honor. In 2001, the magazine the *Diamond Angle* presented him with their F. C. Lane Award in recognition of his excellence in baseball writing, and the *Sporting News* presented him with an award for his research related to the Midsummer Classic. His book *1921: The Yankees, the Giants, and the Battle for Baseball Supremacy in New York* (coauthored with Steve Steinberg) was the winner of the 2010 Seymour Medal, honoring that year's best book of baseball history.